Crem

Jesus is Lord

CHRIST'S DOCTRINE
OF THE ATONEMENT

CHRIST'S DOCTRINE OF THE ATONEMENT

George Smeaton

THE BANNER OF TRUTH TRUST

THE BANNER OF TRUTH TRUST
3 Murrayfield Road, Edinburgh EH12 6EL
PO Box 621, Carlisle, Pennsylvania 17013, USA

*

First published 1870
Second Edition 1871
First Banner of Truth edition 1991
ISBN 0 85151 600 9

*

Printed in Great Britain by
St Edmundsbury Press Ltd, Bury St Edmunds, Suffolk

PREFACE.

THE present volume is intended to be the first portion of a larger whole, which if completed, will exhibit the entire New Testament teaching on the subject of the atonement. I purposed to survey the whole testimony of our Lord and of His apostles; beginning with the former as fundamental. But as the subject grew in my hands, it was found necessary to reserve, in the meantime, the consideration of the apostolic testimony.

In these pages I have examined, according to the rules of exact interpretation, what Jesus taught on the subject of the atonement, and have given a classification of His sayings and an outline of the doctrine. This seems to be urgently demanded in our times. The necessity of correctly ascertaining, by the only means within our reach, what the Lord actually taught on this point, cannot be overstated, when we direct any measure of attention to modern thought, and to the conflicting views, often as ill-digested by their propounders as perplexing to the minds of others, which are at present given forth on the nature, design, and effect of the Lord's death. The one-sided views on this great theme, held not by scoffers at vital religion, but by earnest men, actually though not willingly deviating from biblical truth, are not to be corrected by any human authority, nor even by an appeal to the Church's past, which yet, as the voice of our mother, is entitled to some amount of deference. They can be effectually confronted and silenced only by the explicit testimony of the Church's Lord. The doctrine will stand there, but will stand nowhere else. And every true disciple has this distinctive feature about him, that he hears the voice of Christ, but a stranger's voice will he not follow.

My task in this work has been simply to determine, by strict exegetical investigation, the import of Christ's words, and to reproduce His thoughts by the exact interpretation of language. I have no other desire than to ascertain what He did say, and to abide by it. The principle on which alone it is safe to carry on investigations into doctrine on any point, is, I am fully persuaded, to go to the Scriptures, not for the starting-point of thought alone, but for the substance of thought as well, or for the rounded and concrete development of the doctrine in all its elements: and these will be found in Christ's sayings, if we but patiently investigate them. It is not, then, to the Christian consciousness that I appeal with some modern teachers, nor to Christian feeling and Christian reason with others, but to the consciousness and sayings of the Great Teacher, and of His commissioned servants, employed as His organs of revelation to the Church of all time.

It is the results of exegesis that are here given, rather than the philological process, which would have compelled me to overload the pages with Greek words. With these discussions on Christ's sayings I have been much engaged in my professional work, and here reproduce some of them, with this difference, that I retain only a small portion of the original language, and give somewhat more of elucidation and enlargement than are deemed necessary in the class-room. I have endeavoured to bring out the results of exegetical investigation, not the process, and to put these within the reach of the educated English reader, to aid him in the great work of making himself acquainted with the Lord's mind, through the medium of the language of revelation.

During the preparation of this volume, two things came, of necessity, to be much before my mind. While the main purpose, from the nature of the investigation, was to define and fix the true idea of the atonement as surveyed from Christ's own view-point, a second and less direct object, though not without its importance in the present discussions on the person and life of Christ, came to be frequently presented to the mind: the objective significance of His whole earthly life was presented to my mind, in a manner which the modern biographies of Jesus never touch.

It only remains, that I refer briefly to what has been done on this field by others. In no quarter has the importance of Christ's own teaching on this article been sufficiently recognised, nor its fulness, nor its extent, nor its formative character as regards the apostolic development. To the latter, attention has been mainly and often exclusively directed, as if little could be made of Christ's own teaching on the subject of the atonement; and nowhere has any attempt been made to arrange and classify our Lord's sayings on the subject. It is true that a certain amount of attention has been directed to our Lord's sayings on the nature of His death by writers of an erroneous tendency, with an obvious desire to get His authority to countenance their opinions; and the following may be named as among the ablest who have discussed a number of those sayings in the tendency opposed to the vicarious sacrifice—viz.: Flatt,[1] De Wette,[2] C. L. Grimm,[3] H. Huyser,[4] Hofstede de Groot.[5] A much abler writer than any of these—a keen dialectician and an accomplished exegete—V. Hofmann,[6] in a work which may

---

[1] *Philosophisch-Exegetische untersuchungen über die Lehre von der Versöhnung Gottes mit den Menschen*, van M. C. Christ. Flatt, 1798. He reviews a number of the texts, explaining them in a moral sense, according to the principles of the Kantian philosophy. He held that the death of Christ only *declared* the remission of sins, and only gave an *assurance* of grace.

[2] De Wette, *De Morte Christi Expiatoria*, Berl. 1830.

[3] C. L. Grimm, *de Joanneæ Christologiæ indole*, etc., 1833.

[4] H. Huyser, *Specimen quo Jesu de Morte sua effata colliguntur et exponuntur*, Gron. 1838.

[5] Hofstede de Groot, in the Dutch periodical, *Waarheid en Liefde* for 1843.

[6] Hofmann, *Schriftbeweis*, first edition, 1852. This work has called forth replies from Philippi, Thomasius, Ebrard, Delitzsch, Weber, etc., on the subject of the atonement.

be described as a sort of biblical dogmatics, has canvassed the
sayings of Christ as part of the Scripture testimony on the atonement; which he expounds in the same tendency with the writers
just named, though with far more of the evangelical spirit. I
must also mention Prof. Ritschl[1] of Bonn, who has examined
the principal sayings of Christ in the same tendency. One is
disposed to say of these writers generally, that, with all their
acknowledged learning and ability, they have too much forgotten
the simple function of the interpreter, and deposited their own
unsatisfactory opinions or the spirit of the age in the texts which
they professed to expound.

But there are others who have discussed the Lord's sayings in
a general outline of the Scripture testimony to the atonement,
in a better spirit, and with more success. I refer, first of all, to
Schmid,[2] who treats, in a brief but felicitous way, the scope and
purport of our Lord's teaching on the subject of His death,—only
causing us to regret that his *Biblical Theology* is a posthumous
work, and put together from imperfect notes, his own and others.
A pretty full collection of Christ's sayings, in a chronological
order, and consequently without any attempt to distribute them
into classes, was attempted by Prof. Gess[3] of Basel, some years
ago, in a series of papers which, with much that is worthy of
attention, are defective in two respects. He repudiates the
doctrine of the active obedience, and allows it no place as an
element in the atonement; and then his erroneous depotentia-
tion-theory of the incarnation renders it necessary for him to
assign no influence to the deity of Christ in the matter of the
atonement. I must also allude to a discussion of these sayings
by two learned Dutch writers, who have written with very
different degrees of merit. Professor Vinke's[4] essay, forming

---

[1] Prof. Ritschl, in the *Jahrbücher für Deutsche Theologie* for 1863.

[2] C. F. Schmid, *Biblische Theologie*, 1859 (pp. 229-250).

[3] Prof. Gess of Basel wrote these articles in the *Jahrbücher für Deutsche
Theologie* in 1857 and 1858.

[4] Prof. Vinke of Utrecht, *Leer van Jesus en de Apostel aang. zijn Lijden
etc., in's Gravenshage*, 1837.

one of the publications of the Hague Society in defence of the Christian religion, is a valuable collection of most of Christ's sayings, and also of the apostles' sayings, on the subject of the atonement, with brief comments appended, evincing a warm attachment to the true doctrine of the atonement. It is only too brief, from the nature of his plan, and it attempts no classification. The other Dutch writer, Van Willes,[1] whose work was written for the same society, or at least by occasion of the prescribed theme, is limited to the elucidation of the sayings of Jesus in reference to His sufferings and death. This acute and ingenious writer devotes attention to a number of philological questions connected with the sayings of Jesus, and expatiates, with not a little tact, on the connection between the sayings and the occasion which called them forth. But he does not attempt, in any one case, to bring out the doctrinal import of the sayings which he undertakes to elucidate. He stops short at the very point where we wish him to begin, and gives us nothing but philology or historical construction. It would be going too far to say that he supports a wrong tendency; but he carefully conceals, throughout this treatise devoted to the sayings of Jesus, what the atonement is, or what it effects. He gives us language, not doctrine, or the exhibition of thought contained in language. These are the principal discussions on the subject under our consideration; and I have been at pains to analyze them.

I have only to add, that the preparation of this volume has given me much pleasant meditation; and I send it forth, with the prayer that the Great Teacher may use it to turn men's minds away from unprofitable speculation, to listen to His own voice.

GEORGE SMEATON.

May 1868.

[1] Van Willes, *Opheldering van de Gezegden des Heeren betrekkelijk zijn Lijden en sterven voor Zondaren*, Amsterd. 1837.

PREFACE TO THE SECOND EDITION.

SINCE the appearance of this volume in 1868, the task of surveying exegetically the entire New Testament teaching on the subject of the atonement has been completed. The volume entitled THE APOSTLES' DOCTRINE OF THE ATONEMENT, which appeared in 1870, was the second division of the work. The first volume, from the nature of the undertaking, had to lay the foundations of the doctrine, and to exhibit it both as a whole and in its several parts. The second volume, collecting the testimony of the apostles, is a continuous application of the principles with which the reader is supposed to be familiar from the perusal of the first. The two volumes are thus the complement of each other.

The changes introduced into this second edition leave the body of the work as it was. Some sections have been added, and some paragraphs filled out, so as to supply what seemed defective; and the new division into chapters will render the structure of the whole and the connection of the several parts apparent at a glance.

GEORGE SMEATON.

21st Oct. 1871.

CONTENTS.

CHAPTER I.

THE SOURCES OF OUR KNOWLEDGE IN THE RECORDED SAYINGS OF JESUS,

AND THE MODE OF INVESTIGATION.

CHAPTER II.

THE POSTULATES OR PRESUPPOSITIONS OF THE DOCTRINE OF

THE ATONEMENT.

CHAPTER III.

THE CONSTITUENT ELEMENTS OF THE ATONEMENT.

CHAPTER IV.

THE EFFECTS OF CHRIST'S DEATH.

CHAPTER V.

THE RELATION OF THE ATONEMENT TO OTHER INTERESTS IN THE UNIVERSE.

CHAPTER VI.

THE ACTUAL EFFICACY OF THE ATONEMENT ; OR THE QUESTION FOR WHOM IT WAS SPECIALLY OFFERED.

CHAPTER VII.

THE APPLICATION OF THE ATONEMENT.

CONTENTS.

CHAPTER VIII.

THE ENDLESS HAPPINESS OR WOE OF MANKIND DECIDED BY ITS RECEPTION OR REJECTION.

INDICES.

SAYINGS OF JESUS ON THE ATONEMENT.

PRELIMINARY REMARKS.

THE doctrine of the atonement is put in its proper light, only when it is regarded as the central truth of Christianity, and the great theme of Scripture. The principal object of Revelation was to unfold this unique method of reconciliation by which men, once estranged from God, might be restored to a right relation, and even to a better than their primeval standing. But the doctrine is simply revealed, or, in other words, is taught us by authority alone.

Instead of commencing, according to the common custom, by fixing a centre and drawing a circumference, we wish to proceed historically. We shall not select a view-point, and then adduce a number of proof texts merely to confirm it; and we do so for a special reason. It has always seemed to be a point of weakness in treatises on this subject, that the truth has been so much argued on abstract grounds, and deduced so largely from the first principles of the divine government. The importance of these must be acknowledged, as they rationalize the doctrine, and establish it in the convictions of the human mind, when the fact is once admitted; but they have their proper force and cogency, only when the truth of the doctrine is based and accepted on a ground that is strictly historical. We here inquire simply what Jesus taught. We do not ask what one eminent church teacher or another propounded, but what the great Master said. We turn away our eye from every lower source of knowledge, whether called Christian consciousness, feeling, or reason, to the truth embodied in the consciousness and words of Jesus.

The scope we aim at in the following disquisition, is to gather out of the sayings of Christ the testimony which He bears to His own atonement in its necessity, nature, and effect. And we the rather enter on this inquiry, because the subject, as a separate topic, has never received the prominence due to it; and because, by men of all shades of opinion, the greatest weight must of necessity be laid on those statements which are offered by the Lord Himself in reference to His work. A brief general outline of our investigation, and of the structure of the work, may here be subjoined for the convenience of the reader. The following eight divisions, constituting so many chapters, subdivided into sections as the subject requires, give a skeleton of the treatise:—

I. The sources of our knowledge in the recorded sayings of Jesus, and the mode of investigation.

II. The postulates or presuppositions of the whole doctrine. Under this chapter we shall notice, in separate sections, the great fact of sin for which a provision is made, the necessity of the atonement, the harmony of love and justice, the unique covenant-position of Jesus, and the influence of His Deity in the matter of the atonement.

III. The constituent elements of the atonement, represented under a variety of sections, as consisting of sin-bearing and sinless obedience.

IV. The effects or consequences of the atonement on the invidual Christian, both in an objective and subjective point of view—that is, in respect of the acceptance of His person, and the renovation of his nature by the communication of divine life.

V. The influence of the atonement on other interests in the universe, in reversing the previous order of things, in the conquest of Satan, in procuring the gift of the Holy Ghost, and the like.

VI. The actual efficacy of the atonement, or the question for whom it was specially offered.

VII. The application of the atonement.

VIII. The endless happiness or woe of mankind decided by its reception or rejection; and the influence exercised by this great event on morals and religion.

CHAPTER I.

THE SOURCES OF OUR KNOWLEDGE IN THE RECORDED SAYINGS OF JESUS, AND THE MODE OF INVESTIGATION.

SEC. I.—THE FOUR GOSPELS THE SOURCES OF OUR KNOWLEDGE AS TO THE SAYINGS OF JESUS.

THE Gospels, a record of facts, and of memorable sayings intended to explain those facts, are constructed in the way best adapted to set forth the design of the Lord's death. A brief notice of their constituent elements will suffice for our present purpose.

As no one mind was competent to the task of delineating the divine riches of Christ's life, we have a fourfold mirror presented to us, in order to reflect it on all sides. The four biographies, with each a distinct peculiarity, constitute a perfect harmony and an adequate revelation of the God-man. This explains why the apostles were, during His public ministry, placed in His immediate society. They were to be fitted, according to their divine call, to prepare, as eye-witnesses and ear-witnesses, for the edification of the church, a faithful record of His deeds and words. And intimations of this occasionally occur before they were fully aware of all that was intended (Matt. xxvi. 13; Acts i. 21). The precious record was for nearly thirty years suspended on their oft-imperilled lives. But it came forth in due time, when it could be committed to the Church—already prepared to welcome

and appreciate it as part of the oracles of God. Though some
men presumptuously talk of the entrance of myths, such a supposition is forestalled by the circumstances of the case. What
was at length transferred to writing had been, for near a generation, orally rehearsed by the apostles in the churches which
they founded. The Gospels were the productions of immediate
eye-witnesses, or of men who wrote in their society and under
their sanction. The fact that the apostles still presided over
the churches when the Gospels were issued secured a twofold
result—the authenticity as well as faultless accuracy of the
documents, and their unimpeded circulation. They were simply
received as coming from men who had at once the competency
and the call to digest them into form. And they have, in every
corner of the Christian Church, been reverently preserved as the
oracles of God.

Thus the Gospel of MATTHEW the apostle was received by the
Church as the production of an eye-witness: and it has its own
peculiarity. As evidently appears from the care with which he
digests the Jewish history and traces the genealogy from Abraham, in the descending line, Matthew wrote more especially for
Jewish Christians. He places the life of Jesus in the light of
the Messianic predictions. He does not enter much into detail,
—considerably less, indeed, than Mark and John. But he
groups together a selection of important facts and sayings, with
an ever recurring appeal to the fulfilment of prophecy. The
Gospel of MARK, again, is commonly called the Petrine Gospel,
because it was composed in Peter's society, and embodies
Peter's recollections, as Mark was in the habit of hearing them
rehearsed in the churches. It is not to be regarded as an epi-
tome of Matthew, but as an original Gospel (1 Pet. v. 13). In
recent times not a few think they have warrant for representing it as the first published Gospel. Nor is this without very
considerable probability. Beginning in the style of Peter's
evangelistic discourses (comp. Acts x. 36), it narrates especially
the great deeds of Christ; and was fitted to show that the

Lord's life made the most powerful impression on all who saw Him. It contains few of Christ's discourses, and has few allusions to prophecy. The Gospel of LUKE occupies precisely the same relation to Paul as does that of Mark to Peter, being prepared in Paul's society and issued with his imprimatur. How much it deserves to be regarded as the Pauline Gospel appears by a great variety of topics. Thus, for example, without any distinction of Jew and Gentile, it traces up the Lord's genealogy, not to Abraham, but to Adam (Luke iii. 38). The same Pauline spirit comes to light in the manner in which this evangelist reports the Song of Simeon (ii. 32), the insufficiency of works (xvii. 10), the immediate connection of salvation with faith alone (vii. 50). The fourth Gospel, that of JOHN, the beloved disciple and apostle, was written long after the others had passed away, and was intended to be supplementary to them. His principal object was to show that Jesus was the Christ, the Son of God (John xx. 31); and all this is delineated to a large extent from the Lord's own consciousness, and in a manner not attempted before. For this peculiar description of Christ's person John had a special gift and aptitude. He does not, like Matthew and Luke, commence with the infancy or human descent; and he does not, like Mark, commence with the public ministry of the Lord. He goes back to the Lord's divine pre-existence and eternal Sonship (John i. 1-19).

This brings us to the narrative of the historic facts and sayings in the life of Jesus.

As to the facts, the history proceeds for the most part in the way of simple narrative in its most objective form. The facts, it is true, to be fully understood, require a certain interpretation or commentary; and this is supplied by the Lord's sayings or by the doctrinal comments contained in the Epistles. When the incidents in the suffering life of Jesus are read as a narrative of suffering without this interpretation, they commonly give rise to nothing beyond sentimental feelings or the idle sympathy which the Lord disclaimed in the days of His flesh

(Luke xxiii. 28). The facts and sayings are so connected, that had they stood alone neither could have been understood. The narrative would have been an insoluble enigma without the commentary. The historic incidents of the Lord's suffering life supply what may be termed the realism of the atonement, or the exhibition of it in concrete personal form. The rounded doctrine is given in the apostolic Epistles, where the veil is, so to speak, lifted up, and where we see the divine thoughts or the redemption plan which the narrative embodies in historical reality. And when we put together divine thought and divine fact, plan and accomplishment, the coincidence serves to confirm both. The doctrine renders the history clear. The Gospels are aright studied only when they are read agreeably to this divine plan; and without this men remain on the mere surface of historic fact, content with the bare example of Christ as a model man, or depositing some meagre arbitrary ideas of their own in narratives pre-eminently full of the vicarious sacrifice. When the history is perused by those who have an eye to trace the cause as well as the elements of the Lord's sufferings, they discern in the sphere of fact every aspect of the doctrine. The Gospels, in a word, exhibit on a foundation of fact all the conditions of the atonement, together with all its constituent elements; and the more the history is examined, the more is the correspondence apparent between the sayings and the facts— between the predictions which Jesus uttered and the fulfilment which followed.

When we narrowly examine the evangelists' narratives, we find them peculiarly adapted to the design for which they were composed; and they must be perused agreeably to this design. They aim to bring out on a definite plan that Jesus of Nazareth is the suffering Messiah to whom all the prophets bore witness. Accordingly, their history is so arranged as to bring out—in some more expressly, in others more indirectly—the coincidence between fact and prophecy, but with no attempt to run a laboured parallel between the two. There is a threefold division of prophecy in the Old Testament bearing on the humiliations of Messiah. The first may be described as announcing a suffering Surety; the second, as exhibiting the voluntary subjection of Messiah to the sufferings encountered by Him; and the third sets forth how the tenor of His sufferings leads others to repose their trust in Him for salvation. We find a most impressive coincidence between fact and prophecy.

But still further: the structure of the Gospels, when minutely analysed, brings out all the great elements of the atonement on a basis of historical reality, showing how infinite Intelligence must have presided over their composition. No human reproducer of the Lord's life can approach it. Thus the qualities essentially requisite in the atoning Surety were pre-eminently the following four, and they are all developed on a basis of fact. They must (1) be faultless sufferings, and without challenge, corresponding to the character of Him to whom the satisfaction required to be made; they were (2) to be painful and ignominious to the last degree; they must (3) have an unlimited worth or value derived from the dignity of the sufferer; and they must (4) accurately correspond to the declarations of God.

All these points are brought out in the narrative of the evangelists on the foundation of fact in the most remarkable way. As to the first, the declaration of Pilate and of Pilate's wife, of Herod, and of the traitor, may be mentioned as illustrations of the faultless perfection of the sufferer, brought out in the most natural way. The second point receives its elucidation in what is recorded by the writers as to the scorn and mockery inflicted on the Sufferer, in the indignities done to Him, in the false charges on which He was condemned, as well as in the mode in which the sentence was carried out. The third point, relating to the Sufferer's dignity, receives its confirmation in those touches in the historic narrative which describe His sacerdotal prayers and His sacrifice, as well as the benediction pronounced upon the murderer who was crucified along with Him. In the most simple form of narration, the evangelists record His royalty in prostrating His enemies and in protecting His disciples, in the inscription which by divine providence Pilate, notwithstanding all opposition, must needs write upon His cross, and in the confession to which the centurion gave utterance: "Truly this was THE SON OF GOD." The fourth point receives the fullest illustration in the original threat of death, in the curse of which suspension on a tree was the obvious evidence and emblem, and in the details of the arrest and trial, the crucifixion and ignominy, the sufferings and death, as foreshadowed and foretold in the law, the prophets, and the Psalms, and all recalled as by a touch in those brief records supplied by the Gospels; not to mention little incidents occasionally introduced (John xix. 28, 36).

As to the SAYINGS, they are the expressions of the Lord's own consciousness; and they are accurately given, being retained in the memory of the apostles. These sayings, beyond doubt, utter His own thoughts on the subject of His atoning death; and they announce the design, aim, and motive from which He acted. That the expression of them is according to truth, without overstatement on the one hand, or defect on the other; that they give not only an objective outline of His work in its nature and results, but also a glimpse of the very heart of His activity, will be admitted by every Christian as the most certain of certainties. In this light these sayings are invaluable, as they disclose His inner thoughts, and convey the absolute truth upon the subject of the atonement, according to that knowledge of His function which was peculiar to Himself,—for His work was fully and adequately known only to His own mind. Here, then, we have perfect truth: here we may affirm, unless we are ready to give up all to uncertainty and doubt, that we have the whole truth as to the nature of the atonement, as well as in reference to the design and scope for which He gave Himself up to death for others.

SEC. II.—THE NUMBER OF OUR LORD'S TESTIMONIES TO THE ATONE-
MENT, AND THE CIRCUMSTANCES CONNECTED WITH THEM.

THE number of these sayings, it is true, is smaller than we
should wish; but the amount of information they convey is not
measured by their number, but by their variety, by their fulness,
and by their range of meaning. They are not to be numbered,
but weighed; to be traced in their wide ramifications, not
counted in a series. The comprehensiveness, the force, the
pregnancy of meaning which these sayings, taken together,
involve, are of more consideration than the frequency with
which our Lord touched on the theme. They will be found to
contain by implication, if not in express terms, almost every
blessing that is connected with the atonement; and the apostles,
who are commonly spoken of as expanding the doctrine, will
be found not so much to develop it, as to apply it to the manifold phases of opinion and practice encountered by them in the
churches. Thus the legalism of the Jewish converts required
one application of it in Galatia, and the incipient gnosticism
in Colossæ and Asia Minor, another and a different. We cannot, in this volume, investigate all the applications of it interwoven in the Epistles, so as to exhibit on every side this grand
doctrine, which, in truth, makes Christianity what it is—a
gospel for sinners. We single out at present, for separate investigation, the sayings of Christ Himself,—a field that demands
an accurate survey.

No one could say beforehand what would be the peculiar
nature of Christ's testimony to His sacrifice, nor in what precise
form it would be presented to His hearers' minds. His allusions
to it are for the most part fitted in to some fact in history, to
some type belonging to the old economy, or to some peculiar
title or designation, which He appropriated to Himself, and
which often had its root in prophecy. They are all pointed
and sententious; they are such as are easily recalled; and they

seize hold of the mind by some allusion to ordinary things. He spoke of the atonement according to the docility and freedom from prejudice, or according to the love of truth and the capacity to receive it, on the part of those who came to hear Him. The case of Nicodemus is an instance of this; and the instructions communicated to him had the happy effect of preparing his mind to understand the nature of the Messiah's death, and to take no offence at it when His hour was come.

We often think, indeed, that an allusion to His atoning work is necessary at various turns of His discourse; and we expect to find it. We are surprised that the doctrine which forms the essence of Christianity, and the central topic of the gospel, should be announced with so much reserve. It seems strange that parables, such as that of the publican, that of the two creditors, and the like, meant to teach the gracious way of acceptance, should contain no allusion to the atonement. And hence some, unfavourable to the vicarious sacrifice of Christ, think themselves entitled to draw from this an argument in proof of their position. But a little reflection is enough to satisfy us that He had reasons for the silence. The idea of a suffering Messiah had grown obsolete: His priestly office mentioned in the Psalm (Ps. cx. 4) was ignored; there was none among the people, with the exception of Simeon, Zachariah, and the Baptist, to whom it seems to have been familiar, or, in the least, acceptable.

Not only so: He had to go back a step, and to take up opinion at a previous stage, just as the Baptist did to his hearers, in his preparatory ministry. They must first be taught the spirituality of the law, as He did in the sermon on the Mount. He found it of absolute necessity to awaken a spiritual sense for the divine; to arouse conscience, and to preach repentance, because the kingdom was at hand; to assail their hollow, external forms, and the neglect of weightier matters; to explode their vain trust in Jewish descent, and the futile expectation that they would enter the Messianic kingdom, on

the footing of being Abraham's descendants. He had, in a word,
to turn them away from acting to be seen of men, and from the
desire to cleanse the outside of the cup and platter. They must
learn their needs as sinners; acknowledge their defects; and
have awakened in them a desire for pardon, before they could
learn much of the nature of His vicarious death, or, indeed, be
capable of receiving it.

He had next to announce the kingdom of God as having
come, and to describe its nature and its excellence, the character
of its subjects, and its various aspects in the world. He had
to set forth His divine mission, and to prove it by His many
miracles; His more than human dignity; His divine Sonship;
His being sealed and sent; His unique position in the world
as the Great Deliverer and object of promise; and the long-
desired one of whom Moses wrote, and whom Abraham desired
to see. His first object was to confirm men's faith in Himself as
the promised Christ; to attach them to His person by a bond
which should be strong enough to bear a pressure; and to forestall the hazard of their being offended at that to which every
Jewish mind was most averse. He sought, in the first place, to
bind the disciples to Himself, and to deepen their faith in Him.
This was His paramount and fundamental aim in His intercourse
with the disciples from day to day.

But at this point a new difficulty presented itself. The disciples who were attached to His person, and received Him as
the Saviour, would hear nothing of His death,—they would
not believe it, nor take it in. On the occasion when Peter, in
the name of the rest, declared his belief in Christ's Messiahship,
and in His divine Sonship (Matt. xvi. 16), we should have
expected full submission to every part of His teaching; and
that the explicit statement from the mouth of the Lord Himself as to His death, would have been accepted, in this the
fittest moment, without any doubt. On the contrary, Peter
began to rebuke Him for the language He had held on the
subject of His death,—so possessed were they with preconceived

ideas, and so hard was it to direct the Jewish mind into a new channel. They viewed His kingdom as an everlasting kingdom, on which He was to enter at once without that atoning death which was to be its foundation and ground. They dreamed of places of authority, rank, and honour in the kingdom; and the constant topic of dispute among them, even at the Last Supper, was, who was to be prime minister of state, and fill the post of greatest power. Even His true disciples mingled foreign elements with their conceptions of His kingdom. And hence, to keep His cause free from the risk of those political commotions, to which an open announcement of His Messiahship would have given rise, in a community where the true idea had been lost; and for the farther reason that He must suffer death at their hand, we find that our Lord spoke sparingly, and with reserve; and on one occasion He constrained the disciples to get into a ship, when the excited multitude would have taken Him by force to make Him a king.

To men thus minded, little could be said on His atonement. The two ideas—the Messiahship, and the possibility of death —seemed in the highest degree incompatible. They could not suppose that the universal conqueror could be the conquered, even for a moment. They foreclosed inquiry,—they showed themselves unqualified for further instruction; nor did they, with teachable minds, apply for the information which He would have willingly supplied. He could leave, therefore, a record in their memory, only in a more indirect and incidental way, by means of His sermons in Galilee, and in Jerusalem (John vi. and x.); or by more expressly introducing this truth in connection with events in His own life, or with difficulties in theirs. But it must be allowed on all hands, that while the disciples felt their life was bound up with Him, they evaded the unwelcome fact of His death, although He frequently announced it, by some explanation of their own; nay, though it formed the one topic of conversation on the Mount of Transfiguration between Moses, Elias, and Christ, the disciples contrived, on some plea, to explain away the fact. And when the Lord took them apart, and solemnly announced what was at hand, they were exceedingly sorry; but, as if they had found out some evasion, they are soon engaged in their old dispute again. And the blank dejection into which they were thrown by the actual fact of His death, shows how little they were prepared for it, or understood its meaning. All this tends to prove, that as the disciples could not listen calmly, and without prejudice, to this topic, till they could look back upon the event as an accomplished fact, so His teaching could not possibly have all the fulness and freedom with which the truth could be treated after His resurrection from the dead.

SEC. III.—WHETHER ALL THE TESTIMONIES OF CHRIST ON HIS ATONING DEATH ARE RECORDED.

The question may be put, however, May not Christ have spoken of His atonement more fully and more frequently than is recorded ? As we have not a complete narrative of His words or works, may we not hold that He often alluded to His death, and to the saving benefits connected with it, when He found docile and susceptible minds to whom it could be unfolded ? We have nothing beyond probabilities to guide us here. Plainly, our Lord did not make His sufferings and death the principal topic of His teaching, or taught in precisely the same way as the apostles did, when they referred to the finished work of Christ, and founded churches under the ministration of the Spirit. But this does not exclude the possibility of a larger number of allusions to His death, when He did meet with minds that could receive it, as Nicodemus did, in private. Possibly, the men of Sychar, who received Him with the utmost docility, heard this doctrine from His lips,—a doctrine not withheld from Nicodemus; for they held language in regard to Him as "the Saviour of the world," which seems to imply as much. Not less significant are the words of Christ spoken with reference to the act of Mary of Bethany, when she anointed Him with precious ointment: "She did it for my burial" (Matt. xxvi. 12). She seems to have received instruction from Him on the subject of His death, and ingenuously to have accepted the words in their proper sense. Many will have it, that Jesus was merely pleased to represent the matter in such a light, but that the woman designed nothing of that nature. But that comment is not warranted by the language, which rather gives us a glimpse into her heart, and indicates that her whole loving nature was moved. That groundless commentary has been adopted mainly because her faith was simpler, more enlightened, and more direct than that of the disciples. But why should that cause any difficulty, when faith is not always according to the opportunities? Jesus seems to have instructed her in private as to the nature and efficacy of His death, which she now regards as certain; and she had credited His words with a simplicity and directness which those who dreamed of posts of honour and distinction did not share. This, then, is almost a proof of His having given further statements on His death than are narrated in the gospels.

But after His resurrection our Lord held many conversations on His atoning death, which are not preserved. This seems to have been one of the principal objects of His sojourn of forty days. He spake copiously on that theme, to which they would not listen before; and He said much that is not recorded, when He expounded to them in all the Scriptures the things concerning Himself, beginning at Moses and all the prophets (Luke xxiv. 27). His words to the two disciples on the Emmaus-road were: "O fools, and slow of heart to believe all that the prophets have spoken! Ought not Christ to have suffered these things, and to enter into His glory?" (vers. 25, 26). His great design was to unfold the necessity, nature, and design of His vicarious death, and to open their understandings to understand the Scriptures (Luke xxiv. 45); and we cannot but conclude, when we put all the hints together, that Jesus must then have said more to the disciples on the subject of His death for the remission of sins, than in all His previous communications addressed to them. The work was done, and it could now be fully understood. They knew the fact of His death, and He introduced them into a full acquaintance with its design and efficacy in the light of the Old Testament Scriptures. The full outline of Bible doctrine, as contained in the law, in the Psalms, and in the prophets, concerning Christ, was opened up to their wondering gaze, as it had been fulfilled (Luke xxiv. 44). Who has not often wished to possess these unrecorded expositions of the Old Testament Scriptures? But though they are doubtless embodied in the New Testament, it has not seemed meet to the inspiring Spirit to preserve them in a separate form. The Lord had said, " I have many things to say to you, but ye cannot bear them now " (John xvi. 12); and they could bear them then.[1]

SEC. IV.—THE METHOD TO BE FOLLOWED IN EVOLVING THE IMPORT OF HIS SAYINGS.

Our task will be to expound the import of those sayings which are preserved to us, to collect their import, to set forth what they truly mean. We shall for the present concentrate our attention on the Lord's own testimony to His death for our redemption—that is, on His redemption work, active as well as passive. We cannot wholly isolate these sayings from the old economy which pointed to Christ's coming, nor from the apostolic commentary which points back to what He said; but we place ourselves upon the gospels, and occupy our minds with the Redeemer's thoughts. Of course Moses and the prophets supplied, even to Him, matter which He received into His consciousness, and the practical exhibition of which He embodied in His life; and His words thus received a tincture from the past, as they lend a tincture to that which

---

[1] See note A in Appendix.

was to follow. But still it is the thoughts of Jesus finding expression in words with which our attention is to be occupied. We will insert nothing, we will deposit nothing unwarranted by the prophetic outline of the scope of His coming or by the apostolic commentary on the accomplished fact, but seek only to evolve the Saviour's meaning, according to the force of language. And we wish to withhold whatever can be regarded as ideas foreign to the import of the Saviour's words.

The testimonies of Christ, left to speak for themselves, or only so far elucidated as to bring out their import, will be found to convey such a full and rounded outline of the atonement, as to leave almost no corner of the doctrine untouched; and in discussing them, it will be best to distribute them, and then notice them, as far as may be, singly and apart. This is better than to follow the custom of merely giving them in chronological order, without attempting to digest them under any heads or formulæ which may classify them, and which may be supposed most accurately to comprehend them. The sayings of Christ, however, on this point, are, from their very nature, so vast and extensive, that they are little capable of anything artificial. Our Lord's own testimonies are not only too comprehensive to be easily treated in this way, but are put by Him in such a concrete connection with His mission, person, incarnation, and design, that they cannot well be crystallized in the same way as any other sayings upon some thread of ours which may promise to hold them together. They are, moreover, very diversified, and may be said to bring before us a new field of inquiry wherever He touches on the subject. They each give the key-note, as it were, to a whole series or class of similar sayings in the apostolic Epistles; which may be said to take them up and to continue them, according to the practical necessities of the churches, or the varying phases of doctrinal opinion which threatened them. The apostles take up those diversified sayings, and apply them in all directions; and they give them manifold forms of application.

SEC. V.—THE IMPORTANCE OF BIBLICAL IDEAS ON CHRIST'S DEATH.

It is important to form clear and well-defined ideas of the atonement from the Lord's own words. When we reflect that all His statements are the expression of His own consciousness, the Christian entering into their meaning will say, as the Christian astronomer did when he discovered certain laws of the solar system: "My God, I think my thoughts with Thee." This cannot be a trifling matter in theology. Yet many in these days who exalt the inner life at the expense of true and proper doctrine, are not slow to say that it is indifferent whether the death of Christ be regarded as the procuring cause and ground of pardon, or as the mere assurance of it. They will not inquire how the atonement was effected; they avoid the definition of terms and all biblical precision of thought, as if it could be of little moment to a Christian, whether the death of Jesus is considered as a vicarious sacrifice, or an expression of divine love,—whether it display the evil of sin, or merely stand for a solemn revocation of the Old Testament sacrifices. They will have it, that these points are but theological debates or human speculations, from which they do well to stand aloof in the discussion of the doctrine. That is a process of unlearning, or of leaving all in uncertainty, which does not spring from a commendable zeal for truth, but from a wish to blunt its edge; and it is tantamount to saying, that there is in Scripture no doctrine on the subject. This is the watchword of a tendency which is adverse to clearly-defined views of doctrine or of Scripture truth.

The very reverse of this is our duty. We must acquire, as much as lies in us, sharply-defined ideas on the atonement from the gospels themselves; which, in our judgment, are by this very topic far elevated above all mere human wisdom. Whatever cannot be asserted from the Scriptures, or is overthrown by their teaching, can easily be spared; and we are willing to dismiss it. But we must collect whatever is really taught, comparing text with text, and the less obvious testimonies with the more easy and perspicuous, if we would think our thoughts with God.

Nor is it less common for another school to allege in our day, that the death of Jesus was rather His fate or fortune than a spontaneous oblation, in the proper sense. These writers will make Christ fall a victim to His holy and ardent zeal, while preaching religious and moral truth, and discharging a high commission as the Herald of forgiveness. His death thus becomes a merely historical event or an occurrence; which, however, it is alleged was the occasion of giving a weighty confirmation to that declaration of absolute forgiveness of which He was the preacher. That is an insipid half truth, which is seemingly right and essentially wrong. It will offer a certain spiritual phase to those who are hostile to the vicarious sacrifice, and who will see nothing but love in God. They view Jesus as a mere preacher or herald of salvation, but not as a veritable Saviour in the full sense of the term. They will go farther than this, and will extol Him as the Prince of Life, and as its Dispenser; but it is life unconnected with the price paid, or the ransom offered. And the prominence given to Christ's example, or to the pattern of His life, is never free from a certain influence that operates like a snare. We shall try this view, which has many pretensions to spirituality, by the explicit testimonies of our Lord Himself. But, meanwhile, we indicate the danger from which it is not free. It never brings off the mind from legality, from self-reliance, and self-dependence. It perverts the spiritual life and the example of the Lord to be a ground, if not a boldly avowed argument, for fostering a certain self-justifying confidence. That is the vortex, within the attraction of which every school is drawn irresistibly, that offers no objective atonement, or perfect plea on which the soul can lean. Nothing so effectually carries off the mind from self-dependence as the atonement,—nothing so exalts grace and humbles the sinner; and on this account, God appointed that acceptance and forgiveness of sin should not be given without a Mediator, and without a dependence upon His merits. Hence the jealousy of the apostles and of all Scripture on this point. The apparent spirituality of any tendency will be no compensation for this hazard.

Those also who lay the greatest weight of their doctrine on the person of Christ, or on His incarnation, often make light of His cross in the comparison. Some of them, indeed, concede a little, and say, If any find benefit from the terms PENALTY, PRICE, SURETYSHIP, and SATISFACTION to divine justice, let them take the good of them. But that is said only to call in question their necessity. On the contrary, it will be found that in all true progress in spiritual knowledge, men will make advances in the knowledge of His atonement as well as of His person. The history of the disciples before and after His crucifixion is a proof of this. The more fully we enter into Christ's truly human experience, and trace His chequered course of joy and of sorrow, the livelier will be our apprehension of His curse-bearing life, and of His penal death.

As to the more rationalistic and Socinian phases of opposition to the atonement, they will also be kept in view by us. But we wish to bring out positive truth or edifying doctrine much more than merely polemical discussion,—a considerable part of which may competently, and with more propriety, be thrown into the notes. Our object is, rather, positive truth than refutation of error.

In short, we are not to ask what man holds or has propounded, so much as what Christ has said. The examination of this, and the attempt to enter into His consciousness, must primarily engage our attention.

CHAPTER II.

THE POSTULATES OR PRESUPPOSITIONS OF THE DOCTRINE OF THE ATONEMENT.

SEC. VI.—THE ATONEMENT A DIVINE PROVISION TO PUT AWAY SIN AND ALL ITS CONSEQUENCES.

THE fact of sin with its vast and far-reaching consequences, of which no finite mind can adequately take the dimensions, is seen from every point of our inquiry. The Humiliation of the incarnate Son was primarily planned in connection with a remedial scheme, and is therefore a provision in the Divine counsels by occasion of sin. They who object, on speculative grounds, to the notion that God ever acts by occasion of anything, and who carry out their theory to the incarnation and its fruits, will find nothing in the Lord's words to lend countenance to this opinion (Luke xix. 10).

The terrible fact of sin is assumed and adequately provided for in the Divine plan which we have to survey. The omniscient God took the full measure of the evil. No created mind was competent even in idea to fathom the guilt of sin or measure its consequences—not to mention our utter inability to expiate the one or reverse the other. The Author of the atonement undertook both; and He alone fully knew what were His own claims as the moral Governor of the universe. To this I refer the rather because many, falling a prey to the excessive subjectivity of modern theories, have lost sight of their relation as responsible subjects to a personal God, and, saturated with a mystic pietism, repose on God merely as a fountain of influences, and not as an authoritative Lawgiver. That is a widely different element from Christ's teaching. With a vivid sense of the relation in which men stand to the moral Governor, the Biblical doctrine evolves those truths that stand connected with the authority of law and the guilt of disobedience.

    a. As to SIN IN ITS OWN NATURE, it implies the Divine Law,

THE ATONEMENT A DIVINE PROVISION FOR SIN.

and can only be defined as the violation of that law which mankind were under obligation to fulfil. It is either the omission of a duty required—and, in this respect, to come short of love to God with all the heart, with all the soul, with all the strength, and with all the mind, or of love to our neighbour as ourselves, is a sin of omission—or it is the commission of an act which the tenor of the law has forbidden. And there are no sins venial in their own nature. Nay, he who offends in one point is guilty of all; because the mental state from which the disobedience flows argues an inward contrariety to the nature and will of God (Jas. ii. 10). The only position which can be laid down as to the criminality of sin is this: the guilt of the offence is proportioned to the greatness, the moral excellence, and glory of Him against whom the offence is committed, and who made us for loyal obedience to Himself. Nothing else therefore comes into consideration in estimating the enormity of sin but the infinite majesty, glory, and claims of Him against whom we sin. Accordingly, the terms used by the Lord to designate sin are noteworthy. He calls it DARKNESS (John viii. 12), implying a state of isolation from God, that is an element where God is not. He calls it a TRESPASS (Mark xi. 25), implying a violation of law. He terms it a DEBT (Matt. vi. 12), involving guilt or liability to punishment. He designates it a LIE (John viii. 44), intimating a mental state which either resists or runs counter to divinely-manifested truth.

b. As to the far-reaching CONSEQUENCES OF SIN, these are so manifold and various that they may be said to be the antithesis, or the opposite column, to all the benefits secured to man by Christ's atonement. It is scarce necessary, therefore, to enumerate the evil effects or consequences of sin; because all that is reversed or annihilated by Christ was entailed on us by sin, was caused by sin. When we trace this contrast and look on the different sides, we win breadth and precision of view. Under the effects of sin we may classify a vast number of bitter evils, such as the forfeiture of our right relation or standing before God; the deterioration of our nature and the entrance of death, temporal, spiritual, and eternal; the departure of the Holy Spirit from the human heart, formed to be His temple; the tyranny of Satan; the gulf formed between men and all holy intelligences, and the like. In a word, whatever is restored by Christ was forfeited by sin.

Thus, when Christ, in a memorable passage in John, describes man as the servant of sin, He says: "He that doeth sin is the servant of sin" (John viii. 34). Commentators, in a somewhat superficial way, expound this statement for the most part as intimating that they who addict themselves to any particular sin become enslaved to it. But while it is true that the habit of sin confirms its dominion and the bondage of its victim, another thought is plainly signified by the context, which brings the Son of God before us in all His office as the Liberator. The import is that the freedom in which man was created, and which was forfeited by sin, can be restored only by the Son (ver. 36). The sinner is a servant under guilt and a servant under justly contracted punishment, as well as under the inward power of sin. The words set forth the same personification of sin, as a dreadful potentate, which the Apostle Paul uses throughout three chapters in the Epistle to the Romans (v. vi. vii.). And when the Lord describes men as they are, or IN THEIR SINS (John viii. 21), He brings out, moreover, that death is the doom, wages, or recompense awarded: "Ye SHALL DIE in your sins."

In a word, there is such a correspondence or similarity in an opposite direction between the effects of sin and the effects of the atonement that the comparison of the two serves to throw light on both.

SEC. VII.—SEPARATE SAYINGS WHICH AFFIRM OR IMPLY THE NECESSITY OF THE ATONEMENT.

On several occasions the Lord refers to the *necessity* of His death, but often stops short at the fact that it had been foretold.

Was there any deeper reason assigned by Him? Yes: there are various allusions, direct and indirect, to a deep inner necessity for His atoning work, which we must now evolve. And it is the more important to raise the question, why God could not pass over sin without atonement, and to answer it from Christ's own consciousness or subjective point of view, because not a few regard the alleged necessity of the atonement in no other light than as a semi-philosophical theory, or as a merely traditional doctrine that has come down to us. The necessity of the atonement, or the reason why in the moral government of God, must, as far as possible, be assigned.

Our plan leads us to proceed in an exegetical way, and not to argue from general principles or from mere dogmatic grounds, except as the discussion of the words of our Lord conducts us to the confines of that field. Though our object is to investigate in what way our Lord speaks of the necessity of atonement, yet there are some *à posteriori* arguments which may be noticed at the outset.

We cannot conceive of such a stupendous economy, if it were not necessary. There could be no other reason sufficiently important for God to abase Himself and to be made in fashion as a man, and suffer on the cross; for God would not subject His Son to such agonies if sin could have been remitted without satisfaction. To suppose that all this was appointed merely to confirm Christ's testimony as a teacher, is a shock to reason; for that could have been effected by a martyr's death. To hold that it was meant to impress the human mind with a conviction of God's love, is no better; for the whole historic basis of Christianity would be little better than a mere drama or scenic arrangement, intended to make an inward impression, but nothing real in the moral government of God, if the vicarious sacrifice were not necessary on God's part for the ransom of sinners, and to put away their sin. The facts are too momentous and solemn, and too closely connected with all the attributes of God and all the persons of the Trinity, to be brought down to the level of an imposing representation. To take this roundabout way of making a moral impression, if the death of God's Son was not necessary, would be repugnant to the Divine goodness and wisdom.[1]

Our Lord, in addressing a people familiar with the ideas of sacrifice, did not deem it necessary to dilate on the necessity of an atonement, and for the most part narrowed the allusion to the sacrifice of Himself, assuming the necessity as an undoubted truth. God had from the first sought to develop the idea of SIN among the chosen people, and to keep their consciences alive to the fact that it must needs be expiated by propitiatory sacrifices. Many laws were enacted for the purpose of awakening a sense of want: civil and ecclesiastical privileges were withdrawn for the violation of these laws, and many afflictive visitations were sent. The government of God was ever anew violated by sinful deeds or transgressions of the law, and in all such cases fellowship with God was foreclosed. Every Jew was aware that, in consequence of a transgression, he was liable to the penalty which must follow; and, in a word, that there was no enduring covenant, and no free access to the Holy One, without a complete fulfilment of the law. No approach could otherwise be allowed to God's presence in the sanctuary services; and there was, besides, a conscious guilt, which tended to estrange the sinner from God, and to make him apprehensive. This was an education of the people in the knowledge of sin.

To meet this deep-felt need of pardon, and as a method of remitting the penalty incurred by a violation of the letter, sacrifices were appointed, which operated on the conscience of the Jew in a peculiar way. They gave him a vivid view of the guilt of sin, and of the rectitude and holiness of the Divine government. The whole Old Testament was thus calculated to bring into prominence the necessity of an atonement, and to sharpen the conviction that sin required a higher sacrifice; and the sacrifice, presupposing the sinful deed, showed the inviolability of the law and covenant. If the Jewish worshippers neglected

[1] See Witsius, *De Economia Fœderum* (lib. ii. chap. viii.) ; and the Heidelberg Catechism, question 12, with its expounders.

the sacrifices of atonement, they incurred the curses of the law. If they brought the sacrifices, they were purged from their defilement, and had access reopened to God in the sanctuary service, without impediment from without or fear from within.

With this doctrine of sacrifice the Jewish mind was familiar. They all admitted the necessity of a sacrifice of atonement in order to avert punishment. This was the great idea for the full development of which the nation had been peculiarly separated from other people, and which was to be learned by them in order to be diffused over the earth. They acknowledged these atonements as the method of averting the threatened penalty, however much they perverted them from the Divine purpose for which they were appointed by extending their effects to MORAL TRESPASSES, instead of limiting them, as they should have done, to ceremonial defilement. They held the necessity of expiation; and our Lord, accordingly, in speaking to them, proceeds on this conceded truth. And hence His words take all this for granted, wherever He makes reference to His work. With a deeper reference than was commonly attached to the sacrifices, and sounding the depths which underlay them, He throughout assumed the indispensable necessity of an expiation. All His sayings contain this thought in their deeper relation. Thus, when we read of sin to be borne in a sacrificial sense (John i. 29); of a ransom to be paid for the purpose of liberating captives to Divine justice (Matt. xx. 28); of the law, both moral and ceremonial, to be embodied in a sinless life and exhibited in a sacrificial death (Matt. v. 17); of the blood of the covenant which puts men on a new footing, and in a relation of pardon and acceptance, to be dissolved no more (Matt. xxvi. 28);—all these allusions take for granted that an atonement is indispensably necessary, and that the Divine claims must be discharged in full.

When we survey our Lord's teaching on the necessity of the atonement, we find reference to a subjective and objective necessity, or to the conscience of man on the one hand, and to the Divine rights on the other.

1. Conscience demands a satisfaction or atonement. To this necessity on the side of conscience there are various allusions by our Lord, and all of them full of significance. Thus, when He invites the weary and heavy laden, He plainly alludes to the state of an awakened conscience desiring a satisfaction or atonement which the individual is not able to offer (Matt. xi. 28). The thirsty invited to come and drink are those who are in a similar condition (John vii. 37). They who are described in the Sermon on the Mount as hungering and thirsting after righteousness are obviously those who feel the oppression of conscious guilt, and who pant for that immaculate "righteousness," or atonement which alone can fill and satisfy the wants of human nature (Matt. v. 6). Our Lord's words assume that such is the, harmony between the voice of conscience and the claims of God, or, in other words, between man made in the image of God and the rights of Him whose image he bears, that nothing will satisfy conscience that does not satisfy the perfections and law of God. As God's representative within, it is taken for granted that conscience will acquit only when God acquits, and possess peace only when God has spoken peace through the finished redemption. There is an inner or subjective necessity which must come to its rights.

Thus conscience acknowledges that wherever sin is punishment ought to be suffered. We see in the old economy the intense longing of the heart after sacrifices, and a conviction of their insufficiency in the ceremonial law. Till the waters of reparation and punishment quench it, guilt burns in the human heart, nay, it would continue to burn in the human heart for ever if there were no sufficient atonement; so that they who would have pardon merely by God's retreating from the demand of satisfaction would be followed, even if they had their wish, by the inward pursuer wherever they went. And as their holiness grew, they would still be haunted by a keener sense of guilt, remembering that they were the same person still, and that no reparation had been made. They would be disturbed by self-accusations, by shame, and a gnawing conscience, till they would long to have the faculty of memory destroyed.[1] We read that they who went to heaven before the finished redemption rejoiced when Christ's day came (John viii. 56), and that in some sense, and doubtless in this subjective sense, they were made perfect by sharing with us in that which we enjoy (Heb. xi. 40).

Thus it appears from all history and experience, that conscience is so sensitive, that it will reject everything which may be offered to calm or heal it, till it finds repose and peace in the vicarious death of Christ; and no atonement will avail which is not infinite. Man discovered to himself, and aware of his wants, will fall into despair, if the growing sense of guilt is not stilled by the great redemption of the cross. It is true that mere conscience cannot of itself tell what is an adequate atonement; that it is but a dumb sense of want; and that it often tries false remedies and vain reliefs. The man is a prisoner under guilt, and knows it. God alone knows and provides the adequate atonement; and the unburdened conscience attests that it is adequate when it is found. But no one can persuade conscience that an atonement is unnecessary.

2. There is an objective necessity founded on the divine rights and man's creaturehood. It would require a separate treatise to discuss the question of the necessity of the atonement against all the impugners of the doctrine, and against the pantheistic leaven of our age, which is to us just what the leaven of the Sadducees was in the days of our Lord, which assumes sin as one of the elements of humanity, and virtually holds

[1] Marheinecke, in his *Fundamental Doctrines of Christian Dogmatics*, p. 284, says:—"Man has the choice of committing sin or not, but he has not the choice whether he will possess the consciousness of guilt or not, but himself acknowledges that punishment should be suffered for the sin committed ; and, as is seen in the case of great criminals, he goes out to meet punishment, and feels that he who has sin is not able to free himself from its guilt and punishment." "Even in the grossest sinner, conscience is so sensitive that it rejects everything that is offered to soothe it as a deliverance from punishment, the clemency of the magistrate, etc. The only thing that man can do is to feel a desire after a satisfaction which he is not able to offer—a divine feeling which lives even in the most degraded sinner."

"whatever is is right." But as our present undertaking limits our view to what the great Teacher has said, or, at the utmost, to what His words imply and presuppose, it would carry us into a wholly different field, were we at any length to discuss, on abstract grounds, or in a dogmatic form, the momentous question of the necessity of the atonement. We shall merely glance at some of its elements; or, as Johnson would have said, "shine on the angles of the thought."

The divine *rights*, to which the question of the necessity of the atonement must very much be run up, differ in one important respect from human rights. Men can in many cases recede from the assertion of their rights, whereas the divine rights are inalienable. The Most High cannot allow any infraction of them, any withholding from Himself of that which is His due, or any spoliation of that declarative glory for which the universe exists, and which a personal God has an interest in securing to Himself. The supreme justice, which is no other than the personal God Himself, puts forth its highest exercise in asserting His rights in the universe, which exists not for itself but for its Maker. This follows from the concrete relations of a personal God; who could not denude Himself of His rights, or be without the exercise of His justice from the moment a created being occupies a relation toward Him as its maker, governor, and upholder. He has from that moment rights of which he cannot denude Himself; for the creature exists not independently of Him, but for Him.

A right *anthropology*, that is, a correct conception of the doctrine of man, also shows the necessity of the atonement. The inquirer must read it off from human duty and human will. So far as the conditions of the problem are concerned, the atonement is in reality nothing else than the taking up of man's obligations at the point where the primeval man failed, with, of course, the additional element which his fall had entailed— the awful fact of sin. We may well affirm, then, that a correct anthropology, as well as a due conception of the attributes and rights of a personal God, is indispensable to a correct notion of the necessity of the atonement. This comes to light in the most emphatic manner in certain portions of the Pauline Epistles, where the argument proceeds on the supposition that the second man must needs enter into the position, obedience, and full responsibility of the first man (Rom. v. 12-19). But the same thought is not obscurely exhibited in all those sayings and phrases where our Lord refers to Himself as the Son of Man. He intimates that He entered with a true body and soul into all the conditions of the problem; that after the revolution of ages He took up the task for the reparation of the wrong, and entered into the conflict where the battle was lost.

The point at which the discussion must begin is the relation which a personal God occupies to SIN. As the entrance of sin is a spoliation of the tribute or revenue of honour which the intelligent creature should have rendered to the Creator; as man was made to render this homage by a pure nature and a God-glorifying obedience, such as a moral representation of the divine image in this world alone could render,—a restoration of this honour to the full, nay, to a still larger degree, is only what supreme justice owes to Himself before salvation can be bestowed. Not that the glory of God essentially is capable either of addition or of diminution. But in reference to His declarative glory—in other words, in reference to what He proposed to make of human nature,—God lost when His rights were denied, and God regains when they are restored. Thus the necessity of the atonement is seen to rest on the divine claims, and on the concrete relations of a personal God to the world.

But the atonement must not be considered barely in relation to the consequences of sin, but in relation to SIN ITSELF. And this leads us to see its absolute necessity, on the supposition that a redemption was to be effected. Sin in its magnitude and criminality is a fact for which an actual provision must be made in some way,—a disharmony in His universe who is the

God of order and not of confusion, and that must be dealt with in the moral government of God. One grand lesson taught by the Old Testament economy, which was not an education for one people merely, but for mankind in general, through that single people, was that sin is such a tremendous evil or disorder that there is an indispensable necessity for a satisfaction, or for punishment. Unlike those modern phases of opinion which set forth that sin is nothing positive, but only a law of being, and which owe their origin to a period of speculation when the idea of a personal God and His relations to the world were forgotten or disowned, the doctrine of the atonement, as exhibited in the sayings of Jesus, is based on the magnitude and enormity of sin. It is the very reverse of those men's theory, too numerous in our time, who admit imperfection, but not guilt; who ignore the divine claims as well as the holy anger and moral government of God; who resolve justice into love, and wrath into benevolence.

The entire elements of this momentous question, therefore, are put in their due place, only when a true conception of SIN and of its infinite evil is adequately apprehended. The atonement is not a mere governmental display before creation, as if the principal end of punishment in the government of God were a mere spectacle to deter from sin. So long as men theorize as to God acting before a created public, only to impress and awe their minds, or seek an object apart from God Himself, they are yielding to a course of thought which only tends to subvert or deny His punitive justice. Such a principle may be called into play in human rule, but has no application in the divine government, where the only public worthy of regard is God Himself, and the harmony of His attributes. To hold with certain eminent writers, such as Michaelis, Seiler, and others, that the infliction of punishment, though not absolutely necessary, is yet fitted to serve an important end in deterring other rational beings from sin, is at once destitute of biblical authority, and puts the question on a false foundation. On this supposition, punishment is not an end in itself, but only a means to an end. On the contrary, as Scripture always puts it, God's moral perfections demand satisfaction; justice links the sin and punishment together; and the recompense is uniformly proportioned to what is deserved. We find the statement adduced again and again, both in the Old Testament and in the New: "Vengeance is Mine; I will repay, saith the Lord" (Rom. xii. 19; Heb. x. 30). The meaning of that significant statement is, that punitive justice belongs essentially to God as a perfection of the divine nature; that it belongs to no other but to Himself, except in so far as He has been pleased to delegate it in certain special cases to the magistrate acting as His representative; and that in consequence of this divine perfection, wherever moral evil is committed, natural evil, or punishment corresponding to it, must ensue.

a. But here we are met by the latitudinarian tendencies of the age, which take exception to the necessity of the atonement, on the ground that we are to view God only as occupying the paternal relation to mankind. Not a few repudiate from this supposed vantage-ground, which seems to have a foothold in Scripture, all the representations otherwise given of God as a lawgiver and a judge. They will have it, that we are to conceive of God only as a source of goodness, or as a fountain of influences, but not as the sovereign Lord or moral Governor; that His dominion is only that of a Father; that the divine laws wholly differ from human laws sanctioned by threats and punishments; and that, when God does punish in any case, it is as a father, and not as a judge. By such representations, which are partly the speculations of a false philosophy, partly the afterthoughts of men writing in the interest of a tendency, the modern assailants of the necessity of the atonement would change laws into counsels, and punishments into corrections. They would sunder the link between sin and punishment, on which, as will appear in the sequel, all religion and all morals depend; for nothing could appear more detrimental to human welfare than the circulation of the doctrine that men are irresponsible to a judge.

The only thing that entitles this speculation to any weight is, that it professes to have a biblical sanction. Far be it from our thoughts to ignore the Fatherhood of God and the tender relation formed by grace between Him and His children; but when men come into this relationship, which henceforth exempts them from everything properly penal, that is the privilege of saints, not of natural men. It is a gift of grace, not a right of nature nor a universal boon; for all are by nature the children of wrath (Eph. ii. 3). It cannot be affirmed that it belongs indiscriminately to all men, unless we obliterate the distinction between converted and unconverted men. But God's Fatherhood does not exclude His relation as a lawgiver and a judge. We rather affirm,—without entering into a new question foreign to our undertaking,—that the former rests upon the latter.

But the answer to all these modern theories, which are advocated with the avowed purpose of withdrawing the mind from the judicial relations of God, and so impugning the necessity of the atonement, is, that they run counter to the entire scope and spirit of that ancient revelation in which Jesus was nourished up to manhood, and which He expressly declares He did not come to destroy, but to fulfil. Unless men are prepared to make a violent severance between the Old and New Testament, and bring the one into violent collision with the other, to the obvious injury of both, these notions must be set aside as wholly out of keeping with the Old Testament, and as having no warrant in the New. The expressions which describe divine justice as a perfection proper to the Supreme Being, and prompting Him to punish transgressors, are peculiarly emphatic and strong (Gen. xviii. 25; Ps. xi. 5-7; Ps. xcvii. 2; Ps. l. 21). The divine displeasure at sin, and His holy hatred of it, are forcibly delineated as the impelling cause of punishment (Hab. i. 13; Prov. vi. 16).

When He revealed His name and memorial in all generations, He designated Himself as the God who by no means clears the guilty (Ex. xxxiv. 7); and in the immutable law, which is the transcript of His perfections, He is represented as a jealous God, visiting iniquity upon them that hate Him (Ex. xx. 5-7). There are passages which show that God is not only extolled by His saints on earth, but by the saints above, for the exercise of punitive justice (Deut. xxxii. 43; Rev. xix. 6).

b. It is further urged, in the interest of the same tendency, that the visitations commonly called punishments are only the natural' consequences of sin. This would indeed overthrow the necessity of the atonement, and also its possibility; for the atonement involves the bearing of positive punishment in the room of others. But the whole Scriptures, from first to last, are replete with instances of positive punishments. The deluge, the overthrow of Sodom and Gomorrah; the case of Pharaoh, of Nadab and Abihu, of Korah and his comrades; the expulsion and destruction of the Canaanites; and, in a word, the whole history of God's transactions with His own people and with other nations, contain the most obvious examples of positive punishments,—not the mere consequences or natural concomitants of a course of conduct. We call these *positive* punishments rather than *arbitrary;* which is not so suitable an epithet, nor so applicable.

All the biblical statements argue the existence of positive punishments. Thus, when we read of "the wrath to come" (Matt. iii. 7), which does not follow sin immediately, and by mere natural sequence, we have a proof of positive punishment. When we read of *forgiveness*, what does the term imply but the remission of a certain retributive doom or recompense which is not the mere natural concomitant of sin? Without the idea of positive punishment emanating from the punitive intervention of God, we could not explain, in any adequate sense, the doctrine of *retribution;* for how could there be a retribution or recompense of reward, if sin were followed by no other consequences than such as are but the natural issues or results of a course of conduct in the direct order of sequence? Does this not properly begin, in the full sense, after the great judgment? The evils which are naturally connected with sin, and which are manifold, are, in truth, of a different sort from the punishments which are inflicted by the intervention of the judge. We do not deny that certain results or consequences flow from sin and may be called a penalty. To give the name of punishments, however, to the natural consequences of sin alone, is a fallacious use of language, and contrary to the dictates of a sound understanding. When men express themselves loosely, they may speak of the connection between conduct and experience. But in the strict and proper use of terms we understand by punishment the suffering which is directly and expressly awarded by the sentence of a judge, not that which follows by the mere law of sequence. Hence, when punishment is justly inflicted, as in the case of the great retribution awarded by the sentence of the just Judge, it is for sin committed or for injury done, by which the moral Governor is aggrieved. It thus differs from the natural effects of sin. It differs, too, from *correction* or chastisement, which aims at something prospective in connection with one whom we only seek to impress with a salutary fear, or to deter from a wayward course.

c. But the same impugners of the necessity of the atonement take exception to the above-mentioned doctrine at a point still further back: they argue that God cannot be said to be wronged or injured. They maintain that this language can be fitly enough held when it is applied to an earthly monarch, whose authority is hurt by the violation of his laws and by the dishonour done to him, but that the Supreme God is far exalted above wrong or injury. There could not exist two opinions that this is indisputably true, if it were a question of man's goodness extending to God, or of man's rebellion tending to the prejudice of God's essential blessedness; but it is a question of His declarative glory, and of His relation to the world, existing only to bring back to Him a revenue of praise. The rational intelligences, created to be a mirror of His perfections, bring back this revenue of praise by cordial dependence, by the subjection of their will to the will of God, and by being an eye to trace His wisdom and goodness. Certainly, God cannot be deprived by the sinner of anything that is His. But it does not follow that He does not regard those as offenders who rebel against Him. His relation to the creature is violated by sin, and He cannot be an unconcerned spectator of the conduct of His reasonable creatures; and sin is in proportion to the person against whom it is committed. There is such a terrible power in a human will that the creature can form plans and execute purposes which God regards as hateful. He can do something that is opposed to the divine will. He can, however insignificant, insult, offend, and wrong God.

Hence punitive justice, which is an adorable perfection of the divine nature, and worthy of Him who is infinitely perfect, demands satisfaction for sin. It is as eternal and necessary as anything belonging to His self-existing nature. It must be maintained that God punishes sin as a satisfaction which must needs be made to Himself; that He punishes OUT OF LOVE TO HIS OWN JUSTICE, or because the righteous God loveth righteousness (Ps. xi. 7),—in other words, that He punishes out of love to Himself. Nor, from the very ground that He is possessed of immaculate justice, can the retribution due to sin be omitted; for of God it may be said that He cannot but punish sin, just as we affirm of Him that He cannot lie. God is thus under obligation to no third party, but to Himself and to His own perfections, to exercise punishment; and He cannot forego or renounce His right to do so unless there be an atonement or vicarious sacrifice. But even then, as we shall show in the sequel, sin is duly punished.

But we must further add that, in thus speaking of divine justice, we must take in the full import of the word: we must avoid one-sidedness. There is a PRECEPTIVE rectitude,—that is, justice in that acceptation of it, whereby He demands what is His due, or what He has a right to claim,—as well as a judicial rectitude. There is a PUNITIVE justice, according to which He punishes disobedience; and a REMUNERATIVE justice, according to which He distributes reward,—the two latter being different sides of the same exercise of this perfection. This justice is met in both its aspects—in its preceptive as well as judicial phase—by the active and passive obedience of Christ, or by a subjection to the law in its precept as well as in its penalty. As the rights of God find their adequate expression in the moral law, it is useful to survey the doctrine under our consideration in the light of the divine law, as well as from the more abstract ground of the divine justice. They cover each other: they explain each other.

The objection is often uttered: "Where does Scripture ever use the expression current in discussions on the atonement, 'the satisfaction of divine justice?'" But no one can presume to demand authority for a phrase with which the former may be alternated, and say, "Where do we read of the necessity of fulfilling the divine law?" After the Socinian dicussions began, and principally turned on the point of punitive justice, it became common to speak out on the necessity of satisfying divine justice with more precision than had been used before. What the rationalistic party repudiated, the evangelical Church asserted as a precious and important truth; and in this way the phraseology found its way into the Church's symbols, and into current use. It came in course of time, however, to contract a certain one-sidedness, because the course of discussion was narrowed to the inquiry, whether there was a judicial exercise of justice. But the language ought to comprehend the function of the lawgiver as well as of the judge; and hence it is important to interchange the expression "the satisfaction of divine justice" with the equivalent, but commonly less restricted, phrase, "the fulfilment of the divine law,"—that is, its fulfilment in the positive precept of love as well as in the endurance of the curse. This brings in the law as the true and exhaustive expression of the divine rights. It is a biblical phraseology somewhat broader, and entitled not indeed to supersede the use of the former expression, but to be at least alternated with it.

But we pass now to the inquiry, What express doctrine is there from the mouth of Christ in regard to the *necessity* of the atonement? There are various allusions explicit or indirect to the necessity of His atoning death.

John iii. 14: "*So* MUST *the Son of Man be lifted up.*" As this text must be considered by itself, we limit our attention at present to the import of the *must* here uttered by Christ. Plainly, the necessity is not to be referred to the fact that the prophets had foretold it. Though the faithfulness of God must needs be maintained on account of the type, there was a further reason, which must be traced up to the divine decree, and to the divine justice.[1] It was not a mere necessity to fulfil the type, but had its ground in the purpose of redemption, and in the end to be attained. Some, toning down the language, would represent it as arising from the present condition of the world, as if the cross were only an occurrence befalling Him in a world of rebels, and where all was out of course. But that does not approach the meaning; and the history of Jesus shows that, except in so far as He chose to subject Himself to the course of things, He was exempt from their power, and beyond

---

[1] Though some interpreters limit the δεῖ to the necessity of fulfilling prophecy, that plainly does not exhaust its meaning. Others, in a still more superficial way, as *Hofstede de Groot*, explained it as a *moral must*, on account of the sinful condition of men. He argues that δεῖ differs from ἀνάγκη, according to classical usage. Of course it does: if we were to follow the classical usage in elucidating the difference between the two, ἀνάγκη would bring in the notion of physical necessity or constraint. But according to the language of Revelation, by which alone we are guided in such questions, δεῖ is often used to denote that a thing must be according to the *faithfulness* or *justice* of God, or *word* of God (Matt. xvi. 2; Luke xvii. 25). Valckenaer says in his *Scholiæ in N. T.*: "Ab ista ligandi virtute fluxit ea quæ vulgo viget in δεῖ significante *decet, oportet.*" Marckius says on δεῖ: "Ex eterno et immutabili decreto" (*Hist. Exalt. Christi*, lib. i. cap. 10, sec. 15).

their reach. They could not touch Him till His hour was come. The words here uttered mean, that in order to heal and save, He must needs be crucified,—the *must* indicating a necessity flowing from God's justice, and from His decree, if men were to be saved.

There are other utterances of Christ not less emphatic, though spoken from another point of view.

Matt. xxvi. 42 : "*If it be possible, let this cup pass from Me.*" The argument from this utterance of Christ for the necessity of His atoning work is of the strongest. There can be no reason assigned why the cup did not pass from Him, except that the divine claims required the endurance for the expiation of sin. The only-begotten Son, notwithstanding this request to the Father, who always heard Him, must drink the cup. And to say that the impossibility of removing it did not spring from the divine justice, is plainly untenable. It cannot be supposed that, except on the ground of indispensable necessity, God would be so inflexible as to visit His Son with all that was comprehended in that cup. The suffering was indispensable— the atonement was necessary—that the cup of suffering might pass from His people.[1]

The same thing is proved by passages which describe the irremediable consequences of neglecting the atoning work of Christ. The result of not believing on the crucified Christ is condemnation (John iii. 18).

Mark viii. 37 : "*What shall a man give in exchange* [better, what ransom shall a man give] *for his soul?*" These words occur in a connection which contains an allusion to the rejection or denial of Christ, and are intended to teach that there is a ransom attainable through the reception of Christ, but no ransom to such as neglect the opportunity, or depart this life without finding the only sacrifice. He virtually says, There is no more sacrifice for sin, since they have denied Me, the only ransom or means of deliverance. But this indisputable allusion

[1] See Triglandius, *Antapologia*, cap. 4, p. 73.

to a ransom, takes for granted its necessity,—implying that it is only found in Jesus, who has expiated sin, and paid the ransom in the sinner's place.

The whole question of the necessity of the atonement is also taken for granted in the INTERCESSION of Christ. He pleads on a ground of justice as well as mercy, recognizing a demand which had been made, and pleading a satisfaction which had been rendered.

John xvii. 25 : " *O righteous Father, the world hath not known Thee*," etc. Our Lord bases His intercession on the rectitude or justice of God, when He prays that they who had been given Him might be with Him in His glory. Though there is a gracious reward conferred upon the saints for every work done, these words of Christ cannot refer to any recompense of that nature, because it is not of strict justice. But our Lord can appeal to justice when He asks the eternal glorification of His redeemed and their fellowship with Him where He is; for He merited eternal life for them, and at the costly price of His passion. It is righteous that the people of Christ should reign in life with Him and through Him. As the justice of God was displayed on Christ and satisfied by His atonement; as He had met the demand, " This do, and thou shalt live,"—He can appeal to the rectitude of God that His people may be put in possession of the reward. And this presupposes on the part of God the necessary demand of an atonement.

SEC. VIII.—THE INCARNATION COMES INTO THE REMEDIAL ECONOMY AS A MEANS TO AN END.

Having noticed the provision to be made for sin, we come next to the great fact of the Incarnation as the foundation of the whole work of atonement. The Lord's advent in flesh is uniformly set forth as a means for the accomplishment of a great result: not as in itself an end. Thus, in the Lord's own teaching, He announces that He came down from heaven for the sake of a

people given to Him (John vi. 39); that He came to save that
which was lost (Matt. xviii. 11); that He came to give His life
for others (Mark x. 45). We may represent the relation between
God and man in this way. Between the INFINITE GOD, possessed
of all holiness and justice, and MAN, a rebel and infected with
sin, there is the widest conceivable remove in a moral point of
view. What can bring them together? Who can terminate
the estrangement? The INCARNATION of the Eternal Son supplies
the answer: this fills up the chasm and paves the way to the
rectification of man's relation. But it is equally necessary to
meet the wants and cravings of the human spirit, which ever
and anon exclaims: What would become of me if my Maker
were not my Redeemer? (Is. liv. 5).

.I purpose to touch on this theme in the briefest way. The
modern " Lives of Jesus," though they cannot be accepted as a
satisfactory exhibition of the Incarnation, because they are too
Humanitarian, have rendered a double service. They have
proved that the Incarnation took place in a historic person, and
in one only; and they have established the fact that Jesus came
not to propound an idea, but to do a work, and to become the
Head of a company finding redemption and life in Him. For it
is not too much to say that wherever thought is fixed on the
Incarnation, as the deep ground of union to God and of reconciliation and life, a renovating influence will be shed both over
doctrine and life.

Here I find it necessary to say at the outset that, in all my
references to the Incarnation, I do not take up the doctrine in
the light in which it is presented in too many of the writings of
the present day. I do not share the view so largely adopted by
Continental divines that the Incarnation would have taken place
though no sin had entered to disturb the harmony of the universe.
On the contrary, that view seems to me to go far to vitiate every
department of truth, because it deduces the Incarnation from the
idea of humanity and not from the exercise of free and sovereign
love. The doctrine of sin supplies the *rationale* and ground of

this great truth. But if the Incarnation is represented as the completion of man's creation, or as the realisation of the idea of man, it seems to me that under high-sounding words we introduce a perilous deviation from the truth. If there still remained an extraordinary intervention to supplement the act of creation, this would introduce the most portentous consequences. Man at first would not have corresponded to his idea, and Christ would become the perfected creation. This may suit the Schleiermacher theology, but it reduces all to natural process, and is often meant to avoid the offence of the cross. The Son of God is no longer the Restorer of the lost, but the Perfecter of the imperfect.[1]

On the contrary, according to the tenor of our Lord's teaching, the Incarnation was CONDITIONED BY SIN, and not necessary except on the supposition of redemption. The expiation of sin, the meritorious obedience to be rendered to the law, the vindication of Divine justice, are the objects contemplated by the stupendous fact of the Incarnation, the Incarnation and the cross being inseparable. The words of Scripture announce an incarnation of redeeming love : not of natural process. If we were to accept the latter view, the inevitable result would be that the atonement, instead of being one principal object of the Incarnation, would be reduced to a subordinate and secondary matter in this great transaction. If the Incarnation must be brought about in the course of history, either from a necessity in God, or to give a realization to the idea of humanity, the historic fact in Jesus

---

[1] This favourite speculation of the modern theology is put by Archbishop Trench in the following plausible way : " In this view, the taking on Himself of our flesh by the Eternal Word was no makeshift to meet a mighty, yet still a particular, emergent need ; a need which, conceding the liberty of man's will, and that it was possible for him to have continued in his first state of obedience, might never have occurred. It was not a mere result and reparation of the Fall, such an act as, except for that, would never have been ; but lay bedded at a far greater depth in the counsels of God for the glory of His Son, and the exaltation of that race formed in His image and His likeness. For against those who regard the Incarnation as an arbitrary, or as merely an historic event, and not an ideal one as well, we may well urge this weighty consideration, that the Son of God did not, in and after His ascension, strip off this human nature again," &c.—*Five Sermons before the University of Cambridge*, 1837.

would be but one peculiar mode of what must have taken place in any case. And what becomes of Divine free love in the provision ?

From this view-point we can easily obviate the objection that God never acts by occasion of anything. It is no disparagement to the Incarnation to regard it as brought about by occasion of sin, though it was by no means *caused* by sin. This greatest work of God is still but a free work or deed, not necessary to the Divine felicity, and therefore on the same footing with creation or any other Divine act toward the universe. But, in point of fact, so far is it from being true that God never acts by occasion of anything, that we have only to survey the history of the Incarnation from the Fall downwards to see that all the circumstances of it—its foreshadowing and prediction, as well as the Lord's actual history—were shaped and moulded by occasion of sin. It remains that we view the Incarnation as ushered in to be a MEANS to an end. And this leads us to survey the great provision or problem from a twofold point of view.

a. The first desideratum was : How shall a guilty creature appear not guilty, and how shall the partition-wall raised by the Divine wrath on the one side and human rebellion on the other be removed ? A provision was to be made that Divine love might have free course to mankind, and that sinners might again become the habitation of their Maker. This was to be effected in such a manner that God might appear more glorified in saving than in condemning us. All the attributes of God were, without exception, to be magnified, that grace to sinners might be displayed without limit (Matt. ix. 13). To educe so much good from so vast a ruin ; to place man, once estranged, in such a sphere that in harmony with the Divine claims and the honour of the law, he shall bask anew in the beams of Divine love, realizing nearer intercourse and more absolute dependence than if he had never fallen—was an end worthy of the Incarnation. The Christian redemption is thus a remedial economy, not a natural process to carry on creation to its completion. Every want was to be met, and a more glorious vessel formed with larger capacities of happiness. The remedial scheme contemplated for man a position of greater nearness than if the Fall had never been (John xvii. 20-23). The doctrine of the Divine image, the deep ground-thought of Christianity, is so fully exhibited that the descriptions of Genesis and Revelation seem to touch each other. By the Incarnation the lost image and dominion are restored.

b. A second desideratum, effected by the Incarnation, was the recapitulating of all under a Head (Eph. i. 10; Col. i. 20). The disunion from God and from each other was the fruit of sin. Every person who has reflected on man's original condition must have come to the conclusion on clear grounds of Scripture (Col. i. 15, 16) that, apart altogether from the Incarnation, humanity, according to the constitution of things, had its standing in the Son of God as its Archetype, Head, and Lord. It may be difficult to assign Adam his place, as the counterpart of the second Adam, while contending for the other side of truth—that humanity stood in the Son. We content ourselves with two things too plain to be questioned: (1) the original constitution of all things IN (ἐν) the Son [1] (Col. i. 15); and then (2) that the race was in such a sense in Adam that we are all that one man (Rom. v. 12). Though we do not fashion into a scheme what Scripture leaves indefinite, yet these two points enter into the original constitution of things; and they are found in a new combination in the second man, the Lord from heaven. This sufficiently proves that man was originally created to be an organic unity in a divine Head. The condition of things into which redeemed men are ushered by the historical Christ implies, inferentially, but surely, that what is restored was once possessed, though mutably, in the creation state.

That the Incarnation is a means to an end, is the conclusion to which we must arrive. But this is not to be so put in our

---

[1] Calvin, though condemning the notion of an Incarnation without a Fall (*Insti.* lib. ii. 12, 4), expresses himself strongly on the necessity of a certain mediatorial relation for man as man: "quamvis ab omni labe integer stetisset homo, humilior tamen erat ejus conditio quum ut *sine mediatore* ab Deum penetraret" (lib. ii. 12, 1).

scheme of thought as if the end must needs be greater than the
means.   The Christian consciousness of the Church turning only
to two things—sin and redemption—will not harmonize with
the speculative notion to which we have referred, but rather
oppose a sure barrier to its spread.[1]

SEC. IX.—DIVINE LOVE PROVIDING THE ATONEMENT; OR THE LOVE
OF GOD IN HARMONY WITH JUSTICE AS THE ONLY CHANNEL
OF LIFE.

" *For God so loved the world, that He gave His only-begotten Son,
that whosoever believeth on Him should not perish, but have
everlasting life.*"—JOHN iii. 16.

To a previous saying on the necessity of the atonement
already noticed, this further testimony is subjoined, in order to
make known more fully to Nicodemus the fact of the atonement
and its source in divine love.   That it forms part of our Lord's
address, and is not the commentary of the evangelist, is obvious
to every one who has remarked the peculiar way in which John
appends his commentary on the Master's words.   This is never
left doubtful (see John vii. 39).   The present testimony is introduced by the grounding particle *for*, which shows a continuation
of the discourse, and gives a reason for the final clause in the
previous verse (ver. 15).

The allusion to the atonement, with which we have specially
to do, is obvious in the phrase, "He gave His Son."   Though
some have explained this as if it were equivalent to being sent,
it rather has the sacrificial sense of being delivered or given up
to death.   Here it corresponds to the "lifting up" in the previous context.   This giving of the Son does not go back to the
divine purpose, nor go down to the individual's experience when
Christ is *given to the believer*, but denotes a giving up to death.
It is properly the giving up in sacrifice, because the presenta-

[1] See note E in Appendix.

tion of the victim formed part of the act of sacrifice. The expression, *He delivered*, or *gave*, is not infrequent as a description of God's act of giving His Son to a sacrificial death; and wherever it occurs, whether as denoting the Father's act in giving the Son (Rom. viii. 32), or the act of the Son in giving Himself (Matt. xx. 28; Gal. i. 4), it is always descriptive of the sacrifice which He offered to God the Father. The mistake as to the import of this phrase is enough to show how much of misunderstanding and debate is often due to an inadequate knowledge of language. It is not unworthy of notice, that some time ago it was made a question whether this phrase was to be understood in the sense of giving into actual possession, or in the sense of giving in the gospel offer. The dispute arose from regarding the phrase as simply intimating a gift, with a bestower and a receiver, apart from the received usage of language in a certain connection. In truth, it has neither the one sense nor the other, when used in connection with the death of Christ. For when God is said "to give His Son," or when the Son is said "to give Himself," the language must be understood in the sacrificial sense. Here, therefore, our Lord has in His eye, not so much His sending or His incarnation, though these are involved, as the sacrifice of Himself, when He was lifted up,[1] and was made a curse for us.

There are a few points here mentioned in connection with the atonement to which it will be necessary to advert.

1. The atonement is here described as emanating from the love of God. These words of Christ plainly show that the biblical doctrine on this point is not duly exhibited, unless love receives a special prominence; and that it would be a misrepresentation against which the biblical divine must protest, if, under the influence of any theory or dogmatic prejudice, love

[1] The sacrificial sense of ἔδωκεν may be proved both by the context and by usage. As to the first, ver. 14, referring to the lifting up of the serpent, is linked to ver. 16 by the logical particle *for*. As to usage, I may refer, *e.g.* to Gal. i. 4; Rom. viii. 33. Hence, Bengel says, *gab an das Kreutz* (see note in German version): so too Calvin, Piscator, De Wette, Hengstenberg.

is not allowed to come to its rights.   If even justice were made
paramount, the balance of truth would be destroyed.   As the
text under our notice alludes to both, or describes love as giving
the only-begotten Son up to a sacrificial death—which is just
equivalent to the satisfaction of divine justice,—it is here proper
to define the two.

Love, then, may be fitly regarded as the communicative
principle of the divine nature, or as the diffusive source of
blessing; and it receives different names, according to the
modification of the relation in which His creatures stand to
Him, or the varied course of action He pursues toward them.
Justice, again, may be defined as the conservating principle
of the divine nature or the self-asserting activity of God,
according to which He maintains the inalienable rights of the
Godhead.   It is just run up to this, that He loves Himself, and
cannot but delight in His own perfections; and hence, in describing it, the Psalmist says, "For the righteous Lord loveth
righteousness" (Ps. xi. 7).   In a just conception of the divine
attributes, none of them can be said to predominate; their equipoise being so perfect that it could not be disturbed without
ruin to the universe.   It cannot be wondered at, that the
opponents of the vicarious satisfaction repudiate this equipoise
of justice and love in the work of redemption.   They call it
"the dualism of the divine attributes,"—and they would resolve
justice into love.   But the one can by no means be subsumed
under the other.   They are as distinct as love to Himself, and
love to mankind, or as giving and retaining.   He gives Himself,
in the exercise of love, to His creatures; but He does not give
up, and He cannot recede from, those rights which belong in-
alienably to Himself as God.   And the same principle is
daily practised by the man of active benevolence made in
the image of God, and acting like God in the communication
of diffusive goodness.   He gives or communicates; but when
he communicates, he retains his own proper rights and pre-
rogatives.

With regard to the love of God, several modern writers,[1] in describing the divine attributes, avoid calling love an attribute at all;—chosing rather to call it a definition of God in His whole procedure toward men, or the united concurrent action of all the attributes. There seems no ground for this. But, on the other hand, the selection of this one perfection by an inspired apostle as the most descriptive name for God, furnishes sufficient ground for giving a central place to it, and for investing it, as it were, with all the other perfections, if we would arrive at the most full and accurate idea that can be formed of God in His relation to His church. Were we to invest love with all the natural and moral attributes, and speak of omnipotent and holy love, wise and omnipresent love, we should not mistake the import of the phrase, GOD IS LOVE (1 John iv. 8). Here the love is viewed as self-originated, self-moving, free and infinite; the text before us, as Luther well describes it, being a little Bible in itself. The extent of the divine love delineated in these words of Jesus, may be surveyed from the three points here indicated—the great Giver, the infinite sacrifice of God's Son, and the unworthy objects.

But it must be further noticed, that when Jesus here sets forth the divine love in connection with the atonement, it is not stated simply to assure us of the divine love; for He shows that it mainly consisted in the sacrificial giving of the Son; and this it is important to apprehend. There is a necessity on God's part, as well as on man's. While the death of Christ, as a costly declaration of divine love, removes the slavish fear and distrust which prompt men to flee from God, it does this only as it meets a necessity on God's part, and provides a vicarious sacrifice for sin. The text exhibits the harmony of justice and love—the demand of justice, and the provision of love.

This it is the more necessary to notice, because it is objected, against any prominence to divine justice, that this is at the expense of divine love. The one, however, by no means

[1] *E.g.* Sartorius, *Lehre von der Liebe.*

excludes the other. If a divine provision is made at all, it could proceed from no other source but love; and the greater the difficulty to be surmounted, and the more inflexible the necessity which insists on a satisfaction to justice, beyond the compass of our own resources, the greater is the display of love. If love is in proportion to the difficulties to be overcome, and if redemption could be effected only at the cost of the humiliation and crucifixion of the Son of God, the love which did not allow itself to be deterred by such a sacrifice was infinite. Then only does love fully come to light; and they who do not ackowledge the necessity of the satisfaction can have no adequate conception of love. Thus the cross displayed the love of God in providing the substitute, and was the highest manifestation of its reality and greatness. If the demand or the necessity for such a fact in the moral government of God resulted from the claims of justice, the source from which it flowed was self-originated love.

2. But another point made prominent in this text is the value of the sacrifice from the dignity of the only-begotten Son. As the Lord in the previous verses designated Himself the Son of Man, that is, by the title of His humiliation, He here describes Himself by a title which calls up before us His divine dignity; and it intimates that such a sacrifice was of infinite value, and sufficient to cancel sin, though infinitely great. The divine nature united to the human, incapable of suffering in itself, gave to the suffering of the Mediator an infinite value. The infinite dignity and worth of His suffering, as the atonement of the Son of God, had a perfectly expiatory efficacy for the redemption of all for whom He gave Himself to death.[1]

The design of this saying is to show that the communication of the divine life is attainable only when love and justice coincide in securing the acceptance of the person by the expiation of the Son. All this is plainly put in as the preliminary to life. As to the clause, "He gave His only-begotten Son," the allusion,

[1] See below on the influence of Christ's Deity.

as we have seen, is to the sacrificial death of Christ; the very idea of which, while it involves the utmost conceivable degree of love, implies that it has the effect of pacifying an offended God. The thought to which all these terms point is, that God cannot forego His inalienable rights when He has been wronged, but necessarily punishes, as a satisfaction to Himself; for He cannot deny Himself. This thought is capable of solving several difficulties.

a. The plain meaning of this clause is repugnant to the notion, too widely current in our time, that pure love, without any tincture of wrath, is the sole principle of the divine action toward man; that we are not to speak of punishment borne, or of vicarious obedience rendered; that, in a word, it is not God's relation that is to be changed, but man's. The clause under consideration teaches the opposite, and shows us that the love of God peculiarly appears in this, that He provides the very atonement which puts Him on a new relation to those whose sins had incurred His anger. The two principles, love to the race, and love to Himself, are so far from being incompatible, that they can be placed together in the atoning work of Christ. Punitive justice, which is just regard for His perfections, called for the penalty: love for our race provided the substitute to bear it. What is there of incompatibility in these two?

b. But, it may be further asked, as the atonement is the effect of the divine love according to this testimony, how is it also the cause of the divine favour? Does not love so great imply that He is already reconciled? Here we must distinguish between the moving cause and the meritorious cause. If we look at the prime source of the atoning work, then the incarnation and death of Jesus must be regarded as the fruit of love, and not as its cause. But if we look at our actual acceptance, or the enjoyment of divine favour, and the new relation on which God stands to the redeemed, the atonement is as much its cause as the counterpart Fall was the cause of divine wrath.

c. It may be urged yet further, that God does not hate mankind. But here, again, we must distinguish. It is the sin He hates and punishes: He loves the creature so far as it is His workmanship; but He cannot impart the effects and visitations of His love, while the hindrances caused by sin are unremoved. If men will continue to assert that God, without the intervention of any reparation or atonement, can take them into favour, and that He actually does so in the exercise of pure love, they assert what cannot be deduced from the divine perfections, which are ever in full equipoise. They assert, moreover, what is contradicted by all the divine actions, in sending His Son, and "in giving" Him that we should not perish.

The final clause, introduced by the particle of design, ($ἵνα$), intimates that the channel of divine life is opened only when the divine rights have been secured. It is the same clause which we find in the previous verse, but in a new connection. In the former verse it was placed in relation to the indispensable necessity of the atonement; in the present, it is put in connection with the equipoise or adjustment between love and justice in rectifying men's relation to God; and this clause indicates that the eternal life flows out of it. It is the more necessary to put this matter in the proper light, because all the parts of modern theology are so disjointed, and so much out of their due setting in respect to the whole doctrine of the communication of the divine life.

Our Lord and His apostles commonly adduce the redemption or the remission of sins as the immediate end of the death of Christ. But then the ulterior design of that new and adjusted relationship is to secure a further end,—the communication of divine life. Thus the removal of the guilt of sin opens the way for the impartation of the eternal life, as a further end; and yet it is in causal connection with the death of Christ, through the acceptance of the person. The spiritual life is that to which every man has a right who enjoys the remission of sins; but the immediate link is the acceptance of the person, or the remission of sins, which is in order before the communication of the divine life or the sanctification of the nature.

It must be kept in view, then, that the design of Christ, in offering Himself a sacrifice, was to free us from the power of sin itself. But it is also true that this end is reached only through the acceptance of the person as the immediate fruit of the atonement, and by means of the Spirit of life, for which the death of Christ paved the way. But neither the present, nor any similar passage, represents the spiritual life as the direct and immediate end of the death of Christ. To that a man can possess no right unless the guilt of sin upon the person has been removed. The person is accepted, and then the nature is renewed.

To deduce from this passage and from others similar, as many do, that life is first in order; and that the acceptance of the man and the remission of his sins do not immediately flow from the redemption-work of Christ, but immediately from the possession of life, is to pervert the exposition of language. The final particle used in such phrases is cogent. The argumentation from the tenor of the Old Covenant, " do" and " live," taken up and enforced by the apostles as the competent interpreters of the Redeemer's words (Rom. v. 17), is conclusive. The opposite opinion, too common and too much in vogue, turns all upside down. These modern writers will not have a reconciliation *through* Christ, but *in Him*, that is a reconciliation of a merely mystic nature. They will have it, that God cannot forgive sin but in a way which is in process of effecting its removal. And hence, if the latter has precedence, they argue a previous satisfaction or atonement is superfluous—nay, impossible. But this testimony puts the relation between the atonement and the life quite otherwise.[1]

SEC. X.—SINGLE PHRASES DESCRIPTIVE OF THE UNIQUE POSITION
OF JESUS, OR HIS STANDING BETWEEN GOD AND MAN.

There are phrases and titles used in regard to Himself which argue that He was conscious of a quite unique relation to the

[1] See note C in the Appendix.

world, or, more strictly, to a flock or people whom He acknowledges as His. Of these expressions we shall adduce a few.
The terms commonly used in the doctrinal discussion of the
atonement, and drawn from Bible phraseology, such as SURETY,
MEDIATOR, HIGH PRIEST, ADVOCATE—all representing Him as
our substitute, who appears in the presence of God for us, and
conducts our cause,—are not indeed found in the Lord's own
words descriptive of Himself. But, beyond question, the thing
is there; and He acts as fully conscious that, except through
Himself, as Mediator, God could have no intercourse with man,
nor man with God. He understands and consults the best
interests of His people in every respect: He took flesh, and
knows the infirmities of human nature by personal experience,
that He may sympathize with their condition, and compassion-
ately conduct their concerns: He was lawfully called and appointed to this function. And not only so: the sacrificial
language, which we find Him so frequently using, implies a
Priest, though he does not expressly appropriate the term.

These titles, both numerous and various, imply that He had
a relation to mankind which is unique; that He stood between
God and man; that He was not an individual unit of the race,
as all the negative theology represents Him; but acting in a
representative capacity for it. He assumes a position that no
one but Himself could dare to occupy. Thus, when He calls
Himself THE WAY, in the saying, "I am the Way, the Truth,
and the Life" (John xiv. 6), He means that He is the exclusive
Way; not only paving the way for others, but constituting, in
His own person and work, the only way by which any could
have access to God. That this is the meaning is evident from
the subjoined words, "No man cometh unto the Father but by
Me." Could Christ affirm this of Himself, if He were nothing
more than a teacher, an example, or a merely human founder of a
new religion? Certainly not. It could not be maintained that
there never was any other teacher, or that Moses, David, and
the prophets were in no wise either commissioned or fitted to

point out the way of acceptable worship. Neither could the words hold, if they were interpreted of Jesus as an example or as the founder of a new religion. There are other examples, though by no means so perfect as He; and were He only, like Moses, the instrument or founder of a new religion, men might accept the religion, and without much injury forget the founder. But the Lord says that He cannot be omitted, forgotten, or superseded, and that from first to last no man approaches God but BY HIM. This shows Him to be a Mediator, a High Priest, or introducer on the ground of His person and work, and cannot be affirmed of any prophet or apostle that ever trod the earth.

He on the one hand contrasts Himself with all other men; while on the other He links Himself to the lost and condemned, as their Physician and Deliverer (Matt. ix. 12; Luke xix. 10). And to convey the idea of His unique relation to mankind, He declares, in reference to all who set up rival claims: "All who ever came before Me were thieves and robbers" (John x. 8). He stood where no one but Adam ever stood, acting as one for many; offering a ransom as one for many (Matt. xx. 28); shedding His blood as one for many (Matt. xxvi. 28).

The title of the BRIDEGROOM, which the Baptist ascribed to Jesus, and which the Lord also appropriated to Himself (John iii. 29; Matt. ix. 15), is especially noteworthy, as it exhibits, with definite clearness, the relation which he occupies to the Church, considered as a collective body, as well as to the several individuals who compose it. He is designated the Bridegroom who has the bride, as contrasted with all mere ministers as but ministering to her (John iii. 29); and the designation is one which brings out the tender love of Christ to the Church, as exhibited not only in His whole relation and course of action towards her, but, above all, in the fact that He gave Himself for her; or, in other words, offered Himself sacrificially, that he might put her in this relation to Himself, and array her with all the attractive graces of the Spirit. Michaelis thinks himself warranted to maintain, from a text in Leviticus

(xxi. 4), that the high-priest was called the bridegroom of his people. Were this fully established, we should certainly see a reason why the sacred writers make such frequent use of the figure. But it is not absolutely certain.

We nowhere find, except in the Epistle to the Hebrews, the term priest explicitly applied to our Lord. But that circumstance by no means forecloses the inquiry, whether there may not occur, in the course of our Lord's instructions, titles of similar import, or declarations from His lips, where the idea of the priest and of the priestly sacrifice, though not named in express terms, must be held to lie at the foundation of the thought. And that we do find such sayings as unmistakeably imply the one High Priest between God and man is certain. Thus, when He announces that He came to give His soul or life for many, we cannot fail to notice, whether we fix our attention upon the word LIFE or upon the sacrificial phrase TO GIVE, that He indirectly announces Himself as our High Priest (Matt. xx. 28). The same allusion to a priestly function comes out in connection with the saying that the flesh or sacrifice, which was to be eaten by His followers, for the enjoyment of spiritual life, was to be "given" by Himself, or, in other words, was to be offered for the life of the world (John vi. 51). This priestly oblation, in connection with Himself, and in which He was to be at once the Priest and the Victim, is nowhere more distinctly stated than in the words, "For their sakes I sanctify Myself" (John xvii. 19). I only at present notice these passages as testimonies, explicit enough, though indirect, to His priestly function. They will be considered separately in the sequel.

All the phrases used by Him disclose a full consciousness of His peculiar and unique relation. Thus He represents Himself as standing over against the world, and mediating between God and the world; in the family as one of it, and yet able, representatively, to act for it. He is called the "Saviour of the World"—a title which the Samaritans must have learned from Himself (John iv. 42); the Light of the World (viii. 12); the

Resurrection and the Life (John xi. 25); who came down from heaven with a charge to lose none that the Father had given Him (John vi. 39). And His words indicate that He stood in a representative relation even to the saints who had trod the earth before Him—as appears from His discussion with the Jews as to Abraham's relation to Him (John viii. 53). To the question, whether He was greater than Abraham, their common father, He replied, that the patriarch in two ways rejoiced in Him—(1) in the far past anticipating His day; and (2) in Paradise, when it came. He thus in effect declared that there was no other name given under heaven among men, whether they lived before His day or after it, by which they could be saved; and that there was salvation in no other. This fact proves that His mediatorial work was retrospective as well as prospective, and therefore, that it must be something else than a mere example, however influential, as the latter can only operate prospectively, or after the event, not conversely. He showed, in a word, by many titles and expressions, that He stood in the position of a MEDIATOR BETWEEN God and man, and that if men did not believe in Him they should perish in their sins (John viii. 24). But He abstains, for obvious reasons, from appropriating the title most of all familiar to the Jews,—that of MESSIAH. He used it only once among the simple and docile Samaritans (John iv. 26). The Jews had perverted its meaning; and the use of it among them would not have conveyed the meaning He intended. But not only so : it seems that He could not have used it except at the risk of civil confusion and political complications, from which He would keep His cause clear.

SEC. XI.—SAYINGS OF JESUS REFERRING TO A SENDING BY THE FATHER.

There are few expressions more frequent in the mouth of Jesus than those which refer to His being sent. We find it used by our Lord in connection with all the three offices with which He was invested (John xii. 49 ; Luke iv. 18). But we limit our inquiry, according to the plan prescribed to ourselves, to the sayings which have a reference to His priestly sacrifice, or to His work of atonement; and, considered in this light, it was meant to represent God in the light of the Supreme Director and sole Fountain of the redemption-work. To this view of the sending we shall limit our attention ; and it will be found that, by the use of this phrase, the Lord uniformly intimates that He did not assume or arrogate to Himself the dignity or office of being the Redeemer of sinful men, but that He was appointed to it, or ordained by God to it.

To show what emphasis the Lord laid on this sending, He says, " He that sent Me is true " (John vii. 28),—an epithet which, as the Greek word intimates ($\dot{a}\lambda\eta\theta\iota\nu\dot{o}s$ $\dot{o}$ $\pi\dot{\epsilon}\mu\psi as$ $\mu\epsilon$), does not mean *true* as contrasted with false, but *true* as comprehending everything that constitutes sending in the highest sense of the word, or as exhibiting the highest ideal of a sender. It is noteworthy, too, that the title, " The angel of the Lord," literally THE SENT ONE OF JEHOVAH, is just the Old Testament synonym for this expression. And this phrase, in Christ's mouth, will thus intimate, " I am the Angel of His presence, who appeared to the patriarchs, and who spoke to Moses at the bush ;" who was the Director and Guide of Israel's wanderings, the centre of the Old Testament economy, and now made flesh to usher in the new covenant, and the new order of things."

We do not in this place consider the sending of Christ in connection with the thought that it involves the divine dignity of His person, and thus giving infinite value and efficacy to His whole work of atonement. That latter point is noticed in its proper place. We limit our attention at present to the sending, as evincing that THE REDEMPTION IS OF GOD, and the effect of free, sovereign, and boundless love.

1. If we put together a few of the expressions used by Christ upon this topic, we shall find that He, first of all, leads us, by means of this phraseology, to the counsel of peace, or compact

between the Father and the Son for man's redemption. Thus He says: "*Say ye of Him whom the Father hath sanctified and sent into the world, Thou blasphemest; because I said, I am the Son of God?*" (John x. 36). This is quite of the same import with the declaration of Peter, that He was *foreordained* before the foundation of the world. It is plainly taught there that Christ was appointed by God from eternity to be the Redeemer, or that He was foreordained, and furnished with all that was required for His task. By this phrase He would have men feel that the atonement emanates from God; that it springs from self-moving love; and that He arrogated nothing to Himself when He brought it in. For, on the one hand, it could not have been extorted from God, but must have freely emanated from Him if it was brought in at all; and, on the other hand, it could not have been procured by any finite intelligence. This realization of His sending, to which our Lord so often gives expression, was descriptive of His habitual consciousness; and the phrase implies, that because men were involved in helpless impotence, a divine purpose was formed to deliver them from ruin and condemnation; and that, in the execution of the plan which had this end in view, the Father held in His hand the rights of Godhead, and sent His Son, in the capacity of a voluntary servant, to perform that work of suffering obedience which was necessary for man's ransom. To the same purpose are all those passages in the apostolic Epistles in which the atonement is immediately referred to God, and represented as emanating from Him, or as an arrangement appointed and ordained by Him, for the accomplishment of which the Son was sent as the only Mediator.

2. When we follow the successive steps of this sending—and it is important to do so, according to the Lord's description,—we find Him, first, alluding to a charge, commission, or obligation, laid upon Him, and which it was incumbent on the surety to discharge: "*I came down from heaven not to do My own will, but the will of Him that sent Me*" (John vi. 38). This commission, as the context proves, was of a very extensive nature,

comprehending the end as well as the means, the atonement
and its application to all who were given to Him.   As to the
significance of this sending, it is not quite identical with the
incarnation, but differs from it as former and latter; for God
sent Him to be born (John iii. 17); while others can only be
described as born and sent.   According to biblical phraseology,
we cannot say that He first received His mission after He was
born, and then addressed Himself to its duties; for God sent
His Son—that is, one who already was a person, and who was
the Son; His mission being founded upon His eternal generation.   And though the designation of "the Sent One" was
given to Him anterior to the incarnation—for all the appear-
ances of the Angel of the Lord, or the Angel of His presence,
were only preludes to His coming in the flesh,—the title was
never used irrespective of that atoning work which was to be
brought in by Him in the fulness of time.   Not only so: this
sending of the Son implies a divine counsel or covenant and a
voluntary condescension, but no real inequality between the
sender and the sent.   His mission differs from that of His
apostles in this, that they were sent out as servants, He as an
equal,—an ambassador, indeed, but yet with full equality.   Nor
does it involve local separation from the Father; for He was
STILL IN THE FATHER'S BOSOM, while He trod this world (John
i. 18).   And the official subordination was not of such a kind
as to carry with it a depotentiation in any of His inalienable
divine perfections, but was only a means to an end,—though an
end worthy of such stupendous means.

   3. When we put together some of the many expressions
which fell from Christ's lips upon this topic, in the order of
natural sequence, we find it next said: "*God sent not His Son
into the world to condemn the world, but that the world through
Him might be saved*" (John iii. 17).   This statement, taken in
connection with the allusion in the former verse to the *giving*
of His Son as a propitiation for sin—that is, in the sacrificial
acceptation, as the phrase implies,—intimates that He was *sent*

to be the atonement, and that by this means men are saved; for the sending was the cause of that effect. These two verses mutually explain each other; for the sending comprehended in it, as its scope or intended object, the sacrificial death. And these two express, when viewed together, the plan or commission given, and the end or purpose contemplated,—the giving of His Son for our salvation; which, as we have already seen, can only be regarded as sacrificial language.

4. When we advance in the successive steps of this mission, we next find the Lord Jesus declaring that in no part of His redemption-work was He left alone (John viii. 29): "*And He that sent Me is with Me: the Father hath not left Me alone; for I do always those things that please Him.*" This remarkable testimony, from Christ's own consciousness, intimates that He was continuously upheld as He went from step to step of His high work; and that the constant assistance, aid, or divine solace imparted to Him stood in an ineffable connection with His sinless obedience, and, in fact, was a constantly renewed reward for service done. We here get a glimpse into the heart of Christ as the Mediator, and into the perpetual intercourse between Him and the Father, such as we get nowhere else. He was at every step anew rewarded.

Thus the " sending " intimates that the work of propitiation for our sins was all of God, from first to last. The sanctification or call of such a person for the purpose of being sent into the world (John x. 36); the commandment or obligation imposed upon Him, and which fidelity required Him to fulfil (John vi. 39); the divine presence imparted to Him for the full discharge of His mediatorial work, lest He should fail or be discouraged (John viii. 29; Matt. xii. 18); the repeated recognition of His obedience at different stages,—at His baptism, when His private life lay behind Him,—on the mount of the Transfiguration, when His public ministry was drawing to its close, and when He must stedfastly set His face to go forward to a cursed death,—and in Jerusalem, whither He had come up to die

(Matt. iii. 17, xvii. 5; John xii. 28)—not to mention its final
acceptance and endless reward,—all elucidate the significance of
this sending or mission, the thought of which was never absent
from Christ's mind. And what was in His thoughts came often
to His lips, as an ever present reality.

The great truth intimated by all these phrases is, that the
redemption is of God; that the atonement to which the saints
looked forward who were saved before His advent, and to which
all look back who are saved since, was effected according to the
direction or will of Him from whom the world had revolted;
that the sender was the Father personally considered; and that
the grand object of the sending was to atone for sin. The
sending is thus an expression of authority, and a manifestation
of every divine attribute working together to a definite object.
But it is specially an exhibition of *unmerited love or grace*. The
atonement emanated from sovereign grace, and was an expression of the boundless and incomprehensible love of God's heart
to sinful men; and we may affirm, in reference to this sending,
that there was a twofold object—a proximate and an ultimate,
—first of all to atone; and then, by atoning, to secure the end
that of all whom the Father had given Him He should lose none
(John vi. 39).

5. But the Lord refers also to the reward awaiting Him after
having finished the work given Him to do, when He says, "*I
go to Him that sent Me*" (John vii. 33). This atoning work
received its meed of reward in a twofold sense, which, indeed,
is one: first, in the personal glory on which He entered; and
next, as He is the forerunner, in that representative capacity
which He occupied for the good of others. And it is in this
sense that certain expressions are to be explained, which would
otherwise be far from obvious; and He had the reward always
in view.

It may not be inappropriate, in this connection, to give a
brief elucidation of a passage of considerable difficulty, and
which has received very various expositions. I refer to John

vi. 57: "*As the living Father hath sent Me, and I live by the Father* [or, better, *because of the Father*], *so he that eateth Me, even he shall live by Me* [or, better, *on My account, because of Me*]." An examination of all the Protestant versions, as well as of the patristic commentators, will show the strange perplexity into which they have all been thrown by this language. The Greek fathers refer the first clauses to the eternal Sonship, and to the divine life proper to the Son, by eternal generation. They thus make these words parallel to John v. 26, which undoubtedly has that sense. The Protestant versions, and commentators generally, can make nothing of it, except by altering the force of the Greek preposition,[1] which, when construed with the accusative, means, and can only mean, *because of, on account of*. But the words will not be found of difficult exposition if we only attend to one point, which has always been missed— the *priority* of this sending to the life here mentioned. The life ascribed to the Lord Jesus in this passage is not that which preceded His being sent,—not that divine life, therefore, which belonged to Him as the eternal Son, but that life which followed His being sent; or, in other words, which is the reward allotted to Him on the consummation of His work. The allusion is not to the divine life prior to His mission, but to the premial life which followed it, and which comes out in the passage, "This do, and thou shalt live." And all the mistakes seem to have been owing to not observing the priority of the sending to the life here referred to, which is certainly taken for granted in our Lord's words. There is thus no occasion, as there can certainly be no authority, for altering the force of a preposition to solve a difficulty. The allusion is to the mediatorial reward. Life

---

[1] διὰ τὸν πατέρα. The Greek commentators explain it, for the most part, διὰ τὸ γεννηθῆναι ἐκ ζῶντος πατρός. The interpreters since the Reformation, following Beza, have expounded διὰ here construed with the accusative, in the same way as they would have done had it been construed with the genitive. Beza appeals to Aristophanes' *Plutus*, ver. 470. Lücke quotes the Greek scholiast on it, to the effect that sometimes διὰ with the accusative has the same force as it has with the genitive. We have given the only tenable explanation.

is the reward of the sending, or, in other words, of the work accomplished; and the present tense, *I live,* is just equal and similar to the present tense in "I go to the Father." The verse intimates that He lives, (1) as the reward of His accomplished mission; and (2) lives, too, as the source of life to others, who live only on His account. A similar use of the expression SENT, that is, as involving the completion of the redemption-work, will be found in other passages in our Lord's discourses (see John vi. 44), and also in the Epistle of John (1 John iv. 9).

The phrases, however, referring to the sending of Christ are too numerous to be all noticed in detail; and they are interwoven with the texture of Christ's teaching, so that we can refer to them only in general. They all imply, that in the matter of human redemption, two acting parties are presented to our minds; that the Father deputed, commissioned, or sent the only-begotten Son; and that the Son, in the exercise of a boundless love, which appears at all points, came to give His life a ransom for many.

6. When Jesus refers to the acceptance of His mission by the world, He shows that full confidence in the fact of His sending by His Father is of absolute necessity to a due reception of Him and of His salvation: "*He that receiveth Me, receiveth Him that sent Me*" (Matt. x. 40). If this mission is not credited by those to whom the testimony comes, then they must conclude that He came unauthorized, and that the work on which He entered was planned and executed at His own discretion. He would thus be no Redeemer, called and competent to atone for men; for God, in whose hand they are as prisoners, can alone discharge them, as the competent authority, and only in a way glorifying to His perfections or name. Hence the importance of recognising this mission. It is the badge of true discipleship; for they who believe on Him, believe on Him that sent Him (John v. 24). And the object aimed at by the organization, love, and unity of the Christian Church—at least one great object outwardly—is, as Christ declares, "that the world may believe that Thou hast SENT Me" (John xvii. 21).

SEC. XII.—SAYINGS OF CHRIST WHICH ASSUME THAT HE IS THE
SECOND ADAM, AND ACTING ACCORDING TO A COVENANT WITH
THE FATHER IN THIS ATONING WORK.

In adducing some of those sayings of Jesus which bring out
the idea of a federal transaction in connection with the atonement, I shall limit my attention to those which bear more or
less directly on the vicarious sacrifice. The deity of Christ and
His personal relation to the Father are of course presupposed
in any allusion to the covenant. And here we at once perceive
the persons of the Godhead are found acting according to the
relation of natural order. A brief allusion to this great paction
or counsel of peace will enable us to perceive with greater clearness the sphere in which the surety had to walk.

That there is such an agreement between the Father who
gave a commission involving duty, promises, rewards, and the
Son considered as a public person, who appeared as a representative acting in the name of His people, is put beyond all doubt;
for it is referred to in various testimonies by Christ Himself.
The life of Christ, it is true, presents to us only the phenomenal
part of the mediatorial scheme, as it required certain words to
be spoken, or actions to be done. But all this emanates from a
covenant which proceeds on the ground that a representative
work was absolutely necessary, as man could be saved on no
other principle than on that which is found in connection with
his fall. It takes for granted, too, the donation of a people in
whose name He acted (John vi. 37). Jesus, knowing that He
came from God and went to God, uses various words which show
a commission and announce the second man.

Though the similarity between the first and second Adam
is specially developed by the apostles in the fuller outline of
doctrine which they were appointed to give, our Lord's sayings
constantly assume an express counterpart or analogy between
the first and second man. He appeals to Himself as " the Son

of Man," a title which, as we shall afterwards show, brings out the idea of the second man with a peculiar modification. He announces that He was come that His people might have life, and that they might have it more abundantly (John x. 10); which refers most naturally to that more abundant fulness of divine life which was brought in by the second man, as contrasted with the forfeiture sustained by the first (Rom. v. 17).

To this correspondence or counterpart relation between the first and second Adam it is the more necessary to refer, because almost all the difficulties and objections urged against the atonement at the present time proceed upon incorrect notions of the primeval constitution given to the human race in a single man, or from a denial of that constitution altogether. The doctrine of the atonement cannot be understood at all, except on the principle that the same constitution is laid at the basis of that economy by which we are saved, as lay at the basis of that economy by which we fell. That constitution was to the effect that one man was regarded as the race, and that the race is still the one,—a constitution differing from that which was given to angels, who stood each for himself, or fell each for himself. This seems, clearly enough, deducible from the fact that only a part fell. It does not fall to man to object to such a constitution given to mankind, when it pleased a sovereign God to appoint it for reasons, the wisdom and goodness of which we may not question. Nor does it become us too curiously to inquire into those reasons: God's will is reason enough; and we only incur the risk of darkening counsel by words without kowledge, when we venture on a field beyond our scrutiny.

The objection of self-righteous men against the counterpart provision of the atonement, has generally proceeded from a disposition to challenge the justice or the goodness of that constitution which it has pleased a sovereign God to establish. Of course the world could be redeemed only on the same principle. When men, therefore, argue that if their own virtue cannot save them, they cannot be benefited by the work of another, however excellent, they only misunderstand, or fail to take into account, that peculiar constitution under which the Creator saw meet to place the race. The salvation of many by the righteousness or atonement of Christ as the transaction of one for many, is not out of keeping with the primeval constitution, according to which the race stood related to Adam. The right relation of the man, as such, or of the person, is only in a public representative; and so long as the person is condemned, of what avail are all his actions? So fully are all the individuals represented by that one man, that we may say there have been but two persons in the world, and but two great facts in human history.

They who attach themselves to the new theology of this century ignore this constitution given to the race; or if they nominally acknowledge a representative system, it is of such a character as makes it refer to the NATURE exclusively, not to the PERSON. It comes to be a mere individualism, as if the human race were but a sand-heap or granulated mass, without any public, corporate, or organic unity; and Christ is the mere Lifegiver by means of a mystic union to Himself, without any deed of meritorious obedience as the ground or foundation upon which premially God bestows that life. They take no account of the person as such, nor of the man in his relative standing, no account in fact of a moral governor, of law, of guilt, of acceptance through obedience. All that Paul sets forth in the fifth chapter of Romans is exhibited in the Lord's own sayings, with this exception, that He does not set over against each other, by the same formal comparison, the disobedience of Adam and the surety obedience which He Himself was bringing in. He gives the one side of the parallel, and he leaves us to supplement it, as the apostle has done by the running analogy or counterpart of the other. That we receive the justification of life by Christ, is not once, nor obscurely stated; and that this is of course to be contrasted with being made sinners by the first man, is readily inferred. By the Son of Man we have the ransom

(Matt. xx. 28), the remission (Matt. xxvi. 28), and life (John vi. 51); and this leaves us to infer, as all Scripture teaches, that we have the opposite by Adam.

The same thing appears from the peculiar engagement or covenant between the three persons of the Godhead, by which one person demands the satisfaction, the second renders it, and the third applies it. According to this counsel they have each a different part to act, and a different relation to the sinner. There was a covenant between the Father and the Son in behalf of a peculiar class, who are described as given to Christ, or committed to Him, with a special charge or command that none of them should be lost. Thus He says: " This is the *will of Him* that sent Me, that *of all that He hath given Me I should lose nothing*, but should raise it up again at the last day" (John vi. 39). That language implies, beyond all doubt, a commission on certain conditions, whatever name may be employed to describe it—covenant, treaty, or compact,—the Father on the one side prescribing the duty, and promising the help which should be required; the Son, on the other side, engaging His heart to appear before God in the capacity of a surety. The Gospel of John is so replete with testimonies to this effect on the part of Christ, that unless we take to our aid the elucidation supplied by the idea of a covenant, there are many passages where we can scarcely apprehend the meaning. The whole of His media- torial commission on the behalf of a multitude given to Him, and whom He is charged to keep (John vi. 39); His subjection mediatorially to His Father, who is from this one circumstance called greater than He (John xiv. 29); His declaration that He acted from the Father and for His glory (John vii. 16-18); His explanation of the engagement which bound Him to bring in others who were not of the Jewish fold (John x. 16); and, in a word, His whole intercessory prayer (John xvii.),—proceed so much on the idea of a covenant, and of a people given to Him on certain terms, that we cannot understand the language on any other supposition. And it is evident enough, from reasons drawn alike from God's moral government and from man's inability, that but for such a treaty or agreement on man's behalf, a remedial economy would have been impossible ; for no covenant between God and sinners could have been directly formed. Two parties are plainly brought before us in all these testimonies, —one party imposing conditions, and a second undertaking to comply with certain terms on behalf of a third party. That such a treaty exists, then, in the counsels of the Godhead, cannot be questioned by any one who will do justice to these words of Jesus. And whatever preconceived opinions may be entertained as to what is fitting or not fitting in the Godhead must be overruled, when the word of God, as a sentence in a court of last resort, has actually pronounced upon the point. We must refer to this covenant as His rule of action.

That covenant rested on this basis, that as God at first had created man under a representative constitution, or under a system which was that of one for many, so the surety must come on a footing precisely similar, nay, enter into the very provisions of that first arrangement (Rom. v. 10). Thus Christ and His people stand in the eye of law as one single person. There were, properly speaking, but two persons in the world—Adam and Christ,—in whom the whole seed, belonging severally to these two, must be considered as contained. On the principle just laid down, that Christ and His seed are viewed as one person, it is plain that the salvation of His people was virtually to be wrought out in the obedience and death of the Son of God. The covenant rested on this basis, that the Son of God, condescending to be Son of man, should enter into our covenant of works, and that all who were given to Him should enter into the federal reward. That this may be rendered more clear, it will be necessary to sketch with all possible succinctness the various conditions prescribed to Him.

1. It was necessary, according to that eternal paction, that the Son should take a body as an indispensable preliminary to His subsequent work of obedience,—a humanity that should be

sinless to stand for the sinful, holy to stand for the unholy, and
which could thus hide the stain of our original sin, as well as
lay a foundation for all the work on which He was to enter.
And the Father, who in every part of this great transaction
must be viewed as at once the lawgiver and fountain of the
covenant, prepared for Him a body (Ps. xl. 6-8).

2. The next thing prescribed according to the covenant was
the peculiar work marked out for the righteous servant. He
must be put under the law, and under that law as broken.
Some would make it appear that He was not necessarily made
under the law in the proper sense. But if it was to be a true
obedience on His side, and a true substitution or vicarious
action for others, He must stand under our covenant—that
is, be made under the law of works, both as to precept and
penalty.

3. I pass from the prescription of duty to the promises of
assistance in His work, and promises of reward, when the work
was completed, for Himself, and for all whom the Father gave
Him.   These are numerous; comprehending, among others that
might be named, the promise of unction by the Spirit (Isa.
lxi. 1), of a seed to serve Him (Isa. liii. 10), and of complete
and final victory (Isa. xlii. 1-4).

This covenant on which we have but glanced, exhibiting the
whole economy as springing from the Father's gracious will,
and as a scheme of grace, and nothing but grace, combines in
a vivid way all the doctrines of special saving grace. It is
peculiarly valuable as affording a bird's-eye view of the whole
economy from its commencement to its final consummation.
It is the unrolling of the map of God's procedure; and in
putting together plan and execution, fact and theory, as we
shall proceed to do, we obtain a juster view of the grace which
projected the whole. It is of advantage to study in connection
the scheme and the accomplishment; and when the vast pano-
rama passes in review, we gain in comprehensiveness of view
by the sublime and affecting spectacle in reference to all the

work of Christ, and especially in reference to the great work of atonement.

But the covenant, while glorifying all the persons of the Godhead and all the divine attributes, is peculiarly useful as exhibiting the humanity of Christ in connection with a work given Him to do. The following sections will exhibit Him filling up this plan or scheme as replenished with the Spirit, and as the perfect representative of what humanity should be. Before the Redeemer's MERITS can be fully seen, they must be read off from the covenant, and be viewed in connection with it; nay, it may be doubted whether there could be MERIT in the proper acceptation of the term, except on the ground of a compact or covenant for the performance of a given work.

This brief outline of the covenant will bring us to the consideration of the other postulates of the atonement.[1]

SEC. XIII.—THE INFLUENCE OF CHRIST'S DEITY IN THE MATTER OF THE ATONEMENT.

So close is the connection between the doctrine of the atonement and that of Christ's deity, that they are always found, as history shows, to be either received together or denied together. The one is necessary to the other; and hence the true Church has always in every age confessed to both. The Lord connects the two as the two "heavenly things," on which He lays the greatest stress in His interview with Nicodemus (John iii. 13, 14).

It is the person of Christ, or Himself as a divine person, in the performance of a work given Him to do—and not His teaching, merely, or the republication of lost truth—that constitutes the ransom. But one equal to the task of bringing a satisfaction or atonement for millions must needs possess a divine dignity. A mere man could as little redeem the world as he could create

[1] See note D in Appendix.

the world: the Restorer of man must be the Maker of man.   It
does not fall to our present task to refer at large to the proof
of Christ's deity; for our doctrine presupposes the reality of the
incarnation,—that miracle of miracles, and the grand fact of all
history.   Still less does it lie within our plan to notice the
recent negative speculations which look askance on the whole
miracle of Christ's life on earth.   While they would explode a
particular incarnation as the unique fact of history, in order to
assert a general one, or an incarnation of the race, as they delight to phrase it, their deep error utterly mistakes the vast ruin
of mankind.   And it assumes, too, the possibility of access to
God, and of reunion to Him, without a mediator.

Our Lord, for obvious reasons, lays great stress on His coming into the world, or His coming in the flesh to do a work
which should at once rectify men's relation and bring life (John
v. 24).   His entire teaching proceeds on the supposition that
the primeval harmony between love and holiness in promoting
man's good, which was disturbed by sin, is restored only by
His incarnation and death; not by the incarnation alone—
for then the grain of wheat would have continued to abide
alone,—but by His incarnation and death.   Not to speak of
rationalism, which always assumes that God is willing, without
any atoning intervention, to receive back the lost son to favour,
the more mystic theories of Christ's work, which lay all the
stress upon the fellowship in Christ's life, and the commencement of a new humanity, are not greatly different.   They
presuppose no work for which the incarnation is absolutely
necessary, and which could not as well be done without it.
They seem to say that the incarnation or the person of the God-
man is itself the atonement; and yet it soon appears that for
the production of the new humanity they plead for, the incarnation is superfluous.   That which places the Church upon Bible
Christianity, and severs her from every phase of rationalism, is
the firm belief that the atonement was the work of the incarnate
Son, and that it is a provision offered by the divine love for the

satisfaction of the inflexible claims of the divine holiness and justice.

The point to be noticed here is the influence of Christ's deity in the matter of the atonement. It may seem at first sight that our Lord has said extremely little on the subject of His deity, considered in this light. But the testimonies which touch it are not few when they are all put together; and He has given the germ of all the subsequent statements made by the apostles. If we examine the history of Christ's life, as written by inspired men, we find that the two sides of His person are brought out together in a quite peculiar way; and that the scenes which represent Him in His deep abasement always contain, if we only look for them, discoveries or out-beamings of the Godhead dwelling in Him bodily. The whole person, as divine and human, is in some way brought out,—a peculiarity of the biblical narrative, which is wholly lost in human biographies of Christ. They cannot approach it.

Any system of doctrine looking with an unfavourable eye on Christ's deity or His divine Sonship cannot have a consistent theory of the atonement, as a few words will suffice to show. This will appear whether we have respect to the Arian, the Sabellian, or the Nestorian view of Christ's person.

(1.) The Arian scheme destroys all proper conceptions of His satisfaction. If Jesus were not a divine person and infinitely exalted above all law, He could not act for others. He could not put on a lower nature for the purpose of being made under the law; and there could be nothing of merit in His work for others. Supposing any scheme of attempted satisfaction for others, the mediation of a finite person, it is obvious, could only be of limited value, and could give no peace to a conscience awakened by a sense of sin. With what confidence could we depend on another if He had not power over Himself to give up to death a humanity which He had freely taken into union with Himself, and which was His own? He could have no merit to give away or to rectify man's disordered relation to His maker.

(2.) Nor is an atonement possible on the Sabellian or in-dwelling scheme. This theory, too current in our day, does not admit a proper incarnation, and in fact goes no further than a humanitarian theory of Christ's person. Such a person would have nothing to spare, no superabundance of merit beyond what was absolutely necessary for his own wants. By the sup-position of being merely inhabited by God, He is but a creature necessarily subject to the law, and precluded by the nature of the case from acting vicariously. He could not put Himself under the divine law for others. The utmost that could be done would only be His duty. Whatever a creature has or is capable of rendering, He owes already to His maker.

(3.) Nor is an atonement possible on the Nestorian theory which divides the natures. We meet in all the words of Christ —as was to be expected from Him who is one person in two conjoined but distinct natures—the utterance of one self-conscious I. It has been happily said by a modern writer:— " Considered in a purely exegetical light, there is no more certain or clearer result of Scripture exposition than the position, that the I of Jesus on the earth is identical with the I who was be-fore in glory with the Father. Every sundering of the Son speaking on the earth into two I's, one of whom was the eternally glorious Word, and the other the humanly abased Jesus, is rejected by clear Scripture testimony."[1] We everywhere meet with the conscious utterance of the divine Word made flesh; and there is a communion between the two natures, of such a kind that the properties of either nature belong to the person. Thus the Son of God knows the human nature as His, and speaks of it as His, while the human nature in like manner speaks to us in the person of the only-begotten Son, and regards the divine nature as its own. Hence all that can be affirmed of the one nature can be said of the whole person. And from this flows the infinite value of all He did and suffered. We are warned by the whole mode of speaking followed by Christ, to

[1] Liebner, in the *Jahrbücher für Deutsche Theologie*, p. 362. 1858.

avoid such a notion of the union as thinks of a person who is neither properly God nor man, but an undefined third quantity.

The works of Jesus, accordingly, are the works of the person. The humanity belonged to the Son of God, not to another; and the actions He performed were the actions of the Son of God.[1] This is assumed in all Christ's words; and this guiding principle must be carried with us into the interpretation of all His language. If we ascribe, then, to the person what belongs to either nature, as we may and must, more value attaches to the obedience and suffering of the Son of God than to the sinless service of all creation.

A right view of this important truth will conduct us through all the intricacies of this question; and it may be well to put it in a clearer light from His own expressions. Thus He speaks of the human nature as " My flesh, which I will give for the life of the world," or the flesh of Him who came down from heaven (John vi. 51)—meaning that the humanity is personally united to Himself. If the humanity was not His own flesh, but that of a man existing apart from the Son, and therefore independently of Him, however sanctified, and however occupied by God, it could avail nothing. There would be no merit of more than creature-value in His obedience, no atonement in His blood equivalent to our infinite guilt.

A biblical view of this truth is of the greatest importance for our present discussion; for the foundation of our redemption is overthrown at once by any separation of the natures, or by any Nestorian division of them. When they are looked at apart in this matter, then we may say, as was once said[2] in the hearing of Nestorius: " Mere man could not save: the naked Godhead could not suffer." The humanity of Jesus was not a separate person with a distinct standing, but was taken

---

[1] As the scholastic writers expressed it: *actiones sunt suppositi.*

[2] Thus Proclus expressed himself in the large church of Constantinople in the presence of Nestorius.

into personal union, and existed in the person of the Son, or was the Son made flesh. Hence our Lord commonly expresses Himself in such a way as to show that His humanity was that of the Son of God, and that the actions which were done in it possessed, on this account, an altogether peculiar value. Thus He speaks of "MY body broken for you"—intimating that the broken body of such a person alone could meritoriously wash away sin, and save the sinner exposed to deserved punishment. If that body did not belong to the Son of God as His own, and as assumed into His person, the suffering involved in the breaking of His body, which was but of brief duration, would not have been an equivalent for sin. Again, when He speaks of His blood as "MY blood," the emphasis laid on the person, and on the blood, as belonging to such a person, and not another, cannot be mistaken. The actions are the actions of the person, and hence the blood was of infinite value, because it was the blood of the Son of God.

On this point it must be noticed, too, that in the work of atonement, as well as in all other parts of His mediatorial activity, Christ acted according to both natures. They ever acted conjointly, but in their separate spheres. It is important to keep in mind that they never acted apart in anything that came within the mediatorial function. And this it is the more necessary to mention, because the notion has obtained currency in modern times, that the divine nature was for the most part in abeyance during His humiliation, just as it was formerly maintained, under the influence of other theories equally unscriptural, that the Lord was Mediator only according to one of His natures, not according to both. But it must be laid down as an undoubted axiom, that Christ, from the very fact of the incarnation, did not, *in any part of His mediatorial work*, act as man simply, nor as God simply, but as God-man. With this concurrence of the two natures, however, to the production of the same result, it was not less one act, because the person was one; and He is called one Mediator (1 Tim. ii. 5). It ought to be further kept in mind, that in all His mediatorial action, the Godhead is the regulating principle; and that the humanity, as befits the lower nature, is subservient to the divine, to which it is conjoined. This may be illustrated by the analogy of soul and body. As the soul acts principally, and the body becomes the subservient part, or instrument which the nobler part directs, so in all the official work of Christ, the divine nature was the principal cause.

These are first principles, which must be carried with us to direct the conceptions which are formed, and the phraseology which is used, in regard to any part of Christ's mediatorial action, whether we think of Him during His earthly life, or in His present condition. And hence the atonement is not apprehended according to His own representation of it, unless it is seen to flow from the efficacy of both natures acting each in its sphere. It is the work of the person, which is one; and the atonement, as one work or act, is the result of the concurrent action of the several natures.

Thus the sufferings belonged to the Son of God, just as we should say of a person suffering in his hands or feet, that it was borne by the person. The humanity was His, and so was the agony, though the Deity could not agonize nor die. The intimate connection of the atoning obedience with Himself may be inferred from a more remote union which He also calls Himself, viz. His redeemed people, who are regarded as His body or His members. They were called so by Himself, when He said to Saul the persecutor: "Saul, Saul, why persecutest thou ME?" Now, this is a union far less close and intimate than that of the humanity which He put on. Yet even in reference to this He designates His people the joint heirs with Him, as His body, as Himself. But as His humanity is much nearer and more intimately joined to Him, we may affirm, as Scripture uniformly does, that the humanity is the body of God's Son; and that the obedience, suffering, and death are also His, and, therefore, possessed of all the value and worth that properly attach to Himself.

This brings me more particularly to refer to the influence of the deity of our Lord upon His work of atonement. According to the plan we follow, we aim not to go beyond the limits of exegetical investigation, nor beyond the import and significance of Christ's words. We find three consequences derived from the influence of His person, either directly taught, or easily deducible from His words; and to these we shall allude with as much brevity as shall consist with the exposition of the language.

1. As one effect of His incarnation, Jesus had power over His own life: "I have power to lay it down, and I have power to take it again" (John x. 8). Many doubts, insoluble on mere humanitarian grounds, now disappear at once. We apprehend how one could be an atoning surety for millions, and act a part to which no creature was equal. A mere man, however endowed, could not act this part; for he had no right to offer his own life; and a surety must offer his own, not another's. Hence no one can be the master of human nature who is not supreme God, producing and upholding it by his own power. But having such a nature in personal union with Himself, and therefore in a wholly different relation from that of an ordinary man or unit of the species, He had power to lay down His life, in order to satisfy the law in the room of others. He could offer the life over which He had full authority in man's room.

It is assumed that humanity in this union was exempt from any obligation to punishment or suffering; and when He did incur it, it evidently flowed from some compact, with a view to obtain an end. He who owes nothing on his own account, and yet pays, must plainly be considered as acting in the room of others for the purpose of relieving the insolvent, or of setting free the captive. The price could be given for others, because it was not required for himself; and it was wrought out by such a person only for this end. Our Lord says in the words adduced, that He had authority or right to dispose of His humanity; and He evinced this authority or power when He surrendered Himself into the hands of men, and spontaneously breathed out His life on the cross.

2. As another effect of the incarnation, it must be mentioned that infinite value or merit attaches to Christ's atonement. To this there is an allusion when our Lord says, " God so loved the world that He gave *His only-begotten Son* " (John iii. 16); and the various references to His mission, to His humiliation as the Son of Man, to His coming into the world, point, more or less directly, to the influence of His deity in connection with His atoning work. From this we understand how the obedience of Jesus possessed such a value in His eyes who judges according to truth, as to effect the remission of our sins, and the acceptance of the sinner. It was the obedience of the Son of God. Considered in this light, there are several distinct effects which the deity of Christ must be regarded as producing.

a. Such a knowledge of sin must be acquired as could spring only from a full discovery of all the sins of men, past, present, and to come; and these must stand before His eye at a glance, with a view to be confessed for us, and expiated in our stead. This argues the omniscience of a divine person.

b. Not only so: the endurance of the curse or penalty was wholly beyond the resources of mere humanity. Because the sufferer was God-man, He was able to make atonement for infinitely great sin. This involves the collision of infinitudes— infinite wrath for a world's guilt met by infinite endurance; the curse exhausted in order to be changed into a blessing,—things of such a nature that nothing short of omnipotence could be put into the scale against them. The divine nature did not suffer, and could not; but in virtue of its union to the humanity, the latter was able to encounter and bear more than a mere man could have borne, because it was supported and strengthened for that end. It does not follow, because the divine nature poured out influences to support the human, and to prevent it from giving way, that comforting influences were given in the same proportion. The opposite appears from the events in the garden, and from the desertion on the cross. He knew the infinite hatred of God to sin, and drunk the cup of merited penalty; but the influence of His divine nature supported the humanity in suffering what must needs be borne. He was deserted, yet sustained.

c. But it must be yet further remarked, that the Godhead gave infinite value to the suffering. This was due to His being the God-man. And because His suffering was of infinite value, it was sufficient to satisfy for all whose redemption he aimed at securing. This is the reason why the sufferings and obedience of Christ could satisfy for thousands. If He were a mere man, He could not satisfy for one; but being very God, the dignity of His person not only put the Lord Jesus in a position of suffering what no mere man could ever suffer, but had an influence on the whole obedience. Scripture accordingly fixes our attention on the person to deduce from it the value of His suffering. The sufferings of finite creatures could never offer satisfaction, though their endurance were eternal. But the divine dignity of Christ countervailed the eternal duration of the punishment; for the element of duration is by no means essential to the satisfaction. He who can bear the infinite weight of God's wrath is not subject to its eternal duration. Thus the infinite value of the obedience is traced up to the divine dignity of His person; the act of the Son of God in offering up His humanity being the culmination of His obedience, and constituting merit for others.

3. Another effect of the incarnation is, that the party bought must, by the necessary law of purchase, belong to Him who redeems them. But man cannot be the lord of man. To this proprietary right to His own sheep our Lord refers when He calls them His sheep (John x. 2): He proceeds to argue on the ground of His omnipotence and His Father's dominion, that none shall pluck them out of His hand; and then subjoins the ever memorable testimony to His divine consubstantiality with the Father as well as to His distinct personality: "I and the Father are one" (John x. 15, 27, 30).

Thus, according to His own testimony, the influence of Christ's deity in the matter of the atonement appears in all conceivable respects. The Son of God suffered in our humanity: and in that humanity He was vilified, despised, and crucified; and bore the punishment that must be borne in room of sinners. Thus the Son of God was by the incarnation in the position of sinners for the endurance of the punishment; the dignity of His person supplying what was awanting in the continuance of suf-. ferings limited to thirty-three years,—Christ being no ordinary man, but the Son of God.[1]

CHAPTER III.

THE CONSTITUENT ELEMENTS OF THE ATONEMENT.

SEC. XIV.—CHRIST CONSCIOUSLY FULFILLING ALL THAT WAS WRITTEN IN THE LAW OF MOSES, THE PROPHETS, AND THE PSALMS CON-CERNING HIMSELF.

CONSCIOUS of being the Messiah, the Lord Jesus found allusions in all the Scriptures to Himself. Capable of being influenced by motives, like His people, His sense of the Messianic function was nourished and sustained by all that was recorded in the types, in the prophecies, and in the Psalms; which, indeed, were written for Him—pointing out the sphere in which He was to move and the spirit which He was to breathe—as well as recorded for the Church. Certain modern theologians cannot find Christ in the Old Testament: to them the answer is, the Lord Jesus found Himself in all the divisions of the word already named (John v. 46). That He lived in the word can be doubtful to no one who has reflected on the temptation by which He was assailed; the aim of which was to turn Him away from the word. Nor was this dependence on the word unworthy of the Son of God

[1] See Note E in Appendix.

condescending to be man, or inconsistent with the personal union. The question, however, to which we now direct attention is :· Did the Lord consciously, in the course of His earthly career, fulfil what was written in the Law of Moses, in the Prophets, and in the Psalms concerning Himself? This must be emphatically affirmed. We shall briefly notice the three divisions as they are mentioned by the Evangelist in referring to our Lord's interviews with the disciples after rising from the dead (Luke xxiv. 44).

I. With reference to the types, the Lord, from His boyhood to the close of His career, seems to have wistfully gazed on them with a steady application to Himself (Luke ii. 49; Mark xi. 11). An attentive study of the Evangelists will leave little doubt of this on any mind. We find express allusion by Him to the typical character of the manna (John vi. 32), to the brazen serpent (iii. 14), and to the history of Jonah (Matt. xii. 40); clear proofs that He found Himself in the Old Testament. That He did not in express terms expound the sacrifices with reference to Himself may be explained by the circumstance that the disciples were not yet able to bear it. He speaks of Himself and of the work to which He had devoted Himself under representations which, we may affirm, took for granted, in the most indubitable way, that He was at once Priest and Victim (John xvii. 19; vi. 51-58; Matt. xx. 28). But it was only after His resurrection that the nature of His death could be fully expounded and correctly apprehended, in the light of the ancient types. And accordingly we find that the entire typical system by which His own mind had been fed for thirty years was then explained to the disciples (Luke xxiv. 27). We find these comments of our Lord repeated and interwoven in the texture of the apostolical Epistles, but especially in the Epistle to the Hebrews, which was devoted to this purpose.

II. As to the prophecies, we find the Lord consciously engaged in fulfilling them to the close of His career. One memorable distinction to be drawn between Christ's fulfilment of the prophecies and the fulfilment which they received at the hand

of men and even from His own disciples, may here be specified.
He fulfilled them consciously: they were mere unconscious
instruments in a higher hand.   No one can peruse the record of
the Lord's life without being peculiarly struck with the marked
distinction in this respect between Him and His disciples.   The
latter remembered what they had done to Him at a subsequent
time, and then saw an accomplishment of prophecy (John xii.
16); whereas the Lord Himself, with a wholly different view,
consciously connected past prediction and present fulfilment at
every step (John xiii. 18; Mark xiv. 27).

The Messianic prophecies were so numerous and express that
before this great Person appeared among men no obscurity was
left on anything connected with His person, offices, or work.
And our Lord, in the exercise of His Messianic consciousness,
may be conceived of as living and moving in that sphere marked
out for Him by type and prophecy.   We shall omit, however, the
passages cited by others, and refer to those only which were
quoted by the Lord Himself, and, therefore, spoken from His own
consciousness.   The more general allusions to the Messiah's
sufferings may also be omitted (Luke xviii. 31).   Two passages,
however, are worthy of special notice.

(1). One of these has reference to the servant of the Lord in the
well-known passage which describes the vicarious sufferings of
Messiah (Isa. liii. 12).   Our Lord's quotation is as follows: " I
say unto you that this that is written must be accomplished in
Me, And He was numbered among the transgressors ; for the
things concerning Me have an end " (Luke xxii. 37).   They who
persist in interpreting the designation, The Servant of the Lord
(Isa. liii. 11), either of Isaiah or the people of Israel, involve
themselves in contradictions and insuperable difficulties, and
must content themselves with the most forced interpretation.
Christ interprets that section of the prophet concerning Himself,
and every reverent expositor at once accepts His commentary as
decisive ; for the saying is put by Luke in the mouth of the Lord.
The words, " the things concerning Me have an end," must mean,

as the best commentators interpret them, the things concerning Me have their issue or accomplishment. They emphatically bring out that Jesus was consciously fulfilling prophecy, and that this was the element in which He lived.

(2). The second passage, referring to the smitten shepherd, is equally explicit (Zech. xiii. 7 ; Mark xiv. 27). We must repudiate every exposition of this passage which does not refer it to the violent death which the Messiah, the Great Shepherd of the nation, underwent by God's command. An abbreviated quotation, as the Lord gives it—that is, taken from the first and last portion of the verse—it must be seen in the context; and thus viewed it sets before us with the utmost clearness One who is at once THE MAN by eminence and yet the FELLOW of the Lord of Hosts. When He is further called MY SHEPHERD, the allusion is to the Messiah as appointed by the Father. It is a violence done to the passage to refer it to the order of shepherds generally. And when the shepherd is represented as about to be pierced by the sword of the Lord, but not in the defeat of battle, the issue, as is further stated, is a temporary scattering of the sheep only to be followed by a gathering together to Him, and by God's protecting as well as collecting hand being extended to the little ones.

III. The Psalms, the third division of Scripture expounded by our Lord subsequently to His rising, delineate, in a manner not less expressive, His Messianic history and experience. They were a vehicle prepared to hand, in which the sin-bearing Substitute, when He came, found sentiments and utterances suited to His position. His holy nature of itself breathed the same feelings of complaint, prayer, and submission. But for wise reasons the inner exercises were there outlined by the same spirit which filled His pure humanity, and prompted Him to complete the sacrifice. And perhaps no consideration gives such an impressive view of the necessity of having the word dwelling richly in the human heart, and of men being held by it in all their mental exercises. It does not fall within my present task to discuss the question, confessedly difficult, how far Christ's experience is reflected in the entire Book of Psalms, and to what extent it is warrantable to accept the position laid down by Horsley, Horne, Barclay, and others, that all the Psalms may be so explained. We shall not turn aside to this question: for the plan of investigating the sayings of Jesus limits us to those which He quotes as spoken from His own consciousness. We notice only four Psalms descriptive of Christ's betrayal, and sufferings, and entering into details with an accuracy, which only omniscience could have sketched (Ps. cix., Ps. lxix., Ps. xxii., Ps. xli.). That the speaker in these Psalms is not an ordinary sufferer may easily be proved. Unless the sufferings depicted with such minuteness affected man as man, and related to one who stood in a unique relation to the world, the description would have outrun the reader's sympathy. For why introduce the sorrows of one man, if he were but a man, into the worship of God? To set them forth with minuteness, as if humanity could take such an interest in any hero, however distinguished, would be too exacting, and would only be repelled, unless the sufferer touched humanity at all points, and his fortunes came home to men's business and bosom in all ages. But the enigma is explained when we rise to the idea that the great sufferer was the substitute of others, and that all centuries, till time shall be no more, have an equal interest in the sorrows He underwent. In His woes men see what rescues them from their own.

Psalm cix., more than once adduced (John xv. 25; Acts i. 20), discovers to us how the Redeemer was affected by the treachery of Judas. That the Psalm treats of Judas is proved by ver. 8, as it was expounded by Peter upon the occasion when he assigned the ground or warrant for electing another to the vacant place in the college of apostles. When one of the apostles died in the Lord, or was removed by martyrdom (Acts xii. 2), no election of another ensued, and consequently the number soon passed away. But as there was to be no vacant seat in the twelve thrones occupied by the apostles in the re-

generation, it was provided that another should be substituted
in the room of Judas. The opening words of the Psalm seem
to be an allusion to the calumnies and reproaches heaped upon
Christ when the treachery was concerted, and the Messiah turns
to God as the object of His boast and praise (ver. 1-6). Next
follows a delineation of the fate of Judas; his despair; the
shortening of his days; the ruin of his family (ver. 9); the dispersion of his ill-gotten substance (ver. 11); and Christ's own
trust in God (ver. 21). What seems an imprecation against
Judas is only the infliction of a righteous doom upon the greatest
of sins, and a sublime acquiescence in it.

Psalm lxix., quoted no fewer than six times by the New Testament writers, presents another memorable outline of Messianic
experience. How far the Psalm has a primary reference to
David it is scarcely necessary to inquire; for though that may
generally be taken for granted when the tenor of a Psalm does
not outrun the writer's experience or the facts of his history, a
different canon of interpretation was acted on both by Peter and
Paul, when the words of the Psalm transcend all that could be
said of David (Acts ii. 29-33; xiii. 35-37). The self-consuming
zeal for the house of God (ver. 9); the gall and vinegar given
Him for food (ver. 21); and other elements delineated in the
Psalm, have no application to David. The speaker describes
Himself as sinking in deep mire, as coming into deep waters
which overflowed Him, and continues in this strain to ver.
22, setting forth the complaints of Messiah in His last sufferings. Perhaps we do not err in assuming with Roos, that
Psalm lxix. refers to the time preceding the three hours' darkness which covered the land, and that Psalm xxii. refers to the
period of desertion which followed. This Psalm unfolds to us
how the Saviour during His crucifixion reflected on His present
and previous sufferings, and how He lamented and prayed. He
declares that the reproaches of them that reproached God had
fallen upon Him (ver. 9); that He had been the song of the
drunkard, doubtless when He went about doing good, mighty in

deed and word (ver. 12); and that in the exercise of strict severity, though not too severe, a dread doom was impending over those who rejected their Messiah (ver. 23-29). Bright prospects breaking out from behind the terrible gloom of His sorrows, sustain His soul after these complaints (ver. 30-37); and there is a joyful end to these sorrows both for the sufferer and for all the earth. Under all these woes He was perfectly innocent, sustaining them for others (ver. 5-6); for He restored what He took not away (ver. 4).

We come next to Psalm xxii., which has this in common with Psalm lxix., that it begins with deep complaint and closes with the brightest prospects. That Messiah alone is the speaker throughout this entire Psalm must be evident, we think, to any one who, without prejudice, examines the contents. Though David, the penman, was subject to many bitter trials, and though circumstances in his lot may have been the occasion which suggested or prompted the Psalm, it is evident that throughout the whole tenor of this poem bringing before us the fortunes of one person, we have not David but his greater offspring; one born by a peculiar exercise of Divine power, cast on God from the womb, and occupying a close relation to God (ver. 9, 10). Then we have a description of sufferings unknown to David, for when was David so deserted as to be a worm and no man, recklessly as it were trodden under foot? When were his garments parted among men and lots cast for his vesture (ver. 18)? When did they revile and sarcastically despise him as a pretender or would-be deliverer of the people (ver. 8; Matt. xxvii. 43)? When did they pierce his hands and his feet—a well-known description of suspension on a cross? Our authorised English Version has here done well in so rendering the verse, in deference to the Septuagint and authorities much older than the Masoretic punctuation, which has, either from mistake or by design, introduced a reading which cannot be vindicated. Besides all these arguments derived from the contents, we have the unerring authority of the apostles (John xix. 23; Heb. ii. 12), and

of our Lord Himself when He quoted the Psalm amid the gloom
of the desertion, as finding its full significance in His experience
on the tree.

When we examine the words, we find Him first of all com-
plaining of the sad sense of desertion, and appealing to God to
remember the REASON WHY He was in such a case (ver. 1). As
the reason of the desertion was not due to any personal cause
separating between God and Him, He prayed that it might not
go beyond what was indispensably required for the end contemplated, and might take end in His temporal death. It was
natural, nay reasonable, to spread out before His Father, more
especially as His life hastened to a close, that the cause of His
desertion was man's redemption and the Divine glory in connection with it, and to ground upon this a conviction of being
heard in a way consistent with the Divine rectitude, but leaving
the mode of deliverance with God. When it is added that He
prayed day and night but was not heard (ver. 2), a difficulty has
been started as to the import. But we need go no further than to
the simple fact that during the thickening sorrows of the last day
of His pilgrimage, He had thus prayed amid the agony of Gethsemane and the increasing desertion of the following day, until,
towards the day's decline, He commended His spirit to His Father.

But how, it is asked, are we to apprehend the argument for
deliverance drawn from the fact that He had ancestors in Israel
who cried and obtained deliverance ? There is no difficulty as
to referring this language to the Lord. He might argue, " I am
an Israelite, enrolled as such by the rite of circumcision, and
if the fathers Abraham, Isaac, and Jacob hoped, and were
delivered, a similar deliverance, will be extended to Me" (ver.
4-5): or it may be an argument from the stronger reason, as
follows ; " The believing fathers of our nation, also My fathers
according to the flesh, trusted and were not confounded; and
shouldest not Thou deliver Me, Thy beloved Son, who am the
ground of all that confidence which the fathers exercised, from
this tribulation and perplexity ?"

In the sequel of the Psalm the Lord utters a distinct persuasion as to His death, " And THOU hast brought Me into the dust of death" (ver. 15). When we inquire by whom the Messiah was brought into the humiliation of actual death, we find that though dogs are said to compass Him,—that is heathen soldiers acting against Him; though the assembly of the wicked are said to inclose Him,—that is the company of the chief priests and their faction,—yet Messiah's death is emphatically ascribed to God Himself; " THOU hast brought Me." Properly speaking the Lord was not overcome by His enemies. They could have had no power at all to exercise over Him but for His voluntary undertaking, and the consequent judgment exercised upon Him by the righteous Father. This is put beyond doubt by His own reply to Pilate (John xix. 11), and by Peter's exposition (Acts ii. 23).

As to the concluding portion of the Psalm (ver. 24-32) it means as spoken by the dying sufferer, that subsequently to His resurrection He should be the medium of all the Divine communications towards man, and of all the returns of praise to His Father (ver. 25). Then follows a sublime description of the fruits of His atonement in accomplishing the world's salvation, in emancipating the nations, and in effecting the conversion of the ends of the earth; and we see how much, in the closing hours of His life, He derived comfort from the clearly perceived fruits of His redemption as enjoyed by His people. They who attentively analyse Psalm xxii. easily discern that the great sufferer who complains of the desertion was one who trusted in God from His birth, and the mention of the seemingly incidental parts of the scene, such as the casting lots for His vesture, indicate an extraordinary person, whose fortunes down to their smallest details were foretold, and would touch a chord in human hearts while the world stands. It appears, too, that in all His sufferings God had a hand, and that His enemies did only what God, according to His counsel and foreknowledge, had beforehand determined to be done.

The three Psalms which we have briefly expounded have much in common, and yet are remarkably different. Psalm xxii. makes little mention of His enemies, and not at all in the way of alluding to the vengeance or recompence awaiting them. The sufferer appears as one forsaken, and pours forth in His Father's ear His complaint as suffering the hiding of His face. Here all the suffering appears as coming from the hand of God, and as but a consequence of the great calamity of desertion, under which all else may be reduced. In the two other Psalms the sufferer adverts to the hostility displayed by His people to His instructions, admonitions, and reproofs; and to the way in which they requited His love with reproaches, indignities, and betrayal. It is a commentary on the words of John, "He came unto His own, and His own received Him not" (John i. 11).

These two elements or causes of Christ's sufferings, according to the outline furnished by prophecy, are clearly traced in what befell the Lord. This double aspect of the sufferings of Jesus,—that is, sufferings such as were sent direct from God, and such as were mediately inflicted by the hands of man, were closely connected together. If God had not appointed and sent them, men could not have inflicted ought of suffering. He was beyond their reach. But when God made Him to be sin (2 Cor. v. 21), the sin-bearer, and therefore the curse-bearer, He was placed in a position where He, who in Himself was far beyond all created power, could be seized, and treated with indignity and injustice at the hand of man.

This leads me to notice the prophecy of His betrayal in another Psalm (xli. 9) as quoted by our Lord Himself: "I speak not of you all: I know whom I have chosen: but that the Scripture may be fulfilled, He that eateth bread with Me hath lifted up his heel against Me" (John xiii. 19). The tenor of that prophecy implied that among the intimate friends of Messiah a traitor was to be found. Judas was to carry out his purpose that same night; and the Lord subjoins, that He would have them informed beforehand, that they might not be shaken, but confirmed, in their faith in His Messiahship. They should see that His delivery into the hands of men was no contingent effect of human malice, but the result of the divine purpose or determinate counsel, which He clearly foresaw and announced before it came to pass. Did Judas understand Him? Yes: this quotation and the further exposure of him to the rest of the disciples by the sop (John xiii. 26) rendered it impossible for Judas not to understand Him. But Jesus, knowing that God's plan should be executed and the words of prophecy fulfilled, was not solicitous that the traitor's purpose should be abandoned. In like manner He had, in connection with the parable of the wicked husbandmen (Matt. xxi. 42), intimated to the high-priests that their wicked purpose was well known to Him, and that in carrying it out they only fulfilled an ancient prophecy with which they were familiar—that the stone which the builders rejected should become the Head of the corner (Ps. cxviii. 22). They understood Him, but remained undeterred in their purpose, with the usual blindness of wicked men.

Here the inquiry suggests itself: How could His fellow countrymen continue so completely ignorant as to His Messiahship? He knew it: His disciples knew it: and the entire nation might have known it. But partly from a perverting legalism, partly from prepossessions as to the earthly nature of His kingdom, partly from ignorance of the actual circumstances of His birth, they concurred in rejecting Him. As to their legalism, they misapprehended the true nature of the law and perverted it from its proper use, mistaking the meaning of the sacrifices, as if men were to be justified by the use of them as meritorious works of law. As to the prophecies of Messiah's kingdom, they regarded these as referring to a temporal dominion over subject nations, instead of viewing it as a kingdom based on His atoning death. And as to the circumstances of Christ's birth, they were at no pains to institute any inquiry. The design of Providence in ordering Messiah's lot so that His death should be brought about as it happened, thus unfolds the wisdom of God.

The memorable circumstances of Christ's birth were no longer in men's memory. He had been announced by angels to the shepherds of Bethlehem when He was born. He was visited by the shepherds, and they made known abroad the saying which was told them concerning the child (Luke ii. 7). The Magi from the East had been led by the supernatural guidance of a star to the new-born King, and produced at Herod's court an excitement or sensation so great that it was the occasion of convening an assembly of priests and scribes to determine from prophecy where He should be born. When all this is taken into account, it seems to us at first sight inexplicable that events such as these could have passed from men's memory. But thirty years had intervened between the birth in Bethlehem and the public ministry of Jesus, who was only known as the carpenter of Nazareth. Perhaps few except Mary remained to whom the wonders of Bethlehem were known, or the salutation of Simeon and Anna in the temple. The Magi had not returned to Herod to confirm the impression which their visit occasioned. Then, the utmost perplexity as to the fate of the child was caused by the order of Herod to cut off the infant children of Bethlehem ; the tears of Rachel weeping for her children being largely due to this, that all hope seemed cut off. After returning from Egypt, the long sojourn of thirty years in Nazareth, His mean condition, His manual labour, and the fact that there is not the least trace of His having visited Bethlehem or allowing anything to trans- pire that connected Him with it as the place of His birth,—all tended to fix attention on Him merely as the man of Nazareth. Hence, though He performed innumerable miracles, they had no other effect among the bulk of the community, educated or illiterate, but to win an acknowledgment of Him as a prophet ; but they who admitted this claim concluded that He could not be the Messiah. Their difficulty would have been removed had they known His birth-place and the facts that so marvellously heralded Him into the world. Besides, Jesus did not speak of His Messiahship in public. Hence, notwithstanding His doctrine and miracles, He was taken for a prophet, but not for the Messiah. His humiliation, read aright in the light of prophecy, might have served as a proof that He was the long-predicted Christ. But the doctrine of the Jewish Church was so corrupted that an idea had been formed of the Messiah which could not be harmonized with His actual appearance; and all was so ordered, in adorable wisdom, that the nation might do what they would not have done had the princes of this world known Him (1 Cor. ii. 8). These prejudices prevented men from acknowledging Jesus as the Messiah. How little even His own disciples expected His death is evinced by all His history.

But why was such ignorance and unbelief permitted to prevail? The purpose of God was that He should die as a propitiation for sins, and in order to this be the despised and rejected of men. Hence He must be unknown (1 Cor. ii. 8). The Lord Himself avoided everything that might prevent the execution of the determinate counsel and foreknowledge of God. He neither, in His public instructions, announced His Messianic dignity nor suffered His disciples to make Him known, adding that He must suffer and die (Luke ix. 21). He avowed His Messiahship publicly only before Caiaphas, when the avowal hastened the consummation of His sacrifice. Here, then, we see the infinite wisdom of God.

But, it may be asked, How could they so treat Jesus regarded merely as a prophet? The reason is at hand. Not a few took Him for a prophet with an obscure vague impression that He was something more, and that He might yet declare Himself as the Messiah; but when they heard that He was seized and placed as a criminal at the bar of a human judge, they accepted it as a settled matter that He could have no claim to the Messiahship, and that His reply to the High-priest, when adjured to declare Himself, was a strange and inexplicable claim. They who favoured Him as a prophet were stunned, and many who had previously honoured Him, carried away with the chagrin and disappointment of the hour, joined in the cry, " Crucify

Him!" Nay, the concentrated essence of the reproach which they heaped upon Him took this form: "If He is the Christ, let Him come down from the cross."

The misconception under which the rulers and people rejected Him may be supposed to excuse their conduct. Undoubtedly this rendered their sin, terrible as it was, capable of forgiveness. For had they rejected Jesus, the Messiah and the Son of God, with a full knowledge of His dignity and a full consciousness of their act, we may unhesitatingly affirm that parties guilty of such a crime could find no salvation. This distinction as to their criminality is warranted by the language of Peter in addressing those Jews who had denied the Prince of Life and preferred a murderer: for as showing that salvation was still attainable, Peter said: "And now, brethren, I wot that through ignorance ye did it, as did also your rulers" (Acts iii. 17). Paul speaks of Himself with the same distinction; calling himself a persecutor, blasphemer, and injurious, but adding that he did it ignorantly in unbelief (1 Tim. i. 13). Hence there yet remained a way of salvation open to Israel; and the Gospel was for a generation preached to Jerusalem before its overthrow.

Thus there existed the greatest difference in the amount of knowledge diffused among the people as to the circumstances of the Baptist's birth compared with those relating to the birth of Christ. And in the infinite wisdom of God the Lord's death was brought about by the nation whose Messiah He was, but whom they did not know.

SEC. XV.—THE FIRST CLASSIFICATION OF THE SAYINGS INTO THOSE WHICH REPRESENT CHRIST AS THE SIN-BEARER, AND THEN AS THE WILLING SERVANT.

There are undoubtedly two sets of sayings, or two closely allied but still distinct views of Christ's earthly career, that are presented to our minds as descriptive of the *nature* of the atonement in the sayings which we have now to notice. The Lord represents Himself just as He was represented both before and after His coming, as the curse-bearer, and as the active doer of a work of obedience. Though these two views, as different sides of truth, may be said to presuppose and to imply each other, they must needs be separately apprehended. His position as a sin-bearer is of course involved in the very notion of an atonement. But the other side of His mediatorial work—His position as an active doer of a work of obedience—would have been necessary though man had never fallen; and the fact of the Fall cannot of course exempt man, or exempt Christ as our surety, from the obligation. These two elements may be and must be distinguished by us in idea, but they cannot be disjoined or isolated in this great transaction, as if they were to be represented as separately meritorious. On the one hand, as the mere active doer of man's primeval work of obedience, His incarnation would not have reached our case, or really have availed us, had He not also been, in the fullest sense of the term, a sin-bearer. And just as little would His vicarious suffering, as the sin-bearer, have availed us without the holy promptitude and the cordial delight of the righteous servant in bearing what His Father imposed according to His divine perfections. The two integral parts of Christ's work are not to be considered as if they were separately meritorious.[1]

The element of substitution, that is, of an exchange of places, constitutes the very core of the atonement; and this is also the Gospel in a single word. When mankind had lost a due standing before God, there was, and there could be, no relaxation of the Divine claims or of the original idea of man; and in any scheme of restoration, or method by which grace could be glorified in man's salvation, a mediator must, from the necessity of the case,

[1] These two elements of Christ's work are well delineated in their unity in two recent German works, viz. : Thomasius' *Christi Person und Werk*, 3te Theil, 1859 ; and Philippi's *Kirchliche Glaubenslehre*, iv., 1863. The work devolving on Christ as the surety of men, and of sinning men, is undoubtedly twofold. And yet the obedience, far from being divided into two distinct achievements, is one obedience in the twofold sphere of action and suffering.

enter into man's position and come under his responsibilities both
as to duty to be done and suffering to be endured.   This position,
which we lay down with absolute confidence, is not deduced on
mere abstract grounds from the Divine perfections.   It is
grounded on all those expressions of the Lord and His apostles
in which it is said that He suffered for others (John x. 15; xi.
50-52).   The Greek preposition used in all these phrases either
proceeds on the supposition that He put Himself in the room of
others or expressly asserts this thought (Mark x. 45).   What
renders other senses impossible is the fact that this mode of
speech is alternated with another, which asserts that He suffered
for our sins (1 Cor. xv. 3; 1 Pet. iii. 18).   And in every instance
these allusions to suffering for others are couched in such a way
as implies that the action was competent to Christ alone, and
the language can be applied to none else.   Thus, though apostles
suffered for the Church, and some of them were crucified, Paul
teaches that it would be incongruous and impious to speak of Paul
being crucified for men: "Was Paul crucified for you?" (1 Cor.
i. 13).   The same element of substitution is not obscurely to be
traced in all the passages which set forth Christ as the great
personal Sacrifice, the reality of the Old Testament sacrifices
(John i. 29), or apply to Him the language which describes the
GOEL or Redeemer (Matt. xx. 28).

And for the discharge of this task the constitution of His
person furnished the facility.   I shall not recall what has been
already said in treating of His Deity except to say, that in virtue
of His divine nature He was not only able to render a free
obedience and to have power over His own life which no mere
creature could possess (John x. 18), but also qualified to bear
what no finite creature could have borne, and to give to His
atonement an infinite value.   In this substitution of one for
many the universe for the first time saw perfect sinlessness, the
only one of the race who came up to the idea of man.   Never
did any see aught like it before, and while the present economy
lasts never can such a spectacle of moral perfection be expected
again.

But this substitution was no make-believe, no mere semblance, but a true exchange of places—the most real of facts. He was accounted as the sinner not by a mere *as if* He were so, but because He was made sin (2 Cor. v. 21), and hence was treated as a sinner. And all this was not by a mere Divine permission allowing a free rein to human wickedness, but by God's determinate counsel. That we may have no doubt of this, we shall have to trace in His soul-trouble a direct infliction from the hand of God.

As a curse-bearer Christ is first presented to us. This comes out, as we shall see, very clearly in His own consciousness, His language proving that it was never absent from His mind. But, as this was so essential a point, the Baptist's testimony to Him, spoken in His hearing, and as an objective echo of Christ's consciousness, was added to show that Jesus appeared as the sin-bearer. We shall begin with this, and next take up Christ's own testimony from His own consciousness.[1]

SEC. XVI.—THE BAPTIST'S TESTIMONY TO JESUS AS THE SIN-BEARER.

" Behold the Lamb of God, which taketh away [better, beareth] *the sin of the world."*—JOHN i. 29.

Here the Baptist, looking upon Jesus coming to Him, points Him out to the multitude as the person concerning whom he had a commission to preach, and directs attention to Him as the heaven-appointed sacrifice that was to expiate the sin, not of the Jews only, but of the world. It is a testimony that stands as a heading to the whole series or class of similar sayings which represents the Lord Jesus as bearing our sins in His own body.[2] To whatever occasion we may trace it, whether to the pastoral country where it was uttered, or to the recent baptism of Jesus leading John's mind into a new line of inquiry, or to the passover

[1] See Note B in the Appendix.
[2] *E.g.* 2 Cor. v. 21 ; Gal. iii. 13 ; Isa. liii. 5 ; 1 Pet. ii. 14.

near at hand—and all these occasions have been conjectured,—
the thought itself that one was to be a sin-bearer for others was
familiar to the ancient Church. The identification of the Lamb
of God with Jesus of Nazareth was the only thing in this testimony of the Baptist specifically new; and He is called the Lamb
OF GOD, just as He is styled "the Bread OF GOD" (John vi. 33),
partly because He was graciously provided by God, partly because
He was the truth of the types, or the reality of what was foreshadowed by the Lamb in the old economy; or, it may be, the
Lamb that *belongs to God*[1]—that is, which is to be offered as a
sacrifice to Him.

Whether the entire idea is borrowed from Isa. liii. 7, and ver.
12, is a moot point. While some affirm this, others call it in
question, because Isaiah only likens the servant of the Lord to a
lamb led to the slaughter, but does not call Him a sacrificial
lamb. It is not an express quotation, and therefore the question is not one that calls for a decision. If it did, we might
perhaps bring the two views together by assuming that it was
the sacrificial lamb to which Isaiah too referred; but as it is
not a formal quotation, it is unnecessary to pronounce a positive
decision upon this point either way.

The question is raised, What particular lamb had the Baptist
in his eye? Some hold that the allusion is to the paschal lamb,
while others have referred it to the daily sacrifice. The words
themselves do not decide the question; and the difficulty
encountered in this and in all similar allusions to the lamb is
due to the theories of commentators, and may be said to arise in
large measure, if not wholly, from the too artificial distribution
of the sacrifices to which many expositors have precipitately
committed themselves. Thus, under the spell of too much
system, one earnest advocate[2] of the atonement answers the

---

[1] So Storr and Meyer; the former of whom quotes from the Septuagint, θυσίαι
Θεοῦ (Lev. xxi. 16).

[2] Prof. Doedes, in *Jaarboecken voor Wetenschappelijke Theologie*, p. 305,
Utrecht, 1846.

question what particular lamb is referred to, in this strange way:
—"Not the paschal lamb," says he, "for that had no relation to
the bearing of sin ; not the morning and evening sacrifice, as that
was a burnt-offering; nor could he have thought of a sin-offering
generally, as a lamb was but seldom used for that." This em-
barrassment, denying precisely what should be affirmed, grows
out of the complicated sacrificial system which has been in vogue
for a number of years past. On the contrary, the allusion is
to all those sacrifices where a lamb was slain. The most natural
explanation is, that John alludes not to any one particular offering, but, in a comprehensive way, to all those propitiatory sacrifices where a lamb was used to bear or to take away the penalty
of sin. He first of all included the *paschal lamb*, which was a
sin-offering in the fullest significance of the word. This offering
may be viewed, indeed, as the fundamental sacrifice of the
covenant people. The blood—the principal matter in it—
primarily referred to sin, and was offered to God to make atonement, separating Israel from the world in order to make them
a peculiar people. Next, as to the effect or consequences of
the sacrifice, it secured the safety of their first-born when
divine judgments fell upon the Egyptian idols and their
votaries, as well as gained for the Israelites their safe exodus
from Egypt. Nor were the subsequent passovers mere com-
memorations of what had been : they continued to secure
what was at first conferred, and partook of the same character
with the first.

The Baptist in this testimony no less included the *lamb of
the burnt-offering*, or the morning and evening sacrifice, which
was doubled on the Sabbath. Twice every day a lamb was
thus offered in the temple. That the burnt-offering contained
an atoning element is clear, since it is said to be accepted for a
man to make atonement (Lev. i. 4). As to the difference between it and the sin-offering, it did not lie in this, that the
burnt-offering was not expiatory, as is too often said. It lay in
this, that the burnt-offering was not offered for some sins in par-

ticular but for all;[1] and it was either voluntary or according to divine appointment.

Nor did the Baptist less include *the lamb of the trespass-offering*, which was offered when some defilement excluded the worshipper from the congregation of the Lord. We read that in certain cases a lamb was to be slain as a trespass-offering (Lev. xiv. 11; Num. vi. 12).

Thus, in the threefold distribution of the sacrifices to which we have adverted, we find that a lamb was offered to obtain a legal purification from ceremonial defilement. The assertion often made and repeated in the interest of a certain tendency, that no lamb was offered in sacrifices which were intended to make an expiation or atonement for sin, is thus destitute of all foundation.

But the word in this testimony which has the chief emphasis is that which is rendered, "taketh away." The majority of expositors render the phrase, "beareth sin:" some prefer the rendering, "taketh away:"[2] others, and among these is Calvin, comprehend both. But the one thought does not exclude the other. If we render, "that taketh away," we must understand it thus: *that taketh away by bearing it*. If we render, "that beareth sin," we must understand it thus: *that beareth, in order to take away*. On either view, it is sacrificial language. We prefer *beareth*.

The two clauses of this statement are so closely connected and so mutually interwoven both in point of thought and language, that they cannot be taken apart or construed apart. To give a complete idea, the one clause is necessary to the other; and if we take this guiding principle with us to its interpretation, we shall find that all the one-sided views which tend to alter the true meaning and import of the language can be easily set aside by simply maintaining the connection of the clauses; thus:—

[1] See Oehler, in Herzog's *Encyclop. u. Opfercultus*.
[2] On the phrase ὁ αἴρων, see Meyer on John i. 29, though he prefers the rendering, "who taketh away."

1. Some hold that in this saying we have nothing beyond a figure or comparison, and that the allusion is made simply to the moral innocence and meekness of Jesus. Such a construction might perhaps be allowed, if Jesus were likened or compared to a lamb; but the conjunction of these two clauses cannot be limited to the bare notion of purity or innocence. Plainly, the first clause is not a simple comparison,—it is the use of a type; and such a transfer of names or interchange of language, natural enough in a divinely-instituted type, is out of keeping with the language of comparison. The twofold notion here put together—that of a lamb and that of a sin-bearer—precludes the supposition that we have brought before us nothing beyond the idea of a meek and patient person suffering under indignity and wrong.

2. Nor can we refer the words to the effects of Christ's instruction as a good and gentle Teacher. It is not possible, on any principle of interpretation, to regard these two propositions or sayings as equivalent: " Christ bears the sin of the world," and " Christ has pointed out the way to the world to be on its guard against sin for the future." The Baptist could not mean to say that Christ makes men wiser and better by His doctrine, and that in this manner He takes away or bears the sin of the world. But suppose such a sense could, without violent straining, be put upon the latter clause, it must be remembered that it does not stand isolated and apart. If it were for a moment allowed that the Lord Jesus could be said to bear sin or to remove it by directing men to the pursuit of virtue, and by supplying the motives and warnings, the exhortations and encouragements, which are fully sufficient to turn them away from evil, it must not be forgotten that He is said to do this only as the Lamb of God. The language is plainly borrowed from the Mosaic worship; and it cannot refer to the moral improvement resulting from the instructions of a teacher. It refers to the effect of a sacrifice bearing the merited punishment of sin.

3. Nor will this union of the two clauses, so necessary to the full sense, permit us to refer the language to *inward* deliverance from sin. It is a sacrificial deliverance from sin; and however closely the moral deliverance may stand—and will always be found to stand—in inseparable connection with it, it is not a subjective deliverance alone. And in point of fact who does not see that experience contradicts that moral interpretation and shows its incorrectness? In no such sense has Christ taken moral evil from the world, or removed the weaknesses and imperfections of our fallen nature.

All these comments throw humanity back upon itself, upon its own strength and resources in the last resort, instead of presenting to the mind the adequate object of faith; and therein lies their danger.

The Baptist, in speaking of sin, speaks of it in the singular, "the sin of the world." Not that he had in his eye merely the root-sin,[1] the original sin of the race. Rather, the sins of mankind are viewed as a collective whole, and regarded as a heavy burden; and the Lamb of God is said to bear whatever has the character of sin, or the whole mass and assemblage of sin; the term "world" comprehending men who lived before the nativity of Christ as well as after it. Some have indeed taken the word SIN as synonymous with punishment, but the phrase takes in the notion of sin with the guilt and consequences involved in it.

But the phrase, "to bear sin," demands more particular consideration. Wherever the language occurs, it carries with it the notion of an oppressive burden, or of penal endurance. But let us consider the phrase in examples. It occurs, first, in the sense of living under the frown or punitive hand of God: thus the Israelites "bore their iniquity" according to the number of the days in which they had searched out the land, each day a year (Numb. xiv. 34): it is used as synonymous with being guilty (Lev. v. 17; Num. v. 31): it is found as equivalent

[1] So Beza unhappily expounds it, referring to Rom. v. 12.

to being cut off (Lev. xx. 17; Num. ix. 13): it occurs in the
sense of being punished with death (Num. xviii. 22, 32. Compare also Ex. xxviii. 43 ; Lev. xxiv. 15). In all these instances
it refers to a person bearing his *own* sin. Where the reference,
again, is to the sins of *others*, it means to undergo punishment
for them, or to feel the penal effects and the unpleasant consequences due to the sins of others (Lam. v. 7; Ezek. xviii. 19).
Hence, if we abide by the usage of language, the phrase can
only mean, in this passage, to endure the penal consequences
inseparable from the sins of mankind.

And as to the origin of the figure, it is taken from lifting a
burden in order to carry it, or to lay it on one's shoulders. But
as the language is sacrificial, it points to the victim bearing the
sin which the offerer laid upon it, by the laying on of the hand.
The language, rightly understood, can only mean that Jesus was
put in connection with sin; that He took SIN AS SUCH, and not
the mere consequences of it, or the element of punishment
alone; that He bore sin considered as guilt in its relation to the
moral Governor; that He was made the world's sin, and bore it,
—thus becoming, not personally but officially, the proper object
of punitive justice, and enduring the penalty due to the sins of
mankind. The words prove that the work of Christ was a provision for sin as such,—that is, for sin considered as demerit and
guilt; and only as the atoning work of Christ is adapted to this
end, and divinely accepted, does it reverse the consequences of
sin. A canon of easy application is, that the interposition of
Christ implies that the burden of sin which was transferred to
Him pressed heavily on the world, that mankind could not rid
themselves of it, and could do nothing to remove it; and the
language implies that the Lamb of God made it His—His heritage or property;—bearing in His own person what we had committed.

It must be noticed, further, that the verb *beareth*, which is
in the present tense, is not used as a prophecy,[1] neither as an

------

[1] So Meyer on the verse.

allusion to the constant efficacy of the sacrifice,[1] but as indicating that Jesus was even then the sin-bearer. He never in fact appeared "without sin" during His humiliation (Heb. ix. 28); and His coming in the likeness of sinful flesh was at once a proof that sin was borne by Him, and that this was already a part of His satisfaction. He was, even then, bearing sin, and many of the penal effects of it. It is a mistake to say, then, that the thought of the passage is an allusion to the abolition of sin; for the first idea of a sin-offering was not so much the consuming of moral evil—though that undoubtedly follows, and is a necessary consequence at the next remove—as the bearing of guilt. And an Israelite dreading divine wrath ever thought of the sin-offering in this light, as liberating him from its burden or its pressure.

As to the purpose for which the Lamb of God bore sin with respect to mankind, it is not here distinctly stated in express terms; but it can be easily inferred. With what conceivable object can He be supposed to have placed Himself in men's stead, and to have borne their sin as a piacular victim, but with a view to free or to redeem His people, and to exempt them from their burden,—a burden which He bore in their stead? This is the obvious inference: any other interpretation is intolerable. Nothing can be more forced and unnatural as an interpretation, than to hold that Christ bore the sin of the world for any other object than to set His people free from their merited doom or obligation. The whole burden or penalty and doom of sin must be seen, accordingly, upon the Lamb of God, and as borne by Him for others. He is an adequate and sufficient atonement.

Thus the Baptist, looking into the new economy from his view-point in the Old Testament, fixes attention upon the important place, or rather, the paramount place, which the doctrine of the atonement was to hold in Christianity. To a religious Jew, indeed, looking for the accomplishment of prophecy, and

[1] So Hengstenberg on the verse.

for "the righteous servant" to be the reality of all the types and shadows, the new economy would not otherwise have commended itself. He could not have accepted it unless it had provided for the expiation of sin, to which the whole Old Testament pointed. As the preparatory arrangement of Judaism provided for the expiation of sin annually, so the Baptist's words pointed to what adequately met this expectation,—with this peculiar difference, that it was a provision, not for the Jews only, but for the world. And it was spoken probably in Christ's hearing as well as in His presence.

The atonement was equally important for all mankind; and hence it is that the Baptist announces with so much emphasis, that it was a gracious provision, which comprehended a reference to the world at large, without distinction of nationality. Christ and His apostles were soon more clearly to unfold the universality of this expiation, as a provision equally intended for every tribe and country. And the exclamation BEHOLD ! was meant to direct attention to Him, and to invite all who were either burdened by a sense of sin, or expecting a vicarious sacrifice by which it might be borne. This is incontrovertibly the import of the words according to the significance of language and the connection of ideas.

To all this interpretation, however, a twofold objection has been raised by those who, under the influence of preconceived ideas or philosophical reasonings, have adopted views at variance with the vicarious sacrifice of Christ. One doubt has reference to the supposed extent of the Baptist's knowledge on the subject of Christ's death; and a second exception is taken to this mode of interpretation, on the ground that this sense cannot be held to be the uniform and constant import of the phrase, "to bear sin." We must consider what force, if any, attaches to these two objections.

1. As to the first objection, taken up and repeated in many quarters, it amounts to this: that the doctrine of the atonement, as theologians now hold it, could not possibly have been known

to the Baptist, when so many of his contemporaries were ignorant of it. To this objection it may suffice to answer, that the
vicarious sacrifice of the Messiah was well known to Isaiah,
and to all the ancient believers, who apprehended the nature
and significance of the types, or who saw the bearing of the
prophecies. Not only so: we may argue that John the Baptist
was instructed by his father, Zacharias; and as the redemption
of Israel by a mediator was well known to the latter (Luke i.
77), the Baptist may well be regarded, on this ground alone, as
possessing clearer and more accurate views than were current
among the Jews of his day, on the whole subject of the
Messiah's person and atonement. Besides, the Baptist must
have been well acquainted with the Old Testament Scriptures
generally, and with Isaiah's prophecy in particular (Isa. liii.),
when his very office was to go before Him as His herald and
forerunner. We should have been surprised had no such testimony been given by the messenger who was to go before His
face, and who, according to Christ's own words, was the greatest
of those born of women. It would seem, however, that John
understood this truth, not merely by a study of the law, and
the prophets testifying to it, but also by special revelation.
And though the atonement is not again so expressly mentioned
by him except on the following day (John i. 36), yet all his
teaching assumes it and presupposes it. Nor can any doubt be
drawn from the subsequent message of inquiry, when he sent
from the prison where he was confined two of his disciples, to
ascertain the Messiahship of Christ from His own lips. The
Baptist might desire to meet some new phase of doubt, either in
his own mind or in the minds of the disciples, blinded as they
were by many prejudices.

2. The second objection is based upon the alleged want of
uniformity or constancy of meaning attaching to the words,
"bearing sin," in the fourfold application in which it occurs.
Thus we find it applied—(1) to the sinner; (2) to the sacrifice;
(3) to the priest; and (4) to God Himself. As to the two first

there is little difficulty.   It is common, however, to explain the
two latter applications, but especially the last, as denoting " to
take away or to pardon sin."   With regard to its application to
the priest, there is no cause for deviating from its ordinary
meaning.   They were said to bear sin by eating of the sin-offer-
ings[1] (Lev. x. 17); and the high priest was said to bear the
iniquity of the holy things in virtue of the inscription, HOLINESS
TO THE LORD, as shadowing forth the holiness of Christ engraven
on the plate worn upon his forehead (Ex. xxviii. 38).   The
priesthood, holy by separation and by peculiar rites, partook of
the flesh of the sin-offering in order to point out that they
assimilated or incorporated with themselves the sacrifice or sin-
offering laden with the impurity of the worshipper, and which,
passing over to the victim, was thus consumed by being brought
into connection with a divinely-appointed priesthood.   All this
pointed to a time when priest and sacrifice should be one.   Thus
the phrase, " to bear sin," as applied to the priest, has the same
sense as in all the other applications, though a typical one
adumbrating a coming reality.

The main difficulty, however, connected with the phrase " to
bear sin," is to determine whether we are able to maintain this
uniform sense, or whether we can show cause for abiding by the
same import of the phrase when it is applied to God.   How can
GOD BE SAID TO BEAR SIN ?   And yet what warrant have translators and expositors for deviating from the rendering given to
the phrase here and in Isa. liii., as well as in many similar
passages, with a common consent ?   The general interpretation
of the phrase when it is applied to God, is, that in such a usage
it can only mean, " to forgive iniquity."   The Septuagint led the
way here, and has been implicitly followed ever since.   Alive to
the difficulty which presents itself to every mind, they interpreted
the expression in this application of it: " to forgive iniquity ; "
and all the subsequent expositors and lexicographers in the
Protestant churches, as well as among the Fathers, followed in

[1] See Oehler, *Herzogs Encyklo.* x. p. 649, and Keil on Lev. x. 17.

the same direction. And thus the authorised English version translates the expression, "to forgive iniquity," wherever it occurs in this usage, that is as applied to God. (See Ex. xxxiv. 7; Mic. vii. 18; Ps. xxxii. 5, lxxxv. 3; Isa. xxxiii. 24; Ex. xxxii. 32.) Now, is that a warrantable interpretation? Though it is a question which requires to be weighed with the utmost philological nicety, as well as with the utmost caution in a theological point of view, yet it deserves to be seriously pondered whether preconceived notions as to what is a fitting or unfitting mode of speech as applied to God may not in this case have exercised a misleading influence, and whether that fear did not lead to a wrong decision in the present instance. It is possible that the ordinary solution may turn out to be a wrong one, and may yet come to be repudiated with as common a consent as it has been adopted since the Septuagint led the way in introducing it.

On the other hand, it is held by many writers, ancient and modern, who oppose themselves to the vicarious satisfaction—by the Socinians of a former day, and by some eminent names [1] in our own time,—that the application of this phrase to God decides‘ upon its import wherever it occurs. They will have a uniform and constant interpretation; and, on this account, they vehemently urge and maintain that the phrase cannot in any case mean, *to bear sin, to expiate iniquity, or to satisfy for it*, because God cannot be said to bear sin. The opponents of the vicarious sacrifice or substitution insist on a uniform interpretation, because they think, that by this means they have an incontrovertible argument in their favour.

Most of those who maintain the doctrine of substitution have felt the difficulty of asserting a uniform and constant interpretation, and have distinguished between the sacrifice and the priest, between the sinner and the pardoner. And even those [2] who are

---

[1] See Hofmann's *Schriftbeweis*, vol. ii. p. 285 : "Gott trägt die Sünde, nimmt Sie hin, lässt Sie sich gefallen ohne Sie zu strafen."

[2] See Cocceius' *Hebrew Lexicon* on the word. Compare, too, Stockii *Clavis*.

disposed to abide by some shade of the ordinary meaning, conclude that in the passages where God is said "to bear sin," it can
only mean a forbearance to punish it, as contrasted with taking
vengeance, or a patient bearing of the wrong for a time.

One eminent writer,[1] while discussing the phrase in all its
various applications, contends for a uniform and constant sense
even in those cases where it is applied to God. Œder holds
that, so used in the Old Testament, the phrase must be understood as referring to the Son of God, and to His work as the
bearer of sin. "Ex. xxxiv. 7 is objected," says he, "to our
argument, that the adversaries may not seem to have said
nothing. The purport of their statement is: as the words *to
bear sin*, when used respecting God, do not mean that He laid
them on Himself to satisfy for them, it follows that when we
read the same words respecting Christ, they have not this meaning. But if you inquire whether the Socinians themselves
believe that the signification of the words *take away* in John i.
29 is the same as at Ex. xxxiv. 7, they will most certainly deny
it; for, say they, God took away sin by forgiving it, Christ by
pointing out the way by which we may deliver ourselves. But
yet these men are not ashamed to object to us a passage which
they themselves understand otherwise. But let us come nearer
to the point. I deny, and persist in denying, that the expression,
to bear sin, in Ex. xxxiv. 7, and in such like texts, has any other
meaning than that which is found in so many passages elsewhere.
Nor does that passage treat of God the Father, but of God the
Son, who is truly *the sin-bearer.*" "We have consulted and
weighed with considerable care all the passages which contain
this phrase, and that can be referred to in this sense. They are:
Mic. vii. 18; Ps. xxxii. 5, with which I would compare verse 1
and Isa. xxxiii. 24; Ps. lxxxv. 3; Ex. xxx. 32,—all which are
so beautifully expounded of Christ the sin-bearer, that nothing
can be finer."

This interpretation may not be accepted by all. It may seem

---

[1] Œder in his *Refutation of the Racovian Catechism* (Lat.), p. 802.

to some an incongruous phraseology to apply to God vicarious language of this nature: and it may appear to others too much of a New Testament view to occur to the believers in the remote past. But some expressions, long treated as strong anthropomorphisms, cease to be so when we apprehend them in connection with the Messiah, who was not only the angel of the covenant, but Jehovah, God of Israel. Thus the phrase, "they shall look upon Me whom they have pierced," was regarded by the Septuagint as only a figure of speech, or as an obvious anthropomorphism; and, certainly, it would have been so regarded by every one but for the apostolic commentary [1] upon it. But John's interpretation leaves to the New Testament Church no room to doubt its literal application to the pierced and wounded Saviour. There are other turns of expression and forms of speech, the full import of which is evolved only by the incarnation and by the atonement; and this may be one of them.

We have only further to add, in connection with this interpretation, that when these words are put together, it will be found that the Son of God took sin upon Him, and bore it simultaneously with the taking of the flesh, nay, in a sense bore it even prior to the actual fact of the incarnation. The peculiar character of the Lord's humanity, which was, on the one hand, pure and holy, and yet, on the other, a curse-bearing humanity, plainly shows that in some sense He was the sin-bearer from the moment of His sending, and, therefore, even prior to His actual incarnation. And when it is said that God sent His Son in the likeness of sinful flesh, and for sin condemned sin in the flesh, we have the very same thing. Therefore we may affirm that the phrase, "to bear sin," in its application to God, treats of God the Son; or it may suffice to say that *it refers to the incarnate one, the God of redemption.* There is, I think, ground to hold that the same constant and uniform rendering should be retained even in this connection. This will intimate that sin was borne by the Son of God, not alone in the sense of forbearance, but in

1 See John xix. 37.

such a sense that it was laid on Messiah as the sin-bearer, to be expiated by a divine fact in the true and proper sense. We assert, then, the constant and uniform sense of this phraseology in all its four-fold application; and when challenged to go through with our interpretation, we reply that we do go through with it. And certainly this last usage furnishes no loophole through which its proper force can be evaded, as has been so often attempted by Socinianizing writers, in former as well as in more recent times.

Thus the Lamb of God appeared without inherent sin or taint of any kind, but never without the sin of others. The sin of man was not first imputed to Him or borne by Him when He hung on the cross, but in and with the assumption of man's nature, or, more precisely, in and with His mission. The very form of a servant, and His putting on the likeness of sinful flesh, was an argument that sin was already transferred to Him and borne by Him; and not a single moment of the Lord's earthly life can be conceived of in which He did not feel the burden of the divine wrath which must otherwise have pressed on us for ever. Hence, "to bear sin" is the phrase in God's word for freeing us from its burden and punishment.

Because He bore sin, and was never seen without it, it may be affirmed that the mortality which was comprehended in the words, "Thou shalt surely die"—that is, all that was summed up in the wrath and curse of God,—was never really separated from Him, though it had its hours of culmination and its abatements. Hence, without referring further at present to the character of the suffering, it evidently appears that, as the sin-bearer, He all through life discerned and felt the penal character of sin, that is, the sense of guilt, not personal, but as the surety could realize it. He felt the obligation to divine punishment for sins not His own, but made His own by an official action; and they who evacuate of their true significance these deep words, "that beareth the sins of the world," allowing Christ to have no connection with sin, and only dwelling on His purity and spotless innocence as our example—they who will not have Him as a sin-bearer, who took sin to Himself, and wrapped Himself in it—are the most sacrilegious of robbers and obscurers of His grace. This deep abasement is the glory of His incarnation.

If, then, we put together the elements of this testimony to the Lord's atonement, they are these : (1) It was of God's gracious appointment—" the Lamb of God ; " (2) it essentially lay in the vicarious element of the transaction,—it was the bearing of the sin of others, or of the world; (3) it was a bearing or a penal endurance ; (4) it was sacrificial, being the truth of the shadows in the previous economy; (5) it was without distinction of nationality.

It follows, that if Christ bore sin, His people do not need to bear it. It follows, also, that since God has appointed this way of deliverance, there is no other way.[1]

SEC. XVII.—THE FREQUENTLY REPEATED NAME, THE SON OF MAN, FURTHER EXHIBITING HIM AS THE SIN-BEARER.

This phrase, which has, wherever it occurs, some reference to a work of substitution, is much in our Lord's mouth. Of all the titles He assumed, indeed, it is by far the most frequent. No fewer than eighty instances occur, or, if we deduct the repetitions, fifty-five instances where He announces Himself by this title. And it cannot escape observation, that He makes use of this name not less systematically than He abstains from the title Messiah. The reason of this will perhaps be obvious, when we ascertain the true import of the phrase by which, as will appear, He eighty times, either more or less directly, refers to some phase of His representative work in itself, or in respect to its reward. Not to forestall, however, what must be proved, we shall now proceed to investigate its meaning in the contexts, in the light of the very various comments which it has received. We select only a few of the interpretations for special notice.

[1] See note F.

1. The expression, Son of Man, cannot be limited to a description of His person, irrespective of His office. The patristic writers, and those who follow them, for the most part stop short at this. But the title will be found to be much wider and more extensive in its meaning. The incarnation is in it; but that is not all. It may seem, indeed, that when Christ calls Himself Son of Man (John iii. 13), and in the next verses the Son of God, He means merely to describe His whole person by one of His natures, the only way by which the God-man can be spoken of (John iii. 16). But that, though plausible, will be found to be untenable. The phrase, "Son of Man," is more than a designation of His person described by its human side, or by the humanity belonging to it.

2. Nor is it a mere Hebraism or circumlocution equivalent to the simple expression, *Man*. This sense, though countenanced by many eminent names of the Reformation age, can no longer be maintained. We find that men and the Son of Man are ideas too clearly distinguished and contrasted in many passages by the Lord Himself, to render this interpretation even probable (John iii. 13; Matt. xii. 32). Still less can the phrase be so evacuated of significance as to denote merely *a certain man, this man, or the man here present*,—comments betraying a low exegetical sense, and properly the growth of a rationalistic age. They have only to be repudiated.

3. Nor can we interpret the phrase as denoting, the man by eminence—the most excellent of all men. Modern commentators, with whom this is the favourite view, take it for the most part as a title of dignity and distinction; and they think themselves warranted to deduce this comment from Daniel's vision, where one like the Son of Man is brought near to the Ancient of days to receive dominion (Dan. vii. 13). But we shall find that it is not properly a title of dignity or eminence at all, though the latter idea is often mentioned in connection with it as a reward. And those who limit the allusion to Daniel's vision of His kingdom lose sight of two things,—(1) the foundation on

which this kingdom is reared—His abasement; and (2) the important rule of interpretation supplied to us by the apostle: " Now that He ascended, what is it but that He also descended first into the lower parts of the earth?" (Eph. iv. 9). The first time Jesus called Himself "Son of Man" was, as Bengel remarks, when He had already been recognised by His disciples as the Son of God (John i. 57). Not dignity and eminence, but abasement and meanness, are the ideas expressed by the title. Thus, when God addressed a prophet with the designation " son of man," it was to remind him of his meanness as dust and ashes, lest he should be exalted by the revelations made to him (Ezek. xxx. 2).

We may here make one or two preliminary observations, as elements for directing our iniquiry, or tending to aid us in arriving at the import of the phrase.

1. It must strike every one who attentively examines our Lord's use of this title, that we never find it used after His resurrection. The reason seems to be, that it was not descriptive of His resurrection state; that it belonged only to the days of His flesh; and that when He had left behind Him the servant form in which He appeared among men there was no longer any occasion for using it. This is further confirmed by a striking expression which He addressed to the disciples in the hearing of the Pharisees: " The days will come when ye will desire to see *one of the days of the Son of Man*, and ye shall not see it" (Luke xvii. 22); which can only mean one of those days they then enjoyed, or the days of His flesh. They would wish them back again. This decides on the meaning of our phrase.

2. Nor does He ever use the expression, Son of Man, in His prayers to God,—as if it were not in keeping with the peculiarly close relation subsisting between Him and God the Father. It is descriptive of what is official rather than personal, or of what He became rather than of what He was.

3. Neither does He use it in His capacity of teacher. When announcing any truth, or expounding any principle of duty, He

says, "Verily, verily, I say unto you." It is no exception to this observation, that we find Him saying in the parable of the tares, "The Sower of the *good seed* is the Son of Man." For that allusion is not to the function or office of a teacher dealing with all men indiscriminately, but to the efficacious illumination which the Lord dispenses as the head of His Church, on the ground or basis of the priestly work which He had already finished.

4. Another observation forces itself on the attention of every one who examines the several passages where this phrase occurs. It is a title used almost exclusively by Christ Himself. He is seldom or ever so called by His disciples. He appropriates to Himself the title, Son of Man, as the special definition of His condescending grace; and as displaying to those who heard Him not the divine relation, which was natural and proper to Him, but the new condition which He had taken to Himself, and into which He had stepped down, for the attainment of an object worthy of such abasement. And when Stephen on one occasion uses the phrase, "Son of Man," he nearly quotes our Lord's own words, before the same council, at His trial (Acts vii. 56). And when John, in Revelation, says, "I saw one *like* unto the Son of Man," it may be only a quotation of Daniel.

As to the origin of the title, there seems no cause to doubt that it has a primary reference to the words in Ps. viii. 4: "What is man, that Thou art mindful of him? and the son of man, that Thou visitest him?" The word for *man* in the original does not signify the high and eminent, but the opposite,— the low, despised, and miserable. The same phrase is found in other passages in this acceptation; as, for example, in Ps. xlix. 2, Job xxv. 6. The psalm, as applied to the second man, means that He seemed so utterly neglected and abandoned, that there was no hope of His being ever visited by God or rescued from the doom into which He had sunk as the substitute of others. This is plainly the apostolic comment given in the Epistle to the Hebrews (Heb. ii. 9, 10); and our Lord's use of the phraseology is in harmony with it. The sight of His low condition called forth that language from the Psalmist; and when our Lord applies the language to Himself as the most descriptive of all names, it must be understood as akin to the expressions, " I am a worm and no man" (Ps. xxii. 6); " A man of sorrows and acquainted with grief" (Isa. liii. 3). The expression intimates that He was not only man of man, but that " He made Himself of no reputation, and took upon Him the form of a servant, and was made in the likeness of man; and being found in fashion as a man, He humbled Himself, and became obedient unto death." The phrase, then, is not a mere circumlocution, nor a mere synonym for Jesus: it has a proper significance. We think it will be found, on a full and accurate examination of all the several passages, that the following elements are contained in this title: true humanity or the real assumption of our nature by the Son of God; the idea of the second man or second Adam; the abasement, grief, and shame with which He was acquainted during His earthly lot.

I. The first of these three ideas is accepted by all evangelical men without hesitation, and we do not require to establish it. To the two latter only we shall allude a little more in detail.

2. When Jesus called Himself Son of Man, He plainly taught, under a certain measure of disguise, that He was the second man or second Adam, who was to bruise the serpent's head, or, in other words, to destroy the works of the devil. This allusion to the second man, or second representative man, is wider than a mere relation to the Jews, and goes back to the human race as such. He occupies a similar relation to that of the first man to those who lived before as well as after His coming in the flesh. Against this element of the phrase now widely recognised among a good school of commentators, no valid objection has ever been advanced; we accept it frankly. But by many who accept it, the sense is, we think, unduly extended, so as to take in His glorified state as well.

3. This brings us to notice the other idea already referred to

—the mean condition or the curse-bearing life, which, we think, is essentially connected with our Lord's expression, and contained in it. This idea is perfectly compatible with the other. The two ideas, so far from being discordant, are the complement of one another. He could not, in truth, be the second Adam without being the substitute of sinners. The sense will be then, when we put the three ideas together: the second Adam abased or made a curse for us, and who hid not His face from shame. We cannot but discern this sense in the following passages.

Mark ix. 12: "*And He answered and told them, Elias verily cometh first, and restoreth all things; and how it is written* [or better, interrogatively, *how is it written?*] *of the Son of Man, that He must suffer many things, and be set at nought.*"—These words set forth, with sufficient clearness, two things: that, as the Son of Man, Christ was the subject of prophecy; and that, in this light, He was that great sufferer alluded to in the psalms and prophets, whose sorrows alone were of sufficient importance to mankind to be distinctly foretold. There is here an allusion to Isaiah's prophecy, if not an express quotation of the words, "despised and rejected of men" (Isa. liii. 3). Jesus in substance says, I, as the Son of Man, am the man of sorrows of the prophet.

Matt. viii. 20: "*The foxes have holes, and the birds of the air have nests* [better, *roosting-places*], *but the Son of Man hath not where to lay His head.*"—A certain scribe had offered to follow Jesus wherever He went; and he was told to count the cost, and to dispossess his mind of any secret hankering after worldly wealth or property. Jesus declares that He Himself was without a home or fixed abode, and that He might even be contrasted with the foxes and birds of the air, which have a resting-place in this world, but He had none. Now, as this is said in connection with His being the Son of Man, it is impossible not to observe an allusion to His abasement and to His substitution in our room; for He endured this only as He led a curse-bearing life. He was subjected to the consequences of sin, and was treated as a sinner; because man, having been disinherited, had no claim to ought in the world. He who was rich for our sakes became poor to reinstate us; and thus the Son of Man was never seen without sin while He was here.

Matt. xx. 28 : " *The Son of Man came not to be ministered unto, but to minister.*"—We omit the second clause at present, as our immediate object is to determine the meaning of the phrase, Son of Man. The connection in which it is put with ministering or serving, proves that it is significant of abasement, not of eminence. The Lord frowned on the ambition of James and John, who wished the seats of honour in His kingdom, reminding them of His own example, which must be followed; and that, unlike the kingdoms of men, the fundamental rule of His kingdom was humility. But there is a further thought. Speaking of Himself as the second Adam and the substitute of sinners, He intimates that His work involved the very opposite of ambition,—man's sin having been an aspiring to be more than a dependent creature. The second man came in the form of a servant, and to do a servant's work to the souls and bodies of men. Our phrase denotes, then, the abasement of a substitute.

John v. 27 : " *And He* [the Father] *hath given Him authority to execute judgment also, because He is the Son of Man.*"—As a proof how important it is to apprehend this phraseology aright, it may be noticed that this verse has been generally misinterpreted, because the point of this phrase has been missed. Thus those patristic commentators who construe the verse as we do (for some of them divide it in two, and read the last clause with the following verse), are much at a loss what meaning to attach to it; for, according to their interpretation of this phrase, as only meaning that He had assumed our nature, it seemed to say that His humanity must get this authority elsewhere. Others have put upon it the sense, that man must be judged by man, or by a judge who can be seen. Others interpret the second clause, *as far as He is the Son of Man,* as if it intimated that He acts as man, but that the action is really that of the Father in Him. But that comment misses the import of the causal particle, *because*. Nor does the verse convey the sense: this man saves men, this man judges men. The true explanation is easy when we view the title, " Son of Man," as descriptive of abasement. He receives this authority as a reward: the cross is the foundation of the glory; and the authority to judge, the culminating point of His exaltation, is the recompense of His curse-bearing life. It is just parallel to the words in Philippians, " He became obedient to death; WHEREFORE God also hath highly exalted Him."

Matt. xi. 19 : " *The Son of Man came eating and drinking.*"— This expression is not meant to intimate that our Lord adopted a freer mode of intercourse than the Baptist, as a mere phase of teaching, or as a mere example to His followers; still less does it indicate, as rationalists will have it, that He had a great relish for the hilarities of life. The phrase, Son of Man, intimates that He went there as part of His humiliation, the sinless amid the sinful, in the execution of His office. He used the world as not abusing it, and, by voluntary abasement, entered into all its spheres, even where temptation was most rife, and God had been so much dishonoured. His presence there was a part of His curse-bearing life, but He never was off His guard; and so was sanctifying society to His followers. Hence they called him a gluttonous man and a wine-bibber.

Luke xix. 10 : " *The Son of Man is come to seek and to save that which was lost.*"—This title, as has been already noticed, is always significant, and not a mere expletive or circumlocution. But for the peculiar shade of thought derived from this phrase, which brings in the idea of the surety in His abasement, we might have referred the language more to the application of redemption than to its procuring cause. But the title, Son of Man, with the expression, *is come to seek*, points out what is the design of Christ, and proves that He describes His substitution in the room of others as standing in causal connection with the seeking and saving of the lost: the former is the basis of the latter. The allusion then, is, not to the kingly office alone, but to the second man, the humbled substitute in His representative work,—the ground and basis of the other.

Though we cannot adduce all the passages where the expression Son of Man occurs, we do not hesitate to affirm that, wherever it is found—whether referring to His poverty or to His betrayal—to His condemnation or to His crucifixion,—it alludes to vicarious punishment. The Lord, by means of this expression, utters His own consciousness of appearing in the likeness of sinful flesh, and states that He passed through the various grades of a humiliation, which can only be considered as the steps of a vicarious curse-bearing life. He intimates, by His use of this phrase, that He not only had assumed a true humanity, but stood in the position of the second man; in other words, was the surety self-emptied and abased. We may put it in many other forms, but this is the sense.

The same meaning attaches to the expression when the Lord uses it in connection with a present exercise of authority. To some of these cases it may be proper to refer, as they have been considered by some as adverse to the view already given, and as lending countenance to the opposite opinion, that the phrase rather contains the notion of dignity or eminence. A few instances will serve to prove that they do not invalidate, but confirm the interpretation above given.

Matt. ix. 6: "*That ye may know that the Son of Man hath power on earth to forgive sins, (then saith He to the sick of the palsy), Arise.*"—Jesus seeing their faith, said to the paralytic, as soon as they brought him into His presence, Thy sins be forgiven thee; which only drew down on Him a charge of blasphemy, because He claimed to Himself a power competent to God alone. He uses in reply to them an argument of irresistible cogency. As all disease was acknowledged to be the effect of sin (whether there might be any special sin in the present case or not), the instantaneous removal of the effect will prove that He had power to remove the cause; and He declares that He will prove His authority to remit sin, and its actual remission, by making the man perfectly whole. But the style of language which He uses cannot be interpreted, with one expositor, as but referring to the power which has its seat and source in God; nor can it mean, as another will have it, that He is the authorized representative of God in heaven. The allusion to the Son of Man means something more than the declarative action of a prophet. He means that, as the second man or substitute, He had power on earth, by anticipation or beforehand, to forgive sins,—an authority which He possessed, because He was then in process of expiating sin by His abasement and death. The connection is one of cause and effect. He had authority not merely to promise forgiveness, but to bestow it. Just as He said in relation to the judgment, that He had authority to exercise it, because He was the Son of Man, so He says in reference to forgiveness, that He had authority to dispense it even by anticipation, because He was the Son of Man. The one is the reward, the other is the procuring cause, or the merit by which it is effected; and this is always connected in the closest manner with the second man, the Lord from heaven. Not to mention the general analogy of Scripture, which uniformly deduces all the benefits of this nature from Christ's atoning work, the phrase under consideration is in itself decisive to this effect. Christ's suretyship is the meritorious or procuring cause of them all.

Mark ii. 28: "*The Son of Man is Lord also of the Sabbath.*" —Some have explained this verse, on account of the peculiar connection in which it stands, with the previous verse (ver. 27), as intimating that man, as man, is lord of the Sabbath. But to that interpretation there are two objections: (1) There is always in our Lord's style a sharp and well-defined difference between the two terms, man and the Son of Man. (2) It would be no valid argument to reason as follows: The Sabbath was made for man, not man for the Sabbath; therefore *man* is lord also of the Sabbath. Man, or, to go back to the class who heard

Him, Israel, was not lord of the Sabbath, but servant of it, and bound to observe it; whereas Jesus declares that He was Lord of the Sabbath in a sense in which no other shared. From the occasion on which the saying was uttered, the tenor of our Lord's words bears, that as the Sabbath was not one of the unalterable moral laws, it might be dispensed with in certain cases of mercy and necessity, for the preservation of life and health; for these are of paramount importance; and the Sabbath was made for man, not man for it. That is maintained in the plainest terms. But we find a sudden turn given to the expression in the words of Mark: "Therefore the Son of Man is Lord also of the Sabbath." This train of thought may be easily explained. It is warrantable in cases of necessity to break its rest, on the principle that man was not made for it, but that it was made for man; though he cannot on this account be called lord of the Sabbath, because this very permission is from the Lord. But Christ has a dispensing power over it from a ground which is unique and wholly His own,—because He is the Son of Man. There is no allusion to the other precepts of the decalogue here; nor indeed could this dispensing power be exercised in reference to them—since they are the expression of His own divine nature and divine will—without running counter to Himself and contradicting Himself. But as the abased and humbled substitute consulting for men's salvation and for their highest interests, He has been made Lord of the Sabbath. This is His reward. He had authority to alter and adjust the Sabbath, and to exercise a dispensing power in regard to it, as He deemed best, because He was the Son of Man. There is no word of abrogating it, but only of adjusting it, and adapting it in such a way as would be most conducive to the spiritual interests of His disciples. He, and He alone, had this authority in the very same way as He had authority to pardon and authority to exercise judgment, because He was the Son of Man, or the substitute of sinners, and the second man. And He showed that He was such a Lord of it, when He altered the day of the week. He on this occasion

vindicated the disciples who ate the ears of corn ; and not only
so, He had a dispensing power to give them this permission as
Lord also of the Sabbath.

The passages already adduced, and others to be met with as
we proceed, demonstrate that the idea uniformly attached to the
phrase is humiliation or abasement. Nor is this acceptation
refuted by those texts which at first sight seem to run counter
to it, and involve an allusion to His glory. On the contrary,
they mean that He who then spoke in the abasement of the
curse would appear in His mediatorial exaltation ; and, as was
natural, His thoughts were much directed to the joy that was
set before Him. Thus, when He told the disciples that they
should be rewarded "when the Son of Man should sit on the
throne of His glory," He intimated that His present poverty
and meanness should give place to infinite glory. At His trial
before the Sanhedrim, when He declared to the high priest,
"Ye shall see the Son of Man sitting on the right hand of
power," we have just the same thing. He first avowed His
supreme deity as the Son of God, and then immediately reverted to the view-point from which He usually spake—that
of the despised and rejected of men, the bearer of the world's
curse. And as they set Him at nought in His abasement, He
intimates the majesty and glory in which they should one day
behold Him. And the same explanation must be given of all
the other passages where this title is found in connection with
an allusion to His glory.[1]

The preceding discussion gives us, so to speak, a biography
of the Lord Jesus from His own consciousness, and, in fact, a
wholly different view of the life of Christ, than we should otherwise have been led to form. This language proves that He was
fully aware of the fact that He was the sin-bearer, and called to
lead a curse-bearing life, throughout His whole earthly career.
The human biographies of Christ, which in too many things
betray their incompetence to reproduce that wondrous portrait,

[1] See Note G.

are specially defective here. They rarely take account of this aspect of Christ's earthly life, or find any allusion to it in the Lord's own words. Without this element, however, our whole view of Christ's life is one-sided, and imperfect in the highest degree. Thus the principal use derived from it by many men, otherwise sound in the faith, is limited to His teaching or to His example, or, at furthest, extended to the mode in which the Prince of Life communicates the spiritual life to men, and unites them to Himself. However true and important all these aspects of His life may be, they are still defective. Seen from the true view-point, or read off from the consciousness of the Lord Himself, His life is pervaded from first to last with another element. He is conscious of being the sin-bearer and the curse-bearer; and every utterance that falls from His lips as the Son of Man, discovers that He realized at every step of His arduous work the position of vicarious suffering and abasement.

It is important to notice how He came to occupy this position as the substitute of sinful men, and so to act out that exchange of places which His whole atonement presupposes and implies. With a view to bring out the truth on this point, it may be proper to refer, negatively, to some of the theories current and in vogue on this subject, but without entering very largely into their refutation.

1. He did not first take sin upon Him, or was first made sin, upon the cross. He was not first a man, and at a subsequent period the sin-bearer or the curse-bearer. What has been truly and correctly said as to the assumption of humanity may be equally applied to this. He was not first a man, and then incarnate, or assumed into the personality of the Son; for the humanity never existed but in that personal union. In like manner we may say that the humanity never was without this imputation of sin; for that assumption of sin by which He became the sin-bearer, was IN, WITH, BY, and UNDER the assumption of our nature, though the sin is separable and distinguishable from the humanity. Nay, we should rather say that, according to the order of nature, the

sin was imputed and assumed simultaneously with His mission, and therefore, in a certain sense, prior to the actual incarnation; though it became His, in point of fact, only with the possession of a common nature. They who limit the sin-bearing to the three hours on the cross—a too widely diffused notion—have far diverged from biblical language and ideas.

2. Nor did Jesus become the sin-bearer by any necessity of nature in virtue of taking the flesh. This was the error of Menken and Irving, who thought that He assumed sin simply in virtue of taking humanity; as if sin and humanity were one and the same. Their theory was, that our Lord took to Himself a portion of the lump or mass, and that, in consequence of this, He personally, and not officially, by necessity of nature and not by voluntary consent, came under the obligations of that humanity of which He had assumed a part. This is a confusion of thought, which does not discern the things that differ, as well as perilous theology. But sin is not of the substance of man in such a way that they cannot be disjoined. They are so inter- woven and interpenetrated, indeed, that we may not be able to sunder the workmanship of God, which is good, from the corrup- tion which has tainted it. We can distinguish them, however, in idea; God distinguishes and separates in fact. Redemption, it is obvious, implies this separation: regeneration implies it: the incarnation presupposes it. If it were not so, man's nature could not have been a capable subject of redemption. And the fact that the Son of God entered into humanity by a true incar- nation, is a sufficient proof that sin and humanity are not one and the same; for He could not have united Himself to sin. Christ became the sin-bearer by free consent, not by necessity of nature; by voluntary susception, not in consequence of any indispensable condition adhering to Him in virtue of His birth.

That theory, under any modifications, is a deep untruth, and carries with it consequences that may well repel every Christian mind. Even on the supposition that He took sinless humanity and only assumed the curse, objectively considered, by the necessity of nature, it would still be a theory which no biblical divine could admit or endure. His death, on this supposition, would not be an official act, but a personal doom; not a free oblation, but a due punishment.[1] The guilt would be His own, and the curse a necessary debt, which he personally owed. The atonement, if we could still suppose such a transaction, on that principle, would have been for the race, on a principle of universalism, without selection or distinction. And to come under the curse in this way, He must needs have been Himself in Adam's covenant,—the very thing from which, with all its consequences, the supernatural conception was meant to give Him full exemption. The uniform language of Scripture is opposed to all this, and is a constant testimony to the fact that Christ died solely in the exercise of a priestly oblation, without any personal liability whatsoever. It was as bearing sin not His own in consequence of an act of His will, but not by any indispensable necessity, that the Lord encountered death.

3. It cannot be maintained, however, that the Lord took humanity in all respects as it was in Adam before the fall. That is to ignore all the effects and consequences that man's sin necessarily introduced, and it puts the Lord Jesus outside the family of man. He took human nature distinct and separate from sin, which was no part of its essence; for sin and humanity are separable quantities. He took humanity also apart from the imputed guilt of Adam's covenant, descending to Him individually, as if He were a mere unit in the race. He came as the second man. But He took humanity in such a way as also to assume, by His voluntary act, and at the same moment, the sin of His people, and the curse, which was its sure attendant; which is just what Paul intimates by " the likeness of sinful flesh," or by His appearing at His first coming with sin, as con-

---

[1] The Darbyite dogma, on what is called the Adam-life of Christ, is not much different from Irving's, and certainly not better. It is held that on the cross sin attached to the life of Christ. What would become of substitution or imputation if sin, IN ANY SENSE, attached to His life? (See Darby's *Synopsis* on John xi. vol. iii. p. 454, and *Girdle of Truth*, p. 298.)

trasted with His "appearing the second time without sin" (Heb. ix. 28). He must be regarded as bearing the penalty of sin from the first moment of His incarnation, or even from His sending by the Father. We cannot survey the meanness and abasement of His birth, made lower than the angels; the poverty of His condition; His manual occupation,—earning His bread with the sweat of His brow, according to the doom on all the race; His temptation by the foul spirit; His privations; His endurance of hunger and thirst; the agony and bloody sweat; the arrest; the chains by which He was bound; the trial; the accusation and rejection by His nation; the condemnation pronounced upon Him by the Gentiles; and the shame of a public execution,— without the full conviction that all this was included in our doom, and related to our punishment. All these griefs in the Man of Sorrows tended to the satisfaction for sin, and were comprehended in the primeval threat of death.

Thus the Lord officially appearing on our world as a sin-bearer, and not such a person as was innocent and without sin, must of necessity take a humanity not as He now has it in heaven, nor even as it was in Adam before the fall: "Because the brethren were partakers of flesh and blood, He also Himself likewise took part of the same" (Heb. ii. 14). He assumed humanity in its meanness, abasement, and poverty,—assumed, that is, not a mere body and soul, but the form of a servant under sentence of death. The only difference was, that He took our common nature without any of the individual infirmities found in particular men; that is, without any of the disorderly mental conditions or any of the germs of sickness which are either transmitted or developed in the individual. He was free from disease and free from the incursion of death according to the ordinary course of nature,—the exemption from both being due to the fact that sin and its consequences did not belong to Him as a personal thing, but as they were assumed by His voluntary act.

We now come back to the fact that, as the Son of Man, the Lord Jesus was never from the very first without sin and its consequences. He felt all through His life what it is to be made sin and to be reputed a sinner. And who knows what soul-trouble, agony, and desertion He endured when no eye but His Father's and that of worshipping angels saw Him? These times of agony only, so to speak, crop out here and there in His recorded life; but He was always as the Son of Man, made sin, and always suffering; and all this abasement was owing to the fact that He was the Son of Man.

The Lord's humanity, though derived from Adam through His mother, inherited none of the consequences of sin in itself, because it was not in Adam's covenant. By not distinguishing things that differ at this point, not a little confusion of idea has arisen in certain quarters. Thus some unguardedly have described the common infirmities attaching to the Lord's humanity, when He was among men, as if the sinless consequences of Adam's sin descended to Him, or as if He took by a spontaneous but arbitrary choice the physical infirmities to which humanity had in all ordinary cases come to be reduced. This is by no means the case, as we never find sickness or bodily disease attaching to Him. Though made like His brethren, or sent in the likeness of sinful flesh (Rom. viii. 3), the common infirmities which we undoubtedly find in Him—abasement, the appearance of greater age (John viii. 57), the aspect of a man of sorrows, hunger and thirst, weariness, homelessness, mortality—were not entailed on Him by the necessity of nature, but the effects of another cause. They were the consequences of sin-bearing, and penal therefore in their character, like His other sufferings. The explanation is obvious. Assuming as He did at one and the same moment, that is in the act of incarnation, both our nature and our sin, we have two things distinguishable in idea, but always conjoined during His earthly life. He on the one hand took humanity according to its idea without any PERSONAL connection with sin or its consequences, and on the other hand assumed as our substitute, that is, by His official act, the burden of our sins and their penal consequences in an abased, suffering, mortal humanity.

From the first hour of His earthly life He thus came before men as the sin-bearer, and therefore the curse-bearer, made like unto His brethren. He came within the consequences of sin only because He took sin itself by imputation. But for this, indeed, He might have appeared in a glorious humanity.

Having become man in this way by the two-fold assumption of our nature and our sin, He knew all through life the responsibilities and sorrows which this substitution involved. The idea of substitution involved this consequence, that the Lord should bear wrath instead of His people, or the penal effects of sin. Hence, through every channel which brought sin under His view or made it present to His soul, He seems to have encountered some part of the curse, or of soul-trouble. The exhaustion caused by His miracles, and the soul-trouble into which he was ushered at the time when the inquiring Greeks approached Him (John xii. 21-27), may be taken as instances how His soul was exercised; and the penal consequences of sin struck specially upon His soul.

It does not fall within this topic to describe the nature of this suffering, its ingredients, or its intensity. It may suffice to say, that though the Father while acting the part of a judge did not lay aside the person and relation of a Father, He yet inflicted real suffering, penal suffering, which struck the substitute, because it struck upon the sin which He made His; and there were gradations, too, in this curse-bearing life from the manger to the cross which were just degrees, or descending steps, in His humiliation. The cross was its culminating point; but it was by no means limited to the cross. Though we read little of His private life, or of the way in which His secret hours were spent, He was no doubt in those intervals frequently called to realize, as the Man of Sorrows, that He was on the earth in order to bear the sins of many; and nothing can be conceived more terrible even to the Son of God than to feel the loss of God—the bitterest ingredient in the cup of woe,—or to realize that He was, in the sense in which the sinless One could be so, the object of the condemnation, loathing, and hatred due to sin, or worthy in any sense of receiving it. The Son of Man was treated as if He were the sinners, with whom He had exchanged places before God.

We have seen, then, from the title, Son of Man, and from the allusions which He made to Himself, that Christ's life was from first to last a sin-bearing and a curse-bearing life. This is one essential element of the atonement.

SEC. XVIII.—CHRIST RECEIVING BAPTISM AS THE CONSCIOUS SIN-BEARER.

" *Suffer it to be so now : for thus it becometh us to fulfil all righteousness.*"—MATT. iii. 15.

This testimony is replete with meaning, whether we consider the occasion of it or the import of the terms. It may be called a key to that large class of passages which speak of Christ's obedience as the righteousness of His people, or represent Him as made of God unto us righteousness, because He was first of all made sin for us (2 Cor. v. 21).

As to the occasion which called forth this saying, we find it uttered on the memorable day of Christ's baptism, when he came to the Baptist, the new Elias, the culminating point of the Old Testament prophecy, and its voice. John may be regarded here as the living expression of the law and of the prophets, which had during many ages witnessed to the coming Messiah, and which now, by their greatest representative, were to introduce the Christ into His office. As the Lord Jesus recognised *them*, so they were to inaugurate *Him* as the truth of the prophecies, and as the substance of the types or shadows. So close in every point of view is the connection, rightly apprehended, of the old and new economy, that the one is incomplete without the other. But though Jesus was fully conscious of His mission from the day when the boy of twelve first trod the courts of the temple, and declared that He must be about His Father's business, He would take no steps towards the public discharge of His office till He was formally inaugurated into it by an authorized prophet on the one hand, and by divine testimony on the other; and our Lord well knew that John was sent on this very mission, by means of which a something was to be conferred upon Him that He had not before received.

The Baptist, as a sinner, feeling that it rather became him to exchange places with Jesus, and to be not the giver but the receiver in the interview, refused, for a time, to confer his baptism on the Redeemer. He could not conceive what the Christ had to do with a baptism of repentance for the remission of sins,—what it was to Him, or He to it. But that reluctance was overcome by the explanation which our Lord subjoined:—" suffer it to be so NOW "[1]—that is (for the *now* is emphatic), in my present state of humiliation, and as an action suited only to my state of substitution in the room of sinners. And the plural number, " it becometh us," may either refer, as in some similar cases, to Jesus alone; or, with a greatly modified sense, may include a reference also to the Baptist.

But the Lord subjoins an explanation as to the principle and end for which He sought John's baptism: " For thus it becometh us to fulfil all righteousness." It is not the special act of baptism to which alone allusion is here made. The language is more general, though the occasion was particular. There is nothing to warrant the limitation of the words, which must be accepted in the full force of the phraseology. The Lord had a public confession to make ; and the words here used furnish a key to the whole action. We must then, first of all, notice the import of these His words of confession: *it becometh us to fulfil all righteousness.* The Lord virtually says, " It is not unworthy of the Son of God to go down so far; for it is not a question of dignity or pre-eminence, but of fulfilling all righteousness." The reception of baptism was only a voluntary act, and not a

---

[1] ἄφες ἄρτι.

service personally necessary or required on His own account; for He acted of free choice when He became incarnate. But it became Him to fulfil His undertaking, and in doing so He was not free to omit this or any part of His work; for though he was under no obligation to take the flesh, yet there arose a certain duty from His engagement to the Father, from His mediatorial office, and from the old prophecies. There was a certain hypothetical necessity or propriety which required His acting as He now did, if the end was to be gained. It may be thus put: "It becometh me to appear in the likeness of a sinner, and to fulfil all righteousness."

But, it is further demanded, what significance had baptism for the Christ of God, and what application could it have to Him? This is the very difficulty which presented itself to the mind of the Baptist, and which is still a difficulty to many an expositor in explaining it. It must be borne in mind, in the first place, that, as the surety, Jesus was made under the law; and that sacraments, as prescribed by the second commandment, were among the DUTIES with which He complied. But while that side of the question is clear enough, the difficulty lies in the other aspect of a sacrament: how they could be for Him the outward signs by which the divine promises were sealed and the faith of the receiver confirmed; and they undoubtedly were so to Him.

In this matter it is obvious we must distinguish between the sinless person or individual and the official duty assigned to the surety; the neglect of which distinction has been the chief cause of the difficulty. When we speak of Christ's participation of the sacraments, it must always be on the supposition that He was acting as the Mediator between God and man, and that there is a strict limitation of His actions to a sphere that excludes not only all personal taint, but also all the mental exercises corresponding to this condition,—which, however, are involved in our use of the sacraments of the Church. Impurity of His own He had none. But He had truly entered into humanity, and come within the bonds of the human family; and, according to the law, the person who had but touched an unclean person, or had been in contact with him, was unclean. Hence, in submitting Himself to baptism as Mediator in an official capacity, the Lord Jesus virtually said, " Though sinless in a world of sinners, and without having contracted any personal taint, I come for baptism; because, in my public or official capacity, I am a debtor in the room of many, and bring with Me the sin of the whole world, for which I am the propitiation." He was already atoning for sin, and had been bearing it on His body since He took the flesh; and in this mediatorial capacity promises had been made to Him as the basis of His faith, and as the ground upon which His confidence was exercised at every step.

It is of course obvious that baptism had not, and could not have, the same significance to Him as it has to us. But it had an important significance even to Him,—first, officially, and then, as His faith was thus confirmed and established, also personally. Some writers have perplexed and complicated this whole question by drawing a superfluous distinction between the obedience due by Christ as a rational creature and that which He owed as the Mediator or Surety acting in the name of His people, and between the promises made to Him in the one capacity and those which were made to Him in the other. It is only an embarrassing distinction, which should be dismissed. It is much better to hold that Christ was not made under the law on His own account, and that humanity, existing in the person of the Son of God, came under no law, and was bound to no obedience, except as He spontaneously stooped to become officially the surety of His people. We are not to distinguish here, as some have unduly done, between the man and the Mediator. We meet in this whole scene, an inward offering of Himself, as when the sacrifice was presented at the door of the tabernacle of the congregation (Lev. i. 3), or a full mental dedication to bear the sin of the world, and, in so doing, to fulfil all righteousness. The administration of the rite, accordingly, was a symbol of the baptism of agony which He had yet to be baptized with, and which, with the utmost promptitude, He here, and all through His history, offered Himself to undergo: "I have a baptism to be baptized with; and how am I straitened till it be accomplished!" (Luke xii. 50). This mental dedication ran through all His subsequent career, and gave a tincture to His entire life, till it confronts us afresh as a completed act upon the cross. He had fulfilled all righteousness till now; and this gives us a glimpse into His purpose and resolve for the future. It consisted of these two parts: that Christ, in the likeness of sinful flesh, should condemn sin,—in other words, that He should perfectly fulfil the law of love in heart and action as one for many; and that, according to the same representative system, man should satisfy for man, by fully entering into the lot of sinners under punitive justice. He avowed His prompt and cordial willingness, as the physician of the sick, to take upon Himself their sicknesses and their diseases, though He well knew that He was now at the threshold of His public ministry, and entering on a scene of conflicts and trouble of which Nazareth had given Him no experience.

It might be added, that this merely mental offering of Himself in His baptism was crowned with a divine recognition (Matt. iii. 16). But on this we do not insist, as it does not come within our immediate purpose. It may suffice to say, that this divine act of recognition showed that not only was His past career well-pleasing, but that this dedication, as a thing that was to be daily renewed, was peculiarly so, and would be at the close most gloriously rewarded. The words which our Lord uses at a later period, "I have a baptism to be baptized with, and how am I straitened till it be accomplished!" discovers in what light Christ will have His baptism to be regarded. It was a symbolic representation of those sufferings and sorrows to which He must submit as the voluntary sacrifice in the room of His people,—an emblem of the way in which He was to bear the floods of wrath in bringing in the everlasting righteousness, or in fulfilling all righteousness. We do not need, then, to make two things out of the baptism, but may rest content with the symbol and the reality.

To all that has just been said, however, there are two objections, which must now be obviated. It is argued that we cannot class this passage among those which set forth a meritorious obedience for man, and in man's stead, for these reasons:—(1) because Christ speaks of Himself and of John together, and the obedience of the latter cannot be held to be meritorious for men; and (2) because it refers principally to baptism, which was not received by Christ in man's stead. These objections are easily met and removed.

As to the first objection, that Christ speaks of Himself and of John together, and that the obedience of the latter cannot be meritorious, the answer is at hand. It seems to be, as in many other places, the plural of eminence (comp. John iii. 11). But if the words do include a reference to John, in a certain modified sense, the meaning will be, that he, the Baptist, had duly to fulfil the terms of his commission, and not refuse his baptism to one who sought it at his hand, as our Lord now did upon this occasion.

As to the second objection, I answer; the allusion is not to a single rite or to any one observance which had been appointed by divine authority, and the observance of which was a right thing. That does not by any means exhaust the meaning. The expression used is, that He must needs fulfil all righteousness in a humiliation of which He was not ashamed, and in which John must acquiesce. It can only refer to the sinless One offering in the room of sinners the great atoning act, or to the whole mediatorial righteousness. His greatness and His abasement are equally brought out in the work to be done.

This will help us to understand in what sense it can be said that Christ, by receiving baptism, "fulfilled all righteousness." This is the point of the passage in reference to the subject for

which we have adduced it; and it must be precisely apprehended. The phrase, "to fulfil all righteousness," can only
mean, in this connection, as was symbolized in the rite employed, that the Lord Jesus would bring in an approved fulfilment of the divine law, the work of one for many; that there
must be an exact correspondence between that which is required
and that which is actually rendered,—a coincidence between
the two. Though it is not necessary to refer to the essential
righteousness of God, by which He wills and loves all that
agrees with His perfections, further than to say that the creature's righteousness is to be measured on that attribute, or on
the law which is the transcript of it, yet it is necessary to bear
in mind that this human righteousness is fulfilled only when
men reflect the image of their Maker in their heart and nature,
in their life and actions. As it was not a divine righteousness,
but a creature-righteousness, that was required at our hands, so
it was this that the Mediator rendered,—in other words, it was
the same in kind with ours, though the person who came to
bring it in was possessed of a divine dignity, which gave His
work a validity and value all its own. It consisted in an obedience to the divine law in precept and in penalty, complete in
all its parts, and up to the measure of man's capacity; for as
nothing less was claimed, so nothing less was rendered by the
Mediator, who was made under the law as broken, and who acted
in the room of others. Thus man satisfied for man, and, furthermore, fulfilled the law of love in heart and life.

We cannot limit the phrase to anything short of full obedience
to the law, as the rule of righteousness. And when we look at
the terms here used, it will be found, that as the epithet *righteous*
always carries with it the notion that the person so described is
approved by a competent tribunal as following a line of conduct
which is conformable to the law, so *righteousness*[1] is that quality,

---

[1] This is the meaning of δικαιοσύνη. That the verb δικαιοῦν denotes one who if
acquitted and accepted, is admitted on all hands ; but the mistake too commonly
committed is, that the same meaning has not been carried out to these cognate
words, *e.g.* δικαιοσύνη, δίκαιος.

personal or official, which marks one out as the fit object of that approval. The allusion here is to the righteousness due from the creature, and exhibited in the great sacrifice which was here mentally offered by the Mediator in our stead. That this is the meaning is obvious on many grounds. Expositors have propounded various other explanations, which are not tenable.

We may set aside, then, as faulty and inadequate, (1) the comment that the language is equivalent to saying that Christ fully taught the doctrine of true religion, or that He embodied in His example an outline of all He taught to others. As little will it suffice to say, (2) that the phrase means, "it becomes us to do what is right, or to carry out, even to the smallest duty, that which God has appointed." There is as little ground for the explanation, (3) that humility is the principal part of righteousness. The defect of all these comments is, that they take no account of Christ's mediatorial position in this act, without which we cannot understand His words, or see their proper scope. He was already in this public act MENTALLY OFFERING the sacrifice of Himself to the Father, and so fulfilling all righteousness.

SEC. XIX.—CHRIST, AS THE SIN-BEARER, TAKING ON HIM, DURING HIS EARTHLY LIFE AND HISTORY, THE BURDENS AND SICKNESSES OF HIS PEOPLE.

In the Gospels there are several passages to be found which bring out far deeper views on the subject of Christ's curse-bearing and suffering life than have commonly been adopted, or, at least, than have been taken up in earnest in the Church. Most readers who merely read the narrative of Christ's life as they do a common history, see nothing more in these sufferings than the opposition of ungodly men to the cause of God, or limit the endurance of the curse on the part of Jesus to the hours when He hung upon the cross. But the curse-bearing career of Christ was by no means of that nature, nor limited to that time.

Neither is it enough to say, as the views of others imply, that as Jesus endured the collective elements of the curse on the cross, it serves no purpose to trace it piecemeal and in detail in other spheres and at other times. For on that theory it would not have been necessary for Christ to be an infant, child, youth, and man, if we are to limit attention to the one point which was undoubtedly the climax both of the obedience and of the curse. His previous life, considered in the double light of sinless purity and of curse-bearing endurance, was not less necessary in the divine economy than the cross, and not less provided for in the wisdom of the divine counsels. His entire life was pervaded by the curse; and He encountered it in every sphere where His people were required to bear it. We may trace from His history how He met it in all those spheres and departments where the bitter effects of sin, beyond doubt, assail mankind. The opposite view may seem to have more simplicity in it; but it overleaps the significance of the earthly life of Christ. God's wisdom, however, was plainly different. And this endurance of the curse from the commencement of His life to its close, in every one of those departments or spheres where the bitter consequences of sin had entered, must be viewed as necessary, not only in the way of fitting the Lord Jesus to become a merciful and faithful High Priest (Heb. ii. 17), but as a condition in the moral government of God for the expiation of sin.

As it is easy to err by excess here, many are content to err by defect. Thus Menken and Irving egregiously erred by bringing Christ into the circle of human nature as it now is. But many, on the other hand, have been deterred, in consequence of their mistake, from even venturing to approach the subject. The regulative principle, however, which is by no means to be lost sight of at any point, and which will guide us in our inquiry here, is, that sin is not of the essence of humanity, and that we can distinguish between it and God's workmanship.[1] While

[1] One important thought in connection with the incarnation, and capable of receiving an application to the case in hand, was brought out during the discus-

Christ sustained our persons and entered into our position by a legal exchange of places, He was incarnate in a humanity according to its idea, and not as it now is in us. It was not an exchange of either a physical or moral nature when He officially took our place. The Sinless One took the curse upon Himself, and bore it through life, solely by spontaneous choice, and not by necessity of nature. All this was voluntarily assumed, not taken by the necessity of His incarnation. Hence, viewed in the twofold light of the sin-bearer and of the sinless second man, His entire life was expiatory or atoning. For He was at every moment bearing the curse of that sphere through which He passed, or in which He lived at any given time, and yet fulfilling in it all righteousness, such as man was required to render, or was capable of rendering. He went through all life in a double capacity, and must be regarded at every moment as at once the curse-bearer and the fulfiller of all righteousness. We shall notice some of these spheres, though by no means in an exhaustive way.

Thus Christ's human development took place within the circle of FAMILY LIFE, where the deepest principles of all that is purely human are called into action. And as the curse lies there as well as upon every other human sphere, He lived in it to bear this curse, and also to sanctify by His sinless purity the domestic constitution to all His followers. There are sides of domestic life which often try the mind and involve a deep conflict, all the

---

sions called forth by the theory of Flacius Illyricus, who held that sin had become of the essence or substance of humanity. The churches recoiled in horror from that overdone speculation, and replied that we may and must distinguish between God's workmanship, which is good, and the ruin or defilement which has invaded it. (See *Formula Concordiæ, de peccato originis.*) We can distinguish in idea, and God distinguishes in fact. If it were not so, there could not have been an incarnation. Humanity could not have been assumed except on the ground of such a distinction in point of fact. Christ assumed humanity without its taint ; which indeed was not of its substance, nor essential to it. And this assumption of our nature according to its idea, rather than according to what it has become, is quite consistent with the fact that He took on Him, by voluntary susception, not only all the parts of our curse in all the spheres where it is diffused, but also many sinless infirmities, such as hunger and thirst, weariness and pain, sorrow and death.

more trying because the relations are so close; and from this the Lord Jesus was not exempt. Thus we read that His brethren did not believe on Him, and therefore could not comprehend Him (John vii. 1-7).

He entered also, as we have every reason to conclude, into the PRIMEVAL CURSE OF LABOUR. When we find Him designated not only the carpenter's son, but the carpenter (Mark vi. 3), the language plainly refers to the fact, that during the course of His private life the Lord Jesus followed the occupation of a carpenter. We are constrained, both on exegetical and on dogmatic grounds, to decide for this interpretation. There seems no ground to doubt that Jesus earned His bread by the sweat of His brow, whether we look at the plain words used by the evangelist, or at the necessity devolving on the substitute of sinners of entering into every part of our curse. And He has in consequence transformed the curse of labour into a blessing, and sanctified not only manual and mental labour in every form in which it can be viewed, but also the entire earthly calling to all His followers till the end of time.

During His private life, as well as afterwards in His public ministry, the Lord Jesus, as the sin-bearer, felt, too, in every variety of form, the infliction of the divine wrath.[1] And no mortal man can conceive through what agony and desertion He was called to pass, or what He may have endured on those occasions, when it is said that He went apart, or retired from the society of man, to wrestle with God in secret. We can only figure to ourselves what it may have been, and warrantably conclude that it was similar to the scenes on record. Nor need

[1] It is the more necessary to notice this aspect of our Lord's earthly life, inasmuch as the very best among the biographies of Christ circulating among the churches give no prominence to it, if they even allude to it. Their object is to bring out the active sinless life of Jesus; and they apprehend this earthly life only on this side, while they ignore the sin-bearing element. The language of Ursinus and Olevianus in the *Heidelberg Catechism* is happy: " *eum toto quidem vitæ suæ tempore, quo in terris egit*, præcipue vero in ejus extremo, *iram* Dei adversus peccatum universi generis humani *corpore et anima sustinuisse*." (See Quest. 37.)

I refer to Christ's TEMPTATION in the wilderness, the counter-part of Adam's temptation in the garden, further than to say that the fact of His being the sin-bearer affords the only expla-nation how Satan could obtain such power over Him, or venture into the presence of the Son of God, and appeal to the same elements in human nature, though from a wholly different point of view, in order, if possible, to seduce Him. His position as the curse-bearer can alone explain that marvellous abasement.

There are many other spheres or departments into which the curse had entered according to the judicial sentence of God, such as poverty and pain, hunger and thirst, weariness, reproach, and sorrow. It may suffice to say, in reference to all these parts of the curse, that as Christ's people had given their members instru-ments to sin, and had deserved to suffer, so Christ stepped down into their place, and bore the wrath of God for them in every variety of form.

There is one sphere, however, to which I must more particularly advert ; and the rather, because it has not received in any quarter the attention due to its importance. I refer to the sense in which Christ is said to have taken on Him our SICKNESSES AND DISEASES. The question arises : If they are part of the curse, can it be said that He took them on Himself ; did He bear them, to any extent, and in what way ? If diseases are the effect of sin, and part of the woe which sin has brought into our world, in what sense are we to regard Christ's relation to disease, or explain His interference in the performance of His miraculous cures with the due infliction of this penal sentence ? When we examine His miraculous cures, several things are evident. That they not only fatigued Him, but cost Him much in the way of sympathy, and even of endurance, may be inferred from various incidents, and especially from the fact that He often sighed in the performance of the cure (Mark vii. 34), and was troubled (John xi. 33) ; and from the fact that He was sensibly conscious of virtue going out of Him, as if a mutual transfer, in some sort, took place in every instance of a cure (Mark v. 30).

Now, in the first place, there can be no doubt that the miraculous cures were only a result or effect of that ransom which was to be paid in all the extent to which man was made subject to the curse. If Christ was to annihilate sin as the cause, then the effect, as a matter of course, must disappear whenever He spoke His healing word. He thus removed disease by anticipation, because, as the surety of sinners, He undertook their obligations, and satisfied for all that was the cause of the disease. The effect was virtually removed by the removal of the cause, though in no case was the cure effected without the actual exercise of His omnipotent fiat.

This brings me to notice, in the next place, the additional idea contained in a remarkable apostolic commentary on Christ's miracles. This is exhibited in a somewhat difficult passage in Matthew, where Jesus is said to have taken on Himself our sicknesses. The Lord had, during a day of labour, dispensed blessings to many, and, wearied with incessant activity, He needed rest. But when evening came, instead of a season of repose, there came a new company who had all manner of diseases and possessions, and He healed them all. When Matthew narrates this fact, he subjoins a quotation to the effect that all this was the fulfilment of what had been spoken by Esaias the prophet, saying, "Himself took our infirmities and bare our sicknesses" (Matt. viii. 17). The words of the evangelist must be accepted as an exact quotation of Isaiah's words, and also as a faithful reproduction or transcript of the meaning of the prophet. It is an apostolic commentary, of which the evangelists supply many. The fact that the inspired writer quotes the words in this connection and with his appended explanation, is conclusive as to their meaning. How far the words can bear a wider sense, it does not lie within my present purpose to inquire : but that this is the meaning here, is rendered all the more certain by the formula of quotation, "that it might be fulfilled," which will not admit the application of the theory of accommodation which certain writers use to evacuate a passage of its meaning.

This brings out, then, a new thought, which is quite in harmony with the explanation which has been already given. If diseases were removed by Christ because the sin which was the cause of them was to be expiated by His atoning death, He could say, " Whether is easier to say, Thy sins be forgiven thee, or to say, Arise and walk ?" (Matt. ix. 5). This additional thought is quite consistent with that view. The connection between the atonement and the cure is further illustrated by the fact, of which there is little doubt, that it cost Him something,—in other words, that He suffered in mind and body when He healed all manner of sickness and disease. That He took them upon Himself in some sense, is affirmed by Matthew in that passage. But in what sense ? Perhaps as good an answer as has ever been furnished was offered by Dr. Thomas Goodwin. " Christ," says he,[1] " when He came to an elect child of His that was sick, whom He healed, His manner was, first, by a sympathy and pity to afflict Himself with their sickness as if it had been His own. Thus, at the raising of Lazarus, it is said that ' He groaned in spirit,' etc. ; and so, by the merit of taking the disease upon Himself, through a fellow-feeling of it, He took it off from them, being for them afflicted as if He Himself had been sick. And this seems to be the best interpretation that I have met with of that difficult place in Matt. viii. 16, 17." That Jesus would enter into this department of the curse was only what was to be

[1] See Goodwin's treatise, entitled *The Heart of Christ in Heaven to Sinners on Earth,* vol. iv. p. 138 ; Edin. Edition. Œder, in his refutation of the Racovian Catechism, p. 806 (Francofurti, 1739), has some striking remarks on this topic : " Hic utinam non esset fatendum, in multas vias itum esse ab interpretibus, nostratibus etiam, ut in concordiam redigunt Prophetam et Evangelistam. Namque illum primo, de spiritualibus morbis, h. e. peccatis loqui, existimant, tum vero ea ita suscepta esse a Christo, ut proprie ferret, h. e. pœnas his debitas sustineret, Matthæum contra et de corporis infirmitatibus verba facere, et eas non a Christo toleratas seu in ipsum translatas intelligi velle, sed ablatas sanando, ut medicus non in se transfert febrim, qua medicamentis suis ægrotum liberat. Non satisfecerunt, quod sine vituperatione summorum ingeniorum dictum velim, omnes interpretes omnium religionum." See the best discussion I know of this difficult point in that passage of Œder (pp. 806-820), who maintains that, in some sense, the diseases were transferred by Christ to Himself. The opposite view is maintained by Sebastian Schmid in his commentary on Heb. iv. 15.

expected, because it fills so large a part of human life in the case
of multitudes, and because it extends, in some measure, to every
member of the human family. Though disease could not touch
Him as it assails mankind in general, in the way of contagion,
it needs no proof that this voluntary assumption, or bearing of
it, in some sense, in His sinless body, or the transfer of it to
Himself, was of the greatest moment to us. It was spontaneous,
not constrained. But His miracles alone were so numerous as
to make Him acquainted with all manner of sickness and disease. He took them on Himself for us. And may not pious
minds derive the highest comfort from the fact that the Saviour
took upon Himself not only the sin, which is the cause of
disease, but also the DISEASE ITSELF, in some sense, however
mysterious and undefinable that may be, just as He took poverty
and grief on Himself for us ?   (Comp. Heb. iv. 15.)

SEC. XX.—THE HISTORIC FACTS OF CHRIST'S SUFFERINGS
ILLUSTRATED BY HIS SAYINGS.

The department to which we here allude is too much omitted
by those who handle the sayings of Christ, or who discuss the
question of the atonement. And yet the FACTS and history of
the Lord's passion must needs be correctly apprehended in the
light of His sayings. Their full meaning, indeed, cannot be seen
from the proper point of view, or thoroughly ascertained, unless
the import of His sayings as to the doctrine of the atonement
has been correctly understood. On the other hand, the true
doctrine of the atonement, by the aid of the key thus furnished,
may, and must, be read off from the facts of His suffering and
death, if we are to do justice to either.

When we put together the facts and sayings of Jesus, we find
that men are saved in the same way in which sin entered, and by
a constitution precisely similar, that of one for many (Rom. v. 19).
A way to happiness could be found only by a perfect obedience,
and by a provision to bear sin. And an economy of substitution by a

competent representative entered in the exercise of infinite wisdom and grace.   To apprehend aright what must needs ensue, we have but to trace the history of one who lives and dies impenitent, and compare it with that which the Mediator endured under the penal consequences of sin.   Such a man born a child of wrath is subject to many calamities, and encounters through life many miseries, the common lot of mortals.   He dies, and the departed soul passes into a separate state, where the memory of His deeds gives rise to much anguish and a dread foreboding of a judgment day.   By the union of soul and body the misery is augmented: for the man is raised up to shame and condemnation, and soul and body, which sinned together, are visited together.

Now, the Son of God becoming man of man, not by the common law of natural birth, but in a way which procured for Him perfect sinlessness, undertook to do all devolving on man according to His idea, and to suffer what none but He could suffer in the room of others ; thus entering into an analogous position to that of Adam.   According to this constitution the guilt of men was charged to His account, and the merit of His obedience was deemed theirs.   Sinless, but made their sin (2 Cor. v. 21); infinitely beyond the reach of suffering in Himself, but coming within it, because made a curse for us (Gal. iii. 13), He effected the twofold condition of redemption in the same acts and in the same scenes, all through life.   He fulfilled the condition DO AND LIVE, not precisely for Himself ;—for in virtue of His divine person and His absolutely holy nature, He was already entitled to eternal happiness ; but for the redeemed from among men, who thus have their title in Him.   But elect humanity also bore the curse in Him.   The soul trouble which came direct from the hand of God ; the power over Him given to ecclesiastical and civil rulers, because He was the sin-bearer, and standing in our stead ; the groundless charges of blasphemy and sedition, yet justly preferred against the substitute of sinners ; and the final execution of the sentence, carrying with it tortures from without and desertion from within—were only what His people deserved.

Hence it is that for true Christians the penalty exists no more: nor is there ought of wrath in the sorrows they endure.

There is a double line of inquiry here presented to us. There is one class of facts of a more subjective character, descriptive of Christ's own feelings, and another class more objective in its character, which seems to contain only incidents or events which were permitted to befall Him. But both assume that Jesus was the conscious sin-bearer; and can only be correctly understood from this point of view.

With regard to the more subjective class of facts, we find a few utterances of Jesus in the form of exclamations during His soul-trouble, which bring before us what He felt under the infliction of His Father's hand and the hiding of His Father's face. The whole texture of Christ's life may be said to consist of suffering, sorrow, and bitterness. As the curse had diffused itself through every scene of life, not a sphere can be named, nor a moment thought of, in which He did not, as the surety of sinners, feel, more or less, the bitter ingredients of that cup of woe, which must otherwise have oppressed His people for ever. The bare fact of taking our nature was an acknowledgment of the debt; and as He went about in the likeness of sinful flesh, His entire history was a proof that sin was laid on Him. And these varied sorrows in every sphere in which He moved, and especially in the exclamations of agony which burst from Him on different occasions, only prove that Jesus, in the double capacity of sin-bearer and of sinless second man, was, in part at least, offering the satisfaction in all these scenes, till at last the whole cup of suffering was put into His hand at once. That this is the meaning of this class of facts cannot be doubted or denied.

With regard to the more objective class of facts connected with Christ's experience as the conscious sin-bearer, they are not less significant. We find a series of historic facts connected with the arrest, the trial, the sentence, and execution of the Lord Jesus, which can only be explained on the supposition, that while the Lord was placed before the bar of man, He was really standing before another bar as the sin-bearing representative of His people; and that the transactions of that earthly court only exhibited to the eye of man the foreground of the scene, and gave us the means of apprehending what was taking place, though invisibly, in the court of heaven.

These two series of historic facts in the course of Christ's passion are in the highest degree significant, and must be correctly apprehended, if we would not lose sight of some of the most essential and indispensable elements in the doctrine of the atonement.

SEC. XXI.—THE FACTS AND SAYINGS OF CHRIST, THE CONSCIOUS SIN-BEARER IN PROSPECT OF HIS AGONY, AND DURING IT.

The narrative of the evangelists contains many clear proofs that our Lord from the first looked forward with deep solemnity to the period of His sufferings. Nor, in truth, was He ever without some experience of the curse in the numerous spheres through which it had diffused itself, though these sufferings had their ebbs and flows. They were not always equally intense. Thus, in the first stages of His ministry, He speaks of His death with a certain measure of calmness (John iii. 14; John vi. 51). There can be little doubt, however, that when He did so speak of His approaching death, there is a certain measure of the same experience which afterwards reached its height in the garden and on the cross.

At a further stage His statements are delivered with a greater amount of feeling; and they awaken also more attention among the disciples, as well as a certain degree of fear and awe, because they could not but see a deepening solemnity upon His mind, and the first traces of something more than a mere anticipation of the future (Matt. xvii. 17-22; Mark ix. 31).

It was in the last journey to Jerusalem that He spake out with a distinctness and an amount of feeling that impressed His disciples with fear (Mark. x. 32). This was owing to the way in which He spoke of His death as a cup that He must drink of, and as a baptism that He must be baptized with (Matt. xx. 22). And when He says, "How am I straitened till it is accomplished!" (Luke xii. 50,) He intimates that there was upon His spirit a pressure, anxiety, or straitening, which it may be difficult for us to define, but which must allude to an inner experience akin to the fact that He was the sin-bearer.

The sufferings of Christ may be distributed into those which were an immediate infliction upon His soul from the hand of God, and those in which soul and body alike shared. To the former belong all those exclamations which fell from Him in society or in solitude, without any infliction of pain from the hands of men. There are at least two of this nature, where we cannot but trace the evidences of mental agony,—the soul-trouble manifested in the presence of the inquiring Greeks on the day of His public entry into Jerusalem (John xii. 27), and the agony in the garden of Gethsemane (Matt. xxvi. 38); to which must be added, as a third, the cry of desertion on the cross, which, though accompanied with corporeal suffering, arose mainly from mental distress (Matt. xxvii. 46). One thing is obvious enough in reference to all these three exclamations. They cannot be explained on any supposition which does not fully admit the vicarious death of Christ. We shall notice them separately.

I. *The exclamation of the sin-bearer on His entry into Jerusalem.*—The evangelist John alone records this exclamation of agony and soul-trouble: "*Now is my soul troubled; and what shall I say? Father, save Me from this hour: but for this cause came I unto this hour*" (John xii. 27). The trouble of soul here announced by Christ Himself is not to be explained by the mere recoil of sinless nature from the approach of death. It is to be explained by supernatural causes,—that is, by the divine anger against sin, as it was borne by the substitute of sinners; and the allusion to His death in the previous context seems to have given the occasion for letting in upon His soul, by a special avenue, a sense of the divine wrath.

The next words, " Save me from this hour," convey, in substance, the same petition that comes before us in the Gethsemane scene. This request discovers nature as at a loss, and embarrassed under the pressure of the overwhelming trouble due to us for sin. Some read this clause interrogatively, as if Christ were to be regarded as asking whether He should thus pray, and as if His submission to God lay specially in this, that He did not so ask of God. But it is better to read it without the interrogation, as the latter brings in a train of self-reflection, which is not appropriate to such a scene of vehement emotion. We may suppose one of two explanations. We may either suppose that He does not ask deliverance from the death, but only from the accessories or accompaniments of it, which were so overwhelming, that the horror and anguish seemed to Him insupportable. It will then be a prayer for such a mitigation of the anguish, that He might finish the work of human redemption successfully. Or we may suppose that He prays to be saved from the punitive justice, the cup, or the baptism, within the sphere of which He was now brought. The latter seems the better exposition, though it has far greater difficulties, and brings us up at once to the inscrutable mystery of pure humanity asking with submission, and asking sinlessly, under the stunning sense of present anguish, whether there was no possibility of being saved from that hour.

But the next clause points out in what way His mind returned to its rest: " But for this cause came I unto this hour." He reverts to the vicarious suffering as the design of His incarnation, as the very end of His coming. Those expositors are much mistaken who refer the words to His glorification; as if the Lord meant to say that He came into the world for this cause, that He might be glorified. The immediate context is not that He might be glorified, nor that the world might be saved, nor that He might be delivered,—all which ideas have been offered by commen-

tators as the reason for which He is here said to have come into
the world. The immediate context is found in "this hour," and
the thought is that Jesus came to endure this hour of suffering.

This whole scene discovers the two great features of the
atonement,—sin-bearing and sinless obedience. The exclamation, beyond doubt, is extorted by the pressure of the divine
wrath. Nor is this invalidated, in any measure, by the fact that
the Scripture represents the Lord Jesus as the object of the
divine complacency and love; and the more so, because He laid
down His life for the sheep (John x. 17). It is urged by those
who have inadequate views of the vicarious satisfaction, that the
beloved Son could never be the object of the Father's anger, and,
therefore, that this exclamation could never arise from any such
experience. That objection, urged against the view already
given, proceeds on a mistaken view of what is meant, and con-
founds the personal with the official relation of the Son of God.[1]
In His personal capacity He was, and could never cease to be,
the beloved Son. But in His official capacity He was the substitute of sinners, the sin-bearer and the curse-bearer, who came
into the world to put away sin by the sacrifice of Himself; and
the personal relation in which He stood to the Father lent to
the official all its efficacy and value. Nor is that all.

Such an exclamation as the present cannot be regarded as
worthy of Christ if His sufferings were not vicarious. On the
supposition that Christ's death was but a martyr's death, it
would be a strange and inexplicable enigma. Suppose the death
of Christ to have no higher significance than that of attesting
the truth of His doctrine and of serving as an example, we
should have expected to find in Him a bright example of fortitude and magnanimity, of patience and composure, of calmness
and triumph, without any tincture of dejection or fear; and the
more so, because He was exalted above all other witnesses of the

---

[1] The modern theology denies that Christ, in any sense, bore the WRATH of
God. The question has reference to His official position as the substitute, and
raises the previous question—Is there (ὀργὴ) wrath against sin (Rom. ii. 5, Eph.
v. 6). On this there is no room for two opinions, if we are ruled by Scripture.

truth by the greatness of His person. And on that theory of His work, men may well be astonished to find the opposite. Whence so many signs of fainting, when no infliction came from the hand of man, and only a dim anticipation of something looming in the distance hung over Him on the theory in question? How shall we explain His anguish, dejection, and fear, more than has been evinced by many of His own servants and martyrs? No satisfactory account can be given of His mental anguish and heaviness if Christ were but a martyr or an example of patience; and this gains force if we add, as we must do on that theory, that divine wisdom actively devised whatever would make His example worthy of our imitation.

The only position which we can maintain is, that these exclamations of Christ argue the conscious sin-bearer and a vicarious suffering.

II. *The exclamation of the sin-bearer in Gethsemane.*—The second exclamation, which evinces how Christ's soul wrestled with a heaviness and agony greater far than any bodily pain afterwards inflicted, was uttered in Gethsemane. It is thus given by Matthew: "Then cometh Jesus with them unto a place called Gethsemane, and saith unto the disciples, Sit ye here, while I go and pray yonder. And He took with Him Peter and the two sons of Zebedee, and began to be sorrowful and very heavy. Then saith He unto them, *My soul is exceeding sorrowful, even unto death:* tarry ye here, and watch with Me. And He went a little farther, and fell on His face, and prayed, saying, *O my Father, if it be possible, let this cup pass from Me: nevertheless not as I will, but as Thou wilt.* And He cometh unto the disciples, and findeth them asleep, and saith unto Peter, What! could ye not watch with Me one hour? Watch, and pray that ye enter not into temptation: the spirit indeed is willing, but the flesh is weak. He went away again the second time, and prayed, saying, *O my Father, if this cup may not pass from Me, except I drink it, Thy will be done.* And He came and found them asleep again: for their eyes were heavy. And He left them, and went

away again, and prayed the third time, saying the same words"
(Matt. xxvi. 36-44). Many theories have been proposed by way
of explanation of this scene,—some referring the sorrow on
Christ's mind to a single cause, others referring it to a variety of
concurring causes. It seems more natural to deduce the strong
and vehement emotion of Christ from one cause than from
several; for experience tells us, as well as a right view of the
human mind and of its laws, that very great emotion is never
produced by a variety of concurrent causes.

We must now consider to what the deep agony and sorrow of
our Lord are to be traced. Of the great variety of explanations
that have been given—some of them so shallow and groundless
as not to deserve a moment's thought,—there are three, in particular, that have much more probability. And among these we
must choose.

1. Some ascribe the agony in the garden to the temptations of
Satan. It is argued that Satan, who left Him for a time[1] (Luke
iv. 13), or, as it may mean, till the fit time for renewing the
attack, returned when He was in the garden. It is thought that
there is enough of harmony between the two occasions to lend
countenance to this supposition. But then there are no hints or
intimations of any such thing in the actual narrative of the
evangelists. It does not clearly appear that the tempter, after
being so completely foiled in the first encounter, ventured to
renew the conflict in the same direct way. It may be so; but
it is not recorded. And certainly it would be strange that Luke
should mention the appearance of an angel on the scene, to
strengthen and confirm our Lord, and make no mention of
another agent from the invisible world, if such a hand-to-hand
encounter had taken place. Nor does the language of Jesus on
the eve of His going out to the garden imply a new conflict of
temptation when He says: "The prince of this world cometh"
(John xiv. 30). It seems much more correct to say that the
prince of this world now came through the instrumentality of

[1] ἄχρι καιροῦ.

men, imbued with his spirit, and filled with his influence, to crush the Lord Jesus by violence.

2. Nor can the agony of Christ be traced alone to the vivid view of His approaching crucifixion. This very common explanation assumes nothing but a mere foreboding or anticipation of a dread reality near at hand, but without any higher influence. This comment has been propounded in two different forms, neither of which is satisfactory. The lower theory of the two is, that all Christ's sufferings came from the hands of men, and not from any direct infliction at the hand of God; and, consequently, that He was, and must be, the object of God's delight in such a sense that no mysterious extraordinary power could come from God to aggravate His sorrow.[1] On this theory of Christ's agony in the garden it only remains for expositors to appeal to the fact, that a violent death must have been peculiarly awful to Christ's pure and tender and sensitive humanity. And though the further thought may here be added, that death is the divine sentence against sin, and that Christ realized His death in connection with the *why* and *wherefore* of such a sentence on the world's sin, the whole theory is highly defective. It does not explain the perturbation and sorrow of Christ's mind; it gives no adequate explanation of the bloody sweat; and it fails to give any just account of the other accompaniments recorded in the Gospels.

The other is a deeper theory, but also insufficient, because it goes no further than a mere anticipation or foreboding.[2] This view takes for granted that the Lord Jesus, without anything beyond the exercises of His own mind, was filled with heaviness and exceeding sorrow even unto death, because a lively view was

---

[1] This is the view supported in the two prize essays of Riehm and Van Willigen, published in 1831 by the Hague Society for the defence of the Christian religion, *over het Hooggaande lijden van Jesus in Gethsemane.*

[2] See the exposition of the agony in the garden on this principle, in a sermon by Principal Edwards, of America, which, though it affords a most striking sketch of the Lord's mental agony, is still defective, inasmuch as he regards it as only prospective, not present.

presented to Him of the unutterable wrath of God due to sin, which the surety made His own.   But this second supposition is also defective, because the whole scene on this theory becomes, to an undue degree, a mere subjective impression.   It does not explain the phenomena; it leads to the inference that the mind of Jesus was overwhelmed by a foreboding, which we can scarcely suppose ever rising to such a climax as threatened to master His perfectly-balanced mind; it transfers the actual suffering forward to the hours when He hung on the cross, as if He had none before; and it assigns no adequate reason why an angel came to strengthen Him.   The fact of the angel's appearance for such a purpose implies real and not merely apprehended suffering. And His confirming message, of whatever kind it was, would at least bring something objective before Him, and point to the joy set before Him, as well as promise adequate support.

3. Another and a better explanation than either of the two former is, that the sorrow of Gethsemane was due to the positive privation of the divine presence, or to the loss of God.[1]   Of all the ingredients in the agony of those who encounter the penalty of sin, this is by far the worst element in their cup of suffering. The suffering of Christ in His capacity as substitute was the same in its character, so far as outward causes are concerned, as the penal infliction awaiting the finally condemned.   It was an objective and positive punishment from the hand of God that fell on the Lord Jesus, who occupied the place of our re-presentative; and the exclamation proves that He was the con-scious sin-bearer.   The agony did not visit Him as a just and holy person, but as He was the surety, made sin by His voluntary act.   And it may be added, that these two mental acts—the sense of the divine wrath, and the utmost filial confidence,—

---

[1] This was the prevailing and common view in former times.   I may refer to a remarkable discussion *de agonia et desertione Christi*, on this acceptation of it, by Gisbert Voetius in his *Selectæ Disputationes*, vol. ii. pp. 164-188.   Among the more modern writers, Saurin, *Disc.* t. x. p. 251, Seiler, and others, still take the same view.   The recent exegetes who are opposed to the vicarious sacrifice, object to it as the *vicarious* view, just as a former generation objected to it as the *super-natural* view.   But no other is at all tenable, or can be made even plausible.

though they are distinct, are by no means incompatible. The one was due to His office as the sin-bearer; the other was expressive of His personal relation. Nor are we to suppose that this penal privation of the divine presence was always equally intense, and that no intervals of relief were allowed to Him; for, in the present case, the opposite appears from the fact that He returned in such intervals to the disciples, who were heavy with slumber.

As to the accompaniments of this inscrutable scene, they were the following:—(1) A sorrow unto death, a horror and oppressive sense of sinking (ἀδημονία), till the functions of the mind were well-nigh suspended. It has been likened to the stopping of a clock, not by any intrinsic defect in its mechanism, but by the application of an outward force suspending its motion. (2) The bloody sweat arising from the inconceivable emotions of sorrow, dejection, and fear, so strong as to turn, in a preternatural way, the current of the blood out of its course. (3) The more earnest prayer (ἐκτενέστερον) occasioned by the amazement and deep perplexity of His soul. All this shows what He endured as the conscious sin-bearer from the hand of an angry God, who, while He ever regarded Jesus at His beloved Son, visited sin, when it was laid on Him, with its adequate recompense.

Though these sufferings partook of the same elements with the agonies of the finally lost, in as far as the external cause was concerned, there was also a very wide difference. This comes to light, whether we consider His mental exercises or His personal relation to the Father. It was a holy endurance of the penalty without one flaw or taint of imperfection. His agonies were neither eternal nor accompanied with the worm of conscience,— ingredients in the cup of the finally condemned. But no one can peruse the scene in Gethsemane, without coming to the con- clusion that Christ there suffered immediately in His soul; and that the theory which limits those sufferings to His body, whether advocated by Romanists or by Protestants, is destitute of scriptural foundation. The principal part of the agony fell, without doubt, upon the soul of the Lord Jesus, and comprehended every element of eternal death that could be endured by such a person, or could justly be exacted from Him.

It belonged to the divine plan that He should experience the fear of death for us, which we should otherwise have been obliged to wrestle with all our life long. He must have felt the menaced sentence, and the tormenting execution of it, "Thou shalt surely die." The words of Jesus in Gethsemane were uttered under a heaviness and fear which seemed to intimate that body and mind were alike ready to give way, and for ever to be rendered unfit for discharging the task assigned Him with the fortitude and stedfastness, the patience and endurance, that were required. He felt that humanity could bear no higher degree of sorrow. Though His humanity was strengthened secretly by the support of the divine nature, it seemed to Him that His mind and body could not bear more, without dissolution or wholly giving way under the pressure. He needed an objective something; and the angel's appearance seems to have brought [1] strength both corporeal and mental.

But the difficulty arises, Why did He pray that the cup might pass from Him? Did He wish to get rid of His mediatorial office, and repent of His suretyship? No; but though He knew that He must suffer, the humanity did not know, without direct and actual experience, either the bitterness of the cup, or the extreme to which it must go. As in the former exclamation, so in this scene in Gethsemane, we may either suppose that He prayed for an abatement of the agony and for a speedy termination to it, or that sinless humanity asked with all submission whether the exaction of punitive justice might not pass from Him. The latter, though confessedly the comment that has by far the most difficulties, seems the best adapted to the occasion. When we ask from whence sprung all that agony that weighed so heavily on the soul of Christ, the answer is: from the sin-

---

[1] Bengel remarks that it was not exhortation, but a heavenly power that was conveyed to His holy humanity (see note in his German version).

bearing to which He subjected Himself. No drop of wrath could have visited Him on any other ground. It would have been an incongruity, an impossibility in the moral government of God to allow any penal infliction or suffering to fall on Him, except as He assumed the sin of others by His own voluntary act. But when He became the sin of His people, this was the sure and inevitable consequence.

But how, it is asked, can we maintain the infliction of divine wrath at all when Jesus was the beloved Son? Did He not even here call God FATHER, and pray with filial confidence and affection? To this there is an easy answer. Jesus occupied, by the very fact of the incarnation, a twofold relation,—an official relation as well as a personal relation; and unless He had come to occupy the place of sinners, there was no indispensably necessary cause for His incarnation at all. The personal, however, is the basis of the official capacity; and during the course of His career on earth, these two always presupposed each other. They were not mutually exclusive; they were not incompatible in the one person. On the contrary, Jesus, as the sin-bearer or representative of sinners, regarded God as a righteous judge, who would visit, and could not but visit, for sin. But, at the same time, He was conscious of being the only-begotten Son, and of exercising a filial confidence, which was never abandoned, nor even interrupted, during the severest infliction of wrath due to us for sin. The Gethsemane scene is memorable, just because it brings out these two points so vividly: the exclamation of the sin-bearer, and the unswerving obedience and trust of the Son. His will never turned aside from the straight path of His obedience, but moved in everlasting harmony with His Father's mind and will. But He was very man like ourselves, shrinking as we do from pain and agony and woe: we see the recoil of sentient nature, but an unswerving obedience. Nay, the hotter the trial, the more was the obedience developed and expanded. It was always perfect, but sinlessness is capable of progress; and He learned obedience by the things which He suffered (Heb. v. 8).

III. *The cry of desertion on the cross.*—The third exclamation of the conscious sin-bearer was the cry, "*My God, My God! why hast Thou forsaken Me?*" (Matt. xxvii. 46.) It was like all His sayings, according to truth; and it becomes us carefully to investigate its import and significance. Though it does not fall within my present object to refer to the several sayings on the cross in their order, it is noteworthy, that when Christ had given utterance to certain sayings that had reference to others, when He had uttered the comforting promise to the penitent thief, and had prayed for His persecutors, and had commended His mother to the care of the beloved disciple, He next turned to God alone, as if He had now done with man. The remaining space was to be specially occupied with God alone, as if His work with men was now done.

No sooner were His mind and attention turned away from His relation to men around Him, than a striking phenomenon presented itself. Darkness all of a sudden enveloped the face of nature, and eternal death seemed to seize hold of Him. Whatever view may be given of that darkness, it doubtless stood connected with the chief figure in this whole scene, and with the mental state through which the substitute of sinners was now to pass; and it must plainly be held to be symbolical as well as miraculous. We have not, it is true, any authoritative explanation of its meaning in the Scripture. But as the inner darkness of Christ's soul and that darkness on the face of the earth were simultaneous, no explanation has so much probability as that which regards the menacing gloom, as meant to intimate that our sin had separated between God and the surety, and that our iniquities had hid the Father's face from Him (Isa. lix. 2). That is every way a better explanation than the more current one, that it was meant to convey an impression of the divine displeasure for the indignity offered and the crime committed by the Jewish nation against the Christ. But however we interpret the meaning of this mysterious darkness, it certainly seems to have had one effect. Under the awe which it produced, there seems to have been diffused among the by-standers a death-stillness, which for the time freed the sufferer from the scoffs and mockery of the mad multitude, and left Him alone, and comparatively undistracted, with God. The silence was broken at last, after an interval, by these words of awful import, " My God, My God ! why hast Thou forsaken Me ?" What the Lord Jesus thus uttered was His actual experience ; and as it was from the faithful witness, it was according to truth. He who was the light of the world was under the hiding of His Father's face.

The inquiry into the causes of this peculiar mood of mind, substantially the same as in the two former exclamations, need not occupy our minds so long. The question is much more narrowed in this case; nor is there so much difference of opinion among divines and expositors. The words to which our Lord gave utterance are plainly a quotation from the 22d Psalm, which is unquestionably Messianic, whether it had any immediate reference to the Psalmist or not. As to the interpretation, much depends on the question whether we take the word *forsake* in its full significance, or whether we tone down its meaning to the mere notion of " delay to help." Some even of those who admit that the death of Christ was a propitiatory sacrifice, object to the interpretation that our Lord must be understood as uttering this language as an expression of real desertion, and in a moment of real desertion. And according to them, the words will only mean, " Why leavest Thou Me ?" or, " Why delayest Thou to free Me from My suffering ?" The word *why* is thus an expression of complaint, but involving a petition. In favour of this interpretation, it is argued that God is said " to forsake " one, or to be far from one, when He does not send help, and to " be near " when He delivers. Thus, according to this interpretation, there will be no particular emphasis on the word *forsake*. The whole import of the exclamation becomes flat and meaningless, according to this exposition. And the supporters of it, while they do not deny the atoning sacrifice of Christ, hold merely by one side of the truth,—namely, that the Father surely loved the Son with unabated love, and could not withdraw His favour from His Son; nay, that the Son deserved it all the more when He was bringing His obedience through the deepest humiliation to its highest elevation. All that is true, and not to be questioned in any quarter.

But all this is one-sided, and argues much confusion of idea. It loses sight of the distinction, to which we have already alluded, between the personal and official capacity of our Lord; and it argues as if the supporters of the penal infliction of the divine wrath on Jesus as the sin-bearer also maintained the removal or withdrawal of the divine favour from Him in a personal point of view. That desertion undoubtedly involved the privation of the sweet sense of divine love and of the beatific vision of God, but no loss of the divine favour, and no withdrawal of the grace resulting from the personal union. It was not accompanied with a dissolution of the principle of joy, though it was accompanied with a suspension of the present experience of joy. It was for a time, not for ever. It was not attended with despair or doubt, but with the full confidence of faith, as is expressed in the words, "My God." To sum up all in a few words: it was borne in our name, and not for Himself, —in the capacity of the sin-bearer or surety, and not in that of the beloved Son. It was voluntary, and not enforced; by the imputation of our sin, and not for anything of His own. It was not because He had no power to remove it, but out of love to us. And in that desertion He encountered all the elements of eternal death, as far as they could fall on such a sufferer. It involved the removal not merely of the tokens of divine love, but the privation of God, or that loss of God, which is the very essence of the second death, awaiting the finally lost. Though this departure of God is accompanied, in the case of the sinner, with despair and with the worm of an evil conscience, it could be executed in a somewhat different way on our sinless Lord. But it must needs be executed, if He was to occupy the place of a real substitute and surety for sinful men.

The Lord asks *why*, with a force and significance which bring us to the margin of the inscrutable. It may be wiser to stand and adore than to grope our way into the meaning of this *why*.[1] The language certainly does not mean that the cause of the desertion was unknown to Him as the conscious sin-bearer, who was passing through the flaming fire of the divine wrath for our salvation. But the inquiry, so put, seems to utter a desire that He may not be uninformed, but fully acquainted with the absolute necessity of all these pangs and agonies of desertion. He seems desirous to be assured subjectively, or convinced within His inmost soul, that all this must needs be so. He wishes to rest or anchor His mind in that conviction of its indispensable necessity; and He reminds His Father that it was all endured by a substitute for others, and for the glory of the Father.

The vicarious position of Christ during all these exclamations cannot, therefore, be doubtful to any one who has duly understood them. He bore (1) the soul-trouble, that His people might not bear it; (2) He drank the cup of the garden, that they might not drink it; (3) He was forsaken on the cross, that they might never know that desertion. He felt what sin is, and what it is to be severed from God, that we might never taste it; and He proclaimed with a loud voice the inconceivable agonies of that desertion, that He might convey to those who heard

---

[1] See Thomasius' *Christi Person und Werk*, iii. p. 71, and also Philippi's pamphlet in reply to V. Hofmann on the *Versöhnungs und Rechtfertigunslehre*, p. 39, 1856. From the latter I shall quote the following sentences :—" Indess die Höllenstrafe besteht wesentlich und hauptsächlich in der Gottverlassenheit, und in der positiver Auschliessung und Verstossung ans der Gottesgemeinschaft. Diese objective göttliche That reflectirt sich nur subjectiv bei dem Sünder in dem bösen Gewissen und der Verzweiflung an der Sündenvergebung, kann aber auch ohne diesen subjectiven, Reflex an dem Heiligen sich Vollziehen. Das warum des 22 Psalmes bekündet eine unschuldige Gottverlassenheit bei gutem Gewissen. "

Him, or who should afterwards peruse His sufferings to the end of time, a due impression of the infinite weight of sin, and of the penal desertion it entails. As to the mental condition of the Son of God during this penal loss of God, and retribution for the sin which He made His own, it may be safely affirmed that He then experienced the essence of eternal death, or that sense of abandonment which will form the bitterest ingredient in the cup of the finally impenitent. This was the meaning of the sentence, " Thou shalt surely die."

Had the second Adam been a mere man, there could have been no such vicarious work, because He would have been bound to full obedience on His own account, and that obedience could not have extended to others. But the second man, being the Son of God, rendered a vicarious obedience, and encountered a vicarious suffering, not necessary for Himself, and of infinite value. And, because of His divine person, the brief period of His agony was a fully adequate and perfect satisfaction for the sins of His people, from the infinite dignity and infinite merit of the sufferer.

SEC. XXII.—SINGLE EXPRESSIONS USED BY CHRIST IN REFERENCE TO A WORK GIVEN HIM TO DO.

Under this section we may put together some other expressions which fell from the lips of Christ in reference to the second element of the atonement, that is, to the *nature* of the atonement as a mediatorial work given Him to do. We refer here to a work of active obedience not coincident with His teaching on earth, or with His life-communicating activity in heaven. For both the teaching and the life-giving activity presuppose that mediatorial work, and proceed upon it.

Such a work of obedience, distinguished from the suffering which He bore, may be called the obverse of the titles to which we have already adverted. It is another element or side of divine truth, and may be regarded as the complement of those sayings which represent the Lord Jesus as the sin-bearer. He who bore sin, not on the cross merely, but all His life through, was, regarded in Himself, the sinless doer of a divine work, and one who knew no sin. So little are these two elements disjoined in fact, though necessarily distinguished in idea, that the sinlessness of the Lord is presupposed in His whole work of sin-bearing and expiation. He must be holy to stand for the unholy, pure for the impure, innocent for the guilty. And these two elements taken together—the curse-bearing life on the one hand, and the career of unsinning obedience on the other—furnish the rounded and complete idea of the atoning work which Christ finished in the days of His flesh.

It is the more necessary to bring out this side of divine truth in connection with the atonement, because the whole subject of Christ's excellence, as the realized ideal of humanity, has of late received such copious elucidation. The question, indeed, was canvassed in another interest than that which now engages our attention. The reality of this historic person, as the moral miracle in our world, has been discussed as the life-question of the Church in our age, in opposition to a negation that would, if possible, call it in question. The victory has been won. The reality of His appearance in our world as the loftiest standard of moral excellence has been established beyond doubt or cavil.[1] Men have been compelled to confess that such an ideal could only exist in the conviction of the Church, because the actual reality had appeared. And even minds estranged from the true sense of Christianity have been so overpowered by the moral

[1] We may say that the attacks of Strauss, of the Tübingen school of Baur, and the weak echo of the same tendency in Rénan, have already passed into neglect. The historic truth of Christ's appearance and His ideal moral excellence have been triumphantly established. In the course of the discussion in which Neander, Ullmann, Lange, and many others did good service, the sinless perfection of Christ, and His function as the life-giver, were set in full prominence. (See Ullmann's *Sündlosigkeit Jesu*, 1846.) But the defect in all these delineations was, that they stopped short at this point, as if it were enough to have a faultless pattern.

glory of that character as to acknowledge virtue how lovely, and to express their enthusiastic admiration of it.

But the matter cannot rest there. The character of Christ is not a mere spectacle to be gazed upon as the embodiment of holiness or standard of perfection, without the light of which the world would be dark indeed. Nor is it a mere example to be followed, though the Church of all time will fix her eye upon it, to ennoble, elevate, and purify all her aims. It must be further regarded as underlying all His atonement, and as the work of one for many. The defect in the modern delineations of Christ's character is, that while He is represented as the real-ized ideal of humanity, it is still too much as if He were but a unit in the species. Not so does the Lord describe Himself. It is worthy of notice, that in every context where He mentions His work of obedience, He gives indications, more or less ex-press, that He was conscious of standing in a unique position between God and man, and of mediating between them. And He never leaves His hearers to suppose that He was but *one of many*. He uniformly speaks of Himself as performing a work in a mediatorial capacity, and acting as *one for many*.

Having already referred at large to the utterances of Christ which represent Him as leading a curse-bearing life through His whole course, we have next to notice His sinless obedience through the same extent of time, and in the very same actions. These are the two sides of His one work, and the one is as essen-tial as the other for the expiation of sin. Not that there is a double work, or that these two sides are separately meritorious; but the sin-bearer was necessarily one who knew no sin,— which, however, could not have been had there been any sin of omission or of commission. They concur in the one work of atonement for sin. In entering, then, on this obedience of three-and-thirty years as an indispensable element in the atone-ment, we shall commence at the point where the human con-sciousness of Christ first comes to light, as apprehending His work; and it is descriptive of His whole private life.

"*Wist ye not that I must be about my Father's business?*" (Luke
ii. 49.) This first recorded utterance of the Lord shows that
already, at the age of twelve, He knew His peculiar character.
The fact that the boy lingered in the temple, occupied with
meditations bearing on His office, hearing and asking questions
after the parents had set out on their homeward journey, only
discovered His exalted mind, from which all boyish things were
removed, His deep judgment and quick understanding, and His
ardent desire to be prepared for the high destiny before Him.
When His mother put Him on His defence, asking, with a
certain measure of complaint, why He had so dealt with them,
the reply was, that there was a sacred *must* in it, that His
Father's authority was paramount, and that to Him He owed a
higher obedience. It does not alter the meaning whether we
translate, "in my Father's house," or "in my Father's things,"
as the one involves the other. This may be taken, then, as the
rule or formula of Christ's subjection to man. It was controlled
or regulated,—sometimes, as in this case, suspended by the
higher claims of His Father's service.[1] And He gently reminds
the parents that they should have known this: *wist ye not?*
They might have known it from what had been announced to
them, in many ways. He thus showed paramount obedience to
His Father above what could be claimed by man, as if He
would say, "This is no disobedience to you, but only an act of
higher obedience to my Father." It argues holy zeal, an unreserved devotedness to God, and deep delight in the things of
God.

1. The sinless excellence of Christ was, in one respect, only
the evolution or acting out of His inner nature. As man, corresponding to the idea of man, His nature possessed an intrinsic
purity and elevation before any of His deeds were done. There
must be being before doing; and in this light His deeds and
words only revealed what He already was. But that by no

---

[1] This is the view commonly given by the Lutheran divines, as Luther, Chemnitz, etc., and by Riggenbach, more recently.

means exhausts the idea of the Lord's sinless obedience, which takes for granted that He was to be proved and tested; and hence He is described as learning obedience by the things He suffered.

2. "*I seek not mine own will, but the will of Him that sent Me*" (John v. 30). The single principle that guided that holy life was obedience to the will of God. And never was a step taken or a moment spent but in unconditional subjection to the will of God, which was more to Him than His necessary food (John iv. 34). And, notwithstanding the objection taken by some, and especially by the Romanists, to the idea that Jesus exercised faith, it must be maintained, on the clearest grounds of Scripture, that His whole obedience flowed from faith and love. They were the root of it. Neither are we to imagine that, in a world of sin, the sinless obedience of Jesus could be exercised without a certain measure of conflict with natural inclination. Possessor of true humanity, and with feelings far more susceptible than are found in ordinary men, He naturally recoiled, as we do, from pain and suffering, agony and woe. But His will was ever in subordination to the Father's will, and in harmony with it, notwithstanding the sinless conflict of natural inclination which may be traced in Gethsemane and elsewhere. It only shows, indeed, that He was very man, with human feelings and susceptibilities. But never was one formed purpose, aspiration, or desire either entertained or cherished, that was not in full, everlasting, perfect accord with the will of God. And hence His obedience was ever acceptable and entitled to reward, because it was never a yielding to natural liking, or out of keeping with the appointment of His Father.

3. "*I seek not mine own glory*" (John viii. 56). In this humility lies the foundation of Christ's moral excellence. The humility of Jesus found expression in a constant renunciation of His own honour. It shows that He lived in another element and before another public than that of human opinion, which attaches weight only to that which is ostentatious, or comes recommended

by success or marked superiority in the race of life. His public before which He acted was not human opinion, but the eye of His Father, before whose perfections all the distinctions of man, as well as all their praise and honour, are little and puny indeed. He did not wish to rise, but to abase Himself : " I am among you as one that serveth." Though so exalted and excellent, He was more humble than any creature in the universe.

4. *" I do always those things that please Him"* (John viii. 29). This constant service, uninterrupted in duration and perfect in degree, is described by Him as extending over all the stages of human life, and as filling all its spheres. The history of Jesus of Nazareth brings before us human life in its full-orbed completeness, and in the perfect equipoise of all the virtues. Yet this did not interfere with, but rather helped, the intense activity and energy, in which He passed His life. There was nothing fitful, nothing done by mere impulse ; and even the consuming zeal which led Him to cleanse the temple twice, though it may be called an outburst of zeal, was full of calm, collected majesty. One grace or virtue did not displace or mar another. In the most distinguished saints some graces are more fully developed, while they are for the most part, in a number of points, left far behind by those who have no pretensions to what ennobles them and hence a very different estimate may be made by the Judge of all. But in Christ they are all found, and all complete in measure. The scattered beauties of all the saints are jointly found in Him,—tempered, too, and adjusted to each other in such a way that there is free play for all ; and though we discern in His experience a change of mood or of frame from sorrow to joy, from calm repose to soul-trouble, the harmony is not broken, nor the balance permanently disturbed. And when we look at the social relations, we see Him doing the duty of the citizen and discharging the duty of the family, even to the last hour of life.

5. The moral code required to be embodied in a life, which should not only be an example of virtue to engage and win all

hearts, but prove a work of which the intrinsic value should redound to our account. The life of Christ and the moral glory of His character are not aright understood, if we merely rest in it as an ideal or creative pattern, though in that light it is the most attractive spectacle ever presented to the world, and for all time. But that life was vicarious as much as His suffering, and must be viewed as ours, the obedience of one for many; for perfect obedience in the exercise of holy love was the great task set before man at the first, and that which the Son of God came down from heaven to usher in.

Christ often expressed Himself as conscious of having such a work or task assigned to Him; and He ever kept it in view from His first recorded utterance in the temple to the moment when He said, "It is finished." There is a testimony which we shall afterwards consider, and which very emphatically describes that work: "I have glorified Thee on the earth: I have finished the work Thou gavest Me to do" (John xvii. 4). The same thing is taught under other forms. He calls it a work (John iv. 34), a commandment (John x. 18), the will of Him that sent Him (John vi. 39). All these expressions show that the active cannot be separated from the passive obedience; for voluntary obedience to the Father and ardent love to us concur. This sinless obedience underlies the suffering as the two elements of one work.

6. It may be noticed that there was one special act or culminating point in the obedience of Christ; and this had its counterpart in that testing-point in which the whole obedience of Adam was contained,—the abstaining from the forbidden tree; for it would appear that a sinless nature with the law written on the heart must yet have its loyalty tested by some special act of obedience, in which all the elements of submission may be found to meet, and pure nature fitly express its self-denial and allegiance.¹ The special act of positive obedience imposed on the Lord Jesus was, to die, as that imposed on Adam was, to abstain from the tree by an act of self-restraint,—all the lines of obedience

meeting in that one act, the crowning act, and the culminating point of obedience appointed to complete the work.[1] Hence the constant allusion to the death or blood or sacrifice of the Lord. (Comp. John xvii. 19.)

Having surveyed the atonement in its constituent elements, it only remains that we define with precision what is meant by a satisfaction to God: and a few words will suffice.

Scripture often uses typical and figurative terms on this point, and many who have familiarly used the words from their youth, fail to think out the subject to the end, or to keep the point of comparison fully before them. In answer to the inquiry, what is meant by satisfying God, it is not enough to say that the debt is paid, or that His anger is appeased: for the further questions are raised, How far is sin a debt, and how far is anger to be ascribed to God? nor is it enough to say that by the sufferings of the Lord the divine perfections violated by sin have been glorified, the authority of His law vindicated, and the moral order of the universe maintained. For though all this is true, our explanation, if it went no further, would still place the main scope of the atonement in something external to God. These are ends, but not the sole or the principal ends.

The question recurs: What moved Him to this? and the answer is, His own attributes or perfections. In what relation stood the vicarious obedience and sufferings of Jesus to the divine perfections? This brings up the views propounded by

---

[1] Our Christian poet Cowper well puts this :—

"The Saviour,—what a noble flame
Was kindled in His breast,
When, hasting to Jerusalem,
He marched before the rest !

"Good-will to man and zeal for God
His every thought engross ;
He longs to be baptized with blood,
He pants to reach the cross.

"With all His sufferings full in view,
And woes to us unknown,
Forth to the task His spirit flew,—
'Twas love that urged Him on."

us in speaking of the necessity of the atonement. The Most High, viewing sin in its true nature, punishes it to satisfy an adorable perfection of His nature. The twofold element of sin as an indelible fact or deed committed against God (Ps. li. 4), is defect of obedience and desert of punishment; and against sin, so viewed, God from the excellency of His nature, and His relation as moral governor, must direct His glorious attribute of punitive justice. Only when the divine indignation has been discharged against moral evil, and the tribute of obedience due to God has been restored, can men be taken into favour. The Gospel proceeds on this supposition, and the work of the Lord takes it for granted. When this is attained, all the external objects are also secured. This we see; and further we cannot go : for we cannot give an exhaustive outline of satisfaction—no finite mind can define God's representation of sin to Himself. We must guard against a description of the atonement which portrays another public than God Himself, and which makes the satisfaction bear on some other interest than that of God Himself or external to Him, whether we suppose other orders of being, or man's suspicious nature. These are subordinate at most, and, as we shall notice below, God displayed His perfect satisfaction with the work of His Son by raising Him up from the dead; thus making it evident that they for whom the Lord atoned were viewed as if they had done what He had done (2 Cor. v. 15).

SEC. XXIII.—CHRIST THE SIN-BEARER TESTIFYING THAT HE WAS
    TO BE NUMBERED WITH TRANSGRESSORS DURING HIS CRUCI-
    FIXION.

As our plan directs us rather to the doctrine of the atone-ment than to the history of the transaction, so far as man is concerned, we can bring out the actual history of the crucifixion scene in only a few of its salient points; and in doing so, we shall refer to the cross only in such a way as shall connect the

fact and the doctrine together. The simple narrative of the
scenes of Christ's suffering, as given by the evangelists, is so
limited to the bare facts, and so simply historical in its outline,
that it requires to be read with the commentary supplied by the
prophecy of Isaiah on the one hand (Isa. liii. 1-12), and by the
apostolic Epistles on the other. There we find the rationale of
the whole suffering career of Christ.

But even those outward scenes, where we see Jesus face to
face with man, must be read off, if we would fully understand
them, from the great fact of His substitution in the room of
sinners.[1] It must be kept in mind that He was a sacrifice
from the very commencement of His earthly life, and that His
collective sufferings are to be viewed as belonging to His work
of substitution, and as the one discharge of His mediatorial
work. Hence, even in those historical events, which put Him
in connection with a human judge and with a human court of
justice, we are by no means to dismiss the idea of an exchange
of persons. He was, even then, truly sustaining the person and
occupying the place of the guilty,—that is, was the just in the
room of the unjust, the sinless in the room of the sinful, the
innocent in the room of the guilty. His person was in the
room of our persons; and such was the exchange, that our
punishment became His.

There are several sayings of Christ descriptive of His delivery
into the hands of men, and of the treatment to be received from
them when so delivered, which proceed upon the supposition
of a very deep and peculiar relation. These sayings we now

[1] We have followed the example set by V. Hofmann in introducing a reference
to the historical facts of Christ's sufferings. He sees in these only a *widerfahrniss;* we see in them His vicarious work and sacrifice in process of execution. It
is well remarked by Weber in his work, *Vom Zorne Gottes;* Erlangen, 1862 :
" Mit den selbstaussagen Jesu von der Bedeutung, seines Leidens und Sterbens
vergleichen wir den geschichtlichen Vollzug desselben. Man hat das früher bei
Ermittlung der Frage, in wiefern Jesus durch sein Leiden und sterben uns mit
Got versöhnt habe, unterlassen : aber mit recht hat V. Hofmann in seiner Darstellung des Versöhnungswerkes *die Geschichte* der Passion vorangestellt : denn
an ihr muss es sich bewähren, ob die aussagen über die Bedeutung des Leidens
Jesu richtig verstanden worden sind " (p. 244).

investigate. All the attempts made against Him were, up to a definite time, impotent and wholly futile. He eased Him of His adversaries by retiring with majestic ease beyond the reach of their machinations. Thus He withdrew from the infuriated men of Nazareth, His fellow-townsmen, when they attempted to take Him and to cast Him headlong from the brow of the hill whereon their city was built (Luke iv. 29). They could not touch Him till they received divine permission. The rulers also sent officers to seize Him, and they returned paralyzed and con-science-struck, unable to execute the charge (John vii. 32). At another time the assembled crowd whom He addressed took up stones to cast at Him (John viii. 59), and He passed through the midst of them, and so passed by. In a word, till His hour was come, or, in another form of expressing it, till He spontane-ously consented to be apprehended, He had a perfect immunity from all their violence.

Now the inquiry that confronts us, and which demands an answer, is this: When He was arrested at last, as the first step to the violent death which was to be endured, is this to be ascribed to the ordinary course of events, and to be regarded as His fate? By no means. That is, in modern theology, a too common mode of speech on the part of those who cannot adjust their views to the doctrine of the exchange of places, or to the representative position which Jesus must be regarded as occu-pying. That is the language commonly held at present by the supporters of a tendency. But they who speak of Christ as coming within the ordinary laws of human society and the ordinary incidents of life, and who describe His death as an occurrence in the operation of the common course of history, know not what they say, nor whereof they affirm. They mis-take His position in the world, and they misinterpret the moral government of God.

He had a double immunity from the common incidents of life. He had an immunity, first, as the sinless man on whom the taint of evil had never fallen; and next, as the Son of God, from all those consequences of sin and those ordinary incidents befalling sinful men in a sinful world. No injury could assail Him till He was judicially delivered up as the sin-bearer. He could be seized only when His hour was come. He was to be delivered up only at the time when, having finished His period of sinless obedience for the space of a generation, as read off from the length of human life, and having ended His public ministry, He voluntarily consented as the surety to take our place, and to sustain our person in His trial and condemnation. It was the sinner who was there brought up for sentence. It was not only for sin in a vague, abstract, indeterminate sense that He was delivered up, but in the room of the sinners given to Him, and whose place He representatively occupied. It was only in their room and stead that Jesus was placed at the bar as a criminal. And this was a real transaction before the tribunal of God, not a semblance of a trial. *The sinner was there, but Jesus took his place.* And only in this way can we explain either the prophetical sayings which describe Him as wounded for our transgressions (Isa. liii. 5), or those apostolic sayings which represent believers as co-crucified (Gal. ii. 20), as co-dying (Rom. vi. 8), and as suffering in the flesh (1 Peter iv. 1), when in point of fact the Lord appears to human view single and alone in the historic narrative of the evangelists. He spontaneously took our place, however, and was acting at every step as a public person, or as the second Adam.[1]

Unless there had been this voluntary self-surrender, no earthly power could have apprehended Him. Not to refer to His own divine dignity, which sufficiently secured Him, while He willed it, there could not have happened in the moral government of God such an anomaly as that of a perfectly pure and sinless person subjected to any kind or measure of suffering, except as He appeared to sustain the person of sinners, and was made

---

[1] See the remarkable words of Luther on Gal. iii. 13, where he condemns the Sophists "cum segregant Christum a peccatis et peccatoribus, et eum tantum proponunt ut exemplum nobis imitandum."

sin by His own consent. Nor was this perfect exemption from violence or injury at the hand of men a mere isolated fact. It was part of the general scheme or of the understood relation to human life occupied by Christ. He was not to dash His foot against a stone (Ps. xci.). Disease in the ordinary course, or as it is commonly contracted, could not touch Him, because He did not come within the power of sin in the world; and hence we never read of His contracting any distemper or disease like other men. Nor could death in any of the thousand forms in which it comes to other men, come to Him, till He consented, by a priestly act of self-oblation, to lay down His life. He who was exempt on His own account from any part of the curse, came within its operation in any sphere only by His own consent; and on this footing He came within the curse in every sphere in which it was diffused. On this general ground, no one, till His hour was come, that is, till the appointed time arrived in the Father's purpose, could put forth a hand to arrest Him. This is repeated again and again, as an explanation why His enemies had no power over Him. A judicial act on His Father's part, and a voluntary surrender on His own part, were necessary before He could be delivered into the hands of men.

We find that our Lord brought out this truth very emphatically in reply to an arrogant remark of Pilate laying claim to a power to crucify Christ or to release Him: "*Thou couldst have no power at all against Me, except it were given thee from above*" (John xix. 11). This saying puts our Lord's subjection to human power in its true and proper light. It has been very variously interpreted, and sometimes very superficially. It is not a general statement spoken with reference to the magistrate as the minister and deputy of God. Nor is it an allusion to the general question of providence, as if Jesus would intimate that nothing takes place without the direction of divine providence, and that what befalls the true servants of God takes place only by divine permission. Nor is it a statement of the general truth, that in a world of sinners the righteous, possessing as they do a sinful nature, receive many a wrong and indignity, because they come within the range of those general laws which operate in the world. None of these comments which regard Christ's reply as referring to a general truth, touch the real point of His answer; nay, they pervert it. Pilate had spoken, with a specific allusion to Christ, claiming such judicial authority over Him as was competent to one who had Him wholly in his power. Pilate intimated that it was entirely at his discretion to crucify or to release Him; and the answer of Christ is equally specific.[1] The Lord means that Pilate could have no power at all over Him considered in His proper character as the Son of God, and as the sinless man. He signifies that the power which the Roman governor possessed could be turned against Him, not absolutely, but simply on the ground that our Lord was there in a capacity which properly belonged to others, not to Himself. He intimates not obscurely that He was there as the representative of sinners and as the sin-bearer. Hence the power over Him was given indeed from above to a human judge, but given for an end worthy of such abasement on His part. But because He sustained our person, He is no more to be treated as if He were innocent. Personally sinless, He occupied the place of sinners, and sustained their character by taking their sins and responsibilities upon Himself. We have to notice in this light the arrest of Christ and His trial; for, as we have already said, no power on earth could touch Him till He gave them permission to proceed.

I may here notice another saying of Christ quite analogous to the former, and containing also a deep significance, which can only be apprehended when we read it in connection with Christ's suretyship or representative character. He said, before leaving the upper room, where He celebrated the last supper: " *This that*

---

[1] The remarks on this passage by the profound Lutheran divine, Gerhard, in the *Harmonia Evangelica*, the joint work of Chemnitz, Lyser, and Gerhard, 1628, are well worthy of being read and pondered. He justly argues for the *specific* reference.

is written of Me must [1] *yet be accomplished in Me, And He was numbered among transgressors*" (Luke xxii. 37). Now, are we to regard this remark of Christ, which embodies a quotation from Isaiah's prophecy, as containing nothing more than a description of the opinion entertained by men respecting Him? Does it mean that He was treated as if He had been a transgressor, or in a way which might have led a hasty observer or an undiscerning spectator to conclude that He was, or might be, a transgressor? No; by no means. Our Lord plainly takes the words in all their fulness of significance. He uses them not as denoting a mere *as if*, but as descriptive of the real sentence due to transgressors, and of the doom or punishment consequent on that righteous sentence carried out against transgressors. That is the meaning of the words; and the rationale is supplied by the fact, that the expression occurs in a chapter which, beyond doubt, predicts the vicarious sufferings of Christ, and repeats again and again the great thought, "*that He bore the sins of many*" (Isa. liii.). No candid interpreter, interpreting simply by language, can have any other impression than this, that the righteous servant there named delivers many by a vicarious atonement. And Jesus, by quoting this statement as awaiting its accomplishment in Himself, manifestly applies that whole chapter of Isaiah to His own sufferings and death. We can interpret our Lord's words only in the sense that He was to be judicially numbered among transgressors, that is, numbered agreeably to the execution of a judicial sentence with transgressors. When Mark applies the same quotation to the position assigned to Christ between the two thieves at His crucifixion (Mark xv. 28), he brings out its meaning in all its compass of allusion. But He by no means excludes the preparatory stages of its accomplishment, or that which preceded the fact adduced as its fulfilment. The words,

---

[1] See some interesting remarks by Weber, *Vom Zorne Gottes*, p. 259, on the words δεῖ τελεσθῆναι ἐν ἐμοί, as against the notion supported by V. Hofmann, that Christ's sufferings were merely caused by Satan's influence and opposition, and that they were no more than a *widerfahrniss*, and meant to be but a means *zur Bewährung*.

"He was numbered with transgressors," were accomplished not only when He shared a common lot with the malefactors, but also in all that preceded the erection of the three crosses on Golgotha, and, in fact, from the moment of His delivery into the hands of men. It was thus a judicial numbering of Christ with transgressors.

1. The ARREST of Christ in the garden as if He were a criminal was the first step to the accomplishment of the prediction. He was there treated as a seditious man and as a malefactor in the room of us sinners, who had forfeited our freedom. We are evildoers in so far as our relation to the city of God is concerned, that is, men who had renounced their dependence and allegiance, and who acted in all things as disobedient subjects. That arrest by the hand of justice was a real transaction at the hand of God, —was, in fact, the arrest of the guilty criminal in the person of the representative. And if the veil had been drawn aside, it would have been seen that all this was in the room of the sinner who should have been so apprehended. This is a real, not a symbolical transaction. And if the representative is seized, they whom He represented must go free. There is such a meaning in our Lord's words: "Let these go free" (John xviii. 8). Our Lord deeply felt, indeed, the rude arrest in His tender human feelings when He said: "Are ye come out as against a thief, with swords and with staves to take Me?" (Mark xiv. 48). But He well knew, that though personally sinless, He was there in the room of sinners, and that the officers, acting as the ministers of God, seized Him as the sinner should have been seized. But, at the same time, to show how little human power could have prevailed against Him, unless He had given His consent, it was deemed fitting to let out some display or outbeaming of His majesty; and the utterance of the simple words, "I am He," prostrated the officers and band to the ground (John xviii. 6). Though innocent of the charge of sedition and blasphemy on which He was ostensibly arrested, His people were not; and hence He must needs be seized and bound in His capacity as the

sinner's representative. When we see the Son of God bound in
chains, what does the transaction exhibit but the captivity consequent upon our sin, which He had made His own, or the chain
binding the sinner to the judgment of the great day ? His arrest
is His people's liberty; His bonds are their release.

2. Not to mention all the intermediate points in the successive
steps of Christ's sufferings, we shall notice, next in order, His
TRIAL AND SENTENCE BEFORE THE ECCLESIASTICAL COURT, ON THE
CHARGE OF BLASPHEMY. In this whole transaction, when sentence
of death was pronounced by the high priest, we have but the
visible part of the great assize. He must, as the substitute of
sinners, be found innocent, and yet made guilty,—be proved
personally spotless, and yet be treated by the sentence given as
one who was regarded as officially worthy of condemnation.
And this anomalous trial brings together at all points these two
things. The sentence by which He was condemned only indicated
or announced the sentence passed by God upon the sin-bearer.
The accusation on which He was tried in the Sanhedrim, AS
BROUGHT AGAINST US, is not false. Moses accuses us, that the
revelation given in the name of God has been disregarded and
despised, and that the divine perfections have only been blas-
phemed by us. The accusation is so true and so undeniable, that
there is no need of witnesses. The representative of sinners in
His official capacity is silent, and puts in no plea in arrest of
judgment. But His personal innocence must be apparent. And
it was only His own true declaration of what He was as a divine
person which brought down on Him, in lack of other evidence,
the sentence that He was worthy of death.[1] He thus appears
personally innocent, but representatively guilty ; and unless we
carry with us these two ideas as the key to the whole trial, the
narrative will be inexplicable, and the fact in the moral government of God an impenetrable mystery. That earthly court,
dealing with the charge of blasphemy, or dishonour to the name

[1] Weber says, p. 262 : "Mit ihnen hat er allewege nichts zu thun, als das zu
bekennen und zu sagen, was sie treiben wird, ihn zu verurtheilen."

and works and word of God, sentenced the sinner's surety, and pronounced upon our sin, much in the same way as the shadow on the sun-dial registers the movements taking place in another sphere. He was personally innocent; but as He stood there for. us, He was truly chargeable with all the accusation which was then adduced. His silence at that tribunal opens our mouth to cry, " Abba, Father."

3. The MOCKERY, the shame, and the indignity to which He was subjected, constituted the next part of His vicarious sufferings. They were undeserved by that meek and patient sufferer, but well merited by us, in whose name He appeared, and whose person He bore. The wicked " shall rise to shame and everlasting contempt" (Dan. xii. 2). And from that merited scorn due to sinners from all holy beings the sinless substitute was not exempt. He hid not His face from shame and from spitting.

4. Omitting the desertion of His disciples and the denial of Peter, we advance to the next public act in connection with Christ's sufferings,—THE TRIAL AND CONDEMNATION AT THE BAR OF THE ROMAN GOVERNOR, ON A CHARGE OF REBELLION OR SEDITION. This is very much of the same kind with the trial before the high priest upon a charge of blasphemy, and is to be considered in a similar light. The course of our Lord's sufferings may with advantage be traced, as we have already done, on the sinner's history, and read off from it. The surety encountered, at each successive step, what should have taken place in the history of man's relation to God. For the very same relations, and not merely analogous ones, were occupied by the surety when He was tried, sentenced and condemned. It is noteworthy that at Pilate's bar Jesus was silent[1] (Matt. xxvii. 14). The explanation is to be found in the fact, that though personally sinless, He really, and not nominally, occupied the sinner's place. Hence the silence. He puts in no plea in arrest of judgment or in self-vindication. He was there not in His personal capacity, but in His official capacity, as the representative of sinners and the

[1] " And He answered him to never a word, ὥστε θαυμάζειν τὸν ἡγεμόνα λίαν."

voluntary sin-bearer. He has nothing to adduce in extenuation or in exculpation, since every mouth must be stopped, and the whole world become guilty before God. He accepts the charge of guilt; and as the doom is the sinner's, not His, He submits to it as merited. When Pilate wished to deliver Him, if Jesus would only be aiding in His own defence, the Lord continued silent before His accusers, amid all the accusations adduced against Him. He was then making a real appearance at the bar of God, of which that earthly court of justice was but the foreground. He was personally innocent, and officially guilty. Hence His silence.

We must notice this anomalous trial in connection with the fact that He was sentenced as guilty while pronounced innocent.[1] The examination of the judge was meant to serve the important purpose of manifesting the innocence of Jesus. And the startling fact, that a judge pronounces Him innocent, but condemns Him as guilty, must be historically brought about in the adorable providence of God, in order to exhibit the personal and the official in the Lord Jesus; or, in other words, to discover the sinless one and the sin-bearer. No man could more emphatically testify to Christ's innocence than Pilate. He had examined the accusations; he had heard all that the witnesses could adduce against Him, and was perfectly informed of everything in the case; five times he declared that he found no fault in Him. This was done, too, in public, before His accusers, and in the presence of the vast multitude. And, not content with that public announcement, he, when he yielded at last to the clamour for the crucifixion, confirmed his judicial testimony to His innocence by the significant symbolical action of washing his hands, and declaring that he was innocent of the blood of that just man. It was fitting that all this should be done by a judge, and from the judicial bench, that Christ's innocence might be made apparent; and next, that the inference might be drawn that the

---

[1] See the Heidelberg Catechism, No. 28, and the numerous expounders of it on the reason why Jesus suffered under Pilate,—viz.: "Ut innocens coram judice politico damnatus nos a severo Dei judicio quod omnes manebat, eximerit." See also Calvin on Christ's trial and sufferings.

CHRIST NUMBERED WITH TRANSGRESSORS. 179

doom of the guilty was transferred to Him as standing in a vicarious position. Thus He was personally innocent, though He was by no means to be accounted so in that official and vicarious capacity, in which alone He stood at Pilate's bar. There is no way of elucidating that anomalous trial, which went through the due forms of law, unless we hold that He was truly innocent, but officially guilty.

5. The last step of Christ's sufferings, THE CRUCIFIXION, immediately followed the sentence of Pilate. The intermediate details, such as the mockery, scorn, and indignity inflicted on Him in many forms, we shall omit; though these, too, were vicarious, as appears from the words, "by His stripes we are healed." We shall omit, too, the Lord's words to the daughters of Jerusalem when they wept for Him tears of sympathy, as He toiled along the public way under the burden of the cross,—tears which, He shows them, were out of place as shed for Him. We shall limit ourselves to the crucifixion itself and to the closing acts of His life.

The crucifixion, a Roman mode of punishment, was not only peculiarly painful and ignominious in the sight of man, but was meant to indicate the amazing fact, that Christ, by being suspended on the tree, WAS MADE A CURSE. The words of Moses quoted by Paul are express to this effect (Gal. iii. 13).[1] The Lord Jesus was thus, personally considered, the beloved Son and the sinless man, but, officially considered, the curse-bearer in the room of sinners. The Son of God, truly bearing sin with a view to condemn it in the flesh, was exhibited as made a curse by the very fact of enduring this punishment. We have thus to draw the same distinction, as we already mentioned, between Christ considered personally and Christ considered officially. If there ever was a spot where sin could be laid without entailing the inevitable doom of a righteous condemnation, it was here when

---

[1] The Dutch commentary on the Heidelberg Catechism, translated from the Latin papers of A. Schultens by Barueth, on questions 37, 38, 39, gives some striking views upon this point.

it was borne by the sinless humanity of the incarnate Son; and we see that even there sin was condemned in the flesh and righteously visited. The surety was tried, sentenced, condemned, and made a curse for us, that we might not come into condemnation.

The bitterest ingredient in the Lord's cup was the soul-trouble which He experienced direct from the hand of God. There were indeed actings of His own holy nature which brought with them the deepest sorrow, as may easily be collected from the consideration that One who was inflamed with zeal for His Father's glory, and who breathed the deepest love for holiness, could not but be affected with lively sorrow, when He discerned sin in all its deformity, and furthermore felt that though not His own personally, it belonged in a sense to Him, because it belonged as a personal property to those who were His. And if a mere sight of sin is often painful and well-nigh overwhelming to us though never called to feel its doom, what a hell it must have been to the holy nature of Jesus to see before Him and upon Him by imputation the sins of all the elect. This made Him the man of sorrows. But the most insupportable part of His sorrows was that He had to encounter the frown of an angry Judge, an agony and a desertion which constitute the ingredients of the second death. He tasted death for every one of the many sons who are to be brought to glory (Heb. ii. 9); enduring in a little space what soon overwhelms the lost with unending despair. This wrung from Him the cry in the garden already noticed, and made Him offer up prayers and supplications with strong crying and tears (Heb. v. 7); pressing from Him the bloody sweat, the preternatural character of which testified to a suffering which no other man suffered and no mere man could have borne. This desertion reached its climax on the cross: but faith was kept in lively exercise in His human soul amidst it all.

During those awful hours on the cross when made a curse for us, the Lord Jesus sustained that desertion, which was just the endurance of the death of the soul, when sin separates between

God and the soul, and when God hides His face from us. To this it is not necessary to refer further, after what was said in a previous section. The actions of the Lord Jesus when He hung on the cross, were in the highest degree momentous and significant. These expiatory sufferings, " an offering and sacrifice to God for a sweet-smelling savour" (Eph. v. 2), were so efficacious that they were made the ground of two signal displays of grace, while He was on the cross. The one of these was the salvation of the dying malefactor, who was made an eminent trophy of His redemption work, and enabled to recognise Him as a sufficient Saviour, even in that deep abasement and humiliation. The other was the prayer for forgiveness to His crucifiers, which had a prevailing efficacy, whether we regard the scope of the prayer as comprehending the individuals then before Him, or as extending to the preservation of the Jewish nation.

After these hours of inconceivable sorrow and desertion on the cross, under a darkness which just resembled the blackness awaiting the lost, the Lord felt that His work was accomplished; and He gave utterance to that saying which has brought light, rest, and liberty to so many minds : " *It is finished*" (John xix. 30).[1] He meant that the expiatory sufferings had reached their climax, and were sufficient; that the guilt of mankind was fully atoned for; that there was nothing left undone; that God and man were reunited and reconciled; and now He had but to resign His spirit into His Father's hands. As PRIEST AND VICTIM, He had now only one act to perform,—to lay down His life by the priestly act of commending His spirit to God. Nature was not exhausted, nor did life ooze away; for He still

---

[1] τετέλεσται. This cannot refer merely to the fulfilment of all the prophecies, as many yet remained to be fulfilled, but specially to the fulfilling of all the vicarious suffering and meritorious obedience necessary for man's redemption. This is better than the comment of the modern exegetes, of whom the recent lexicographer, Cremer, *Wörterbuch der N. T. Gräcität*, 1868, may be taken as a representative, and who writes : " τετέλεσται : welches sich somit auf die Vollständige ausführung dessen, wodurch die Schrift erfüllt wird bezieht, nicht erfüllen." On the contrary, Wolfius, with much more accuracy, said in his *Curæ*, 1741 : " Interpretes hactenus omnes verbum illud de consummatione omnium, quæ ad salutarem perpessionem pertinebant acceperunt."

had power over His own life, and no man took it from Him (John x. 18). After having done all and endured all, He deemed it fitting, without more delay, to resign His life or spirit into His Father's hand as an acceptable sacrifice. It was the High Priest offering up His soul to God that said, " Father, into Thy hands I commend my spirit." And He uttered it with a loud voice, to show that strength still remained in Him, and that, by His own authority, He released the spirit from the lacerated and wounded body.[1]

The curse was, " Thou shalt die ; " and now it was exhausted, and sin annihilated. Now heaven and earth were reunited ; God and man were at one again.

SECTION XXIV.—THE CONNECTION BETWEEN THE LORD'S ATONEMENT AND HIS RESURRECTION WITHOUT SEEING CORRUPTION.

The Lord's Resurrection, the Christian's boast, the pledge of all our hope, is in a special sense the foundation of our religion, because it is the evidence that the atonement was at once complete and accepted. On several occasions the Lord foretold it to gainsayers and to His own disciples—to the former as a sign of His divine mission and analogous to that of the prophet Jonas (Matt. xii. 40 ; John ii. 19)—to the latter as an event awaiting Him on His path to glory (Matt. xvi. 21 ; Mark ix. 10). Mark, who accurately reproduces from Peter's recollections many impressions and circumstances bespeaking the eye-witness, informs us that the disciples questioned among themselves what the rising from the dead should mean.

This great fact was always viewed as connected in the closest

---

[1] The removal of the desertion and the return of light to Christ's soul before He expired are affirmed by many great divines. That return of light is not improbable, though it is not more than a probability. (See Weber, *Vom Zorne Gottes*, p. 266 ; Dods on *Incarnation;* Hulshoff, *Sermons*, etc., who affirm it.) The desertion may have terminated with the darkness spread over all nature. But there is one caveat necessary where this is held : the curse was not, and could not be, fully exhausted till death ensued—the wages of sin.

manner with the expiation—necessarily distinguished from it, indeed, but not to be disjoined. The resurrection of the Lord does not enter into the meritorious part of the Redeemer's work, that is, into the element which divines call the impetration of redemption. A certain class, remarkable for only crude think-ing, have begun to speak of the Lord's resurrection as the ground or basis of justification: but this is an error of the most obvious kind, arising out of an utter misconception of the text on which it professes to be based (viz. Rom. iv, 25),[1] and tending to the subversion of the entire Gospel. The atonement and resurrection stand to each other in the relation of service and reward, of cause and effect.

When we examine the interpretation put by the apostles on the fact of the Lord's resurrection, we find it said that He could see no corruption (Acts xiii. 35); that He could not be holden of death (ii. 24); and that our deliverance is so inseparably connected with it, that if Christ be not raised, our faith is vain, and we are yet in our sins (1 Cor. xv. 17). These three state-ments are so important, that it seems necessary to give an elucidation of them.

With regard to the statement that the Holy One should not see corruption, it is plain that a return to dust—the common lot of fallen humanity—could have no place in connection with one who was personally sinless. He could not, in consistency with divine justice, linger in the grave or return to the dust (Ps. xvi. 10). It is not so with believers whose body is corrupt and unfit, till radically changed, for inheriting heavenly glory. Had Christ returned to dust, the reason would have been that His humanity, like that of other mortals, had been tainted by sin, and in that case He would neither have been competent to act the part of a

---

[1] The Darbyite doctrine that our justification is not the result of the work which Christ finished on the cross, but is accomplished by union with Him in His resurrection, is a piece of ignorance arising from a mistake of the import of διὰ with the accusative (Rom. iv. 25). (See *Apostles' Doctrine of the Atonement*, where I have explained it.)

mediator, nor actually to present Himself as having expiated sin. The legitimate inference would be as follows: if Christ is not raised without seeing corruption, then no atonement has been made. Had He not risen without seeing corruption, His disciples could have had no assurance that sin was annihilated. Nay, on the contrary, they would have had certain evidence that guilt was not taken away. But having expiated sin and put it away, He could see no corruption: for the cause being removed, the effect must cease. He could remain no longer in the grave than for such a period as was necessary to give an assurance to the church of the actual death and actual resurrection.[1]

As to the second statement—that He could not be holden of death—we remark that it is rather an allusion to rectitude than to omnipotence. Having satisfied for His Church, and bought the flock of God, He could not remain in the state of death, but must needs be raised by God. The nature of the case required it, as will readily appear to every inquirer. The Lord's humanity being perfectly holy, must be in itself blessed and immortal. To subject a perfectly holy nature to either misery or death runs counter to the divine rectitude, and could not have occurred in the moral government of God, except by mutual agreement in the prosecution of a great plan. Yet the Lord was a sufferer. He died by His voluntary consent, allowing the sins of His Church to be charged to Himself. Though absolutely holy He was accounted guilty, and treated as guilty by the Supreme Judge. In a word, He came by His own act within the scope of the sentence: *thou shalt surely die* (Gen. ii. 17). But when the satisfaction was complete, the sinless Surety must needs rise from the dead: it was not possible that He should be holden of death (Acts ii. 24).

The last statement which we adduced was: "if Christ be not raised, your faith is vain; ye are yet in your sins" (1 Cor. xv.

---

[1] Another of the crude Darbyite doctrines is, that there was no blood in the Lord's resurrection-body.

17). This contains a twofold declaration. When it is said that were the resurrection not a fact our faith would be vain, the import is, that in that case faith would be unavailing or worthless for the purpose on account of which it is exercised, and the object of that faith would be false. When it is further added, that we should still be " in our sins," this means we should still be under their guilt, or in a state of condemnation. The phrase cannot refer to the lingering remains of sin in the redeemed (1 John i. 8).

Now the important question here presents itself: On what ground does the apostle thus reason ? What is the connection between the resurrection and those consequences which are deduced from it by Paul ? This will at once appear if we go back a step and survey the principal topics of the Christian system. Of one thing there can be no doubt: the apostle's reasoning would not have force on the supposition that Christ was but a model man, a mere teacher or prophet, or even a head of spiritual influences. For on any of these theories man is supposed to attain his end, by personally conforming to an example, or complying with a prescribed rule and standard, and not by something in the events or fortunes that entered into the history of Jesus. A good or virtuous man, according to these theories, attains his reward by following a rule, or filling up a prescribed course; and how can the objective fact of Christ's resurrection come into account at all ? The reasoning in that case should rather have proceeded according to this tenor: " All depends on a good or virtuous life, and not on the objective fact whether Christ is risen from the dead or not. As God loves all good men, the question whether men are objects of the divine favour, and no more in their sins, depends simply on leading a virtuous life, or complying with the rule to which they must needs be conformed." The apostle's reasoning would not hold on this theory.

To discover the grounds on which the apostle reasons, we must take to our aid what is said in other passages of the divine word.   When the whole world had corrupted its way, God appointed a Mediator to do and suffer what the law demanded of man the sinner.   He entered into the same relation that Adam occupied, and thus took upon Himself, as the condition of salvation, obedience to the law and satisfaction for the penalty. By taking the sins of His people He suffered as the second Adam, and they are supposed to have suffered and died in Him. Hence we are represented as having satisfied in Him, as having suffered and died in Him (John vi. 51-57; Rom. vi. 1-11; Gal. ii. 20).

This reasoning, as we have brought it out, demonstrates the vicarious character of the atonement.   The suretyship of Christ is presupposed, and the argument is: Since He occupied the place of His people, and took their responsibilities, they are justified in their representative, and no more in their sins.   Not only so; redeemed humanity, raised from the dead in their living Head, and having life judicially awarded to it, cannot be holden of corruption, in soul or in body; for their whole persons are redeemed, and indissolubly united to Him.   But it is premial life.[1]

CHAPTER IV.

THE EFFECTS OF CHRIST'S DEATH.

SEC. XXV.—THE CLASSIFICATION OF CHRIST'S SAYINGS AS THEY REPRESENT THE EFFECTS OF HIS DEATH, AND, IN THE FIRST PLACE, AS THEY SET FORTH HIS DEATH AS THE GROUND OF THE ACCEPTANCE OF OUR PERSONS.

The Lord's sayings describe His death in connection with manifold RESULTS, EFFECTS, or ENDS which it was appointed to

---

[1] The Darbyite theory is, that in resurrection the Lord had a new life to which righteousness as distinctly attached as did sin to the life He laid down ! But that is not premial life, the only scriptural view of the matter (Rom. vi. 1-12).

effect. These effects are either objective and immediate, or sub-jective and mediate; and we must now consider these in detail. Some refer to the acceptance of our persons, others to the com-munication of inward spiritual life. Without following the pre-cise chronological order in which the testimonies were uttered, it will serve our object best to notice first in order some of those testimonies which bear on the acceptance of our persons; and after discussing those objective fruits of the atonement as set forth in the first three Gospels, we shall be able to follow more closely, though by no means chronologically, the order in which the other sayings are found in the Gospel of John.

With regard to the IMMEDIATE and direct effects of the atone-ment, in the first place, they are those which relate to the acceptance of our persons. There are three sayings in particular which may be adduced as peculiarly comprehensive and im-portant: (1) where He speaks of giving Himself a ransom for many; (2) where He speaks of His blood as the sacrifice of the new covenant for the remission of sins; (3) where He speaks of the fulfilling of the law for righteousness. All these stand in relation to a counterpart want in man; and it is important to trace them, if we would see their full significance and adaptation, on the dark background of human misery.

Upon this question whether any causal connection exists be-tween the Lord's death and the acceptance of our persons, the two schools of theology part company, as they have ever done since the rise of Socinianism. By all biblical divines it was always maintained on sure grounds of Scripture, that the atone-ment is the cause or meritorious antecedent to manifold effects, both relative and internal. The school opposed to substitution allows no such direct or immediate effects of Christ's death as the remission of our sins and the purchase of a people to Him-self (Acts xx. 28.)

According to this latter theory man is still, as at the Creation, possessed of power and natural resources to render himself acceptable to God by the practice of piety. If he deviates by moral trespass, it is not necessary to subject him to punishment, or to insist on any expiation in order to forgiveness. The principal aim of Christ's mission, according to this school, was to restore natural religion by doctrine or example, and to teach men what duties are to be done. The entire Gospel is consequently nothing but the restored law of nature by a divine messenger. It follows, according to this theory, that any effects ascribed to the sufferings of Christ,—such as the remission of sins in an objective respect, or the communication of life in a subjective respect, must be taken as mere figurative language, adapted to men's taste, according to the sacrificial worship with which they were familiar. All that Christ did will amount simply to this, that He confirmed the doctrine by His death. This doctrine, sometimes more boldly Socinian and rationalistic, sometimes dressed out in the mystic phraseology descriptive of the divine life, finds many friends and advocates among writers of taste, who, while extolling the ethics of the Gospel and the perfect example of Jesus, subvert the foundations of the atonement. Attention is wholly turned away from that element of the Gospel which represents the Lord as the high priest and sacrifice.

Before we examine which theory deserves the preference, it may be meet to notice that the doctrine of the atonement not only does no injury to the practice of virtue, or to the comfort of a Christian, but alone effectually secures both. And assuming for a moment—though it is not the case—that men could expound the sayings of Jesus, according to one or other theory, there would still remain the question, which exposition is most in harmony with the divine purpose, and with the entire economy of God in connection with the Mediator's person and offices. We know that God chooses the best means for the proposed ends. But were the restoration of natural religion or a mere moral redemption—as men at present phrase it—the only scope of Christ's mission, could we for a moment suppose such a disposal of providence as to the fortunes of Jesus, or would this illustrate the divine wisdom? Were He a mere messenger to inform men of a moral redemption, or the mere medium by whom the spiritual life was to be ushered in, but in no respect its meritorious cause, what need was there for His despised life and ignominious death? If all this could be absolutely given without purchase, why this costly expenditure of means to an end which could be won without it? Had this been all, He would have found more access to men's minds by the advantages of birth and the power of working miracles.

It is alleged indeed (1) that he suffered to awaken His followers to a patient submission, and also that He might from His own experience learn to exercise sympathy. To this we answer: unless He had been under obligation to suffer from another cause, these ends, confessedly subordinate, could have had no place. Death or suffering could not by possibility have approached the sinless One, apart from sin-bearing. They who adduce this text (Heb. ii. 17), omit all those other passages which bring out the scope and effects of His death. It is alleged, too, (2) that He suffered to confirm His doctrine. But on the supposition we impugn—that He came only to restore natural religion—His mission would have been more confirmed by the evidence of miracles and by being translated, like Elijah, without tasting death. His death was rather a stumbling-block, and must be so till men have come to realize guilt and substitution. But in point of fact the Lord was so far from confirming the principles of natural religion by His death, that there was no dispute between Him and His enemies on that point. Rather, the charge on which He was condemned was His claim to be the Messiah, and His open avowal of it in the council, when the high priest adjured Him to declare Himself. In a word, they who deny substitution and expiation, are wholly at a loss for any tenable explanation of His fortunes.

But on the other supposition all is plain. The divine justice, wisdom, and goodness, are all equally glorified. And from the ENTIRE EFFECTS or consequences resulting from the atonement, we may argue back TO ITS NATURE. If it effects the remission of our sins and the acceptance of our persons, that can only be, because by the nature of the transaction, a substitute occupied our place and discharged the obligations in the same way as a debtor is discharged by another party putting the debt to his own account. It was necessary in order to maintain the glory of the divine perfections, to display justice and truth in visiting sin with adequate punishment: and because man Himself was not in a condition to satisfy divine law and justice, a substitute or mediator entered into our position and obligations, not in name, but in deed and in truth; that those for whom He obeyed and suffered might have all the effects or consequences which justly followed in the train of expiation. Thus the atonement and the numerous effects or consequences which we now trace in detail from the Lord's sayings, stand related to each other as cause and effect, or as merit and reward.

SEC. XXVI.—CHRIST DESCRIBING HIMSELF AS DYING TO BE A RANSOM FOR MANY.

" *The Son of Man came not to be ministered unto* [to be served], *but to minister* [to serve], *and to give His life* [His soul] *a ransom for* [better, in room of] *many.*" (Matt. xx. 28.)

This saying furnishes a key to a large class of passages descriptive of Christ's death as the price or purchase of redemption.[1] Though they may seem to be Old Testament allusions, they must also be regarded as based on this text.

As to the occasion of this condensed saying, we find that our Lord, during His last journey through Perea, took the disciples apart to tell them of the certainty of His death. While He was doing so, the train of His remarks was harshly interrupted by an ambitious request on the part of Salome, to the effect that the two seats of honour in the Messianic kingdom might be

---

[1] *E.g.* 1 Pet. i. 18, 19; 1 Cor. vi. 20; Gal. iii. 13; Rev. v. 9.

given to her two sons, James and John. The Lord Jesus replied that the chief places were not to be bestowed on such a
principle of arbitrary choice, but on wholly different grounds.
Then calling His disciples to Him, He took occasion to refer to
His own voluntary abasement, as an example of the spirit to
be breathed by His followers, and thus led back the conversation to His death. He sketches, at the same time, a brief but
comprehensive outline of the doctrine of the atonement: "The
Son of Man came not to be served, but to serve, and to give His
soul a ranson in room of many." Every word in this condensed
passage is replete with meaning.

I shall not dwell on the designation, "Son of Man," which has
already been explained as implying that He who was Son of
God in His own right condescended to become the abased,
curse-bearing second Adam, and the representative of the sinner.
I shall not refer to it further than to say that the curse-bearing
abasement of this divine person is here emphatically placed in
connection with His redeeming work. This thought is the
prominent one: that only the Son of Man, or the Son of God
incarnate and abased, could in reality give the ransom, and be
sufficient to give it. He says that He came not to be ministered
to or to receive service at the hand of others, but to render service,—a phrase which comprehends His whole humiliation and
His voluntary abasement. The last clause, referring to the
nature and purpose of His death, is attached to the first clause
in such a way as to interpret to us what that service consisted
in—viz. that He so ministered or served, that He gave His life
for others. As to the word translated *life*[1] in the authorized
version, it may be interpreted SOUL or LIFE or PERSON; and it
matters not in which of the three senses the word is here actually
taken. But the rendering "*soul*" may be fitly enough retained
as the literal meaning of the term.

We must next notice the scope or design of His coming.
The commencing words of the sentence, "The Son of Man came,"

[1] ψυχὴν.

is connected with the last clause, " came to give His life a ransom," and sets forth in the clearest manner both the fact and the purpose of Christ's coming in the flesh. The great design of the incarnation, or the object which it was intended to subserve, was the expiation or propitiatory death of the Messiah. Though Christ's doctrine comes also within the scope of His mission, He in these words connects His coming with His redemptive death in such a way that we must regard this latter as the principal design of the incarnation, and as the principal object of our faith; for we cannot interpret the words as denoting merely " to expose His life." He could not affirm more unambiguously than He does in this passage that He came into the world to act on the behalf of captives, and with the definite purpose of dying for the redemption of sinners. Thus His death must not be considered as an accident, nor as the result of the miscarriage of another plan, nor as the mere experience of the world's enmity to what is good, but as the very design of His coming. He came to give His life a ransom; and hence it appears that not our merits but our misery brought Him.

In this passage the Lord enunciates three weighty truths which, though they are all to be distinctly apprehended by us, must be regarded as only integral parts of one great thought. The elements of the statement are, (1) that of His own free choice He came to give up His soul or His life; (2) that He gave it as a ransom, or in order to have redemptive effects; (3) that in its true character this surrender of His life was a substitution in the room of others. These are the three predicates; and it is plain that either of the latter two would have sufficed to bring out unmistakeably the great idea of a vicarious death. It would have been enunciated by the use of the term RANSOM singly, or by the preposition IN ROOM OF,[1] as it is here used singly. The combination of these three ideas, however, expresses the doctrine with a fulness, a force, and an emphasis which completely remove every shadow of doubt. We shall first consider them apart, and then combine them.

---

[1] ἀντί.

1. The Lord came to give His soul or His life. The language, however, implies that He acted from the free bent of His own will, without compulsion or constraint of any kind. And this is a side of truth necessary to give completeness to the doctrine of the atonement, and especially to other passages which speak of a work laid upon Christ, and of the Father's sending Him and giving Him. But what is the precise import of " giving His soul " or His life ? At first sight it seems merely to signify, " to die." But it has a much greater significance when the language is viewed as adapted to the Hebrew ideas. The term *soul* is emphatic; and the reason for declaring that He came to give His soul will at once appear from the sacrificial language of the law : " For the *soul* of the flesh (or the life of the flesh) is in the blood ; and I have given it to you upon the altar, to make an atonement for your *souls* : for it is the blood that maketh an atonement for the *soul*" (Lev. xvii. 11). Thus the reason why the atonement was effected by the blood was, as is stated in the first clause of that verse, because the soul or life was in it; and, accordingly, whenever the blood was offered, it was understood that the soul of the sacrifice was meant to stand for that of the offerer ; that one soul covered another; that what was executed on the one was only what the other had incurred. One life was thus offered in the room of another. This was the fundamental idea of sacrifice. The words of Christ, considered in this point of view, represent Him as a Priest, offering to God an atoning sacrifice, and in this vicarious way giving His life for the life of men. There were reasons, doubtless, why our Lord did not directly apply to Himself in express terms the designation Priest during the days of His flesh, while He openly assumed the title of Prophet and King. But in the present passage, and in others similar to it, He beyond question supplied the germs of all the copious sacerdotal phraseology which we find applied to Him in the Epistle to the Hebrews. He speaks of Himself by implication, though not in express terms, as at once the Priest and the Sacrifice.

2. The giving of His soul or life was intended to be a ransom

or a price (λύτρον) paid for the redemption of captives. Thus the idea of a sacrifice passes over into that of a ransom. The one idea becomes a sort of transition to the other; and it is important to notice this, that we may not confound two things which are certainly distinct. The word does not mean the redemption itself, but the price of it, or the price given to redeem another. And it will be found that the term "ransom," wherever it is used, involves a causal connection between the price paid and the liberation effected—that is, a relation of cause and effect. It is deliverance, not by a mere remission, in the absolute sense, but by a redemption-price, that the term invariably suggests wherever it occurs, either among classical or Jewish writers.

Thus among classical writers the word always denotes the price paid for the liberation of a prisoner of war or the price paid for a slave, on condition that the holder shall forego his rightful authority or claim to the party in his power. Classical usage so indelibly stamped this meaning upon the word, that it became the paramount idea, and could not be separated from it, even when the word was used by Jewish writers.[1]

---

[1] λύτρον. Every diligent student of the Septuagint will readily discover that the translators, in their use of this term, felt themselves controlled by a fixed usage, and used this word only in those cases where the notion of a price could be naturally attached to it. But they resorted to another Greek word when a different idea was to be expressed, even though the original might have the very same term. This is decisive as to the fixed usage of language in this case. They felt that the language would not bend. We have referred to this fixed meaning of the word λύτρον, because a great amount of needless discussion and groundless refining has been indulged in by several writers, who, not content with a comparison of the Septuagint and Hebrew, argue back again from the wider meaning of a Hebrew term, as if that alone could warrant a different acceptation of the Greek λύτρον. On that groundless theory the notion was taken up in certain quarters, especially since Grotius led the way (see Grotius, *De Satisfactione Christi*, cap. viii.), that the word RANSOM might mean *a victim or propitiatory sacrifice*. But it does not in any case signify immediately the victim or the sacrifice : it is rather an advance upon the latter idea. The notion of sacrifice rather passes over into that of the *ransom*. Nor can this theory be argued, as Grotius has done, from the import of the Latin word *lustrare* (see Grotius, *l. c.*) ; as if a proof could be drawn from a word of similar origin in a cognate language. Hofmann, in his *Schriftbeweis*, argues from the Hebrew word בֹּפֶר, which is translated λύτρον by the Septuagint in several passages (Prov. vi. 35 ; xiii. 8 ; Ex. xxi. 30), that we may render the Greek word *Deckung*. And Ritschl, in *Jahrbücher für Deutsche*

Not to speak, then, of the redemption of things (Lev. xxv. 14), and confining our attention to persons, this word, as employed by the Septuagint, is found to be used for " the ransom " by which a maid was redeemed from slavery (Lev. xix. 20); for "the ransom" of a prisoner of war (Isa. xlv. 13); for "the ransom" of a person who might go into voluntary servitude and sell himself till the year of jubilee (Lev. xxv. 51); for "the ransom" paid to the judges to expiate a fault, of which one very notable instance occurs in the case of the owner of a pushing ox (Ex. xxi. 30). If such an ox occasioned death or happened to kill a human being, the law pronounced death both upon the ox and its owner; and, to be delivered from the punishment threatened in the law for such a casualty, the owner might, in certain cases, pay "a ransom" or a pecuniary fine to save his life. On the other hand, it was provided that " no ranson " should be accepted for the life of a murderer, nor for one who had fled to his city of refuge (Num. xxxv. 31, 32).

The same term ($\lambda \acute{v} \tau \rho o v$) is used to denote the price paid for the liberation of a man from imminent danger, or the money given to induce another to recede from the merited or expected infliction of punishment, injury, or death. Thus it is said, " The ransom of a man's life are his riches " (Prov. xiii. 8)—a statement referring to the events of common life, and intimating that, by the payment of "a ransom," the rich not unfrequently free themselves from the dangers, exactions, and oppressions to which they would otherwise be subjected, or that by means of these they procure defenders for themselves in courts of law. Of an

Theologie, ii. Heft, 1863, maintains that it may be rendered *Schutzmittel*. But both argue incorrectly from the broader meaning of the Hebrew word, as if that were enough to control the meaning of the Greek $\lambda \acute{v} \tau \rho o v$. In point of fact, the Greek word was fixed and inflexible. Just as little can it be argued that the term *ransom* is capable of being understood of a deliverance which is considered as absolutely irrespective of the idea of a price ; for however men may speculate as to the possibility of such a meaning, no example of that usage of the word is to be found either in a Greek writer or in the Septuagint version. In referring to the Alexandrine translation, therefore, we shall not complicate the inquiry in the manner already mentioned, but limit our references to those passages where the same Greek word ($\lambda \acute{v} \tau \rho o v$) is used that is here rendered *ransom*.

injured husband, for example, it is said, " He will not regard any
ransom" (Prov. vi. 35), meaning that he will not be pacified by
any ransom when his resentment is inflamed against the violator
of domestic purity and honour.   These are instances of the use
of the term ($\lambda\acute{\upsilon}\tau\rho\sigma\nu$) in man's relation to man.

But the same term, with the same sense, is also used in
reference to man's relation to God.   The first-born of the family,
for instance, was exempted from attendance on the sanctuary
only by the payment of "a ransom" of five shekels (Num. xviii.
15).   So, too, we find that on the occasion when the tribe of Levi
was accepted in room of the first-born of Israel, and the attendance
of that tribe taken in exchange, "a ransom" was to be paid for
all those persons exceeding the number of the Levites who took
the place of the first-born.   And "a ransom" was paid, accordingly,
for 273 persons for whom no substitute was found provided by
the 22,000 Levites (Num. iii. 49).   But of all the instances of a
ransom in money, by far the most significant and familiar was
the redemption-money paid by every Hebrew male whose name
was registered or entered on the muster-roll or census of the
congregation.   This ransom was a half-shekel—the rich not
giving more, and the poor not giving less.   It was intended to
signify that all who were of age were thus enrolled as the
redeemed of the Lord; and the phrase, "redeemed or ransomed"
of the Lord is a common and familiarly used Old Testament
phrase (Ps. cvii. 2).   It seems to have been paid as an annual
tax or tribute in all the best times of Jewish history.   Though
many writers assert that it was not annually paid, there is no
sufficient ground to warrant the opinion of those who would limit
it to the first occasion.   The allusions to this tribute or didrachma,
which our Lord on one occasion was asked to pay, and which He
paid (Matt. xvii. 24), suffice to prove that it was claimed from
every male annually, or at least once, when he was enrolled
among the chosen people (2 Kings xii. 4; 2 Chron. xxiv. 9; Neh.
x. 32).   Every Israelite seems annually to have given that half-
shekel or didrachma as a ransom for his soul.   And we know

that, as a ransom, it averted the Divine displeasure; whether this was owing to the fact that it was set apart for the service of the sanctuary, or as it was a sovereign and independent arrangement. And it showed that sinful men could not come nigh a holy God, or stand before Him, except upon the ground of a ransom paid for every worshipper (Ex. xxx. 11). These instances show that a ransom was necessary in that typical economy which was to find its reality in Christ.

Now, as to the application of this term to Christ, one thing is obvious at first sight. The redemption price is to be traced up to something which is done by another, and not to any personal merit on the part of the redeemed; and it is described as the act of one for many. There are two questions here to which an answer, if not expressed, is implied: To whom was the ransom paid? and with what was it paid?

1. As to the first question, who is the imprisoning party, or the party demanding the ransom? the answer is furnished by a correct idea of God's relation to His creature, and of the violated rights and law of God. The captivity is primarily to divine justice, and only in the second instance is it a captivity to Satan, death, and hell; and, accordingly, a satisfaction to God's injured law and honour terminated the bondage, the ransom being paid to God, not to Satan.[1] The captivity presupposed by the use of the term "ransom" has various elements. The Judge, by a just sentence, reduced the sinner to a state of bondage, because every attribute of the Godhead demanded vindication against Him. He was made a captive primarily to divine justice, and then, secondarily, to Satan, death, and hell. The curse affixed to sin was death, or separation from God's countenance and favour. And not only so: Satan obtaining possession of mankind, and holding them by right of conquest, could be dispossessed only when the necessary ransom had been paid to that

[1] With the exception of Hasenkamp and Menken, few moderns have followed Origen and his school in this notion. But it was common among the Fathers, as I have pointed out in *Apostles' Doctrine of the Atonement*, Appendix.

primary fountain of justice and law which pronounced the separation between God and man as right, and left the conqueror to
hold his conquest. That captivity is capable of being reversed
only by an interposition which, remounting to the original cause,
altered the relation on which God stood to sinning man; and,
accordingly, when the law was fulfilled, and the curse exhausted
by an adequate ransom, the bondage terminated. The same
Judge who had pronounced the sentence awarding captivity,
reverses it in the behalf of all for whom that ransom was paid,
and who put their trust in it, or in Him who brought it.

2. As to the second question, viz., with what the ransom
was paid, it cannot be every sort of act, but only a vicarious
death. The captive was held by the inflexible grasp of justice;
and the ransom could only be a death which should be a proper
punishment, or an adequate infliction of all the curse which
was comprehended in the divine sentence. In other words, a
full equivalent was paid by the Son of God, made the second man,
and appointed by the divine commission to act as the representative of man. This is just life for life. The ransom, then, is
a penal infliction in its full significance, and spontaneously
undergone. No ransom could be found but in the death of
Jesus; or, personally considered, the ransom of the human race
is just the dying Saviour representing us and acting in our
stead.

3. The third element in this proposition is, that it is said to
be *in the room of many* (ἀντὶ πολλῶν). With what are we to
construe these last words? They are referred by some to the
acting party, or to the subject or person spoken of. They are
connected by others with the object of the proposition, and
placed in apposition to the term "ransom." I rather think
that there is a threefold idea in the proposition, as has been
already hinted, and that the notion (1) of the sacrifice, and (2)
of the ransom, must be both connected with the words, "in room
of many." As the one idea passes over into the other,—as our
Lord intimates that He offers a priestly sacrifice, and then adds

the idea of a ransom which delivers from captivity,—it is clear that we must construe the words, " in room of many," with both the ideas. This threefold distribution of the proposition is lost by both the modes of construing the words to which we have above referred. The Lord offered a sacrifice as a priest in the room of many. He paid a ransom also in the room of many. The former thought passes into the other as an advance upon it, or an extension of its meaning; and in both modes of representation the thought unmistakeably is, that the Lord Jesus was acting in a vicarious manner.

The true import of the phrase here used, as every scholar interpreting by language at once admits,[1] is, *in room of many*. To adduce a few instances, it may be noticed that it is the same preposition ($\dot{a}\nu\tau\acute{\iota}$) occurring in the phrases, " an eye *for* an eye " (Matt. v. 38); " who *for* one morsel of meat sold his birthright " (Heb. xii. 16); " will ye *for* a fish give him a serpent ? " (Luke xi. 11;) " recompense to no man evil *for* evil " (Rom. xii. 17); " Archelaus reigned *in his stead* " (Matt. ii. 22). In these instances, and in every other where the preposition is not used to signify *against*, the notion of substitution is the uniform and undoubted sense of the phraseology. The words here used convey the idea, that Christ gave Himself as a substitute ; that He gave His soul in room of others; and that this surrender of His life for others was further accepted, or regarded as the price or ransom by which the deliverance was effected. It is not enough to say that the death of Christ was for the good of others in some vague, indefinite, indeterminate sense ; for that is not warranted either by the meaning of the preposition used, or by the connection of the sentence. If we would apprehend the Lord's thought without offering violence to language, we must accept it as conveying the idea of a vicarious provision, and allow that the Son of Man underwent the very death that others

[1] See Meyer's commentary on this preposition as denoting substitution. Hofmann tries to escape from this, by confounding $\pi\epsilon\rho\grave{\iota}\ \pi o\lambda\lambda\tilde{\omega}\nu$ with $\dot{a}\nu\tau\grave{\iota}\ \pi o\lambda\lambda\tilde{\omega}\nu$. (See his *Schriftbeweis*).

had incurred; submitting to the penal infliction which they had deserved, and dying in their room that they might be rescued from the punishment. If it was only for the good of others in a general, indefinite, and abstract sense, the same thing might be said of any apostle or martyr. But if He gave His life vicariously, or surrendered His life in the room of others, what else does this convey but that He offered Himself to give death for death, and that He frees others by taking the punishment upon Himself? The Son of Man, very God and very man, came to do this in the room of many.

And as to the *many* referred to in the phrase, it must be noticed that He does not say *all*, which might have been considered as limited merely to all the disciples present, who were not many. He speaks not of them alone, as if the efficacy of His death were confined to the disciples then present; nor of their nation alone, but of a seed out of every nation, countless as the stars, or as the sand upon the sea-shore. And He calls them *many*, either because He contrasts Himself with them as acting one for many—and so we find a similar phraseology in Rom. v. 19,—or rather because He has His eye upon the multitude out of every tribe and nation who were given Him by the Father; in other words, to the elect of God, the truly saved, the redeemed from among men, for whom He offered Himself.

I would now say something by way of obviating the exceptions taken to the sense which we have just put upon the passage. These objections are principally two, and they are directed either against the reality of the substitution or against the reality of the ransom.

1. With regard to the objection made to the reality of the substitution or exchange of persons, it is sometimes of a more evangelical strain. Thus one modern writer[1] thinks himself warranted to object to the idea of substitution as not expressing Christ's relation to humanity, because " He is not ' another '

---

[1] Hofmann, in his *Schriftbeweis* on the passage.

alongside of humanity and outside of humanity, but the Son of Man, in whom humanity finds its second Adam." He adds, " It is also not barely a vicarious act by which He reconciled us to God,—it is not barely through Him, but in Him, that we are reconciled." This objection may be said to express the strain of the new theology, or the mystic theory of the atonement so much in vogue, with all its one-sided and subjective bias. But in the words before us we find the Lord Himself, with unmistakeable precision, declaring that the surrender of His life was a vicarious act in room of many. And a death which redeems another under death, and is declared to be in the room of others, is properly vicarious, if language is to be the interpreter's guide; and a redemption merely by the communication of the inner life, or by union to the person of Christ, without any provision legitimately to reverse the divine sentence pronounced against sin, or to remove the actual curse, argues a very defective view of the relation occupied to mankind, both by the first and second Adam. It is to make no account of the necessity of personally standing in an accepted righteousness, or of the reversal of the inflicted curse. It is to ignore the objective relation of our persons, which is as necessary as the inner nature, and it merges all that is relative or personal in the spiritual life.

The older Socinians, again, with nothing of the evangelical sentiment which we have just mentioned, repudiated the vicarious element, or the substitution of Christ, on wholly different grounds. It would be tedious to mention, and to refute in detail, all their overdrawn inferences, and all their exaggerated difficulties. But to some of them we must refer. Thus they argue, that in the exchange of prisoners to which the language must primarily allude, both parties are freed and restored to their friends. This of course is true, when both are in the same condition, and no reconciliation is indispensably required, as is needful in the sinner's case. But we meet all these exaggerated and overdone details at once, by observing, that in all comparisons, just as in all parables, it is only one point in common, or a certain *tertium quid*, which challenges attention; and in this case it is the exchange of captives. And when it is still further rejoined, that in such an exchange Christ must have remained a captive, the reply is at hand, that He was certainly a captive, nay, all His life long a captive, till the ransom was completely paid, but that He redeemed us in such a way as to lead captivity captive, and to set us free. All these objections are nothing but the urging of inferential exaggerations.

But the chief argument of this class of writers is, that the question is somewhat different from an exchange of persons, and turns not so much on an exchange of persons as on a commutation between a thing or a price and a person. On the contrary, the preposition here employed, and the whole language of Christ in reference to His death, implies a commutation of one person for another,—that is, of one person's suffering for what another should have borne and suffered. It is the exchange of one person's suffering for another person's suffering, and therefore an exchange of persons, according to that representative system which must be accepted in the mediatorial economy, whether we look at the first Adam or at the second Adam.[1]

2. With regard to the second objection already mentioned, which denies the reality of the ransom, and reduces all to a mere figure of speech, it is easily obviated. It has always been maintained by Socinian expositors that this whole phraseology, which is taken from the redemption of a captive, is only a metaphorical use of language, derived from the custom of redeeming prisoners of war, but that it means no more than simply this, that we are discharged. To this we give a general and a particular reply.

As the language used in reference to a ransom or price has a well-defined significance, invariably involving the idea that it was necessary to pay a price for a captive, it were in reality tantamount to evacuating the import of Scripture and the proper

---

[1] See Stillingfleet's sermons, *On the True Reason of the Sufferings of Christ, wherein Crellius' Answer to Grotius is considered*, pp. 440-450, London, 1669.

sense of words, to reduce its meaning to a mere figure of speech. And let this principle be fully carried out, as it has been to its legitimate consequences in modern mythism, and it will reduce Christianity to a system of mere ideas, dissociated from fact or from any historic basis in actual reality; and on this principle of disconnecting Christianity from the underlying facts, all becomes notions and ideas and a mere world of thought. To be consistent, they must hold a figurative or metaphorical Christ, a figurative or metaphorical mediator, a figurative or metaphorical salvation. On the contrary, there is nothing in the language expressed in the passage that is not literally true. All is reality, not semblance or figure,—fact, not comparison or similitude. So much for the general reply to this objection.

Again, to meet this objection more particularly and more in detail, it must be maintained, that as men are in a real and not a figurative bondage, so they are delivered by a real and not a figurative ransom. If the Redeemer gives His life for others, and gives it, too, as a ransom or as a price for captives, it follows, that if the first is a literal and real captivity, the other is not less a literal and real ransom for their deliverance. Nor will it avail to argue, that as the language is unmistakeably taken from the ancient sacrifices and only accommodated to Christ, it cannot be pressed any further. To this I reply, the types take their colour from the actual event, or from the reality reflecting its light upon them, not conversely. It was the coming event that cast its shadow before, and gave its colour to the type. It was not the type which gave a metaphorical representation to the fact.

The allegation is frequently made, too, that the writers of the New Testament use the term *ransom* for deliverance simply, without the accessory notion of a price; and warnings are frequently addressed to the expositor as to the risk of insisting more upon the figure under which the truth is represented than upon the thing itself. But, plainly, we should run counter to all the canons and guiding principles of strict interpretation, were we to deal with the term *ransom* either as if it had not been used at all, or as if it had no precise and definite meaning. This would introduce the most arbitrary licence of interpretation, and it would make men expound not by language, but by preconceived ideas. Some men of name in theology[1] have recently expounded the phrase as if nothing else were to be found in it but an allusion to the influence of Christ's doctrine confirmed by His death. And what is that but to reduce Christ to the level of a mere teacher or prophet? It is very little different from this to urge, as some others have done, that Christ, in the use of such language, merely points to men's liberation from the bondage of the Mosaic law, and refers to the fact that He was to set up a purer worship, and to preach to all mankind the absolute and unbought forgiveness of sins. The laws of sound interpretation will not allow any man to indulge in such wayward licence. The usage of language, and the full significance as well as connection of the thought, will allow an allusion only to the actual and real issue of Christ's death. The term *ransom* denotes not the deliverance itself, but the price of it; and the thought is, that mankind are discharged from bondage by a vicarious atonement,—the bondage and the ransom being equally real. They who contend that the passage announces redemption but without any allusion to a redemption price, while the discharge is held to be not less sure than if a price were actually paid, not only violate Christ's doctrine, but also the laws of language. And as to the interpreter's fidelity, it may be added that he has no arbitrary discretion to change the meaning of Christ's words. There is no more arresting thought to him than this, how he shall answer for it at the bar of Christ, if under any influence or tendency he has been led on to pervert the meaning of Christ's teaching, and to evacuate the proper force and import of His language. And many do so on the precon-

---

[1] See De Wette, *De Morti Christi*, p. 139. Ritschl, again, in the *Jahrbücher für Deutsche Theologie*, 1863, p. 222, sees no more in it than a sort of protection against death for those who fulfil the condition under which alone this can be available to them.

ceived idea that a satisfaction to divine justice is absurd. But I ask, is it absurd to maintain that the divine law must be fulfilled in precept and in penalty, which is all that is implied in that statement that justice must be satisfied?

The other objections to the above given interpretation of this verse, are only trifling and sporadic; and they may be here omitted, as they have been anticipated in the previous exposition of the words. As to the objection, however, that the notion of a ransom is untenable because no one can be shown to whom it was paid—and it cannot be supposed now-a-days to have been paid to Satan,—the answer is at hand. It is not simply the case of a creditor receiving a pecuniary payment, but that of a criminal guilty of a capital crime, and deserving a penal infliction by which the authority of law is maintained. It is paid to God, the Judge of all. (Comp. Eph. v. 2; Heb. ix. 14.)

We may put together the elements of this passage as follows: (1) the humiliation of a divine person, which gives value to His work; (2) the priestly act of self-oblation; (3) the assumption that men are captives to death; (4) the ransom, with its redemptive efficacy; (5) the persons for whom He was a substitute; (6) the necessary effect,—deliverance from death by the death of such a substitute.

Having determined the import of the ransom, there is little else calling for remark. We may notice, finally, as to the significance of this testimony, that the notion of delivering a captive by ransom or commutation is not alien to the thinking or customs of any people; that it underlies all theology; and that it commends itself to all minds.

The ransom is described in these words without any ambiguity. The sacerdotal offering of Christ's life as the culmination of His obedience is further represented as the ransom; and it has a direct or causal connection with present and future deliverance from divine wrath. The surrender of life for life is the only price or compensation to be offered for the sinner; and we are taken

to hear the expression of Christ's consciousness to this effect from
His own lips.   There is a causal connection between the ransom
paid and the redemption or deliverance effected.   This deliverance
or redemption has so wide a scope, that believers are " redeemed
from all evil," present and to come.   The ransom is the meritorious cause of the deliverance, just as sin or the fall was the
meritorious cause of the captivity.[1]

I may add, the entire penal evil consequent on sin is denoted
by the term, death, as taken in its full significance.   The Lord
gave life for life, or, in other words, encountered death in all its
breadth of meaning, considered both as temporal and eternal,—
thus depriving it of its sting.   It henceforth ceased to be death
in the proper import of the word to those who believe on Him
(John viii. 51),—that is, because the Sinless One has died.   It
might seem, indeed, as if the atonement, considered as a ransom
from captivity, had no reference to physical evil, because this is
still found in the matter of it entailed upon believers after their
acceptance as well as upon others.   But though physical evil and
death are not removed, the change which the atonement merits
and actually produces is so great in every respect, that in truth
it ceases to be evil when that which is penal is altogether removed.   The ransom changes the entire relation of the Christian
to everything in the moral government of God ; and with regard
to our relation to physical evil and temporal death, there is no

[1] It would be tedious to enumerate all the different writers who have discussed
this text against the various schools and tendencies which have impugned the
proper notion of the atonement.   Thus, against the Socinian school I may mention
Hoornbeck, Calovius in *Socinismus Profligatus*, Maresius, Arnold, Essenius,
Turretin, Stein, *De Satisfactione*.   In recent times this text has received a very
satisfactory treatment from Philippi, Delitzsch on Hebrews (Appendix), Weber,
Keil, in the discussions caused by Hofmann's *Schriftbeweis*.   I shall notice it more
fully in the Appendix to this volume.   But I may here quote the happy words of
Tittmann, *Opusc. Theol.*, p. 445 : " Igitur in verbis Christi quando dixit se vitam
ponere pretium redemptionis, tria insunt : (1) Christum mortuum esse nostro loco,
nostra vice ; quam dicere solemus mortem Christi vicariam ; (2) Christum mortuum esse eo consilio, ut nos redimeret, peccatorumque veniam Christi jure nostro
meritoriam appellamus; (3) Christum solvisse pretium sufficiens, hoc est, mortem
Christi sufficere ad impetrandam veniam peccatorum, nec opus esse ut aliquid ad-
datur a nobis."

ONCHRIST'S BLOOD THE NEW COVENANT.
207
207207207207207207207207207207nav207207207207207207

more curse in them, nay, not a drop of wrath, but only fatherly
discipline and a means of education.[1]

SEC. XXVII.—THE TESTIMONY OF CHRIST, THAT HIS DEATH IS THE
SACRIFICE OF THE NEW COVENANT FOR THE REMISSION OF SIN.

The words of Matt. xxvi. 26-28, Mark xiv. 22-24, Luke xxii.
19, 20 (comp. 1 Cor. xi. 23-25), may be harmonized as follows:—

> " *And as they were eating, Jesus took bread; and having given
> thanks and blessed it, He brake it and gave it to the disciples,
> and said, Take, eat, this is My body which is given* (or
> broken) *for you; this do in remembrance of Me.   And in
> like manner, after supper, He took the cup; and when He
> had given thanks, He gave it to them, and said, Drink ye
> all of it; and they all drank of it.   For, said He to them,
> this cup is the new covenant in My blood, which is shed for
> you* [and] *for many, unto the remission of sins.*"

Of all the sayings which our Lord uttered on the subject of
His death, there is none which can be regarded as either more
important or more express than that testimony which He uttered
at the institution of the Supper.   He had previously called His
death "a ransom;" He had called His crucified flesh "meat indeed;" and in the present passage He calls His blood *a covenant.*
This phraseology may be considered as a key to all those passages
which announce a reconciliation to God through Him; and also
a key to all those passages in the Epistle to the Hebrews, as
well as elsewhere, which speak of a covenant people as separated
and sanctified, as saints and holy ones, or speak of the Church of
God according to the new covenant relation in which believers
stand.

With regard to the occasion of this saying, it requires no remark.   As our Lord drew near His death, His language constantly

---

[1] See note H.

became more explicit and clear in reference both to the fact of His death and to its nature. A memorial was to be instituted to commemorate that great faet, which takes Him wholly out of the class of mere instructors, and which gives Him a place apart, and a position wholly unique, among mankind. He used words which, no doubt, recall the language and the position of Moses at the founding of the Sinaitic covenant, but which are of a description such as no mere teacher could ever have ventured to utter. He intimates that all ages onward to the end of time should have an interest in His death still more than in His words; that He instituted the Supper as the commemoration of a fact which should be fraught with the most important consequences; and that in His death He aimed at an object such as neither His doctrine nor His example contemplated. He deemed this symbolic action so important for all ages, that He did not leave it to His disciples to institute it after His departure, as He left many other things for them to found. He Himself instituted this memorial of His historic life and death. The better to inform the Church of His design, and to cut off every exception from future cavillers, who are ever ready to affirm that His disciples made several unwarrantable additions to His doctrine, and to declare that some undue and exaggerated importance came to be attached to His death by those who went forth to preach His gospel, our Lord instituted this memorial Himself, with His death full in view, on the night of His betrayal.

With respect to the words used at the institution of the Supper, they are four times given, with only slight variations, and should be accurately compared in the form in which they are given by the three evangelists and by Paul, as they convey the most important instruction both on the nature and on the scope of the Saviour's death. They concur with the memorial which was then instituted to set forth the design and the effect of Christ's atoning death.

The saying is two-fold; and a certain interval of time must have elapsed between the utterance of the two. This, with other reasons which might be adduced, serves to show, that while they properly come within the category of parallel passages and under the appellation· of parallel passages, there is a somewhat extended sense or further meaning attaching to the last of them. The one prepared the way for the other. Both together, in some sort, interweave a historical reference. The first of the two sayings undoubtedly alludes to the paschal lamb, which was, according to the divine idea, regarded as at once a ransom to redeem, and as a spiritual food to nourish the receiver. This is set forth in the words, *This is my body given for you* (Luke xxii. 19); *broken for you* (1 Cor. xi. 24).

This second saying, again, is, *This cup is the new covenant in my blood, shed for you, and shed for many* (Luke xxii. 20).

This second saying, which adds an additional or further thought, goes back to another event in the history of Israel, posterior or subsequent to the passover, and yet closely connected with it. It alludes to the Sinaitic covenant, which was to be superseded, in due time, with all its typical arrangements, and to give place to the better covenant. An obvious enough link of connection bound these two events together—the institution of the passover and the founding of the Sinaitic covenant —in the history of the chosen people. As the direct issue of the passover, or as the immediate effect consequent upon it, the Israelites, delivered from the destruction which. fell on Egypt's first-born, were led on to Sinai to be taken into a covenant relationship as a nation; or, in other words, to enter, in a manner competent only to a redeemed and cleansed community, into a recognized relation to God, such as none else ever enjoyed. That people was now to be admitted into the privilege and dignity of being the peculiar people of God. That was, on the one hand, a true relation to God, but at the same time, too, a figurative history, which was in both respects to be reproduced in the fulness of time with a deeper significance and with a wider and fuller meaning—that is, with the real sacrifice, and not with the mere type. And it is this second thing that is represented, as well as the first, in the memorial of the Lord's Supper, instituted for the Christian Church. Thus, the sole ground of God's covenant with men is the great atoning sacrifice by which sin is taken away; for God could admit no sinner to His fellowship, or to a participation in the standing of His own covenant people, without an atonement or satisfaction for sin.

Considered in this light, the two sayings are parallel; and yet they are not simply coincident. They do not precisely cover each other. The second is rather an advance upon the first, and passes over into a wider and more enlarged meaning. And the two taken together announce that Christ gave Himself for the disciples, with the ulterior purpose or design that they might be taken into a new covenant relation and be God's peculiar people.

As to the first saying, I need not further advert to it, except to say that the words, *my body given for you*, as it is in Luke, or, *my body broken for you*, as it is in Paul, must be taken only in the acceptation that it is sacrificial language. We are not to understand this peculiar style of language as merely signifying a gift *to us*, but to interpret it as denoting a sacrifice given *for us*, or as denoting a victim delivered up to death for us. No doubt, if we were to expound the proper import of these sacramental emblems, and to set forth what is represented in the sacramental invitations, we should have our minds directed to the other point, and find a gift *to us*. But in the present elucidation of this testimony I purpose not to deviate from the question of the atonement; and I shall therefore limit my attention to the peculiar import and bearing of the testimony here emphatically borne to it. When Christ speaks, then, in the present passage, of His body given or broken for His disciples, the allusion is obviously to the fact that the Father gave Him for us, and that He spontaneously surrendered or gave Himself, as an atonement or paschal sacrifice, for the salvation of His people. And once offered, He becomes thereafter to His people, onward to the end of time, their spiritual food, as they partake of His crucified flesh by faith.

It is on the second saying, however, that the chief emphasis may be said to rest in relation to the doctrine of the atonement; and it is this to which our remarks will be directed. This is the more full and copious saying of the two, describing, as it does, the blood of Christ as the basis or condition of the entire new covenant. The words here used by Christ are peculiarly suggestive, as they recall the blood of sacrifices offered at the dedication of the Sinaitic covenant, when Moses sprinkled both the book and all the people, saying, "Behold the blood of the covenant" (Ex. xxiv. 6). That covenant at Sinai was founded on the blood of a typical atonement, and could have had no place without that blood. And in the far deeper sense contained in the reality as contrasted with the type, the one true and perfect sacrifice of the Son of God must be viewed as the foundation of the latter covenant. Christ here describes His blood, then, from a threefold point of view: (1) as shed or poured out for His disciples; (2) as the procuring cause of remission of sins; (3) as the fundamental condition of the covenant. And we shall briefly advert to each of these points in order.

1. His blood was shed or poured out for many. Though the Greek construction in Luke is irregular and somewhat peculiar, plainly the participle *shed* or *poured out* is connected with the term *blood*, just as it is put in Matthew and Mark. There can be no doubt that this is the connection in point of thought, if not also in point of language.[1] It is a sacrificial

---

[1] Luke xxii. 20: Τοῦτο τὸ ποτήριον ἡ καινὴ διαθήκη ἐν τῷ αἵματί μου, τὸ ὑπὲρ ὑμῶν, ἐκχυνόμενον. This abnormal structure is differently explained. Thus, some refer the words τὸ ὑπὲρ ὑμῶν ἐκχυνόμενον to τὸ ποτήριον (Euthymius, Calovius, De Wette, Winer Gram.). But every one is sensible of the harshness and unnaturalness of the interpretation, "the cup which is poured out for you." However we explain the grammatical difficulty, there is no doubt that Luke, in point of thought, meant the participle clause, τὸ ἐκχυνόμενον, to be referred to the αἵματι,

phrase, recalling how the priest was wont to shed the victim's blood, or to pour out the victim's blood, at the ratification of the covenant. Blood was shed on the great occasion when the covenant was first formed, and whenever it was subsequently to be confirmed and upheld, just as on the day when it was first founded. It was the blood of sacrifice expiating the sins of others. Some have alleged, indeed, that it is by no means of absolute necessity to view that class of sacrifices as expiatory which were intended only as the basis of a covenant, and that they may be regarded as but a covenant sacrifice. But the answer is obvious: Whenever an occasion occurred for God to enter into covenant relations with sinful men who were relatively severed and estranged from Him, it always was, and it could only be, upon the footing of a sacrifice of atonement. This is based on the relation between sinful men and a holy God.

We need not here discuss the question whether the best rendering is, *shed for many,* or, *poured out for many;* that is, whether it relates more to the slaying of the victim or to the sprinkling of the blood. We may omit this discussion, because, in point of fact, there was no sacrifice where either of these elements could be omitted; the sprinkling, as the more advanced step, having a special reference to the application of the atonement. And the remission of sins here mentioned plainly shows that the allusion to that latter point of the sacrificial arrangements is not excluded, but really comprehended. That which makes the second saying wider and more comprehensive in its scope, however, is the unmistakeable allusion which is contained in it to the Sinaitic covenant, which here gives place to the new and better covenant.

As to the persons with whom the new covenant is understood to be made, they are no further alluded to than merely as

---

though, in strict philology, we should have expected ἐκχυνομένῳ. (See Bleek, *Synoptische Erklärung der drei Ersten Evangelien,* vol. ii. p. 415, 1862; and Meyer's *Commentary.*)

they are Christ's recognized disciples. It makes no difference in this respect whether they were directly in His immediate fellowship during His earthly career, or in subsequent times are regarded as belonging to a peculiar company who are His own, His sheep, and here designated MANY. And the Lord says absolutely nothing of any condition to be performed on their side, or of any prerequisite to this covenant relation; thus leaving it to be inferred that the covenant is wholly gracious and unconditional.

2. The Lord Jesus declares that His blood was shed or offered in order to obtain for others the remission of sins. And in declaring that it was *for*, or rather *unto*,[1] the remission of sins, He affirms that His blood, or dying obedience, is the procuring cause, and remission the effect,—that the one is the direct result of the other. That these words are genuine, though found only in the narrative of Matthew, is a point beyond suspicion or challenge, because they occur in every manuscript and ancient version.[2] And since they contain Christ's own declaration as to the scope and effect of His death, they prove that His death was intended to be, and therefore that it truly was, the cause of the remission of sins. This is the undeniable and obvious import of the language, if we are content faithfully to interpret words. We have only to observe the connection and the true force of the preposition *unto* or *for* (εἰς), which expresses the object which the Lord had in view, to perceive that remission of sins is the effect, and that the blood of Christ is the cause. And no mind unbiassed and free from prejudice can fail to admit, that according to the natural construction of language, a causal connection between the two is signified.

As to the import of the term *remission* (εἰς ἄφεσιν), it uniformly refers to the remitting of merited punishment, whether

[1] εἰς ἄφεσιν ἁμαρτιῶν.
[2] The doubts of rationalists and of the laxer school, on mere subjective grounds (*e.g.* De Wette, *De Morte Christi*), are unworthy of any attention.

that be temporal or eternal. It is a judicial term; and all the various modifications of phraseology and of expression by which forgiveness is denoted, uniformly bear this sense. The special point to which the phrase relates, is deliverance from all the punishment due to us for sin, rather than deliverance from its inward power, whether past or present. The Greek term rendered "remission" points out much better than our English word the immediate effect of the atonement; implying that the sin was cancelled, and no more found, and that the person upon whom the sentence of acquittal is pronounced is again without guilt or charge, because it was put away, and therefore annihilated by the sacrifice. That the death of Christ is the direct, sole, and immediate cause of the remission of sins, without any other intermediate ground, is proved by the general tenor of biblical language on this head, by the analogy of the bloody sacrifices to which this text alludes, and by the express terms of the present passage.

3. The Lord Jesus, furthermore, speaks of His blood as the new covenant, or as constituting its fundamental condition. The sole ground upon which a covenant in any case is, or can be, constituted, is that of sacrifice; without which a sinner could not be allowed to stand in any friendly relation toward God. We find it was enough to institute a typical sacrifice for the temporary covenant, but the true sacrifice was indispensably necessary for the abiding covenant. At the founding of the two covenants, it appears that something similar took place; and we can easily gather from the peculiarities of the typical covenant, that the blood of Christ must be viewed in the same light and as serving the same purpose that the blood of bulls and goats subserved in the institution of the covenant at Sinai. The blood was not a mere martyr's blood to confirm his testimony, but the blood of sacrifice. It does not merely seal Christ's doctrine as true. There is no allusion, indeed, in these words of Christ either to His doctrine or to the sealing of His doctrine; for a covenant is not to be viewed as

consisting in bare doctrine. Rather it is the founding or erection of a new relation between God and man; and in the present case it was a divine economy, order, or arrangement, by which, on the ground of Christ's atoning blood, as shed for the remission of sins, God becomes our God, and we become His people.

As to the peculiar nature of this covenant, it had its objective foundation and basis in pardon; and in its internal character it is in several passages contrasted with the economy of the outward letter, and is specially delineated in the prophet Jeremiah. The prophet says, " Behold, the days come, saith the Lord, that I will make a new covenant with the house of Israel, and with the house of Judah; not according to the covenant that I made with their fathers, in the day that I took them by the hand, to bring them out of the land of Egypt; (which my covenant they brake, although I was an husband unto them, saith the Lord;) but this shall be the covenant that I will make with the house of Israel; after those days, saith the Lord, I will put my law in their inward parts, and write it in their hearts; and will be their God, and they shall be my people. And they shall teach no more every man his neighbour, and every man his brother, saying, Know the Lord: for they shall all know Me, from the least of them unto the greatest of them, saith the Lord: for I will forgive their iniquity, and I will remember their sin no more." (Comp. Jer. xxxi. 31 with Heb. viii. 8.)

The special difference between the two covenants, distinguished into old and new, was, that the Sinaitic covenant did not effectually provide for personal forgiveness; and that it was, besides, rather national and Jewish than universal,—rather mundane and external in its blessings and promises than spiritual and transforming.

This new covenant, so called because replacing a previous one, is not to be regarded as equivalent to the federal transaction between the Father and the Son. We do not call in question the biblical foundation of that valuable scheme of thought.[1] The language before us, however, does not contrast the two Adams, or recall to us, as some say, the difference between one covenant made without blood, or with man in his integrity, and another covenant made with blood, or with man as fallen. Rather it is the twofold method of administering the one covenant—to which allusion is made in the words before us,—with a special antithesis between the typical or preparatory economy on the one hand, and the reality or truth as come at last on the other. The former had for its object to prefigure or foreshadow the blood of the covenant. The blood of the new covenant is an allusion to a people purified by an atonement, and thus permitted to enter on the enjoyment of full forgiveness, which constitutes the substance, in no small measure, of the covenant, or at least its basis and its indispensable condition on God's side. It is a covenant of union, or the formation of a new relation, first based upon the privilege of reconciliation, and then involving, as a further step, the inward renovation of the nature, or the writing of the law upon the heart. At the erection of the old covenant there was a manifold and repeated sprinkling of blood,—first the paschal blood, and then the blood of bulls and goats at Sinai; and besides all this, the annual pouring out and sprinkling of blood upon the great day of atonement as well as in the daily sacrifice. But the new covenant has but one blood of atonement, or one sacrifice, perfect and complete for ever, by which the covenant is at once founded, maintained, and perpetuated.[2]

I must now, however, obviate the current perversions in reference to both these last-mentioned truths,—the remission of sins, and the new covenant.

1. The first point—the remission of sins, as here put—has

<hr>

[1] See before, at sec. xii.

[2] Gess happily refers to the one blood of the new covenant as contrasted with the various forms of blood-shedding, which stood connected with the founding and perpetuation of the old economy. (See his articles in *Jahrbücher für Deutsche Theologie*. 1857, 1858.)

the greatest moment in the light of current thought. The Lord
Jesus, in thus speaking of the remission of sins as the direct and
immediate effect of His death, did not state, as some will have
it, that He contemplated only an ethical result, or that He had
before His mind no other than a moral redemption. Neither
does He say that His religion proclaimed an absolute remission
of sins apart from any expiation by blood. He lends no countenance to the supposition that pardon is so dispensed to us, or
that His death was meant only to confirm the truth of what He
taught, and thus merely to ratify the promise of an absolute
forgiveness. For language cannot be more express, that Christ's
death was a sacrificial death to obtain for us the forgiveness of
sins. Neither can the Lord be represented as laying all the
weight of His teaching on the mere possession of spiritual life,
while the atonement occupies, in comparison, an altogether subordinate place.   Though many put it in that light at present, it
cannot be proved that Christ ever spoke as if His dying was
not of any further moment than merely as it tended to perfect
Him to be the Prince of Life, and to make Him the source of
all divine communications to His Church; while remission of
sins only comes in at an after stage, and but as an incidental
thing or accessory boon, for which no express provision was
either made or required.[1] The words of Christ in this passage
are so explicit in their announcement of the vicarious sacrifice,
that they contain the very opposite of such a notion, and are

[1] Usteri, a follower of Schleiermacher, and a representative of the new theology
to which so many now confess, thus puts the remission of sins in connection
with inward renovation, or with the power of love in the heart, and not with the
sacrificial death of Christ : " Wenn wir nun Keines von beiden annehmen wollen,
so kommen wir darauf zurück, dass die Sündenvergebung sich auf die in der
Gemeinschaft Christi und seines Leibes, der Gläubigen (verg. Joh. xx. 23 ; Matt.
xvi. 19, xviii. 18), durch die Kraft der LIEBE entweder schon hervorgebrachte
oder noch im Werden begriffene Sinnesänderung und Umwandlung ($\mu\epsilon\tau\acute{a}\nu o\iota a$ und
$\kappa a\tau a\lambda\lambda a\gamma\acute{\eta}$), des Menschen beziehe und diesem nach massgabe seiner Liebe (Luke
vii. 47), bewusst werde (verg. Schleiermacher's Predigt über den Zusammenhang
zwischen der Vergebung und der Liebe. Dritte Sammlung, Nr. xi.). In diesem
Sinne werden wir also auch das Wort Christi fassen müssen, dass sein Blut ver-
gossen werde für Viele zur Verzeihung der Sünden (Matt. xxvi. 28, etc.)." (See
Entwickelung des Paulinischen Lehrbegriffes, p. 132. 1851.)

wholly incompatible with it. Far from speaking of the remission of sins—according to the defective teaching of that school of modern theology which does not call attention to the acceptance of the person or the acquittal of the sinner, but only to the communication of life—as if pardon were a mere accompaniment or an attendant blessing which goes along with the later and riper stages of the Christian life, the Lord Jesus here puts remission of sins in immediate and causal connection with His death. He makes remission of sins a boon of primary importance, and the first in order; nay, every true partaker of the Supper is supposed to possess this remission of sins, and to be conscious of enjoying it.

Remission of sins, then, is not dependent on the renovation of the nature or on Christian love, however closely and inseparably they may and must be connected in the human mind. These words of Christ emphatically prove that remission is an immediate and direct fruit of Christ's atoning death, and not an effect procured or caused by those amendments. Remission of sins rather precedes them as their cause; for the statement of our Lord, as given in this testimony, explicitly declares that Christ's blood was shed in order to effect remission of sins, and that the latter is the immediate fruit or consequence or purchase of His death.

We think this conclusion may be safely left to every truth-loving mind, taking Christ's words as they stand, and to the judgment of every unbiassed interpreter desirous only to discover what is the undoubted truth of Scripture. The death of Christ is undoubtedly represented in these words as the immediate antecedent or cause of the remission of sins. Nothing even specious has ever been opposed, or can ever be opposed, to this biblical doctrine; for this is an explanation from Christ's own lips both of the nature and effect of His atoning death. The Lord Jesus was given for this purpose, as the great manifestation of the divine love and rectitude for the remission of sins; and we find nothing involving any difficulty, when we deduce from this language that remission of sin is attainable only through the cross, and that God would not, and could not, confer this pardon but through the expiatory death of Christ, regarded as the appointed and accepted substitute of sinners.

2. As to the second point, the nature of the new covenant, there are many very superficial comments in circulation as to the foundation of this covenant, many of which are replete with error. Thus it is alleged by some interpreters [1] that the language only implies, " this cup is the new religion in my blood, or that by which I seal the new religion." It is held by not a few averse to the vicarious sacrifice, that Jesus simply meant to say that He died in confirmation of His doctrine. These are all shallow interpretations, and are utterly defective and faulty. They ignore the great idea contained in the Saviour's words; which intimate, with all the perspicuity with which language can say it, that His blood was shed really, and not typically, to expiate sin; and that the new covenant was based on His death, or, in other words, causally connected with it. The covenant was founded, then, with all its provisions, in Christ's atoning blood. The blood of Christ is the fundamental condition on which it rests. And they who take the emblems into their hands at the Supper do not view Him as a martyr merely, or as dying simply to confirm His message. They recall the great fact that Christ's atoning blood was offered, not in a vague, general, abstract way, but specially and vicariously for them; and that they become in consequence a covenant people or peculiar people.

Thus Christ's blood is the blood of the covenant, not simply as it attests or confirms the truth of the Gospel, but as it has an atoning character; and the idea is not that Jesus died to confirm to us the truth of the promises, or to seal them, or to ratify them. Moses did not sprinkle the blood to ratify the promises, but to cleanse the people by his atonements. And

[1] So De Wette, *De Morte Christi*, p. 141.

the disciples, in like manner, hearing of a new covenant founded
and set up by the shedding of blood, naturally and necessarily
reverted to the erection of the Sinai covenant. Christ was the
mediator of the new covenant in a higher sense than Moses was
or could be in that covenant which was but typical and transitory; and yet the typical mediatorship was all based on. the
blood of the covenant (Ex. xxiv. 6). These shallow comments
on the new covenant are faulty in two respects. They would
make the words convey no more than an allusion to a new way
or method of procedure which God introduced among men by
Jesus Christ, without any objective ground or basis on which it
can be seen to rest. They all tend, too, in a legal or semi-legal
way, to throw men back upon themselves and upon their own
resources, will, or strength, instead of leading them away from
self-dependence. For if the human heart does not lean on
Christ's propitiation, it inevitably falls back, in some phase of
it, upon self-dependence. Certainly it is but mediæval mysticism at the best without liberty.

With regard to the purport of this most important testimony,
then, we must understand Christ's language in the following
way. The means by which the new covenant is formed with
any individual or class of persons, is the real introduction of
the indispensable condition on which it is based,—the true
sacrifice for sin, which pacifies the conscience and purifies the
heavenly things themselves. For as to the mere cup, it could
neither be nor make the covenant. The covenant is here explicitly said to be based or set up in the remission of sins, as
effected by Christ's blood. God did not found the covenant by
merely proclaiming or publishing the promise of pardon, irrespective of the blood of atonement. It is the latter alone that
could put them in the place of a peculiar people or holy nation.
This discharges us from the old covenant; and the one true
eternal sacrifice for ever keeps up and maintains the covenant,
which would otherwise be daily violated.

This memorable testimony of Christ, then, decides on certain points of the greatest moment, to which it may be proper to advert a little more fully.

a. The Lord, speaking from the conscious purpose which was in a few hours to be accomplished, puts the remission of sins in immediate causal connection with His blood or sacrificial death. What is the biblical idea attached to the phrase, "the remission of sins?" It will be found to denote, wherever it occurs in the Old Testament, or in the New, deliverance from the due punishment of sin. And all the figurative terms employed to set it forth—and they are numerous and varied,—such as, "to pass by" (Mic. vii. 18), "to cover" (Ps. xxxii. 1), "to blot out" (Isa. xliv. 22), "to hide His face" (Ps. li. 11), "not to impute sin" (Ps. xxxii. 2),—convey the same thought. It implies wrath, or liability to punishment, which would be inflicted if no provision were made—such as the sin-offering in the old covenant, and the great atonement of the cross in the new covenant —to effect the removal of the penalty threatened in the law. Our whole investigation is at present exegetical; and *à priori* reasonings, outside the pale of revelation, do not affect or retard our present inquiry. The cavil only too common in these days, as it was a century ago, that the Deity did not need to be pacified by the bloody death of a victim, does not affect us in simply investigating what the Saviour taught. We abide by the import of His language; and remission of sins is here described as the design and effect of His death. Nothing is plainer than that the forgiveness of sins is here put in the closest connection with the death of Christ, that is, as effect and cause.[1] That His

---

[1] The words of Morus on this passage, in his *Dissert. Theol. et Philol.*, vol. ii. p. 100, 1798, are very striking: "Hæc autem verba . . . hunc sensum habent, eas res fieri hoc consilio, ut ἄφεσις sequatur et contingat: sic usurpatus de hac morte idem loquendi modus eundem sensum teneat necesse est, nisi usum loquendi velimus per arbitrium mutare. Quod si hunc utique sensum tenere debemus: exstat vere in sacris libris hæc doctrina, Jesum eo consilio et fructu vitam depossuisse, ut ἄφεσις cum suis bonis sequeretur et contingeret, et hunc una cum suis bonis contingere propter illam mortem cum respectu ad eam. Præterea hæc verba, αἷμα ἐκχυθὲν εἰς ἄφεσιν ad hanc conclusionem ducunt: ergo ἔχομεν τὴν ἄφεσιν διὰ τοῦ αἵματος. Si ex illa propositione hæc conclusio ducitur: sequitur, illa pro-

death is a sacrifice, has been fully proved, and cannot be impugned.   And when we place ourselves on the view-point of
the old sacrificial worship, it cannot be doubted that the forgiveness of sins or the remission of the penalty is effected by
Christ's death without any other intervening cause.   His blood
is the immediate cause of remission, and not a mere mediate
cause; that is, it was not dependent for its efficacy on the
amendments which are the concomitants or attendants of a
religious life.   When Christ, therefore, represents His blood as
shed for the remission of sin, He must be understood as saying
that He bore the penalty of sin in order to set us free from it
as a deserved doom.   This remission, consisting in nothing else
than in the liberation of the man, or in personal liberation from
any liability to punishment, is here meritoriously connected with
His sacrificial death as its procuring cause.   It is not denied,
but rather assumed and implied at every step, that the remission of sins is a benefit to be traced up to God's grace, or to
His gratuitous favour.   But it is not the less affirmed that it
is bestowed only because the atonement was offered by Christ
as its procuring or meritorious cause.   And remission by this
means takes for granted that God was not a mere indifferent
spectator of human guilt, but animated by just resentment till
sin was expiated by atonement.

   b. But a further inquiry confronts us : How do sufferings and
trials that seem to come to us under the guise of punishment,
remain after the full and complete remission of sins ? why are
the consequences of sin suffered to remain, if sin is thus completely cancelled ?   This fact does not invalidate the full remission of sins, which takes place at the moment one believes.
The man is perfectly forgiven, and the person fully accepted,
and all that is strictly penal in the consequences of sin is
brought to an end and terminated for ever.   These effects of sin

---

positione describi mortem, propter quam sequitur et contingit venia, aut quod
idem est, cui hanc acceptam ferimus, sine qua hanc nunc quidem, re sic instituta,
non nanciscimur, cujus respectu hæc contingit."

are transformed into a course of discipline. The sickness, suffering, and death which come to us in the ordinary course of things, and which could not be altered without a miracle, still remain to the Christian, but they are wholly changed in their character. They are no longer penal, no longer part of the curse, which was quite exhausted on Christ, but means of spiritual improvement, or a part of the Christian's education in patience and hope. Though physical suffering is allowed to remain in the history of the redeemed, it is no longer an infliction of wrath or a channel of vengeance, but a fatherly chastisement or a salutary discipline, and through divine grace richly made available for our growth in holiness. For we must always distinguish between correction and punishment in the proper import of the term; and constant prosperity is so rarely advantageous, that an alternation with the opposite is found profitable to the Christian.

c. Another point demanding attention is, that the remission of sins is here represented as the ground or reason of the other blessings contained in the covenant. This comes out not only in the saying under consideration, but in the words descriptive of the covenant, as they are given both by Jeremiah and in the Epistle to the Hebrews. Forgiving grace is set forth as the source of every other benefit. "This is the covenant that I will make with the house of Israel after those days, saith the Lord; I will put my laws into their mind, and write them in their hearts; and I will be to them a God, and they shall be to Me a people: and they shall not teach every man his neighbour, and every man his brother, saying, Know the Lord: for all shall know Me, from the least to the greatest. For[1] I will be merci-

---

[1] Heb. viii. 12 : ὅτι ἵλεως ἔσομαι. On this clause let me refer to the Commentaries of Seb. Schmidt, Alting, D'Outrein, and Piscator. The latter makes these happy remarks : " *Observandum tamen illa tria apud prophetam proponi ordine inverso.* Naturalis autem ordo hic est *quod primo omnium Deus electis remittit peccata propter satisfactionem Christi;* deinde donat eis Spiritum Sanctum; qui primum illuminat mentes eorum cognitione gratiæ Dei per satisfactionem Christi acquisitæ, deinde vero renovat voluntatem ad studium gratitudinis pro beneficio liberationis seu redemptionis per Christum. *Etsi enim remissionem peccatorum postremo loco commemorat tamen illam præcedentibus annectit per conjunctionem causalem inquiens, ero enim,*" etc. ὅτι ἵλεως.

ful to their unrighteousness and their sins, and their iniquities will I remember no more." The use of the grounding particle *for* (ὅτι) intimates that the promise of forgiveness is not appended at the close as an additional blessing. On the contrary, forgiveness is represented as the REASON why the other benefits are conferred, or as the CAUSE, source, and origin from which they flow. It is as if it were said: "The reason or ground of all these other blessings, viz. regeneration, illumination, and fellowship, is to be traced to the remission of sins. That is the connection; and it is not hard to trace the link between the two. It was sin that made the separation between God and man (Isa. lx. 2), and the remission of sin paves the way for the new covenant relation. Before any are received, their sin must be, once for all, forgiven. And not only so; as there are daily sins and violations of the covenant, there must be a provision for a daily reconciliation.

SEC. XXVIII.—CHRIST FULFILLING THE LAW FOR HIS PEOPLE, AND THUS BRINGING IN A RIGHTEOUSNESS OR ATONEMENT FOR THEM.

" *Think not that I am come to destroy the law, or the prophets: I am not come to destroy, but to fulfil. For verily I say unto you, Till heaven and earth pass, one jot or one tittle shall in no wise pass from the law, till all be fulfilled. Whosoever, therefore, shall break one of these least commandments, and shall teach men so, he shall be called the least in the kingdom of heaven: but whosoever shall do and teach them, the same shall be called great in the kingdom of heaven. For I say unto you, That except your righteousness shall exceed the righteousness of the scribes and Pharisees, ye shall in no case enter into the kingdom of heaven.*" (MATT. v. 17-20.)

This passage brings under our notice the active obedience of Christ, to which we already referred in a previous section

(section 22); but with this peculiar difference, that it is here put in relation to the divine law, and in connection with the previous economy or arrangements of God. The former economy was, from the beginning, only a pledge of something yet to come, or an outline unfilled up, whereas the present is its fulfilment. And this saying of Christ implies that for this event the whole previous history of man waited, and the history of Israel was in fact a pledge or preparation for its appearance. He virtually declares that all previous ages looked forward to this day, and that the whole divine economy was constituted and arranged only with a view to it. This saying emphatically shows that the event here referred to—the coming of the Son of God to fulfil the law—was the centre-point of the world's history, and therefore carrying with it retrospective as well as prospective consequences.

The testimony under consideration is worthy of attention, too, as expressing from Christ's own consciousness the great design which His incarnation had in view in reference to the law. It proves that if His whole career was, as we have seen it was, a curse-bearing life, it was not less a sinless career, or a life which had for its scope, at every step, to fulfil the divine law by a course of active obedience; and it was this in a vicarious sense, or in the room of others. This testimony may therefore be called a key to all those passages, both numerous and varied, which describe Christ as the end of the law (Rom. x. 4), or as the counterpart of Adam in his act of disobedience (Rom. v. 19); and also to all those passages which represent the acceptance of our persons as effected by the work of Christ, and as irrespective of the works of the law (Rom. iii. 28). It is a pregnant saying, indicating in few words the distinctive features or the nature of His whole mediatorial work, which must have been obscure to those who first heard Him, but has now become, since its fulfilment, clear enough to all who can survey it from first to last upon the outline of the divine law and prophecy.

As to the occasion of this testimony, it may be referred rather to the calumnious accusations of Christ's enemies, who regarded His mode of teaching as subversive of the law, than to the neutral state of some of His disciples desirous to escape from the yoke of the law.   And the Lord enters upon the subject by a sudden break in the body of His discourse,—such as He sometimes uses when He breaks the continuity of His discourse and addresses Himself to the state of mind which His omniscient eye detected as prevailing among His hearers.

When we inquire in what sense the words of this testimony are to be understood, it will be found that the interpretation of them varies according to the idea which may be formed of the authority with which Christ contrasts His own authority, and of the peculiar teaching to which He opposes His own teaching. Thus, it has been held by Socinians and rationalists, with a general consent, that the teaching with which Christ in this passage contrasts His own statements, is that of the Mosaic law itself, or the teaching of Moses.   They will have it, that in the sequel of this chapter the Lord Jesus partly corrects, partly cancels and abrogates, the teaching of Moses, and that He puts a better legislation in its place.   They would thus make Christ a legislator, not a Saviour, and regard Him as coming to usher in a new law.   And, accordingly, they render the 17th verse in in this way: " I am not come to destroy the law or the prophets: I am not come to destroy, but to fill out or to expand them."[1]   And the same interpretation of the words is held, though sometimes in a considerably modified form, by several English as well as German interpreters, who deserve to be regarded generally as interpreters of an evangelical tone and

___

[1] This very incorrect rendering is supported by Alford, Meyer, De Wette, Olshausen, and others ; as if our Lord only meant to say that He came to set forth the ideal import of the law, or to give a deeper and holier sense to it.   This comment of the modern school is well refuted by Bleek in his *Synoptische Erklärung*, 1862, p. 248, and also in the *Studien und Kritiken* for 1853.   Nor can we regard with any more favour the comment of Vitringa, who interpreted πληροῦν *docere*, from the usage of a Chaldee-Talmudic word.

sentiment. They will have it that Christ in this section contrasted Himself with the confinement and narrow political form
of the Mosaic law, or with the stand-point of law as such;[1] and
they contend for the translation, " to fill out."

But that interpretation cannot be maintained, whether we
look at the immediate context in which the word occurs, or at
the import of language generally; and a few words will suffice
conclusively to show this.

1. The immediate context is opposed to that interpretation.
It would be a flagrant self-contradiction, if in one verse the
Lord Jesus were to announce that He did not come to destroy
the law, or, in other words, to subvert its authority, and then,
in the sequel, proceed to correct and modify it in many points
of the greatest importance,—nay, go so far as to abrogate and
change it both in its principle and in its details. But He sub-
verts the teaching to which He refers in the sequel (see ver. 43).
That cannot, therefore, be the divine law which He overthrows
at so many points and in a way tantamount to destroying it;
for He expressly declares that it was no part of His mission or design to destroy the law, but rather to fulfil it. It
must, then, have been the traditions of the elders which He[2]
overthrows.

2. The usage of language is opposed to that interpretation
which here adopts the rendering, *to fill out*, in preference to *fulfil*
($\pi\lambda\eta\rho\hat{\omega}\sigma\alpha\iota$). No example of such a usage can be adduced when
the verb is applied to a law or to an express command contained
in the spirit of the law; in which case it uniformly means, " to
fulfil." Thus it is said, " He that loveth another hath fulfilled
the law " ($\nu\acute{o}\mu o\nu\ \pi\epsilon\pi\lambda\acute{\eta}\rho\omega\kappa\epsilon$), (Rom. xiii. 8). The inflexible usage
of language rules the sense in such a phrase, to the effect that
Christ must be understood to say that He came not to fill out

---

[1] So Neander puts it.

[2] Lechler shows this from the fact that Jesus does not say in any of the six
examples which He adduces, " Moses said," but always, " ye have heard." (See
Studien und Kritiken for 1854, p. 804.)

or to supplement the law by additional elements, but to fulfil it by obeying it or by being made under it.

But there are other arguments, not less strong, which may be urged from different points of view against that mode of rendering. And it may here be proper to adduce them with as much brevity as we can.

3. We add, then, as another conclusive argument, which may be adduced against the interpretation already mentioned, that such a sense as "fill out" is inadmissible as applied to the second term or object of the verb; for Christ did not come to *fill out* or to expand the prophecies, but simply to fulfil the prophecies. Wherever, indeed, the word here used is applied to anything prophetical, it is always found in such a connection that it can mean only, "to fulfil;" and hence we must by no means deviate from that meaning here.[1]

4. Another strong argument may be drawn from the grounding verse which follows; for the 18th verse must be regarded as grounding or giving a reason for the statement in the previous verse. Now, what sort of reason would be given for the 17th verse, if we were to render the connected verses thus: "I come to fill out or to supplement the law; *for* verily I say unto you ($\dot{a}\mu\dot{\eta}\nu$ $\gamma\dot{a}\rho$ $\lambda\dot{\epsilon}\gamma\omega$), till heaven and earth pass, one jot or one tittle shall in no wise pass from the law, till all be fulfilled?" This would be illogical and inconsequent in the highest degree; and no reverent interpreter will willingly ascribe such logic to the Son of God.[2] The perpetual duration of the law mentioned in the 18th verse could not ground the 17th verse, if we were to interpret the latter by the rendering, "to fill out;" and hence that meaning must be held to be untenable.

5. We may argue to the same effect from the nature and peculiar scope of our Lord's personal ministry. He did not come

---

[1] Bleek well argues that the rendering, "to fill out," is possible only on the supposition that the $\pi\rho o\phi\dot{\eta}\tau as$ refers to the legal or moral elements in the prophetical writings.

[2] See Philippi's treatise, *Der thätige Gehorsam Christi*, 1841, p. 30.

in any peculiar sense to preach the law, at least as the main or prominent object of His teaching. But the rendering we impugn would imply that He came on the errand of filling out or enforcing and expanding the domain of the law, or of making the law the burden of His ministry; whereas His errand was, as every one knows, of a different kind—to usher in and to announce an economy of grace. And this very passage, rightly understood, will be found to preach not law, but grace. (See John i. 17.)

But another inquiry confronts us at this point: What is the LAW here mentioned, and in what sense is it to be distinguished from the *prophets?* Many expositors are disposed to take these two words, "the law or the prophets," in the sense of bearing reference to the ethical elements of the Old Testament, of which the Decalogue was the source and the prophets the expounders, just as when the Lord Jesus said in regard to an ethical principle, "This is the law and the prophets" (Matt. vii. 12). But that is contrary to the peculiar language used, and is here wholly inadmissible; for here the two terms are not put together in such a way as to comprehend a unity, or as merely indicating the spirit of the law by another word. The two terms are here put together by the *disjunctive particle,* OR, and therefore must each indicate distinct ideas familiar to the hearers.[1] It has been alleged, indeed, that as there is no further allusion to prophecy as such in the entire Sermon on the Mount, this distinction between the law and the prophets is not to be admitted. But whether we have regard to the proper significance of the terms, to the disjunctive particle which separates them, or to the import of the *fulfilling* spoken of in these two verses, it is sufficiently proved that prophecy in the proper sense is here meant. And the design of Christ, therefore, was to intimate that

---

[1] The disjunctive particle ἤ, disjoining the law and the prophets, is utterly opposed to the notion that we can take the two terms as intimating the moral elements common to the law and the prophets. It is true, "the law AND the prophets" are elsewhere put together in this sense (Matt. vii. 12 ; Luke xvi. 16), but they are here disjoined as distinct ideas.

the whole Old Testament, in all its parts and elements, referred
to Himself, and was accomplished in Himself.

As to the law, again, the Lord means the whole Jewish law.
We are warranted to affirm that our Lord and His apostles were
not in the habit of distinguishing, as we commonly do, between
what was permanent in the law and what was transitory, but
that they accepted it as a whole; the moral law constituting the
centre of it, or its core.   That the allusion here is to the moral
law primarily, may be argued from this, that the subsequent parts
of the Sermon on the Mount directly and mainly refer to it.
But we must add that the allusion is also to the types or to the
law of sacrifice, and specially to the sin-offering; for it might
well have been asked, if there had been no direct fulfilment of
the sacrificial types, what had become of all the references in the
law to the propitiatory sacrifices generally, and to all the typical
system ?   If Christ had not fulfilled them and offered the reality,
they would have been an unfulfilled prophecy or pledge.   The
language of sacrifice, in fact, gave a sort of prophecy or pledge of
a coming 'reality.   The meaning of the passage, then, is this :
The Lord Jesus came to fulfil the law and the prophets by an
appropriate deed.   It was pledge and type before, but became
reality in Christ's obedience.

Nor must we omit to notice the significance of the phrase, " I
am come to fulfil."   It must be regarded as setting forth the end
of Christ's coming into the world, the design and purpose of the
incarnation.   This fulfilling of the law was for man an absolutely
necessary, though an undischarged duty.   To Christ it was a free
act.   The perfect harmony of the human will with the law of
God, or the constant exercise of holy love in the sphere of human
obedience, was the great goal which was set before the race of
mankind.   And to keep this thought alive in the human consciousness, we find an express appointment to the effect, that the
law which had grown dim and scarcely legible in the human
heart should be afresh republished by the hand of Moses.   Hence
it is that the Lord of Life here announces that, in His capacity

of Mediator, the special end for which He came was to fulfil the law and the prophets. He thus points out the grand design or scope of His whole work, and couches the description in a few simple words, intimating that He stands in the midst of a sinful world as the living law or the embodied law, which might be regarded, so to speak, as walking before men in the one unique and sinless life that had appeared in the world's history. The law of God has thus, in the person of the incarnate Son, been once fulfilled upon the earth; and this is the one great event which has had a far more important bearing on human destinies than any other that ever occurred,—a fact which, though accomplished in a remote corner of the world, was for all time. All previous ages had looked forward to it, as all after ages lean on it. This FULFILMENT OF THE LAW is the second fact in human history, as SIN was the first, and it is the corrective as well as the counterpart of the dire catastrophe which sin brought in. It underlies the world's renovation; it is its second creation.

We may here give a sketch or outline of the sequel of this context before exhibiting the import of the passage in a doctrinal point of view. Our Lord proceeds, then, to declare fully (ver. 18), that the law is immutable, and that it must needs be fulfilled; which was only done, however, by His own obedience, as He indicated in the previous verse (ver. 17). He then subjoins the statement (ver 19), that whosoever shall break one of these least commandments shall be called the least in the kingdom of heaven,—language which implies the perpetual and inflexible obligation of the law during the whole course of the kingdom of heaven. There are two senses or interpretations in which this verse has been taken by expositors. It may either be supposed to mean that one is called the least because he is not deemed worthy to have any part at all or any real inheritance in the kingdom of Christ and of God; or it may mean that this person shall be contemned, or held in such low repute and estimation by the fellow-citizens in the kingdom as to be esteemed and called the least. To this latter comment, which explains it of the New Testament Church, I rather incline. And if we accept this as the correct interpretation, then this just shows that the teachers and members of the Church or kingdom of heaven shall all imbibe and shall perpetually hold this deep conviction of the immutable nature of the law.

But the next verse, introduced by a grounding particle ($\gamma\grave{\alpha}\rho$), makes an important addition (ver. 20); and the inquiry is, What does it ground? It may either ground a tacit thought such as this: " and do not think that a pharisaic externalism is any fulfilling of the law; FOR I say unto you." Or He may append another reason why He came to fulfil the law,—a reason taken from the nature of the kingdom into which none could enter without a perfect righteousness. Either of these modes of explaining the grounding particle FOR ($\gamma\grave{\alpha}\rho$) may be adopted. One thing is clear, our Lord argues from the nature and demands of His kingdom, that none can enter it without a RIGHTEOUSNESS ($\delta\iota\kappa\alpha\iota$-$o\sigma\acute{v}v\eta$), which shall at once accord with the claims of the law, and be much more *abundant* than the righteousness of the Pharisees. To what does He refer in the sequel? That our Lord does not refer to the pure ideal of righteousness, or to the perfect transcript of the divine holiness exhibited and taught by the Decalogue itself, but to the low, traditional exposition of the law which was usually given by the Pharisees, as delivered to them by the elders, may be established by many arguments. We shall limit ourselves to the argument that may be derived from the language used. The Lord does not say in any of the six examples which He quotes and amends, " Moses said," but, " ye have heard that it was said by them of old time."

It must be further noticed that our Lord's great aim in this portion of the Sermon on the Mount is not so much to teach us Christian ethics, or to adduce a number of practical duties, to be followed out under the force of Christian motives, such as we find enumerated at the end of the apostolic Epistles, as to awaken the conscience of these somewhat legal hearers to whom He addressed Himself. For while the former use has been legiti-

mately made of the Sermon on the Mount by the Church of all
times, our Lord's view-point and scope are somewhat different.
It cannot be said that He takes so much for granted; His Church
was not yet founded. Rather, He expounds the law on this
occasion, as He does in several other passages, in order to convince and awaken men to feel their need of a perfect righteousness. (Comp. Luke x. 25; Matt. xix. 17.) It was the ignorance
of the law that was the true parent or source of Pharisaism, for
they claimed to fulfil it in the outward letter; and our Lord in
this sermon aims to awaken conscience, by enforcing its true
import and requirements.

It will be found, accordingly, that the Sermon on the Mount
perpetually returns to one main thought, which is again and
again applied with various modifications and peculiar turns. It
aims to awaken in men a sense of need, and to shut them up to
the righteousness which is of God.[1] This object could be attained
only by the spiritual application of the moral law, or by enforcing its inviolable import and the indispensable strictness of its
demands. This alone convinces men that they need a righteousness which emanates from a divine person, and which much
exceeds that of the Pharisees; and hence, to awaken this sense
of need, we find that the Sermon on the Mount returns again
and again to this one central thought in many forms and applications which are variously modified. (Comp. Matt. v. 28, v. 44.)

According to this design, which is the key to the whole discourse, we may affirm that the 20th verse is to be regarded as
materially or substantially the sum of all that follows. It is the
great principle or ultimate goal to which this entire exhibition
of the divine law is to be run up. Here, then, the question
arises, What is this righteousness ($\delta\iota\kappa\alpha\iota\sigma\sigma\acute{\nu}\nu\eta$) which our Lord
declares must needs be more abundant than that of the Phari-

[1] The only writer known to me who even hints at this view of the Sermon on
the Mount is Harnack, in his separate treatise on this text, entitled *Jesus der
Christ oder der Erfüller des Gesetzes und der Prophetie,* 1860. But the longer I
reflect on the scope of this discourse of Christ, the more certain does this view
become.

sees ? That the allusion is not to inherent righteousness, but to justifying righteousness, that is, to the righteousness which meets the awakened sense of need, which it is the object of the whole discourse to produce, may be proved by various arguments. Thus (1) the whole phrase plainly refers to ver. 17, and has a very close connection with the statement that Christ came to fulfil the law: (2) it is the righteousness which is spoken of as the necessary condition or ground, on the footing of which a man is to enter the kingdom of heaven; and therefore it is not the evangelical righteousness which is the fruit of our acceptance; —it is rather the righteousness which is the ground of our acceptance, or the righteousness which is of God by faith: (3) it is that which far exceeds the pharisaic righteousness, and which is much more abundant in dignity, worth, and excellence: (4) it is the same righteousness after which the awakened hunger and thirst; and therefore it is the surety-righteousness, rather than that which is personal and inward. And if it is alleged, as an argument against this interpretation of the word, that the Lord's purpose in the Sermon on the Mount was not to treat precisely of the article of justification, or to show in what the justifying righteousness peculiarly consists, the answer is obvious.[1] Our Lord's words expressly treat of a righteousness which is necessary and indispensable as the ground or condition on which men are to enter this kingdom; and the entire discourse, as we have already seen, has, for its object, to produce a sense of need.

Having elucidated the words and scope of this memorable passage in the Sermon on the Mount, it remains that we put together the doctrinal import of it in relation to the subject of the atonement.

1. In this fulfilment of the law and of the prophets, the Lord

---

[1] This interpretation of δικαιοσύνη, for which we contend, was maintained by the divines near the Reformation age,—such as Calovius, Quensted, Perkins in his Exposition of the Sermon on the Mount, Van Til, and others. But it came too soon to give place unduly to the subjective interpretation, which has long become general.

Jesus must be considered as acting in the capacity of a surety or substitute; and the obedience in both lights was, beyond doubt, vicarious. Hence His active obedience is for us, and reckoned to our account, not otherwise than if we had fulfilled it. The entire obedience of Christ was a compliance with the will of God as expressed in the law. And His conscious aim in His mission, as He here expresses it, was to fulfil the law. If, according to the federal agreement, the law was the special sphere of Christ's earthly work, it is obvious, that without a clear conception of the law, not only in the extent of its claims but also in the extent of the curse which it entails, we cannot adequately know His obedience in our room. Hence we must look at the usual threefold division of human duty, in relation to God, to ourselves, and to our fellow-men, if we would adequately apprehend the extent and breadth of this obedience.

With regard to the duties towards God, the whole life of Christ shows that He was animated by supreme love to God (John xiv. 31); that a desire to glorify God was His grand aim in all things (John xvii. 4); and that, from love to His Father, He followed with an undeviating purpose the will of God in all things (John xv. 10). He gives expression to this at the threshold of the greatest trial: "But that the world may know that I love the Father; and as the Father gave Me commandment, even so I do. Arise, let us go hence" (John xiv. 31). The trust which He reposed in the Father, the prayers, and the thanksgivings, recorded in His history, all suffice to show this.

The second class of duties are those which we owe to ourselves. And these, too, Jesus fulfilled in a perfect purity of conduct, in a self-denial which distinguished Him as the meek and lowly One (Matt. xi. 29), and in that marked feature of His character by which He pleased not Himself (Rom. xv. 3).

As to the third class of duties, again, those toward our neighbour, and which are summed up in the love which Paul designates the fulfilling of the law, the Lord Jesus speaks of it when He says, " Greater love hath no man than this, that a man lay

down his life for his friends" (John xv. 13). This He did; and
He went about during all His previous life doing good (Acts x.
38). It was in the exercise of this love that He made intercession for His own (John xvii. 9), and prayed for His enemies
(Luke xxiii. 34). And among these duties must be comprehended that obedience to His parents to which there is an early
allusion (Luke ii. 51), and which shone out so brightly on the
cross, just before the earthly relation toward His mother was
dissolved for ever (John xix. 26).

Thus at every step we can trace the most prompt and undeviating fulfilment of the divine law. It was no common
obedience, however, which was necessary to constitute the
ground of our acceptance, but one which must needs pass
through unparalleled difficulties and sorrows, which we can but
faintly conceive of, and which must possess a value, on account
of the dignity of His person, such as is nothing short of infinite.
The grand commandment laid on Him, and the culmination of
His whole obedience, was, to die; and hence it was in the spontaneous oblation of His life that the greatness of the obedience
was peculiarly displayed.

2. It is one undivided obedience; for Scripture knows of
only one service or work in which all the elements of submission or obedience meet. It was not a double obedience. The
entire life of Jesus must be apprehended as one connected deed.
But the obligation was twofold, including the perfect obedience
of His life, as well as the suffering of death, or the obedience
unto death. The right formula, then, is not "to obey OR
suffer;" for the claim to a service of love with all the heart
still unalterably devolves upon man as man, just as it did in
man's primeval state. Not only so: the person who expiates
sin must of necessity accept the curse with the utmost alacrity
and adoring love, and with a full sense that the infliction of it
is to the glory of God. These two elements enter into the
Lord's obedience, and neither could be omitted. Hence only a
person free from all moral defilement, and therefore not needing

to satisfy for personal defects, was in a position to undergo the inconceivable suffering due to sin. What He did concurred with what He suffered, to satisfy the divine law, and to place man in the position which he occupied before the fall, or, rather, in a higher relation, because in a premial state, and in a state of confirmation.

Had the Church been left to herself without the attacks of error, the two elements of Christ's obedience probably would not have been so much sundered as they have often unduly been. We may distinguish, but not divide, the parts of that obedience which is one.[1] But the obedience of Christ before His final sufferings, and during them, or, as it has been called, the active and passive obedience, may be vindicated, as two distinct but connected elements, in His propitiatory work. The active obedience belongs to the atonement, and is an essential part of the satisfaction to divine justice, in the wide and proper acceptation of the word justice. This is a question that has been canvassed long and earnestly; and we the rather refer to it in connection with this passage, because the tendency to deny the element of the active obedience is so strong in modern theology. The question is not, whether the holiness and active obedience of Christ were necessary to sanctify His sufferings, which no one will call in question, but whether they were available for this alone. Nor is it the question, whether Christ's passive obedience is the ground of our salvation, but whether the one can be regarded as valid or efficacious without the other. It is not, whether Christ's holy obedience was necessary to His person as a due prerequisite to that atonement which He offered, but, whether Christ, in His entire obedience as well as in His expiatory work, won an unchallengeable title to life for such as are willing to be dependent on Him, and who

[1] The theory of Karge among the Lutherans, and of Piscator among the Reformed, who both limited the atonement to the sufferings of Christ, and set aside the idea that Christ's active obedience was vicarious, has no biblical warrant; and it is based on a false assumption, as we shall notice at the end of this section.

were unable personally to meet the law's demand: "This do, and thou shalt live." The consequences of denying the active obedience of Christ are these: Either God must be supposed to recede from His rights, which would just be tantamount to saying that He denied Himself, or man must be held to procure a title to heaven by some services of his own, which are imperfect in their nature. Either supposition is inconsistent with the gospel. If, however, we dismiss all scholastic terms, the matter may be put in the following biblical way, to which no exception can be taken: "The law must be kept, and sin must be punished; and divine wisdom and grace provided a man, that is, a God-man, who was in a position to accomplish both, and did so."

3. Christ's people are thus, through faith in Him, considered as if they had always fulfilled the divine law. This is the SECOND fruit of Christ's satisfaction, as sin-bearing is the FIRST. Thus, according to this essential element of divine truth, the Lord Jesus not only bore sin, but fulfilled all the claims of the divine law, and so put His people in possession of a perfect and immaculate righteousness, and secured for them its due reward. For as God could not have ceased to demand punishment at the hand of sinners, from the very perfection of His nature, so He cannot but confer a reward from the same rectitude of His nature, when His law has been fulfilled for them in so complete a way, and by a person so excellent.

But to all these biblical views of divine truth not a few objections have been taken, and some of them of a nature that seem, at first sight, plausible and staggering.

a. Thus, it is asked, Was not Christ, as man, bound, in common with every rational creature, to render obedience to God on His own account?[1] The answer to this is not difficult. A right view of Christ's humiliation will suffice to show that He

---

[1] This was Piscator's and Karge's argument against the vicariousness of Christ's active obedience. And too many have conceded this first principle, when it is but a fallacy.

did not owe obedience on His own account, and that He was not under the law by any necessity of nature. He owed obedience, not precisely because He took humanity, but because He willed to be made under the law for us. The law was not given for the human nature in union with a divine person, except as He condescended to be abased, and was made under it by voluntary susception, as a means to an end. Christ became man for no personal object of His own, but only to be a Mediator for others, and in that capacity to fulfil the law. But for this, He would not have come into the world, or have become man. Hence the obedience which He voluntarily discharged was only for His people, not for Himself; and Scripture never deduces His active obedience from any natural or inevitable obligation, but always regards it as the end and scope of His mission. Nor can we regard the Lord Jesus as a mere man. He was still the Son of God, neither bound to assume humanity, nor to submit to the laws of humanity, nor to encounter any of those numerous temptations by which His obedience was to be exercised. And He did all this spontaneously and vicariously in a humanity which He had assumed, not to be a separate person, but merely as a rational and intelligent instrument or organ, by means of which that great work of vicarious obedience could be accomplished.

b. But it is asked again, How can one be righteous, because another was obedient? The answer is obvious. The entire constitution of our race, as contradistinguished from that of other orders of being, was of this nature, that it stood or fell in a representative; and Christ is the second man. Men may quarrel with this arrangement, and destroy themselves by proud and petulant rebellion. But it will stand, notwithstanding. Believers are treated in Christ as perfectly righteous, and as if they had done all that He did. The race is saved on the same principle on which it was placed at first; and we who believe are the fulfillers of the law in the second man, the Lord from heaven.[1]

[1] See note I.

Here I may allude to a crude tenet, of an antinomian stamp, which finds favour at present in some quarters. The Gentiles, it is said, whether considered before or after conversion, have nothing to do with the law. "Where is it stated," says one of this school, "that I, a sinner of the Gentiles, was bound to keep the law?"[1] To this reckless assertion I allude only as it bears on the atonement.

The law of nature is still traceable as written on the human heart (Rom. ii. 14, 15). And though the Decalogue was dispensationally imposed on the people of Israel, while other nations received it not, it was but the republication of the law originally given to man as man and written on his heart. To affirm that any human being is exempt from the application of the law, either in its precept or its curse, is to betray a sad misconception of the moral make or primeval constitution given to our race and of the mould in which man was cast. The apostles proceed on the opposite assumption. Thus, when Paul teaches the guilt of mankind, it is brought out that all are condemned by the law (Rom. iii. 19-31), whether they were Israelites or not. The same thing holds true of the doctrine of justification, which in its very nature is forensic, and therefore must have a relation to the law. As to the atonement, the meritorious ground of all God's judicial sentence, this is expressly set forth as the endurance of the curse of the law on the part of Christ (Gal. iii. 13). And when we reflect on the other expressions used by Paul, what can be meant by the Christian being dead to the law if he had never been under any obligation to that from which he is set free?

[1] This Darbyite doctrine is the antithesis of reformation doctrine, which laid the law at the basis of all theology. See Chemnitz (*Loci Communes*, ii. p. 20): "Lex moralis primò est æterna et immota regula justitiæ in Deo : Secundò in ipsa creatione mentibus hominum inscripta : tertio ab initio semper in ecclesia voce divina patefacta et repetita : quæstio est non indigna consideratione, Quare Deus post tot annos Decalogum publico et solenni testimonio iterum promulgârit et digitis suis describere voluerit?"

SEC. XXIX.—SAYINGS WHICH REPRESENT THE DEATH OF JESUS AS
HIS GREAT ACT OF OBEDIENCE, AND AS THE RIGHTEOUSNESS
OF HIS PEOPLE.

As we noticed in the former section the testimony of Jesus,
that He came not to destroy the law or the prophets, but to
fulfil them, in order to bring in the true righteousness, it is
proper to consider, next in order, some of those sayings which
set forth the righteousness of God from a somewhat different
point of view. There are sayings which connect it with the
death of Jesus as His great act of obedience. One testimony, as
we have seen, refers it to His fulfilling of the law, while another
refers the same benefit to His death. These two modes of representation, however, are by no means inconsistent with each
other; nay, the one presupposes and involves the other whenever allusion is made to either. And it will be necessary to
bring together two classes of sayings, with a view to establish
these two distinct but mutually connected truths,—that the
death of Jesus was the climax of His obedience, and that it was
also the true righteousness of His people.

1. With regard to the first point, that the death of Jesus constituted His great act of obedience, it must be borne in mind,
that while we trace the element of suffering in the death of the
Lord, we are by no means to lose sight of the element of obedience. Willing subjection underlay the whole of His suffering,
and that, too, of the most active character. Indeed, suffering in
itself, and considered merely as pain, is no obedience; for a man
may suffer, and not be obedient. But when he encounters
suffering with his full consent, and evinces, during the course of
it, a steadfast and inflexible tenacity of purpose, that cannot be
turned aside from the straight path of obedience, what is that
active fulfilment of duty or observance of the divine will, but
patience? And no virtue is of a more active character than
patience; while none in the catalogue is more worthy to be

called the queen of the virtues.[1] We may affirm, respecting obedience generally, that it must needs be tested by some special or positive injunction, whether that may be presented in the form of restraint, or in the form of endurance; the former being the test imposed on the first man, the latter being the test to which the second Adam was subjected. Thus it appears that even sinless nature, without a taint of defilement or imperfection, can have its obedience tested only in some such way; and, accordingly, the Son learned obedience by the things He suffered (Heb. v. 8). When the Lord Jesus was required to display the reality and extent of His obedience by His act of self-oblation, and to go through life with this formed and definite resolve in His mind, we see pure humanity, with the divine image inscribed upon it, and with the law in His heart (Ps. xl. 8), summoned to its highest act of obedience. The great commandment laid upon Him was, to die, just as Adam's special commandment was, to abstain from the forbidden fruit.

In speaking of Christ's great act of obedience, we shall not turn aside to the numerous references found in the sayings of Jesus, to the work of teaching also imposed upon Him by the Father (John xii. 49). We here allude only to His redemption work, and to that, too, merely as it is presented to us under the guise and designation of obedience.

The first saying which we shall adduce in this connection is the announcement just before He went out to Gethsemane: " *Hereafter I will not talk much with you: for the prince of this world cometh, and hath nothing in Me. But that the world may know that I love the Father, and* [that] *as the Father gave Me commandment, even so I do. Arise, let us go hence*" (John xiv. 30, 31). These words, spoken on the threshold of His arrest, intimate His promptitude and readiness to undergo what lay before Him, or His firm and inflexible resolve to give Himself an offering

---

[1] See some valuable remarks by Ernesti in his refutation of Töllner's treatise, which was directed against the active obedience of Christ (Ernesti, *Neue Theologische Bibliothek*, ix. Band, p. 920).

and a sacrifice to God for a sweet-smelling savour (Eph. v. 2).
He first announces that the prince of this world was approaching and on the point of assailing Him with all the violence
which united ingenuity and malice could either invent or inflict,
through the medium of human power.   But He adds, " *He hath
nothing in Me;*" which may mean that Satan would find nothing which could be called his own,[1]—nothing which could be
charged against Him, or that could give the adversary any
legitimate power over Him; and He intimates that, far from
desiring to withdraw from the suffering that awaited Him, He
was on the alert to meet and to undergo it.   The words, " But
that the world may know that I love the Father, and that I do
as the Father gave Me commandment," must imply some such
tacit thought as the following: "therefore, I will not withdraw."
This, or some equivalent supplementary idea, is required for the
sense.   Jesus intimates that He was about to surrender Himself to the impending sufferings with His full consent; and He
adds that He did so, in order that mankind might know that He
both loved the Father, and unreservedly complied with His
commandment.

A second testimony to the same effect is found in the declaration, that the Father loved Him because He spontaneously laid
down His life for the sheep at God's command: " *This commandment have I received of my Father*" (John x. 18).   He thus
evinced the highest act of obedience, when at the divine command He voluntarily laid down His life.   Having fulfilled the
whole law to the utmost measure, He closed His career by a
priestly act of self-oblation, which was the culmination of His
work; for it is said that He was obedient unto death (Phil.

---

[1] We nowhere else find this mode of speech either in the Old or New Testament, though we find what some think similar and equivalent phrases,—such
as ἔχειν τι κατὰ τινὸς (Matt. v. 23 ; Apoc. iv. 14–20), and ἔχειν τι πρὸς τίνα (Acts
xxiv. 19, xxv. 19 ; 1 Cor. vi. 1).   But here it is, ἐν ἐμοὶ οὐκ ἔχει οὐδέν.   There
may, as Calvin thinks, be an allusion not only to Christ's purity, but also to His
divine power.   We have given, in preference, the happy comment of Olshausen,
who says that Jesus means, " Er *besitzt* in meinem innern nichts, er kann nichts
sein nennen."

ii. 8). Thus the final surrender of His life must be emphatically called the highest act of obedience. This thought, which shines through our Lord's words in many of His sayings, receives its fullest illustration in the·memorable antithesis drawn between the disobedience of Adam and the obedience of Christ in the Epistle to the Romans (Rom. v. 19). While we cannot allow that the obedience of Christ as there described is limited to a single act, as is commonly affirmed by those who object to the doctrine, that the whole sinless life of Jesus was vicarious and redounding to our account, it is very evident that the death of Jesus is always represented by Himself and His apostles as the great deed in which the whole lines of His obedience met, and that by which His obedience was tested. This is the truth upon the point.

2. The second topic to which we must advert is, that the Lord Jesus represents His death as the true righteousness of His people in the following testimony: "*And when He is come, He will reprove the world of sin, and of righteousness, and of judgment: of sin, because* [better, that, or to the effect that, in respect that[1]] *they believe not on Me; of righteousness, because* [better, that] *I go to My Father, and ye see Me no more*" (John xvi. 8, 10). The interpretation of the phrase, "I go to My Father," must be, first of all, ascertained. And of all the comments that have been given, by far the simplest and most natural is that which explains it of His meritorious sufferings and death as the pathway by which He returned to the Father.[2] That this is a mode of speech by no means infrequent in the Gospels, is proved by many things in our Lord's own style of address, and not least by

---

[1] The ὅτι is best interpreted here as the ὅτι indicative ; that is, as showing wherein the sin and righteousness and judgment consist. (So Lücke, Meyer, Hengstenberg).

[2] Luther's comment, as given by Gerhard on this passage, is, " Demonstrabit per meum abitum, hoc est per meam passionem, mortem, resurrectionem, etc., veram fidelibus restitutam esse justitiam." Gerhard adds, " Inter cœteras causas Christus passionem et mortem suam ideo vocat *abitum ad Patrem*, ut significet, se passione et morte sua Deum reconciliasse" (*Harmonia Evangelistarum*, pars tertia, p. 330).

the fact, that when Moses and Elias conversed with Jesus upon the Mount, they are said to have talked with Him about His departure or exodus, which just means the atoning death by which He departed to the Father. This language, so understood, proves that the true righteousness of which the Comforter convinces men, and which plainly means the divinely-provided righteousness of God by which our persons are accepted, consists in the sufferings and death of Christ.

Thus, that great act of obedience constitutes the atonement or righteousness of Christians. The great reason why the Lord Jesus assumed our humanity, and offered it by an act of self-oblation, was to bring in this everlasting righteousness; or, to put it in a personal form, more adapted to the phraseology of the last-mentioned saying, the righteousness of Christians is the Son of God dying on the cross and going to the Father. Christ Himself is our righteousness or propitiation, which avails with God for the complete acceptance of our persons. Thus, the righteousness of God, viewed in this personal aspect, coincides with the position that the dying or crucified Christ is the righteousness of His people, or made of God unto us righteousness; and that not by a make-believe, but because what He did, His people are considered to have done in Him.

SEC. XXX.—CHRIST OFFERING HIMSELF, THAT HIS FOLLOWERS MIGHT BE SANCTIFIED IN TRUTH.

" *And for their sakes I sanctify myself, that they also might be sanctified through the truth* [better, sanctified in truth, or, truly sanctified.]" (John xvii. 19.)

This saying brings out another effect of the atonement, which may be said to be supplementary to the former. This effect belongs to the sphere of worship, or to that peculiar element which may be called the priestly character of Christians. It presupposes pardon and acceptance; taking up the thought at the point where the reconciled come before God in the free access of true worship. It is thus, in a certain sense, an advance upon the judicial or forensic idea; presupposing the latter, and also essentially comprehending it. Access to Israel's holy God, or worship from a people made nigh through blood, is the great idea with which the whole Old Testament is replete. And as the entire Old Testament was formed to bring a people before God in an act of worship, and as ever-recurring causes of separation necessitated sacrifice, and were ever removed in order to make way afresh for typical access, we naturally expect to find in our Lord's utterances some allusion to the true worship, with the true Priest and the true sacrifice.

The occasion of this saying was fitly furnished by our Lord's own prayer or act of worship. Nowhere could we expect to find this subject more naturally introduced or more fitly expressed, than when we find Him referring in this last prayer to His followers left behind Him in the world, and interceding for them, that they might be kept apart from the evil in the world. He is thus led, in the first place, to speak of the atonement as that which actually set them apart, or dedicated them as a holy people. The section begins with the appeal, " Holy Father" (ver. 11): the word " sanctify" occurs once and again; but the whole privilege of this priestly separation to God is here based upon Christ's act of self-oblation. We must first investigate the meaning of the phrase, " I sanctify myself for them, or for their sakes," and then consider their sanctification.

1. The word SANCTIFY, which is properly an Old Testament expression, denotes, in its common acceptation, to set apart, or to dedicate, from a common to a sacred or religious use. Hence arose other significations, such as, " to purify." But the most common signification arising out of that primary idea was, " to offer sacrifice," from the frequent necessity of atonement in the ancient worship. That is the proper signification of the expression here; and so the Greek exegetes correctly interpret it.[1]

---

[1] Thus Chrysostom, in his commentary on the passage, puts the question, τί ἐστὶν, ἁγιάζω ἐμαυτὸν; and answers the question as follows : προσφέρω σοι θυσίαν.

It is an expression for Christ's act of self-oblation, He being at once the priest and the sacrifice. Jesus could say with truth of the present activity in which He was engaged, " I sanctify myself," inasmuch as He was then in the act of executing the work devolved upon Him by the Father ; and He puts it in the present tense, because He was still occupied with it, and because His obedience was to last till it was consummated by death.

There are other interpretations of a different import, of which we may say in general, that they cannot stand examination. Thus some will have it, that our Lord had merely in His eye His consecration to be a teacher;[1] which is obviously quite untenable, on two grounds. It would represent Him as saying that He came self-commissioned, whereas He always describes Himself as sent; and the present tense is thus altogether lost sight of. Nor can the language refer, as others think, to such a sanctification of Himself as should aim at forming men to be apostles and teachers.[2] The great objection to both such comments on the ground of language is, that at the present stage, and within a few hours of His death, that teaching work lay behind Him ; and the Lord refers to it in the context only as to a past thing (vers. 11, 14, 18, 21, 23). But this expression in the present tense, while it cannot be referred to the work of teaching or of moulding teachers, with which He had been occupied from the first, may be referred to that sacrifice of Himself which had just been figured forth by the emblems of the Supper, and which was now filling His mind as near at hand,— the climax of His obedience, the priestly self-oblation. And, naturally, it is spoken of as a present thing.

The expression, " I sanctify myself for them," is thus a priestly word,—the same word that many times occurs in the Old Testament ritual.[3] It is to be understood of the sanctification which the Lord executed in Himself, when He offered to

---

[1] So Kuinoel.

[2] So Tittman on the passage, and also Nösselt.

[3] See J. Alting, *Opera Theol.* iv. p. 98, who says that it is segregare . . . ut foret hostia pro peccato.

God the sacrifice of Himself as a sin-offering. The language is by no means rare in the Old Testament. Thus we read of sanctifying the paschal lamb (2 Chron. xxx. 17). And the sanctifying of the first-born of beasts is alternated with another similar expression, that of offering them (Deut. xv. 19-21). The phrase does not intimate that our Lord sanctified Himself for any new work of practical activity in the world; for that was ended. Rather it means that He sanctified Himself to be made sin, or, in other words, to make an exchange of places with us, and to offer Himself, by an act of self-oblation, as the great sin-offering.

Here we distinctly perceive the two sides or aspects of truth which we developed at large in former sections,—sin-bearing and sinless action ; but not the one without the other, or isolated from the other. The one could not avail without the other in this great transaction. They constitute, when taken together, the two essential elements of the atonement, and are inseparably conjoined in the production of one result. Not that we are to represent these two elements as separately meritorious ; for they are, from the very nature of the problem, concurrent. Hence, as sinless nature must, from the liabilities of those in whose room Christ acted as a surety, be subjected to a test, or tried, He learned obedience by the things He suffered (Heb. v. 8),—the meaning of which remarkable statement is, that His obedience increased ; in other words, that it was not fully expanded at the first, but became more energetic and vigorous as the trial advanced. Not that His life wanted the character of obedience at any moment, but it rose with the occasion, till it triumphed over every obstruction and hindrance, as we can distinctly trace in the garden. And all this is in full consistency with His moral perfection, and only proves that His obedience was ever complete, but capable of increase with the trials to which it was subjected.

Thus the import of the saying on which we are commenting is, that the Lord Jesus sanctified Himself to be made sin, and to exchange places with us as the great sin-offering. And we may regard Him, accordingly, as here repeating, in His own words, and in language still more emphatically sacerdotal, what by the mouth of David He had long before announced: "Lo, I come to do Thy will, O my God" (Ps. xl. 8). The whole tenor of this language, together with the issue to which it leads, is just another mode of announcing that He took our place, that we might be set apart to occupy His place, and to stand in His relation before God.

The next question is, What is intimated by the preposition here rendered, *for their sakes* (ὑπὲρ αὐτῶν)? It means, *for the good of, for the benefit of.* Though the preposition, in point of strict philology, does not exactly mean, in such a construction, *in room of,* it cannot be denied, that in several passages it not only may but must be accepted, in connection with several expressions employed in reference to the atonement, as denoting *instead of.* That latter thought, indeed, lies not so much in the preposition itself, as in the whole idea of substitution which is interwoven with the thought in such passages. The phrase, "to do something for one," may be employed to mean, *for another's advantage,* or, *for another's good* (Eph. iii. 1). But it cannot be denied by any one acquainted with the phraseology of Scripture, that it never was said of any mere man that he suffered or died for others in the sense, and to the extent, in which Christ is said to suffer and die for us.

Hence, when the apostle, in one definite passage of much significance, takes occasion to reason on the subject of one dying for another, and concedes what could by possibility occur in common life, he leaves us in no doubt as to the sense in which he would have the preposition to be understood (Rom. v. 7). The idea of spontaneous self-oblation for the sake of others, and, from the nature of the case, *in the room of others,* is, according to his explanation, plainly contained in that expression;[1] and the

---

[1] Some philologists put this in a form to which no exception can be taken. While they abide by the conclusion, that ὑπὲρ means *for the benefit of,* they admit

whole phraseology implies that Christ offered Himself, of His own proper motion, not constrained by any outward influence, and not overborne by enemies. Moreover, when the innocent suffers for the guilty, it is plainly with the intention of delivering the guilty from the penalty which impended over him as his due. Thus substitution is involved. The preposition FOR, or, FOR THE SAKE OF, carries with it, therefore, the following significance: that when the one representative of the children of God died for all, all died in Him, and were all judged to have suffered in Him (2 Cor. v. 15). He did this once for all, and it had everlasting efficacy.

2. But we now notice the effect of this self-oblation, or the design and end which the Lord had in view in offering it: "that they also might be sanctified in truth." We decidedly prefer this rendering, because the definite article is awanting in the original.[1] The phrase may be regarded as equivalent to TRULY, or, IN TRUTH; and so we find it in other passages (1 John iii. 18; Phil. i. 18; John iv. 24). They for whom Christ sanctified Himself, are thus set apart as the true worshippers of God in the highest sense.

With respect to the word SANCTIFY as applied to the disciples of Christ, it is necessary to keep before our minds a distinction which is not always observed, and which, in popular theological language, is too much disregarded. There is a sanctification of the Spirit by which we are inwardly made holy; and there is, as contradistinguished from the former, the separation or sanctification of the person to God by Christ. It is in the latter sense that the word "sanctify" occurs here; and this unquestionably lays the foundation for the other, which is more subjective, and

---

that, from the nature of the transaction, the ὑπέρ implies the ἀντί. Windischmann, in his Commentary on Galatians, 1843, p. 15, says happily: "Man hat sich bemüht in dem Gebrauch dieser Präpositionen [viz. ὑπέρ and περί] den Begriff eines stillvertretenden Todes, ohne zu bedenken dass dieser in der Sache und nicht bloss in den Worten liegt.

[1] ἐν ἀληθείᾳ. The article, found only in some single MSS. and in a Greek father, has no claim to be inserted in the text.

follows in the order of nature after it. The question to be clearly settled in connection with this passage is, Whether are we to regard the sanctification here mentioned as the moral and spiritual renovation effected in us by the Spirit, and therefore the same with what is elsewhere called "the sanctification of the Spirit" (2 Thess. ii. 13), or, to interpret it as a direct fruit of the atonement? Is it objective or subjective? Is it a part of the Spirit's work, or an immediate fruit of Christ's sacrifice? It must be specially observed, that in this clause the Lord does not allude to the sanctification of Christians in the *moral* sense, or in the sense of *inward renovation*, but according to the acceptation of the word in the old Mosaic worship, and according to its import in the Epistle to the Hebrews[1] (Heb. xiii. 12, ix. 13). It would be a wide departure, indeed, from the true meaning of our Lord's words, if we should interpret this clause of the inward renewing by the Spirit. The word SANCTIFY, as it occurs in the Old Testament ritual, has primary reference to those appointed rites used for consecrating the whole people, or any individual, to belong to the theocracy in due form. This was a standing won and retained chiefly by sacrifice. And the apostle to the Hebrews explains that, in like manner, the sanctification of Christians, or the dedication of them to belong to the true people of God, and to share in their services and worship, was effected by the sacrifice of Christ. To apprehend the precise meaning of the word "sanctify," it will be necessary to trace its usage in the ancient ritual of Israel.

The two words frequently occurring in the old worship, *sanctify* and *purify*, are so closely allied in sense, that some regard them as synonymous. But a slight shade of distinction

---

[1] The words of the acute J. Alting, *Opera Theol.*, 1686, vol. iv. p. 98, are very precise and accurate: "Ipse sua ista sanctificatione segregatus fuit, et [ut?] ipsi quoque segregantur sed diversimode: ipse segregatus est ut esset reatus et peccatum: ipsi autem ne essent reatus et peccatum." (Compare Storr, *Dissertatio exegetica in Librorum N. T. Historicorum aliquot loca*, pars altera, p. 57; Lang, *Zusätze zu Teller's Wörterbuch d. n. Testaments*, art. *Heiligen*.) Schleusner, Lex. on ἀγιάζω.

between the two may be discerned as follows. It is assumed
that ever-recurring defilements, of a ceremonial kind, called for
sacrifices of expiation; and the word "purify" referred to those
rites and sacrifices which removed the stains which excluded
the worshipper from the privilege of approach to the sanctuary
of God, and from fellowship with His people. The defilement
which he contracted excluded him from access. But when this
same Israelite was purified by sacrifice, he was readmitted to
the full participation of the privilege. He was then *sanctified*
or *holy*. Thus the latter is the consequence of the former. We
may affirm, then, that the two words, "purify" and "sanctify,"
in this reference to the old worship, are very closely allied; so
much so, that the one involves the other. This will throw light
upon the use of these two expressions in the New Testament
(Eph. v. 25, 26;[1] Heb. ii. 11; Tit. ii. 14). All these passages
represent a man defiled by sin and excluded from God, but readmitted to access and fellowship, and so pronounced holy, as
soon as the blood of sacrifice is applied to him. That is the
meaning of the word "sanctify" in this verse.

a. Hence, when we trace the connection of sanctification as
here used with the atonement, it is a causal connection. It is
placed in direct and immediate relation to the atonement. The
immediate sequel to a state of personal reconciliation is the
sanctification here referred to, or the access to be a people near
to God, or to be a theocratic people. Christ is thus said to
sanctify us, as He makes His people free from defilement and
from the estrangement flowing from defilement, and restores us
to the divine friendship; and His people are said to be " sanctified in truth," because reality is contrasted with shadows, and
the permanent with the transitory. They are set apart to God,

---

[1] The two words, ἁγιάζειν and καθαρίζειν, both referring to the idea of a sacrifice,
and so nearly equipollent that the one involves the other, are put together in the
phrase : παρέδωκεν—ἵνα αὐτὴν ἁγιάσῃ καθαρίσας (Eph. v. 26). Morus would put
into a parenthesis the clause beginning with καθαρίσας. But, at all events, the
participial force of καθαρίσας in the aorist must be maintained ; and this will
sufficiently indicate the relation between the two verbs.

and made a peculiar people, or a kingdom of priests, by the remission of sins.

b. Under this head it is necessary to refer a little more to the teaching of the Epistles; for the meaning of this significant phrase is not exhausted, till we add from the Epistles, that they who are thus "sanctified in truth" by the atoning death of Christ are further regarded as *consciously near to God.* They are described as worshippers once purged, and having no more conscience of sin (Heb. x. 2); and it is the same standing which Paul delineates in the Epistle to the Ephesians, when he shows that they who are saved by grace through faith are now made nigh: " But now in Christ Jesus ye who sometimes were far off are made nigh by the blood of Christ" (Eph. ii. 13). This is real, not typical nearness. The old Mosaic worship sanctified only to the purifying of the flesh (Heb. ix. 13); whereas they who have the application of Christ's atoning blood, have their consciences purged from dead works (ver. 14). They are purified, in other words, from an accusing conscience or an evil conscience, in order to be filled with the peace of God, and so brought into a state of conscious nearness to God by the sacrifice of Christ; or, to quote another form of describing it: " By one offering He hath perfected for ever them that are sanctified" (Heb. x. 14). Thus, what was typically done in the old Mosaic worship, is now done in truth by the self-sacrifice of Christ.

c. But, furthermore, it is *a nearness to serve,* or to act as priests; and they who so stand before God are purged in conscience to serve the living God (Heb. ix. 14). They are sanctified, or dedicated, as the ancient priests were, to a holy service, by which everything is done as in the sight of God. It must be added, that their dedication to be a people near to God carries with it the further accompaniment, that all life becomes an offering, and all its activity a worship. Thus, a human life may become a hymn of praise, when it is passed in the presence of God, and done to Him, even to its minutest details. This is the natural result or sequel of being dedicated in truth. And not only so: the defilement, still inevitably adhering to all the actions of these sanctified ones, is constantly cleansed and covered by Him whose offering dedicated them (1 John ii. 1, 2). Their service as priests unto God is presented faultless, and acceptable unto Him by the continued intercession of our great Advocate on high (1 Pet. ii. 5); they live in the holiest into which they have boldness to enter (Heb. x. 19); and they stand in the grace into which they have access or introduction (Rom. v. 2).

Thus it clearly enough appears that this expression on which we have been commenting is not to be interpreted of a moral amendment, or of a spiritual renovation, though that of course immediately follows, but according to the sacrificial and priestly phraseology of the old Mosaic worship.[1] The meaning, as we have seen, is simply this: that the Son of God dedicated Himself in that act of self-oblation, that they who are far off, aliens and strangers, might be made nigh; or that He was sanctified and set apart to be a sin-offering, to take our place, in order that we might be put in His place. Thus it is the atonement which sanctifies us in truth, or makes us a people near to God, not typically, but really, or a kingdom of priests to God.

SEC. XXXI.—SAYINGS RELATIVE TO THE SUBJECTIVE LIFE-GIVING EFFECTS OF CHRIST'S DEATH.

We have already noticed several of the sayings of Jesus which refer to the more objective effects of His death, or which have respect to the acceptance of our persons and the remission of our sins. There is another class of sayings, which we shall,

---

[1] Compare Zechariæ's *Biblische Theologie*, vol. ii., *Verrede*, where there are some just remarks on ἀγιάζειν, mingled with observations which are questionable; Vinke, *leer van Jesus en de Apostel aang. zijn Ltjden*, 1837, p. 76; Herwerden on the passage, *over het Evangelie van Johannes*, 1798; Lotze, *over het Hoogepriesterschap van Jesus Christus*, 1800, p. 104.

next in order, adduce, referring more to the inward or sanctifying fruits of His death. The former, as we have seen, are to be
regarded as the immediate results or fruits of the atoning work
of Christ; the latter are rather the mediate effects of His atoning death, and presuppose the former. The acceptance of the
person, or the right relation of the man, is communicated first
in the order of nature; for the " doing," according to the tenor
of the law, is in order to the " life" (Rom. x. 5). It is important to notice, that of all these subjective or sanctifying effects
of the atonement in men, there are none which are not to be
regarded as following upon the liberation of our persons from
the curse of the law. They all presuppose this; so that the
spirit of life, which comes to renovate the nature, is sent only
on the ground of this acceptance to occupy the heart; or, to put
it in Pauline language, the disciples of Christ are delivered from,
or dead to, the law, that they may be married to another, that
they may bring forth fruit unto God (Rom. vii. 4). Nor are the
inward effects merely those which follow in the way of motive,
or as an expression of gratitude. For however powerful the
death of Christ is as a motive to influence the heart, there is
another ground based upon the merit of His atonement which is
much stronger, and exercises an influence, not on the human
mind merely, but also on the government of God.

Among the sayings of Jesus which refer to the subjective
effects of the atonement, there are several in John's narrative
which speak of life: (1) the allusion to the brazen serpent; (2)
the allusion to His crucified body as the bread of life; to which
might be subjoined another already mentioned, the harmony of
love and justice, as opening up the channel for the gift of life
(John iii. 16). All these are subjective and mediate effects of
Christ's death. The teaching of our Lord and of His apostles
proves, that as truly as the fall brought into the world death
and bondage, so truly does the atonement bring life; and that
there is thus the closest connection between the atoning death
of Christ and the spiritual life of the soul, as the end or object
to which the atonement always had respect.

It is the more necessary to notice this, in opposition to the modern school which puts the life first. They will have it, that the acceptance of the person does not directly flow from the death of Christ as its immediate result, but, conversely, that remission of sin flows from our grateful love.[1] This is a perversion of all Scripture; it does not make pardon result immediately and directly from the cross; and it differs little from mysticism, or legalism, or Popery. On the contrary, the communication of life and of growing sanctification is regarded by our Lord as the result which follows at the next remove, or as the further aim of the acceptance of the man, and of the remission of his sins. They who are liberated from the curse of sin are next liberated from the power of sin by the spirit of life. But our Lord's sayings put life in connection with His death, as the reward, fruit, or purchase of the atonement.

One of Christ's titles frequently mentioned in John is THE LIFE (John xiv. 6); presupposing that men are dead in sin. And when we determine from Scripture how life is dispensed, we find that the connection between the atonement and life, or between righteousness and life, is the connection between work and reward. Where no righteousness is, in other words where sin is, which may be taken either as omission or commission, there is death; but on the other hand, where righteousness is, there is life (Rom. viii. 10). This connection between the atonement and life may be discovered in numerous passages of Scripture (Rom. vi. 1-12; Gal. ii. 19-21; 2 Cor. v. 14, 15; Col. iii. 1-6). There are three distinct conceptions which may be traced in such passages as follows:—

a. The right to life is based on service rendered or atonement offered. This is expressed by the apostles under the terms co-crucifixion, co-dying with Christ, or being co-planted with the Lord in His death. This act is viewed as their act, and accordingly His people are to *reckon* themselves to be dead with Him unto sin (Rom. vi. 11).

[1] So Usteri puts the matter, according to the Schleiermacherian representation. *Entwickelung des Paulinischen Lehrbegriffes*, p. 131.

b. The redeemed Church, even while conflicting with sin, is sitting with Christ in a risen life (Eph. i. 6), and has a life hid with Christ in God (Col. iii. 3). This carries forward our conceptions to the incorruptible life of glory, of which the pledge and warrant are already found in Christ's resurrection-life. The members are one with the Head, and even now live together with Him; and so joined, as Gambold expresses it, that He will not be in glory and leave them behind.

c. A further thought is the perpetual supply of spiritual life, because Christ lives in us (Gal. ii. 20). His people are to be replenished with all His fulness; He ever imparting and they ever receiving (John i. 16). The Lord's design is that His life may reappear anew in His people or be reproduced in them; and that there may be such a symphony, so to speak, that His people shall promote on earth the great object for which He lives in glory. The life of love and active service which He lived on earth is to be renewed and reproduced in all His people. And when we inquire how this is attained, we find that the tide of resurrection life flows into His people, in proportion as they keep before them His abasement, atoning death, and resurrection as the great themes of faith and the great springs of action (Gal. ii. 19, last part). Hence, when the Apostles would have us live over again the humility, the forbearing, meek, unretaliating life of Christ, they commonly fix attention on His coming from His pre-existing glory to abasement (Phil. ii. 7), or on His patient endurance as the voluntary sin-bearer (1 Pet. ii. 22-24).

SEC. XXXII.—CHRIST CRUCIFIED THE ANTITYPE OF THE BRAZEN SERPENT, AND THE LIFE-GIVER.

" *And as Moses lifted up the serpent in the wilderness, even so must the Son of Man be lifted up; that whosoever believeth in Him should not perish, but have eternal life.*" (John iii. 14.)

This significant saying points out the inseparable connection between the cross of Christ and eternal life, and the indispen-

sable necessity of the former to the latter. The occasion on
which it was spoken demands particular attention. It forms
part of the Lord's address to Nicodemus, when He opened up
to him the nature of spiritual religion, step by step meeting the
difficulties of the Jewish teacher. After drawing a distinction
between "the earthly things," among which the new birth is
classified, and which is so named because it is a blessing enjoyed upon the earth, and thus a thing of human experience,
and "the heavenly things," so called because they belong to
what is divine and heavenly, and which must be regarded as
included in the counsel of redemption, He proceeds to name
two of the latter—His own deity (ver. 13), and His atoning
work (ver. 14). They are put in connection with the new birth,
and delineated as its indispensable prerequisites on God's part.
By means of this type, which was intended to utter a language
that should speak to all time, our Lord convinced Nicodemus
that He must needs be crucified. And we find, accordingly,
that when He actually died on the cross, it was less of a shock
to Nicodemus than to any of His immediate disciples; for he
went along with Joseph of Arimathea, who also seems to have
been prepared, by means of private intercourse with Jesus, for
the fact of the crucifixion, and begged the body of Jesus (John
xix. 39). The import of our Lord's words here may be correctly
represented as follows: "You see a mean man, or the Son of
Man, who must needs be abased still lower, and even lifted up
upon the cross, as the antitype of the brazen serpent, for men's
salvation" (Num. xxi. 9).

But the question is raised, Did Christ really refer to His
crucifixion when He thus spoke of being "lifted up?"[1]   All
doubt as to the import of this verb, at least as it is used by John
in connexion with the work of Christ, is completely set at rest
by the apostolic commentary appended to one of the passages

---

[1] ὑψόω is always so used by John. It is a Johannine peculiarity; for we find
other sacred writers use the same verb of the exaltation. (Comp. ὑψωθείς, Acts ii.
23, v. 31.)

where it occurs: "This He said, signifying what death He should die" (John xii. 33). Some, and among these Calvin, have expounded the "lifting up" as containing an allusion to the preaching of the gospel, as from a high and elevated place, and in the eye of all. But that comment, though supported by several great names, is forced and far-fetched; it loses the point of the comparison; and we can only wonder that any have adhered to it, when the Apostle John has explicitly settled the question. Others, again, have expounded the words, "so must the Son of Man be lifted up," as referring to Christ's exaltation to heaven.[1] But that, too, is inadmissible, as it cannot stand a moment against the authoritative apostolic commentary of John, who, speaking with infallible inspiration, tells us what the language really meant in the mouth of Christ. And even though we should doubt whether Nicodemus at the time fully understood the words, such a testimony, based on a fact of Jewish history, otherwise inexplicable, would be afterwards of use to Nicodemus personally, as he doubtless understood it, when the event arrived.

To this well-known fact, the last of the miracles of Moses, and performed by him at God's command and direction, towards the close of the forty years' wanderings, it is not necessary more specially to refer, except to say that it was meant to be a type, and that our Lord adduces it as such. He does not make it a mere groundwork of a comparison.[2] The word *as*, with its correlated *even so,* will not permit us to rest satisfied with the comment, that here we have nothing but a mere similitude or comparison; for the one is deduced from the other in such

---

[1] So Beza, Lampe, and some of the fathers mentioned by Suicer in his *Thesaurus*, on this word. That comment is untenable. As little can be said for another explanation supported by Luthardt and Hofmann, that the words only mean that Christ, as crucified and as exalted, should be the object of faith. John's comment is decisive (John xii. 33).

[2] This view, that it is only a comparison, supported by Bloomfield, and by Webster and Wilkinson in their notes, is untenable. It wishes to simplify the sense by dismissing the type, but makes a greater difficulty. The καθὼς and οὕτως are opposed to this.

a way as indicates that, according to divine appointment, the fulfilment must needs be because the future event was shadowed forth, and in a manner predicted, by the preparatory type. It was a proper figure of good things to come, having the same relation to the substance that a picture has to the reality. The points of resemblance lay in the things themselves, according to the divine intention. If the reality had not been appointed to appear, indeed, in the fulness of time, we may certainly conclude, according to the relation between the two, that men should never have seen its shadow or rude outline. It was, like the sacrifice, intended as a foretokening of a coming atonement, though differing from these in one obvious respect —that the material was brass, and the whole appointment, in the utmost degree, sovereign, positive, and even arbitrary. The whole arrangement, however, shows the wisdom of God in providing for a clear and accurate idea of the atonement in the fulness of time, and in leading the Jews to hail and welcome the hope of its realization.[1]

The question is not, how many of the Jewish nation rose to such anticipations, nor what ideas were formed of this type by the nation generally; for God dealt with that elect nation, all through its history, on the principle of a remnant or inner election (Rom. ix. 11). The question is, whether the believers among them were not led to harmonize it with the divine design, as they did in the matter of the sacrifices; and also, whether it was not in a sense ministered, not so much to them, as to us who have the gospel preached to us (1 Peter i. 12).

The Lord chose this singular instrument of cure, because the people were to see the sovereign hand of God, and not ascribe the effect to any intrinsic efficacy in outward things, apart from the direct interposition and power of God. They who saw no congruity between the means and the end to be effected, would

[1] See F. Turretinus, *Disp. Miscell. Decad.* Disp. x. ; Marckius, *Exerc. text* viii. part iv. ; Deyling, *Observ. S.*, part ii. Observ. xv. ; Witsius, *Egyptiacorum*, lib. i. ix. 6.

naturally, if they gave the rein to reason, feel a great difficulty, and be disposed even to ridicule the idea of being healed by looking upon a piece of brass. They must necessarily take offence, if they did not bow to the sovereignty of God. But there were also weighty reasons for the commandment given. The people were to see, not only an image of the punishment of sin, but also an image of a vicarious economy. I cannot say whether we find any further allusion to this fact in the Old Testament besides the allusion to the idolatrous perversion and abuse of this relic which had crept in during Hezekiah's reign (2 Kings xviii. 4). Isaiah's phrase is not unlike it: "by His stripes we are healed." But we cannot doubt that Jesus, in His interpretation of the type, meant to show that He was appointed to become a vicarious sufferer, to be made a curse, on whom was to be manifested the divine vengeance against sin, that others might escape, and be healed.

The various points of comparison between the type and antitype may be enumerated as follows:—

1. The raising of the brazen serpent on the pole or banner-staff, and the lifting up of Christ upon the cross. These two are related as shadow and substance—the one being prophetic of the other. Nor is this by any means to be regarded as a subordinate point, as certain expositors suppose. For, in the first place, the repetition of the verb "lifted up" in the two contrasted clauses, and then the correlation of the two particles, *as* and *so*, unite to prove that the one is to be viewed as type, and the other as antitype.[1]

2. The two objects here named were, in two different respects, according to the appointment and command of God, to be regarded with a trustful and confident look. Men were directed to look to them with unhesitating confidence, according to the divine appointment, for salvation.

[1] The use of καθὼς and οὕτως shows an intended type; and there are many similar interpretations in the mouth of the Lord, such as the *manna* and *Jonah*. The whole fact in Jewish history, in all its details, is conclusively and authoritatively pronounced to be an intended counterpart or type to His historic work.

3. The instant effect of that look was to bring deliverance and health. This is the direct and obvious point of comparison, into which the whole statement is naturally to be resolved. It takes for granted believing confidence in the divinely appointed remedy, but implies that there is an instant communication of life in connection with a look at the crucified One.

4. It is a moot point whether we are to add, as another element of resemblance, the fact that the brazen serpent was only made like the poisonous serpents, yet without their poison, and that Christ was in all points made like unto His brethren, yet without sin.[1] It is not only warrantable to add this further point of resemblance with many of the best commentators, but it is necessary. It is true, the great point (or the *tertium quid*) of the comparison is, that the lifting up of the brazen serpent healed the wounded Israelite, and that Christ crucified delivers perishing men from eternal death. But we must also take in this point. The serpent was only in appearance like the noxious creatures that had caused lamentation and woe in the camp of Israel, but not one of them; and, in like manner, Christ was made in the likeness of sinful flesh, or made in all points like the brethren, yet without sin. Some make the analogy to lie more in the circumstance of the lifting up, than in any accessory or accompanying allusion to the serpent itself. There seems no difficulty, however, in the supposition that the brazen serpent represented Christ in the sense that He took the place of sinners, and specially of the sinner, by whom death and all our woes were disseminated and passed over unto all mankind. It would have been a real difficulty had one of the true serpents, and not the mere resemblance or figure of them, been put upon the pole.

But, in adding this fourth point of analogy, we must, by all means, be careful to disencumber it of a further allusion to Satan, who is so often described in Scripture as a serpent, and

---

[1] This was strongly brought out by Luther in his sermons, and in his German comments on John, by many Lutheran divines, such as Chemnitz, after him, and by Gomar among the Reformed ; also by more recent writers, such as Bengel, Lechler in the *Studien und Kritiken*, 1854, and others. Lücke opposes it.

who is supposed by many to be necessarily referred to here. A great difficulty would certainly be presented, if it were necessary to accept this widely received view, that there must be a further reference to Satan, either in the allusion of the original fact, or in our Lord's quotation and reference to it. For how could the crucified Christ in any sense be represented by an emblem of the devil, or be compared in any sense to the serpent with this additional allusion ? It is not denied that ingenuity may discover, and has often satisfied itself with thinking that it has discovered resemblances; representing men, for example, as the brood of the serpent, and therefore that Christ was made sin in the form of the seed of the serpent. But these are mere fancies that cannot be tolerated here. And there are no traces that Christ meant to teach that the serpent, with this further reference to Satan, was a type of Himself. That is so incongruous, that, to avoid it, we must rather make the point of comparison be merely in the lifting up. But there is no allusion to Satan at all; and the mistake arose from not discerning that the serpent, in one respect, at least in the brazen figure of it, may as well be employed to represent Christ as the various other animals, which were used to represent substitution, or were offered to God in the way of a typical vicarious sacrifice.

This brings me to notice another exposition which was much in vogue a century ago, and which is still advocated in some of its phases—that we have not here a direct type of Christ, but an allusion to the old serpent triumphed over on the cross.[1]

[1] This comment originated with J. D'Espagne, an ingenious French pastor, who laboured in London, 1659, and is found in his *Opera*, tom. ii. p. 214. It was adopted by the celebrated F. Burmann, *Synopsis*, lib. iv. cap. 32 ; by Vitringa, *Observ. S.*, lib. ii. cap. 11 ; and it reappears, with some modifications, in Menken's treatise, *über die eherne Schlange*, and also in Olshausen's commentary. This interpretation was refuted energetically by Marckius and by Deyling. Lingering remains of this interpretation reappear, and may be traced in the remarks of even recent exegetes. It arose from the mistaken notion, that, according to the analogy of Scripture, the serpent must have some reference to Satan, and that therefore there was an obvious impropriety in making the serpent, so viewed, a type of Christ. And there certainly would be, if that accessory notion were included at all, which, however, we have seen, is by no means to be taken in.

This explanation starts from the same mistaken notion that there must be an allusion to Satan, and was suggested by the obvious impropriety of representing Christ by an emblem of Satan. According to this view, our Lord's words are identical with the apostle's statement, that Christ made a show of him openly, triumphing over him on the cross (Col. ii. 15). That, however, makes a greater difficulty; and, as a comment, it is wholly inadmissible, as will readily appear from the following considerations :—

(1.) The types are not meant to be adumbrations of the adversary in any respect, but of Christ; and the notion on which this interpretation proceeds, that the symbols must always have the same allusion in every connection, is not confirmed by fact. Thus the serpent is referred to in a light wholly different, when the Lord tells His disciples to be "wise as serpents." The goats, too, which were used on the day of atonement, were meant to be a representation of the vicarious sacrifice, while they are elsewhere referred to as the emblem of the wicked. And there is nothing, therefore, to prevent the interpretation of the brazen serpent as setting forth a type of Christ, the substitute of sinners.

(2.) The similarity between the type and the antitype is preserved, only if we regard the brazen serpent as a type of Christ. The condition of the Israelites at that time gives us a vivid picture of the guilt and spiritual misery in which all sinners are involved; and the act of lifting up can only refer with any fitness to Christ, who was lifted up upon the cross in the infliction of an accursed public death. This is one point of analogy; and His body was like the sinner, too, only in fashion, and as having a common nature, but without the life of sin. The analogy consists further, in the fact that He was appointed by God, and that He acted as the one Mediator between God and man.

(3.) This was not a trophy of victory, but a means of cure. It was not one of the actual serpents, living or dead, but only a resemblance, having nothing in common with them but the form, and having wholly different effects. The one wounded, the other healed; the one killed, the other made alive; the one destroyed the works of the other; and hence it was not a figure of Satan, but of Christ.

(4.) The look of the sufferer also was certainly to be directed to Christ alone as its proper object, or to the type of Christ, and not to the adversary; and as immediate healing was imparted to the wounded dying Israelite by a simple look at the brazen serpent, so life eternal is communicated to every one who turns a believing look to Christ. There was life for a look then, and there is life for a look now. But Satan, from whom we flee, cannot, with any modification of the idea, be regarded as the terminating object of faith. It was not a look at the actual serpents, nor at Moses, nor at the pole, but solely at the figure of the serpent; and it is solely at Christ, as the true object, that faith now looks.

To return, then, to the fourth point of similarity, it must be held that the Lord Jesus, the sinless substitute, had an external resemblance to man in all points, or was in all points made like unto the brethren, but was wholly exempt from their life of sin (Heb. ii. 17). It is not without reason that He was typified by the brazen serpent; for·He was a curse-bearer, and yet a Saviour. By this striking type He described to an Israelite, in the most vivid way in which the idea could be put, that He was not come as a mere earthly king, but as a sufferer, and that in His sufferings He was not a mere martyr, but the Redeemer of men, coming in the guise and receiving the treatment of the greatest of sinners. They who are not ready to say, that Christ only plays, in the most arbitrary way, with emblems and historic facts, must admit that the brazen serpent is typical. That hideous image of sin and its effects represented the Son of God in the likeness of sinful flesh, and as made sin, to condemn sin in the flesh. The entire type had a deep enigmatic meaning, though it was dark to a Jew, and indeed is obscure to every one ignorant of the substitution of Christ. But it is no more obscure to us who know the vicarious atonement.

Thus the historic fact implies, when considered in its true significance, that men are saved by a method similar to that by which they were undone; that by man came death, and that by man came the redemption from death. Till the mind is enlightened by the wisdom of God, this seems a remedy running counter to all natural congruity and fitness; for who would expect deliverance from a piece of brass fashioned after the shape of the Destroyer? and, in like manner, who would look for salvation from one carried out to a public execution? But when we apprehend substitution aright, it is a most significant and suggestive type.

As we have already noticed the necessity of the atonement or crucifixion, it is the less incumbent to enlarge on the words, " So must the Son of Man be lifted up." The MUST here expressed, bringing out what is indispensable, is not to be limited to the mere carrying out of the type, but has a deeper ground in God's purpose of redemption, and in order to finish the curse. That the punishment of sin must be borne and exhausted on the cross was already indicated centuries before by the brazen serpent raised upon the pole. Plainly, the necessity here alluded to is a deep inner necessity. It is not due merely to the fact that it was foreshadowed: rather it was foreshadowed because it must needs take place on moral grounds. Though the faithfulness of God must be maintained in carrying out the types and prophecies, it was not they that conditioned the crucifixion, but, conversely, the deep necessity in the moral government of God that threw back its shadow upon them.

As the punitive justice of God, or the necessity for the atonement, with the evidence that goes to establish it in our Lord's teaching, has been noticed in a previous section of this volume, we forbear to adduce the evidence which goes to illustrate it. Let it suffice to say that the *must* here uttered by our Lord is connected with the communication of divine life and perfect healing, and that "no cross, no healing" is the purport of this testimony. When sin entered into the world, God's moral perfections rendered it indispensably necessary that it should receive its recompense of reward, and that a satisfaction for sin should be required before divine life could be diffused through the race. The Most High owes this to Himself—it being a *must* in the Divine government as well as a necessary provision for the relief of mental anxiety and dread. He owes this to Himself, because He loveth righteousness (Ps. xi. 7). It was not brought about to make a mere impression on the moral universe, in order to deter them from sin; and as little was it done because God was acting before a vast public composed of all spiritual intelligences. The necessity of punishment, and of expiation, is irrespective of any aims or considerations that refer to a public apart from Himself. His perfections are the only public before which He acts; and He punishes sin only because of the demerit of it, as calling for punishment, and because He is under obligation to Himself, or, in other words, from love to His rectitude, which is just love to Himself (Ps. xi. 7). This punitive retribution is commonly called vengeance; and the Most High claims it as His own prerogative: "Vengeance is mine: I will repay" (Rom. xii. 19; Deut. xxxii. 35). Hence, when moral evil has been committed, natural evil, suited to it, must needs ensue; and we may lay down with confidence the position, that the creatures of God, in the moral government of God's world, suffer only what is due, and never more than their due. Hence, to bear this infliction in a manner which should expiate the sin and exhaust the curse, was the reason of Christ's crucifixion, and gives the explanation of the *must* which He here expresses.

It must be specially noticed, however, that the atonement was intended, in the divine economy, to open the way for the dissemination of the life. The words are introduced by a final particle:[1] " that whosoever believeth in Him should not perish, but have eternal life;" and bring out a twofold end,—life as the ultimate end, and faith as the intermediate end, or the instrument of reception. This much is indisputable, that the death of

---

[1] ἵνα is always telic. (See Winer, Fritzsche on Matthew, and Meyer.)

Jesus was an indispensably necessary matter, in order to attain
this eternal life. It is to His death, according to Christ's own
testimony, that men owe deliverance, healing, and life; and it is
by faith in His crucified person that men are put into the actual
possession and enjoyment of these benefits,—the faith which
presupposes the finished work of Christ, and which relies upon
His death, or upon Himself as crucified and lifted up.

But it is important to notice also, that the atoning death stands
in a causal connection, or in a meritorious connection, with the
eternal life considered as a present inheritance. This LIFE is
spoken of as the end, effect, or reward of the crucifixion.[1] The
design of all these passages, which put life and sanctification in
connection with Christ's death, is not, as the modern theology
will have it, to show that the life is first, and that the acceptance of a sinner does not flow immediately from the death of
Christ, but only mediately from life. That theory is totally
without scriptural warrant; and, carried out to its legitimate
consequences, it makes another gospel. The life and the progressive sanctification are to be considered only as a reward, or
as the further aim, or the consequence of the acceptance of our
persons. It is by no means proved by such passages, that we
are to regard sanctification, or the communication of the divine
life, as the immediate aim and scope of Christ's death. Life is
the reward of the atonement, and is always represented by our
Lord and by His apostles as premial life, on the ground of a
righteousness or atonement (Rom. viii. 10).

It is the more necessary to apprehend precisely the scope and
tendency of this school of interpretation, because it has obtained,
in our day, such wide diffusion, and so much acceptance; and it

---

1 Vinke, in his *Leer van Jesus en de Apostel aang. Zijn Lijden*, notices several
antitheses in which ζωή stands; *e.g.*:—

ζωή and κρίσις or θάνατος (John v. 24).
ζωή and ὀργὴ τοῦ Θεοῦ (John iii. 36).
ζωή and ἀπώλεια (Matt. vii. 13, 14).
ζωή and τὸ πῦρ τὸ αἰώνιον (Matt. xviii. 8).
ζωή and ἡ γέεννα τοῦ πυρὸς (Matt. xviii. 9).
ζωή αἰώνιος and κόλασις αἰώνιος (Matt. xxv. 46).

has, perhaps, in some degree, its rights, and also its advantages, as against a frigid orthodoxy.   But it is no higher than mediæval mysticism ; and its one-sidedness is hurtful, while its exhibition of the gospel is highly defective.[1]   It puts life first, and pardon next ; and the former, in a directly unbiblical manner, is made the pathway for the latter.   It does not base acceptance directly and immediately on the cross, but on the previous possession of the divine life.   The relations of truth are reversed and disorganized.   The whole attention is turned to communion with Christ in His life ; and thus the gospel remedy is turned away from its proper object.   The subject-matter is disjointed, and the message is turned upside down.   All the great doctrines connected with God as an authoritative lawgiver and moral ruler, with guilt and punishment, with atonement and acceptance, fall into the background, while all prominence is given to the truths which stand connected with Christ as a fountain of life.   It is thus an interpretation essentially the same as mediæval mysticism, limiting its view to Christ *in His people*, but stopping short at the point of giving the prominence which is due to Christ *for His people*.   In a word, this school of interpretation does not connect the communication of the divine life with Christ's vicarious death, or with the righteousness of the law, which is the only purchase or cause of the life,—as Paul puts it in the Epistle to the Romans.   Nay, a distinction is attempted between the one as a Johannine, and the other as a Pauline, mode of

[1] This is the mystic theory of the atonement, which, emanating from Menken and the Schleiermacher school, has found champions or adherents in all the various Protestant Churches.   Its one-sidedness appears in this, that it makes the gift of the divine life *absolute*, and makes no distinction between the person and the nature, or between the relative standing of the man and his inner nature.   It has a very defective view of the original constitution given to man in a representative, and it has a tendency to throw men back upon mere mediæval mysticism, and therefore into a semi-legality, most adverse to the doctrine of a free acceptance and to the liberty in Christ, in which the Christian is to stand fast (Gal. v. 1). We shall more fully refer to this school in the notes appended to this volume. But all who are in the habit of reading German works should be aware that this is the theory of the atonement maintained by Menken, Hasenkamp, by Schleiermacher and all his school, by Nitzsch, V. Hofmann, Rudolph Stier, Rothe, Lange, Martensen, Baumgarten, Klaiber, Schöberlein, etc.

thought. This whole theology is contradicted, however, by the present passage, and by other sections of John's Gospel. It will be seen that all the communications of the divine life are connected, according to the teaching of this section, just as they are in the Pauline statements, with the meritorious obedience, the wounds and the blood of Christ, as the price by which they were purchased. God looks at that purchase, when He imparts the divine life, as the sole exclusive ground of His divine supplies of life. And men, too, must also have regard to that purchase as the foundation of all their confidence, and the meritorious cause of all the daily communications of that divine life which they receive.[1]

SEC. XXXIII.—CHRIST GIVING HIS FLESH FOR THE LIFE OF THE WORLD.

" *I am the living bread which came down from heaven. If any man eat of this bread, he shall live for ever : and the bread that I will give is my flesh, which I will give for the life of the world. The Jews therefore strove among themselves, saying, How can this man give us his flesh to eat? Then Jesus said unto them, Verily, verily, I say unto you, Except ye eat the flesh of the Son of Man, and drink His blood, ye have no life in you. Whoso eateth my flesh, and drinketh my blood, hath eternal life; and I will raise him up at the last day. For my flesh is meat indeed, and my blood is drink indeed. He that eateth my flesh, and drinketh my blood, dwelleth in me, and I in him. As the living Father hath sent Me, and I live by* [on account of] *the Father, so he that eateth Me, even he shall live by Me* [on account of Me]." (John vi. 51-57).

This saying is more explicit than the former as to the connection between the vicarious sacrifice of Christ, and the com-

[1] See note K.

munication of spiritual LIFE. It plainly announces that the atonement stands in causal connection with life. The crucified flesh of the Lord is represented as possessing a life-giving influence, and constituting the new and sole fountain from which life can be derived. This passage may be regarded as a key to all the numerous texts in the epistles, which delineate the atoning obedience of Christ as the cause of life to others (Rom. v. 18), or which describe co-crucifixion with Him as the procuring cause of life to His people in and with Him (Rom. vi. 1-11), or speak of His living in us (Gal. ii. 20).

With regard to the occasion of this memorable saying, it may suffice to say that it forms part of a discourse which naturally arose out of the miracle of the loaves. Our Lord had retired from the enthusiastic multitude who were bent on proclaiming Him king, but was again brought in contact with them on the following day in the synagogue at Capernaum, and then led to disclose to them the whole truth. He declares that He should be cut off by violent death, but that His flesh was to be the world's life. They see His meaning, though a certain obscurity was still suffered to rest upon the language, for the obvious purpose of letting history take its unimpeded course. He warned them to seek not the perishable bread, but that bread which endureth to everlasting life, and which He added was to be found by faith alone (ver. 29). He next proceeded, on the ground of a remark which fell from the multitude, to contrast the temporary manna, which the Israelites partook of in the wilderness, with the true bread, or with Himself. He then described the two main elements of the true or essential bread as compared with that which was typical,—showing that (1) it comes down from heaven, and (2) that it gives life to the world (ver. 33). The second element, the life-giving property belonging to it, is further explained as rendering those who eat of it partakers of eternal life, and no more liable to death. This bread is first identified with His own person, and furthermore described as satisfying the hunger of His people, and as quenching their thirst (ver. 35).

Then, after meeting several cavils of the multitude, He takes up the same thought, but makes an advance upon it, by connecting the life with His atoning death (vers. 51-57). He had connected the life with His person ; He next connects it with His atoning work, or with Himself as crucified. The whole section is thus in the highest degree important; setting forth that the bread of life is the Lord Himself as crucified, or Christ presented to us and received in the capacity of an atoning substitute for others.

As the exposition of these verses is very various, and discussed in the interest of different tendencies, we must define their import. The controversies carried on in reference to the Supper brought them under discussion in a sacramental light from the earliest times. Hence it will be necessary to show, before we advance, what they do not mean, as well as what they do mean, that we may guard against such comments as either unduly limit, or pervert and misstate, the force of the words.

1. The expressions cannot refer to the Lord's Supper, which, indeed, was not yet instituted. The symbolic language used in both is very similar : the underlying thoughts are also the same ; and therefore the tendency was by no means unnatural, especially at a time when men began to over-magnify the Supper, to describe its symbolic actions as finding their truth here, and coinciding with these deep references, which exhibit the spiritual mind acting itself out upon Christ crucified.[1] But it is by no means probable that Jesus, when He stood before this unbelieving multitude in the synagogue of Capernaum, and replied to their manifold cavils, had the Supper in His view.

The eating and drinking are adduced as figurative actions, and the terms give no warrant for the exaggeration of sacramental language, as if there was, or could be, any oral eating of the flesh of Christ. The whole previous context is a bold use of apt and significant figures ; and it would be against all the laws of connection and analogy, were we to adopt the literal sense at this point, when the discourse flows on continuously. When we com-

---

[1] This patristic comment has descended through the Greek and Romish churches.

pare these verses with the language held by our Lord at the institution of the Supper, there can be no doubt that they both refer to the vicarious sacrifice, and exhibit that crucified flesh as the food and nourishment of His people. But the allusion here is not to be interpreted in a sacramental sense.

2. Some refer these words, " I am the living bread," to the doctrine of Jesus.[1] But it needs few words to prove that our Lord, in this passage, is not giving a confirmation of His doctrine, but directly referring to His sacrifice, or to the atonement offered for sin in the room and stead of others. They who view the death of Christ in no other light than as an attestation to the truth, are of course compelled to make the doctrine of Jesus, and not His death, their sole nourishment; or they add, perhaps, the example of His perfect human life. But, underlying this comment, is a low view of Christ's person and mission, and a decided tendency to regard His death as not embraced in the grand purpose of redemption, the objective counterpart to our subjective faith, but as the casual result of those efforts which He put forth in His capacity as a great teacher. And an equally shallow notion is entertained as to the LIFE here mentioned, which ought to be interpreted as nothing short of a new creation. To meet all such perversions, it may suffice to state, that, in the context, the Saviour roundly sets forth, not His doctrine, not His example, not His system of ethics, but His flesh offered in sacrifice as the life of the world.

3. A third interpretation is that which refers this language to the incarnation as the sole channel for the communication of life. Life is thus regarded as the one design of His mission, and as an absolute gift. Those interpreters who maintain that a new principle of life stands connected with the incarnation, will have it, that there is no immediate reference in this passage to the death of Christ, but only an invitation to partake of Him by faith in the entire saving manifestation of Himself in the flesh.

---

[1] So Grotius on ver. 51. And the argument is taken from the style of the Jewish teachers, who call it doctrine bread.

According to this view, which is the expression of a widespread modern school, which calls itself believing, Christ's death is not vicarious, but merely the condition for the communication of the saving efficacy of His divine life.[1] It is only the last step in His own preparation or personal self-sanctification to be the life-giver. Thus, not the death of Christ, but the fulness of the divine life residing in Him, and communicated absolutely, becomes the nourishment of His people to life eternal. According to this interpretation, the language is not an expression for His death, but for His whole appearance in the flesh for the life of the world. And the Lord's death comes into consideration, in no other light than as the climax of His holy dedication to God. But this is opposed to the whole phraseology of the passage, which assumes that there is a violent death, separating flesh and blood.

4. Having noticed in order these defective interpretations, it remains that we fix the true interpretation of the words, and especially their reference to His atoning work. The Lord opens the section by a phrase, which, in the original, means that something is said in an explanatory way, while yet the statement is marked out as something new.[2]

As the multitude whom our Lord addressed were the same persons who had witnessed His miracle of the loaves, and as they were going up to the passover (v. 4), it is probable that He drew this peculiar style of address from the sacrifice of which they were going to partake. He intimated, in effect, that He was the reality of the sacrifice, that the paschal lamb was but the shadow, and that they must, with much more eagerness than they looked forward to the passover, eat His flesh and drink His

---

[1] Lücke and De Wette support this interpretation ; and it is held by all who support the mystic theory of the atonement, mentioned by us in the previous section.   But they are not entitled to claim Clemens and Origen as supporters of it.

[2] καὶ δὲ has this meaning.   See Tholuck, Lücke, Winer.   Again, as to the words ἣν ἐγὼ δώσω, which are awanting in Cod. ℵBCDTLT, they are not to be suspected, as they have sufficient evidence in their favour.   The omission of them arose, probably, from the previous ὃν ἐγὼ δώσω, some transcriber thinking them a repetition.

blood. The declaration that they must drink His blood must
have sounded strange in the ears of a Jewish company, accustomed
to look with peculiar awe on blood. But the difficulty is much
diminished, when we reflect that they were on their way to offer
the paschal sacrifice, and that He virtually said to them, " I am
the substance or reality of that type." The passage, thus viewed,
conveys a series of arguments as to the connection between the
atonement and the divine life. They are to be pondered in their
connection as well as in their isolation, as separate statements.
The first announces the necessity of eating His flesh (ver. 53);
the second shows that it is effectual in every case (ver. 54); the
third brings out the truth that His crucified body is the true
bread, or bread indeed (ver. 55); the fourth portrays, that in consequence of eating it, a vital union is maintained between Christ
and all His people (ver. 56); and the fifth shows that His disciples,
eating of His crucified flesh, enter into His reward, and participate
with Him in His premial life (ver. 57). But a few preliminary
remarks may be necessary here in order to place the subject of the
divine life in its proper light and to trace it in its organic connection with that which must be regarded as its meritorious cause.

a. The inquiry into the proper import of the term LIFE, as
used by Christ, is in the highest degree important, in the
present state of exegetical research. That it holds a primary
place in Christ's teaching, and belongs to the fundamental truths
of Christianity, must be evident to all who have devoted any
attention to the words of Christ or His apostles. Little aid, it
has been well remarked, is supplied in this investigation by the
lexicographers of the New Testament language, as they too
much deposit in the words only the opinions of modern times.[1]

---

[1] Thus Olshausen expresses himself, after pointing out the superficial explanations of ζωή given by Schleusner, of whom he says :—"At omnino virum
doctissimum ignorasse, quid sit ζωή interpretationes passim ab ipso propositæ
aperte docent." See Olshausen, *de notione vocis ζωή in libris N. T.*, in his
Opuscula Theologica, 1834, p. 185 ; also Brückner, *de notione vocis ζωή quæ in
N. T. libris legitur, Commentatio*, Lips. 1858. I may also refer to the brief
Exegetisch-Dogmatische Entwickelung der N. T. Begriffe von ζωή ἀνάστασις und

The doctrine of Jesus, as derived from this and cognate sayings, may be given in a few words, though the subject is too wide to be fully entered upon in the present discussion. He presupposes man as without life, in the high and proper sense of the term, nay, as alienated from the life of God. The language which Jesus holds on the subject of spiritual life takes for granted that we are involved in death; the term employed by Him to designate that separation from God which sin involves (John v. 24), and which is defined as the condition where men have not the love of God in them (John v. 42). This leaves the heart vacant for any sinful substitute. The fact that life is procured and imparted by the Lord, presupposes a condition of spiritual death. For, according to a canon, of easy and universal application, constantly applied by Augustin and Calvin in their interpretation of the divine word, whatever is freely provided and bestowed by God, is a something of which man is destitute, considered in himself.

b. As to this spiritual life which the Lord came to restore, it consists in reunion to God, and in that inward renovation or new creation which is consequent on reunion to God, the fountain of life. The incarnate Son, having life in Himself, as the Father has life in Himself, and able, on this account, to act the part of a mediator (John v. 26), interposed between a dead humanity and its Creator, in order to be a new source of life. The eternal life was manifested (1 John i. 1-3); and that which had been intercepted by sin was again communicated. The

---

κρίσις, by Dr. A. Maier, Freiburg, 1840; and to Rauwenhoff's treatise, *De Vita in homine æterna, peccato oppressa a Christo restituta*, Leidæ, 1857. But more important and profound than any or all of these is Vitringa's sketch of the spiritual life, in his *Typus Theologiæ practica sive de Vita Spirituali*, Franeq. 1716. It is the more necessary to refer to these discussions and treatises on this subject, as the whole current of modern theology runs in this direction, and all depends on the true idea of LIFE, which, after all, is of a superficial character in the Schleiermacherian theology. One sentence of Vitringa may be quoted to show how strongly he insisted upon the point ignored by the new theology : "Primus respectus in vita spirituali est causæ ejus meritoriæ quam Scriptura ostendit esse obedientiam Filii Dei ab ipso secundum leges æterni pacti cum Patre initi præstitam ad mortem, imo ad mortem crucis." (Cap. iii. p. 27.)

term LIFE denotes much more than deliverance from misery. It means, as used by our Lord and His apostles, the restoration of something that had been forfeited, nay, something higher than the primeval life of Adam. Nor will it suffice to say that it implies no more than a restored right to life. For though some identify *forgiveness* and *quickening*, as used by the sacred writers (Col. ii. 13), an accurate examination of the passages where the words occur, will satisfy every man that life is consequent upon forgiveness, or the reward for a service rendered. It is the accepted person that has passed from death to life (John v. 24).

Christ describes Himself as the life (xiv. 6), and as having life in Himself (v. 26). And He has become incarnate for the purpose of imparting the Life which He has and which He is (xii. 50). He describes Himself accordingly as dispensing the bread of life (vi. 35) and the water of life (iv. 10); and they who abide in Him and follow Him, are described as having the light of life (viii. 12). He thus nourishes those who partake of the bread of life. But it was not by His incarnation or by His personal appearance alone that He became the Life of the world. He is the resurrection and the life to unnumbered millions of redeemed men (John xi. 25), only as He laid down His life that He might take it again (x. 17). That He might be in a position to give life to those whose persons were under condemnation and whose natures were alienated from the life of God, He must needs give His flesh for the life of the world (vi. 51). As the Righteousness and Life, He was able to overcome sin and death : but He must needs subject Himself to the penalty of death by taking on Himself the guilt which had been the cause of separating between God and man. It is as the Lamb of God that He gives life to the world (i. 29). Only the Good Shepherd who gave His life for the sheep (x. 15) is in a position to bring back life to those who are dead in trespasses and sins. Many are the passages and various are the terms which are used by Him to express the same idea. He has presented Himself to us as the great personal sacrifice who in His twofold capacity as

priest and sacrifice, sanctified Himself for His own (xvii. 19);
as the friend who with greater love than human friendship ever
knew laid down His life for His friends (xv. 13); as the true
Paschal Lamb sacrificed for us (xix. 36); as the grain of wheat
which falling into the ground and dying cannot abide alone
(xii. 24); as the Saviour of the world (iv. 42); as the substitute who was in the divine purpose to die not for the Jewish
nation alone, but that the children of God might be gathered
into one (xi. 51); as the only-begotten Son who was given
up to death to deliver others from death and bring them to
everlasting life (iii. 16). He commends Himself to us as the
eternal life personally considered, as the meritorious cause of
life, as the dispenser of life; and he who believes in Him hath
everlasting life (John v. 24). Faith is, in one aspect of it, the
outcome of this new life, and in another the means or instrument by which it is received. Life, in a word, is, in its divine
side, nothing but the immanence of Christ, or the abiding presence
of Christ in a believing heart; and the life develops itself in
love, and light, joy, and holiness. But this testimony of the
Lord emphatically declares that the supply of life, far from
being an absolute or an unpurchased gift, was possible only by
means of His atonement; that it was secured by a work of
obedience; and that it is forfeited no more. Not only the
primeval life which was enjoyed in fellowship with God is
restored, but the premial life which awaited man after a period
of probation, and which would have been conferred had he continued in his first estate, is procured and conferred by the atonement of the incarnate Son in the room of sinners. In securing
this result, the Prince of Life encountered death, and rendered
an equivalent for the guilt of mankind; for the dominion of
death could give place to a reign of life in no other way. And
they who, through the influence of modern speculations, regard
Christ only as a great teacher, or a mere example, have never
understood the impediment to be surmounted, nor the reversal
of the curse which was required.

The Lord expressly declares, that He GAVE HIS FLESH by an act of self-oblation for the life of the world; and the uniform sense of the expression denotes a priestly act of oblation (Gal. i. 4; Eph. v. 2). Hence we may say, that, as the fall brought death, so the atonement has brought life; and that the restoration of life, forfeited by sin, was the express design or end of Christ's atoning work. The atonement had specially in view, among other objects contemplated in the divine counsels, to quicken those who were alienated from the life of God, and thus to confer a premial life. Thus God pours in a new life upon dead humanity from the crucified flesh of Christ, to be forfeited no more.

c. But the Lord Jesus next proceeds to speak of the "eating of His flesh" and of the "drinking of His blood." That the language is metaphorical, scarcely needs to be proved. The expressions, the *eating of His flesh* and the *drinking of His blood*, are used interchangeably with believing in the previous context (vers. 35, 40, 47), and they must be so accepted here. These figurative terms imply that men are to believe on Him as giving His flesh for the life of the world, and that they are to receive the atonement with the same eagerness with which a hungry man partakes of food. The doctrine of Christ's sacrifice is the principal matter in the way of procuring the donation of spiritual life; and it is never ignored in any of those inward blessings of renovation, love, growth, zeal, and strength, which are comprehended in the spiritual life, and go to make up our idea of this life. It is unwarrantable, then, to interpret this figurative "eating" as the general reception of the truth, without any special appropriation of the atoning death of Christ. On the contrary, it is Christ's atonement, or His crucified flesh, with which faith is first occupied, for the purpose of attaining this inner life. And the Lord virtually says, "By this sacrifice of mine I procure Life; and, not only so, I become, the true Bread of Life; and every one who will live appropriates my atonement as offered for the life of the world."

This language implies, that the atonement not only holds the most important place in the moral government of God, but that, in an individual point of view, sin must be atoned for, and the person accepted, before there is, or can be, free course for the communication of life. It is not only an expedient in the general scheme of God's moral rule, but a personal necessity as well. And this latter point of view, too much omitted or merged in the general one, is the special truth on which the emphasis is laid in this testimony of our Lord. Thus the words, " eating the flesh and drinking the blood " of Christ for life, announce that we do not bring, but receive ; that we do not work for life, but enter into a finished work, the already accomplished death of Christ.

But as faith is figuratively represented by eating and drinking, we may ask, How is the analogy between the two to be defined ? It is as follows : As food has a nourishing property, and effectually acts upon the life, the crucified Christ stands in the same relation. The most nutritive food cannot avail, unless we partake of it ; and no one is benefited by Christ's death, unless we believe on Him as crucified for us. Faith has, in this way, the same relation to the spiritual life that the eating of bread has to the temporal life ; for faith is the means of receiving and enjoying the life-giving property of His death ; and no figure could more strikingly set forth the necessity of faith.

Enough has been brought out to show that the atonement of Christ is offered for the life of the world, and that, to have life, men must eat that crucified flesh ; in other words, must believe that redemption and acceptance are effected by His atoning death. This is put in a personal rather than in a general light in the passage under consideration. As to the subsequent verses, as our object was only to gather up this testimony into a focus, we shall but briefly notice them.

(1.) In the saying, " He that eateth my flesh HATH eternal life," the emphasis is laid specially upon the present tense. The firm and secure possession of life is founded on what He obtained by His atonement for His people.

(2.) This crucified flesh of Christ, and His blood poured out, are designated true bread and drink, or that essential food that comes up to the idea (ver. 55). Or if we apply the allusion to the food of the sacrifices, it will mean that He was their great antitype or reality. Whatever can be affirmed of food may be affirmed in a still higher significance of Him; for if food is the God-appointed means for sustaining natural life, that crucified flesh was the only means for imparting and sustaining, in the higher sense, the spiritual life.

(3.) This participation, furthermore, brings union of the closest kind (ver. 56). The passage intimates that the Lord becomes united to His people in the same way as he who eats is united to the food he eats. And Christ, on His part, most closely unites Himself to them. They are so joined in their life and fortunes as to be for ever one, not only in this world, but in the world to come. Plainly, the figure is continued; and the allusion intimates that food, so assimilated, sustains the receiver's life.

(4.) The Lord winds up the passage by the remarkable utterance already explained by us in a previous section; "he that eateth Me, even he shall live on account of Me" (ver. 57). The statement is, that His people live because of Him, or on His account, as the possessor of a premial life, which is conferred upon Him as the due reward of His mission. "He that eateth Me shall live on my account," is the proper translation of the words; and they will bear no other sense.

A few words will suffice to exhibit the peculiar character of this life of God. Thus in one passage the Lord puts life and the knowledge of God in a connection which demands a strict investigation; "this is life eternal, that they might know Thee the only true God, and Jesus Christ, whom Thou hast sent" (John xvii. 3). What does that passage mean? Many accept it as meaning that the knowledge of God and of His Christ is the way to eternal salvation. They think this exposition simple and obvious, and argue that no reason exists for accepting another interpretation of the passage, as it forcibly contrasts the Christian religion, both with the folly of the Gentiles in worshipping many gods, and with the error of the Jews in refusing to acknowledge Jesus as the Christ. It is not denied that we may give the passage a sufficiently appropriate sense on this acceptation, if we understand a knowledge which produces a salutary influence on the heart and walk. But confessedly this gives no exact meaning to the final particle (ἵνα). Nay, it ignores the particle of design altogether. Hence another exposition may be accepted which is more strict and faithful to the import of the words, as follows: " This is life eternal, that they may (are destined to) know Thee." According to this interpretation, which is preferable, we conclude that eternal life consists in a clear and purified knowledge of God, and of His Son who was sent into the world to save sinners. The truth imperfectly known here shall hereafter be fully perceived by the saved, and God shall be fully glorified by them. The main scope of Christ's labours was to make men know God, and to fill them with the homage and adoration due to Him; but as this knowledge should ever be defective here, a perfect knowledge of the Father and of Christ, and of the near relation between them, awaits them hereafter.

This life may be defined on the one side by the in-being of Christ in His people (Eph. iii. 17), and by their inseparable union to Him (John xiv. 20). And to know this in an increasing measure constitutes no small portion of their vital exercise. Ushered into the gracious presence of their God who is the fountain of life, they receive a divine life, which unfolds itself even here below, in an enlightened understanding, in an ardent love, and in a joyful hope.

The new life is seen in the understanding, the eye of the soul, as it finds scope for unwearied contemplation on the perfections of the Creator,—on the person, offices, relations, and works of the Redeemer,—and on the mission of the Comforter. And though at first touching but the surface of things, the mind is step by step enlarged, and led to survey the treasures of wisdom and knowledge in the Lord.

Another degree of the divine life may be discerned in the ardent love which fills the soul as with a penetrating flame. This stimulates them to embrace and extol the glorious Father, who Himself is described as love. They come, in part, to live the life of God who is love (1 John iv. 16).

And from all this arises an unspeakable joy, another aspect of this life in God; for as sorrow is the death of the soul, so joy unspeakable and full of glory is the soul's life.[1]

CHAPTER V.

THE RELATION OF THE ATONEMENT TO OTHER INTERESTS IN THE UNIVERSE.

SEC. XXXIV.—TESTIMONIES SHOWING THE RELATION OF THE ATONEMENT TO OTHER INTERESTS IN THE UNIVERSE.

HAVING considered the sayings of Christ, which show the effects of the atonement on the individual, both in an objective and subjective point of view, we have next to consider it in its bearing on other interests and relations in the universe. It must be regarded as a narrow and unbiblical theory, which limits the whole effects of the atonement to man. Though the objective acceptance of our persons, and the inward renovation of our natures, together with the provision for a life of worship, which we have already exhibited from particular sayings of Jesus, may be considered as the proximate results, as they may be said to be the first and main concern of sinful creatures, yet these are by no means all the effects that were contemplated by the atonement, or are accomplished by it. It will be found that our Lord constantly spoke, with His eye upon all the relations of the universe, and with the consciousness that His work had a reference to them all. Those utterances from His lips emphatically show that He realized them all, and that He

---

[1] See the last chapter of Vitringa's excellent treatise, *De Vita Spirituali.*

lived amid these various relations, in a way very little apprehended by us.

The atonement—the great central fact in the history of the
world—had a perceptible influence on all the relations which
may be said to meet on the earth, or to have any connection
with mundane things.   Thus, (1) the atonement has an intimate
connection with the overthrow of Judaism and the temple-
worship, to pave the way for Christ's kingdom being set up in
its new form on the earth.   The cross is the basis or the sole
foundation of His throne; for it was not upon His teaching, or
upon His example, that His kingdom was reared, but upon His
atoning work.   (2) This atonement was the great foundation of
Christ's relation to the sheep ; it giving the Shepherd a flock,
and laying the basis of the whole relation between His flock and
Him.   (3) The atonement makes a pathway for the communication of the Spirit, which a fallen race could not otherwise
have possessed.   (4) The atonement of the Lord, or the finished
work of redemption, glorifies God on the earth, or gives the
supreme God the glory due to His name, as the tribute or
revenue from His creatures.   (5) The Lord Jesus, by means of
His humiliation unto death, opened heaven, and brought men
and angels, heretofore separated and estranged, into a new relation.   (6) The atonement is called the judgment of the world,
and the victory by which the Lord overcame the world.   (7)
The atoning death of Jesus is declared to have judged and cast
out the prince of this world.   (8) It overcomes the power of
death and the fear of death.

Thus, the atonement is represented by our Lord as having a
most decisive influence upon all these various interests.   In a
word, it is the central fact of God's present procedure or moral
rule in the universe, and that on which all depends.   Its effect
is felt also to the widest circumference and ramification of
mundane relations.   The fall and the atonement thus constitute
the two facts or pivots of human history,—they are the turning-
points of the world's destiny; and as there are but two repre-

sentative men, as well as two facts in history, and two families under these two heads, the deeds of these two, in their representative position, may be said to decide upon the fortunes of all connected with them ; that is, may be said conclusively to determine their lot.

We shall briefly notice, but not quite in the above-named order, the effect or influence of the atonement on all these other interests in the universe.

SEC. XXXV.—THE DEATH OF CHRIST IN CONNECTION WITH THE
RAISING OF THE TEMPLE OF GOD.

" *Destroy* [break down] *this temple, and in three days I will
raise it up.*"   (John ii. 19.)

The allusions which were made to His death in the early part of our Lord's ministry were, for the most part, darker and less obvious than they afterwards became. It was His aim, during the course of His teaching, not to anticipate unduly the historic course of events, but rather to furnish matter which might serve to enable His disciples, after the accomplishment of events, to compare His sayings with the fact of His atoning death.

The passage under our consideration has not been sufficiently viewed, as it should have been, in connection with the doctrine of the atonement. It will be found, however, when understood aright, to contain a most important testimony, whether we look at the nature or at the effects of Christ's redemption-work. It declares not only that Christ had power to lay down His life and to restore it, but also that His death should found a new theocracy and a new worship. It is much akin, therefore, to the saying, spoken in connection with the institution of the Supper, that His blood, shed for many for the remission of sins, should found the new covenant. These two testimonies have much in common ; and this passage may be called a key to all those sayings, both diversified and frequently recurring, which either describe Christ as the head of the corner (Acts iv. 11), or display a spiritual temple (Eph. ii. 21), or set forth a new gospel worship (Heb. viii. 13). But it will be necessary, first of all, to ascertain the exact meaning of the words, and to apprehend the proper point of them, before we consider their import or scope as a testimony to the atonement.

The occasion which gave rise to this declaration was as follows : The Lord had purified the temple by a very arresting display of holy zeal for His Father's house, the first time He appeared in it after the commencement of His public ministry. The Jews of all classes, as well as the actual desecrators, had been paralyzed and awe-struck by this display of zeal; but they no sooner recovered themselves, than they demanded from Him some sign or miracle to warrant this assumption of authority; seeming to indicate that they would not call it in question, if He could show His authorization, or furnish evidence that He came with a divine commission. Our Lord gave them a fit sign, though a future one,—a sign not foreign to His Messianic work, but constituting its very essence, and which, when it should occur, would fully vindicate His authority for the step which He had just taken. But He couches the remark in highly typical language, and takes for granted that the hostility of the Jews, then indicated for the first time, would never cease till they had compassed His death.

This was a saying of which the Jews could never afterwards get rid. They well saw, that though they could not penetrate into its full significance, the statement contained a deeply mysterious meaning, and one that foreboded the overthrow of their temple. We find that, three years afterwards, the false witnesses at the trial of Jesus bring up this remark in an incorrect form, —one witness alleging that He said, " I will destroy" (Mark xiv. 58); another representing Him as saying, "I am able to destroy" (Matt. xxvi. 61). A second time we hear it in the taunting words addressed to Him as He hung on the cross: " Thou that destroyest the temple, and buildest it in three days,

save Thyself, and come down from the cross" (Mark xv. 29).   A
third echo of it we discover in the precaution to set a watch at
His grave, because He had foretold His resurrection on the third
day (Matt. xxvii. 63).   A fourth time it is recalled, in connection
with the trial and martyrdom of Stephen (Acts vi. 13, 14).   In
a word, they could not shake it off.   And the narrative of John,
written subsequently to the other Gospels and filling up what
was awanting at many points, gives us the original saying to
which all these references are made.

To these words of the Lord the evangelist appends his inspired
commentary : " He spake of the temple of His body ; " which
must be held to be conclusive as to the true significance and
import of the saying.   The perverted meaning or false construction put upon the saying by the Jews would seem to need no
refutation as running counter to John's narrative and comment ;
and we should have thought that every Christian would at once
reject it.   But, strange to say, not a few modern interpreters[1]
have ventured to go so far as to call in question the correctness
of John's comment, to repudiate his explanation, and to put
upon the words of Jesus a meaning which is very much akin to
the false interpretation of the Jews, who sometimes blindly, and
not unfrequently by design, were wont to pervert His language.
But there cannot be two opinions, on the part of any man imbued
with adequate ideas of inspiration, as to the authority of John's
commentary, as to the unwarrantableness of expounding the
Saviour's words after this rationalistic fashion ; that is, of expounding them merely to the effect that He was going to break
down the old form of religion, and to erect in its room and stead
a better and more spiritual religion within a short space of time.
That exposition, to which some devout minds[2] have unhappily
adhered, is untenable in every light in which it can be regarded,
whether we look at the words themselves, which will not bear

1 Herder was the first to begin this false interpretation.
2 This lax view is held by Neander in his *Life of Jesus*, by Lücke on John, and
by Bleek. On the other hand, Oostersee, in his *Leven van Jesus*, p. 61, strongly
maintains the opposite.

it, or at the authority of the evangelist, as a few remarks will suffice to show. (1) The Lord Jesus does not speak of a short space of time, but of the three days between His death and His resurrection; (2) He does not speak of one temple broken down, and of another and a different one raised up, but of His own body; and then, (3) as to the accuracy of the evangelist, we must hold that, writing, as he did, under the plenary guidance of the Spirit, he unquestionably gives us the true scope and import of the words.

But while we must abide most strictly by the comment of the inspired evangelist, as literally accurate, this by no means precludes all other reference to the stone temple as a type; and this ulterior reference must, we think, be included, if we would expound it aright. There was a one-sidedness in the view of almost all the older commentators, at least thus far, that they forbore to connect any further meaning with the words; and that, while correctly enough expounding them according to the leading thread supplied by John, they stopped short at a point, where the sense is not exhausted. They saw no allusion to the material temple. They satisfied themselves with a supposed metaphor,—some accepting it, as did the patristic writers, as a fitting figure or metaphor to portray the incarnation,[1] others bringing together similar phrases descriptive of the human body, either from Jewish or classical antiquity. They thus lost sight of the type, and omitted the link between the shadow and the substance. But we are warranted to hold that the Lord connected a further meaning with His words; and this interpretation is absolutely necessary, if the sign or miracle given to warrant Christ's assumption of authority on that occasion was to have any connection with the act which it was meant to sanction.[2] It will not do to assert that Jesus does not elsewhere call

---

[1] Thus, in the Nestorian discussions, it was much canvassed whether the person of Christ was only the inhabited temple of God, or ναός.

[2] The modern commentators are generally disposed to take in this additional idea, e.g. Hengstenberg, Luthardt, Schmid, *Biblische Theologie N. T.* p. 223, Lange, Stier, Riggenbach; and it is necessary to accept some such further reference, from the fact we have stated above.

His body the temple (see, however, John i. 14). It cannot be forgotten that the one was the type, and the other the reality— as much a type as was the lamb,—a pledge, too, and a symbol of God's continued habitation in the midst of the Jews, and also of the acceptance of their worship. Thus He said on one occasion : in this place is one greater than the temple (Matt. xii. 6). The fate of that temple, and the fate of the religion that stood connected with it, and was, in a manner, based upon it, was decided by the fate of Christ's body. There was a deep connection between the two, though unintelligible to the Jews.

Nor was this an unheard of consummation, of which no intimation had been given. Christ had been foretold in prophecy as the builder of the temple of the Lord (Zech. vi. 12); and the present passage shows that He laid its foundation in His atoning death. The atonement stood related to it as cause to effect,— no atonement, no temple or dwelling-place of God among men. But here God and man meet—here heaven and earth are joined; this is the gate of heaven for man, and this the place of condescending revelation and communication for God; for in Christ, as the true temple, dwells all the fulness of the Godhead bodily (Col. ii. 9).

All this is made more obvious by the allusions to the tabernacle or temple; which had been a visible pledge of God's covenant relation to Israel, and of His actual residence among them, not indeed in the local sense—for in that sense He is not confined to heaven itself,—but in the sense of free and gracious manifestation. The temple had been the place of revelation, the audience-chamber where He received His people's supplications, and heard them, and to which they turned, when far away from it; the seat of rule from which He governed; the place of worship where His people communed with Him, and He with them. All this had been due to one fact, that there was instituted in it a blood-sprinkled mercy-seat, or propitiatory; and there He dwelt between the cherubim. Now, it is on this same ground, and for this same reason, that Christ is to mankind

the true temple or the dwelling-place of God. His body crucified and risen, is the one medium of communion between God
and man, as well as between man and God; and the acceptance
of all gospel worship depends simply on its relation to Him as
the sole atonement for sin, and temple of God.

We have next to notice, however, how far this text may be
regarded as supplying a testimony to the atonement, both in its
NATURE and EFFECTS.

1. The words before us, setting forth the voluntary surrender
of Christ's life, and the crime of men as accessory to that death,
bear witness to the *nature* of the human instrumentality used
in the matter of Christ's atonement. It is not put as a bare
future, nor as a merely hypothetical statement, when our Lord
says, "destroy,"—it is a permission, in the course of providence,
or a judicial and permissive imperative. That is the true meaning, as intimated by the word here used in the imperative,[1]
"destroy." The meaning is not "if you destroy this temple:"
they as a people would not lift a hand against the temple, the
centre of their worship. But the meaning is: "Go on in your
course of action and accomplish that deed which will prove the
overthrow of the theocracy and of the temple, which is its visible
symbol and pledge." The theocracy was to go down in the overthrow or dissolution of the temple; and when we inquire by
what act this was to be consummated, the answer is, not by increasing and renewed profanations, such as the buying and sell-
ing which Jesus checked, but by the rejection of the Messiah.
This was intimated in Daniel and Zechariah in terms sufficiently
express. Thus Daniel speaks of Messiah being cut off, and the
destroying of the city and the sanctuary (Dan. ix. 26). Zechariah describes the ruin of the nation under the emblem of devouring fire, and the cause of the destruction is there mentioned,
the rejection of the Christ, and the price at which they prized

---

[1] The verb here used, λύσατε, is plainly much more than, *if you destroy, 1 will
raise up;* it is a permissive imperative, like πληρώσατε τὸ μέτρον (Matt. xxiii. 32),
ποίησον τάχιον (John. xiii. 27).

Him (Zech. xi. 1-13). To kill the Prince of Life, and to destroy the theocracy and the temple, were thus synonymous and coincident. By cutting off the Messiah, their national covenant-standing was to cease, and the kingdom of God was to be taken from them and given to a nation bringing forth the fruits thereof (Matt. xxi. 43).

The whole phraseology implies that the Lord possessed a full and independent dominion over His own life; that the Jews could not break down that temple of His body without receiving leave or permission from Himself; and that both its dissolution and its re-erection were equally at His own disposal. The argument is cogent, and it is obviously this: If He could raise up that temple by His own divine Sonship, or by the omnipotent fiat of His divine nature, it indisputably follows, that His life, without leave from Himself, could not have been taken from Him. The "I" is necessarily different from the temple, and also distinct from the human soul; plainly alluding to Him who was in the beginning with God. So voluntary was the Lord, indeed, in every step connected with the atonement, that nothing befell Him, or could befall, which He did not perfectly foresee, and cheerfully consent to undergo. Of all the beings in the universe, He alone had perfect and unchallengeable power over Himself, whether respect is had to His giving up to death the body which He had taken into union with Himself, or to the fact of raising it up again.

But the words contain, too, a further reference to the flagrant crime of the Jews in putting Him to death. This allusion requires no little delicacy and precision in our exposition. To what peculiar phase of Jewish guilt is allusion here made? Our Lord does not refer in this place to the fact that He was appointed to be cut off by violence at the hand of men as contrasted with dying on His bed, or with being struck down by the bolt of God. Though the atonement specially consisted in what was inflicted upon the substitute by the hand of God, it is always taken for granted—whether we look at the terms of the first promise in the garden,[1] or at the language of all type and prophecy—that He was to die by a violent death, and die by human hands. But that is not to be regarded as the precise idea of the passage. Nor is the remark designed to show merely the enormity or virulence of sin in general; though the treatment of the incarnate Son shows that sin is of such a character, that it rises even to Deicide when a proper occasion occurs, and that instead of hailing perfect virtue in its human ideal, and adoring the fulness of the Godhead bodily, the human heart only discovers all the more its deep enmity. It is true, sin here abounded in its highest conceivable degree, and grace much more abounded in overcoming it. But neither is that the thought. Rather, it is the peculiar sin of the Jewish people in the national rejection of their Messiah, the God of Israel, to which our Lord refers. He intimates a progressive profanation of all that was holy, culminating in the rejection of their divine Messiah; and He bids them fill up the measure of their profanation.

We may here trace the various steps of this national rejection. He was the despised and rejected of men, from the very day when He came officially to His own. They could not bear their own theocracy embodied and realized in Jesus. They said, in the language of the parable, " This is the heir; come let us kill Him." This comes out unmistakeably at this first passover, as the context proves. And when Pilate, by a higher guidance, gave a true interpretation or voice to their violence, saying, " Shall I crucify your King ?" they only clamoured the more for His speedy execution, and desired a murderer to be granted to them in preference to their Messiah, the Prince of Life. In this text, then, our Lord, with a full appreciation of their national rejection already indicated and begun, virtually says, " As you have already desecrated the type, go on to break down the reality (λύσατε); that is desecrate the temple of your Messiah's body, which is the grand antitype to which the tabernacle and temple

---

[1] " It shall bruise thy head, and thou shalt *bruise* his heel " (Gen. iii. 15). The same violent death was adumbrated by the sacrifice, which *must be killed*.

alike pointed, and which gave to this stone temple all its significance and value." The fate of these two was connected, in the
most close and indissoluble manner, as type and antitype; and
hence the rejection of the Christ, ending in His death, was of
necessity followed by the outward dissolution of the stone temple,
which was now no more the house of God, or the centre of unity for
all true worshippers. Our Lord, accordingly, when He took final
leave of the temple, to tread its courts no more, calls it *their house*
—not His Father's: "*your* house is left unto you desolate " (Matt.
xxiii. 38). But not only so : the fate of that temple was also
connected with the national rejection of Israel as the theocratic
people who had long been in national covenant with God. Henceforth, the Sinaitic covenant was to be at an end, and Israel as a
nation cast off, till the fulness of the Gentiles should enter (Rom.
ii. 25). The kingdom of God was henceforth to be taken from
them, and was no more, during the ages of their rejection and
dispersion, to have a peculiarly national footing among them.
Jerusalem, as well as the Mosaic worship, was to perish in the
fall.

2. This passage, moreover, alludes to the *effects* of the atonement, as well as to its nature. With regard to these effects or
fruits of Christ's atoning death, they are general as well as personal; and here we have presented to us a new temple, a new
people of God, and a new theocracy, not bounded by the narrow
limits of a single nation, but co-extensive with the number of
believers out of every tribe and people. The mode of restoring
the temple, or of raising it up, must be in keeping with the
mode of its dissolution. The temple was the habitation of
Jehovah, God of Israel, in a symbolic sense. The Lord's body
was the true tabernacle which the Lord pitched, and therefore
the dwelling-place of God in its highest meaning, the meeting-
place between God and man. His resurrection body realizes
the idea of what was symbolically portrayed in the stone
temple.

Thus the death of Christ, considered as the adequate atonement for sin, laid the true foundation of the universal Church, exploding the narrow particularism of Judaism, and breaking down the middle wall of partition (Eph. ii. 14, 15); while the material fabric, though it continued to stand for forty years alongside of the new order of things, had in fact ceased to have any value or validity, and in truth was now become a common place. The person of Christ crucified, the atonement for sin, and risen from the dead, was henceforth to become the great centre of unity, and not the stone temple; and the Lord virtually said, "I will, by my atoning death, and in my resurrection life, erect the true temple of God, which shall, in the first instance, be my risen body, and shall, in the next place (because also called my body), be that great redeemed company of which I am the head and centre." There was thus formed a new temple, and a new people of God, in the midst of which God was henceforth to dwell as in His true sanctuary, and where He was to have His perpetual abode. If the old theocracy was dissolved, and the old national covenant ended as it was made at Sinai,[1] this was only that it might be replaced by a new and a universal one.

SEC. XXXVI.—THE ATONEMENT OF CHRIST DECIDING THE JUDICIAL
PROCESS TO WHOM THE WORLD SHALL BELONG.

*" Now is the judgment of this world : now shall the prince of this
world be cast out."*   (John xii. 31.)

This pointed and sententious saying brings out the idea that the atonement was to decide the grand question, or the judicial

---

[1] Ebrard says (*wissenschaftliche Kritik der Evangelischen Geschichte*, p. 287) that our Lord understands, by the re-erection, the founding of a *new covenant* effected by His resurrection. I may further add, that this dissolution of the Sinaitic covenant, which was only a temporary economy, did not disannul the promises made to Abraham (Gal. iii. 17), and leaves untouched all the questions as to the constant remnant (Rom. xi. 5), and of their being a holy root (Rom. xi. 17), and beloved (ver. 28), and their final reingrafting, and the new covenant to be made with them (vers. 24-27).

process which had long been pending, as to the party to whom the world should be awarded. It is assumed that this had, as it were, been long under litigation in a court of law, and that it was now to receive its final and irreversible decision in connection with the atonement.

As to the occasion on which these words were spoken, it was when the Lord made His entry into Jerusalem, and after that soul-trouble by which He had been moved and well-nigh overborne,—a trouble which interrupted His train of thought, and brought home to Him the sense of divine wrath. The terror of death, armed as it was with all the sting and curse of the violated law, and confronted as a very different enemy from what He is to any of His people, could not turn Him aside from the path of obedience. When repose and composure returned, He announced, with the calm consciousness of an already anticipated victory, that various results or fruits stood in causal connection with His death. A whole series of sayings are uttered by Him, not only descriptive of His triumph over the world and over Satan, but also setting forth that His mediatorial dominion and the attractive power by which He should draw sinners to Himself, are all based on His atoning death. Up till now the world had belonged to one who was undoubtedly its lord, and who is called by Christ the prince of this world, in as far as he held it by right of conquest. Not that our Lord, in so speaking, meant to acknowledge His title as either legitimate or irreversible. He meant that He had succeeded, in virtue of a successful usurpation, in becoming the world's actual potentate, and in making men His lawful captives. But a new and just adjudication was at hand. This text may be taken as a key to all those passages which represent Christ as the appointed heir of all things (Heb. i. 2), and as Lord of all (Acts. x. 36), and as having power over all flesh (John xvii. 2).

With regard to the expression "the world," we must understand it generally. This appears from the fact, that it was uttered by Christ in connection with the arrival of the Greeks or Gentiles, who desired to see Him. It is a general name, as here used, taken simply for the world of mankind, irrespective of its condition, or of the usual accessory idea of its being the evil world, whether Jewish or Gentile. Those expositors who limit the allusion to the idea that it is the world rejecting Christ and serving sin, have been swayed by the interpretation which they put upon the word *judgment* as meaning condemnation. But for that interpretation there is no good ground, as we shall immediately show. As the sense depends, however, on an accurate apprehension of the term *judgment*, we must, first of all, determine its meaning as used in this verse.

1. Some will have it, that the term *judgment* in this passage must be taken as denoting condemnation or punishment.[1] They argue, with a certain amount of plausibility, that as Jesus frequently uses both the noun and the verb in that acceptation, the word must be so understood in the passage before us (compare John iii. 19, John v. 24, John xii. 47, 48). But it must be further observed, that the expositors who so interpret the term are, in great measure, influenced by the sense put upon the conjoined word, "the world," which they regard as the Christ-rejecting world. Sometimes they argue from the word "judgment," in order to prove that the term "world" must here mean the Christ-rejecting world. Sometimes, again, they argue from the latter term, understood as has been mentioned above, in order to prove that the judgment must be condemnation.

2. The judgment here mentioned has been regarded by other expositors as denoting the just sentence executed upon sin, but not upon the sinner himself.[2] An attempt has been made by some able advocates of the atonement, in the true sense, to prove that, in the present passage, the allusion is to the sentence of condemnation upon sin vicariously endured, inasmuch as the death of Christ was in reality a witness of the divine justice,

---

[1] So Vossius, Vinke, etc.
[2] So Gess, in his article on the atonement. He makes it a display of justice, but on Christ, not on the world.

and He bore sin in His own body on the tree.   However true
and precious that doctrine is, and however clearly taught in
other passages of Scripture, plainly it is not the truth in this
verse.   Though the sin of mankind was condemned in Christ's
flesh during His humiliation, it would be a violence to language,
or an imported and deposited idea brought from another connection, were we to force that meaning upon the words here.

3. Other eminent expositors will have it, that when our
Lord speaks of the judgment of the world, He refers to the
reformation and deliverance of the world.[1]   They argue to this
effect from the Hebrew usage of the word, as well as from the
fact that the world was to be restored to its legitimate order,
and that it was the death of Christ that causally or meritoriously inaugurated this new state of things.   They hold that the
allusion, therefore, is not so much to a single and separate result,
as to the continuous effect of the death of Christ in all those
results connected with the renovation or deliverance which we
daily see around us.   But, however much this interpretation
may approximate to the true meaning, it puts a quite incorrect
meaning on the words which our Lord employs.

4. The true meaning is, that the hour had come, when the
grand adjudication of a judicial process was to take place, that
should decide at once and for ever the question to whom the
world should belong, as its prince.[2]   In the judicial process
which was pending at that moment before the court of last
resort, the great decision or sentence was immediately to be
given; and our Lord in substance says, " It is now to be finally
determined to whom this world shall rightfully belong,—whether
it is to remain in the hand of its present prince, or belong to Me
as its owner and its heir for ever.   The final award on this

---

[1] So Calvin, and also Grotius, who says, *in libertatem vindicare.*

[2] This is Bengel's happy comment, both in his *Gnomon* and in his notes to his
German version of the N. T.   In the former he says : " est genitivus objecti ;
judicium de hoc mundo, quis post hæc jure sit obtenturus mundum."   In the
latter, his brief note is : "ein gerichtlicher Process und Urtheil wem die Welt
gehöre mir, oder ihrem bisherigen Fürsten."

great process is now to be given." The language is thus unmistakeably taken from a cause in court, and describes a
judicial process, awaiting its final and irreversible adjudication.

When our Lord says, "*Now* is the judgment of this world,"
the immediate context demands consideration. It shows, as
may easily be gathered from the passage, that the direct allusion
is to the soul-trouble, the commencement of His agony, and the
prelude of His death, which was destined to accomplish that
result. The *now* must be taken as referring to His present
anguish in connection with the crucifixion. That this is the
meaning, and that the decision of this great cause took place at
the completion of Christ's vicarious sacrifice, is put beyond
doubt by the next clause. In a word, the world passes into
other hands; another prince enters into rightful possession. It
is more a question of legitimate title, than of actual possession,
to which our Lord here refers; though He received at once
power over all flesh when He ascended, that He might exercise
unlimited authority in every corner of the globe, for the pro-
motion of His cause. The same thing is plainly taught by our
Lord in another passage, when He describes the function of the
Comforter, who takes of the things of Christ, and shows them
unto us: "*He shall convince the world of judgment, because*
[better, to the effect that] *the prince of this world is judged*"
(John xvi. 11). The meaning is: the Comforter, when sent
forth by the ascending Jesus, shall convince mankind that Satan
has lost his cause, that is, the legitimate power previously belonging to him, and that he is virtually denuded of all the
authority of a prince, which he so long and so universally
exercised on the earth. No one is now compelled to remain
under his power, unless, with his own resolve and purpose, he
chooses darkness rather than the light. The passage intimates
that the Comforter convinces men that Satan has lost the cause,
that the decision is against him, and that Jesus is the rightful
Prince and Saviour, to whom they may and ought to swear
allegiance.

This text, then, putting all this result in indissoluble connection with Christ's atonement, intimates that the world is no more Satan's, but Christ's; or, in other words, that the second man has, by His obedience unto death, received a divinely-conferred right to be heir of all things. He can claim the world as His own, and dispossess its former prince, because He has endured the curse and fulfilled the conditions which put Him in possession of a claim to the reward. His disciples are freemen in the world, and well aware that they can serve their Prince with a good conscience, in every sphere and in all the positions where they are placed by His providence. This sense is put beyond doubt by the precise and definite language of the next clause: "Now shall the prince of this world be cast out." In a word, the world passes into other hands: one prince yields his dominions, and another enters into rightful possession. Having announced in the present tense "now IS the judgment of the world," the Lord adds in the future tense, "now *shall* the prince of the world *be cast out*." This ejection begins and advances. Satan must yield ground wherever the atonement takes effect, till he shall resign the whole globe and be cast into the lake of fire. The title which Satan derived from his victory over the first man is lost; and the new title which is founded on the cross, and exercised by the only begotten Son, is paramount and irreversible. Not that Christ must be understood as speaking of an immediate *de facto* occupation: it is more a question of *de jure* sovereignty. But He has power over all flesh, and exercises unlimited authority in every corner of the globe, according to His sovereign will, for the advancement of His cause. In the other passage, where our Lord delineates the work of the Comforter, the revealer of Christ (John xvi. 11), the meaning is: the Spirit subjectively convinces men of the objective fact alluded to in the saying under consideration—that Jesus is now the rightful Prince and Saviour, on the ground of His atoning sacrifice, and that He is the Lord to whom we owe obedience.

This text, important in many aspects, is capable of being viewed in many applications. It throws a steady light on the great and momentous doctrine, that the world is, in consequence of the vicarious work of Christ, no more Satan's, and that Christ's people are now to be far from the impression that they are only captives in an enemy's territory, and unable warrantably to occupy a place in the world, either as citizens or magistrates. On the contrary, this testimony shows that every foot of ground in the world belongs to Christ, that His followers can be loyal to Him in every position, and that in every country and corner where they may be placed they have to act their part for their Lord. The world is judicially awarded to Christ as its owner and Lord.

SEC. XXXVII.—CHRIST, BY MEANS OF HIS ATONEMENT, OVERCOMING THE WORLD.

" In the world ye shall have tribulation; but be of good cheer: I have overcome the world." (John xvi. 28.)

This saying of Jesus, spoken on the night of His betrayal, a little while before He went out to Gethsemane, shows us His victory over the world, from a point of view different from that which was developed in the previous section. It will not be necessary to do more than briefly notice it, as adducing a consideration or a motive drawn from the atonement, to confirm the disciples of all ages amid the troubles and persecutions that are to be encountered in the world. The Lord, speaking in the perfect tense, with a special reference to His atoning sacrifice, says, I HAVE OVERCOME the world and its prince. He reminds us how His disciples may at one and the same time have tribulation and peace—tribulation in the world, peace in Him. They may have a peace or good cheer amid the greatest dangers, and even glory in tribulation through the cross (Rom. v. 3). Our Lord does not bring out here a mere example, however animating, from which we may learn how to follow His footsteps, but calls attention to an obedience or merit, which has power with God, and constitutes a foundation on which the Christian's faith may lean. We are by no means to view this saying as referring only to the victory subsequently to be achieved in the world by the preaching of the gospel, but rather to consider it as alluding to what was won by Christ for all His people by His atoning death.

· To understand this testimony, then, it must be borne in mind that the allusion is here to Christ's representative act, intimating that His victory is also ours; in other words, that that act of Christ, comprehending His whole earthly life and work, considered in its vicarious character, avails with God, and emboldens us to fight the good fight of faith. This memorable saying, important as it is to the militant church of all ages, may be regarded as a key to that numerous class of passages which speak of Christians as more than conquerors through Him that loved us (Rom. viii. 37); of a world overcoming faith (1 John v. 45); and of overcoming by the blood of the Lamb (Rev. xii. 11).

When we inquire, in the first place, how the Lord Jesus overcame the world, an accurate investigation of the passage will show that the emphasis must specially be placed on the person who speaks. He would have all eyes turned upon Himself when He says, "*I* have overcome." He virtually says, "Turn your eye away from the world's hatred and persecuting rage to the consideration of my person and of my finished work of atonement, as constituting the grand victory over the world." He may be said to have overcome the world, partly as He vicariously and in our stead withstood from day to day the world's allurements and temptations, and was not to be turned aside by them—partly as He was faithful in His capacity of surety to His undertaking amid the hatred of the world, that would have sought to put down His cause; but, above all, as He bought by His obedience not only a people in the world, but that world itself, that He might be the heir of all things.

This representative act of Christ, then, lies at the foundation of this saying, His act being the act of one for many. Thus all our victory lies in the merit of Christ. It may seem strange, at first sight, that the Lord should direct His followers to take encouragement from the thought that He overcame the world; which looks much as if a man of large resources should say to the poor and needy, " I am rich and powerful; " for that seems to bring neither aid nor comfort to others. But the announcement changes its character the moment it is understood that His means are possessed in common with that other, and made available for that other more than for Himself. The Lord bids the disciples realize His act as theirs, and His victory as achieved for them, or, in other words, to take the assurance that He identified Himself with them to such a degree that He overcame the world for them more than for Himself. He virtually says: I have by my sacrifice effected this result, That the world, with all its violence, cannot really injure you. The victory of Christ, our High Priest and Head, is ours.[1] Indeed, He needed not, on His own account, to have come down from heaven; and He acted only for His people, for whom His victory was made available. He virtually says, " I have overcome not for myself, but for you." It is Christ's work that constitutes all His people's victory; and hence, when the Apostle John says, " This is the victory that overcometh the world, even our faith " (1 John v. 4), the language must not be understood as referring to two victories, but as intimating simply, that in and with the exercise of faith upon the Son of God, this full victory over the world is obtained through means of Christ's victory accounted ours.

Thus, the disciples of Christ accustom themselves to triumph in the triumph of Christ, inasmuch as the true victor did all that was needed to atone for sin, and to open heaven on the behalf of His saints; and what remains for them but only to enter into His victory ? The battle was won by Him, and they

---

[1] See Cocceius *in loc.*

have but to enter into His work, and so tread death and hell
under feet. And as they realize this victory in Him, they are
" of good cheer," for they virtually hear Christ say, " I won the
fight, and ye reap the victory;" and thus all the rage, enmity,
and persecution of the world are only but the impotent death-
struggles of vanquished enemies.

The Lord here speaks in the near prospect of death, as if the
victory were already won for His people, because it was won in
His purpose. Hence, while all the powers, ecclesiastical and
civil, supposed that He Himself was crushed, and that His cause
was in ruins, His own language shows that He was only in process of leading captivity captive. And when we inquire in
what sense Christ's victory is the Church's victory, and how it is
fitted to fill Christians with good cheer, several distinct points
may at once be named. Thus, He bought a people to Himself;
He obtained power over all flesh; He acquired for them the
inextinguishable power of the divine life; He puts into them
the bold courage of a world-overcoming faith; and He bridles
the power of evil in such a way that it cannot prevail so far as
to overwhelm them (1 Cor. x. 13). I shall only notice, however,
one or two of those results which directly flow from His representative act.

1. Christ's people get boldness to overcome the world, and
the world's lord, through the blood of the Lamb. They feel that,
feeble as they are—nay, as sheep killed all the day long—they
can still say, " Who shall separate us from the love of Christ ?
We are more than *conquerors, through Him that loved us*"[1] (Rom.
viii. 37). The words there used, if we exactly interpret them,
will be found to point to Christ's one redemption work as the
great procuring cause of His people's victory. The martyrs,
loving not their lives unto the death, are said to overcome by
the blood of the Lamb (Rev. xii. 11); which means that the
death with which they were threatened by their persecutors had

[1] The aorist participle ἀγαπήσαντος, as Meyer well observes, marks the eminent
act of love which Christ performed by offering up His life.

no terrors for them who had washed their robes in the blood of the Lamb; and they were fully aware that, if their lives must needs be forfeited, they could say "we shall sup with Christ to-night." Under this bold assurance and confidence derived from the cross, they felt that the world could as little devour or really injure them as it had been able to swallow up their Lord, and that their more abundant entrance into their rest was only hastened, and their crown made so much the brighter by their martyr-death. What though the world took away life, honour, and goods ?—they were going to more than they left.

2. They get, through the atonement of the cross, the victorious power of a divine life, to rise superior, both to the world's allurements and to its frowns. The redeemed Church is assured that she owes all the grace which she receives to the blood of the Lamb; that the Lamb overcomes His enemies in virtue of His atoning blood, inasmuch as this not only deprives Satan's accusations of their point, but brings the power of an invincible divine life into the heart. Our victory depends on the victory of Christ; and hence the apostle, looking round on all the enemies that threatened Him, bade them defiance with a bold and joyful confidence, whether they came in one form or another: they could not separate him from the love of Christ (Rom. viii. 35). The faith which appropriates Christ's atonement is thus full of divine strength to overcome the world's allurements, as well as its enmity; and when they conquer through faith in Christ, they overcome by the power of the atonement, or by the blood of the Lamb.

SEC. XXXVIII.—THE ATONEMENT OF CHRIST DENUDING SATAN OF HIS DOMINION IN THE WORLD.

"Now shall the prince of this world be cast out." (John xii. 31.)

Our Lord, in His last discourses, makes various allusions to Satan, and three times mentions him under the title of the Prince of this world. That the allusion is to Satan, and not, as

some have fancifully thought, to the Jewish high priest, is too
obvious to require proof. He comes to the Christ on the last
night, but finds nothing in Him; that is, nothing which properly belongs to him which he can call his, or which is in any
way allied to his kingdom (John xiv. 30). He is represented as
judged (John xvi. 11); and, last of all, it is said that he is
about to be cast out.[1]

The Lord's language in reference to the personality of Satan
is too express to leave room for doubt. The attempts that have
been made, on exegetical grounds, to explain away the import of
His words are little worthy of notice. But that we may leave
nothing behind us to which exception may be taken, we shall
adduce a few testimonies which are unmistakeable. The question is: is Satan a personification of the principle of evil? and
can our Lord's words be so understood? a few passages will
supply the answer.

Only a person can be meant when our Lord, in addressing a
warning voice to Peter, said: "Satan hath desired to have you,
that he may sift you as wheat" (Luke xxii. 31). Here personal
feelings, aims, and devices, are ascribed to Him. With as little
warrant can any one maintain, that it is a mere personification
of evil when our Lord said, "when a strong man armed keepeth
his palace, his goods are in peace; but when a stronger than he
shall come upon him and overcome him, he taketh from him all
his armour" (Luke xi. 21). When our Lord describes the sentence to be pronounced by Him at the day of judgment on those
at the left hand, He is equally explicit; "Depart from Me, ye
cursed, into everlasting fire, prepared for the devil and his
angels" (Matt. xxv. 41). When we turn to the gospel of John,
we find language which, in many respects, unmasks and exposes
the false spiritualism of our day, which labours hard to trans-
mute stern realities into shadows or figures. Our Lord calls
Satan the murderer from the beginning (John viii. 44). He
describes a personal being, a friend of falsehood, and its author

[1] ἐκβληθήσεται ἔξω.

who, through all ages from the beginning, has been the murderer of the human race, and the lie is his own or native to
him. In the passage at the head of this section (John xii.
31), our Lord speaks of a suit or judicial process carried on against
the Prince of this World. This implies a person;[1] for a legal
process cannot be carried on against an abstraction, a personification, or a spectre of the mind, as certain modern writers
permit themselves to speak in referring to the doctrine of Satan.
No man who honestly interprets Scripture as an inspired docu-
ment, and takes God's word in earnest, can entertain any doubt
as to the personal existence of Satan, and the reality of his
kingdom. The doctrine of Satan has an influence on every
department of doctrine or ethics. Thus, when we think of the
doctrine of man, we may affirm that he is a capable subject of
redemption, only as he was the victim of the tempter's lie ; for
he is a liar, and the father of it. When we think of the doctrine
of sin, it stands out as something absolutely evil in consideration of its origin. When we think of redemption, it is described
as a proceeding on the part of the Son of God to destroy the
works of the devil (1 John iii. 8), not that the ransom was paid
to him, as many of the fathers and some modern theologians[2]
have imagined. But this does not prevent us from maintaining
that the Son of God was necessary as the only mediator who
could break the power of Satan over the human family by
means of His atoning sacrifice. In a word, when we run our
eye over the history of Satan from his attempt upon our first
parents, to the day when he shall be cast out and shut up in
chains of darkness, we see a conflict extending through all
earth's history, and the grandeur of a divine plan, destined to
put him to shame. We see a personal devil, not a personification of the principle of evil.

[1] A marked feature of theology during last century was the denial of Satan's
personality. The most powerful writer who has assailed it in this century is
Schleiermacher. See Sartorius, Philippi, Sander, and others in reply to him.

[2] The school of Origen among the Fathers, and Hasenkamp and Menken among
the moderns.

This terrible adversary of the human race was overcome by the second man who came into our place, and entered the lists with Satan, where the battle had gone against us before. Satan fell by pride, and infused this poison into our first parents, and the mystery of the incarnation began with abasement. By humility the Lord advanced to all His work of expiation. His meritorious sacrifice, and His willing subjection to suffering, wrested the dominion from Satan, and bruised the serpent's head. Before the work of expiation was accomplished, Satan had a right to man whom he had conquered, and to the world which he had won. But Christ reversed all this, and led captivity captive.

As to the title here given by our Lord to Satan, "the Prince of this World," it aptly applies to him as the head of all who attach themselves to that natural life which lies in estrangement from God, or who set themselves in banded opposition to the Christ of God. How fitly the name applies to the world in its moral and intellectual condition under ungodly influences which come from the evil one, the first cause and father of corruption, scarcely requires to be pointed out. Thus a kingdom is ascribed to him (Mark iii. 26); the wicked are regarded as his children (John viii. 44); the tares in the parable of the sown field, a term by which our Lord means ungodly men, are said to be sown by him among the wheat (Matt. xiii. 38); the plucking away of the good seed is his work (Matt. xiii. 19); the act of Judas in betraying Christ is referred to Satan entering in and taking possession of the man (John xiii. 27); and when the ecclesiastical authorities combined to put Him to death, and were allowed to execute their purpose, Jesus said, "This is your hour, and the power of darkness" (Luke xxii. 53). Satan tried subtlety first, and violence afterwards, and was signally baffled in both attempts, as a glance at both will suffice to show.

1. In the first conflict with our Lord, when he assailed Him with all the resources of cunning and artifice, he was signally defeated. Our Lord took up the combat, as the nature of His

suretyship required, at the very point where the battle had been
lost by the first man, and withstood the adversary, in presenting
temptations and allurements, as well as dissuasives, which had
everything in common with those seductive baits by which he
had made an easy prey of our progenitors.   That temptation is
by no means to be regarded in the light of a mere example, how
to conduct ourselves in similar scenes, and how to meet and
overcome him; for, though it must be regarded as an example,
as all Christ's life will ever be to His people, it was also a meritorious deed in our room and stead, of which His people reap the
reward.   If we limit it to the mere example, it can inspire but
little ardour or confidence of victory into us, in following His
footsteps.   But the case is altered when we regard Christ as the
atoning surety satisfying for Adam's sin, and meritoriously overcoming in our place the tempter that had so easily triumphed in
the former case, and held the universal race as lawful captives.
Thus the temptation of Jesus stood in necessary connection with
His whole atoning work, not in the sense that it was but a
preparation for His atoning work, but rather as it was an integral
portion of the work itself.   The victory won over the adversary
was to be in a way of rectitude, not by the mere exercise of
power.   The Son of God must needs, as man and as a substitute,
enter the lists with the adversary, and deliver the race in whose
room He stood, and for whom He constantly acted, in a way of
right and justice.   He took up the controversy just where it had
before so disastrously ended.

To the temptation itself, and the several points of attack comprehended in it, it is not necessary more particularly to refer.
Let it suffice to remark, that the tempter's aim from the beginning was directed to the one point of suppressing or of destroying, in the most effective way in which it was possible, the
human nature of Jesus, or to render it unavailing as the instrument in which man's redemption was to be accomplished.   He
sought, as much as in him lay, to create a discordance between
the two natures of our Lord, and thus to frustrate the design of

their union. He would destroy, if possible, the harmonious connection between them, by tempting Him, under the influence of
his taunting words, to usurp the prerogative of the divine, and to
deviate from the lot appointed for Him by God.   Then he sought
to infuse a false confidence.   And when baffled, once and again,
in this audacious attempt, he offered Him the world, the subject
in dispute between the two, without a trial or a conflict—a
temptation all the more subtle, as our Lord foresaw, with His
enlightened mind, the long and painful conflict before Him.   To
induce Him to comply, and thus accept the kingdoms of the
world, he showed Him how easily the world might be put at
His disposal at once.   There was a terrible coincidence in this
threefold temptation, well fitted, had there been the smallest
tinder on which the spark of temptation could fall, to set all
within into a conflagration.   But it signally failed.

2. Satan having vainly tried subtlety next tried the fury of
persecution.   But the Lord was equally proof against both, and
learned obedience by the things He suffered (Heb. v. 8).   The
evil one, by stirring up the hatred of the rulers, and infusing
into them the utmost pitch of rancorous malice, thought to make
Christ waver and recoil; or, if he could not draw Him into distrust of God and actual rebellion or apostasy, he aimed at least
to accomplish an object much desired by him—His removal from
the world,—and so to remain master of the field.   He little
thought, in the machinations of blind rage, that he was but a
tool in the hand of Omniscience, and that he was carrying out,
as a passive slave, what the counsel and foreknowledge of God
hath determined beforehand to be done (Acts iv. 28).   The
death by which the Lord should die for men's redemption, was
to be a violent or sacrificial death, but, from the peculiar relation
He occupied, neither immediately inflicted by the hand of God,
nor an immediate resignation of His own life.   It must be
through the intervention of man.   The malice of Satan only
served to give effect to this foreappointed purpose ; and the
wrath of man was made to praise Him.   That violent death was

the way through which the Lord, by a sublime priestly self-oblation, was to atone for the human family. By this means divine
justice was to be satisfied, a sufficient atonement offered, the
divine favour won, and the lawful captive delivered.

It is noteworthy that our Lord in the two clauses of this verse
twice uses the emphatic word *now*. He refers to the nearness
and efficacy of the atonement, within the circle of which He
was now come. The language implies that Satan's dominion
rested upon the fact of sin. And as he occupied a secure and
impregnable position so long as the vicarious sacrifice was not
offered, so the vantage ground from which he had long ruled the
world was lost the moment divine justice was satisfied. In the
first clause of this verse, as was already noticed, the Lord refers
to a formal process then pending, which was finally to decide to
whom the world should be adjudged,—whether to Christ or to
Satan, its former prince. When we put the two members of the
verse together, the language intimates, that the judicial process
as to the right of property, or the legitimate title, was then to be
decided. And when sin was expiated, and the curse borne,
Satan's right to the sinner was annihilated, and his sovereignty
over the world overthrown. The Lord could say, "Now shall
the prince of this world be cast out," because the ground of this
victory was first to be laid in law and justice, or meritoriously
secured by that atoning death which was soon to be undergone,
and which was to destroy the sin which gave Satan his dominion
in the world. He virtually says: "My death shall be the
destruction of Satan's dominion." There are a few separate
sayings of Jesus to this effect, demanding more particular elucidation; and to these we shall advert.

1. The first word by which our Lord sets forth the approaching termination of Satan's authority, is, *the prince of this world is
judged* (John xvi. 11). It is plain that our Lord does not intend
to speak of a judgment upon Satan for his own fall from God,
nor refer to a judicial sentence to be passed on the deceiver, for
tempting men at first to become allies with him in his revolt

from God. He speaks of a judgment which should strike him as the head of a hostile confederacy in banded opposition to God and His anointed. The meaning is, that the right which Satan had acquired to rule over men, and to treat them as his lawful captives, in consequence of sin, was now to be taken from him, and that his power was now to be broken; for he is said to be *judged*, when his legal, though usurped, right to dominion is terminated.

And how did Christ's sacrificial death subvert his empire? In a twofold way. As sin was put away by the sacrifice of Himself (Heb. ix. 26), and as the curse was fully borne, the supreme Judge discharged the guilty. Nor could the accuser, on any plea of justice, either accuse them, or demand their condemnation, that is, a doom similar to his own (Rom. viii. 1). Besides, the legitimate authority which the tempter had previously possessed, to keep men in death and spiritual estrangement from God, was for ever at an end. The Mediator's death, the winding-up of His active and passive obedience, destroyed him that had the power of death (Heb. ii. 14), and destroyed the works of the devil (1 John iii. 8). The captivity to which men had hitherto been subjected by divine justice, could be reversed only by the death of one who was more than man. By this means Satan was overthrown in point of law, and the way was paved for the annihilation of his sway.

2. The next saying which we adduce respecting the victory over Satan, mentions *the binding of the strong man, and the spoiling of his goods* (Matt. xii. 29). This result follows upon the judgment pronounced upon him. Men are called "his goods," the property which belongs to him, and which he is said to hold in peace (Luke xi. 21), till they are effectually called by a high and holy calling. They are then translated into the kingdom of God's dear Son (Col. i. 13). This second step, in the execution of which Christ interposes, as stronger than the strong one, to bring His sheep into the fold, and rescue souls from the grasp of the destroyer, is simply an act of power by which He quickens men

when dead, enlightens them when blind, and gives near access to those who previously were far off.

3. It is further said, "the prince of this world shall be cast out." This follows as the legitimate result of that judicial process which has adjudged the world to Christ. Satan is to be cast out of the world; and in due time bound in chains, to the judgment of the great day. He is not, even at present, lord *de jure* of one foot of earth; but his usurpation lingers, and is permitted to continue, on many accounts, into which it is not our present business to inquire. He is to be ejected, in point of fact as well as right, to exercise no more power or authority either over single men or communities of men, by means of any of those systems on which he has expended, for centuries, the utmost refinement of his subtlety. These shall melt away like the mists of the morning. But even now the church has, on the ground of Christ's atonement, to go in and take possession of the world from which its prince has been legally cast out, and from which he will ere long, in point of fact, be fully ejected (Luke x. 18).

The synonymous phrases which occur in Scripture are numerous. Thus it is said of Christ, that He led captivity captive (Ps. lxviii. 18); that He takes a prey from the mighty (Isa. xlix. 24); that He was appointed to bruise the serpent's head (Gen. iii. 15). This last expression, familiar to the Old Testament Church from the beginning, was the figure under which God was pleased to convey to man the earliest notion of a deliverer, and was, in fact, the first proclamation of the Gospel. The serpent had already overcome our race, and held humanity, not only as it existed in the first pair, but as far as it should be multiplied under his galling yoke. No one could measure himself against the prince of the world, who was in fact armed with the sharp sting of the divine law, of which he was the executioner. The first promise or primeval gospel intimated the advent of a person of greater power than the conqueror, yet one with true humanity, whose heel could be bruised. That was done upon the cross, and there practically the victory was won which is carried out in the history of the Church. Satan is now simply dispossessed by power; a word can conquer him; and God shall bruise him under the Church's feet shortly. Our Lord does not mean that the kingdom of Satan was to be all at once overthrown; for the tense, " shall be cast out," intimates a future ejection.

SEC. XXXIX.—CHRIST'S VICARIOUS DEATH TAKING THE STING OUT OF DEATH, AND ABOLISHING IT.

Among the sayings of Jesus which set forth the effects of the atonement, there are some which represent Him as the conqueror of death. One class of sayings declares that His people never die (John viii. 51). A second class of sayings represents the vicarious death of Christ as bringing in a more abundant life, which effectually abolishes death, and will in due time swallow it up in every form, corporeal as well as spiritual (John x. 10, 11). That the element of incorruption or of resurrection-glory must be included in the term LIFE, will be admitted by every one who does justice to the interpretation of the word as it is used by our Lord. This, however, is delineated as a fruit or effect of the atonement.

Our Lord very frequently uses the term DEATH, which He understands as that complete destruction, spiritual and corporeal, which follows upon man's estrangement from God, and which will remain as the inevitable doom of all who reject the provisions of divine grace. And no diligent student of Scripture can fail to see that death was a much more terrible fact to mankind in general, and even to believers, previous to the atoning death of Christ, than it has been since. The reason of this is on the surface. It was more formidable than after the death of Jesus, partly because the ancient saints had not, as we have, the great fact of a dead substitute and surety before their eye, partly because death was not then, as it is now, swallowed up in victory (Job vii. 21; Ps. vi. 6; Isa. xxxviii. 3-14).

Our Lord, as we have above noticed, does not formally contrast Himself with the first man, in reference to the influence
which they severally have on the fact of death in the world
(Rom. v. 12; 1 Cor. xv. 47-56). An analysis of our Lord's
teaching sufficiently shows that ample room is left by Him for
the introduction of the other member of the contrast. But He
leaves this to His apostles. When we investigate the meaning
of the apostle's words, it is evident that the entrance of death to
which the apostle refers includes the idea of temporal death.
But while we cannot exclude physical death, a limitation of the
meaning to that idea must be held to be quite unsatisfactory;
for it comprehends the entire ruin caused by sin, whether spiritual
or temporal. The objective existence of death is unmistakeably
traced to sin (Rom. v. 12); and the destruction of death is no
less clearly referred to Christ, who has abolished death, and
brought life and immortality to light, by the gospel (2 Tim. i. 9).

That the redeeming death of Jesus has the effect of destroying
death, and depriving it of its sting, is not obscurely indicated in
the Lord's own words: "He came to give *His life* a ransom *for
many*" (Matt. xx. 28). The one death was in room of the death
of many, but with the ulterior view of ushering in a reign of life.
Nor can we fail to see the same truth in the special connection
of the clauses, which bind together another statement in reference
to the Shepherd giving His life for the sheep: " I am come *that
they might have life,* and that they might have it more abundantly.
I am the good Shepherd: the good Shepherd *giveth His life for
the sheep*" (John x. 10, 11). The giving of the more abundant
life is there, beyond doubt, put in the closest causal connection
with the surrender of His own life. The vicarious sacrifice may
be regarded as the death of death, and the cause of life; and thus,
by His own deep humiliation, Christ won a triumph over death
for all His followers. To obtain this, however, He Himself of
necessity became the prey of death, and bruised the serpent's
head, by being bruised in His heel.

There are three remarkable sayings of Christ, which agree in

declaring that the Christian's death is not death; that is, he
never sees death, because it is not coupled with eternal death:—
" Verily, verily, I say unto you, He that heareth my word, and
believeth in Him that sent Me, hath everlasting life, and shall
not come into condemnation; *but is passed from death unto life* "
(John v. 24). Again (John viii. 51), " Verily, verily, I say unto
you, If a man keep my saying, *he shall never see death.*" Again
(John xi. 25, 26), " I am the resurrection, and the life: he that
believeth in Me, though he were dead [better, though he die],
yet shall he live: and *whosoever liveth, and believeth in Me, shall
never die.*" These three sayings must be applied not only to
eternal death, but also in a sense to temporal death. It may
be urged: " How do they not die whose bodies we see day after
day descending to the tomb, and returning to dust ? " Jesus
declares that they never die, not even a temporal death, if we
fully fathom the depths of Christ's words. In what sense ?
Because they are not subjected by temporal death to any such
changes as are really their destruction, having the principle and
seed of immortality within them. They, in truth, never see
death, however much they may seem to men to die. The fear of
death, by which they were once haunted and held in bondage, is
also removed by the Lord's vicarious death. The phrases used
in those verses to which we have referred—*shall never see death,
shall never die, hath passed from death to life*—intimate, that
believers, though passing through temporal death, never undergo
death with the dire penal results consequent on it; that they
never encounter death properly so called; that they are already possessed of life, and will be raised up in incorruption.[1] The allusion cannot be to the actual abolition of death,
inasmuch as that still continues, and will be the last enemy
destroyed. But the fear of death, or death with its sting

[1] It does not fall to us to explain here Christ's profound explanation of the words,
" I am the God of Abraham, Isaac, and Jacob " (Matt. xxii. 32), to the effect that
He is not the God of the dead, but of the living, and that this relationship secured
the final resurrection of the saints. But of course it presupposes the atonement
as its ground.

agonizing the human mind, in reality exists no more to a Christian. This allusion, however, is not to mankind as such; for the sting, the fear of death, remains with the unbelieving, who receive not the gospel; and the sting of death is sin, making every unpardoned man afraid to die, while the strength of sin is the law. The words mean, then, that a true disciple never dies, inasmuch as death has ceased to be penal, and is no more dreaded. Not only so: the atonement of Christ requires that the body shall be again associated with the soul, and that death shall thus be swallowed up of life (2 Cor. v. 4).

There is a memorable passage in which Satan, the Prince of Death, is contrasted with Christ, the Prince of Life (John viii. 44). The Lord there tells the Jews that they were of their father the devil, who was a murderer from the beginning. The words are not to be interpreted, as some have done, of Cain, but of Satan, whose seduction of the first pair brought death into the world, and all our woe, and who is therefore said to have the power of death (Heb. ii. 14)—a power which he wields, and which must be said to belong to him, in a certain sense, so long as the human race dies, and of which he will be fully denuded at the second advent. On the contrary, the honour conferred on the Lord Jesus by the Father, as a reward for His loyal obedience or humiliation unto death, is that He is constituted the Prince of Life, and that His disciples shall never see death. This is the direct antithesis of all that belongs to him that hath the power of death, and who was a murderer from the beginning. If Satan is a murderer from the beginning, the Lord Jesus, on the contrary, is the Prince of Life; and His followers receive, as the reward of His abasement undying life, and shall never see death (ver. 51).

But a difficulty presents itself: why do believers undergo temporal death at all, if divine justice has been fully satisfied? To this the ready answer is, that the death of the Christian is not in any sense a proper punishment of sin, and that he is as perfectly accepted through the atonement of Christ, as if he had

not committed a single sin. The importance of this question
appears from the fact, that whenever the temporal death of
believers is regarded as the penalty of sin, in however small a
measure, the perfect satisfaction of divine justice by Christ
cannot be maintained. It is urged, that as we can judge of the
extent of the atonement only by its effects, so, in point of fact,
the extent of its effects can only be inferred from its results, and
that believers, therefore, are not delivered from all the consequences of sin.[1] But that is a very ambiguous mode of presenting the question. The one point is: Are the consequences of
sin, in the case of true Christians, still to be regarded, as in any
sort, a punishment by which they pay something to divine
justice ? And the answer must be emphatically in the negative.
But again, it is asked: Can there really be a consequence of sin,
which is not a punishment of sin ? To determine this, we must
consider what reference it has to God, who dispenses it; and
since we find that He sends temporal trials and afflictions as well
as temporal death, not in wrath, not as an avenging judge, but
as a wise and loving father, they cannot be termed proper
punishments, though they are the consequences of sin; Christians
having wholly passed from a state of wrath into a state of grace.
The Epistles, accordingly, dwell upon the fact, that Christ, by
His death, destroyed him that hath the power of death, and
unstinged it for all His people (Heb. ii. 14; 1 Cor. xv. 1-58).

But why, it is still further asked, do the consequences of sin
remain, if the acquittal is complete, and justice fully satisfied ?
We may explain the anomaly by a parallel case. A rebel may
have been arrested and imprisoned, and up to a certain point
treated as a criminal worthy of death: he may, through the
mediation of another, have obtained a full pardon and discharge,
but still have to carry with him, for a considerable time, the
wounds inflicted on him during his rebellion, or the sores and
bruises of his chains and imprisonment. But, plainly, the latter

---

[1] So Roellius, in his discussion with Vitringa, put it ; maintaining that the
Christian paid a something of the penalty.

are not any longer regarded in the same light as before,—they are not now a part of his punishment, nor a part of what he has to pay to the justice of his country. While they remain, they may remind him, indeed, of what he was; but they are wholly altered in character, and no more foretokenings of something worse that must ensue. They have, in a word, ceased to be punishments.[1] Such is temporal death to a Christian, and such are all his present trials and afflictions. They are altered in their character; they have no wrath in them; they are salutary, paternal discipline; they bring him home.

The Lord's sayings in reference to this point are fully expanded by the apostles. Thus the apostle Paul (1 Cor. xv. 54-56) adduces two quotations from the prophets to show that death was swallowed up in victory (Isa. xxv. 8), and that its sting is removed (Hos. xiii. 14). The Pauline theology here brings together in the most striking way DEATH, SIN, and THE LAW, as three enemies which must needs be encountered, but which are now disarmed. The first statement is: "the sting of death is sin;" an announcement which gives us to understand that had there been no sin death could have had no power to assail us and no terror to alarm us. For what could death do to an innocent and holy man, who was without sin, and therefore exempt from every part of the curse? In such a case death could have no weapon, no sting. But when the apostle thus speaks of sin, he seems to have in his view the inward sense of sin which has revived in the soul (Rom. vii. 9), and brought along with the knowledge of its existence an alarm and dread which nothing but the death of a suffering substitute can calm.

But whence has sin this power? The apostle adds: "The strength of sin is the law" (v. 56). This means that sin would not awake in this manner were there no law to accuse and condemn us. But the Lord by His substitution has blotted out the handwriting of ordinances that was against us, and contrary to us, nailing it to His cross; and now death is unstinged. The

[1] See Vitringa's Dutch reply to Roellius.

Christian sees his death, as he sees his sins, on Jesus, and meets the approach of the last enemy with calm triumph, because in the cross of Christ death itself has died. It is no more a penalty, no more the expression of the curse, but the pathway to endless rest. Hence the early Christians, as Athanasius informs us,[1] exercised themselves in this arena, and were so conscious of their victory through Christ's substitution that women and children, in the times of persecution, derided death as dead.

There is a further prospect on the same foundation. The Lord has a paramount claim to His people because He purchased them with a price (Acts xx. 28). On this ground He will have them to be with Him, that they may behold His glory (John xvii. 24); and not only must the most fondly cherished earthly tie, but every sphere of labour terminate here below, when He who has the keys of the invisible world and death asserts His rightful claim. The redeemed are to be for ever with the Lord, and no plea can be weighed in the balance against His will. Hence when life must be resigned, or cherished friends surrendered, His higher rights are paramount: for He bought them with His blood.

SEC. XL.—CHRIST LAYING DOWN HIS LIFE FOR THE SHEEP, AND
THUS BECOMING THE ACTUAL SHEPHERD OF THE SHEEP.

" *I am the good Shepherd : the good Shepherd giveth His life for
the sheep. But he that is an hireling, and not the shepherd, whose own the sheep are not, seeth the wolf coming,
and leaveth the sheep, and fleeth : and the wolf catcheth*

---

[1] None of the writers of antiquity laid more stress than Athanasius on the subject of death in connection with the atonement. See his entire treatise on the Incarnation. Thus he says (c. 27) : πρὶν πιστεύσουσιν οἱ ἄνθρωποι τῷ Χριστῷ, φοβερὸν τὸν θάνατον ὁρῶσὶ καὶ δειλιῶσιν αὐτόν. Ἐπειδὰν δὲ εἰς τὴν ἐκείνου πίστιν καὶ διδασκαλίαν μετέλθωσι τοσοῦτον καταφρονοῦσι τοῦ θανάτου, ὡς καὶ προθύμως ἐπ' αὐτὸν ὁρμᾶν καὶ μάρτυρας γίνεσθαι. The allusions of Luther to the unstinging of death are equally copious and emphatic. See for example his letter *ad Hard-
mannum à Cronbergh.*

*them, and scattereth the sheep. The hireling fleeth, because
he is an hireling, and careth not for the sheep. I am the
good Shepherd, and know my sheep, and am known of mine.
As the Father knoweth Me, even so* [better, and] *know I the
Father: and I lay down my life for the sheep. And other
sheep I have, which are not of this fold: them also I must
bring* [better, lead], *and they shall hear my voice; and
there shall be one fold* [better, flock], *and one Shepherd.
Therefore doth my Father love Me, because I lay down my
life, that I might take it again. No man taketh it from
Me, but I lay it down of myself. I have power to lay it
down, and I have power to take it again. This commandment have I received from my Father."* (John x. 11-18).

This saying of Jesus is peculiarly important, because it exhibits,
with the utmost vividness, various aspects of the atonement not
usually put together, and elucidates the whole transaction as a
divine provision, whether we view it with respect to its nature
or to the special effects which it produces. This testimony may
be considered as the key to all those allusions contained in the
apostolic Epistles, which bring before us the office of the Shepherd,
as well as the care and watchfulness which He exercises in that
capacity in behalf of the flock (1 Pet. ii. 25, v. 4). While it embodies most of the essential truths involved in the atonement, so
far as its peculiar character or nature is concerned, the special
points which it establishes in connection with the effects of
Christ's death, are these: (1) that it sets forth the deliverance
thus effected; and (2) portrays the legitimate right and claim
which Christ acquired, in point of purchase, to become the actual
Shepherd of the sheep.

The occasion on which the Lord uttered this memorable saying, was as follows:—The Pharisees, who always resisted His
teaching, had just evinced the utmost hostility in connection with
the cure of the blind-born man, and He was led, by their
opposition, to contrast their pretensions with such teachers as are

called and commissioned from above, whom alone the sheep will hear, and, above all, to contrast them with Himself, who is the Shepherd, by way of eminence, or "the good Shepherd" (ver. 11). As these men had not entered by the door, which He explains as equivalent to a belief in Himself, and a commission from Him, and as they were only perverters of the people, Christ describes Himself as the good Shepherd, because He is the ideal of all that the office implies, and the long expected Shepherd whom all the ancient prophecies announced under that title (Zech. xiii. 7; Ezek. xxxiv. 23; Ps. xxiii.).

As this memorable section can be apprehended as a testimony to the atonement in its nature and effects, only when its profound phraseology and bearing are fully surveyed, it will be necessary, for the purpose which we have in view, to give a succinct outline, at least of the salient points, though by no means a full commentary, of the words, in the connection in which they stand.

This entire passage yields the most important results for the elucidation of the atonement. According to the classification which we have adopted, it is adduced specially to show that the death of Christ was considered by Himself as giving Him the right to be the actual and legitimate Shepherd of the sheep. But we also notice that the Lord Jesus here enters more fully than in almost any other passage into the nature of the atonement as a voluntary sacrifice; employing language which, from its very nature, implies that one party is rescued by another's death. He states that He not only did not stop short at confronting danger, and exposing Himself to death, which is all that some expositors see in the words, but that He, of His own free choice, subjected Himself to death, because the sheep were to be rescued in no other way. To those who will have it that the section says nothing definite on the vicarious sacrifice of Christ, it may suffice to say that the Shepherd found the sheep in peril, and died to rescue them from it, which was only to be done by a vicarious death (ver. 12). When it is further argued that one acting in the capacity of a shepherd does not seek death, but rather avoids

it, as far as in him lies, and that the same thing must necessarily
have been done by Christ, the answer is at hand. Comparisons
agreeing in only one point of resemblance must not be too far
pressed; but here the Lord says, in the most express terms, that,
far from avoiding danger, as is commonly done, it was not so with
the good Shepherd, who spontaneously laid down His life.

This testimony sets forth the legitimate claim or right which
Christ acquired, in point of purchase by the atonement, to become the Shepherd of the sheep. It is the key to all those
allusions which we find in the apostolic Epistles, and in the New
Testament generally, to the office of the Shepherd, as well as to
all the assiduous care and watchfulness which He exercises in
behalf of the flock (1 Pet. ii. 25, v. 4). In contrast with the
Pharisees, He designates Himself "the good Shepherd;" which
three words may be thus resolved: (1) a *Shepherd*, because He
evinces the realized ideal of whatever that office signifies; (2) a
good Shepherd, because, whatever can be predicated of good or
excellent is found in Him; (3) *the good Shepherd*, by way of
eminence, because He was long expected and predicted in all the
ancient prophecies under that title (Zech. xiii. 7; Ezek. xxxiv.
23; Ps. xxiii.).

The peculiar and distinguishing act, nay, the unique act,
which the good Shepherd[1] here mentioned performs, is thus
announced: "I am the good Shepherd: the good Shepherd
giveth, or lays down, His life for the sheep" (ver. 11). We
must, first of all, determine the force of this expression, *giveth
His life for the sheep*, which is again and again repeated in the
sequel of this section. That it implies a condition of danger on
the part of the flock, is evident from the allusion to the wolf.
But we by no means interpret the words aright, or exhaust their
meaning, if we expound them, with many, as denoting merely
that the good Shepherd exposes His life to hazard. The Saviour

---

[1] ὁ ποιμὴν ὁ καλός. καλὸς intimates, in such phrases, that the person or thing
is all that it behoves to be, excellent, pre-eminent in his kind (Gen. i. 4; Matt.
iii. 10; 1 Tim. iv. 6).

means, much more, a self-surrender, a spontaneous oblation. The modern theories, deviating from the full acknowledgment of substitution, or of a vicarious sacrifice, commonly allege that Jesus, from the very nature of His position, must come within the laws of moral evil in the world, and perish by their operation, like ordinary men. That is the current representation given forth with much force at present, both abroad and at home, by all such as are opposed to the vicarious atonement. As the opposite has already been proved, I shall not in this place enforce a second time, either the general arguments or the historic facts presented to us in the life of Christ, which fully disprove that view of God's moral government of the world. But this utterance of Christ may, for all reverent interpreters, be accepted alone as absolutely conclusive: "I am the good Shepherd: the good Shepherd giveth His life for the sheep." He in substance says that His death, though a violent one, and necessarily inflicted by other hands, would not be against His will, but His own spontaneous act; that He could ward it off if He pleased; but that He would voluntarily submit to it for the sake of His sheep, and to secure His right to them. When He says that He giveth His life for the sheep, He intimates that, in His capacity as a substitute, and as the High Priest, who was called of God, He would lay down His life for His people, by a voluntary act of self-oblation.[1] And He announces in the sequel, as we shall see, that He had full authority over Himself, and was about to do what was competent to no created intelligence, to none but a divine person, to die for His fellows, or, as He sacerdotally expresses it, to lay down His life for the sheep.

He intimates that He was not to risk His life merely as does a patriot in the defence of his country, but actually, and of design,

---

[1] Compare Matt. xx. 28, which intimates the same thing. (See Tittmann on the passage.) It does not satisfy the force of this phrase, τὴν ψυχὴν τίθησι, to interpret it as meaning, to hazard or expose His life as a hero does for his country. (So Grotius.) τιθέναι ψυχὴν ὑπὲρ is a Johannine phrase (John xiii. 37). We need not be surprised that the phrase does not occur beyond the pale of revelation, for the idea is not found elsewhere.   Matthew has δοῦναι (Matt. xx. 28).

to lay it down.   That this is the only true import of the phrase,
is evident from the subsequent verses, where the Lord, in the
most express terms, contrasts the laying down of His life, and the
taking of it again (vers. 17, 18); from which we may argue, that
if the latter is to be interpreted as the spontaneous resumption of
life, the former can only signify the voluntary resignation of it.
Thus the antithesis between the two clauses determines the
meaning of the phrase, and puts it beyond all reasonable doubt,
that our Lord intends to express a voluntary death, which was
to be undergone, in order to obtain the salvation appointed for
His people.   This phraseology, then, from its very nature,
intimates that the Lord Jesus offered up His life, or died, in such
a sense that another is delivered in consequence of His substitution.

This leads me to advert to the preposition here employed:
"The good Shepherd giveth His life *for* the sheep."   The phrase
indisputably means, *for their benefit, for their good*.   Nor must
it be omitted, that when the clause in which this expression
occurs, denotes *instead of*—which it frequently does—this latter
idea is to be regarded as rather involved in the nature of the
transaction, than derived from the preposition itself.   When He
says, therefore, that He died or laid down His life for the sheep,
the phraseology implies, that from the nature of the case, He
suffered in their room and stead.[1]   The statement that He laid
down His life for the sheep, carries with it these two important
thoughts: that He acted from spontaneous choice, or from His
own proper motion, and not necessitated by any outward constraint; and that this substitution secured the safety of the
sheep.   Our Lord thus represents Himself as laying down His
life to save theirs from the danger and destruction which inevitably impended, or as dying to separate His sheep from those
that were exposed to the destroyer, and ready to be devoured.
From the fact that such a surety laid down His life, it follows,

---

[1] ὑπὲρ τῶν προβάτων.   The ὑπὲρ implies the ἀντί, as we noticed before in
section xxx.

by necessary consequence, that His people shall be saved with everlasting salvation.

Not only so: the whole connection of the words on which we have been commenting, leads us to the further thought, that He died to purchase them by His substitution, or to put them under His protection, and to make them His own. They are considered as not only rescued from danger, but as rescued to be His. That this is the full thought, of which we are not to stop short, is evident from a right interpretation of the passage as it stands. And hence, though Christ was called the Shepherd in virtue of His designation to this office, and though they also are designated the sheep in virtue of being given to Him by election, yet, in point of fact, He becomes the Shepherd, and they the sheep of His fold, only in virtue of the accomplished fact of the atonement. The Lord acquires an actual or purchased right to them as His sheep by His death. They are bought to be His, only by a price (Acts xx. 28. Compare Rom. xiv. 9).

As a consecutive commentary on this important passage would require us unduly to extend our remarks under this section, we shall limit our attention to two points: (1) the statements which elucidate the nature and character of the atonement; (2) the effects which are described in connection with it, as procuring for the Lord, not only a purchased right to His people considered as His sheep, but also the actual exercise of all those functions which belong to Him as the Shepherd. The second of these two is represented as the effect, fruit, or reward conferred on the Lord Jesus in virtue of His work of expiation. I shall refer to them both in order.

1. With regard to the words here used, which more particularly elucidate the nature of the atonement as a divine provision on the Father's part, and as a work accomplished on the part of the Son, He fixes our attention, in the first place, on the commandment of His Father: " This commandment have I received of my Father." This at first sight seems to run counter to the absolute authority in His own right, to which the previous

clauses emphatically lay claim; and this I notice first, as being first in the divine order of action. We have merely to settle the relative position of the two clauses, to discern all the sides of this important truth. How can we harmonize these two things, apparently incongruous—the receiving a commandment to lay down His life, and the possession of intrinsic power to dispose of His life as He pleased? In other cases a command presupposes a want of this authority in him to whom it comes. But it is not so in the case of Jesus. He was at once Lord and servant, one with the Father (John x. 30), and yet obedient to Him. He both fulfilled the commandment and exercised His own inherent authority. It was only because Christ had an inherent divine right to dispose of His humanity at discretion, that He received this commission or command of the Father to lay down His life in the execution of a paction or covenant, which takes for granted all that inherent right, and proceeds upon it. That is the relation of the two propositions. The converse would involve error of the worst description. The supreme deity of Christ indeed shines through all these sayings. The word COM-MANDMENT, here used, is not to be interpreted *authority*, as it was by the old Socinians and modern Humanitarians. It refers to that covenant or counsel of peace, according to which the Lord Jesus, as a divine person, was appointed to act an impor-tant part in the restoration of the lost family of man, or required to suffer death for the redemption of the human race. A wide difference obtains, however, between a command imposed upon a creature, and a command imposed on Christ. In the former case, the command is absolute and binding, whether we will or not. In the case of Christ, the commandment applies only on the supposition that a work was to be done according to a divine paction, for the salvation of the human family, and that He, of His own proper motion, undertook to finish it, for the welfare of the Church. The phraseology implies that God appointed the arrangement, and is pleased to allow the substitution to redound to the account of others. This commandment He received from

the Father, or, in other words, He came into the world charged
with this momentous commission from the Father.[1]

Hence, all that was to be accomplished in our Lord's life after
the incarnation, was undertaken and carried on according to the
commandment of the Father. Whether we have regard, therefore, to the surrender of His life, or to the resumption of it, He
acted at every step only in obedience to the commandment of the
Father, who so loved the world, that He gave His only-begotten
Son, and required the atonement at His hands. This naturally
leads back our thoughts to other statements, to the effect that the
Father loved Him on His own account, and then loved Him on
this account, that He accomplished the work given Him to do
(ver. 17). The present verse raises our thoughts to the origin
of the covenant or pact between the Father and the Son for
man's redemption ; and the other declaration shows that Christ
on account of the fulfilment of the great undertaking, becomes,
in a new sense, the object of the Father's love and complacency;
and herein especially does God manifest His love to us men, that
He gave the commandment, and rewarded the surety for performing it.

2. The Lord here declares, in the most unconditional and unrestricted use of the terms, that no one took His life from Him,
and that the sacrifice was absolutely self-moved and voluntary.
No language could be more unambiguous, as addressed to hostile
minds before Him, and to all ages, ever ready to take up some
imperfect notion as to the spontaneous sacrifice of Christ. He
declares that no power from any quarter could exercise any constraint upon Him ; that He was exempt from the malice and
power of men, except in so far as He chose to surrender Himself into their hands. Immortality belonged to Jesus by a
double right. He was immortal, first of all, in virtue of a sinless and perfect humanity, in which no taint was to be found ;
and He was immortal, still further, in virtue of the fact that
His humanity was the flesh of the Son of God.

---

[1] This is the proper meaning of the ἐντολή.

To make this point still more clear and indubitable, He subjoins the additional statement, that He had power, in His own right, to lay down His life, and to take it again.[1] This saying no merely human personage could arrogate to himself. In the case of a martyr, for instance, who, in a certain sense, lays down his life in attestation to the truth, such an expression would be improper; for he only discharges an incumbent duty which he owes to God, and has no discretion to conserve or to retain his life—an idea which our Lord's words comprehend and imply. The death of Christ was so absolutely voluntary, that He had full-power to withhold the sacrifice or to offer it.

They who do not frankly accept Christ's true deity, are reduced to the necessity of making reservations as to the proper force of His language. They argue that the words, " to lay down His life," mean " to receive death willingly;" and that " to take it again," is to receive it from the Father's power. But that is not the import of the phraseology. The element of spontaneity and divine authority or power over His humanity must be discerned in both phrases; and hence there is a wide line of demarcation to be drawn between Christ's position and that of a created being. The words mean that it was in Christ's power, as a divine person, to resign His life, and that it lay within the resources of His omnipotence to resume it at His discretion. All this is contained in the language : " No man taketh it from me, but I lay it down of myself. I have power to lay it down, and I have power to take it again. This commandment have I received of my Father" (ver. 18). This passage is meant to be an exhaustive exposition of the priestly self-oblation of Christ. We may affirm that all one-sided opinions on the proper nature of the atonement, and especially that the modern theories, are shattered, and go to pieces upon this text; which uses every form of expression to bring out the

---

[1] The old Protestant commentators correctly interpreted the ἐξουσία as referring to the power of the Son of God to let the humanity expire, and by the same exercise of power to resume it. This is better than the comment of the moderns.

fact that our Lord, on the one hand, acted of His own proper
motion, and, on the other, according to a commandment, pact, or
agreement with the Father. It may serve to exhibit the full
force of this language, if we consider the third proposition.

3. The Lord next speaks of His reward for His self-oblation:
" *Therefore* doth my Father love Me, *because* I lay down my
life, that I might take it again" (ver. 17). The Jewish nation,
already seeking to compass His death, were not to conclude,
when they had gained their end, that Jesus was an involuntary
sufferer, or that His public execution was fatal to His Messianic
claims. They were not to think that He had been abandoned
by God. On the contrary, He here declares that, far from
incurring the position of one abandoned of God for ever, His
voluntary oblation was only the special ground of the Father's
love to Him, as is here expressly declared, or the procuring
cause of this great reward. The Lord means that He was
to be the special object of the divine love, and of the highest
possible exaltation, because He was to finish this work of atonement in His capacity as surety; or, in other words, He was to
receive this love, and all the reward which that love could confer,
and especially the glory and office of being the chief Shepherd,
only on this ground.

But before developing this thought, I must notice that our
Lord adds, that He laid " down His life, that He might take it
again." His death was, according to the express intention of
the offerer, to be succeeded by His resumption of life. This
is not the mere result or consequence of His death,—the language expresses design or intention. It is best to understand
it as intimating " on the condition that I take it again."[1] It
will thus intimate: He who cannot overcome death by tasting
death for others—that is, he who is not of such dignity as to
atone for the sins of men by dying, and yet able to take life

[1] Of all the four different expositions given of this phrase, τίθημι ἵνα, that of
Calvin, *hac lege ut*, is much to be preferred. It cannot refer to the mere issue
or result of His death apart from the intention or design, as ἵνα is the particle
employed.

again, cannot be, or be called, the Shepherd of the sheep. Christ intimates that He, from His own inherent dignity and resources, could do this, and that He laid down life, because He was one who could exhaust the curse, and not be destroyed by it. He alone could give His life, because He alone could take it again. A mere creature could do neither. This was an indispensable condition. It was necessary that He should not abide in death, but so lay down His life, that He could take it again; and He could not have been a Saviour, if He could not have taken His life again.

But let us return to Christ's reward. It may at first sight seem strange that the beloved Son, who in His own right dwelt from everlasting in the Father's bosom, should here describe Himself as the object of divine love, because He laid down His life. How could He so speak, when He was the Son of His love from all eternity? But the reward of Christ, to which this language points, is always based on the work of atonement or humiliation to which He stooped, and is correspondent to it; and the love of God, in the sense in which our Lord here uses the term, is peculiarly displayed in advancing Him to the office and dignity of receiving a multitude of redeemed sinners, and of being the chief Shepherd of the sheep. There is the same connection between the *because* and *therefore* in this saying that we find elsewhere expressed, when a connection is pointed out between Christ's work and His reward. It is the very same as when it is said, for instance, by the Apostle Paul: "He became obedient unto death, the death of the cross; wherefore God hath highly exalted Him" (Phil. ii. 8, 9). Some, whose opinions lead them to regard the cross as only a display of love, without any other element, regard this utterance as merely intimating that the Father's love to men found its full expression and manifestation on the cross.[1] But that notion is inadmissible on the ground of language which will not admit such an inter-

---

[1] Thus Stier expounds the words, but incorrectly; for the διὰ τοῦτο ὅτι will not bear such a meaning. (See Meyer.)

pretation, nay, on every ground, whether we have regard to philology or doctrine. The only meaning which the words will admit is, that the Father loved the Son with the love of recognition and reward for His voluntary sacrifice, and that He rewarded Him with all that exaltation, authority, and glory which are comprehended in the office of "the great Shepherd of the sheep." The laying down of His life was thus the reason why the Father loved Him in this sense, and made Him the object of His complacence and regard.

Thus it appears that Christ has won the sheep to be His by right of purchase. Accordingly, His exaltation to be Lord of all is uniformly put in connection with His death, and viewed as the reward of His atonement (comp. Phil. ii. 9). Not to mention the universal dominion which He exercises over all flesh, He has a peculiar authority over the Church, or over that flock for whose welfare He laid down His life,—being constituted the Lord of His people, the head of His Church, the Shepherd of the sheep, on the ground of His vicarious death. His dominion is based upon His sacrifice; and all Scripture, as well as this present section, is one consistent testimony to the fact that He was exalted because He was obedient to the Father's will.

Thus His death did not redound to the injury of the sheep, as it would have done in the case of the earthly shepherd. On the contrary, the surrender of life, and the resumption of it on Christ's part (ver. 17), were both conducive to the highest welfare of the sheep, and gave Him the legitimate right to become, in the full sense of the term, their Shepherd in point of fact. There was no cause to fear, lest, by the death of Christ, the sheep should be deprived of His protection, interest, and care. He took His life again, to be their everlasting Shepherd (ver. 18).

I may only further refer, for a moment, to the statement made in reference to the sheep. They are described as known by Christ, and as knowing Him (vers. 14, 15). The correct

mode of construing these two verses, is not to separate them by
a full break in the sense, but to connect them by a comma;[1] the
thought being that the mutual knowledge which obtains between
Christ and His people, has its counterpart in the mutual knowledge between the Father and the Son. The relation between
Christ and His people is thus like that which is between the
Father and Him. The thought is, that the Lord Jesus knows
His sheep, and that He is known of them with a knowledge
which has its analogue in the mutual knowledge between the
Father and the Son. They are here represented as His, because
given to Him from of old, and because bought with a price.
Hence He adds, a second time, that He laid down His life as a
vicarious sacrifice, in order to gain a right to the sheep (ver. 15).
But He adds furthermore: " And other sheep I have, which are
not of this fold: them also I must bring [lead], and they shall
hear my voice; and there shall be one fold [better, one flock],
and one Shepherd" (ver. 16). When the Lord states that He
had other sheep, and that they were equally His, He unmistakeably refers to the vast outlying Gentile world. Plainly,
our Lord does not refer to the danger to which His first disciples were exposed, on the occasion of His arrest and trial. He
means that other sheep were given to Him of another fold, and
that, in consequence of His atonement, He should lead or feed
other sheep, who should be accounted His, wholly irrespective
of nationality, and united under Himself as the chief Shepherd,
who should feed them all with equal love. The allusion is not
to the Jews of the dispersion, but to the gathering together of
all nations to Him; and His death was to be the grand uniting
power (comp. Eph. ii. 16). It was God's design and plan to
bring them together, and to unite them in one flock, every partition wall being broken down, and thus to make, not many
flocks, but one, under one Shepherd.

---

[1] See the translation which we have given at the commencement of this section.
The authorized English version, making καθὼς begin a new sentence, violently
severs the sentence, and loses its point.

It only remains to add, that the Lord announces two things in this section which deserve special notice,—how He acted in respect to the devouring wolf, and next in reference to the sheep.

a. As to the wolf, by which we must understand the great destroyer of men, the Lord contrasts Himself with the hireling who consults but his own safety, and leaves the sheep to their fate. On the contrary, He would not shun the certain death which He saw before Him, although He easily might have done so in the exercise of His inherent power. He might have found a refuge on earth, or translated His sinless humanity to heaven (John xii. 24). But He would spontaneously lay down His life.

b. As to the case of the sheep, to which He next refers, they are His own, known as such and loved as such (ver. 14). Our Lord, in describing this mutual knowledge and acquaintance, compares it to that which subsists between the Father and the Son. What finite mind can adequately measure this analogy, which our Lord announces as a something divinely constituted and actually existing in the sphere of fact? The knowledge, love, fidelity and care of which the Lord Jesus was the object has its analogue in the Shepherd's relation to His sheep. The terms imply that He is not only acquainted with all their outward and inward condition, but that they are the peculiar object of His love and care. He had received them as a donation from His Father, and was at the moment when He spoke in the process of offering the ransom which was to secure their safety. They, again, on their part, knew Him in His relation as Redeemer and Lord, the object of their confidence, the owner to whom it was their privilege to belong for time and eternity; and as they heard His voice they were led out and in to green pastures.

SEC. XLI.—SAYINGS WHICH REPRESENT CHRIST'S DOMINION, BOTH
    GENERAL AND PARTICULAR, AS THE REWARD OF HIS ATONE-
    MENT.

We shall in this section consider those sayings which describe
Christ's unlimited dominion in the universe, as based on His
redemption work. So constant are the allusions in the Epistles
and in the Acts of the Apostles to the universal lordship of
Jesus, and to the fact that the atonement is the basis on which
it rests, that we naturally expect to discover some express testimony of Jesus to the same effect; and we find, accordingly,
most explicit statements from His own mouth, that the exaltation awaiting Him was due to the fact that He was humbled as
the surety, and that He became obedient to the Father's will.

The Lord's dominion rests for its foundation partly on the
covenant between the Father and the Son, partly on the price
actually paid, or the meritorious obedience of the surety. A
brief allusion to these two elements will here suffice. The covenant takes for granted that certain conditions are to be fulfilled
before the full possession of this dominion is enjoyed. When
allusion is made to the actual donation of unlimited authority
conferred on the Son, this is clearly described in numerous passages as the result or effect of the covenant. Thus it is said:
"The Father loveth the Son, and hath *given all things* into His
hands" (John iii. 35): "Jesus knowing that the Father had
given all things into His hands, and that He was come from
God and went to God" (xiii. 3). The divines who maintain the
federal theology illustrate this point copiously in all its aspects.

The actual dominion stands connected with the express fulfilment of the terms or conditions on which the reward was to
be conferred. They who dislike the thought that He bore our
penalty, forget that this is the true ground of His mediatorial
glory. In order to possess the dominion, the atonement must
needs be consummated by the great High Priest ; and the

deeper the abasement, the greater the real honour. He acquired a title to become the Lord or Ruler of a ransomed people only by His blood (Acts xx. 28; 1 Cor. vi. 20; Rev. v. 9; 1 Thess. v. 9). He not only purchased redemption for His people by satisfying for their sins, but obtained a right to the possession of themselves as a peculiar people (Titus ii. 14), that He might be admired in all them that believe. The import of the term LORD as used of Christ implies that He has a purchased right to His people, and that they acknowledge it in the use of this term. Not only so: He has a dominion over all flesh (John xvii. 2), over all rational intelligences (Col. i. 20), being Lord of all— King of kings and Lord of lords.

1. To begin with an early testimony, we hear from Him the announcement that God gave Him authority to execute judgment, because He was the Son of Man (John v. 27). The meaning of this saying, according to the import of the title *Son of Man*, as already explained, is, that He should be exalted to the utmost conceivable dignity, and to the authority of pronouncing the irreversible sentence of the judgment day, because He had become, by voluntary abasement, the second man, and the atoning surety of sinners. That is the import of the title; and the whole passage proves that, in virtue of His atonement, Jesus was, in the first place, to be invested with supreme dominion, and to receive the authoritative exercise of all judicial functions, as the climax of His exaltation.

2. That the atonement is the foundation of Christ's dominion, considered in its particular bearing, will appear still more clearly, if we apprehend correctly the saying of Jesus, where He delineates the merits of His atonement for the conversion of others, by comparing Himself to a grain of wheat, which dies, and brings forth fruit. "*Verily, verily, I say unto you, Except a corn of wheat fall into the ground and die, it abideth alone: but if it die, it bringeth forth much fruit*" (John xii. 24). Here the influence of the atonement on the cause of Christ in the world is further described. As to the occasion, we find this saying

uttered in connection with the request of certain inquiring Greeks, who, under the force of religious impressions, wished to see Jesus, and to be introduced to Him. Their coming was a prelude to the vast multitudes who were soon to attach themselves to Him, and constituted a proof or evidence to the Lord, that the hour of His sacrifice was now come. No one can reasonably doubt whether our Lord here alludes to His death; and the formula, "verily, verily," commonly used when uttering some weighty truth, not finding a ready assent in the mind of His hearers, was meant both to convince His first disciples that it was no earthly dominion that He was setting up, and to show all ages that His death was no fortuitous event, but the great end of His coming, and destined to have decisive issues for multitudes.

The figure borrowed from nature is intended to display the indispensable necessity of Christ's atoning death, if a people were to be gathered to Him. He represents His death as the sowing of seed-corn, from which a harvest was certainly to be reaped in due time; and He says, the grain must die first. On the physical fact that a grain of wheat first dies before it fructifies, it is not necessary here to enlarge (comp. 1 Cor. xv. 36). The well-known Haller, who so fully met the exceptions taken by the sceptical writers to this language, points out that the visible parts of the grain, from the moisture of the soil, do suffer decomposition, and die; and that the germ, which alone lives, receives a new form, as the direct consequence of that decay. But what does our Lord mean by the language here used, when He represents the dying as being the antecedent to the much fruit? Some expositors will have it that the Lord had His eye on the fruit, which His death would yield to Himself in the glorification which was before Him. Others regard the fruit as the remission of sins, or as the benefits of salvation that accrue to His people.[1] But though these are results of the atonement, according to Scripture, they are, neither of them, the

[1] See Tittmann on the passage.

truths in this passage. Our Lord plainly refers to the multiplication of believers, or to the bringing of many to faith. This is by far the best commentary on the words; it harmonises with the figure. It is confirmed by the circumstances and by the occasion.[1] The meaning will thus be: that if He had not died, He never could have gathered a people to Himself, nor organized a Church; that the vast multiplication of subjects who were soon to come to Him, as these Greeks were already coming by anticipation, was to be the fruit of His atoning death. These words, then, intimate that His death was as indispensable to the erection of His kingdom, as the germination of the grain for the harvest. In a word, without His atoning death, He would have remained alone—a solitary unit, a sinless, perfect individual,—who would have gone to heaven alone. But there would have been no multitude to follow Him—no harvest.

3. Christ's particular dominion as to its specially attractive power, is founded on His atoning death. This comes out in the words: "*And I, if I be lifted up, will draw all men unto Me*" (John xii. 31). We may say that this whole section, beginning as it does with the visit of the inquiring Greeks, brings before us a series of sayings descriptive of the effects of the atonement in different points of view. He had just said that, by the adjudication of a pending process, the atonement gave the world to another proprietor or master, the consequence of which should be the ejection of its former prince; and here He adds, that the atoning sacrifice, now about to be offered, and nigh at hand, was to lay the foundation of His own dominion, and to constitute the ground or warrant of all that attractive power or subduing grace by which He should deliver men from the service of Satan, and draw them to Himself. The words emphatically prove that the cross is the basis of His sway over all whom He brings out of Satan's empire, and draws to Himself, as Lord. The phraseology employed, "and I, if I be lifted up," shows

---

[1] See Nösselt, *Opusc.;* Usteri, *Entwick. Paul. Lehrbeg.* p. 231; Hengstenberg on the passage.

plainly enough, as has been already proved, that the Lord has in His eye, not His glorification in heaven, but His abasement on the cross. This is the import of the phrase, "if I be lifted up." But, to obviate all doubt on this head, the evangelist subjoins his own inspired commentary: "This He said, signifying what death He should die" (ver. 33). The meaning, then, intended to be conveyed by our Lord, is simply this: that, in virtue of His atoning death, He should draw all nations equally to Himself. When we examine this pregnant passage, a certain measure of reserve is, beyond doubt, apparent in the language, arising not so much from a wish to conceal aught, as from the fact that the persons to whom He spoke could not yet receive the full import of the communication. But several points are made plain, partly by direct statement, partly by implication.

With respect to Christ's crucifixion, which is here considered in the light of a special and efficacious atonement, He speaks of it as the antecedent or cause of the erection of a kingdom, which is plainly contrasted with that dominion which Satan possessed, and which was to be founded on its ruins. He unmistakeably intimates, too, that the foundation of all that drawing power by which He should bring men to Himself, in His capacity of a King, invested with authority and dispensing divine life, is the propitiatory death of the cross. All this is contained in the connection of the clauses. The antecedent and consequent emphatically intimate this.

But He next refers to the personal exercise of this drawing power when He says, "*I* will draw." He thus, clearly enough, intimates that, though crucified, He was not to abide in death, but was soon to live, and set up a kingdom, drawing subjects into it; that is, that men were to be drawn to Him as the King. *He* was to draw men, and to draw them to *Himself;* and when He says *all men*, this must be interpreted in the light of the visit of these inquiring Greeks, who were Gentiles,. or as referring to the totality or definite company of the elect. He rather refers to men of every nationality and culture: "I will draw *all* unto Me." Not that all this was instantaneously to follow the crucifixion; but, as all were to be drawn, so the ground or warrant was, in every case, furnished by the cross.[1]

4. As to the more general dominion of Christ, we find that, subsequently to His resurrection, He reminded the disciples that His sufferings were the pathway to His power: "*Ought not Christ to have suffered these things, and to enter into His glory?*" (Luke xxiv. 26). This was a truth which they might have learned from Isaiah (Isa. lxii. 14, liii. 12), and from the prophecies and Psalms, which had long before sufficiently exhibited both the suffering and glorified Messiah, and set forth that the abasement only paved the way for the glory (Isa. lii. 14-53; Ps. xxii.; Ps. cx.). The dominion on which Jesus was to enter, was to be nothing but the reward and fruit of that expiation for sin which was offered upon the cross; and He was crowned with glory and honour, as the reward to which He was entitled. Thus the kingdom of Christ has its foundation, not so much in the truth He taught, as in the humiliation to which He descended, and in the redemption work which He finished. This kingdom was promised to Him as the reward of this finished work, for the world's redemption. On this foundation His kingdom was to be erected; and dominion was actually imparted to Him over His own purchased property, and also over all things, without limitation or exception, for the execution of His wise and gracious designs toward all who obey Him. After the consummation of His work, He received, as a reward for all His previous abasement and indignities, a condition of glory, in which the human nature of Jesus participates in a way which is far above our comprehension.

Questions are here raised as to the capacity in which Christ

---

[1] Another striking though little noticed saying of our Lord of the same import is: "No man can come to Me except the Father who hath sent Me draw him" (John vi. 44). The phrase *who sent Me* is sometimes so broad and comprehensive in its meaning as to include the whole finished work of the commissioned servant. Compare what we said on *sending* as used by John (John vi. 57 ; 1 John iv. 9). Here the atonement or *sending* is delineated as the basis of the *drawing*.

exercises His dominion, and whether we are to regard Him in this His regal authority as *God*, or as *man*, or as *Mediator*. Some, having regard exclusively to the divine power of the Lord, and to the perfections needed for the due discharge of this dominion, ascribe the kingdom to Him as God. Others, discerning that man's dominion over all nature was his primeval privilege, and that this was a dignity awaiting the second man on the completion of His work, are ready to refer all this rule and authority to Christ as man. But, more correctly, we must view this dominion as His due reward as Mediator: "To this end He both died and rose and revived, that He might be Lord both of the dead and of the living" (Rom. xiv. 9). We are not, then, to separate His human nature from His divine in any act of His dominion. The design to be attained was the world's salvation, and to prevent the sentence of condemnation from swallowing up mankind.

5. There are numerous sayings of Christ on the subject of His dominion, which delineate a general economy of gracious forbearance, during which men are brought to Him as individuals.

To exhibit the general nature of this dominion in a sinful world in some of its aspects, we must listen to our Lord's delineation of it. "The Father judgeth no man, but hath committed all judgment unto the Son" (John v. 22). His dominion, based, as we have seen, on the atonement, allows an economy of forbearance which could not otherwise have existed. How are we to expound, in a manner worthy of God, the words, "the Father hath committed all judgment to the Son?" Plainly, the Father does not recede from His inalienable function as the supreme Lord and Judge of rational beings, for that would be too human a mode of contemplating this transaction. Though we must hold, as a first principle, that there is no will in the Father which is not also in the Son, and conversely, still the kingdom of Christ, or the dominion of grace which is maintained in the earth, removes the distance between God and man in such a measure that, during the course of this dispensation or

economy, grace, remission of sins, and invitations to repentance
are constantly announced to mankind on the part of God. It is
a dominion which can have place only where there are sinners,
and which is sustained simply through grace, and aims at the
remission of sins; pointing also to a consummation where the
perfections of God shall at last be manifested in a renewed
humanity and in a purified earth. It was erected only on the
ground of Christ's expiatory death.

This dominion is, from its peculiar nature, adapted only to the
world in its present state of imperfection, and as corrupted by
sin.[1] It would be no rule appropriate for heaven, where sin
never enters, nor for hell, where forgiveness is never proclaimed,
and is only adapted to man in his present condition. Not that
Christ's merits only usher in a bare possibility of salvation,
while the application of His finished work depends, in whole or
in part, upon men themselves; for where true conversion takes
place, this result is ascribed to Christ's merits and to the operation of the Spirit. But the representation given of that dominion
is to the effect, that when the Lord had by Himself purged our
sins, He sat down on the right hand of God, and sent forth the
proclamation of remission to all nations in His name. The
expiatory death of Christ alone procured and established that
kingdom; and He was crowned with glory and honour, that He
might manifest, in the most signal way, a gracious dominion
among men, and overthrow the dominion of Satan. Thus God
restores many a forfeited privilege, and even prolongs the existence of the race, which, but for the atonement, would have been
forfeited, according to God's just sentence.

The statement has often been made, and still is made by
rationalistic writers, that Christ's kingly sway is nothing more
than the influence of truth upon the minds of men; by means
of which a new kingdom of truth and virtue is founded in the
earth, the members of which are those who embrace the truth,
with loyal subjection to its claims. They thus make Him

---

[1] See Royaards' *De waare aart van Jesus Koningryk*, Utrecht, 1799.

nothing but a king of truth, or a teacher of truth. Nor is that opinion warranted by the passage on which it is professedly based (John xviii. 37), for the Lord does not say that He is called a king only as bearing witness to the truth, and that, besides this, He has no other proper dominion. The Lord, in answer to Pilate's question whether He was a King, roundly affirms it, notwithstanding Pilate's obvious wish to hear Him disclaim such pretensions: "I am a king;" and the subsequent statement grounds His unambiguous and bold confession, as if He would say, "I will not dissemble; for this end was I born, and came into the world, that I should bear witness unto the truth."[1] The passage says nothing, then, about His having no other dominion but a subjective dominion of truth. Nor is that thought in the passage. That interpretation gives Christ no other dominion than such as apostles and teachers would have in common with Him. But to Christ alone is a kingdom ascribed; and no one shares it, or can share it, with Him, except as He graciously exalts them to sit with Him on His throne.

Thus the dominion of Christ, whether we view it in one aspect or in another, is founded on the atonement of the cross.

SEC. XLII.—THE INFLUENCE OF THE ATONEMENT IN PROCURING
THE GIFT OF THE HOLY GHOST.

There are several sayings of Jesus which point out the close connection between the gift of the personal Holy Ghost and the atonement of Christ. These I purpose briefly to elucidate in the present section. We find the Lord affirming, in a variety of passages, that it was He who, by His vicarious sacrifice, obtained for His Church this great gift. And, in discussing this point, it will be necessary to carry with us the canon of interpretation, which has already been frequently applied,—that whatever is

---

[1] The phrase, "to bear witness to the truth," occurs elsewhere, meaning, to declare the truth (comp. John v. 33); and this very passage is adduced by Paul in proof of the fact that Christ witnessed a good confession (1 Tim. vi.). It certainly does not mean that Christ is a king of truth, and in no other sense.

graciously conferred on man through Jesus Christ, was wanting in our natural condition. The Spirit, whose absence is thus taken for granted as in the other blessings, forfeited by sin, and no more within the compass of our own resources, is represented as restored or graciously provided by the Mediator between God and man. Our Lord's language, correctly interpreted, announces that the presence and operations of the Spirit were procured by His atoning sacrifice for a fallen world; and furthermore, that He is sent by Christ, and leads men to Christ. Not that the Spirit was unknown in the ages which preceded the incarnation and the redemption of the cross; for we see that He not only acted as the Spirit of inspiration in the case of spirit-filled men, such as Moses, the Judges, David, and the prophets generally, but came upon many, as an animating power, for the work of conflict or endurance to which they were called. But that preparatory work of the Spirit, as well as the personal enjoyment of forgiveness, was owing to the atonement, which had a retrospective as well as a prospective efficacy, and thus had an influence on all times. That supply of the Spirit enjoyed by the Old Testament saints was dependent on the atonement or meritorious work of righteousness, which was, in due season, to be brought in by the Lord Jesus. And the reason why the Spirit was not more largely given in the previous ages, was because this gift stood in causal connection with the atonement, and because the link between the two must unmistakeably be established, and appear in deed as well as in word. The actual effusion of the Spirit, in the fulness which distinguishes the Christian from the Jewish Church, was reserved for the day when Christ sat down on His mediatorial throne, filled with a plenitude of the Spirit, given to Him as the reward of His atoning sacrifice.

To understand aright our Lord's sayings on this point, it is obvious that we must regard Him as the second Adam. His work, as is everywhere assumed by Himself, and declared by His apostles, was the counterpart of Adam's disobedience; and

as the result of the fall appeared, among other things, especially
in this, that the Spirit was, in the necessary exercise of divine
justice, withdrawn from the human heart, which was thus left
not only without its great inhabitant, but a prey to all those
influences of a natural and visible kind which, in the absence
of the Spirit, inevitably draw the affections away from God,—
so the atoning work of Christ, not less influential for good than
was Adam's act for evil, brought back the Spirit in His fulness
to all for whom Christ was accepted as a representative, with
this further or additional security, that He was to be forfeited
and withdrawn no more. It is in the highest degree important
to regard the redemption work of Christ as the ground or meritorious cause, in virtue of which the Spirit was restored to man.
The Spirit was given only after the atonement was finished.
Not only so: He is given in connection with the preaching of
Christ crucified (Gal. iii. 3). God has respect to the cross in
communicating the Spirit; and believers, and the church in
general, in expecting His powerful operations, must fix their
undiverted gaze on the cross.

The sayings of Jesus on this point are explicit enough, and
leave no doubt that there is a special connection between His
atoning work and the gift of the Holy Ghost—such a link, in
fact, as is established between merit and reward. The connection in which the effusion of the Spirit stands with the atonement of Christ on earth, and with His intercession in heaven,
as founded on it, demands a special study; and when this is lost
sight of, everything is presented in a false light. Though the
Spirit, as a divine person, comes in the exercise of free and condescending love, He yet comes as the representative of Christ
and the Spirit of the risen Surety, according to the tenor of
Christ's prevailing intercession, and on the ground of the atonement. This intercession is never ineffectual, because it is founded
on the work which was finished on the cross; and it consists in
presenting before the Father that crucified humanity, in which He
accomplished man's redemption. The mission of the Spirit is

thus the fruit of Christ's atonement,[1] and one of the greatest fruits of His mediation in behalf of a fallen world.

We shall now notice more particularly a few of Christ's sayings, which serve to bring out this causal connection between the atonement and the donation of the Holy Spirit.

1. The first saying of Jesus on this subject was the promise uttered at the feast of Tabernacles, when He invited every one who had the sense of thirst, to come to Him and drink: "He that believeth on me, as the Scripture hath said, out of his belly shall flow rivers of living water. (But this spake He of the Spirit, which they that believe on Him should receive; for the Holy Ghost was not yet given; because that Jesus was not yet glorified.)" (John vii. 38, 39.) The special application of this text to Christ's glorification, which is immediately appended by the inspired evangelist, is the point which here demands our attention. But it will be necessary to ascertain, first of all, what our Lord signified by these words, and the rather because they are so uniformly misapprehended. The rivers of living water, described as flowing from the Christian are commonly understood to mean the communications of the Spirit which one Christian is made the channel of dispensing to another. To that interpretation, however, there are great objections: (1) It introduces an idea foreign to that which our Lord had expressed, which was the quenching of thirst; (2) it represents one Christian, as in some sense a fountain of the Spirit to others, which is not a biblical mode of representation. A better comment, and serving to maintain the unity of the figure, is to view the saying as of the same nature with the promise of Christ as to thirsting no more, for there should be the well of water within,[2] springing

---

[1] Whether we say with Owen and the Puritans that Christ PURCHASED the operations of the Spirit, or prefer another phrase, every biblical divine must hold that our Lord procured the Spirit by His atonement.

[2] The only exegete known to me who gives this interpretation, is Baumgarten-Crusius, who says, p. 308, "Das heisst sein Gemüth wird aus der Tiefe heraus unendlichfort Erquickung, Befriedigung haben, ganz wie A. O. 4, 14." Though Meyer condemns it, it is far the preferable comment, and gives consistency to the whole.

up to everlasting life (John iv. 14). It is thus a promise of full satisfaction and abundant refreshment to the thirsty themselves. This is the best comment on the words.

John next adds that the Lord spoke of the Spirit, who was not yet given, because Jesus was not yet glorified (ver. 39). The language literally is, "for the Holy Ghost was not yet."[1] This of course does not mean that there was no personal Holy Ghost before Christ's ascension, but that He was not yet dispensed, as He was afterwards given, to the Church. The commentary of John, setting forth the two points, that all who believe should receive the Spirit, and that the Spirit was not yet given, demand some elucidation. The metaphor may refer to the Old Testament prophecies and to the passages in Isaiah, Ezekiel, Joel, and Zechariah, where the gift of the Spirit is frequently expressed under the figure of pouring water on him that is thirsty, and floods on the dry ground. Commentators largely refer these words to the diversity between the two economies in regard to the measure of the Spirit, and to the amount of spiritual liberty or assurance conferred. But that by no means exhausts our Lord's words, even though that antithesis were maintained by the interpreter as the true point of the saying. The language sets forth that the Spirit's presence and operations could only be consequent[2] on Christ's vicarious satisfaction, and His exaltation to the mediatorial throne. The word *glorified* is intended to denote the way and the end, the atonement and the exaltation, but not the latter irrespective of the former. He in fact intimates that the donation of the Spirit is a fruit of the everlasting righteousness brought in, or of the vicarious sacrifice offered, of which this glorification was but the reward and proof. However men may interpret the word

---

[1] οὔπω γὰρ ἦν Πνεῦμα ἅγιον. Tholuck says this is the πνεῦμα Χρ. as contrasted with the πνεῦμα δουλείας. Lücke says that the difference between the Old and New Testament lay in the smaller and larger measure of the Spirit. Olshausen appeals to the relation of the different persons of the Trinity. These do not exhaust the meaning.

[2] See the quotation from Gerhard at the end of this section.

glorified in this passage, they must comprehend way and end, antecedent and consequent, merit and reward, cause and effect. The best Greek[1] interpreters lay the emphasis on the cross, and many modern interpreters expound it of Christ entering on His glory by means of that vicarious suffering on which the effusion of the Spirit was to follow as a fruit.

2. Another important saying of Christ on this point is: "It is expedient for you that I go away: for if I go not away, the Comforter will not come unto you; but if I depart, I will send Him unto you" (John xvi. 7). Various reasons have been assigned by interpreters why it was expedient that Christ should go away, and why the Spirit could not come unless the Lord departed. These reasons have been expressed sometimes in one tendency, sometimes in another, and sometimes on grounds that have little, if anything, to support them. Thus, some have alleged, as the reason why it was expedient that He should go away, that a belief in His divinity could not consist with His visible presence. Others have explained the reason of His departure, from the consideration that the disciples, while they clung so much to Christ's corporeal presence, were not in a state of mind which was fully capable of receiving the Spirit. These grounds are merely of a subjective character, and quite faulty. Another explanation, which is also subjective, alleges that the Comforter could not, in point of fact, act the part of a comforter, if there were no deep necessity for consolation, such as was supplied by Christ's departure. It would be tedious to enumerate and to discuss all the various opinions which have been given; and I shall content myself with stating what seems to be the obvious meaning of the words.

When Christ speaks, in this passage, "of going away," the

---

[1] Thus Chrysostom says, δόξαν καλῶν τὸν σταυρόν. So Euthymius, following Chrysostom. Theophylact's beautiful comment to the same effect might be quoted in full, but it is too long. He says, οὔπω οὖν τοῦ σταυροῦ παγέντος οὐδὲ τῆς ἁμαρτίας καταργηθείσης εἰκότως οὐκ ἐδόθη ἡ δαψιλὴς τοῦ Πνεύματος χάρις. To the same purport are Hengstenberg's words on this passage: "in der Thatsache der geschehenen Versöhnung wurzelt die Potenzirung des Geistes." The latter quotes, as a proof, Jer. xxxi. 31.

language plainly means His return to heaven, but comprehends a further reference to the expiation of sin, or to that pathway of atonement and obedience by which He was to go. In a word, the Spirit could not come without the vicarious sacrifice of the cross; and Christ's departing to the Father by such a way— that is, in the accomplishment of a course of obedience—was indispensably necessary, if the Spirit was to come. It is just another mode of stating that He had merited the donation or supply of the Spirit by His sufferings.[1] He intimates that the gift of the Spirit, who comes as a personal inhabitant to the human heart, and who brings, when He so comes, the communications of life, light, and divine supplies, can be received and possessed only when the guilt of sin has been cancelled, and the entire curse under which men were held has been fully and righteously reversed. Thus Christ's return to the Father includes the way as well as the end; or, in other words, designates His departure by means of the atonement, or expiation of sin, which is thus represented as the only channel by which the supplies of the Spirit could be communicated in every variety and form.

It must be further noticed, that the Lord in this passage gives the necessary prominence to the Spirit's operations, without removing the Church's eye from Himself as the crucified One, and as the Lord our righteousness. What was to accrue to men from this mission of the Spirit, is expressly taught in the words immediately subjoined; intimating that when He is come, He shall convince the world of sin, of righteousness, and judgment. By the first He understands *the sin of unbelief*, as He explains it

---

[1] The Greek exegetes, Chrysostom and Theophylact, already quoted on the former saying of Christ, are most explicit to the same effect here. Luther adopts their comment; and Gerhard, *Harmon. Evangel.* iii. p. 324, after quoting, with approval, the Greek comments, says: "Quæ præbet utilem doctrinam, quod donatio Spiritus Sancti sit salutaris fructus passionis et mortis Christi ac congruit phrasi, qua Christus utitur, quia per abitum suum ad Patrem non tantum intelligit ascensionem in cœlos, qua venit ad Patrem, imo ad dextram Patris consedit, *sed etiam viam mediam*, per quam eo venit, nempe iter passionis et mortis."

(ver. 9). By *righteousness*, He intimates, not the justice of His cause, but, as we already proved, the righteousness which He wrought out, in His atoning death, for His people (ver. 10). By *judgment*, He understands that the adversary has lost his cause in the great judicial process, and therefore all lawful claim to the property which he formerly possessed. All this is won through the expiation of sin effected by Christ (ver. 11).

The Lord had promised the Comforter, as the author of a two-fold work: (1) to testify of Himself: and (2) to qualify the disciples for the great office of planting His gospel in the world (John xv. 26, 27). The former was a more immediate work of the Spirit: the latter should be effected through the medium of the Spirit's operations on the minds of the disciples. The former is explained first (John xvi. 7-12): the latter is subjoined, and specially points out how the apostles' minds should be enlightened, regulated, and directed by the Spirit for the work of bearing witness to Christ (v. 12-15). On these points it falls not within our plan to expatiate. Let it suffice to say that the Comforter was promised to lead the disciples into all the truth, and therefore not only into a clear perception of the *rationale* and connections of the truth already known, but also into parts of it which hitherto could not have been borne (v. 12, 13). It was further promised that the Comforter should not, like the seducing or erring spirit which leads men's mind astray, speak of Himself, but in fellowship with the Father and the Son (v. 13). Whatsoever He should hear He was to speak—which means that the Spirit, in a way to us inscrutable, hears from the Father and the Son; knowing the mind of God, and searching the deep things of God. The truth imparted by the Spirit to the disciples was thus to emanate from the Father and the Son: and what was spoken should have special reference to the counsel of peace. He was to take of Christ, that is of His divine dignity and glory, and show them things to come, or make them prophets; and all the New Testament books are replete with and breathe the prophetic spirit.

To understand the evangelist's references, we must remark, that whenever John adduces our Lord's words as alluding to His departure, or to His return to the Father (John xvi. 28), there is uniformly comprehended in His words such a going or return as is consequent on the accomplishment of the finished work of redemption. Now, as it was only at the glorification of Christ, that is, at the time when God and men were reunited by the completed work of atonement, or by the payment of the ransom, that the Holy Ghost could be legitimately given to man, and come forth on His mission in the sense described in the New Testament,—so the actual sending of the Spirit, as our Lord further shows, is only to be by means of a Mediator who has passed through death, and made an end of sin, and sat down on the throne of glory.

3. Another saying may be adduced, pointing out the relation in which the gift of the Spirit stands to the death and intercession of Christ: "I will pray the Father, and He shall give you another Comforter" (John xiv. 16). When the true High Priest entered heaven, and appeared in the presence of God for us, on the ground of His finished work on earth, one part of that ever-active intercession, as He here declares, was to ask the Spirit for His people, that is, to ask what God had promised to bestow, according to the merit of His death. It was indeed to be no small part of His reward, that He should acquire a right to ask the Spirit, and to send Him, in consequence of giving His life a ransom for many.

Such is the connection between the gift of the Spirit and the mediation of Christ. They must be apprehended together; and the isolation of the Spirit's work from the cross and crown of the Redeemer is always of doubtful tendency, and calculated to divest the theology, to which it gives a tone, of its evangelical liberty. It speedily engenders a legal element; and hence, according to this view of the connection between Christ and the Spirit, it is necessary to fix a steady gaze on Christ's cross, as the Lord our righteousness. The living personal Saviour, the true

foundation of life to humanity, gives the Spirit, thus won or procured by His death.

As our object, in this section, is only to point out that the gift
of the Spirit has a *very close relation* to the great fact of the
atonement, it is not necessary to refer specially to the Spirit's
work as carried on in the heart. Let it suffice to say that He is
called the Spirit of Life (Rom. viii. 2), by whom sinners, alienated
from the life of God, are quickened and renewed; the Spirit of
Faith (2 Cor. iv. 13), because the author and cause of faith; the
Spirit of Adoption, by whose aid the timid come boldly to God
(Gal. iv. 6); the Leader, by whom the Christian is led (Rom.
viii. 14); the Helper of their infirmities (Rom. viii. 26); the
Sealer, who seals them as the inviolable property of Christ, to
the day of redemption (Eph. iv. 30); the earnest of the inheritance (Eph. i. 14); the originator of all spiritual fruit, called
fruits of the Spirit (Gal. v. 22); and who abides in them for
ever (John xiv. 16).[1]

SEC. XLIII.—CHRIST'S ABASEMENT AS THE SECOND MAN OPENING
HEAVEN, AND RESTORING THE COMMUNION BETWEEN MEN AND
ANGELS.

" *Verily, verily, I say unto you, Hereafter ye shall see heaven*
open [better, opened], *and the angels of God ascending and*
descending upon the Son of Man." (John i. 51).

This saying of Jesus points out the intercourse between angels
and men, and the foundation on which it rests. It may be called
the key to all those numerous allusions which are found in the

---

[1] There are two phrases used in reference to the Spirit: παρ᾽ ὑμῖν μένει, and ἐν
ὑμῖν ἔσται. The phrase, ἐν ὑμῖν ἔσται (John xiv. 17), occurs only once in Christ's
sayings, but it significantly represents Him, not as an objectively operating
power, but as a subjectively present power, given by God, and for ever dwelling
in the Christian. The other phrase, παρ᾽ ὑμῖν μένει, seems to refer more to the
preparatory work of the Spirit before Pentecost; that is, while Christ was still
with them.

Acts, and in the apostolic Epistles, to the ministration of angels (Acts xii. 7; Heb. i. 14), and to their being gathered together into one, and recapitualed, along with redeemed men, under one head (Eph. i. 10; Col. i. 20).

As to the occasion of this saying, it was spoken to Nathanael at the time when he was first brought into Christ's presence. Nathanael may have been meditating in secret on the second Psalm, for he uses the two titles of the Lord contained in the Psalm, in giving expression to his sense of Christ's dignity and office, "Rabbi, Thou art the Son of God, Thou art the King of Israel." The Lord, having given a convincing proof of His more than human knowledge, by referring to exercises—probably religious inquiries—under the fig-tree, said that he should see greater things than these, which had just called forth his adoration and religious homage; and then, according to His manner, when referring to Himself, He immediately begins to speak from the view-point of His incarnation and humiliation, as the great display of His grace, calling Himself " Son of Man." The explanation already given of this title, in a previous section, contains sufficient evidence that it uniformly alludes to Christ's abasement as the second Adam, or to some of the fruits or consequences arising from that obedience unto death, to which it always refers.

The centre of the whole announcement is this title of Christ, " The Son of Man."[1] And the promise here expressed, in connection with it, shows that there is a causal or meritorious link between the blessing and the humiliation of the second man, the surety of sinners. The title placed in immediate connection with the promise, implies all this. Not only so : the fact that this is the precise title, appropriate to the occasion and utterance, is of itself sufficient to convince us that the promise, whatever

---

[1] The mistakes in the interpretation of this difficult text come from not apprehending the phrase, ὁ υἱὸς τοῦ ἀνθρώπου. Calovius' and Gomar's erudite discussion on the passage fail, on this account ; and so, too, Marckius, *Exerc.* xxv. 1. N. T.

may be its special import, refers to an angelic ministry, or an angelic fellowship with men, and that, though it may seem to be directed in the first instance to the Lord Himself, it is more to be referred to the disciples, for whom He acted, in this capacity as the Son of Man.[1]

That the words refer to Jacob's vision in some sense is admitted by almost every expositor of any note. On the question whether the ladder indicated Christ, there was little difference of opinion among the older divines, such as Calvin and others, who all affirmed it. Most is to be said in favour of the view, that our Lord referred to Jacob's ladder as the figure of Himself, and therefore, that the Son of Man is the uniting link of heaven and earth. The vision, in its application by Jesus to Himself, implies that, as the true Mediator between God and man, He opens a way, and keeps it open, between heaven and earth, by His humiliation unto death. That this is the import of the words, is generally maintained by the best interpreters. But the emphasis which the passage gives to the atoning work of Christ as the foundation of all those blessings delineated in the promise, has not been sufficiently adverted to, from the fact that commentators have so much failed to exhibit the proper import of the title, " The Son of Man."

Another widespread inquiry was propounded, Might not our Lord mean to represent Himself, not as the reality and truth of what was figured forth in the ladder uniting earth and heaven, but rather as the Lord who stood above it ?[2] They who adopt this latter view will have it, that Christ describes Himself as the Lord, not only of men, but of angels. They suppose that this is intimated by the ascending and descending *to* the Son of Man ; for so they translate the preposition *upon* ($\epsilon\pi\iota$).[3] The

---

[1] Meyer incorrectly makes it, "symbolische Darstellung des permanenten lebendigen Wechselverkers zwischen dem Messias und Gott."

[2] So the celebrated French preacher, Du Bosc, explained it. See Witsius, *Meletem Leidensia de Aperte Cœlo*, p. 213 ; and also Muntinghe, *Gescheid.. der Menschheid*, ix. Aan 41.

[3] The preposition $\epsilon\pi\iota$ here denotes, not *to*, but *upon*, and refers equally to the *ascending* and the *descending*. As Lücke well observes, the ascending and descend-

idea, according to this interpretation, is, that as Jehovah, in
Jacob's dream, was seen at the top of the ladder directing the
angels to do His pleasure and execute His will, this is Jesus the
Son of Man sending forth the angels, whose Lord He is (Heb. i.
6). They suppose our Lord to say that He sends the angelic
intelligences to execute His commands in all the realms of
nature, and in every variety of errand connected with His
kingdom, and that this is a greater thing than that which
Nathanael had yet seen. Hence, the words are referred by
many to the future of the Messianic kingdom, the Millennial
period; or to gathering in the elect at last from the four
corners of the globe, or to the carrying of departed spirits home.[1]
And the more this class of expositors identify the Son of Man
with the Lord, who stood above the ladder in Jacob's vision, the
more are they persuaded that it is descriptive of Jesus commis-
sioning or sending forth the angels, of whom He is the Lord.
But this comment proceeds upon the supposition that " The Son

---

ing of the angels is to be comprised in the one idea of *uninterrupted intercourse*,
—the ascending standing first both in Genesis and here ; and we may say with
Tholuck, that it means, they return to heaven to receive new commissions. We
cannot refer the words to the angelophanies in Gethsemane and at the Lord's
resurrection, as Witzius, Grotius, and Chrysostom interpret the words.

[1] There is no good ground for cancelling ἀπ' ἄρτι, with Lachmann ; but it must
be understood as qualified by the phrase, " Son of Man." Aright understood, it
gives no warrant for the argument of Witsius and others, that the reference is to
what immediately took place. It refers rather to what follows, or is consequent
upon the work of *the Son of Man*.

We cannot refer this language to the miracles of Jesus in which He used angels
(so Piscator), or make it a vague generality to denote miraculous manifestation
(so Lightfoot, Michaelis), or make it mean God's help and providence, which
Christ was to experience (Morus). Much more happily, Chemnitz, *Harmon.
Evangel.*, p. 239, says : " Docet igitur Christus officium suum esse cœlum aperire,
et cœlestia rursus conjungere cum genere humano, quod per peccatum et a Deo
et a sanctis angelis avulsum fuerat, ut simus cives sanctorum, et angeli jam
descendant super humanam naturam assumptam a Filio Dei, et propter caput
etiam jam emittantur, scilicet ad ministerium electorum (Heb. i. 14) : emissio
enim ad ministerium per descensum et ascensum describitur. Nam angeli emissi
descendunt et rursus sistunt se Deo ascendendo, injuncti ministerii rationem
reddituri (Job i. 6 ; Zech. i. 11)." The only thing awanting here, is the connection between this ministry and the title " Son of Man," correctly understood.

of Man" is a title of dignity, whereas we have fully proved that it is a title of humiliation and service.

The starting-point in this inquiry is, What is the significance of the title *Son of Man*, which is not used as a mere expletive, but as intimating the foundation or ground on which the angelic agency here mentioned rests ? As this has been discussed and established in a separate section, it is only necessary to refer to the conclusion at which we arrived. The work of the sin-bearing second Adam is the point or import of the title ; and one of the effects which that atonement ushers in, as here stated, is the restoration of the long-forfeited intercourse between men and angels, who are brought together as two branches of one family in Christ, or gathered together under one Head—the reconciler of all things in earth and heaven (Col. i. 20). If the partition wall between Jews and Gentiles is removed by the cross, and the enmity slain thereby, the same thing holds true in reference to angels and men; and all that the promise here mentioned contains, stands in causal connection with the abasement of the second man. Moreover, the expression *Henceforth*, is an incontrovertible proof that, however far the provisions of this promise extend, and however long they may be carried out, they all took their origin from His surety work and His obedience unto death.

1. The first part of the promise shows that heaven, once shut, is now opened. It sets forth, according to the canon frequently applied by us, that the opposite obtained before, and that through the humiliation of Christ there is now an open intercourse with heaven, together with the free supplies and rich communications of divine grace. The heavens were opened at the baptism of Jesus (Matt. ix. 16) ; and again, on the Mount of Transfiguration (Matt. xvii. 3-5), announcing what was soon to be effected by the completion of His atoning work, to which all these scenes pointed ; a third time, when the voice came from God to the suffering Jesus (John xii. 27) ; and at Stephen's martyrdom we see what may be taken as the special privilege of all the Christian Church (Acts vii. 5, 6).

2. The second part of the promise announces a restored communion between angels and men, who had long been widely estranged by sin. Angels were, previous to the death of Christ, separated from all fellowship with our race; and though we read of many Old Testament angelophanies, it is not the less true, that any ministry on which they came, before the incarnation, was based on that atonement which was to be accomplished on the cross. But now, says Christ, *Henceforth* peace shall be restored between angels and men, the partition wall being broken down. They are now both reduced, or, as it has been rendered, recapitulated under one Head (Eph. i. 10), and are only separate departments of one family and household. Thus, all that angelic ministry, which we find so often mentioned in the Acts of the Apostles, and doctrinally set forth in the Epistles (Heb. i. 14; Col. i. 20), depends, as this testimony fully proves, on the atonement of the cross, or on the fact that the Son of God has become the Son of Man.

As to the ministration of angels, it is spoken of as a fact, and in such a way as intimates that the Lord sends them forth on various errands during all the Christian's pilgrimage. The two special works recorded as belonging to their ministry, are the conveying of the souls of the departed to their place of bliss, and the final gathering or collecting of the elect on the resurrection day. But these presuppose, as going on at present, ministrations of every varied description, such as the Scripture records in multitudes of instances; and Christ's people are warranted to believe that angels encamp around the Church and her individual members; and the foundation of the whole is the cross, which makes both the families one under one Head.

SEC. XLIV.—SAYINGS OF JESUS WHICH REPRESENT THE ATONEMENT
AS GLORIFYING GOD.

Various intimations are conveyed in our Lord's sayings, to

the effect that His redemption-work glorified God; and these demand an accurate examination. To understand them aright, it will be necessary to go back a step, and to read them off from a similar and opposite state of things. We must start from the fact that sin had dishonoured the divine majesty, and robbed Him of the declarative glory due to Him, according to the relations in which a personal God stands to the world.

It is the more necessary to place this point in a proper light, because it is precisely the element which is too readily dropped or displaced from the prominence that properly belongs to it. I shall not adduce all the sayings that might be collected together on this point, but content myself with a few of the most emphatic. Nor shall I inquire whether the glorification to which our Lord's language points, refers more to His conscious design and purpose, or to the effect which His atoning death subserved, and to which it tends; for, in truth, these two, however capable of being distinguished in idea, were never dissociated in His mind, nor disjoined in His actual walk. In handling those testimonies which represent God as glorified by means of Christ's atonement, it seems to me that there are two different aspects in which this matter is presented,—one rather exhibiting Christ's act as the representative of the creature, and a second rather exhibiting the Father's act. They are not to be confounded, though they must necessarily be united, if we would see the whole matter in a biblical light, and as reflected from Christ's own consciousness.

1. First of all, I shall notice a remarkable saying belonging to the first class just named, found in the Lord's intercessory prayer: *" I have glorified Thee on the earth; I have finished the work Thou gavest Me to do "* (John xvii. 4). The meaning of these two clauses, when put together, is, that the one is the means or pathway to the other,—that the glorifying of God on the earth was attained by the work given Him to do, and now finished. That, beyond doubt, is the relation in which the one clause stands to the other, as an examination of the passage will suffice to prove.

There is in these first verses an allusion to a twofold activity of Christ, and to a double glorification of the Father. Thus the Lord declares that He *had* glorified the Father (ver. 4), and also intimates that His ascension was to be made the means by which He, the Son, *should* glorify the Father (ver. 1); which can only refer to the revenue of glory which should redound to God by means of the Gospel, by the existence of a Church, and by the final perfection of the saints: for a tribute of glory redounds to God from all those results which subsequently stand connected with the ascension or the glorifying of the Son (ver. 1). But in this passage which we have quoted, Christ speaks of glorifying the Father by means of a work finished on the earth; and it is the finishing of that work which glorified the Father.

The interpretation of this language is by no means difficult. From these words some have concluded that all that Christ had to do according to the divine plan, consisted in His instructions as a teacher, or, as it is put in the context, in the manifestation of God's name, and that when that was done, His work was finished. But we cannot limit the words to His work as a teacher, especially when we find that the Lord grounds His request to be glorified with the Father (ver. 5) on His work done, which can only be His priestly self-oblation; for only when that work was done, could He expect with confidence His due reward. He must suffer and be obedient unto death (Phil. ii. 8); He must voluntarily lay down His life according to the commandment received from His Father (John x. 18); and then be exalted to the place of supreme dominion, and to have power over all flesh, to give eternal life to as many as the Father has given Him. This was His crown of glory and high reward. In this sense we must understand the words; they affirm that He finished the work, and now enjoys the reward. He first makes mention of a work to be done, and then announces that it was finished, or as good as finished, because it was already accomplished in His purpose. It is not difficult to perceive what that work is to which our Lord refers. The description of it, in the first place, as a work assigned to Him, and then the reward of glorification for which He prays in connection with it (ver. 5), suffice to show that the allusion is to the atonement or vicarious work of the Mediator, so far as it must be finished on the earth. He alludes to the work given Him to do as the surety of others, and which was well-nigh finished. The word here used sometimes means to bring to an end, and at other times denotes the measure and degree of perfection to which a thing is brought. And our Lord could testify of His work, with the greatest emphasis, that it was perfected; not only that it was brought to an end—for He was already mentally offered,—but that He perfectly and completely performed it in all its parts, so that it was every way complete and without defect.[1] In other words, there was nothing lacking, nothing left undone in His mediatorial undertaking. And if it is asked, how could He say that His priestly work was done, and perfect in its measure as well as in all its parts, when the most arduous part of His task lay before Him ? the answer is at hand: He was come to the last day of it—the morrow would see it done; and hence He speaks of it as already accomplished and wound up.

We have adduced the passage, however, to show that the finished or perfected obedience of Jesus, both in action and in suffering, redounded to the glory of God, and this in design, as well as in tendency and effect. The matter of His obedience flowing as it did from a lively sense of God's greatness and perfections, was to the glory of God. There was in the active obedience such a glorifying of God as could not be found in any creature, and which was amply proportioned in point of merit, to procure for men eternal life.

This view proceeds on a just conception of the divine claims, and presupposes deep views of sin on the one hand, and of the divine adaptation of the atonement as a remedy for sin on the

---

[1] τὸ ἔργον ἐτελείωσα ; and the aorist is used, as the Lord views it as already done, or, as Alford well puts it, "looks back on it all as past." (See Gerhard's *Harmon. Evangel.*, and Charnock, ii. p. 184.)

other. It is a mode of surveying the atonement, which is not only of the utmost importance in itself, but so comprehensive in its range, that it takes in all the more definite statements which may be made on the subject of the divine law. It involves the necessity of the magnifying of the divine law to make it honourable. We cannot admit, then, when we trace these allusions of our Lord Himself to the restoration of the divine honour, that the theology which grounds itself on this notion is worthy of being called, as it has been called, an outward stand-point of abstract reflection. Nor will it do to say, with such a testimony before us, that the referring of the work of Christ to the divine law, according to the representation current in the evangelical Church, is not only much more conformable to the type of Scripture doctrine, but much more practical, living, and experimental than this reference to the divine honour;[1] for in point of fact they do not exclude each other. The one is from the view-point of Christian experience; the other is from that of the divine throne. The view of the atonement, which surveys it in connection with God's declarative glory, is not only biblical in its import, but necessary in an experimental point of view.

First, as to the biblical warrant for the position, that the divine honour has been taken away, and must needs be restored as an indispensable condition of forgiveness, the Apostle Paul plainly exhibits it in the broad outline which he gives of redemption in the section of the Epistle to the Romans, where he brings together two things: the fact that men come short of the glory of God, and the consequent necessity of an expiation for sin (Rom. iii. 23). The sense of that passage, when taken in connection with the context, involves incontrovertibly the idea of rendering to God His honour, or the tribute of declarative glory due to the Creator from His intelligent universe. What is the glory of God there spoken of, and of which all men come short? Of the different modes of exposition which have been given, the com-

---

[1] Thus Philippi expressed himself against Anselm's principal position in his *cur Deus homo*. (See Hengstenberg's *Kirchenzeitung* for 1844.)

ment which refers the phrase to the divine image once possessed, but lost by sin, approaches nearest to the apostolic thought.[1] It involves the idea of rendering glory to God, or of giving Him His honour, by a pure nature, and a God-glorifying obedience. When Christ glorified God, He did it as the Mediator representing man, and in the way of creaturehood in its perfection, learning obedience by what He suffered (Heb. v. 8). If it is said of Peter that he was to glorify God by a martyr's death (John xxi. 19), and if renewed men are changed from glory to glory (2 Cor. iii. 18), much more did the sinless Mediator glorify the Father by His perfect work.

And as to the necessity of this view in an experimental respect, conscience cannot be satisfied with any method of atonement that does not secure the divine honour. Far from feeling satisfied with a defective scheme, conscience asks with wistful eagerness, whether, by the way propounded, God's honour suffers no eclipse, and His majesty no stain; and if conscience, as God's vicegerent, is pacified only when God's honour is restored, it is not difficult to see, that without this view the glorious liberty of the saints would be forestalled, and give place to inextricable bondage. Thus the principle to which we have been referring, far from propounding a mere abstract reflection, is derived from the centre of biblical and experimental truth, and is but an echo of this saying of Christ. This will aid us in perceiving a correct exposition of Christ's words in reference to the glory that redounds to the Father from His work. He undertook to restore the glory due to the divine majesty withdrawn by man's sin, and for which a reparation must be made, although that could not be effected by angels or men; and this

[1] The four interpretations of δόξα proposed by different commentators, are these: (1) that it refers to the future glory (so the Greek exegetes, Beza, Bengel); (2) glorifying before God (Luther); (3) honour, as at John xii. 43 (so Stuart); (4) the created image of God (so the old Lutheran expositors, Chemnitz, Calov, Schmidt; also among the Reformed, J. Alting; and so, too, Olshausen). This last comment is every way to be preferred, and shows that the image of God is the glory of God, and that this, carried out in all things, is the true and only way in which God can be glorified by a creature.

part of the Lord's mediatorial obedience had such value and dignity, that it was fully adequate to this end. There was that in the work of Christ which fully satisfied the insulted majesty of God.

2. A second class of testimonies contains a declaration of that which God does to glorify His name by the atonement. There are two sayings of Jesus which here demand elucidation.

The first is that passage where He appealed to the Father during His soul trouble or anguish: "Father, glorify Thy name. Then came there a voice from heaven, saying, I have both glorified it, and will glorify it again" (John xii. 28). There is a reference to a past act of glorifying His name on the part of God, and a promise of another yet future. This is very note-worthy; but what precisely does it import? Plainly, the words intimate, that up to that moment the human life of Christ, to which the language must refer, had been a continuous glorifying of God, both in purpose and effect; that as man by his apostasy had trampled under foot the declarative glory of God, not rendering the glory due to His name, so the second man brought what is the due tribute to God. But the words, descriptive as they are of God's own act for the glorifying of His name, intimate, especially in connection with the plan of redemption, that God had already glorified Himself, and that He would do it again, in as far as the events connected with the cross would exhibit and commend the divine wisdom in the contrivance of redemption, His mercy in sending His Son as the Saviour, His veracity in fulfilling the promises, His justice in requiring the due satisfaction for sin according to His law, and His power in carrying His counsels into execution. Much was already accomplished. But the Father would again glorify His name in completing the work and accepting the sacrifice. In what still remained of His redemption work, God's name should again be glorified to the utmost measure. And the Father says, that as He had glorified His name by Christ's coming into the world, and by the work done in it, so He would glorify it "again" by the mode of His departure from the world, and by accepting the sacrifice which He offered.

Another testimony to the same effect was the saying which Jesus uttered in the presence of the disciples, at the moment when Judas went out to betray Him: " Now is the Son of Man glorified; and God is glorified in Him" (John xiii. 21). The title, *Son of Man*, which, as we have already seen, is uniformly descriptive of Christ as the curse-bearing second Adam, leads our thoughts to a right understanding of His words. In speaking of the Son of Man being glorified, He has in His eye that exaltation which was to be the reward of His atonement, or the joy set before Him. Though the opinion of many commentators, that the Lord's glorification may here simply mean His sufferings, is scarcely tenable—for His sufferings alone are never presented to us precisely under the notion of His glorification—yet the idea of the atonement, as the foundation and pathway to His glory, is undoubtedly implied.

First, as to the saying in reference to Himself, " *Now is the Son of Man glorified*," it is an instance of the endurance to which He submitted for the joy set before Him (Heb. xii. 2), or with His reward in view. He did not use this language when He received the voice from heaven at IIis baptism (Matt. iii. 17), nor after the transfiguration scene (Matt. xvii. 5), nor after the commendations of the people (Mark vii. 37), nor after the Hosannahs with which He was saluted on His entry into Jerusalem (Matt. xxi. 9), but after Judas' departure to betray Him.[1] The work is, in His purpose at least, and in His voluntary submission, already a consummated fact, and He grasps the crown as already at hand, and given only for the abasement of the cross. And when He adds, " God is glorified in Him," the allusion is to that exercise of His attributes, or display of His declarative glory, which the Father evinced by means of the atonement. He intimates that His atoning work manifested all the attributes and vindicated all the rights of Godhead, and

[1] See Wolfburgius, *observationes sacræ*, on this verb.

so glorified Him. But how was this ? If we survey the relation of God to His creatures, or take account of His perfections, the mode in which His name was glorified at this time will readily appear. Thus, if we take account of the divine *law*, it received a greater glory from the subjection of such a person to it than by the faultless obedience of all the universe. The *authority* of God was more fully disclosed and exercised in connection with the incarnation and abasement of the Son of God than it was, or could be, in any other sphere. The *holiness* of God, which leads Him to hide His face from sin, and to withdraw from all fellowship with it, was exercised and displayed in a more extraordinary way, and therefore glorified more fully, by the desertion of His Son, when made sin for us, than in all that exercise of it which will be displayed on the finally impenitent in the blackness of darkness. The *love* of God was displayed, and therefore glorified,[1] to the utmost by an infinite gift to creatures most unworthy. His punitive *justice*, whereby He shows that He cannot bear evil, and must punish it out of love to Himself, was never exercised at such a cost as on Christ. In a word, the divine perfections, that is, all the revealed attributes of God, were exercised, and therefore displayed or glorified, to the utmost by the atonement.

Thus the redemption, consisting in the obedience and death of Christ, is the great work of God, the centre of all His ways, which most brightly displays all the divine perfections, especially His grace and holiness ; and hence the Lord said, with a peculiar emphasis, " Now is the Son of Man glorified; and God is glorified in Him."

---

[1] When God glorifies Himself, the action differs little from acting out or exercising His own perfections, though the further notion of other beings thinking honourably of Him is not excluded.

CHAPTER VI.

THE ACTUAL EFFICACY OF THE ATONEMENT, OR THE QUESTION
FOR WHOM IT WAS SPECIALLY OFFERED.

SECTION XLV.—THE EFFICACIOUS CHARACTER OF THE ATONEMENT,
OR THE SPECIAL REFERENCE OF THE DEATH OF CHRIST TO A
PEOPLE GIVEN HIM.

THERE is a considerable number of the sayings of Jesus which
bring out, with unmistakeable precision, the efficacious character
of the atonement, or that the death of Christ had a special reference to a people given to Him.   The redemptive efficacy of
His death is described as taking effect within a given circle, and
as bearing upon a given company of persons.   What is that
circle, or who are the parties described as participating in the
fruits of Christ's death ?   The Lord's sayings on this point are so
express, that we are not left in any doubt whether the atonement was offered specially for the persons who receive the benefit
of His death.   He indicates that they for whom it was offered
and accepted, were the persons who had been given to Him, and
to whom He had united Himself in the eternal covenant.

All who have a biblical scheme of doctrine, understand, by
Christ's dying for His people, A DYING IN THEIR ROOM AND
STEAD.   They attach no lower sense than this to the expression.   They hold that Christ underwent the penal suffering
which was their due, that He occupied their place as the
sin-bearer and curse-bearer, and that He rendered the full
obedience which was required; and they hold that it was a
real and valid transaction—as much so as the fall, of which
it is the counterpart, and as the curse, of which it is the
reversal.   This brings us to the real point of the investigation,
and away from the disguised, and sometimes fallacious, mode
of presenting it.

The proper nature of the atonement must first be ascertained before we can advance, with any precision, to define its extent; and when that point is settled, there is but one step to an accurate definition of its extent. Without entering here into a recapitulation of its constituent elements, as already set forth in the previous sections of this work, let it suffice to state, that the atonement, as a fact in history, is as replete with saving results and consequences, as the fall of man, with which it must ever be contrasted, is replete with the opposite. Its extent coincides with its effects. In the Scripture mode of representing it, we find it placed in causal connection with man's salvation, as a fact not less real than the fall, and not less fraught with consequences (Rom. v. 12-20). The words intimate, that if the fall was fruitful of results for man's condemnation and death, the atonement is not less so for man's restoration.

Now this of itself decides on the extent of the atonement. No one doubts that the extent of the fall is coincident with its obvious and manifest effects. If a causal connection obtains between one man's disobedience and the sin, judgment, and death in which the world is now involved, a causal connection obtains, too, between the second man's obedience and the saving benefits in which all Christians participate. If the fall was pregnant with consequences which cannot be gainsaid, and which ramify so widely, that they are everywhere apparent, the atonement of Christ in like manner produces, and will continue to produce, results which are as real, and shall ramify as widely, through time and through eternity.

They who regard Christ in no higher light than as a teacher come from God, as a distinguished pattern of virtue, or as a faithful witness, who did not shrink from confirming His doctrine by His death, cannot mean that He died, in any sense of the word, for those who lived before His coming. The very idea of an example implies that it is but prospective, and that it is fruitful of consequences or results worthy of the name, only where the knowledge of His doctrine extends. On that theory of Christ's death, its scope or reference cannot be supposed to go further than the knowledge of His life and character.

In investigating what Jesus said, we direct attention to the question, whether the Lord's sayings do or do not assign a special reference to His redemption work. The testimonies of this nature, when put together, are by no means few or doubtful; and it is impossible to canvass them with due attention without coming to the conclusion, that He assigned to His atonement a definite reference, and that He acted, all through His history, with a special regard to a certain class of men, whose person He sustained. A few of these expressions, or turns of phrase, we shall now adduce.

1. He calls them *many*, when He speaks of those for whom His blood was shed, and who were the objects of His redemption work (Matt. xxvi. 28, xx. 28). The natural interpretation of this expression in both passages, as we have already explained them, is, that He refers to those who are elsewhere represented by Him as His own, as given to Him. The mere use of the word *many* would not suffice to prove this of itself, without the additional circumstance, that they are described by marks which are by no means universally applicable.[1] A theory was propounded, two centuries ago, of a very perilous kind, to serve as a sort of guiding principle, or canon of interpretation, in reference to such phrases. It was held by the Arminian school, who were opposed to the special reference of Christ's death, that when He was said *to die for all*, the language meant what was done to win or procure redemption; and that when He was said *to die for many*, or for the Church, it described the actual par-

---

[1] The remark of Jerome is happy: "non dixit pro omnibus, sed pro multis, id est, pro iis qui credere voluerint." I may notice that Amesius' *Coronis ad Collationem Hagiensem* meets all the arguments of the Arminian school on this point, and on the five points generally, and supplies a most pointed, felicitous, and biblical refutation of that style of thought. See, too, Witsius, *de œc. Fœd.*, lib. ii. cap. 9; and Gomar's biblical discussion, *an Christus pro omnibus et singulis mortuus sit*, p. 453.

ticipation of redemption. *It is an artificially contrived theory in the interest of a tendency, and cannot, without violence, be applied to any of these texts. Plainly, our Lord describes the actual offering of the ransom, and not its application alone. The language had its full truth in the actual atonement, and sets forth what was His own and His Father's purpose, when He offered Himself.

2. Our Lord calls the objects of His atonement *His sheep* (John x. 15). The same remarks are equally applicable here. They are already called His sheep, because they were given to Him in the divine decree, and known as His own. So necessary was it that some link of connection should be formed between Christ and the objects of redemption, such as obtains between shepherd and sheep, head and members, that without it an atonement could not have been made.[1] According to the divine paction, there must be some union or conjunction. This phrase thus involves two things : (1) that Christ did not die in a merely indeterminate way and in uncertainty whether He should have a flock, but with special objects of redemption before His mind, to whom He was already knit by a tie necessary for the redemption-work; (2) that they are also His purchased property, the result or fruit of His atonement. This latter truth enables us to obviate the cavil against our interpretation, as if it assumed that certain persons were already the sheep of Christ before He died. They were so in the divine purpose, and in Christ's undertaking, though not actually His till the ransom was paid for them. He declares that He died for the sheep, which, as appears from the context, were the elect given to Him (John x. 26). The special reference of the

---

[1] See Amesius' *Coronis*, p. 112. It is noteworthy that Grotius, when compelled to meet the objection of Socinus that there was no connection between Christ and us, argues with as much point for the affirmative as any Calvinistic divine could use : "dici hic posset, non esse hominem homini alienum, naturalem esse inter homines cognationem et consanguinitatem, carnem nostram a Christo susceptam ; sed longè major alia inter Christum et nos conjunctio a Deo destinabatur. Ipse enim designatus erat a Deo ut caput esset corporis, cujus nos sumus membra." (*De Satisfactione Christi*, cap. iv.)

atonement, and the further thought that the vicarious sacrifice secures the conversion of those for whom it was offered, are incontrovertibly intimated in the words, " Other sheep I have which are not of this fold: them also I must bring" (v. 16). They are first called His sheep; then they are described as the objects of redemption, for whom He laid down His life, that is, for whom the atonement was actually offered; then they must needs be brought, or rather led, as a shepherd leads his flock.

3. The persons for whom the atonement is offered are called *His people*—a name which indicates that they were already Christ's in the divine purpose : " Thou shalt call His name Jesus; for He shall save HIS PEOPLE from their sins " (Matt. i. 21). If He saves His people, they were His by divine gift already; and this obviates the allegation that the atonement would have been equally complete, though no one had been saved. That is plainly incompatible with this text, which declares that He was the Saviour of His people. The objections taken to this interpretation, which involves the special reference of the atonement, are, (1) that the phrase, *His people*, may be referred to the Jews,—and so Calvin interpreted the words;[1] (2) that the language does not refer to the purchase of redemption, but to its application. Both statements are easy of refutation. As to the first, the answer is, that God's people are twofold, according to the double covenant,—the Jews as the people whom He foreknew (Rom. xi. 2), and the true people of God, who belong to the class that are given to the Son (John vi. 37). And as to the second allegation, that the allusion is to the application of redemption, the answer is, that these were both in the divine purpose and intention.

4. They are called the *children of God scattered abroad* (John xi. 52). This phrase occurs in connection with the divine oracle uttered by Caiaphas, and forms part of the inspired commentary of the evangelist. The high priest of the year on which the

---

[1] Calvin does not limit the phrase to the Jews, but extends it to all nations, who were to be inserted into the stock of Abraham.—*Vid. in loc.*

great atonement was made, was employed, in the marvellous
sovereignty of God, to embody the import of the entire Mosaic
worship, of the temple, the priesthood, and the sacrifices, when
he said, " It is expedient for us that one man should die for the
people, and that the whole nation perish not " (John xi. 50).
He thus unwittingly prophesied, and gave a voice to Judaism,
much in the same way as the Urim and Thummim of old gave
forth intimations of the will of God or of His mind.   To this
oracle the inspired evangelist appends his commentary, to the
effect that this was a prophecy, and that it conveyed the important truth that Jesus was to die for that nation ; and not for
that nation only, but that also He should gather together in one
the children of God that were scattered abroad (ver. 52).   Now,
the objects of redemption are here called " the children of God
scattered abroad," because they were so in the divine purpose,
though not yet actually ransomed.   The evangelist intimates that
they were already the foreappointed children of God, and in
some sense worthy of being so called before the death of Christ;
then, that they were the objects of the vicarious sacrifice ; and
that the atonement was to carry with it the certain issue or
result that they should be gathered into one, that is, united to
Christ and to one another in Him.   The special reference of the
atonement cannot be called in question here.

5. They are called by the Lord *His friends*, for whom He laid
down His life in the exercise of a special love : " Greater love
hath no man than this, that a man lay down his life for his
friends " (John xv. 13).   Unquestionably, the emphasis falls on
the special love which He cherishes toward His people, here
termed His friends.   The design and end for which He laid
down His life are not here mentioned, because the recent institution of the Supper, and the explanation appended to it, that
His blood was to be shed for the remission of sins, sufficiently
expressed both the purpose and effect of His atoning death ; and
as He meant to inculcate on His disciples mutual love, according
to His own example, He points to the greatest proof which could

be given of His love—His vicarious death.[1] But the language
clearly enough indicates that His death was to be for the behoof
of others, and in their stead. He assumes that it is the case
of one offering himself to rescue another from danger. But,
apart from the use of the term *friend*, the special love[2] to
which our Lord here refers in connection with laying down His
life, comprises these two things, which are always to be viewed
together, and not apart—that He not only procures salvation,
but also applies it. This special love wins its object, finds its
object, and rescues its object.

The answer to the inquiry, who are the special objects of
Christ's atonement? would have been simple, if men had con-
tented themselves with Scripture statements, and with ideas
derived from Scripture. Whatever be the infinite value of the
atonement, considered as a divine fact, as well as a human transaction, yet, in point of saving efficacy, *it does not extend beyond
the circle of those who believe in Christ.* Though in intrinsic
worth it could save the whole world, and a thousand worlds
more, if there had been such worlds of human beings to be saved,
yet the redemption-work does not extend, in point of fact, beyond
the circle of those who approve of it as a fit and proper method
of salvation; or, in other words, who, by a faith which is the
gift of God, are led to accept it as the ground of reconciliation
with God. It is simply co-extensive, as to saving effects, with
the number of true believers. Of that there can be no doubt,
when we examine the words of Christ, and abide by His teaching. And in this conclusion, as the positive truth on the point,
all might have rested, and probably would have rested, with
perfect satisfaction, but for the theories and philosophical reasonings of men who, not so much under religious conviction as
under speculative tendencies, deemed it necessary to extend the

---

[1] The τίθημι does not mean *to expose to danger*, as Grotius puts it, but *to lay
down;* and the ὑπὲρ is to be understood as implying the ἀντί (see above).

[2] Calvin says on the passage : "Christus vitam suam pro alienis exposuit, sed
quos jam tunc ipse amabat, mortem alias pro ipsis non subiturus.

atonement to all alike, whether they were saved by it or not, whether they believed it or not. They would not be content with regarding it as co-extensive with its EFFECTS—the only true measure by which its reference can be known, and that which makes it the counterpart of Adam's fall,—but must needs contend that it was co-extensive with the race, and for all equally. It soon appears, however, that it is in reality a question as to its nature. This will be evident by a brief allusion to these universalist theories.

a. Thus, under the influence of plausible reasonings, not a few in various countries go so far as to assert, that in virtue of Christ's work all men will finally be saved. That theory of a universal salvation has at least this in its favour, that it is consistent, and is carried through to its logical consequences. It was propounded in early times by Origen, and is, under an evangelical garb, at present more widely diffused than it ever was.[1] It has been principally based on the position that the divine benevolence embraces all alike, and that the actual restoration will be co-extensive with the ruin. This speculation overlooks divine justice, and looks simply at the point, that the ruin and the remedy may presumably be held to be co-extensive in their actual results, as well as analogous in the provision. Though it is unscriptural, and even directly opposed to Scripture, it is at least consistent, as it goes through with the idea of the universality of the provided remedy.

b. Much less consistent is another theory of universal grace—that of the Arminian and semi-Pelagian school, though tracing its rise to the same speculative reasoning and plausible comparison between the ruin introduced by Adam and the remedy brought in by Christ.[2] They hold that the atonement made on Christ's side and accepted on God's side was co-extensive with

---

[1] This is the common doctrine of the Continental rationalistic school, and of some of more biblical sentiments.

[2] What Coleridge so happily said of another scheme of thought, may equally be applied to this : " It is not a religion, but a theory."

the human family, whether men believe it or not, whether they
reject it or not. They look only at one side of the question, and
they undermine the atonement as a really valid fact. They
maintain that on God's side the remedy is as universal as the
disease. But what they thus gain in compass or breadth is lost
at the centre. The apparent advantage is more than countervailed at another point: it is stripped of its efficacy; and this
brings me back to the position, that the true question is no
longer, how far does it extend, but is it a real counterpart of
the fall, and does it render a perfect satisfaction to every claim
of justice, and fulfil the law in the room of any?

We find, accordingly, when we examine the opinions of these
disputants, and ascertain the sense in which they take the
phrase, " to give His life FOR many," that the question turns not
so much on the point for whom Christ died, in the sense of a
true and valid transaction, as on the point whether He died for
any in the proper acceptation of the term. It is not a question
as to its extent. Rather it is, What was the design and object
which God had in view in giving His Son to die for us, and of
the Son, in giving Himself? It is not whether Christ died for
all and every one, but whether He died for any, with valid consequences or effects as certain and efficacious as in the great
counterpart transaction of man's fall. This will appear to every
one who will make a full survey of these opinions.

The Arminian contends that Christ's death only renders
reconciliation possible, and gives God a right to make a new
covenant, of which this shall be the tenor: that Christ shall
give eternal life to all who obey Him, and persevere to the end.
The semi-legality of this opinion is on the surface. It throws
men back upon themselves and upon their own resources. Not
only so: from the very nature of the theory, he cannot maintain
that such a covenant has ever been propounded to all who have
lived at any given time; and obviously it can only be prospective not retrospective. It is not true to itself.

c. The Amyraldist view, or the theory of universal grace, differs
in some respects from the former, but is nothing beyond a half-

way house. It sets forth that God, moved by a certain love to fallen men, appointed Christ as a mediator for all and every one, and that by this means all barriers on the side of divine justice have been removed. It propounds the theory of salvation made possible, but adds a condition that transfers the application to the sovereign will of God: it is for all if they believe. This, it is obvious, entirely alters the nature of the atonement. The theory sets forth that Christ, according to His own intention and His Father's purpose, died for all and every one; that a salvation was procured for all though not applied to all; nay, that the atonement, though not actually securing redemption or faith, in the way of causal connection, rendered it possible to bestow salvation on any whom the divine good pleasure might select, and to form a new covenant of grace with mankind in general. It is thus a new expedient which may become effectual in any case where it may seem good to apply it. But it is not a valid transaction in its own nature, involving a covenant or substitution and SECURING its own application.[1]

d. There is still another mode of putting the universality of the atonement, adopted by others in various churches, which is comparatively innocuous—amounting, in reality, to little more than a roundabout way of representing the universal call of the gospel. They are content with saying, that Christ died for all, without ever tracing the ramifications of the statement, or thinking out the position to its logical consequences; and they only mean that the invitation comes to all alike. Thus many good men express themselves in different churches under the somewhat confused and unexamined impression, that the universal call must, in some sense, which they never investigate, have a universal provision equally broad underlying it. They never reflect, as every one thinking out this matter must do, that to the completeness of the atonement, as an accomplished fact, it is indispensably necessary that all the three parties concerned in the transaction shall concur—the Father, the Surety, and the man needing the salvation. There must be a consent

[1] See note L in the Appendix.

of all the parties concerned; and the exercise of faith on the sinner's part must be viewed as his approval of this method of salvation, and his consent to it. There must needs be such an approval of this provision as may be traced in the Jewish economy, when the worshipper laid his hand on the head of the sacrifice, intimating his consent to this mode of expiation and confessing his sins on the victim.

The class of divines last named sometimes allege that, to believe in Christ is equivalent to believing that Christ died for us. But these two acts of the mind are by no means to be regarded as one and the same. The former describes that mental act which apprehends a sufficient Saviour. The latter is an inference, though a sure and certain one. No one is summoned, in the first instance, to believe that Christ died for him, any more than he is required to believe that his sins are pardoned before he believes.[1] And as to the responsibility of rejecting the gospel, the condemnation consequent on this is due to the fact that the unbeliever will not accept of a sufficient Redeemer, nor approve of such a way of salvation. He rejects it in its *idea and contrivance*, whereas faith is just the approval of it.

But the sinner must signify his concurrence, before the vicarious death of Christ can be to him an accomplished fact, and faith, therefore, is just that approval and consent by which he signifies his concurrence, though given by the believer after the lapse of centuries. He by faith signifies that he cordially approves of this way of redemption, and wishes to be saved by no other way. Then all parties concur in it. They who plead for an indefinite atonement make the whole a completed transaction, without man's consent; and we are at a loss to see what conceivable advantage can be gained by making the atonement wider than the number of those who approve of it, and are willing to be saved by it. Of course it is applied to unnumbered millions of infants, who are saved by it in a different way.

[1] See Polanus, *Syntag.* lib. 6, cap. 18.

All these various theories go to pieces when we bring out from the words of Christ the true nature of the atonement; for in reality, as we have already remarked, it is more a question as to the character of the atonement, as an actual transaction, than as to its extent. Whether we look at the covenant, which lies at its foundation, or at the fact that the purchase and application of the atonement are co-extensive and necessarily connected with each other, or at the nature of Christ's intercession, we are left in no doubt as to its extent.

1. One proof of this is contained in the nature and provisions of the covenant.[1] I have only to advert to the unity of the Surety and of those whom He represented, to prove the extent of the atonement. It is a unity or oneness so close, that we may affirm of the second man, as well as of the first, " we were all that one man." The thought that lies at the foundation of our participation of the federal blessings, is union, or oneness. We may thus call in the idea of organic union, as well as the idea of a covenant, for they are not exclusive of each other, but rather supplementary. The idea of unity may be said to run through the whole declarations on the subject of Christ's saving work, whether they were given forth by the Lord Himself or by His servants. On this principle, then, that Christ and His seed are viewed as one, just as Adam and his family were one, the redemption work by which we are saved was incontrovertibly finished by His obedience, and must be held to have been at once offered and accepted in the room of all for whom He acted the part of a surety (John vi. 39). This, however, decides on the scope and extent of the atonement.

2. The purchase of redemption and its application are co-extensive. The salvation is not won for any to whom it is not applied: the Christ will not lose one for whom He died. All our Lord's sayings assume this, and take it for granted (John x. 15). To suppose the opposite, would imply that a costly price had been paid, and that those for whom it was paid derived no advantage from it; which could only be on the ground that

[1] See before, at sec. xii.

He wanted either love or power. Not only so: a concurrent action and perfect harmony must be supposed to obtain among the three persons of the Godhead. There can be no disharmony between the election of the Father, the redemption of the Son, and the application of the Spirit.

3. Christ's intercession is based on the atonement, and could have no validity or ground but as it referred to that finished work of expiation, which needs no repetition. Now, we see from the explicit statement of the Lord, that the intercession is not for the world, but for those whom the Father gave Him: " I pray for them: I pray not for the world, but for them whom Thou hast given Me; for they are Thine" (John xvii. 9). This decides upon the scope and destination of the atonement for any available purpose; for it will not be argued by any divine biblically acquainted with the nature of our Lord's priesthood and intercession, that any one ever was or ever will be effectually called but on the ground of that all-prevailing interposition (John xvii. 20).

To those who allege, in the spirit of the Arminian school, that the love of Jesus consists only in applying the redemption, but not in procuring it, it is enough to say, that love, in the proper meaning of the term, is anterior to both. It would not be love if it were dissociated from the purpose and design of conferring on its objects every conceivable good which can either be procured or applied. And whenever Scripture speaks of the divine love, either in connection with the Father or with the Son, this is the import of the term. This fact, that love is only love to persons, and that the divine love finds out its objects over all impediments, enables us to obviate the two-fold love which the Arminian writers suppose, and for which they argue in the interest of their views,—one preceding faith, and another following it. The former, they allege, is to all alike, and there-fore cannot be regarded as in itself efficacious to any;[1] the

---

[1] Many writers have laid, and still lay, stress on the term *world*, which fre-quently occurs in those passages which describe the death of Christ. It is a

latter they describe as an increasing quantity, and as a sort of complacential approbation of a state of mind or mental act which is acceptable to God. But the redeeming love of Christ, as the source of all saving benefits, does not, properly speaking, receive additions or increase, though there may be, and doubtless are, ampler manifestations of it, as well as a keener sense of it on the mind. This is emphatically brought out by Paul, when he sets forth the immutable constancy and omnipotent efficacy of the divine love in a remarkable argument à fortiori (Rom. v. 5-11). He argues, that if God could set His love on the saints when we were yet sinners and enemies, without strength and ungodly, much more shall that love be continued to them when they are justified. The argument is, that if God's love found an outlet to us when we were aliens and enemies, much more will it be continued now that we are friends. But the foundation of the whole argument is, that His love is special and redeeming love, and directed to individuals, whom God will never abandon or let go.

The text on which we already commented demonstrates the special love of Christ (John xv. 13). They for whom He died were the objects of supreme and special love, which of necessity secured their ultimate salvation. For them He must be considered as acting at every step ; their names being on His heart in the same way as the names of the tribes of Israel were on the high priest's breastplate. And the same special reference confronts us in every form. Thus He is described as loving His own

term commonly used in contrast with Jewish limitation, and in this usage commonly designates men of all nationalities. That it is not conclusive as an argument urged in favour of general redemption, will appear from such phrases as these : "The bread of God is He [better, that] which cometh down from heaven, and *giveth life unto the world*" (John vi. 33) ; "that the *world* may *believe* that Thou hast sent Me" (John xvii. 21). As it denotes, (1) either a great multitude (John xii. 19), or (2) men of all nations (Rom. xi. 12), it is plain that no argument can be urged in favour of a universal atonement, from the mere occurrence of this word. Hales tells us that he was carried over to the Arminian opinions at the Synod of Dort, by Episcopius' argument from John iii. 16. But though that is the chief argument of the Arminian school, it is a fallacious argument, and not borne out by the *usus loquendi*.

that were in the world (John xiii. 1), which cannot be affirmed of all and every man, without distinction, and in precisely the same form. We have only to recall such phrases as co-suffering (1 Pet. iv. 1), co-crucifixion (Gal. ii. 20), co-dying (Rom. vi. 8), co-burying with Christ (Rom. vi. 4), to perceive that He bore the person of a chosen company, who are spoken of as doing what He did at every important turn of His history. It was for His own that He was incarnate (Heb. ii. 14); and He must be regarded, all through His history, as uniting Himself to His own, or as loving His own that were in the world, and loving them to the end (John xiii. 1). This special love, according to which He acted in the name of a chosen company, and laid down His life for them, is a love that finds them out over every impediment or hindrance. And it were to think unworthily of Christ, to suppose such a conjunction established between Him and the objects of redemption, as is presupposed in the very nature of this transaction, without the certain effect that salvation is secured to many by His death. It were as absurd as to suppose a king without subjects, a bridegroom without a bride, a vine without branches, a head without the members.

But here a question arises: How is the special atonement to be harmonised with the general invitations of the gospel propounded to mankind indefinitely? Both these have abundant evidence in Scripture: and sometimes a difficulty has been felt where none should exist. It would be tedious to enumerate all the disputes which have been carried on, sometimes on the one side, and sometimes on the other. Thus it has been made a question, whether God offers the eternal life, or the salvation procured by Christ to all men indiscriminately, or only to those who are the objects of special love? and then, a further difficulty is started on the ground that an atonement specially provided for some cannot be propounded indefinitely to all.

These are merely exercises of human reasoning on themes which, from the nature of the case, the finite mind must rather accept as facts than presume exhaustively to explore. The

sufficiency of the atonement for ALL NATIONS and ALL MEN must
be affirmed, and therefore no one can have any doubt as to the
possibility of its being extended to them if they have been
awakened to a sense of need, and if they penitently wish to share
in it.   It is as infinite in value as is its divine Author.[1]

That the offer of salvation is to be made to all men is the con
clusion to which every one must come who duly considers that
Christ so preached.   Though He knew all those that were His, all
that were given Him by the Father, He yet invited sinners indiscriminately (Joh. vii. 37), nay, complained of their reluctance and
refusal when they set at nought His proposals of love (Matt. xxiii.
37; John v. 40).   A special atonement and invitations sincerely
made on the ground of it to mankind indefinitely are quite compatible.   They will be found to meet at some point though their
junction be beyond our present line of vision.   And our Lord and
His apostles, by their mode of preaching, give us an example
how to proceed.   They brought motives and expostulations to
bear on men as if no hard question were in the way.

SEC. XLVI.—THE ATONEMENT EXTENDING TO ALL TIMES IN THE
WORLD'S HISTORY, AND TO ALL NATIONS.

The position which Christ ascribed to Himself in the world,
sufficiently indicates that His death was, in the divine purpose, a
provision for all times and nations, and that there was to be no
repetition of the sacrifice.   We shall briefly adduce His testimony
to both these points.

1. With respect to all times, the sayings of Christ imply that
He was the centre-point of the world's history, to whom all

[1] The memorable language of the Synod of Dort is as follows (c. ii. § 3, 4, 5):
mors filii Dei est unica et perfectissima pro peccatis victima et satisfactio infiniti
valoris et pretii, ABUNDE SUFFICIENS AD TOTIUS MUNDI PECCATA EXPIANDA.—
Ceterum promissio Evangelii est, ut quisquis credit in Christum crucifixum non
pereat, sed habeat vitam æternam.   Quæ promissio OMNIBUS populis et HOMINI-
BUS, ad quos Deus pro suo beneplacito mittit Evangelium, promiscue et indiscriminatim annunciari et debet proponi CUM RESIPISCENTIA et FIDEI MANDATO.

previous ages looked forward, and all subsequent ages look back. The saints who lived under the time of the first promise, to whom the advent of the woman's seed was revealed, or who expected Abraham's seed, in whom all the families of the earth were to be blessed, were saved by the retrospective efficacy of His atoning death, and not in virtue of a typical expiation, which was but a shadow of good things to come (Gen. iii. 15, xii. 3). The pardon, or, as some have preferred to call it, the preterition,[1] which extended to unnumbered multitudes during the ages preceding the birth of Christ, was due to the blood of atonement about to be shed in the fulness of time.

The fact that the death of Christ is set forth in its retrospective, as well as in its prospective, influence, shows the vast superiority of the blood of the new covenant as compared with that of the old covenant. The one was merely for the Israelites, the other was "for many;" which may be interpreted for men of all times and generations, even for those who were long dead, but had faith on Him who was to come. This may warrantably be held to be there taught by our Lord (see Matt. xx. 28, xxvi. 28; John vi. 57). I shall not here adduce the statements in the Epistles, to the effect that the atonement had an influence of a retrospective nature, but content myself with saying, that this is set forth with peculiar emphasis in several passages (Rom. iii. 25; Heb. ix. 15). Our plan leads us to abide by the sayings of Christ. And we have more than stray hints from the mouth of Christ, that His vicarious death was retrospective as well as prospective in its influence. When we consider how He described Himself in contrast with all who ever came before Him, and condemned as thieves and robbers such as came with rival claims to His (John x. 1–7); when we hear Him speaking of the necessity of His death for the world's salvation, as well as declaring that Moses,

---

[1] The distinction between πάρεσις and ἄφεσις—the former referring to the Old Testament saints, the latter to the New Testament—was first made by Beza, and carried out to an extravagant length by Cocceius and his school. Some distinction of a subjective nature, must be allowed, whatever opinion may be formed as to that distinction drawn between πάρεσις and ἄφεσις in Rom. iii. 25.

the prophets, and all the holy oracles testified of Him (John v. 39, 46); when we find Him here declaring that Abraham rejoiced to see His day (John viii. 56),—we have intimations which imply that He was the central figure of both economies, and that His incarnation and death had a relation to them who lived before His coming, and that their salvation was not less due to Christ's atoning blood than ours. The scene on the Mount of the Transfiguration, moreover, when Moses and Elias appeared to converse with Him on His exodus or decease, about to be accomplished at Jerusalem, affords confirmatory evidence that the scope of that death had an application to all times. It was that on the ground of which they had been saved; for Christ was the atonement or sin-offering for the transgressions under the first covenant (Heb. ix. 15).

2. With respect, again, to the bearing of the atonement on men of all nations, Christ gave no dubious announcement that it was not limited to Israel, but had an influence which extended to those who were not of that fold (John x. 11), and that, in a word, it was irrespective of national distinctions. Thus He declared, on the occasion of the inquiring Greeks approaching Him with an express desire "to see Jesus," and whose inquiries He regarded as the prelude or first-fruits of the wide in-bringing of the Gentile nations, that if He was lifted up or crucified as an atoning sacrifice, He would draw all nations to Him (John xii. 32). The same wide and universal reference of the scheme of redemption to all tribes and nations, wholly irrespective of the narrow limits of nationality, comes out in the other sayings of Christ where He alludes to the world and to the scheme of redemption in its bearing on mankind as such; who are addressed by the Gospel message, and summoned to the exercise of faith just because they are comprehended within the class for whom the atonement has been provided (John iii. 14–16). Hence the Lord directed His disciples to preach, with the most unrestricted universality, the remission of sins to all nations, and to announce it in His name as crucified and risen,—in other words, as the

crucified Saviour, who offered an atonement for a people given to Him, without respect to nationality (Luke xxiv. 47). Christ may thus be designated the official Saviour of mankind, as men are contrasted with fallen angels, for whom no such provision is made; and on this ground the invitations of the Gospel, with all that is comprehended in them, are equally and without distinction made to all nations. Thus, irrespective of national distinctions or class distinctions, the invitation to accept a crucified Saviour applies equally to all tribes and ranks of men, and is offered indefinitely to all to whom the message comes.

CHAPTER VII.

THE APPLICATION OF THE ATONEMENT. '

SEC. XLVII.—SAYINGS WHICH PARTICULARLY RELATE TO THE APPLICATION OF THE ATONEMENT.

As we endeavoured in the previous sections to distribute the sayings of Jesus according to a classification which seemed the best fitted to give a full outline of the atonement in its nature and effects, it only remains for us to notice such testimonies as refer to the mode in which it is appropriated and applied. A brief and condensed statement of the import of these is all that is now required.

The previous elucidation of the doctrine renders a very succinct sketch of the mode of applying the atonement quite sufficient. We commenced by exhibiting the presuppositions of the whole question, or the grounds on which this great fact may be said to rest. We next considered the constituent elements of the atonement, as consisting of sin-bearing and sinless obedience. We further proceeded to survey the proper effects of this divine fact on the individual Christian, both in an objective and in a subjective point of view; that is, in respect to the acceptance of his person and the renovation of his nature. We were next brought, in order, to set forth the influence of the atonement upon other interests in the universe, which, as we have seen, are at once numerous and various. We were thus naturally led to discuss the actual efficacy and extent of the atonement, or the question for whom it was rendered.

These topics pave the way for the only remaining division of our Lord's sayings on the atonement, viz. those which contain an allusion to the mode of its application. These are not so numerous ; and they may be discussed within a limited compass : (1.) This classification of our Lord's testimonies brings under our notice the objective presentation of the atonement, by means of ecclesiastical institutions and ordinances, which are, first of all, based on this accomplished fact, and next intended to commend it to the acceptance of others.   (2.) But if there are objective appointments which aim at the application of this divine fact to susceptible minds, there are also means of a subjective character, and especially the exercise of faith, which is the divinely constituted instrument, for receiving and appropriating what has been provided.   (3.) The responsibility and doom of not accepting the provided remedy comes naturally into consideration in this connection.   (4.) In addition to all this, the effect of the atonement on all religion and practice is a point of such moment that it cannot fail to attract the attention of every mind that has duly learned to regard the atonement as the grand distinctive peculiarity of the Christian religion.

On these points, it might be interesting and important to enlarge. But as our object is brevity and condensation, as far as may be consistent with perspicuity and completeness, we shall content ourselves with a brief outline on this division of the subject; and the rather, because it touches on a department on which it does not precisely fall within our present plan' to enter.

SEC. XLVIII.—THE PREACHING OF THE ATONEMENT AND OF FORGIVE-
NESS AS BASED OF THE ATONEMENT.

There are sayings of our Lord which bring out a divinely
constituted connection between the atonement considered as an
accomplished fact, and the proclamation of it by His servants,
—a connection which it is the part of every Christian, as far
as possible, to understand, but which, after all our inquiries, is
rather to be apprehended as a fact, than fathomed in its nature
and mode.

When we come to the preaching of forgiveness, we find that
the Lord commanded the disciples to preach forgiveness in His
name to all nations, beginning at Jerusalem (Luke xxiv. 47);
and His ambassadors, faithful to the charge imposed on them,
carried the message during their lifetime far and wide through
the known world, proclaiming repentance and forgiveness as the
two topics which they were to preach in Christ's name, and as
the principal elements of the new covenant,—repentance on man's
side, and forgiveness on God's side.   Christ meant to signify by
that memorable saying, that the disciples were to preach forgiveness as a benefit won by His death, and imparted by Him as the
Risen One, to all who repent and believe.   He intimates that
He obtained by His death the authority and right to give the
remission of sins.   This comes out in connection with the circumstance that the disciples were to preach this message IN HIS
NAME; which may either mean, as many interpret it, at His
command, or, according to others, the express naming of His
name, in the light in which He is mentioned as the crucified and
risen Mediator[1] (ver. 46).   The preaching "in His name" could
only have place when the expiation was finished.   The pro-

---

[1] ἐπὶ τῷ ὀνόματι αὐτοῦ.   Winer, 6th ed. p. 350, makes it refer to Christ's command : "d. h. sich dabei auf ihn als Originallehrer und Abordner beziehend."
Luther, again, interprets the phrase of Christ's *merits* as the ground of remission ;
Meyer and Vinke make the phrase refer to the utterance of Christ's name in
preaching as that on which it rests.   The two latter views may be combined.

clamation of this message could not have been made if He had not died. The message is announced only on the ground of the finished work.

There are two points which here summon our attention. The first is, that there is a connection between Christ's death and the immediate remission of sins ; and the second is, that the entire preaching of forgiveness, as well as the office of the ministry itself, presupposes the atonement, and is ever directly connected with the atonement. Both points may be fitly considered under this section.

1. With regard to the first of these points, we had occasion to notice, in a previous section, that the Lord puts the forgiveness of sins in causal connection with His death.[1] He very emphatically, at the institution of the Supper, placed the pardon of sin in causal connection with His own atoning death, or with His blood shed for many (Matt. xxvi. 28). The guilt which suspended merited punishment over mankind, and which stood in the way of their acceptance, was removed only by the atonement. This is a point on which His teaching is so unambiguously clear, that if men would come to it without preconceived opinions, mistakes would at once be obviated.

It may be proper to define, before we proceed, the sense in which we are to take the term forgiveness, so as to get rid of the confused and incorrect opinions entertained in many quarters as to its meaning. And here I may premise, that a right notion of SIN determines the import of forgiveness. Wherever sin is regarded merely as imperfection or disease, not as guilt or the violation of the divine law, a different notion of forgiveness of necessity prevails. Sin in that case is not considered judicially, or in the light of the divine tribunal ; nor is forgiveness.[2] But, according to the biblical idea, sin always stands related to a lawgiver on the one hand, and to a judge on the other; and as

---

[1] See before, at p. 207.

[2] This rationalistic idea of forgiveness, common at the beginning of this century, was well refuted by Lotze, *over de vergeving der Zonden*, 1802. (See Storr also on Hebrews, in Appendix.)

God not only threatens positive punishments beyond the mere consequences of actions, considered in their ordinary issues, or according to the natural course of events, but inflicts positive punishment out of love to His perfections, and because He must do so from what He owes to Himself, a wholly different notion of forgiveness must be adopted. When we compare the biblical notion of it as used either in the Old or New Testament, it will be found to involve in every case the idea of deliverance from punishment; and the notion of deserved punishment for sin is so universally accepted, that it belongs, as the apostle shows, to the beliefs of natural religion, ineradicable from our nature (Rom. i. 32).

To bring out this fact, we have but to recall any portion of our Lord's teaching where He uses the word *forgiveness*. Thus the petition, "Forgive us our debts, as we forgive our debtors" (Matt. vi. 12), when we trace how it is more fully explained in the subsequent verses, contrasts our forgiveness of man's offences with forgiveness vouchsafed to us by God. If the one denotes a non-avenging of ourselves upon a fellow-man, or an abstaining to punish an injury inflicted, the other must mean an acquittal on the part of God, or a complete liberation from the punishment we deserved. Nor is the phrase ever used in any other sense by our Lord. Thus, when He said to the palsy-stricken man, "Thy sins be forgiven thee" (Matt. ix. 5), we cannot, with some, understand the language as equivalent to his restoration to health. On the contrary, the passage unmistakeably compares two benefits derived from Christ, and asks which of two things it was easier to say. The forgiveness of sins cannot, therefore, be interpreted as intimating no more than recovery or restoration from a bodily disease. The cure was meant to prove that He had power to forgive sin; and the words of Christ must be understood of the man's deliverance from the merited punishment of sin.

Again, when we examine the words of Christ used at the institution of the Supper, it is evident that He intimates a meritorious or causal connection between His death and the remission of sins.[1] The words, " My blood shed for many unto the remission of sins," can bear no other sense. Nor could the disciples, accustomed to the idea of sacrifice, understand the words in any other sense than as intimating that He was to die, that He might deliver men from deserved punishment by His death. The forgiveness of sins consists in this, that a man, notwithstanding his real guilt, is treated as if he had not sinned, or, in other words, goes free from punishment.

Thus, forgiveness is nothing but exemption from punishment; and as to its procuring cause, it is directly effected by the death of Christ. The meaning of this statement, rendered into other words, is simply this: that God exacts no more punishment, because Christ has exhausted it, and offered that on the ground of which God is actually gracious. Our Lord unmistakeably deduces pardon and deliverance solely from His death (Matt. xxvi. 28, xx. 28). If we keep in mind this notion of the sufferings of Christ, we readily understand why He sometimes mentions merely the removal of punishment (John iii. 15, 16). The atonement of Christ, in a word, aimed at this—to change men's relation toward God, and their condition, for eternity.

And this leads me to add that, as our Lord describes it, the effect of the atonement is by no means limited to those sins which were committed before the reception of the Gospel. When we inquire to what sins the atonement of Christ referred, the answer obviously is, that sins after conversion, as well as before it, were, without exception, expiated by His blood. If, indeed, provision were not made for the remission of all sins, great and small, for daily recurring sins during the course of the Christian's life, as well as for sins committed during the time of

---

[1] I would refer specially to Storr, in the Appendix to his commentary on Hebrews, to Vinke, and Lotze, for the best demonstration of this immediate causal connection.

impenitence, what would the atonement avail?[1]   The Lord meant His blood was shed for all sin.

But we must further inquire, If forgiveness means exemption from punishment, what is the kind of punishment? The answer is, that punishment is remitted of every kind, and specially future punishment, with all its consequences, because all sin is forgiven. Many of the natural consequences of sin, such as sickness and death, are not at once reversed by the reception of forgiveness; but a provision is made for their ultimate removal, and, as we have already pointed out, they are, from the moment of forgiveness, altered in their character. They become part of a paternal discipline, or of a system of training for the inheritance; but there is no wrath in them.

2. But the special topic brought before us in this section is, whether the PREACHING OF FORGIVENESS was to be immediately and directly based on Christ's atoning death. Was it a simple announcement of a free boon, based on the accomplished fact of the atonement, irrespective of any intermediate condition? The commission there stated shows that the Lord Jesus, in describing His atoning death, required that the preaching of the forgiveness of sins should be connected with it in the closest way; and the question arises, In what way? Is it a direct or indirect connection, an immediate or a more mediate connection? This momentous inquiry goes to the root of the modern tendencies, and divides into two parties or schools the believing divines of the present time, who, according as they maintain a direct causal connection between the blood of Christ and pardon, or hold a mediate connection, may be designated biblical expositors, or the adherents of a rationalistic tendency. This question goes very deep into the character of preaching, and it is felt in the inmost experience of the Christian.[2] The subject of the forgiveness of

---

[1] It is not necessary further to refute the opinions of such men as Löffler, Bretschneider, Rückert, and Reiche, who limit the pardon to sins prior to conversion.

[2] The whole spirit and style of the pulpit may be said to be conditioned by the opinions entertained on the question, whether forgiveness is to be preached as the *very first thing* in the Gospel message to sinners. The opinion, which puts life or any thing else first, makes another gospel.

sins, indeed, stands in the fore-front of the articles of religion as a question closely connected with men's highest interests, and stands in the fore-front of all preaching; and the subject is kept alive by the constant opposition which it encounters in some form.

As to the inquiry, whether forgiveness is to be preached as standing in immediate or mediate connection with the death of Christ, it may be affirmed that all who abide by any form of spiritual religion are agreed on one point: that among the grand ends contemplated by the death of Christ, must be pre-eminently classed the spiritual and moral improvement of mankind. But the debate is, whether, according to Christ's testimony, the primary and principal design of His death is to be sought in the spiritual improvement of men, that is, whether the forgiveness of sin is to have place only in so far as that first point is realised; or, conversely, whether forgiveness is to be preached as a benefit, in the first instance, directly effected by the death of Christ, and whether the moral improvement follows as the inseparable effect of the forgiveness. Not a few in all countries have accepted the theory, flowing from a very inadequate notion of law and sin, that they must preach a message, which lays stress on the fact that Christ's design was only to implant a new life among mankind. They speak as if the impediment or difficulty to be overcome did not at all lie on God's side, but only on man's side, who had yielded himself up to selfishness, and whose leading would be completely effected by regaining the inclination or bias to what is holy. They add, that just in the proportion in which their recovery is advanced, does the forgiveness of sin ensue; for with them sin is a calamity rather than a crime—a disease rather than a fault. Though they allow that there are in Scripture passages which appear to derive the forgiveness of sins directly from the blood of Christ, they yet assert that these are counterbalanced by others which connect the design of Christ's death with our moral improvement (Gal. i. 4), and that the former are to be explained by the latter; and some of these writers contend that their theory is even more scriptural than the exposition which asserts the direct connection between the death of Christ and pardon. That position is not only exegetically baseless, but makes another gospel (Gal. i. 4-10).

The twofold answer to all this is obvious. (1) The positive declaration of Christ, that His blood was shed for many for the remission of sins, indisputably points to an immediate connection (Matt. xxvi. 28). On no other ground can we explain the way in which Christ connects His blood with the remission of sins. He announced a direcct causal connection between the two. This appears, too, from another mode of expression. If one dies in another's room, and, by dying, effects deliverance, what can that mean but an immediate and causal connection between the sacrifice and the deliverance or remission? The Jewish mind was quite familiar with this notion by means of sacrifices, and they easily connected together the victim's death and the worshipper's direct liberation from punishment in virtue of it. (2) The commission as to the way in which this forgiveness was to be preached proves the same thing. It was to be preached, not sold; and the simple announcement of His death, and of present forgiveness by means of it, to sinners as they are, was the sum and substance of the commission with which the first teachers of Christianity were invested.

The whole office of the ministry, as it is here delineated with the commission, given by our Lord, has for its object the proclamation of repentance and forgiveness. And, hence, the apostles describe their office as a ministry of reconciliation (2 Cor. v. 18), and as instituted to tell of Christ's ransom for all (1 Tim. ii. 5-7); while the word is called the preaching of the cross (1 Cor. i. 18).

Thus our Lord emphatically sets forth the immediate connection between His blood and forgiveness (Matt. xxvi. 28); and the great work of preaching, as well as the great design of the gospel ministry, is to announce or proclaim this fact.

SEC. XLIX.—THE PLACE WHICH CHRIST ASSIGNS TO THE ATONEMENT IN THE CHRISTIAN CHURCH.

The prominent rank which our Lord gives to the doctrine of the atonement in the founding of the Christian Church, and in all its solemnities, deserves our particular attention, as a proof of its being a divinely provided fact, and as an evidence of its vast importance. Everything connected with the Church, and with its solemnities or services, presupposes the historical fact of Christ's atoning death. This circumstance takes Christ out of the category of a mere teacher. The influence of the Lord's sacrifice may be traced on every institution, on every doctrine, and on the whole outline of Christian experience. Had our plan led us to indulge in personal reflections, or to expatiate on the practical fruits and consequences of the atonement, these might have been set forth at large. But as we limit ourselves to an expository outline or statement of our Lord's sayings, we notice only what He has marked out as the due position of this truth in the institutions and services of the Church, which are all based upon the cross. When we have done this, we shall apprehend correctly in what light the Bible leads us to survey the doctrine.

1. The blood of atonement is the basis of the entire new covenant. On this point it is the less necessary to enlarge, because we noticed, in a previous section, some of the topics connected with it.[1] Our Lord, in referring to the new covenant, so called as contrasted with that national covenant which was made with Israel at Sinai, declares that it was founded in His blood, or on His atonement. This new covenant, into which all believing disciples are taken, whether Jews or Gentiles, rests on the true sacrifice, just as the Sinaitic covenant, with which it is contrasted, was founded on the typical sacrifices which must needs be offered at its institution.

[1] See page 207.

I shall not here enlarge again on the nature and provisions of the new covenant, as my present object is only to show that the atonement lies at its foundation. The term *covenant* does not denote a mere doctrine, but implies an actual relation formed between God and man—the atonement being the basis on which it rests. No atonement, then no covenant and no Church. The more precise nature of it will appear when we read it off from the provisions of the typical economy, which preceded it. The blessings were to be individual as well as national, so that, instead of the national theocracy, the members of the new covenant should also be individually in covenant with God, and have the law written on the heart (Jer. xxxi. 31). The new covenant was to stand on the foundation of a full and everlasting remission of sins, which, again, according to Christ's words, was derived only from the blood of atonement. Thus the entire new covenant recognised the death of Christ as its foundation. It may be added, that in this covenant, differing as it did from the former, by being universal, Jews and Gentiles participate in equal privileges, being reconciled to God in one body. On the other hand, the new covenant ceases to have any place where the doctrine of the atonement is not received, either under the influence of philosophical reasonings, or of a legal bias; and the terrible judgment of God, called by our Lord dying in their sins (John viii. 24)—a doom much more severe than that of dying for disobeying Moses' law—falls upon all who despise the blood of the covenant (Heb. x. 28). This involves more, by many degrees, than the mere neglect of Christ's words or teaching. He was but the prophet or teacher of His own salvation, so that He is rejected in both respects.

2. The atonement is described as the substance of the sacraments. They have neither significance nor value, except as they presuppose the great fact of a vicarious sacrifice for sin; and to keep the atonement perpetually before the eye of the Church, as the one fact on which our entire salvation rests, not only at the commencement, but also during the course of

the Christian's pilgrimage, the Lord deemed it fitting to institute these two sacraments in the Church. Thus the Christian
disciple sees the atonement everywhere, and finds it in every
Church institution. It is the one great fact from which he
starts, and to which he ever returns.

a. We shall notice this fact, first in connection with baptism, which is by no means limited to the idea that it is a sign
of reception into the Christian Church. If nothing further than
this were implied, there could be no reference to the atonement.
But it involves much more. Not to adduce the subsequent
statements of the apostles, which affirm that they who are
baptized into Christ are baptized into His death (Rom. vi. 3),
the Lord's own sayings upon the point are not obscure. Thus,
when He speaks of His disciples baptizing in His name, as well
as in the name of the Father and of the Spirit, He plainly
alludes to a peculiar relation to Himself in His official capacity[1]
(Matt. xxviii. 19); and when He said, "I have a baptism to be
baptized with; and how am I straitened till it is accomplished!"
(Luke xii. 50), He gave His own authoritative exposition of the
meaning and import of John's baptism, as it was administered to
Himself. It was a symbol of the way in which Christ was to
pass under the heaviest sufferings; and He submitted to the
symbol as a token of the readiness with which He submitted to
undergo the reality. The baptismal water was an emblem, in
Christ's case, of the punitive justice of God, under which He
passed.[2] Christ, the surety, was baptized in His official capacity,
and His people are considered to have undergone this punishment in Him for the remission of sins. The water of baptism is
a symbol of the shed blood of the crucified surety on whom the

---

[1] βαπτίζοντες αὐτοὺς εἰς τὸ ὄνομα (Matt. xxviii. 19) intimates, in the first place,
faith and a confession, and, in the next place, a certain relation, as intimated by
εἰς. But what I refer to is, that *the name* is not an allusion to the mere Trinitarian relation, but also to the official redemption work, and so to the name of
Jesus in this respect as well.

[2] See this idea, developed by the well-known A. Schultens, on the Heidelberg
Catechism, as translated from his papers by Barueth.

curse no more rests. It is blood that has passed through death and the application of which takes away the guilt of sin. The symbol can mean nothing else but this, that His death was ours; the only difference between John's baptism and that of the Christian Church being, that the former was a baptism for a suffering yet future, while the latter is a baptism into that which is finished. Baptism intimates a fellowship with Christ in His death. The grand fundamental idea of baptism, though not to the exclusion of other allusions, is, that His death was a propitiatory death, and that His people died with Him; and this is specially developed by the apostles (comp. Rom. vi. 4; 1 Pet. iii. 21).

b. The same thing holds true of THE LORD'S SUPPER, intended to keep alive, through all the ages till the second coming of Christ, the great fact of His expiatory death. Its primary design was not to commemorate His office as a teacher, but to commemorate and to symbolize His great sacrifice, when He died to put away sin by the sacrifice of Himself. The words used by Him in connection with it are so express and clear to this effect, that no doubt as to their meaning remains on any mind interpreting words according to their precise significance. They who have a right to the Supper eat and drink spiritually of the body and blood of the Lord, not as He was still laden with the guilt of sin and still under obligation to fulfil the divine law, but as having purged our sins and now entitled to all the glory which falls to Him and His redeemed as the reward of His agony. They identify themselves with Him as passing through death for them. When Christians receive the bread and wine by faith, they are supposed to be made partakers of His vicarious death, and are regarded as united to Him, and as having undergone, in and with Him, all that He endured.

Thus, according to the purpose of Christ, both these symbolic actions of the Christian Church refer to the atonement; and they are meant to attest it, whenever they are solemnized. As they perpetually return in the services of the Christian Church, they keep before the eye of believers this great fundamental truth till the Lord come. The meaning of the atonement, its nature, and effects of every kind, the utility of the atonement and its necessity, are all proclaimed anew by every repetition of these sacraments, which are appropriate to the different stages of the Christian life,—the one to its commencement, the other to its progress. These provisions keep up a constant remembrance of the cross, shewing that the eye is never to be turned away from the crucified substitute, and are accompanied with the word given to explain them. Hence we may see the rank and place that belong to the atonement.

SEC. L.—CHRIST'S SAYINGS WHICH REPRESENT FAITH AS THE ORGAN OR INSTRUMENT OF RECEIVING THE ATONEMENT.

The relative place of faith becomes evident, when it is viewed as that mental act on which the whole application of redemption on man's side depends. The term *faith* means a spirit-given trust on the divine mercy and on a personal Saviour, as opposed to man's native self-reliance. This is its uniform signification, according to Scripture usage. Though some have thought that, in a considerable number of passages, it must be taken in an objective sense, denoting the doctrine[1] of the Gospel (as Gal. i. 23; 1 Tim. iv. 1; Jude 3), yet the best modern expositors explain these passages in the ordinary sense; from which, indeed, we are not required to depart in a single instance.

The important position which faith occupies appears when we consider that it is the means by which redemption is appropriated. It presupposes Christ's atoning work, which it receives, and is so closely connected with repentance, that the one is never in exercise without the other. It is saving only, as it is receptive of Christ's finished work; and this is the point to which

---

[1] The commentators of the Reformation age, and afterwards, took up this idea of πίστις, or rather inherited it from mediæval times. It is now given up by all good exegetes. (See Winer, Meyer, De Wette, Fritzsche, *passim*.)

primary attention must be directed. Faith in its proper nature is the reception of a gift, and saves, not as it involves obedience, but simply as it is receptive of Christ and His redemption.

There are passages in Scripture, indeed, where we find the phrase, "the obedience of the faith," denoting a compliance with the divine authority in accepting the gift (comp. Acts vi. 7; Rom. i. 5, x. 3). Though these passages have been explained by some as denoting the obedience which follows faith, they really mean obedience in accepting the divine gift. The personal Saviour, as the surety of sinners in the discharge of His official undertaking, which involved an obedience unto death and the acceptance of His work, is the proper object of faith; which is by no means limited to a bare act of the understanding, but also an exercise of the heart. There are several sayings of our Lord, describing faith as the one means of receiving the atonement. Faith, in the sense attached to it by Christ, involves a trust in His person, and gives a relation to His person. It denotes a God-given reliance on an all-sufficient Mediator. Nor is it a reliance on His person irrespective of His office; for faith uniformly looks to what He officially did and suffered for our salvation.

To apprehend the connection between faith and the Saviour, we must investigate the sayings of Christ. We shall limit our attention to the function of faith in obtaining the participation of the ransom, the atonement, or righteousness which Christ brought in; as it would turn us away into a line of inquiry different from that we are pursuing, were we to enter on the doctrine of faith in all its aspects and bearings. Our one object in this section is to set forth from the words of Christ, that a divinely originated faith is the receptive organ or hand by which the believer is made partaker of the atonement. I shall not refer to those passages where it is interchanged with the phrase, "to receive His testimony" (John iii. 11, 12). I shall omit, too, the frequent use of the term in connection with the miraculous cures wrought on the bodies of men, though, both in their conscious need and in the persuasion of Christ's sufficiency, this exercise of faith was analogous, though not precisely the same with that which receives the crucified Christ for salvation.[1] In a word, faith is the hand by which the graciously provided ransom is received by the captive, and the complete righteousness is put on by the destitute; or, to use another mode of representation, it is that bond which attaches us to Christ, and thereby to the Father. It makes Christ and His disciples one, in such a sense that they are no more two, but one person, in the eye of law and before God. By faith, the person is put on a right footing of acceptance; the standing before God is adjusted; the relation of man towards God is rectified. There is nothing else by which men can be connected with the Saviour. Without it, there is no relation to Jesus, and the atonement would be offered in vain. But when any avail themselves of His mediation, the way, the truth, and the life, they have access to God by Him (John xiv. 6). There is thus an immediate connection, without any intervening steps between faith and the acceptance of the person or the forgiveness of sins.

In our Lord's sayings, moreover, it will be found that faith is put in direct antithesis to work of any kind, or to any moral virtue, which might become a ground of confidence before God. His sayings leave us in no doubt that faith leans on the person of Christ alone, with a full repudiation of all the righteousness of works. Thus on one occasion He replied to the self-righteous multitude, demanding, "What shall we do, that we might work the works of God?" in a manner which was fitted to repress such legalism: "This is the work of God, that ye believe on Him whom He hath sent" (John vi. 29). It is only by a kind of paronomasia that He calls faith a work, as if He would say, "If this language is to be introduced at all, this is the work of God, the divinely appointed injunction, that ye believe on Him whom He hath sent."

[1] See an interesting biblical, as well as dogmatic, discussion of this doctrine by Superintendent Cless, *über den N. T. Begriff des Glaubens.*

Faith is thus the hand by which we receive all that Christ has done. This will appear, if we recall our Lord's sayings on this point. Thus, in that striking delineation given of faith in His conversation with Nicodemus, He defines it as an exercise of the soul, corresponding to the looking of the wounded Israelite to the heaven-appointed means of cure (John iii. 14, 15). In both the verses where He speaks of faith as the means of cure, it is spoken of as trust or reliance on the incarnate Son crucified or "lifted up" (ver. 14), or "given" in the sacrificial acceptation of the term (ver. 16). The looking of the wounded Israelite, as the means by which he was healed, is parallel to faith on the crucified Christ. Thus the proper import of the term "faith" is limited to this peculiar relation which is always presupposed between a sinner and a Saviour. As in the case of the Israelite it was not the reception of a moral doctrine, nor fidelity in the observance of the laws of Moses, but a confiding look to the brazen serpent, that constituted the means of cure, so faith is nothing but reliance on the crucified Jesus. For what did that figure serve? and why was that figure peculiarly selected? It was for the purpose of showing that faith presupposes the finished work of atonement, a divine provision, and a human want. As human necessities are many and great, faith clings to the crucified Son of God as the God-appointed and sufficient remedy. The atonement is the means of putting sinful men on a right relation to God, a provision for the greatest necessity that can be named; and as the atoning death of Christ is the centre-point of all His benefits, so faith is the centre-point of Christ's doctrine.

Our Lord represents the same thing under another figurative description—that of eating the bread of life which came down from heaven (John vi. 32-53). To apprehend the force of this figure, we must attend to the point of comparison. Between the bread and the crucified Christ there is one analogy; between the act of eating and the exercise of faith there is a second. With reference to the first of these, the comparison must be made only with reference to the nourishing property of food, thus: food has a nutritive quality, and the death of Christ has the same relation to our salvation. His death is the cause of our salvation in the same way as food is the cause of sustaining life. But here the second analogy, or point of comparison, presents itself. The most nutritious food could not avail to any who did not make use of it; and, in the same way, the death of Christ will not benefit any who do not believe in Him. According to this simple and perspicuous figure, faith stands to our salvation in the same relation that the partaking of food does to this temporal life.[1] Faith is thus the appointed means, and the only means, by which any man can enjoy the saving efficacy of Christ's atoning death; and no words could more forcibly point out the indispensable necessity of faith for a participation in the saving efficacy of Christ's atoning sacrifice. This is the one means of reception. He who believes receives the saving blessings which Christ's death procured, and has a right to the fulfilment of the promise. He who receives with the heart the gift of the crucified Christ, has a right to pardon, and can claim it.

We do not here develop the doctrine that faith is an inward work of God, produced by the operation of divine grace; for we are directed by our theme to faith, as that by which men please God, and find the acceptance of their persons before God. Christ tells us that a man is saved, not by working, but by believing on Him whom the Father sent (John vi. 29). It is as if He said, " Have done with working; begin by believing on a God-appointed Mediator, as containing in His person and redemption-work the only sufficient ground of acceptance." Salvation is to him who ceases from working; or, as it is put by Paul: " To him that worketh not, but believeth on Him that justifies the ungodly, his faith is counted for righteousness " (Rom. iv. 5); and this proves that faith constitutes the primary, principal, and most important duty.

---

[1] See Lotze, *Hoogepriesterschap van J. C.*, p. 145.

The same thing is proved by those sayings of Jesus, where He declares that they who believe not, perish in their sins (John viii. 24). All depended on this, that they took Him for what He was. That language referred to His person and office, not to His doctrine, and it shows what stood connected with faith on His person, or the opposite. They who would not receive Him as the sin-bearer, or as the Lamb of God, must therefore perish in their sins.

CHAPTER VIII.

THE ENDLESS HAPPINESS OR WOE OF MANKIND DECIDED BY THE RECEPTION OR REJECTION OF THE ATONEMENT.

SEC. LI.—ENDLESS HAPPINESS, OR IRREMEDIABLE WOE, DECIDED BY THE MANNER IN WHICH MEN WELCOME OR REJECT THE ATONEMENT.

THOUGH we embrace in this section two opposite classes of sayings, we deem it best to put them together, partly because the one suggests the other, by contrast, partly because men's destiny hinges simply on the acceptance or non-acceptance of Christ's atonement. I shall refer a little more fully to the second point just mentioned, that is, to the remediless doom of those who refuse the propitiation of the cross.

1. Christ's vicarious sacrifice alone, apart from any accessory work or merit of a supplementary description, secured for His people a place in the heavenly inheritance: "I go to prepare a place for you. And if I go and prepare a place for you, I will come again, and receive you unto myself; that where I am, there ye may be also. And whither I go ye know, and the way ye know. Thomas saith unto Him, Lord, we know not whither Thou goest; and how can we know the way? Jesus saith unto him, I am the way, and the truth, and the life: no

man cometh unto the Father, but by Me" (John xiv. 2-6).
This saying, understood according to the deep significance
which our Lord commonly attached to the words, *depart* and
go away, comprehends not only the departure, but the mode by
which He went; that is, the vicarious sacrifice by which He
returned to the Father. This, as we have already proved, is
the import of Christ's language in such a connection. The
words intimate that heaven, once shut against mankind, is reopened by the satisfaction of the Son of God, and that His
entrance secures that of His people. The text is thus a key to
all those passages which describe Jesus as the new and living
way (Heb. x. 20), as the leader of our salvation (Heb. ii. 10),
as the forerunner who has for us entered (Heb. vi. 20), and
also to another class of passages which speak of sitting in
heavenly places with Him (Eph. i. 3).

It is a superficial comment, which interprets the words as
referring only to doctrine, and as intimating merely that He
pointed out the way to happiness. No mere teacher ever expressed himself as the Lord has here done. It is true the
disciples might not at the time discern the full meaning of the
words, and might understand Him as if He represented Himself
in the light of a traveller, who goes to a certain place Himself,
and makes certain preparations also for the reception of His
friends. Many interpreters see little beyond this in the words.
But they imply much more. They intimate that Jesus was to
be the procuring cause and ground of our endless felicity, and
not the mere messenger to announce it. He represents Himself
as the one cause of man's happiness, and as accomplishing what
meritoriously prepared a place for His disciples. He calls His
death or vicarious sacrifice *a going to the Father*, and delineates
it as the means or cause of preparing a place for His people
among the many mansions. No one is warranted to explain
these words in a metaphorical way, when it is evident, from the
whole scope and connection of the passage, that He would have
them apprehended in their strict and proper import.

According to the principle of interpretation which we have applied several times already, the words of Jesus imply that men had forfeited their position in the house of God, and that Christ has restored it by His atoning death. A place was prepared for the disciples by Christ, first, by annihilating the cause of the estrangement, or putting away sin by the sacrifice of Himself; and next, by taking possession of the inheritance in His people's name, as their representative and Head. Thus, apart from any supplementary work of man, or any merit of our own appended to the work of atonement, Christ's going to the Father prepared a place for the redeemed; and His disciples enter heaven simply on the footing of His atoning sacrifice. This is more than a teacher's function, and more than to follow a mere example.

2. This leads me to consider, in the next place, the opposite class of testimonies, which set forth the irremediable woe and endless punishment awaiting those who reject the redemption work of Christ. The general question of final retribution and of endless punishment of sin as such in all its wide bearings, does not come within our present purpose. But one important aspect of it—that connected with the rejection of the atonement, or the non-acceptance of the divinely-provided remedy— demands attention, as a large number of testimonies uttered by our Lord has express reference to the endless and irremediable misery of those who reject His sacrifice. To these we must refer, and the rather, because at present, doubts as to the eternity of future punishment are more widely diffused than at any previous epoch, among those who in other respects accept the truths of Christianity.

When we consider the constant and uniform teaching of our Lord as to the future destiny of men, we find two periods mentioned,—one of preparation, which is of brief duration; and one of retribution, which is fixed and endless. Thus, faith is required in this life, and urged with the distinct announcement, that otherwise men are condemned already (John iii. 18), and that the wrath of God *abideth* on them (John iii. 36). The same allusion to the endless endurance of the divine displeasure comes out emphatically in a passage of which the point is much missed. "For whosoever will save his life shall lose it: and whosoever will lose his life for my sake shall find it. For what is a man profited, if he shall gain the whole world, and lose his own soul? or what shall a man give in exchange for [better, as a ransom-price for] his soul?" (Matt. xvi. 25, 26).[1] This implies that the payment of a ransom was indispensably necessary in order to liberate men from captivity, but that it has been neglected; and the point of our Lord's inquiry is, what other expedient or ransom, to satisfy God and to effect man's liberation, can be given? It is tantamount to the declaration that there remaineth no more sacrifice for sin, no second ransom, when the soul has been lost by the rejection of the one sole expedient devised for this end. The rejection of Christ's atonement is a new transgression, the enormity of which far outweighs all other sins, whether we think of the greatness of His person or of the fact that it is a sin against the remedy. It shuts the door of mercy. The figurative terms, too, by which these future punishments are expressed—such as "the unquenchable fire" (Mark ix. 45), and the "way that leadeth to destruction" (Matt. vii. 13)—convey thoughts that are wholly out of keeping with the idea of restoration or deliverance.

Before noticing single testimonies, we may adduce, as a ruling instance, the case of Judas Iscariot, of whom our Lord said, "Woe unto that man by whom the Son of Man is betrayed! it had been good for that man if he had not been born" (Matt. xxvi. 24). This mode of arguing from a ruling case, employed by Paul, for the establishment of such weighty truths as justification by faith alone (Rom. iv. 1-23), election (Rom. ix. 10-23), and the liberty of those who are children of the promise (Gal. iv. 22-31), may be used to prove the truth of eternal punishments. Here is a ruling instance in the moral government of

---

[1] ἀντάλλαγμα τῆς ψυχῆς.

God.   It is noteworthy, that the objection of greatest weight
to certain minds is, that it would have been better for such
persons that they had not been born; and that is the very inference drawn by our Lord in respect of Judas.   He allows it;
He asserts ,it.   But this language could not have been used if
there were any termination to the retribution awarded, or any
ulterior felicity and rest;—a proof, this, which cannot be evaded,
and before which all must stand silent!   If a pause to suffering
should follow, or a period of felicity should enter, to be at last
a relief or compensation, such words could not have been used
by the omniscient Saviour, whose eye minutely surveyed all
future, as well as all present, relations.   It would have been
good for Judas to be born, if, even after innumerable ages of
punishment, however long continued, he should at last enter on
the inheritance of rest, peace, and glory; for the intermediate
torment, how protracted soever, would bear no proportion to the
unending rest of eternity.   On the contrary, this case demonstrates that there is no outlet, no repentance, no hope; and a
ruling instance of this sort is conclusive.

They who doubt the eternity of future punishment must
explain away our Lord's words on some preconceived theory,
and by a non-natural interpretation (John viii. 24).   Certainly,
their usual position, that Christ taught nothing but love, is
refuted, not only by the woe pronounced upon Chorazin, Beth-
saida, and Capernaum (Matt. xi. 21-23), and upon the Scribes
and Pharisees (Matt. xxiii. 1-33), but also by the distinct announcement with which He sent forth His apostles: " He that
believeth not *shall be damned* " (Mark xvi. 16).   Without going
into an exhaustive discussion of this question,[1] it will serve the
purpose which we have in view, to adduce one or two sayings

---

[1] On the subject of eternal punishment, I may refer to the anti-Socinian
writers, such as Hoornbeek and Calovius.   As against the rationalists I may
mention specially Michaelis, *über Sünde und Genugthuung*, p. 260 ; also an able
discussion in Mosheim's Sermons, Lampe's Dissertations, Schultens on Heidelberg
Catechism, Muntinghe, Van Voorst, etc.

of Jesus which conclusively establish the fact, that endless woe
awaits those who reject His atonement.

In sending out the twelve on their first evangelistic tour, He
said, " Rather fear Him who is able to destroy both soul and
body in hell" (Matt. x. 28). I shall not refer to the comment
given in some quarters to the effect that the person here referred
to is Satan ; for that cannot be made even probable. Plainly, it
is God to whom our Lord refers as able to destroy both soul and
body ; and the words, contain the notion of unending destruction
as the second death. Finality is wholly out of keeping with
our Lord's words ; for that notion would argue purification and
preparation for a better lot, not the destruction of both soul and
body in hell, which is affirmed. Not less express is the statement in the parable of Lazarus, that there is a great gulf fixed,
and impassable, between those in bliss and those in misery, by
which they are for ever separated (Luke xvi. 26). The language
implies, that if the blessed never fall from their felicity, the lost
never escape from their misery.

The same awful truth is brought out when our Lord speaks of
everlasting punishment, using the same word with which He
speaks of life eternal (Matt. xxv. 46). To those who argue that
a different meaning may be assigned to the same adjective in the
two contrasted clauses of the same verse, it is enough to say that
the admission of such a diversity of meaning would be to violate
all the rules of just interpretation. It is to no purpose to allege
that the word here rendered *everlasting* and *eternal* sometimes
denotes nothing beyond a definite time[1] (Gen. xvii. 13 ; Eph. iii.
9). However men may argue from other passages where the
word denotes enduring as long as a certain economy or institution continues, that does not touch the antithesis of this verse.
It still remains that the same word is equally applied to
the heavenly blessedness and to the future misery ; and

---

[1] It is not denied that, in certain connections, αἰώνιος denotes what lasts during
a given epoch, or αἰών. (See J. Alting on Rom. xvi. 25.) But the connection
shows, in all languages, what is meant by *for ever*. I may refer to a discussion
by Moses Stuart on αἰών and αἰώνιος, in Clark's *Biblical Cabinet*, vol. 37.

on no principle of interpretation can an expositor be allowed to give a different sense to the same word in two contrasted clauses.

One of the strongest proofs for the eternity of future punishment is found in the words descriptive of the condemned: "where their worm dieth not, and the fire is not quenched" (Mark ix. 46). They who contend for the finality of punishment have no refuge from the cogency of this passage, except in the desperate peradventure of annihilation, to which, indeed, without any evidence, they sometimes appeal.

The theme on which we have been commenting is awful in the extreme, and one which no one can approach without a bleeding heart. But the question to be determined, apart from all other considerations, is, What has Jesus said? does He assert the finality of punishment or proclaim its unending duration? and no faithful expounder of His words can maintain that He has even left this matter doubtful. As to the further question, On whom does this unending doom strike? His words are not less clear. They are the men, who, like Judas, or the Jewish nation, or Capernaum, refuse His redemption work, and reject His great salvation (Matt. xxv. 46; John iii. 36; Matt. iii. 12); and the frequency with which our Lord refers to this theme is a merciful forewarning, intended to shut men up to the all-sufficient atonement.

SEC. LII.—THE INFUENCE OF THE ATONEMENT, CORRECTLY UNDERSTOOD, ON THE WHOLE DOMAIN OF MORALS AND RELIGION.

The doctrine of the atonement, which it was our aim to establish in the foregoing pages, and to put in its true light, from the view-point of Christ's consciousness, is so interwoven with all the other essential doctrines of Christianity, that they stand or fall together. Nothing important can keep its ground, if, indeed, anything of paramount moment can be said to remain, where the atonement is abandoned, or no longer held in some form. It is this that gives coherence, meaning, and consistency to the entire fabric, which must otherwise collapse.

But it is not so much the place of the atonement in Christian doctrine, as its influence on morality and vital religion, to which I here allude. The plan we have pursued does not lead us to the Epistles, where we find perpetually recurring references to the fact of the atonement, and to all the spiritual benefits which stand in intimate connection with it, but to the Lord's own words, as the basis and groundwork of all the applications which the apostles make of it. But we find His own sayings explicit enough on the subject of our present inquiry.

We shall consider the influence of the atonement on the domain of morals and true piety. The common objection to the method of acceptance by the satisfaction of divine justice, or by the work of another, is that it has a tendency to make men rest in what has been done by a substitute and to be indifferent to purity of heart. This is the old cavil to which the apostle alludes (Rom. vi. 1-7). On the contrary the participation of the saving benefits flowing from the atonement yields the strongest of all motives that can influence the human heart, not to dishonour, but to glorify, the ineffably gracious Giver of such blessings. If we were to enumerate the securities for vital religion supplied by the atonement, we should have to distribute them into two classes—one having its basis in the moral government of God, a second in the sphere of motives. To the former, indicated in our Lord's allusions to the premial life consequent on the reception of the atonement (John vi. 51), and fully developed in the apostolic Epistles (Rom. vi. 4; Gal. ii. 20), it is not necessary again to refer, because the subject was under our consideration when we discussed the renovating and transforming effects of the divine life, as it takes possession of the human heart. It is only to the motives furnished by the atonement, that it is further necessary to allude.

A scheme of thought which runs counter to the atonement, if

carried out to its logical consequences, is destructive to religion, and subversive of morality. The peace and security of mankind depend on a true knowledge of God, not in one attribute, but in all the perfections of His nature. The position too widely maintained at present, that God is nothing but a fountain of goodness, who sacrifices everything to the happiness of His creatures, destroys all religion, because it takes no account of the subjection, love, and reverence due to God. The thinkers who at present would strike out the atonement from the creed of Christendom, agree in maintaining that love was the only motive in the divine mind in creating the world, and in legislating for it, and that He had no other object or design but the communication of happiness. Though this scheme of thought is not formally connected with any philosophy, as it was within the Leibnitzian or Wolfian philosophy, last century, it comes to substantially the same result, viz. that the supreme Being sacrifices everything to human happiness and to the best world. It is argued that He is too highly exalted to be injured by human transgression, or angry at men's impotent opposition; and that He indulgently connives at this, if they do not injure or destroy themselves. It is held that the Most High never punishes but for men's good, and generally not at all, if they render this unnecessary by repentance.

This at once banishes all moral aims from the divine government, and, in a word, so completely reverses the relations of things, that, on this principle, the creature can scarcely be said to exist for the Creator, but conversely. This theory disconnects happiness from moral excellence, which cannot any longer be regarded as possessed of intrinsic value. Nay, it gives way at every point where physical happiness is threatened or imperilled. This is a low view of the divine government. On the contrary, God could not rest with complacency in even the happiest world, if men did not seek after their Creator, and acknowledge His rights. And all religion is at once subverted, as well as all right ethical action—supported as this is on the natural relation which we bear, as reasonable beings, to the Creator—the moment men maintain that God aims at the natural happiness of His creatures as the chief end.

The effect of this theory on morals and religion, if no other elements came in to countervail or check it, is obvious. All those duties, which terminate in God, would fall to the ground, for there would be no motives drawn from our relation to Him. And if some duties would at once fall to the ground, others, such as joy and delight in Him, would be so much deteriorated that they could scarcely be said to partake of a moral character, because they would not differ in kind from joy or delight in insensate things, which please or profit us. God would not be made the end of human action, and self-interest would predominate.[1]

On the contrary, the atonement, as we have developed it from the words of our Lord, is based on the fact that God vindicates His rights, and that He cannot recede from the legitimate claim —based not only on His relation as Creator, but also on His own moral excellence—to the love and confidence, the reverence and homage, the subjection and adoration, of every creature made in the image of God. He demands this from His intelligent universe, and cannot connive at rebellion without the infliction of due punishment. This is the first principle of His moral government; and the atonement is its recognition on the part of the substitute, as well as its enforcement on the part of the Creator.

The virtue, which takes its tincture from Christ's atonement, is perceptibly different, too, from that which disregards it. Experience shows that the virtues of such persons as plume themselves on their morality, apart from any dependence on the atonement of Christ, are of a hard, arrogant, and censorious character. On the contrary, where men feel themselves to be imperfect sinning creatures, daily confessing errors, and standing

---

[1] On the influence of right ideas of the atonement, I may refer to two Dutch champions of the truth : Hulshoff's *Philosophische Gesprekken*, 1795 ; and Wynpersse, *over de Straffende Gerechtigheid*, 1799.

before God in a Mediator's merits, they possess a virtue which is mild, meek, patient, humble, and attractive in the comparison.[1]

2. Having already adverted to the influence of the atonement on the whole domain of morals, it remains that we briefly notice its effect on the field of true piety or vital religion in its various phases. To begin with FAITH, the organ or instrument of reception, we readily perceive that, without the atonement, it would have wanted its adequate and proper object. Under various modes of representation, metaphors or analogies from common life, it is described as the hand or instrument by which men are made partakers of the atonement (John iii. 15, 16, v. 36). As faith does not merely accept Christ as a teacher or approve of His moral code, but depends on Himself, it could have no object without the atonement.

Not only so : as many passages in our Lord's teaching connect the atonement more or less directly with almost every spiritual benefit and every phase of vital religion, it is obvious that this central truth, the key-stone of the whole structure of a religious life, cannot be removed without irreparable ruin. Thus, to enumerate a few of these blessings, we find that our Lord, on the eve of His arrest by the hand of men, spoke of a *peace* which He should leave with His disciples as the fruit of the atonement (John. xiv. 24); for the whole context indicates that He refers to the peace of conscious reconciliation flowing from His vicarious sacrifice. Many other privileges—more numerous, indeed, than can here be mentioned in detail, belonging to the essential elements of true religion—stand in precisely the same relation : the *freedom* with which the Son makes His people free (John viii. 36); the hearing of *prayer* (John xvi. 23); *rest* for the weary and heavy laden (Matt. xi. 28); the satisfaction of a felt hunger and thirst (John vi. 35, vii. 37); a more abundant life (John x. 10); and a coming to the Father with boldness of access (John xiv. 6). It may seem, at first sight, as if these

---

[1] Compare the ethics of Epictetus, Antoninus, or Kant with the delineations of Christian ethics by Melancthon, Mosheim, Fenelon, Sailer.

passages stood in no direct connection with the surety-merits and atonement of Christ; but every one will be constrained so to connect them, when he compares them with the general statements of the New Testament, or puts them in their organic connection with the system of biblical doctrine. The titles which Christ assumes, especially that of the Saviour of the lost (Luke xix. 10), elevate Him far above the rank of a teacher or messenger of salvation.

3. It only remains for us to notice the influence of the atonement in the sphere of religious motives. Its influence is as powerful and efficacious in the domain of spiritual motive as we saw it was in the sphere of morals, and first in order. Thus, to adduce a few of the constituent elements of all true piety, the atonement is peculiarly adapted to imbue men with *reverence* for God. The rational creature can revere and stand in awe of God only when He is known as venerable; and what can more fill the human mind with reverence than a due discovery of the majesty of God, and of the inviolability of the divine law in the atonement of the cross? Even in other orders of being, who obtain a knowledge of it, and who look into these things, the same feelings are awakened (1 Pet. i. 12). Then, as to the *dread of sin*, nothing is so calculated to infuse it, as a right view of the atonement, especially when we apprehend the infinite dignity of the substitute, who must needs be made the object of the divine wrath. With regard, moreover, to the *aversion to sin*, essential to all true piety, nothing is more calculated to make the memory of sin bitter, and its allurements repulsive, than the agonies of Christ in connection with the sins that caused them.

Nor does the constraining motive stop short there. We may survey the influence of the atonement over the entire sphere or cycle of man's duty. In reference to grateful *love*, nothing so much tends to fill the heart with this emotion as the believing realization of Christ's redemption work—nothing so melts the heart; and no purer love to God can be imbibed. Nor is this a service which either allows room for self-dependence, or warrants men to plume themselves on merit; for if we should describe it, we could only say that the redeemed are not less jealous of mixing their own holiness with the Redeemer's meritorious propitiation, than afraid of a fruitless faith or dead profession. There is no motive to a holy life so powerful and efficacious as that which is drawn from the propitiatory work of Christ, who, after meeting the demands of the law and bearing its curse, makes *that same law a rule* to direct our steps; and Christians learn to take it from the Mediator's hand.

The manifold and various motives derived from the cross are enforced in all the apostolic epistles. The final purpose which we are there told the atonement was meant to effect, according to the divine plan, becomes to believers a guiding principle in the sphere of motive. Thus when the redeemed apprehend that they are not their own but bought with a price, they are directed on this very account to glorify God with their body and spirit (1 Cor. vi. 20). When holy fear is inculcated on Christians during the time of their sojourn, it is enforced by the consideration that we are redeemed by precious blood (1 Pet. i. 18). The Christian thus falls in with the ways of God. The ground and motive for holy duty, for inflaming and increasing the true fear of God, and for expelling misleading aims or tendencies, as seen in almost every point of practical religion, will be found in the apostolic epistles, traced up to the atonement of Christ. The Christian calls on his soul to remember this, whether he discovers in the death of his Lord indications of divine holiness or of compassionate love. And he contemplates the doctrine of the atonement, in order to find motives for the discharge of sacred duties, for the cultivation of love, fear, and confidence. He investigates the source from which these graces can be most effectually derived, and he finds all this in the doctrine of reconciliation effected by the atoning blood of Christ.[1]

[1] See note M in the Appendix.

APPENDIX

OF

NOTES AND HISTORICAL ELUCIDATIONS.

NOTE A, p. 15.—*Number of the Sayings on the subject of His Death.*

IN speaking of the limited number of the Lord's testimonies on the subject of His atoning death, I allude to several elements in the public opinion of the age, which go far to explain the amount of reserve. Among other circumstances may be mentioned the fact that few of the Jews at that time retained a right idea of the atoning work or function of the Messiah, as it is represented in Isaiah's prophecy (Isa. liii.).

The Jews in the time of Christ do not seem to have retained the belief of a suffering Messiah, or of His priesthood (Ps. cx. 4). Nay, the prophetical office, too, was swallowed up in the one notion of a temporal prince (see John i. 21, compared with Deut. xviii. 18). BORGER, in his *Disputatio contra Eberhardum*, quotes writers who assert, and also writers who deny, that the Jews in the time of Christ still had the idea. The evidence from the Gospels, that the idea had well nigh perished from the Jewish community, is almost conclusive. The Jews seem to have expected nothing but a temporal dominion, and a Messiah who should overthrow the power of Rome, and give to the Jewish people an ascendency among the nations. Their words at Jerusalem, "We have heard out of the law, that Christ abideth for ever" (John xii. 34), are decisive. The offence, too, which the multitude took at Capernaum, as De Wette and Meyer correctly show, must, in a large measure, be ascribed to His declaration, that He was to die as a suffering Messiah (John vi. 60). (See also Vinke, p. 164.)

The apostles were not exempt from the prejudices of their contemporaries, but rather shared in them in a double measure. This appears from the fact that they expected to receive places of honour, distinction, and authority in the Messianic kingdom, from their language, and from incidents in their history. If they understood the import of Christ's words, they misinterpreted His allusions to His death, by foregone conclusions derived from the prophecies which announced that the Messiah should reign for ever, and that His government should have no end (Isa. ix. 7). These prophecies they understood as declaring that He should never die. Christ promised them the Comforter, who was to lead them into all truth, or rather "into all the truth" ($\pi \hat{\alpha} \sigma a \nu \ \tau \grave{\eta} \nu \ \grave{a} \lambda \acute{\eta} \theta \epsilon \iota a \nu$), and especially into the full doctrine as to His atoning death, which they could not bear while He was still among them (John xvi. 13, 17).

These causes go far to explain the reason why our Lord said less on the subject of His atoning death than might have been expected. But the supposition is highly probable, that He uttered many things on the subject of His death which have not been recorded; for we have only a small portion recorded of what He said and did (John xx. 30, xxi. 25). Thus the Apostle Paul adduces one memorable saying of Christ, not recorded by any of the evangelists (Acts xx. 35). It is a remarkable feature of the Gospels, that we commonly find a narrative of the discourses and actions of the Lord as He appeared in public, and came in contact with those who could not hear the whole truth as to the nature of His mission, history, and fortunes. We have not the record of His private interviews to any large extent, if we except such incidents as His interviews with Nicodemus and with the family of Bethany (Luke x. 38). It would be too much to affirm with *Van Willes,* that Jesus did not, in the proper sense of the word, publicly *preach* His sufferings and death; for, though the allusion to His death in His public discourses is commonly introduced after something else (comp. John vi. and x.), no one with these two chapters before him, as specimens of His Galilean ministry and of His ministry in Jerusalem, is entitled to say that He did not, in appropriate and fitting places, make His death and its effects one of the principal points of His preaching. But of *His words in private* we have very little recorded, such as we now desire to possess. A number of references to His death may have been made on many occasions of which we have no record. The explanation of John as to the mode in which the Gospels were composed serves to explain this reserve (John xxi. 25). We may infer that the men of Sychar, who evinced a docility and freedom from prejudice little found among the Jews, received an outline of the necessity, nature, and effects of His atoning death, such as susceptible minds were in a position to hear and accept from His lips. They call Him THE SAVIOUR OF THE WORLD; and the words of Christ about Mary of Bethany, who anointed Him for His burial,—though exegetes such as Grotius, Kuinoel, and Fritzsche, repudiated the notion of a conscious purpose on her part,—argue a belief in His death, and imply private instruction from Himself on His vicarious sacrifice. Another instance of a secret disciple who seems to have received instructions from our Lord in private on the subject of His death was Joseph of Arimathea, one of the members of the Sanhedrim. The fact that he was not offended by the death of Jesus, but confirmed in his attachment to Him, and went in boldly to Pilate to beg the body (τολμήσας, Mark xv. 43), argues that he must have received instruction on the Messiahship of Jesus; which he could get from only one of two sources—the prophecies, or the personal teaching of Jesus. There is much probability in the supposition that he received the information from the Lord Himself, as one of the "many" chief rulers who believed on Him (John xii. 42). He appears to have been more prompt than Nicodemus, though they went in together (John xix. 38). Plainly, he was a disciple before this. Many of the explanations and instructions communicated during the forty days of the resurrection are left unrecorded. In the course of those TEN recorded interviews which they were permitted to enjoy, some of which were more private, while some were more public, their attention was specially directed to the subject of His death,—to its nature, rationale, and effects; and to the types and prophecies which went before (Acts i. 3-8; Luke xxiv. 44-49).

NOTE B, SECT. VII. pp. 36, 94.—*The Satisfaction to Divine Justice necessary.*

At present, when the judicial or forensic aspects of theology are widely impugned, deep importance attaches to the inquiry, whether a satisfaction to divine justice was imperatively necessary. The course of thought on this question is worthy of attention.

Several patristic, mediæval, and post-Reformation divines affirmed, on high transcendental grounds, that God could have given salvation to sinful men without any satisfaction for sin. This speculation was innocuous, so long as they maintained that, in point of fact, salvation was only to be found, according to divine appointment, through the actual incarnation and atonement of the cross. Divines in former centuries sometimes spoke loosely on this point from the view-point of the divine sovereignty, and of the absolute dominion. Thus ATHANASIUS; AUGUSTIN in some passages, though not always; CALVIN (on John xv. 13, where he unhappily says, "poterat nos Deus verbo aut nutu redimere, nisi aliter nostra causa visum fuisset"); ZANCHIUS (*Incar.* iii. 11), and others asserted this position, but they all zealously preached the forensic or judicial side of theology. The same may be said of MUSCULUS, VOSSIUS, TWISS, RUTHERFORD, to whom OWEN

replied in his treatise on Divine Justice. The arguments were undoubtedly all in favour of the conclusion, that the exercise of punitive
justice was necessary when sin had entered into the world; but the
practical necessity of maintaining this position was not so apparent to
them. Hence, when we consult the great divines of the post-Reformation period, we find, that in handling the priestly office of Christ,
or the meritorious ground of justification, under which section most of
them discussed the atonement, they do not raise the question of the
necessity of Christ's atonement. They are content with a statement of
its reality, with an assertion of the fact, which they call its *veritas*.
This holds true of the Lutherans, GERHARD, QUENSTEDT, BUDDEUS, who
scarcely allude to the indispensable necessity of the atonement, while
they powerfully assert the reality of the atonement.

But in proportion as the Socinian leaven spread through the
Protestant churches, with its persistent tendency to set aside the
satisfaction to divine justice in every form, and with the avowed
declaration, uttered by Socinus himself, that if they could get rid of
punitive justice, they would overthrow the doctrine of the atonement,
divines felt that they must express themselves in a different way. A
new attention came to be devoted to the inquiry, whether a satisfaction
to divine justice was not absolutely necessary. They now used more
caution (see the statements of the *Synopsis Purioris Theologiæ*, by
Polyander, Rivetus, Walæus, and Thysius, 1642). They were fully
convinced that the question of the atonement must be ultimately run
up to the necessity of satisfying divine justice; and very generally
they came to assert, that on the entrance of sin, justice must needs be
exercised, and that the atonement was necessary for salvation.[1]

A modified opinion, or an opinion which deserves to be called a
middle way, was propounded by GROTIUS in his able work, *De
Satisfactione.* While he strenuously maintained the reality of the
atonement, or the fact that it was offered, he put it not on the ground
that it was of absolute necessity in order to satisfy divine justice, but
on the ground that it was a spectacle calculated to deter other rational
intelligences. Ravensperger immediately replied to this part of
Grotius' book; and to him, again, Vossius replied, re-asserting the
views of his friend Grotius. In this view, GROTIUS was followed by a
very large number in all the Protestant churches during the two last
centuries. Thus MICHAELIS, *On Sin and the Atonement*, Gottingen,
1779, and SEILER, *über der Versöhnungstod Christi*, Erlangen, 1782,
strongly take up this ground. The view which this theory introduced
on the subject of suffering, however, was new, and somewhat startling.

[1] See our Historical Appendix to the *Apostles' Doctrine of the Atonement.*

Men began to speculate on the salutary effects of punishment, which was no longer regarded as an end or as a penal infliction, which must be awarded because sin deserved it, and because God owed it to Himself. It came to be spoken of as a means to an end ; nay, some began to speak of suffering as having a tendency to augment the happiness of the universe. This theory was but a half-way house, and made insoluble difficulties. Punishment was thus regarded as an arbitrary device, and not as a necessary visitation for a crime, wrong, or insult, which must be avenged by the Divine Majesty. It did not render justice to the word, " Vengeance is mine ; I will repay" (Deut. xxxii. 35). The effect of this modified opinion was only to foster doubts and objections, and to lead men step by step to modify and apologise for, and finally to abandon, punitive justice as an attribute unworthy of God, and unnecessary for the vindication of His honour. In a word, wherever punishment is represented as inflicted merely before some other public or some other end than the satisfaction of God's perfections, we may say that the matter in dispute is really given up, and the fortress surrendered into the hands of the enemy. If we maintain with Michaelis and Seiler, sincerely attached though they were to the doctrine of Christ's satisfaction, that the principal end of punishment is to furnish a spectacle to deter men from sin, this is far from satisfactory as applied to the atonement of Christ. Such a principle may be applicable to the government of human states—though not universally and absolutely applied as a rule even there,—but it cannot be applied to the divine government. On this theory, all the inflictions unknown to others—such as the anguish of conscience, and the secret consequences of vice, considered as a retribution for sin—fall to the ground. But, above all, on this theory, what purpose will punishments serve in the future life ? Who are to be deterred by them, if that is their intention ? It will not satisfy any one to say with Michaelis : to deter other rational beings. Nor can any maintain that the deterring punishment, in this life, always follows the offence, or that it is uniformly in proportion to the offence.

As little will another explanation avail, that God punishes for the glory of His justice. This may have two senses : (1) it may mean that God, as supreme ruler, punishes, with a political and prophetic design, or in order to maintain the authority of His government and promote reverence among His subjects—an end which cannot be attained without severity ; or (2) it may mean that the exercise of punishment takes place, in order to convince men that God will not be regarded as indulgent and tolerant of evil. But this is wholly insufficient ; for the question still arises : Why does God wish to impress this sentiment, and how does it tend to the glorification of His perfections ? We must go further, and affirm something more : for no opinion would glorify Him, if it did not harmonize with truth. And the only position that can be maintained in reference to punishment, is, that punitive justice is an essential, eternal, necessary attribute of God ; that its exercise is necessary on the entrance of sin ; that God is such a Being, that out of love to Himself, and delight in Himself, He loves all that coincides with His perfections, and hates all that is in collision with them ; that His love leads Him to bestow happiness, and His hatred or anger leads Him to send the reverse. The supreme God, insulted by sin, and wronged, if not personally injured, by the irreverence of free creatures, punishes to satisfy the perfection of His nature. This is the reason why He punishes ; and no other explanation is satisfactory to any mind. And hence, due consideration must be given to proper punishment, to vengeance, and retribution for ill-desert. (See Hulshoff's *Philosophische Gesprekken over de Voldoening*, Amst., 1795—an able Dutch writer,—and Wynpersse's *Betoog dat de Strafoeffende Gerechtigheid Gode Waardig is*, Amst., 1799, who very much follows the former.

During last century, the evasions by which the philosophizing divines eluded the arguments for divine justice from the Old Testament, were such as these : that it was a defect in Judaism to regard God, not in the light of a loving Father, but in that of a severe Lawgiver and Judge, who avenged sin, and was to be pacified only by the sight of the blood. The most repulsive language was used against Judaism on this account, as if it were only an expression of the lowest and most unformed religious sentiments. But Christ, as we have seen, uses the same style of speaking about God. Men may allege that the severe ideas of divine *wrath*, and *sacrifice*, of *punishment*, and *atonement*, current among the Jews, were erroneous. But they have still to encounter the question, that Christ holds the same language. If their theory were true, why did Jesus not correct these representations, when the only begotten Son came from the bosom of the Father to reveal Him, and to correct error ? It is in vain to urge, in explanation of this, that it was hard to recall the Jews from these notions, and that it was not attempted.

On the necessity of satisfying the divine justice, the writers against the Socinians may be consulted—that is, the anti-Socinian writers generally who do not take up Grotius' view ; e.g. HOORNBEEK, *Contra Socinianos*, vol. ii. ; ESSENIUS, *De Satisfactione*, 1666 ; CALOVIUS, *Socinismus Profligatus*, 1668 ; STEIN, *De Satisfactione*, 1755. I may also mention these three writers in Dutch—HULSHOFF'S *Dialogues*,

1795 ; WYNPERSSE, *On Justice*, 1799 ; VAN VOORST, *On Punishments*, 1796,—who have ably written on this point against the philosophizing theology at the close of the last century. But of all who have handled this theme, no writer has more powerfully vindicated divine justice in the matter of the atonement than Anselm, in his celebrated treatise, entitled *Cur Deus Homo*, written in 1098 during his exile from England, and intended to meet speculative objections in his day, not unlike those of our age. In an article for *The British and Foreign Evangelical Review*, October 1859, on Anselm's great work, I gave several passages, literally rendered to exhibit his views, from which I shall give the following extracts :—

" CHAP. XI.—WHAT IS SIN, AND A SATISFACTION FOR SIN ?—*Anselm*. We have now to examine by what method God remits men's sins ; and that this may be done with greater clearness, let us first see what it is to sin, and what it is to make a satisfaction for sin.—*Boso*. It is yours to expound, and mine to attend.—*Ans*. If angels and men always rendered to God what they owe, they would never sin.—*Bo*. This cannot be gainsaid.—*Ans*. To sin, therefore, is nothing else but the not rendering to God His due.—*Bo*. What is the debt we owe to God ?—*Ans*. The entire will of a rational creature should be subject to the will of God.—*Bo*. Nothing surer.—*Ans*. This is the debt which angel and man alike owes to God : he who pays it does not sin ; and every one who does not pay it, commits sin. This is the righteousness or rectitude of the will which renders men righteous or upright in heart, that is, in will ; this is the sole and whole honour due to God, and which He requires of us. For only such a will, when it is able to work, performs actions acceptable to God ; and when this is not within its power, it is of itself and alone well-pleasing, since there is no acceptable work without it. *He who does not render to God this due honour, withdraws from God what is His, and dishonours God; and this is to commit sin.* Now, as long as he does not pay what he took away, he abides in guilt. Nor is it sufficient to restore merely what was taken away, but for the indignity inflicted he must render more than he took away ; for as it is not enough for one who does an injury to another's health merely to restore his health, without some recompense for the pain and injury inflicted, even so it is not sufficient, when one has hurt a person's honour, merely to restore the honour, without making some satisfactory reparation to him whom he dishonoured, for[1] the pain inflicted by that indignity. Nor must it be forgotten, that in repaying what was unjustly taken away, he ought

[1] *Secundum* is here used for *pro*, a mediæval usage. (See Vossius.)

not to give in reparation something which could already have been required, though he had never committed that injury. *Thus, then, every sinner must repay the honour which he took from God; and this is the satisfaction which every sinner must make to God.*—*Bo.* In all this, though you somewhat alarm me, I find nothing to which I can take exception.

"Chap. xii.—Whether it becomes God, without any payment of the debt, to forgive sin in the mere exercise of mercy.—*Ans.* Let us return and consider whether it becomes God, without any reparation of His violated honour, to remit sin by mere mercy.—*Bo.* I do not see why it is unsuitable.—*Ans.* To remit sin in this manner is nothing else than not to punish it; and since the due maintenance of order[1] in reference to sin, where no satisfaction is offered, consists solely in its punishment [it follows that], if it is not punished, sin is remitted, without any provision being made for the maintenance of order[2] in the universe.—*Bo.* What you say is reasonable.—*Ans.* But it does not become God to leave anything disordered in His kingdom.—*Bo.* If I were to say anything contrary, I fear it would be sin.—*Ans.* Therefore it is not suitable for God to forgive sin thus unpunished.—*Bo.* That certainly follows.—*Ans.* But something further follows, if sin is thus remitted without punishment: the guilty and the innocent will be alike in the sight of God, which is manifestly not befitting God.—*Bo.* It cannot be denied.—*Ans.* Consider this, moreover: every one knows that man's righteousness is under a law by which the measure of the recompense from the hand of God is proportioned to its magnitude.—*Bo.* So we believe.—*Ans.* Now, if sin is neither atoned for (solvitur) nor punished, it is subject to no law.— *Bo.* It is not possible to view the matter otherwise.—*Ans.* Then unrighteousness, if remitted by mere mercy, is more free than righteousness, which appears to be in the highest degree unbefitting. To such an extent even would this incongruity extend, that it would make unrighteousness like God; for as God is subject to no law, so would unrighteousness.—*Bo.* I can urge nothing against your argument; *but when God commands us absolutely to forgive those that trespass against us, it seems a contradiction to enjoin us to do what He cannot with*

---

[1] This pregnant sentence cannot be rendered literally. Anselm maintains that every sin must be followed by satisfaction or punishment. This is his alternative. Though the phrase is sometimes mistaken, it will be clear that "recte ordinare peccatum sine satisfactione non est nisi punire" is just one side of the alternative.

[2] Inordinatum dimittitur. Vossius shows that inordinatio was used by the mediæval writers for ἀταξία, perturbatio ordinis.

propriety do Himself.—Ans. In this there is no contradiction ; *for God just enjoins us not to arrogate to ourselves what is the prerogative of God alone.* For vengeance belongs to none but to Him who is Lord of all ; for when civil authorities exercise this function aright, God Himself, by whom they are ordained for this very purpose, executes it as His own act.—*Bo.* You have obviated the contradiction which I thought involved in it ; but there is another point to which I desire your answer. It is this : since God is so free that He is subject to no law, and to no man's judgment ; and since He is so good that nothing more kind can be conceived ; and since nothing is right and proper but what He wills, it seems strange to say that He from whom we are wont to ask pardon, even for the injuries we do to others, will not, or cannot, remit an injury done to Himself.—*Ans.* All that you state regarding His liberty, His will, His goodness, is true ; but it is reasonable that we should so apprehend them as not to have the appearance of trenching upon His dignity. For the liberty is only for what is advantageous or proper ; nor is that any more worthy of the name of goodness which does what is unbefitting God. Now, when it is affirmed that what He wills is right, and what He does not will is wrong, this is not to be understood as implying that, were God to will anything improper, it would be right because He willed it ; for it would not follow, that if God willed to lie, therefore lying would be right,—rather the inference would be, that he who does so is not God ; for a will can by no means be disposed to lie, unless it be a will in which truth has been corrupted, nay, corrupted by abandoning truth. Therefore when it is said, If God willed to lie, it is just tantamount to saying, If God were of such a nature as willed to lie ; and therefore it would not follow that a lie is right, unless[1] it be so understood as when we speak of two impossibles : If the one is, so is the other— neither the one nor the other being true ; as if one should say, If water is dry, then fire is moist ; for neither is true. Therefore, of those things only, not unsuitable for God to will, can we say with truth, if God wills them, they are right ; for if God will that it shall rain, it is right ; and if God will that a certain person shall be killed, his death is right. Wherefore, if it does not become God to do any-thing wrong, or in violation of order, it does not fall within the sphere of His liberty or goodness or will to discharge unpunished a sinner who does not repay to God what he has taken away.—*Bo.* You remove every objection which I thought could be made to you.—*Ans.* Consider yet another reason why it does not become God to act in this way.— *Bo.* I willingly listen to your discourse.

[1] We think Anselm refers to the whole proposition.

"CHAP. XIII.—THAT THERE IS NOTHING MORE INTOLERABLE IN THE ORDER OF THE UNIVERSE THAN THAT THE CREATURE SHOULD TAKE AWAY THE HONOUR DUE TO THE CREATOR, AND NOT RESTORE IT.—*Bo.* There is nothing more clear.—*Ans.* Now, nothing is more unjust than the toleration of what is most intolerable.—*Bo.* Nor is that doubtful. —*Ans.* I suppose, then, you will not affirm that God should tolerate what would be the summit of injustice, namely, that the creature should not restore to God what it takes away.—*Bo.* Nay, such a position, I think, should be absolutely denied.—*Ans.* Furthermore, if there is nothing greater or better than God, it follows there is nothing more just than the *justice which maintains His honour* in the arrangement of all things—the supreme *justice, which is nothing but God Himself.* —*Bo.* That is certain.—*Ans. There is nothing which it is more just for God to maintain than the honour of His majesty.*—*Bo.* This must be granted.—*Ans.* Do you think He would preserve it inviolate, if He should permit it so to be withdrawn from Him that there should be no reparation, no punishment inflicted on the offender?—*Bo.* I dare not affirm it.—*Ans.* It is necessary, then, that either the glory[1] withdrawn from Him shall be restored, or punishment ensue, otherwise God will either be unjust to Himself or impotent for both purposes; which it is impious even to suppose.—*Bo.* I think nothing more reasonable can be said.

"CHAP. XIV.—HOW FAR THE PUNISHMENT OF THE SINNER IS THE HONOUR OF GOD.—*Bo.* But I desire to hear from you, whether the sinner's punishment is His honour, or how far? For if the punishment of the sinner is not His glory, then God so loses His glory as never to recover it, when the sinner does not repay what He took away, but becomes the subject of punishment; which seems to stand in opposition to what has been already advanced.—*Ans.* It is impossible for God to lose His honour; for either the sinner voluntarily pays what he owes, or God takes it from him against his will. For either man, by voluntary choice, offers to God due subjection by not sinning at all, or by offering an atonement for the sin he has committed; or God reduces him to subjection by force, and against his will,—thus showing Himself as his Master; the very thing which the man himself refuses voluntarily to confess. In this matter it deserves consideration, that as man by sinning robs God of what is God's, even so God, by inflicting punishment, robs man of what is man's; for not only is that said to belong to an individual which he already possesses, but that,

---

[1] Anselm obviously intends by *honour*, God's declarative "glory;" and we use them interchangeably.

too, which it lies within his power to possess. As man, then, was so created, that he could attain to blessedness if he did not sin, and as he is deprived of blessedness and of every benefit on account of sin, he repays, though reluctantly, of his own for the crime which he had committed. For though God does not turn to His own advantage what He takes away, as man converts to his own profit the money taken from another, yet He renders it subservient to His glory, by the very fact of its removal; for He proves, by that very removal, that the sinner, and all that is his, is subject to Him.

"CHAP. XV.—WHETHER GOD WILL SUFFER HIS GLORY TO BE TARNISHED EVEN IN A SMALL DEGREE.—*Bo.* I assent to what you say; but there is still another point to which I have to request your answer. For if God must so preserve His honour, as you prove, why does He suffer it to be tarnished, even to a small degree? For what is suffered to be hurt to some extent, is not maintained entire or perfect.—*Ans.* The honour of God, as far as relates to Him, is not capable of addition or diminution; for He is to Himself His own incorruptible and immutable glory. But when every creature, whether by natural instinct or rational conviction, maintains its own, and, as it were, its prescribed order, it is said to obey God, and to honour Him; and this is peculiarly the case with a rational nature to whom it is given to understand what duty is. When this creature wills as it ought, it honours God, not because it confers anything upon Him, but because it spontaneously subjects itself to His will and disposal, and thus maintains, as far as lies in it, its order in the universe, and the beauty of the universe; but when it does not will as it ought, it dishonours God, as far as relates to it, because it does not spontaneously submit to His disposal; and thus disturbs, as far as lies in it, the order and beauty of the universe, though it does not by any means hurt or tarnish the power or dignity of God. For if any of those things, bounded by the circuit of the heaven, wished to be no more under the heaven, or to be removed[1] to a distance from the heaven, they could not be but under the heaven, nor remove from the heaven but by again approaching it. For whencesoever, whithersoever, and in whatever way they might go, they would still be under the heaven; and the further they might remove from any part of heaven, the more would they approach the opposite part. Even so, though a man or evil angel be unwilling to subject himself to the divine will or disposal, yet he cannot flee from it; for if he would flee from under the preceptive will, he falls under the punitive will of God. And if you inquire in what way he makes the transition, the answer is, only under His permissive will; and that

[1] Elongari, a mediæval usage. (Vossius.)

very perverse will and action are made subservient, by supreme wisdom, to the order and beauty of the universe, already mentioned. For, irrespective of the fact that God brings good out of every kind of evil, the very voluntary satisfaction made for perversity, or the exaction of the punishment from him who offers no satisfaction, occupy their own place in the same universe, and possess the beauty of order. And if these were not added by divine wisdom, when perversity threatens to disturb the right order, there would arise, from the violation of the beauty of order, in that very universe which God must maintain in order, a certain hideous deformity; and it would bear the appearance as if God failed in carrying out His arrangements. And as these two are as unbefitting God as they are impossible, it is indispensably *necessary that every sin should be followed either by a satisfaction or by punishment.*—*Bo.* You have satisfied my objection.—*Ans.* It is plain, therefore, that[1] God, as He is in Himself, can neither be honoured nor dishonoured[2] by any one; but an individual seems to do this, as far as lies in him,when he subjects his will to the will of God, or withdraws it from Him.—*Bo.* I do not know what exception can be taken to this.—*Ans.* I have something further to add.—*Bo.* Say on; it will not weary me to listen. . . . .

"CHAP. XIX.[3]—THAT MEN CANNOT BE SAVED WITHOUT A SATISFACTION FOR SIN. . . . . .—*Ans.* Let us suppose the case, that a certain rich man held in his hand a costly pearl which had never been touched by any defilement, and which no other party, without his permission, could remove from his hand; and he appoints it to be laid up in his treasury among the dearest and most costly articles in his possession. —*Bo.* I fancy it as it were before us.—*Ans.* If he should suffer that pearl to be struck out of his hand into filth by some envious person, when he could have prevented it, and then taking it from the filth should deposit it, all defiled and unwashed, in a clean and prized spot, to be ever afterwards preserved in such a state, would you account him wise?—*Bo.* How could I? For would it not be better to keep and to preserve his pearl clean than covered with defilement? *Ans.* Would not God act in a similar way, who held man in His hand in paradise, destined to be associated with the angels, and permitted Satan, inflamed with envy, to cast him down into the filth of sin, though not without His own consent—for, had He wished to prevent Satan, the latter could not have tempted man,—would He not, I say,

---

[1] Palam qui; a later Latin or patristic phraseology.

[2] Exhonorare (see Vossius).

[3] In these omitted chapters, Anselm introduces a fanciful theory, taken from Augustin, about the angels; but it is an episode.

act in a similar way, were man brought back, at least to the paradise
from which he had been driven out, stained with the defilement of
sin, and always to continue so without any purification, that is, without any satisfaction? *Bo.* If God were to act in such a way, I durst
not deny the similarity of the two cases; and therefore I do not concur in the notion that He could act in such a way; for it would wear
the appearance, either that He could not execute what He had purposed, or that He had repented of His good intention,—neither of
which can obtain with God.—*Ans.* Therefore hold fast the position
that, without a satisfaction—that is, without the voluntary repayment
of the debt—neither could God leave sin unpunished, nor could the
sinner come to happiness, even of such a kind as he possessed before
he sinned; for in this way man would not be restored even to the
condition which he occupied before the entrance of sin.—*Bo.* I cannot at all refute your arguments. *But what is the import of that
prayer to God, 'forgive us our debts?' and every nation, according to
its creed, prays to God to remit their sins. For if we pay what we
owe, then why do we pray for forgiveness?* Is God unjust, to exact a
second time what has been paid already? And if we do not pay, why
do we vainly request Him to do what He cannot do, because it is
unbefitting God?—*Ans.* He who does not repay, in vain cries
'Forgive;' while he who does pay, rightly offers prayer, since the
very supplication forms part of the payment that is due; for God is
not indebted to any one, but every creature is indebted to Him; and
therefore it is of no avail to deal with God as an equal with his fellow.
But on this point it is not necessary at present to give a further
answer; for when you shall understand why Christ died, you will
perhaps solve the question for yourself.—*Bo.* I am content, then, for
the present with the answer you have given to this question. You
have so plainly proved, however, the position that no man can come
to blessedness with sin, or be released from sin without repaying
what he took away by sinning, that I could not, though I would,
doubt any longer.

"CHAP. XX.—THAT THE SATISFACTION MUST BE COMMENSURATE WITH
THE SIN, AND THAT MAN CANNOT RENDER IT OF HIMSELF.—*Ans.* Of this,
too, I suppose you will not entertain a doubt, that the satisfaction
must be proportioned to the measure of sin.—*Bo.* Otherwise sin would
remain, in some respects, unreduced to order,[1] which, however, cannot
be, if God leaves nothing disordered in His kingdom. But this is
fore-ordained, because the smallest thing unbecoming in God is impos-

[1] Inordinatum maneret peccatum.

sible.—*Ans.* Say, then, what will you render to God for your sin?—
Bo. Repentance, the contrite and humble heart, abstinence and manifold bodily labours, acts of mercy in giving and forgiving, and obedience.—*Ans.* In all this, what do you give to God?—*Bo.* Do I not
honour God when, for the fear and love of God, I cast away the joys
of time in the exercise of heart-contrition, when I scorn[1] delights and
live laborious days of abstinence and toil, when I bestow what is my
own in the way of giving and forgiving, and when I subject myself to
Him in a course of obedience?—*Ans.* When you render something
which you already owed to God before you sinned, you must not
reckon that as the debt which you owe for sin. Now, all that you
have mentioned you owe to God already; for so great must be the
love and the desire cherished in this earthly life of attaining the end
for which you were created, and to which all prayer tends—so great
the sorrow that you are not yet there, and the fear of not reaching it,
—that you should feel no joy, except in those things which furnish
you either with the help or the hope of reaching that consummation.
For you are unworthy of possessing what you do not love and desire
for its own sake,[2] and about which you have no feeling of grief, because it is not yet attained, and because, moreover, there is a great risk
of losing it. It belongs to this state of mind also to spurn that rest
and those worldly pleasures which recall the mind from the true rest
and satisfaction, except in so far as you know them to be helpful to
your earnest endeavour to reach that consummation. As to giving,
again, you must expressly consider this as your duty, as you are aware
that what you give is not derived from you, but from Him whose
servant you are, just as he is to whom the gift is bestowed; and nature
teaches you to do to your fellow-servant, that is, to do as man to man,
what you wish him to do to you; and that he who will not give what
he has, ought not to receive what he has not. With respect to the
forgiving of injuries, again, I have briefly to say, that vengeance
belongeth not to thee, as we said before; for neither are you your own,
nor is the offender yours or his own—you are both servants of one
Master, and created by Him out of nothing; and if you take vengeance
on your fellow-servant, you proudly arrogate a judgment upon him,
competent only to the Lord and Judge of all. In your obedience,
again, what do you give to God which you do not owe Him to whom
is due all you are, and have, and can perform?—*Bo.* I cannot any
longer affirm, that in all these things I could give God what I owe.—
Ans. What, then, will you pay to God for your sin?—*Bo.* If I owe

---

[1] Delectationes et quietem hujus vitæ calco.
[2] Non enim mereris habere quod non secundum quod est amas et desideras.

Him myself, and all I can perform, when as yet without sin, that I may not be involved in sin, I have nothing to render Him for sin committed.—*Ans.* What, then, will become of you? How shall you possibly be saved?—*Bo.* If I consider your arguments, I do not see how? but if I have recourse to my faith, I hope it is possible for me to be saved in the Christian faith, 'which worketh by love,' and because we read, 'If the unrighteous man turn from his unrighteousness, and do what is right, all his unrighteousness shall be forgotten.'[1] —*Ans.* That is said of those only who either waited for Christ before He came, or who believe on Him since He came. But we assumed that Christ and the Christian faith had never been, when we purposed to inquire by reason alone, whether His advent was necessary to man's salvation.—*Bo.* We did so.—*Ans.* Let us proceed then, by reason alone.—*Bo.* Though you are leading me into some perplexing difficulties, yet I very much desire you to go on as you have begun.

"CHAP. XXI.—THE MAGNITUDE AND WEIGHT OF SIN.—*Ans.* Let us suppose the case, that you did not already owe all that you recently affirmed could be paid by you for sin, and let us consider whether they could suffice for the satisfaction of one sin, so small as a single look contrary to God's will.—*Bo.* Were it not that I hear you proposing this as a question, I should suppose that such a sin could be deleted by one single act of contrition.—*Ans.* YOU HAVE NOT YET CONSIDERED THE MAGNITUDE AND WEIGHT OF SIN.—*Bo.* Point it out to me, then.—*Ans.* If you considered yourself in the presence of God, and an individual said to you, 'Look in that direction,' and God said, on the contrary, 'I will not have you look,' ask your heart what there is in the entire universe for which you should cast that look contrary to the will of God.—*Bo.* I find nothing for which it should be done, except, perhaps, I may be placed in such necessity as compels me either to do that or a greater sin.—*Ans.* Put aside the case of necessity, and reflect, in reference to this sin alone, whether you could do it even to redeem yourself.—*Bo.* I plainly see that I could not.—*Ans.* Not to detain you longer; what, if it were necessary that either the whole world, and everything, except God,[2] should perish and be annihilated, or that you should do so small a thing contrary to God's will?—*Bo.* When I reflect on the action itself, I consider it extremely trifling; but when I reflect what is involved in its being contrary to the will of God, I regard it as extremely weighty, and not to be compared to any sort of loss; but we are accustomed sometimes to act against a person's will without incurring blame, that his property may be pre-

[1] Ezek. xxxiii. 14-18, xviii. 27.
[2] Et quicquid Deus non est.

served; and afterwards the step is agreeable to him against whose will we acted.—*Ans.* This happens to man, who sometimes does not understand what is for his advantage, or who cannot restore what he has lost; but God stands in no need of any man, and could restore all things if they were to perish, just as He created them.—*Bo.* I must needs confess, that even for the preservation of the entire creation, I should not do anything contrary to the will of God.—*Ans.* What if there were more worlds full of creatures such as this one is?—*Bo.* If they were multiplied to infinity, and they were all presented to me in a similar way, my answer would be the same.—*Ans.* You could give no correcter answer; but consider, too, if it should happen that you cast that look contrary to the will of God, what could you offer as a satisfaction for this sin?—*Bo.* I have nothing greater than what I have already mentioned.—*Ans.* Thus grievously do we sin every time we knowingly do anything, how small soever, contrary to the will of God; for we are always in His sight, and He always commands us not to sin.—*Bo.* We live, as I hear, all too perilously.—*Ans.* It is evident that God demands a commensurate satisfaction.—*Bo.* It cannot be denied.—*Ans.* Therefore, you give no satisfaction unless you render something greater than all that for which you should not have committed sin.—*Bo.* I see both that this demand is reasonable, and that it is utterly impossible.—*Ans.* God cannot admit any one to blessedness who is in any measure chargeable with the debt of sin, because he should not.—*Bo.* A heavy sentence.—*Ans.* Hear yet another ground why the reconciliation of man to God is not less difficult. —*Bo.* If faith did not give me consolation, this alone would drive me to despair.—*Ans.* Yet listen.—*Bo.* Say on.

"Chap. xxii.—What indignity man did to God in permitting himself to be overcome by Satan, for which he cannot render satisfaction.—*Ans.* Man, created in paradise without sin, was, as it were, placed for God, between God and Satan, that he might conquer Satan, by not consenting to his persuasive allurements to sin. This would have redounded to the justification and glory of God, and to Satan's confusion, when the weaker on earth would not sin after all the persuasion of that very Satan, who, while the stronger, sinned in heaven without any persuasion at all; and though man might easily have accomplished this, he, though constrained by no force, voluntarily permitted himself to be overcome by persuasion alone, at Satan's will, and contrary to the will and honour of God.—*Bo.* At what do you aim?—*Ans.* Judge for yourself, whether it is not contrary to the honour of God, that man should be reconciled to Him with the reproach of this indignity done to Him, without first restoring to God

His honour, by a victory over Satan, just as he dishonoured God when vanquished by Satan. Again, the victory should be of such a nature, that just as he readily consented to Satan's allurements to commit sin, when strong and arrayed in the power of immortality, and hence justly incurred the doom of mortality, so he should overcome Satan, and resist every temptation to sin in the weakness and mortality which he drew upon himself. This could not be, so long as he was conceived and born in sin, in virtue of the wound of the first sin.—*Bo.* Again, I must say that reason proves your position, and that it is impossible for man as he is.—*Ans.* Hear one thing more, without which man cannot be justly reconciled, and which is not less impossible.—*Bo.* You have already placed before us so many requirements to be done, that whatever you superadd, cannot greatly terrify me.—*Ans.* Yet hear.—*Bo.* I listen.

" CHAP. XXIII.—WHAT MAN TOOK AWAY FROM GOD WHEN HE SINNED, AND WHICH HE CANNOT RESTORE.—*Ans.* What did man take away from God, when he permitted himself to be overcome by Satan?—*Bo.* Say on, as you have begun, for I know not what could add to the evils you have already unfolded.—*Ans.* DID HE NOT TAKE AWAY FROM GOD WHATEVER HE HAD PURPOSED TO MAKE OF HUMAN NATURE?—*Bo.* It cannot be denied.—*Ans.* Now direct your attention to strict justice, and judge, according to it, whether man can satisfy God in proportion to the sin unless he shall, by conquering Satan, restore that very thing which was taken from God, in permitting himself to be overcome by Satan ; so that, as by the fact of man's defeat, Satan took away what was God's, and God lost, even so by the fact of man's victory, Satan loses, and God regains.—*Bo.* Nothing can be conceived more strictly just.—*Ans.* Do *you suppose that supreme justice can violate this justice?—Bo.* I dare not think so.—*Ans. By no means, then, should man receive, nor can he receive, what God purposed to bestow upon him,* WITHOUT RESTORING THE WHOLE OF WHAT WE TOOK AWAY FROM GOD ; so that God regains by him, as He previously lost by him. This cannot be accomplished in any other way than that as by the vanquished man the whole of human nature was corrupted, and, as it were, leavened by sin, in which God can receive no one to complete His heavenly kingdom ; so by the victorious man, as many men are justified from sin as will fill up that number for the completion [1] of which man was made. But that is by no means possible for man, a sinner, because a sinner cannot justify a sinner.—*Bo.* Nothing is more just, but at the same time more impossible ; but from all this, the mercy of God, and the hope of man, seem equally to be destroyed, so

[1] This is the theory of Augustin, elaborated by Anselm.

far as relates to that blessedness for which man was created.—*Ans.* Have patience yet a little longer.—*Bo.* What have you further?

"CHAP. XXIV.—THAT SO LONG AS MAN DOES NOT RESTORE TO GOD WHAT HE OWES, HE CANNOT BE HAPPY NOR IS HIS INABILITY EXCUSABLE. *Ans.* If a man is termed unjust who does not render to his fellow-man what he owes, much more unjust is he who does not render to God His due.—*Bo.* If he can, and does not, render it, he is indeed unrighteous; but if he cannot, how is he unrighteous?—*Ans.* Perhaps he might in some measure be excused, if there were no cause of this inability in him; but if the guilt is in the very inability, then, as it does not mitigate the sin, it does not exculpate the man who does not render what is due. For if, for instance, one should enjoin a certain piece of work upon his servant, and require him to be upon his guard against casting himself into a certain pit, which he points out to him, and from which there is no escape, and that servant, contemning the charge and warning of his master, should voluntarily cast himself into the pit previously pointed out, so that he cannot do the work enjoined upon him, do you think the inability would in any measure be valid as an excuse why the work enjoined was not performed?—*Bo.* Not at all, but rather it would be to the aggravation of the guilt, since he caused his own inability. He doubly sinned, because he did not do what he was commanded, and he did what he was commanded not to do.—*Ans.* Thus man is without excuse, who has voluntarily involved himself in a guilt which he cannot atone for, and by his own fault plunged himself into such an inability, that he can neither pay what he owed before the sin, namely, not to sin, nor what he owes in consequence of sin; for that very inability is guilt, because he ought not to have it (non debet eam habere), nay, ought to be without it (debet non habere)," etc.

NOTE C, SECT. IX. p. 51.—*Harmony of Love and Justice in the Atonement.*

The principal objections to the atonement at present, however variously expressed in words, commonly resolve themselves into this, that love alone marks all God's relations and ways to men. The Socinians of a former age denied punitive justice, and the modern mystic theory sees only love. I may refer to the history of opinion on this theory of the atonement.

At the close of last century, as a result of the Wolfian philosophy, a speculation arose, which laboured to classify or subsume *justice* under *goodness*, and defined it as "goodness exercised with wisdom." Ac-

cording to this theory, divine punishments were only paternal chas-
tisements, or wise applications of evil for the improvement of man.
(Thus Steinbart, Eberhard, Teller, during last century, expressed themselves.) This of course struck at the foundation of the vicarious satisfaction, and removed the very ground of the atonement. The effect
of these opinions was disastrous in the highest degree, wherever they
were adopted in the churches. To make good their position, the most
common method was—and it has been recently revived—to caricature
the old doctrine, to supply quotations of extravagant and incautious
phrases used by orthodox writers in their practical writings, and to
give a violent misrepresentation of the terms "wrath" and "punishment," as if that phraseology necessarily represented God as a fierce,
vindictive, implacable tyrant. And, contrasted with this, they drew the
portrait of an affectionate Father. The great aim of those who assailed
the atonement as a vicarious satisfaction in that age, was to overthrow
the necessary exercise of divine justice, as if this opinion were merely
grounded on a comparison of God with worldly princes. They maintained that the infinitely good God can do nothing which is to the
injury of any; that He is only love; and that the evil consequences
which follow sin by a natural law, and never as a punishment, are
only directed to men's good. This scheme of thought was lasting and
disastrous.

A much more evangelical theory, but agreeing with the former in
reference to the divine justice, arose about the beginning of this century. It enrolled among its defenders some of the most active men
who appeared at the close of last century and the beginning of
the present—such as HASENKAMP, MENKEN, LAVATER; R. STIER,
author of the *Words of Jesus;* SCHLEIERMACHER and his school;
NITZSCH, V. HOFMANN, of Erlangen; the GRONINGEN THEOLOGY in its
more recent phase; the followers of M. MAURICE, and much of the
BROAD SCHOOL THEOLOGY, in our own country. They agree in one
thing, that nothing is to be seen in the atonement but love.
With all their complexional diversities, whether in a more or less
advanced stage towards evangelical theology, they hold that God is
represented in His redemption work as simply exercising love. They
allow no element but love in the atonement. Hence Nitzsch, in his
system, calls it "the revelation of holy love to human life." Under
the influence of this notion, Schleiermacher announced, as the title of
a sermon, "That we have to teach nothing of the wrath of God" (2d
vol. of his Sermons, p. 725).

The elaborate work of J. Macleod Campbell, formerly minister of
Row, in the Scottish Established Church, entitled *The nature of the*

Atonement, and its Relation to the Remission of Sins and Eternal Life, Cambridge, 1856, strongly supports the same position, from a wholly different starting-point. It is noteworthy that this production should be so much an authority among the adherents of the Broad Church School. Mr. Campbell says : " The first demand which the gospel makes upon us in relation to the atonement, is, that we believe that there is forgiveness with God. *Forgiveness, that is, love to an enemy surviving his enmity,* and which, notwithstanding his enmity, can act towards him for his good,—this we must be able to believe to be in God toward us, in order that we may be able to believe in the atonement." He further states : " This is a faith which, in the order of things, must precede the faith of an atonement. If we could ourselves make an atonement for our sins, as by sacrifice the heathen attempt to do, and as, in their self-righteous endeavour to make their peace with God, men are in fact daily attempting, *then such an atonement might be thought of as preceding forgiveness and the cause of it.* But if God provides the atonement, then *forgiveness must precede atonement,* and the atonement must be the form of the *manifestation of the forgiving love of God, not its cause*" (pp. 17 and 18). The notion which he has of justice is as disjointed ; he explains it thus : " Justice, looking at the sinner not simply as the fit subject of punishment, but as existing in a moral condition of unrighteousness, and so its own opposite, must desire that the sinner should come to be in that condition—should cease to be unrighteous—should become righteous ; righteousness in God craving for righteousness in man with a craving which the realization of righteousness in man alone can satisfy" (p. 30). This is tantamount to confounding the divine perfections, instead of exhibiting their harmony in the scheme of human redemption. Nay, Mr. Campbell goes on to say, " How can it be otherwise, seeing that the law is love ?" (p. 31). That is to make a new vocabulary, instead of accepting the plain rigorous use of biblical words. I may add, the same scheme of thought comes to light in two works of Mr. Baldwin Brown—the first entitled *Divine Life in Man,* Ward and Co., London ; the second, *The Doctrine of the Divine Fatherhood in relation to the Atonement.* The praise which he bestows on M. Maurice, and on the Rev. J. Macleod Campbell, of whose work he says that he does not know any book in which the subject is discussed with such deep thought and deep experience, and which he advises his readers to study, sufficiently indicate his viewpoint and tendency.

It is obvious that, on this theory, we have no more a legal atonement, but only what Mr. Campbell calls " a moral and spiritual atonement." Of course these notions sweep away the judicial and forensic side of theology; and the whole question of the sinner's objective relation towards God, disordered by nature, and calling for reparation, is a total blank in this theology. We have nothing but mystical representations of the divine love and of the inner life, and pardon is either made absolute, or regarded as a mere sequel and accompaniment to the exercises of the spiritual life.

If man's nature and moral conformation, as originally constituted by God, did not offer a daily protest against any theory which represents God only as a source of influences, and not as a moral Governor or Lawgiver in any sense of the word; if conscience in men did not loudly reclaim, there would be but one step to a terrible deterioration in religion and morals; for all religion and morality depend upon a right recognition of authority and law, of divine justice, and a system of punishments and rewards. We do not deny the good connected with the school to which we have referred, that it often depicts the Saviour as the source of spiritual life and light in most glowing terms, and expatiates on the privilege of union to Him. But with all this, it has two deleterious influences wrapped up in it: (1) it throws men back on a certain legality or semi-legality, never taking them beyond themselves; and (2) it undermines the whole rectoral administration of God, the nature, perpetuity, and sanctions of the divine law, and the wrath of a righteous God against sin. It makes God a source of life or influences, but no moral Governor, Lawgiver, or Judge.

The glaring imperfections of this school, which neither gives revelation its rights, nor man's conscience its place of authority, have driven many to go beyond it, and to advance to better views. Thus CHALYBÆUS and DORNER, among the German thinkers, have advanced far beyond the mystic and subjective theories of the Schleiermacher school. They maintain that there is in God not only a self-communicating element (das selbst-mittheilende), but also a self-maintaining, self-asserting element (das selbst-behauptende)—the former being love, the latter justice. This was what was expressed in the scholastic period by the phrase, *communicativum sui*, the definition of love, and *conservativum sui*, the definition of justice. Justice is an attribute worthy of God, and necessary to the welfare of the universe; and they who assail the exercise of justice, really overthrow the foundations of the gospel. Punitive justice is, in reality, an amiable attribute, worthy of God, and indispensable to the moral welfare of mankind.

I shall not notice the arguments of these schools in detail; nor is it necessary, when the principle on which they are based is overthrown.

But I would obviate two of the most common. Thus it is, (1) maintained, from the parable of the prodigal son (Luke xv.), and of the unmerciful servant (Matt. xviii. 23-35), that God forgives sin absolutely out of pure compassion. This is a misrepresentation of the grace-aspect of the gospel, which, it must never be forgotten, is grace to MAN, through a propitiation offered to GOD (comp. Rom. iii. 24). It is a recognised canon, however, in the interpretation of a parable, that attention is to be fixed on only one point, the *tertium quid* of comparison ; and that we are not warranted to make a running parallel in all points, as in an allegory. These parables were never meant to teach the ground of forgiveness. The argument from the parable of the prodigal son is not derived from the words, but from the silence or want of reference to satisfaction ; and we are not warranted so to construe silence. The Redeemer's object here was not to point out the ground or principle of forgiveness, which He elsewhere does plainly (Matt. xxvi. 28), but to exhibit His love to lost mankind—the great thought in the three parables contained in the chapter (Luke xv.). (2.) Again, it is demanded, Can there be love and anger at once in the divine mind, to the same object? This objection ignores the fact of sin ; whereas man is considered, in a double capacity, as a creature and as a sinner. This meets all difficulties. This has its analogue in a father's relation to a wayward rebellious son, where we trace love and anger at once to the same object.

It is further argued, that as man must imitate God in the free forgiveness of wrongs, it follows, that God forgives without atonement. That were to overthrow plain texts by a mere inference. But neither is it true that man, in his JUDICIAL RELATION, simply forgives. These divines only speak of man in his social relation to his brother man, or in his paternal relation, forgetting that man, made in the image of God, presents a manifold analogue to the divine relations; that he has the LEGISLATIVE AND JUDICIAL as well as paternal relation ; and that if he acted in the latter capacity according to mere mercy, he would neither be God's vicegerent, nor maintain the justice, order, or moral welfare of human society.

NOTE D, SECT. XII. p. 69.—*Christ acting as the second Adam, or according to a covenant with the Father, in the whole of His atoning work.*

This idea must be carried with us, whether we consider the fundamental presuppositions of the atonement, as stated in some of the first sections, or discuss the special reference and extent of the atonement, as exhibited in section xlv. (p. 365). The doctrine of the atonement cannot be understood without the idea of a conjunction between Christ and His people, whether it is called a covenant or not (*pactum salutis*), and whether we use the terms of the federal theology, or prefer others. The whole scheme of thought relating to the covenant occupied at one time an important place in the Reformed Church, and even in some portions of the Lutheran Church, though it never became general in the latter.

Of various elements which may be said to have concurred, if not to originate, at least to turn attention to this scheme of thought, the two following may be particularly named ; the cavils of Socinus, and the subsequent rise of the Arminian controversy. As to the first of these concurring forces, I may mention that one of the objections against the satisfaction on which Socinus laid stress, was, that there ought to be at least some conjunction between the guilty and him that is punished ; and he would not admit that there was any such conjunction or bond between Christ and us. This drove the defenders of the truth to assert the affirmative, and to define it. They maintained that Christ was united to us, not only as a partaker of our humanity by becoming one of us, our brother and friend, but also as He entered into a still closer conjunction as the Bridegroom, Head, Shepherd, Lord, King, and Surety of His people. Grotius, in his treatise, *De Satisfactione*, chap. iv., is particularly emphatic in asserting this close conjunction, on which the possibility of an atonement depends. Thus, in opposition to Socinus, Grotius says, " It might be said here that man is not without relation to man, that there is a natural kindred and consanguinity between men, and between our flesh assumed by Christ. But another much greater conjunction between Christ and us was decreed by God, for He was appointed by God to be the Head of the body of which we are members. And here it must be observed, that Socinus erroneously confined to the flesh alone that conjunction which is sufficient for laying punishment upon one for another's sins, since here the mystical conjunction has no less power. This appears principally in the example of a king and a people. We cited above the history of the Israelites punished for the sin of David." A little afterwards, Grotius adds that this conjunction lays the foundation for vicarious punishment: " Therefore the sacred writings do not at all favour Socinus, declaring, as they do, that God did the very thing which he undeservedly accuses of injustice ; but neither has he any greater defence from right reason, which it is wonderful that he so often boasts of, but nowhere shows. But that all this error may be removed, it must be observed that it is essential to punishment that it be inflicted for sin, but that it is not likewise essential to it that it be inflicted on him who sinned; and that is manifest from the similitude of *reward, favour*, and *revenge*,—for *reward* is often wont to be conferred upon the children or relations of a well-deserving person, and *favour* on the kinsman of him who conferred the benefit, and *revenge* upon the friends of him that offended. Neither do they, on that account, cease to be what they are—*reward, favour*, and *revenge*. Add to this, that if it were against the nature of punishment, then this very thing would not be called unjust, but impossible. But God forbids a son to be punished by men for the father's fault; but impossible things are not forbidden. Moreover, injustice does not properly happen to a relation (such as punishment is), but to the action itself, such as the matter of punishment is. And here the true distinction must be inquired into, why it is not equally free to all to punish one for another's sin, and to bestow a favour or reward for another's merit or benefit; for an act which contains in it a reward or favour is a benevolent act, which, in its own nature, is permitted to all; but an act which has in it punishment, is a hurtful act, which is neither allowed to all, nor against all. Wherefore, that a punishment may be just, it is requisite that the penal act itself should be in the power of the punisher, which happens in a threefold way; either by the antecedent right of the punisher himself, or by the legitimate and valid consent of him about whose punishment the question is; or by the crime of the same person. When the act has become lawful by these modes, nothing prevents its being appointed for the punishment of another's sin, *provided there be some conjunction between him that sinned and the party to be punished.* And this conjunction is either natural, as between a father and a son; or mystical, as between king and people; or voluntary, as between the guilty person and the surety. Socinus appeals to the judgment of all nations; but as to God, the philosophers doubted not that the sins of parents were punished by Him in the children." I shall not quote further from this memorable chapter of Grotius, in which he overwhelms his opponent by the testimony of all classical antiquity. I have adduced this discussion, only to show how men came during the course of it to adopt and maintain a certain necessary conjunction between the Redeemer and the redeemed, which involved something more than a community of the same nature, and, in a word, the elements of a covenant.

But another cause concurred with the former. When the Arminian debates arose, and the five points were debated, many were led, during the course of this discussion, more and more to the conclusion that there was a given party in whose behalf all the provisions of redemption were contrived and carried into effect. Thus Amesius, *Coronis*, p. 112, expresses himself: " Addam etiam insuper, si nullo modo versabatur ecclesia in mente divina, quum unctus et sanctificatus fuit Christus ad officium suum, tum caput constitutus fuit sine corpore, ac rex sine subditis ullis in præsentia notis, vel omniscio ipsi Deo : quod quam indignum sit thesauris illis divinæ sapientiæ qui in hoc mysterio absconditi fuerunt, non opus est ut ego dicam. Hoc unum perpendat cordatus Lector satisfactionem illam Christi pro nobis nocentibus susceptam valere non potuisse, nisi aliqua antecedente inter nos et Christum, conjunctione ; tali scilicet qua designatus est a Deo ut caput esset corporis, cujus nos sumus membra ; ut Vir cl. Hugo Grotius, relictis remonstrantibus, quos alibi defendit ingenue concedit.—*Defensionis fidei Catholicæ*, pagina 66." Hence the doctrine of the covenant was the concentrated essence of Calvinism, and appeared especially in a formed and concatenated system, after the Synod of Dort. Cloppenburg maintained it immediately after that Synod.

Thus these two elements above named led many of the greatest divines of the Reformed Church to bring out, and to lay stress upon, a *pactum salutis*, or *fœdus*, as necessary to a full understanding of the atonement. This doctrine has fallen out of the prominence it at one time occupied in theology. But whatever view may be held as to that scheme of thought, there is no room for two opinions as to the scriptural character of the doctrine. There must be a certain conjunction between Christ and the redeemed.

It is due to the federal theology to state, that it was only meant to ground and establish the undoubtedly scriptural doctrine of the two Adams (Rom. v. 12-20 ; 1 Cor. xv. 47). These are by no means to be regarded as two different lines of thought, or two mutually exclusive modes of representing truth. They proceed on the same principle, and they come to precisely the same result,—the one from the viewpoint of humanity, the other from the counsels of the Trinity. No one can doubt, who examines the federal theology, that the design of those who brought that scheme of thought into general reception in the Reformed Church for two centuries, was principally to ground, and to put on a sure basis, the idea of the two Adams ; that is, to show that there were, in reality, only two men in history, and only two great facts on which the fortunes of the race hinged. The leading federalists were CLOPPENBURG, DICKSON the Scottish divine (who developed it so early as 1625—see *Life of Robert Blair*, in the Wodrow publications—several years before the work of Cocceius, *De Fœdere*, appeared in 1648), COCCEIUS, BURMANN, WITSIUS, STRONG,

PETTO, OWEN, etc. etc. It became a magnificent scheme of theological
thought in the hands of these men, and of others who took it up with
ardour. That foreign thoughts afterwards came to be introduced into
it, and that it became complicated by many additional elements,
brought in to give it completeness, but which only lent it an air of
human ingenuity and artificial construction, cannot be denied. But
as to the point already referred to, there is no doubt that they intended
to establish, by this mode of representation, that Christ and His people
were to be regarded as one person in the eye of law ; and that, properly speaking, there were only two heads of families, and only two
great facts in history—the fall and the atonement.

Against this whole scheme of thought, a reaction set in a century
ago. Nor can this be wondered at, when we remember that it was
overdone, and that the reaction was only the effort of the human
mind to regain its equilibrium—as is always the case when anything
is carried too far. It was overdone, and now it is far too much
neglected.

But it is by no means to be repudiated, or put among the mere
antiquities of Christian effort. This, or something like it, whether we
adopt the federal nomenclature or not, must occur to every one who
will follow out the revealed thoughts uttered by Christ Himself to
their legitimate consequences. The only objection of any plausibility
is, that the notion of a covenant presupposes a twofold will in God.
To meet this objection, springing from an exclusive regard to the
unity of the Godhead, it may be remarked, that the supposition of a
council or covenant, having man's redemption for its object, has no
more difficulty than the doctrine of a Trinity. Each person wills,
knows, loves, and exercises acts to one another and to us ; and as
they are personally distinct in the numerical unity of the divine
essence, so, according to the order of subsistence, they each will,
though not apart and isolated. Accordingly, Dr. OWEN remarks
against BIDDLE, in his *Vindiciæ:* "Because of the distinct acting of
the will of the Father, and of the will of the Son, with regard to each
other, it is more than a decree, and hath the proper nature of a covenant or compact."

Whatever view may be taken, however, of that scheme of thought,
the one important matter on which no doubt can be entertained by
any scriptural divine, is, that as Adam was a public person,—the
representative of all his family, according to the constitution given to
the human race, as contradistinguished from that of other orders of
being,—so Christ, the Restorer, stands in the same position to His
family or seed. The world could be redeemed on no other principle

than that on which it was at first constituted. Augustin's expression, *ille unus homo nos omnes fuimus,* as applied to the first man, is perhaps the very best formula ever given; and the same formula may be applied with equal warrant to the second man, the Lord from heaven. As applied to the atonement, this principle of a covenant, or a conjunction between Christ and His seed, is simple and easily apprehended. The conditions being fulfilled by the second man, His people enter into the reward.

Thus Christ was commissioned to do a work for a people who were to reap the reward. The Father laid on Him the conditions given to Adam, with the additional one derived from guilt, and claimed satisfaction from the Son undertaking to act as a surety for a seed given to Him. Man could be redeemed only on the principle or constitution on which God placed him at first, not on one altogether different; and the one aim of the federal theology was to base or ground this biblical truth.

NOTE E, pp. 44, 79.—*The Influence of Christ's Deity or of the Incarnation on the Atonement.*

Less prominence has been given in recent times than in former ages to the doctrine of Christ's deity and of a proper incarnation in connection with the atonement; and various causes will readily occur to explain this fact.

For the first four or five centuries occupied with discussions on Christ's person, it may seem as if little attention were spared for canvassing the influence of the incarnation on the atonement. But it is not so. The importance attached to the solution of the questions bearing on the person of Christ—whether the Docetic, Arian, Sabellian, Nestorian, or Monophysite controversies—arose, in large measure, from the conviction that they had a direct influence on the atonement of the God-man. The patristic divines sought indeed the absolute truth; but their solicitude was largely due to the effect which they saw was exercised by these questions on the actual faith of the Church. This is well brought out by THOMASIUS in his *Beiträge zur Kirchlichen Christologie,* Erlangen, 1845. We may take an illustration from the Nestorian and Monophysite discussions. Cyril on the one side, and Theodoret on the other, bring the argument from the atonement into all their debates. Thus Nestorianism was objected to, as leading, when legitimately carried out, to Humanitarianism or Ebionism, and by consequence to the subversion of the atonement, because it was felt that the death of a mere man, however inhabited by God, or made the temple of God (θεοφόρος), could have no world-wide significance. Eutychianism, again, was objected to, because it led, when legitimately carried out, to *Docetism*—a principle on which we could have but the semblance of an atonement (δόκησις). Hence the Synod of Ephesus assigned, as the reason for condemning Nestorius, that he ascribed the work of salvation to the humanity of Christ, or to His flesh alone.

When we come down to the theology of the Reformation, we find, both in the Lutheran and in the Reformed Churches, the greatest emphasis laid on Christ's deity, as absolutely necessary to His work of atonement. They held that Christ's deity was indispensable to the atonement, and that His office as Mediator was correctly understood, only when it was maintained that Christ acted everywhere and in every scene according to both natures. Hence, when Osiander, in order to repel the Romish doctrine, asserted that the Lord Jesus was Mediator only in His divine nature, and Stancarus, on the other hand, in opposing him, asserted, in an equally one-sided way, that Christ was Mediator only in the human nature, the spiritual instincts of the Church, enlightened by the divine word, recoiled from both, and felt that they both deviated from the truth. The position firmly taken up in both divisions of the Protestant Church, was, that Christ, in every meritorious work, acted according to both natures, and that His whole mediatorial activity comprehended both.

The infinite value of the atonement, viewed in connection with the incarnation of the Son of God, is exhibited forcibly by QUENSTEDT, *Systema Theologicum;* WESSEL, *Nestorianismus confutatus;* and GROTIUS, *De Satisfactione.* The latter is peculiarly fresh and clear on this point. Socinus would allow nothing to the dignity of the person; and Grotius says, "We believe otherwise, that this punishment was to be estimated from the fact, that He who suffered the punishment was God, though He suffered not as God." He quotes 1 Cor. ii. 8, 1 Cor. ii. 27, and Heb. ix. 14; and adds, "Socinus objects, because the divinity did not suffer. It is just as if he would say that it is the same thing whether you strike an unknown person or a father, because strokes are directed to the body, not to the dignity of the person; which gross error Aristotle long since confuted, and the common judgment dissents from Socinus." On this point, see also Seed, *Sermons*, vol. ii. p. 391.

The value attached by the Reformation divines to the influence of Christ's deity in the atonement will appear, if we consult the ecclesiastical confessions of the period, the theological systems and compends, or the catechisms prepared for the churches. I may refer to the Heidelberg Catechism, and its host of expositors (Questions 14, 15,

16, 17); and the mere fact that Socinianism and Rationalism have always assailed Christ's deity and His atonement together, unmistakeably shows how inseparably they are connected.

Two modern theories on the incarnation are in a high degree unfavourable to a full estimate of the influence of Christ's deity on the atonement; and it is necessary to advert to them both.

I refer, (1) to the depotentiation theory—a widespread tendency or school in modern theology—asserting that, during Christ's humiliation, there was an actual self-denudation or depotentiation of His divine attributes on the part of the Logos. To an English mind, untainted by modern speculative tendencies, this appears an impossibility and an absurdity; but it is held by many eminent evangelical theologians abroad—viz. by SARTORIUS, GESS, EBRARD, LIEBNER, LANGE, SCHMIEDER, STEINMEYER, HAHN, KAHNIS, DELITZSCH, V. HOFMANN, GAUPP, KÖNIG. The best refutation of this theory will be found in DORNER's work, *On the Person of Christ*, and more especially in a paper of his in the *Jahrbücher für Deutsche Theologie*, vol. i. An echo of the same theory is found among a class of divines, who, since Irving's days, have confusedly spoken of the divine nature being in abeyance during the Lord's humiliation. Whether surveyed in the German form, or in the English form last mentioned, the theory has a tendency to represent the Lord Jesus in a too humanitarian guise, and as only acting in a humanity replenished and aided by the Holy Ghost;—a truth, but by no means the whole truth. My object in referring to these theories, is to say that they operate unfavourably on the doctrine of the atonement, inasmuch as Christ is not supposed to act as the God-man in His mediatorial works, and is represented too much as the man, and too little as the God-man. In GESS' *Articles and Contributions on the Doctrine of the Atonement*, accordingly, the writer is silent on Christ's deity in coi nection with the atonement. It could not be otherwise, if he was consistent. He carried out the abeyance theory or the depotentiation theory to its utmost extreme, maintaining that the Lord denuded Himself of His omniscience, omnipresence, and omnipotence, and eternal holiness (see GESS, *die Lehre von der Person Christi*, Basil, 1856); and hence he is only consistent with himself in making no allusion to the influence of Christ's deity in His work of expiation. His articles on the atonement are good, if we deduct this important omission (see GESS, *der Geschichtliche Entwickelungsgang der N. T. Versöhnungslehre*, in the *Jahrbücher für Deutsche Theologie*, 1857, etc.). No man, on his principle, can assert, as must be asserted, that Christ, as Mediator, acted in both His natures in the work of atonement.

2. Another theory on the incarnation, which has recently risen to a prominence—such as it never before attained in the Church's history —is, that the incarnation is irrespective of the fall, and would have taken place apart from the fall. The German divines largely confess to this theory—viz. DORNER, EBRARD, MARTENSEN, LIEBNER, LANGE, ROTHE, EHRENFEUCHTER, CHALYBÆUS. Archbishop Trench, in this country, adopted it, and holds strong language in its defence in *Five Sermons preached before the University of Cambridge*, London, 1837. Its great advocate is DORNER, in his work, *On the Person of Christ*. I shall not here enter into the discussion of the question, having done so some time ago in *The British and Foreign Evangelical Review*, Jan. 1861. My object in referring to it here is to say that it imperils the doctrine of the atonement. It puts Christ's mission on new and non-biblical ground. If, according to this theory, we deduce the necessity of the incarnation, either from the *nature* of God, or from the *idea of humanity*, and not from God's free and sovereign love to sinners, we deviate from the Scripture representation of it (comp. Matt. xviii. 11 ; Gal. iv. 4 ; Heb. ii. 14 ; 1 Tim. i. 15). Scripture exhibits the ATONEMENT for the fallen human race as the chief end, nay, as the one *only revealed* end, of the incarnation (Matt. xx. 28 ; John iii. 16). We do not by any means need to affirm that no other ends existed in the πολυποίκιλος σοφία of God. But this is the *only revealed end ;* and the tendency of this theory, without doubt, is to reduce the atonement to the rank of a subordinate and accidental accompaniment of the incarnation. The atonement is no longer the great end of His coming, the counterpart of the fall of man, the re-adjustment of the disordered universe. The incarnation is thus made an *end in itself*, not a *means* to the stupendous end of the world's salvation. The whole effect of the theory is to depreciate the atonement.

NOTE F, p. 110.—*The Lamb of God bearing sin.*

Though most of the words in this pregnant saying of the Baptist were noticed in the text, some of the points which could not be conveniently introduced may be referred to in a supplementary note.

De Wette and Weiss, on the one hand, maintain that the entire idea contained in this testimony is borrowed from Isa. liii. 7 and 12 : Hengstenberg and Hofmann, on the other hand, hold that this cannot be accepted because the prophet introduces the allusion to the lamb only in the way of a comparison. Perhaps a middle way may be adopted, which is better than either. The prophet may have taken his comparison from the sacrificial lamb; and thus both views may be harmonized. But as there is no formal quotation, no necessity exists for this discussion among exegetes at all.

As to the question which we found it necessary to discuss, what peculiar lamb is here referred to, I may refer to an excellent note of Huther, in his commentary on 1 Pet. i. 19, which forms a part of H. A. W. Meyer's *Kritisch Exeget. Commentar.*, and also to some comments of Cocceius in his *Anecdota*, vol. ii. p. 457. Both these commentators extend the allusion here made to the lamb beyond the paschal lamb, and make it a more general reference. Thus Huther on 1 Pet. i. 19 uses these words : " Zu der Bezeichnung Christi als des Lammes ist der alttestamentliche Typus hier nicht blos das Passah Lamm (wie 1 Cor. v. 7), sondern allgemeiner : das Lamm we es in dem Jüdischen Opferwesen überhaupt." Cocceius, too, says : " Christum agnum dici non tantum indiscriminatim respiciendo ad 'omnia sacrificia expiatoria ; sed etiam in specie ad sacrificium juge, et illa quæ pro delicto offerebantur (nam delictum est peccatum opinor) et holocausta, quæ expiatoria esse docet Ps. li. 18, imprimis verò ad agnum paschalem, qui exeuntibus ex Ægypto instar omnium sacrificiorum erat."

As to the participial clause, ὁ ἀμνὸς—ὁ αἴρων, it must be noted that the article and participle in such a phrase uniformly points out a well-known relation, or a noteworthy peculiarity for which one is distinguished. It corresponds to *is qui, quippe qui* (see Winer's *Grammar*, sec. 20, *c ;* Matthiæ's *Grammar*, sec. 269, *obs.*).

The two words which require an accurate and precise exposition are, αἴρειν and ἁμαρτίαν.

(1.) With regard to αἴρων, it must be noticed that the verb means, primarily, " to lift up ;" but according as that is done with various intentions, we find derivative senses arising out of it. Thus (1) he who lifts anything upon the way, lifts it, perhaps, to take it for himself, and so takes it away ; and if one appropriates it, he takes it away from another : hence the meaning, " to take away." But (2) one may lift it also " to carry it," or to bear it as a burden or load. Hence αἴρεσθαι is used by the Greek writers, and αἴρειν by the Hebraizing writers in the sense of " to bear," " portare." The principal thought is not always that of carrying from place to place, but often that of taking upon one's self a burden or load. And it is in full accordance with this usage of the word, when Christ is regarded as the Lamb. (See an article by Storr in *Flatt's Magazine für Dogmatik und Moral*, ii. St. 1797, p. 206.) STEIN, *De Satisfactione*, p. 338, on this point, thus writes : Joan. Georgius Dorscheus, Pentadecad. Dissertat. Disp.

xi. p.m. 380, sec. 43, loca ultra quadraginta profert ubi τὸ αἴρειν *portandi* significationem habet proprie, quod cum primis e loco, 1 Joan. iii. 5, confirmatur." C. L. W. GRIMM (*De Joan. Christologiæ indole*, p. 106) maintains, that though the verb αἴρειν both in the LXX. and in the N. T. involves the notion of *bearing, sustaining, taking on one's self,* and occurs particularly in reference to bearing burdens, Gen. xlv. 23, Lam. iii. 27, Matt. xxvii. 32, and in Job xxi. 3 (though the reading here is doubtful); yet, when it is joined with the word ἁμαρτίαν, or its cognate, ἁμάρτημα, it always has the idea of "taking away," "removing," never of *bearing,* 1 Sam. xv. 25, xxv. 28. To the same effect is the later conclusion of Grimm, in his edition of Wilke's *Lexicon of the N. T.* The answer to all this is, that the translation of the Septuagint is no conclusive argument; and that there is reason to conclude that the same Hebrew phrase was differently given by the Septuagint, because the translators were plainly at a loss to see how a constant rendering could be carried out in all the four applications in which the phrase occurs. They translate in one way when it applied to the sinner or the victim (viz. φέρειν, ἀναφέρειν, λαμβάνειν), and in another way, when it is used with reference to the priest, or applied to God (ἀφαιρεῖν, or ἀφιέναι). This whole subject must be discussed afresh. Here I would take occasion to express my conviction, that the Septuagint rendering of the Hebrew phrase, "to bear sin," demands an ampler and more rigid investigation. These translators draw a line between certain applications of the phrase which they regard as conveying the meaning "to bear," and certain other applications which they understand as denoting "to take away." In the first of these two translations they render the phrase by these Greek verbs: φέρειν, ἀναφέρειν, λαμβάνειν, ὑπέχειν (Ezek. iv. 4, xviii. 19; Lam. v. 7; Ex. xxviii. 43; Lev. v. 1, 17; Num. ix. 13; Lev. vii. 18; Num. v. 31; Lev. xvii. 16). In the second of these two translations they use the verb, ἀφαιρεῖν, ἀφιέναι (Ex. xxviii. 38; Ps. lxxxv. 3; Ex. xxxiv. 7; Lev. x. 17; Num. xviii. 1, 23, xiv. 18). Now it is plain, that in deciding on the translation to be given in any given passage, the Septuagint translators were guided by certain *à priori* considerations which, whether right or wrong, were derived from some other quarter than the bare signification of the language which they translated. They appropriated the rendering φέρειν, (1) to the individual worshipper, and (2) to the sacrificial victim; and they appropriated the other rendering, ἀφαιρεῖν, (1) to the priest, and (2) to God. This is undoubtedly the conclusion or result to which every thorough investigator into the peculiarities of the Septuagint will be forced to come.

But as it is by no means a faultless version, the further inquiry forces itself on our attention : Were they correct in this interpretation of the language ? were those *à priori* grounds, which directed them, and taken from what they deemed fitting and appropriate, correct and unchallengeable ? The Church of the patristic age and of the Reformation age accepted the rendering of the Septuagint, as if in this matter it gave us the ultimate truth. I say that there is a call for a fresh investigation. And whether Œder, to whom I have referred, has brought out the truth or not in reference to the import of the phrase " to bear sin " in its application to God, of one thing there is no doubt. The priest may be regarded as " bearing sin " (see Keil and Hengstenberg on Sacrifices). Deyling (*obs.* i. 45, 2) says, " incorporabant quasi peccatum populique reatum in se recipiebant ; " and as this takes away one of the renderings of the Septuagint, further investigation may not less convincingly remove the other.

I have indicated an inclination to accept a uniform translation of the phrase for a plain reason. We are challenged by the Socinians, and by the more erudite and exegetical opponents of the vicarious sacrifice, to accept a uniform rendering, or give up asserting the reference to the phrase αἴρειν ἁμαρτίαν to anything like penal suffering. I have said that I think there is sufficient warrant to maintain the uniform rendering ; and I am ready to abide by it. But one caveat is necessary. The phrase, *in the passive voice*, naturally assumes a shade of meaning slightly different. This I notice, lest any one should feel the apostle's rendering of the phrase, *in the passive voice*, as opposed to all that has just been said : μακάριοι ὧν ἀφέθησαν αἱ ἀνομίαι (Rom. iv. 7).

(2.) As to ἁμαρτία, it denotes *sin*, with all the demerit and consequences involved in it, such as guilt and punishment. The rationalistic Gabler explained ἁμαρτία by *vitiositas, pravitas*, and put this interpretation on the phrase : " He patiently bore the wrongs and injuries of every kind inflicted on Him" (see Meletem. in *Joan.*). But had the Baptist intended to express that idea, we should doubtless have had ἀδικίαν, or κακίαν, as De Wette, *De Morte Christi*, has well pointed out. I may notice that Grotius, in a former age, carried exegesis very much away in the direction of considering the atonement only in connection with punishment. But while the Bible phraseology takes in all this, it goes deeper, and puts the death of Christ in connection with SIN itself.

NOTE G, p. 121.—*The Title, Son of Man.*

The two points discussed in this section are both of great import ance for a right understanding of the doctrine of the atonement, viz. (1) the title, Son of Man; and (2) the peculiar mode in which the Sin-bearer took flesh. Little requires to be added in this place, except a reference to the literature connected with the discussion of the import of the designation or title, " Son of Man." Among the many different views and comments which have been propounded, there are several that demand some further literary notice.

1. The Fathers, for the most part, saw in the title nothing beyond an allusion to the fact that He who is Son of God became man ; and they understood it as denoting the whole person as designated by the humanity. Thus Chrysostom, in his commentary on John iii. 13, says : υἱὸν δὲ ἀνθρώπου ἐνταῦθα, οὐ τὴν σάρκα ἐκάλεσεν· ἀλλ' ἀπὸ τῆς ἐλάττονος οὐσίας ὅλον ἑαυτόν, ἵν' οὕτως εἴπω, ὠνόμασε νῦν. To the same effect are the comments of most of the other Greek Fathers, when they elucidate the phrase. Thus Theodoret, on Dan. vii. 13, having occasion to expound the precise import of the phrase, says : τὴν δευτέραν σωτῆρος ἐπιφάνειαν προθεσπίζων υἱὸν μὲν ἀνθρώπου σαφῶς ἀποκαλῶν δι' ἣν ἀνέλαβε φύσιν. Euthymius Zigabenus says on Matt. xiii. 37 : υἱὸν ἀνθρώπου ἑαυτὸν ὀνομάζει διὰ τὴν φαινομένην ἐνανθρώπησιν αὐτοῦ. To the same purport are the statements of Epiphanius, Eusebius, Theophylact ; though we occasionally find the word ἀνθρώπου interpreted with a more particular reference to Mary, the mother of our Lord. Thus Euthymius Zigabenus, referring to the fact that ἄνθρωπος may refer to male or female, says on Matt. viii. 20 : ἄνθρωπον δὲ νῦν λέγει, τὴν μητέρα αὐτοῦ· ἄνθρωπος γὰρ λέγεται οὐχ ὁ ἀνὴρ μόνον, ἀλλὰ καὶ ἡ γυνή. But we may affirm of the patristic interpretation of this phrase, that the Fathers commonly, if not invariably, limited the allusion to the idea of the incarnation, and understood the language as descriptive of the whole person of Christ by one of His natures. The phrase was held to mean, in a word, according to the Fathers, that Jesus is the eternal Son incarnate ; and, in the same way, the phrase is commonly understood by all who, like Suicer, Pearson, Bull, and Waterland, simply content themselves with reproducing the patristic theology in their interpretations of the Scripture phraseology. We may say with confidence, that this interpretation does not exhaust its meaning, nor explain all the peculiarities connected with our Lord's mode of using the phrase. Thus He never uses it when appealing to His Father. And then this interpretation cannot be said to offer any explanation of the fact that Jesus constantly used it in alluding to His betrayal, rejection, sufferings, and death.

2. Another interpretation, which obtained currency in the age of the Reformation, was to the effect, that the phrase " Son of Man" intimates

only that He was man, or that He was in the likeness of man. I
might quote Calvin, Bucer, Musculus, Piscator, and many of that age,
in proof of this current interpretation. Thus Calvin says on Acts vii.
56 : " vocat filium hominis, ac si diceret, hominem illum, quem morte
abolitum putatis." Again, Musculus says, on John v. 27 : " esse
filium hominis, more Scripturæ nihil est aliud, quam esse hominem ;"
and Bucer says, " notandum autem diligentissime, quod Christus filium
hominis, id est, hominem (Ebraismus enim est), sese ubique appellat."
Thus Camerarius and Piscator express themselves on Matt. ix. 6.
This mode of explanation carries an air of much simplicity ; but it is
defective, and cannot serve the purpose of a key to unlock the import of all the passages where the phrase occurs, or to explain the
peculiarities of our Lord's use of it. It does not explain the fact that
Christ alone employed it, and that His followers did not. Nor does
it throw any light on the passages where men and the Son of Man are
expressly contrasted and distinguished. And I may add, that the
limitation of the phrase to the sense that He was a man, would only,
in fact, have announced what no one doubted,—what all saw and be-
held with their own eyes.

Other senses allied to that just mentioned, and current in the
rationalistic period, are unworthy of being mentioned. Thus even
Hess, in his *Leben Jesu*, interprets it, *this man, I who am before you.*
These shallow comments, which limit it to such senses as *a certain
man, I, one, some one,* are not deserving of notice. It was interpreted
the *archetypal man* by Herder, Neander, Olshausen.

3. The interpretation most in vogue among exegetes at present is
that which expounds it as a name or title of Messiah glorified, or in
His dignity. They deem it equivalent to the title of the reigning
Messiah, as if it were taken from the vision of Daniel, where the
Messiah appears as the Son of Man in the exercise of authority and
dominion. This comment, proposed by Beza, was supported by sub-
sequent expositors to a large extent,—by Cameron, Capellus, Abresch,
Storr ; and in recent times, by Stier, Tholuck, Weiss on John's
Lehrbegriff, Meyer, and, in a word, the great majority of modern interpreters. This is the view advocated by Scholten (in his *Specimen
Hermeneuticum Theologicum, de appellatione* τοῦ υἱοῦ τοῦ ἀνθρώπου,
Utrecht, 1809), by Heringa and others, as the only correct view. But
this interpretation, however it may explain some of the passages, and
especially those which describe Christ as the Son of Man sitting on
the right hand of the power of God (Luke xxii. 69), fails to explain
the references to His abasement ; and the Messianic glory was but the
reward of the humiliation.

4. A fourth interpretation is that which expounds the phrase of the second Adam. The celebrated philologist Heinsius, who led the way in this interpretation, which has found many supporters, says, (Exer. on Matt. viii. 20): "cum ubique Dominus servator υἱὸς τοῦ ἀνθρώπου, dicatur, primi hominis respectu sine dubio, qui אדם sive ὁ ἄνθρωπος vocatur. Ut ὁ ἄνθρωπος sit homo primus: υἱὸς τοῦ ἀνθρώπου, qui post illum sic ἐξόχως, dicitur, idem qui *secundus Adam* dicitur." This opinion was followed by Leigh, Lightfoot, Bengel in part, who says on Matt. xvi. 13 : "ut Adamus I. cum tota progenie dicitur HOMO, sic Adamus II. (1 Cor. xv. 45) dicitur filius hominis, cum articulo ὁ υἱὸς τοῦ ἀνθρώπου." The same view was adopted by J. D. Michaelis and Zachariæ, and also in substance by Morus. That this view, so far as it goes, is well founded, there seems no ground to doubt. The objection which Scholten makes to it—that our Lord never makes the smallest allusion to Adam—assumes the whole matter in dispute. This is the allusion. We know that our Lord was wont to go back to man as he was at first, in some of those discussions which He carried on with the men of His time. Thus, in regard to marriage and divorce, we find Him going back to the beginning (Matt. xix. 6-8); and in this phraseology we have just the same thought that lies at the basis of Paul's comparison of the first and second Adam (Rom. v. 12, 20 ; 1 Cor. xv.).

5. Another interpretation is to the effect that the title " Son of Man" denotes the *mean, despised, and miserable condition* of our Lord in His capacity as surety. This interpretation, propounded chiefly by Grotius, found, in a former age, very considerable acceptance in the Church. The phrase was held by a large class of divines, who in this matter followed Grotius, to refer, not to Christ's dignity, but to His abasement and humiliation. This opinion was adopted by Walæus, Van Til on Matthew, by Wolfburgius, by Beausobre et L'Enfant, Rosenmüller, and others ; by Heumann in 1740, and by Less in 1776, who both, in separate treatises, discussed the title *filius hominis* in the same line of thought with Grotius, and clearly proved that it is not a title of dignity. Undoubtedly this last thought is contained in the phrase as our Lord employs it. The allusions to His abasement, as we have attempted to prove in the text, are so express and emphatic, that we think they cannot be mistaken. Heumann maintains correctly, that in the Gospel of John, this title is always used as the antithesis of Christ's divine majesty. Let me refer the reader to Scholten's interesting treatise on this title, though its main position has been proved to be untenable.

The three thoughts contained in the phrase, then, as we sought to bring them out, are these: (1) true humanity ; (2) the second Adam ;

(3) abased curse-bearing humanity. Nor can any one object to this as
too composite, because it expresses what the surety must needs be, and
what His work must needs embrace.—And His one work comprehended as a unity all these three elements; and with this phrase, so
understood, we can interpret all the passages where the title occurs.

The next point noticed by us relates to Christ's *voluntary susception*
of the curse. The SECOND thing discussed in this section has reference
to the mode in which Christ, as the sin-bearer, took the flesh. The
problem here is to show that Christ took sin and the curse along with
the assumption of humanity, and that He never appeared without it,
χωρὶς ἁμαρτίας (Heb. ix. 28). Our aim here was to show that, in
some sense, He was the sin-bearer *in*, *with*, and *under* His assumption
of humanity,—nay, before the flesh was prepared for Him; and it in
some measure bears the indubitable marks of the curse upon it. Our
object was to show that it was not the flesh of sin, and yet ἐν ὁμοιώματι
σαρκὸς ἁμαρτίας (Rom. viii. 3),—not sinful flesh, for that would have
incapacitated Him to deliver us, but the likeness of sinful flesh. And
all that followed in the way of suffering was entailed on Him, not because He took a portion of the common lump or general mass of
humanity, but only as a part of the voluntarily assumed curse taken
on Him by His own free susception, or assumption.

NOTE H, p. 207.—*The Son of Man giving His life a ransom
for many.*

We have so fully canvassed the import of the term λύτρον, that
little here requires to be added. As the notion of redemption, however, by a price paid, or by a ransom offered to God by Christ, involves
the whole notion of an atonement in the room and stead of others,
and runs counter to an absolute deliverance, every effort has been
made, since the days of Socinus, to make good the point, that redemption may mean *deliverance without any price.* But as biblical language contains both the idea of *deliverance* and of a *price*, and as they
are commonly put together (Eph. i. 7; Col. i. 14; 1 Pet. i. 18, 19),
no one can warrantably doubt that we have in these passages the
mention of deliverance, and of the ransom as the special way of deliverance, irrespective of anything done or attempted by men themselves.
It is well remarked by Chapman, in his *Eusebius, or the True Christian's Defence*, 1741, vol. ii. p. 290: " We have this expressed here as
clearly and strongly in the phrases above as the Greek language could
express it; and if it had been the full design of our Saviour and His
apostles to express thus much, they could not in Greek have done it

in plainer or less ambiguous terms—there being no instance, I believe, in antiquity where δοῦναι λύτρον or ἀντίλυτρον are used in any other sense ; and therefore, to resolve these words with Socinus or Crellius, by a figure of their own inventing, into a bare deliverance, without any causal price of it, interposed antecedently by Christ, but only such in respect of the reformation of mankind—which His doctrine or example or exaltation after death might produce in the world—is such trifling and arbitrary expounding of Scripture, without regard to the usage and sense of words, as no reason and criticism will endure.   In their way of commenting, besides the total want of authority, there is this further absurdity, that they turn the words λύτρον and ἀντίλυτρον into metaphor, without making any sort of analogy in the case,—there being evidently no proportionable similitude between giving a λύτρον without any kind of ransom or price, and giving one altogether with it,—whereas every true metaphor always carries a plain analogy or proportion between the proper and improper usage of words ; as Aristotle (*Rhet.* 3, 10, 11), Tully (*Cic. Orat.* 3, 38, 39, 40), and Quintilian (*Inst.* 8, 6), have resolved long ago, and the nature of the thing requires ; and therefore the metaphor which they talk of in these passages is wholly without foundation, and absolutely unwarrantable."

The exact import of λύτρον must be ascertained.   This is the more imperative, as the notion gained ground in many quarters, especially since the times of Grotius, and was asserted not only during all last century, and up to a recent day, that λύτρον may be taken in the sense of a *sacrifice*.   That is a sense put on the word, neither in keeping with classical usage, nor with the language of the Septuagint.

1. As to the classical use of the term, we find it used in the singular, but more commonly in the plural, λύτρα, to denote the price or compensation for which captives are redeemed from those who have taken them prisoner.   Thus Thucydides, Book vi. 5, says that Hippocrates, tyrant of Gela, received the territory of the Camarinæans as a ransom for some Syracusan prisoners : λύτρα αἰχμαλώτων λαβὼν τὴν γῆν τὴν Καμαριναίων.   Xenophon, *Hellen.* vii. 16, says that the Phliasians gave liberty to Proxenus without a ransom: ζῶντα λαβόντες ἀφῆκαν ἄνευ λύτρων.   In Demosthenes, 1248, 45, we find εἰσενεγκεῖν αὐτῷ ἐκέλευέ με εἰς τὰ λύτρα : " to contribute to the ransom or price of his deliverance from captivity."

The undoubted meaning of the term λύτρον, as it occurs in the classics, is a price paid to deliver a prisoner from captivity, or recover something lost, or perhaps stolen.   Though many argue, in the interest of a tendency, that the term may also be taken for any sort of deliverance, irrespective of the price paid for it, yet no example of such

·usage is found in point of fact. I shall here quote the accurate statement of the meaning of the term given by Bishop Pearson in his *Exposition of the Creed*, article 10: "What is the true notion of λύτρον will easily appear, because both the origination and use of the word are sufficiently known. The origination is from λύειν, *solvere*, to *loose;* λύτρον quasi λύτήριον, *Etymol.*—θρέπτρα τα θρεπτήρια, ὥσπερ λύτρα τὰ λυτήρια. Eustath. λέγει δὲ θρέπτρα (*ita. leg.*) τὰ τροφεῖα ἐκ τοῦ θρεπτήρια κατὰ συγκοπήν· ὡς λυτήρια λύτρα, σωτήρια σῶστρα. *Iliad*, Δ, 478. λύτρον, *igitur quicquid datur ut quis solvatur.* ἐπὶ αἰχμαλώτων ἐξωνέσεως οἰκεῖον τὸ λύεσθαι· ὅθεν καὶ λύτρα τὰ δῶρα λέγονται τὰ εἰς τοῦτο διδόμενα. Eustathius, upon that of Homer, *Il.* A, 13, λυσόμενός τε θύγατρα. It is probably spoken of such things as are given to redeem a captive, or recover a man into a free condition. Hesych. πάντα τα διδόμενα εἰς ἀνάκτησιν ἀνθρώπων (so I read it—not ἀνάκλησιν). So that whatsoever is given for such a purpose is λύτρον; and whatsoever is not given for such an end, deserveth not the name in Greek. As the city Antandros was so called, because it was given in exchange for a man who was a captive," etc.

Thus the λύτρον or τὰ λύτρα was the price of a captive's deliverance. The scholiast on Homer renders ὃς ἄποινα φέροι by the words ὁ κομίζων τὰ λύτρα. Polybius mentions that Hannibal, after the battle of Cannæ, sent ten of the prisoners to Rome to treat περὶ λύτρων καὶ σωτηρίας, making the λύτρον three minæ a man.

Here I must obviate the statement of Socinus and Crellius, that λύτρον is properly used only of the redemption of captives. On the contrary, it means whatever deliverance was effected by a gift or service. Thus, if a slave purchased his liberty, the money payment, consisting of his earnings, was called λύτρα; whereas a slave obtaining his liberation for good conduct, was said to get it προῖκα. Not only so: the word was used to denote the price of deliverance from punishment (Josephus' *Wars*, ii. 14).

This is indisputably the meaning of λύτρον; and it may be added, that even in the more *metaphorical* or derivative senses given to λύτρον by the poets, there is always something corresponding to the idea of a price, or at least of compensation. It is never the absolute idea, irrespective of a price paid. In Pindar we find the metaphorical or secondary sense of the word (see Heine), in the acceptation of a certain *compensation* for some evil or hardship that men may have endured. Thus the poet calls the marks of honour paid to Tlepolemus, λύτρον συμφορᾶς οἰκτρας γλυκυ, *a sweet compensation for his sad disaster* (*Olymp.* 7, 141). He also uses the phrase, λύτρον εὔδοξον καματων, *a glorious reward of toils* (*Isthm.* 8, 1). (See Muntinghe's *Geschiedenis der Menschheid*, vol. ix. Anmerk 96.)

I may here refer to the passage in Ælian, which Kypke quotes on this verse of Matthew in his *Observationes Sacræ*, as follows: "*Ælianus, Hist. An.* lib. 10, c. 13. Asserit quod conchæ, margaritis exemptis, liberæ dimittantur, οἱονεὶ λύτρα δοῦσαι τῆς ἑαυτῶν σωτηρίας, *hoc veluti liberationis suæ pretio dato.*" It is plain that Ælian describes the pearls which the oysters contain, as in some sense the λύτρον which is paid to secure their liberty. According to Ælian's representation of the matter—whether true or false, is not the question—the oysters are caught, and then, when deprived of their pearls, are liberated, as if the pearl were in some way the ransom or the price of freedom; and he uses an *as it were* (οἱονεὶ), to intimate how he would have his language understood. (Comp. Storr's Essay, appended to his commentary on Hebrews, p. 436.) We must hold, then, if we are to be guided by the *usus loquendi*, that λύτρον designates only a ransom or a price paid to set one free who is a prisoner, or in distress and danger.

There is thus no ground for the interpretation given by Grotius, that λύτρον may be held to denote a sacrifice. There is no well-ascertained instance where it is so used. De Wette says, correctly, "at vocabulum λύτρον neque apud Græcos, neque in Vers. Alex. de piaculis in usu est." (*De Morte Christi*, p. 140.) No doubt Kypke quotes the passage from Lucian's *Dialogues of the Dead*, where Ganymede says to Jupiter, "*quod si me dimittes, polliceor* σοὶ καὶ ἄλλον παρ' αὐτοῦ κριὸν τεθύσεσθαι λύτρα ὑπὲρ ἐμοῦ, *tibi et alium arietem ab ipso immolatum iri, in pretium redemptionis pro me.*" This by no means proves that λύτρον denotes a sacrifice, as the meaning is not that the sacrifice of a ram is a piacular offering, but that it is the price of his deliverance. The only argument that Grotius can produce for his position, that λύτρον may mean a sacrifice, is taken from the cognate Latin word *lustrum :* "Latini veteres quorum lingua tota Græcæ erat depravatio, litera una interposita, λύτρον lustrum dixerunt et λυτροῦν lustrare. Lustrare ergo urbem est eam a pœna liberare per lustrum, hoc est, per pænam succedaneam, quod et piaculum dicitur." (Grotius, *De Satisfactione*, cap. 8.) But it is a very uncertain mode of proof, to argue from the meaning of a word of probably cognate origin in one language to the meaning of a word in another. This can never overthrow the *usus loquendi* as to λύτρον. On the contrary, the classical usage was so fixed, that it could not bend or pass into any other sense but that of *ransom* or price in order to deliver a prisoner from captivity.

2. The *usus loquendi* of the Septuagint in reference to the term λύτρον, is equally definite and precise. Though men may speculate as to what might or might not have been, this point is unmistakeably evident, that the word is never used by the Septuagint in any other

sense but in that of *ransom*. The word is uniformly used in the Septuagint, to denote a price, compensation, or payment, with a view to
deliver a prisoner from captivity. It is the translation for several
words, viz. כפר, גאלה, פדיון ; and it is the term used to intimate generally, that something is given or offered to deliver a person, or to
obtain the surrender of a thing (Ex. xxi. 30, xxx. 12 ; Prov. vi. 35 ;
Num. xxxv. 31, 32). (Compare Schleusner on the word ; also Borger
on Gal., p. 154.) We may confidently conclude, then, that the word
λύτρον does not mean a sacrifice, but carries with it the notion of a
price or compensation for a captive. It is an advance on the idea of
a sacrifice ; or, more precisely, the one idea passes over into the other.
(See Œhler, under the word *Opfercultus*, in Herzog's *Real Ency-
clopädie*, and Keil on Exodus.)

The notion that λύτρον may denote deliverance generally, without
the idea of a ransom, was often expressed in former days as it is also in
modern times ; but it is wholly without foundation. On this point
the celebrated Ernesti expressed himself, *Neue Theologische Bibliothek*,
vol. v., 1764, as follows : "Hiebey macht der Hr. V. eine lange
Anmerkung darinne er saget, dass diese Worte entsetzlich übel verstanden und ausgeleget worden sind, und sich verwundert, dass
Männer die griechich verstunden und vorgaben, denken zu können,
dieses Wort durch eine Erlösung übersetzen, und von einer Loskaufung,
die durch ein Lösegeld geschehen, erklaren können, und durch eine
Genugthuung für die göttliche Gerechtigkeit. Wir sagen dagegen,
dass wir uns wundern, wie der Hr. Verf. der mit den alten Schrift-
stellern so bekannt seyn will, und so viele Jahre sich mit Augslegung
derselben abgegeben hat, so übersetzen und erklären können, und das
ohne allen Beweis aus der Sprache und Parallelstellen. Denn dass er
saget : wussten denn die Leute nicht, was die Gerechtigkeit Gottes
sei ? Gerechtigkeit bestehet in einer weislich eingerichteten Güte u.
s. w., damit ist gar nichts gesaget. Freilich wussten die Leute vor
Hr. Wolfen nicht, dass die Gerechtigkeit eine weislich eingerichtete
Güte sei ; ob sie gleich wohl wussten, dass Gott nicht wider die
Gerechtigkeit seine Güte beweise. Aber kann man dagegen sagen,
weiss denn der Hr. Verf. nicht, dass ἀπολύτρωσις nicht Lossprechung
heisset, noch heissen kann, und dass es noch kein Socinianer hat
beweisen können, wie er es auch nie beweisen wird ? Weiss er nicht,
dass an andern Orten stehet, diese ἀπολύτρωσις sei durch das Blut
oder den Tod Christi geschehen, dass sein Tod deswegen ἀντίλυτρον
heisset ? und was soll denn nun dass ἀντίλυτρον seyn, wenn der Effect
davon eine Lossprechung, d. i. eine nachricht von der göttlichen Lossprechung ist ?"

The term λύρτον, therefore, can be taken in no other sense than in that of a ransom. It must be added that λύτρον, as the translation of the Hebrew *copher*, is employed in the Septuagint to designate the price paid, in the Mosaic law, to deliver any one from threatened or merited punishment (Num. xvi. 46, xxxv. 31); and our Lord here expresses the *very price* which He was to give for man's salvation, viz. *His life.* He could mean nothing else by this saying, but that the giving of His life is the only price or ransom by which the redemption of His people was effected, just as the liberation of a prisoner of war was effected by the λύτρον.

Not to lengthen out this note unduly, let me refer the reader to the expositions of this text that have recently been given by Delitzsch on Hebrews, p. 732; by Philippi, in his controversial pamphlet against Hofmann, p. 61; by Keil, in his articles on Sacrifices in *Zeitschrift für Lutherische Theologie*, 1857, p. 449; by Thomasius, *Christi Person und Werk*, vol. iii. p. 89.

I may again refer to Chapman's *Eusebius, or the True Christian's Defence*, 1739, ii. 4, sec. 9, note E, where he shows, from Greek writers, that λύτρον intimates a special mode of redemption, by the payment of a ransom. He remarks : " if Christ and His apostles had specially intended to declare this with the most appropriate and strongest expressions, they could not have found in the Greek language words more plain and unambiguous than those which they employ."

NOTE I, p. 239.—*Christ fulfilling the Law, and bringing in a Righteousness.*

These two sections were meant to show that the fulfilling of the law, not less than the endurance of the curse, is of the essence of the atonement. Some, under the influence of prejudice or one-sidedness of view, object to imputed righteousness or the vicarious fulfilment of the law, alleging that it is an ecclesiastical conception (so Meyer on Gal. iv. 4); others, on the ground that Christ, as man, was under obligation to fulfil the law for Himself (so Piscator); others, because the atonement is deemed enough for pardon (so the Wesleyans); others, because the law was only for the Jews (so the Plymouthists). These are all one-sided theories, which will at once be exploded by every one who will either remount to man's primeval position before sin entered at all, and recall the task of obedience which was imposed on him before his confirmation could be conferred, or correctly apprehend the nature of sin, with which the atonement has to do, as containing the element of omission as well as commission; for even if the guilt of transgression were removed, there would remain the element of omission, which would equally be sin; and with both elements the Mediator must deal.

1. Let me first establish the true import of δικαιοσύνη. This is all the more necessary, because the precise import of it is now so generally missed. As to the exact meaning of the term, I may notice that the utmost importance attaches to an exact definition of it, because the whole argument in the Epistle to the Romans and Galatians, as well as the import of many other sections of the Pauline Epistles depends on it; and the true business of an interpreter is accurately to ascertain the force and import of terms as used by the sacred writers, without intermingling foreign elements. To save space, and not unduly to swell this note, let me refer the reader to a discussion of the import of δικαιοσύνη Θεοῦ, in an article which I wrote on the Pauline doctrine of the righteousness of faith, in the *British and Foreign Evangelical Review* for January 1862, in which it is discussed at length. In that article I endeavoured to prove, (1) that the phrase cannot be regarded with Reiche as a description of the divine attribute of righteousness; (2) that it cannot mean, as Neander, Olshausen, and Lipsius contend, an inward condition of righteousness; (3) that it cannot denote faith itself as counted to us for a righteousness, as the Arminians, Tittmann the younger, and Nitzsch put it; nor (4) be interpreted with others, such as Wieseler, Moses Stuart, and Dr. John Brown, as the divine method of justification. On the contrary, it is proved in that paper, by an analysis of Paul's language, that this δικαιοσύνη Θεοῦ is a substantial reality, not less a fact than sin, and not less productive of results in an opposite direction; that it is a complete, prepared, and perfect righteousness; that it *consists in an obedience to the divine law, which is its standard and measure;* and that it is a righteousness in our stead, or of a vicarious character. I shall not repeat what is there brought out as to the objective and vicarious character of Christ's obedience to the divine law, as that alone by which we are made righteous (Rom. v. 19).[1]

This view of Christ's active and passive obedience, as two concurring elements in one joint work, viewed as a unity, was accepted by all the Protestant Churches as the expression of their Church-consciousness: and more weight attaches to the public symbols and confessions, in which whole Churches embody their convictions, than to the individual sentiments of any teacher, however eminent. That this view

[1] See the section entitled "the Pauline doctrine of the righteousness of God" (p. 106) in the *Apostles' Doctrine of the Atonement.*

of the righteousness may fitly be called the Church-consciousness of all the Protestant Churches, will be evident to every one who will consult the Lutheran symbolic books and the various confessions of the Reformed Churches; and among the latter the articles and homilies of the Anglican Church. (See Art. 11 and Hom. on Faith.) I may also refer to Bishop O'Brien's excellent work on justification, and especially to Note Z, where he appends some well-grounded remarks, philological and doctrinal, in refutation of Mr. Knox's interpretation of δικαιοσύνη.

Before passing from the philological meaning of δικαιοσύνη, I would refer to the confused and unsatisfactory opinions entertained in many quarters on the meaning of the word from the days of Grotius, who interpreted the δικαιοσύνην Θεοῦ the *loving-kindness of God, benignitas Dei,* on Rom. iii. 5, 25, 26. The same notion was taken up by Schoettgen in his Lexicon, by Schleusner, Koppe on Rom. iii. 25, Michaelis, Carpzovius, Storr, Pott, Tittmann, and others. This is a sense of δικαιοσύνη and of δίκαιος, which has no warrant in philology, and which, doctrinally, tends only to bring all into confusion. And no argument of any weight has ever been, or can be, adduced in its behalf.

But another opinion, not much better, is, that δικαιοσύνη denotes *the Christian salvation itself.* This view was supported by the celebrated Vitringa on Isaiah xlv. 24, lix. 9; by J. A. Turretin on Rom. i. 17; by Koppe in an excursus on Galatians; by Rosenmüller, and others. But every one who weighs the force of words will discover that, in the Epistles of Paul, σωτηρία is the wider term, and δικαιοσύνη the narrower, and that they do not cover each other. (Compare Rom. i. 16, 17, x. 10; Titus iii. 5-7; Rom. v. 9.) Others have supposed that δικαιοσύνη may mean remission of sins, and the state of happiness or acceptance. But nothing can be said in defence of this acceptation, save only that it is thought to fit in to some passages. But that is to guess a meaning; that signification has no warrant in language; and the Septuagint lends it no countenance. Carrying out these views, which have a close connection with each other, Morus makes it, " favorem et misericordiam Dei quæ est in danda venia ; " and J. V. Voorst, in discussing its import in a separate treatise, *Annot. in loc. select.*, 1811, translates it thus, " Singularem benignitatis Dei demonstrationem, sive ex benignitate proficiscentem Dei erga homines favorem." All these views naturally flow from Grotius' deviation from the true sense of the term.

On the other hand, several exegetes, at the close of last century, adopted a modification of the old Protestant view of δικαιοσύνη, by expounding it, *innocence* or *guiltlessness*. Thus Noesselt, *Opusc.* i. p. 74, says, δικαιοσύνην Θεοῦ eam esse quam Deus ita nobis tribuit, ut non tanquam rei, sed innocentes ac justi habeamus. So Heinrichs, Phil. iii. 9, and Doederlein, in his *Instit. Theol.*, secs. 262, 263. That is undoubtedly in the right direction, though it is somewhat too negative. But it cannot be denied by those who intelligently compare the passages where δικαιοσύνη occurs, that it is the opposite of *reatus* or *guilt*. It is put in such connections as prove it to be a relative term, descriptive of the relation in which man stands to approval or reward, and presupposing obedience as its essence (Rom. v. 19). (1) It is not the divine attribute ; nor (2) is it descriptive of what is merely inward. But it is a relative term, implying a rule or a law, and a conformity to it of such a kind as entitles the δίκαιος to a re-ward. We do not approximate to a due apprehension of its meaning, if we start either from the classical notion of δικαιοσύνη as a human quality, or from the tenets of any philosophical school. The apostle, in announcing that the δικαιοσύνη was witnessed by both the law and the prophets, carries us back to the Old Testament, and leads us to apprehend that a *person who is righteous in the Old Testament sense, is one who not only corresponds to the God-appointed rule*, but is recognised as *entitled to a reward*. Thus the observance of the divine precepts was to be to the Israelite a righteousness (Deut. vi. 25). Very noteworthy is it, that Israel never corresponded to the idea, and that God promised to bring nigh His righteousness (Isa. xlvi. 13 ; Jer. xxiii. 6) ; and it is brought in and brought nigh by Him who is the end of the law for righteousness to every one that believes (Rom. x. 4).

2. Christ was vicariously made under the law for His people. The widespread objections to the active fulfilling of the law in our stead can only be obviated by the direct testimony of Scripture ; and for this purpose a single text may suffice : " God sent forth His Son, made of a woman, made under the law, to (ἵνα) redeem them that were under the law, that we (ἵνα) might receive the adoption of sons " (Gal. iv. 4, 5). If it could be made out, according to an interpretation proposed by Teller and others during last century, that the phrase " made under the law " means no more than " born a Jew "—and the same comment is repeated by Meyer, Alford, and Ellicott,—an ostensible reason could be given for denying the proof from this text. But that is a very partial and incomplete exhibition of the idea, as a few remarks will show. (1.) The phrase, " to be made under the law," occurring several times in Paul's Epistles, is always equivalent to being *subject to the law*, with the accessory idea of something burdensome and

oppressive connected with it (comp. Rom. iii. 19, vi. 14, 15 ; Gal. iv. 5, 21, v. 18; 1 Cor. ix. 20). Thus, in Rom. vi. 14, the "being under the law" is contrasted with being under grace ; and in 1 Cor. ix. 20 we should have a needless tautology, if nothing more were indicated than "to be born a Jew." That is mentioned immediately before ; and the manner in which the phrase is introduced in the Pauline phraseology shows all too plainly that it cannot be a mere circumlocution for a Jew. But (2) the connection between the two verses in Galatians is opposed to that exposition. For if the telic particle ἵνα (ver. 5) is connected with γενόμενον ὑπὸ νόμον, and leans on it, more must be contained in the phrase than is conveyed by the idea of being born a Jew, as this would make no relation between the cause or the meritorious means and the purposed end. And that there is such a connection, is obvious enough from the repetition of the same word, made *under the law*, to redeem *them that were under the law*. Or if we suppose that the commencing words of ver 5, ἵνα τοὺς ὑπὸ νόμον ἐξαγοράσῃ, could be immediately connected with the words, "God sent His Son," then the intervening words would be idle and super-fluous. (3.) To be consistent, they who adopt this mode of exposition should interpret the words in ver. 5, τοὺς ὑπὸ νόμον, "to redeem the Jews ;" for if the one clause has that meaning, the second, closely related to it, must have the same. And on that principle, what would be the import of the whole ? It would yield this strange and incom-prehensible thought, as the ultimate end contemplated by the second ἵνα clause: "Christ was born a Jew, to redeem the Jews, THAT we (the Gentiles) might receive the adoption"—thus making the redemp-tion merely affect the Jews, and representing the Jewish redemption as the cause of our adoption. This is a sufficient *reductio ad absurdum*. On the contrary, the simple meaning is, " God sent His Son, and put *Him under the law ;* that He might *redeem them that were under the law.*" The Gentiles having the law written on their heart, and being concluded under sin (Gal. iii. 22), are equally with the Jews redeemed by Christ's vicarious subjection to the law. As we were bound to two things—(1) to the "do this, and thou shalt live" (Gal. iii. 12) ; and (2) to the curse of the law as violated—He must be regarded as made under the law in both respects. This passage therefore, strictly interpreted, implies that Christ, thus vicariously made under the law, fulfilled all the claims which it had upon us, to the full extent of our relation to the law.

The point which these sections establish, is simply that Christ's vicarious fulfilment of the law constitutes an essential element in the atonement, in consequence of which His people are treated as if they had rendered that obedience : and are thus not only exempt from condemnation, but possessed of a right to the reward. The two elements, not very happily termed *the active and passive obedience*, are jointly concurring causes in the one atoning work—not the one to the exclusion of the other. It would have been well if divines had not been compelled to separate what is represented as one obedience (Phil. ii. 5). But they were challenged to answer the question, "If the Mediator reconciled us to God by His death, of what avail was His active obedience ?" They are not to be sundered, however, as if they were separately meritorious, or represented as if the passive obedience put men anew in the state of innocence, and the active merited the blessings to be earned by men in innocence, by a career of perfect obedience. For though these two ideas are distinguishable, and must be distinguished, the two elements, in point of fact, were always together and inseparable. (See, on this point, Spener's *Evangelische Glaubensgerechtigkeit*, p. 1135 ; Seiler's *Versöhungstod*, i. p. 274 ; Philippi's *Kirchliche Glaubenslehre*, iv. p. 143 ; Hutter's *Loc. Com.*, p. 450 ; Thomasius, iii. 307 ; Hollaz, iii. 1, 3, 78; Gerhard, secs. 56, 63.) The fact that sin is not only commission or trespass, but omission, implies the necessity of the active as well as of the passive obedience.

On the text in John xvi. 8-10 in sec. xxv. (p. 202), I refer to Luther's comment. He says (see vol. xii. p. 116, in the Erlangen edition of his German works, 1827): "Was ist nun das für Gerechtigkeit, oder worin bestehet sie ? Das ist sie, spricht er, dass ich zum Vater gehe, und ihr mich hinfort nicht sehet. Das heisset ja undeutsch, und vor der Welt lächerlich genug geredet. Und so das erste fremd und dunkel ist, das diess der Welt Sünde sey, dass sie nicht glaubet an ihn : so lautet diess viel seltsamer und unverständlicher, dass diess allein die Gerechtigkeit sey, dass er zum Vater gehet, und nicht gesehen wird. . . .

" Denn diess Wort : dass ich zum Vater gehe, begreift das ganze Werk unsrer erlösung und Seligung, dazu Gottes Sohn vom Himmel gesandt, und das er für uns hat gethan, und noch thut bis ans Ende ; nämlich sein Leiden, Tod, und Auferstehnng, und ganzes Reich in der Kirche. Denn dieser Gang zum Vater heisst nichts anders, denn das er sich dahin giebt zu einem Opfer, durch sein Blutvergiessen und Sterben, damit für die Sünde zu zahlen. . . .

" Siehe das heisst und is nun der Christen Gerechtigkeit vor Gott, dass Christus zum Vater gehet, dass ist, für uns leidet, auferstehet, und also uns dem Vater versöhnet dass wir um seinetwillen Vergebung der Sünde und Gnade haben ; dass es gar nicht ist unsers Werks noch Verdienstes, sondern allein seines Ganges, den er thut um unsertwillen. *Das heisset eine fremde Gerechtigkeit, darum wir nichts gethan, noch verdienet haben, noch verdienen können, uns geschenket und zu eigen gegeben, dass sie soll unsere Gerechtigkeit sein, dadurch wir Gott gefallen, und seine liebe Kinder und erben sind."*

NOTE K, p. 270.—*Christ as the Brazen Serpent and Lifegiver; and Christ giving His flesh for the Life of the World.*

These two sections allude to the question which parts the two great schools of theology in our day, viz: whether the life of Christ is given as an immediate and absolute gift, or whether it is purchased by His atoning death. The whole opposition to the vicarious sacrifice of Christ turns at present on this point, just as, a generation ago, it turned on the question whether pardon was absolutely given. The present is, beyond question, the most evangelical phase which opposition to the vicarious satisfaction ever assumed; and there is little doubt that it will be overcome, as other phases have been, by the word of Christ's testimony. With much that is said by the adherents of this tendency as to the nature and manifestations of the divine life, as well as in reference to that fellowship with Christ which is represented as its sphere and essence, every spiritual mind will sympathize. There are exceptions, indeed, far from unimportant, to an unreserved approval of the representation of the divine life, given by this school, —such as an incorrect idea of a fall; the universalist features it has contracted; the want of definite allusion to the mental exercises of repentance and conversion connected with the impartation of this life; and its readiness to ally itself to hierarchical and sacramental views. But no evangelical divine will simply condemn it, but rather accept much that it has of good, and seek to supplement its defects. Its founder was mainly Schleiermacher, whose impress it still bears. And as it arose in a time of prevailing spiritual death, its adherents were more solicitous about the introduction of spiritual life than of orthodox doctrine. Its watchword is the *Lebensgemeinschaft mit dem Erlöser*, or fellowship with Christ in His life; and the essence of Christianity is not regarded so much as any objective thing, whether it be the Trinity or the atonement, as the communication of a new life with which man's nature must be imbued from its centre, and by which all his powers are to be sanctified and ennobled; and Jesus of Nazareth is represented as communicating that life to sinful humanity. The principal and perilous defect is, that the atonement is not exhibited as the purchase of this life, or as having any causal connection with it. My object in this note is to add some further remarks, which shall

bring out the biblical representation of the meritorious connection between the atonement and the life. I shall notice some of those
passages where the eternal life stands connected with the performance
of a work done, or with righteousness as its price ; for life is its
promised reward.

But it may be proper in the first place to point out, in the words of
some of the prominent supporters of the new theology, how they
describe the communication of the divine life apart from the atonement. They ignore the whole forensic side of theology, or deny it.
They take no account of the right relation of the *person*, of his standing or title, and set forth merely the renovation of the *nature*. Thus
V. Hofmann says in his *Abweisung*, in reply to his opponent, p.
188: "das Verhältniss des Vaters zum Sohne nunmehr ein Verhältniss
Gottes zu der im Sohne neu beginnenden Menschheit ist, welches seine
Bestimmtheit nicht mehr von der Sünde des adamitischen Geschlects
sondern von der Gerechtigkeit des Sohnes hat." The writer makes
the incarnation of the Son to be the immediate reunion of fallen man
to God, and the commencement of a new humanity, without any
expiation. He asserts the mere exercise of holy love, as producing
this result without any atonement, and simply postulates a new starting-point, from which the race runs on anew. How like this is to
Schleiermacher, who makes Christ the completed creation of the human
race, will be apparent to every one. As this entire school owes its
rise to Schleiermacher, and repeats his positions, scarcely altering his
phraseology, I shall here quote a few sentences from him on his view
of the atonement. Schleiermacher says (*der Christliche Glaube*, vol.
ii. p. 94): "His [Christ's] act in us can only be the act of this sinlessness and perfection, as conditioned by the in-being of God in Him:
hence, both the one and the other must become ours, as otherwise it
would not be His act that becomes ours. Now, as the individual life
of every man is spent in the consciousness of sin and imperfection, we
can find ourselves in communion with the Redeemer only in so far as
we are not conscious of our individual life, but as He gives us the impulse to regard the source of His activity as the source of our activity,
and as a sort of common possession. This is uniformly the sense in
which Scripture speaks of the in-being and life of Christ in us (Gal. ii.
20 ; Rom. viii. 10 ; John xvii. 23 ; 2 Cor. xiii. 6), of the death to sin
(Rom. vi. 2, 6, 11 ; 1 Peter ii. 24), of the putting off the old man, and
putting on the new (Col. iii. 10 ; Eph. iv. 22-24). Now, as Christ
can direct His consciousness of God (Gottesbewusstsein) against sin,
only in so far as He, by entering into the collective human life, had a
consciousness of it as a fellow feeling, and as a something to be overcome

by Him, this, too, becomes the principle of our activity by His working in us. . . .

"If all activity in Christ proceeds from the indwelling of God in Him, and if we know no other activity than the creative, in which the sustaining is included, or, conversely, the sustaining in which the creative is included, we must so regard the agency of Christ. But as we do not exclude the human soul from creation, though it cannot be expected of us to understand the creation of a creature with free agency and liberty in connection with a greater whole, and though we can rather apprehend than comprehend this in our mind, so is it with Christ's creative agency, which has wholly to do with the province of freedom ; for His receptive agency is creative, while that which it produces its entirely free. As, then, the indwelling of God in Him is eternal, while all its manifestations are conditioned by the form of human life, He is able to act on that which is free, only according to the order in which it enters into His sphere of life, and only according to the nature of that which is free. His receptive agency, in taking us into fellowship with Him, is thus a creative production of the wish to receive Him ; or rather—for it is only a receptivity of His agency as in communication—a consent to the operation of this agency ; and that agency of the Redeemer is conditioned by the fact, that individuals enter into His historical sphere of action, where they perceive Him in His self-revelation. Now, though this consent cannot be imagined otherwise than as conditioned by the consciousness of sin, yet it is not necessary that this should precede the entrance into the Redeemer's sphere ; rather, it may just as well arise in it as an effect of the Redeemer's self-revelation, as it, at all events, comes to full clearness only through the view of His sinless perfection. The original agency of the Redeemer will thus be best conceived of under the form of a causal agency, and which is apprehended by its object as an attractive agency from the freedom with which it turns, just as we ascribe an attractive power to every one to whose formative intellectual influence we willingly yield ourselves. Now, since all the Redeemer's activity proceeds from the indwelling of God in Him, and since, at the origin of the Redeemer's person, the divine creative agency which established itself as the indwelling of God in Him was the only active power, so all the Redeemer's agency must be considered as a continuation of that divine influence on human nature forming His person. For this causal activity of Christ cannot occupy an individual without also becoming person-forming (person-bildend) ; all his actions, nay, all his impressions, being different in consequence of the operation of Christ in him. Hence also his personal self-consciousness is different. And as the creation had not a reference to what was individual—so that each creation of what was individual was a separate act,—but when the world was created everything individual was created in and with the whole and as much for the rest as for itself,—so the Redeemer's agency is formative for the world (welt bildend), and its object is human nature, in which the strong sense of God (Gottesbewusstsein) was to be implanted as a new principle of life. He takes possession of individuals with a reference to the collective body, when He meets with those in whom His agency will not only remain, but also operate on others through the revelation of His life. And thus the entire operation of Christ is only the continuation of the divine creative act from which the person of Christ took its rise." (Sec. 100, 1, 2.)

This modern theology to which so many confess in our day, is so unbiblical, that it disconnects the life from the cause of life, expatiating on life apart from the atoning death. Christ Himself puts the matter differently, as we have proved in the above-named sections. To show how widely different this mode of exhibiting the divine life is from that representation with which Scripture in every portion of it makes us familiar, I shall briefly review the allusions to LIFE, both in the law and in the gospel.

1. The idea of *life* was explicitly announced in the law as the promised reward held out to those who should comply with its terms. Thus it is said (Lev. xviii. 5), " Ye shall therefore keep my statutes and my judgments ; which if a man do, he shall live in them : I am the Lord." Compliance with the requirements of the law was the condition or ground on which the promise of *life* was made, as will appear from the very frequency with which these words were quoted in connections of which the import is not doubtful (Ezek. xx. 11, 13, 21 ; Neh. ix. 29). As the legalists, with whom the Apostle Paul had to carry on a controversy as to the way of acceptance, drew their confidence from their supposed compliance with the law, and plumed themselves on this legal promise, in the expectation of a reward, we find him appealing, on two several occasions (Rom. x. 5 ; Gal. iii. 11), to this reward of the law. The apostle's design in quoting the legal promise of life in both these passages, was to contrast the legal promise connecting work done with life in prospect, and the economy of grace. Thus He sought to bring out and give prominence to the essential difference between law and grace, works and faith. *Life* is set forth as the goal in both economies,—in the one as an unattainable prospect ; in the other, as a free gift. That the law was εἰς ζωὴν, is asserted by the apostle (Rom. vii. 10), and proclaimed by Christ Himself (Luke x. 28). But that which was unattainable by the law is provided for by

an economy of grace for the helpless. Accordingly, retaining the idea of righteousness as the essential prerequisite or condition, the apostle says (Gal. iii. 21), " If there had been a law given which could have given LIFE, verily righteousness should have been by the law." Without minutely analyzing this language, the broad sense of the passage, obvious to every mind, is a denial that the law can give life, as the promised reward for work done. The very opposite result is ascribed to the law : it was found to be unto death (Rom. vii. 11). That Paul conceives of life as the proposed reward, cannot be doubtful.

2. But the actual ζωή comes by a wholly different economy. By re-taining the word righteousness, however, when he speaks of the believer's participation of life, the apostle makes it plain that he still preserves the idea of the *legally* promised life. Thus, in Rom. v. 18, we find the righteousness of one redounding εἰς δικαίωσιν ζωῆς. Again, in Rom. v. 21, it is expressly called a *righteousness unto life eternal*. Again, in Rom. viii. 10, we have the phrase, ζωὴ διὰ δικαιοσύνης. The apostle thinks of life, then, as the proposed reward, whether he sets forth the terms of the law, or the provisions of an economy of grace. This comes out in the antithesis which he some-times employs between death the penalty of sin, and life by righteous-ness (Rom. v. 17). Nay, so far as the legal Jews connected this glorious life, as the promised reward, with the exact fulfilment of the terms of the law, the apostle does not say that this was a mistake on their part as to the connection between the two, if they were able to comply with the condition : he only denies, that such a result was attainable in the actual condition of men (Rom. viii. 3). But God has made this life accessible to men, as men, without distinction of nationality, by faith (Rom. i. 17 ; Gal. iii. 11 ; Heb. x. 39, where he quotes Hab. ii. 4).

3. One great defect of the modern mystic speculation on the atonement is connected with an imperfect recognition of the representative system, by means of the two Adams. Thus they who regard Christ as the Prince of Life, irrespective of any proper atonement or meritorious obedience, have crude and incorrect ideas of the whole representative constitution given to the race. The life they plead for so earnestly, or the new humanity which they suppose to begin with the incarnation, and to run on from that starting-point, ignores any deed of meritorious obedience which secures and obtains that new life. Theirs is a theory not thought out ; and it makes no inquiry how the counterpart of the life (ζωή) entered into the world, by the previous entrance of SIN (ἁμαρτία) as its cause (Rom. v. 12). If death entered by sin, then, in like manner, LIFE entered by RIGHTEOUSNESS (Rom. v. 12-20). Where

this is not apprehended, there cannot be a biblical view of the atonement. This decides upon the mystic theory so much in vogue at
present, which resolves the entire work of Christ into the communication of life. It is forgotten that this life is given to the second Adam,
only for a work done, only for a δικαίωμα, which is a counterpart of
the first man's παράπτωμα. It is thus an inconsequent speculation to
speak of the mere dispensation of life to run on from the incarnation,
irrespective of a ὑπακοή (Rom. v. 19).

The Schleiermacher theology, as represented by Usteri, would
indeed have a certain consistency here. (See Usteri, *Entwickelung
des Paulinischen Lehrbegriffes*). He will have ἁμαρτία refer, not to a
primeval deed of sin, but to sinfulness originally deposited in the constitution of the first man, that is, to original imperfection. And he
argues that the παράβασις or παρακοή was only original imperfection
expressed in conscious act, which Usteri supposed to have come into
the world, as man was by nature " earthy " (1 Cor. xv. 47). But
such a notion of humanity as involves the admission of imperfection
in his very nature, is untenable, not only on dogmatic grounds, but on
exegetical grounds. The connection of the section (Rom. v. 12-20)
shows, indisputably, that we must suppose an active, and not a passive, relation in this matter. The whole language there shows, that it
is by one man as sinning that sin came into the world, and not by one
man as created with sinfulness. The words τῷ τοῦ ἑνὸς παραπτώματι
(ver. 17), and διὰ τῆς παρακοῆς τοῦ ἑνὸς ἀνθρώπου (ver. 19), will admit
no other sense. There was no mere passive origin of sin in the race
of man, and just as little is there any mere passive derivation or origin
of ζωή apart from a ὑπακοή. There is thus a full and express counterpart between the way of the fall by Adam and the way of the recovery
by Jesus Christ. This will suffice to show that the mystic theory of
the atonement, as emanating from love alone, and consisting in the
communication of life alone, is utterly baseless.

The words of Jesus on the connection between His death and this
premial life, are unambiguous ; and they have been so fully discussed
in the text that it were superfluous to renew the discussion here. The
locus classicus is John vi. 51, etc., to which John iii. 14 and John x.
10 may be added. And when we enter into the Epistles, we find that
the connection between the vicarious DEATH and the divine LIFE is so
explicitly set forth that no one can question it on exegetical grounds.
The connection is one of work and reward, of righteousness and life.
This is the key to all the sections in the Pauline Epistles, often much
misunderstood, where the Christian is represented as dead, crucified,
and buried with Christ, in that one representative act of His. Ful-

filling the law and exhausting its curse, He laid the foundation for all
that life, regarded as the fruit and reward of His sacrifice, into the
possession of which His people enter as their rightful heritage. For
if we died with Christ, we shall also live with Him. It is premial
life. (Comp. Rom. vi. 1-11, 2 Cor. v. 14, 15, Gal. ii. 20.)

Note L, p. 374.

I had occasion to describe Amyraldism in the historical sketch
appended to the *Apostles' Doctrine of the Atonement*, and it is unnecessary to do more in this place than to add a few supplementary remarks
on the literature of the subject. The theory, strictly speaking, was
an artificial middle way between the sentiments of the Arminians and
of the strict Calvinists. But, as commonly happens in such cases of
compromise, it betrayed a considerably greater inclination or bias to
that party to whom the approximation was to be made, than to the
party out of which they came, and to which they still professed to
belong. Cameron, who gave rise to the theory, declared in unambiguous
terms : " the death of Christ, on condition of faith, belongs EQUALLY
to all men" (on Heb. ii. 9). Amyraldus, his scholar and admirer, propounded the same views as Professor of Theology in Saumur, and in
two separate treatises on UNIVERSAL GRACE and on PREDESTINA-
TION. The theory was but a more subtle form of Arminianism,
expressed in somewhat ambiguous phraseology : special efficacious
grace was replaced by a vague and plausible universalism. Very considerable excitement for a time was occasioned by the new theory.
But when the two Synods of Alençon in 1635, and of Charenton in
1647, acquitted the advocates of these opinions of heresy, some of the
most eminent divines of France, such as Capellus, Testard, Placeus,
Dallæus, Blondel, Le Blanc, Claude, Gautierius, Mestrezat, unhappily
adopted them. The consequence of this facility and vacillation on
the part of a church, once eminent for the soundness of its doctrinal
views and truth, was in the last degree calamitous. The remarks of
the late Dr Cunningham on this fact are worthy of consideration.

" The position of the French Church," says he, " in regard to the
great Arminian controversy which raged in the beginning of the
seventeenth century, and the Canons of the Synod of Dort, was this :
It was desired that the Synod of Dort should represent the whole
Reformed Church—that is to say, all the Protestant Churches except
the Lutheran. The French Church, therefore, appointed four men to
attend the Synod ; but from some misunderstanding, or suspicion, the
king would not allow them to leave the country, and they did not

take a formal part in the Synod. But at the next National Synod, held two years after, in 1620, they unanimously adopted the Canons of the Synod of Dort, and required all members of the Church to make a solemn declaration to maintain them all. We find however, soon after this, that unsoundness and impurity of doctrine began to show itself in the Church of France. Very soon we find a countryman of our own, Cameron, an able and ingenious man, did a good deal in the way of sowing the seeds of a kind of intermediate system, between Calvinism and Arminianism, which exercised a most injurious influence on the Reformed Church of France. The truth is, that Cameron and Amyraldus, and the University of Saumur which went with him, occupied very much the same position in regard to the spread of pure doctrine in the French Church, as Professor Simpson and the Divinity Hall of Glasgow occupied in our country. The Synod of 1637 manifested a considerable amount of unfaithfulness to God in connection with these doctrines, and the unfaithfulness did not fail to reappear in the Synod of 1645—the one only seventeen and the other twenty-five years after the solemn adoption by the National Synod of the canons of the Synod of Dort. The National Synods and purity of doctrine seem very much to have gone down altogether ; as it is remarkable that the one became more impure as the other grew rarer. In point of fact, so far had the Synods come short of faithful testimony to the truth of God, that the most elaborate book in defence of the universality of the atonement, in a Calvinistic point of view, by Daillé, is literally entitled as an ' apology for the two Synods.' This impurity of doctrine must be viewed, I think, in connection with the revocation of the Edict of Nantes. That revocation was, no doubt, a great crime on the part of the government, and was attended with most important effects on both the temporal and spiritual condition of France ; but one view ought not to be overlooked among others—for there are many others—and that is, that it must be regarded also in connection with the growing impurity of doctrine, which, for two generations, had been growing up in the Reformed Church of France, and had been eating into the sound doctrine originally professed, and was God's final and judicial dealing with them on that account. With all our abhorrence of Popery, with all our sympathy with the sufferers, who bore their trials in a way that shewed they were not even then without a large measure of sound doctrine and true piety, yet in spite of all that, we cannot but regard the subversion of French Protestantism, partly also as a punishment for the large departure of the Reformed Church from purity of doctrine." (Speech in the General Assembly of 1859 on the occasion of the Tricentenary of the French Synod.)

The theory which the Saumur divines had contrived formed a very crude and incongruous system, as must be apparent to every one who surveys the impossible task to which they had committed themselves —the endeavour to combine universal and special grace. Though by no means holding a uniform language on the atonement, they agreed in the statement that the Lord died for all and every man. They meant by this, as Cameron and Amyraud explicitly declared, that the death of Christ was for all men EQUALLY. But when the Synod of Alençon forbade that phraseology,—that is, discountenanced the doctrine that Christ died for all men equally, whether they receive Him or reject Him, a new style of language was adopted, but it was equally untenable. They supposed that it might be possible to assert a double and diverse satisfaction, one for all mankind, and one specially for the elect, and in this phase the theory was imported by Polhill into England, and by Venema into Holland ; but the entire expression *to die* FOR *one* comes in this way to be ambiguous and to have a twofold sense. As applied to the elect, it means IN THE ROOM OF ; as applied to the mass of mankind, it means FOR THEIR GOOD. It becomes a mere fencing with words, or a paltering in a double sense. Not only so ; the further question is immediately presented to our minds, What becomes of the three ideas which lie at the foundation of the whole provision for an atonement, viz. the covenant, substitution, and the vicarious endurance of the curse as valid facts ? How could punishment light on Christ, except as bearing imputed sin ? How could justice reach Him except as a surety, a substitute, and a sin-bearer ? The question is, Does the atonement effect anything by its own potentiality, or is it a mere expedient which may or may not become valid by other things extrinsic to itself ? The Scriptures represent it as purchasing a people (1 Cor. vi. 20) as purchasing the Church (Acts xx. 28). The analogy between the fall and the atonement, the only two great facts in the world, is conclusive on this point. The one carries terrible consequences to mankind wherever they are, the other *carries saving consequences to all for whom it was offered.* The whole Amyraldist theory was without a foundation, and its absurdity was increased by the fact that these divines formed a new arrangement of the divine decrees, making the atonement universal, and the election special.

My object however, in this note, is rather to refer to the literature connected with the discussion of these questions. Shortly after the publication of Amyraud's work on Predestination, a masterly reply to his main positions appeared from the pen of Rivetus in a work entitled *Synopsis de Natura et Gratia* (Rivet. *Opera*, tom. iii. p. 831). In this treatise Rivetus reviews the French sermons of Amyraud, as well as the topics contained in his formal theological treatise, and also notices the *Irenicum* of Testard, which was replete with the same views. The great work, however, on this subject, is Frederick Spanheim's exercitations on *Universal Grace*, 1646. Here every point is calmly and lucidly reviewed, with little of the acrimony of controversy. Of this great work an outline or condensed summary was given to the public by G. Reveau, under the assumed name of Gregorius Velleus. The Dutch divines, as well as the Swiss divines, aware of the danger to which they were exposed, from their proximity to France, showed a great anxiety to keep their churches free from the contagion of these opinions. Maresius wrote his treatise entitled *Epicrisis Theologica ad Quæstiones de Gratia et Redemptione Universali.* Francis Turretin, who well knew the corrupting tendency of these opinions from personal observation—for he had studied at Saumur, as well as at Geneva, Leyden, Paris, and Montauban—exposed their groundless and subverting character in the most unsparing manner. His admirable refutation leaves nothing to be desired (Loc. xiv. Quæs. 14). The *Formula Consensus Helvetica*, the last of the confessional documents, was prepared by the Swiss divines, Heidegger, Hottinger, Turretin, Werenfels, and Zwinger, in 1675, for the express purpose of protecting their churches from the invasion of these universalist opinions.

Among the testimonies of eminent theologians, I may refer to a very interesting and remarkable letter of Cocceius to the same purport with those already mentioned. Spanheim had sent him a copy of his work on Universal Grace, with a request that he would communicate his sentiments on the important subject, and especially on the new method which Amyraldus had propounded. Cocceius, in reply, (Ep. cxxv.) expresses himself in the most decided manner, first in commendation of Spanheim's work, as written with singular care and remarkable moderation, and next in dissatisfaction with Amyraud's opinions. The letter is too long to translate, but it is admirable as showing the absurdity of an indefinite and conditional suretyship. He says,—" This substitution we cannot make common and extend to the reprobate, unless we also make common the suretyship of Christ, or of that will by which we are sanctified, and the grace of the Father and the Son which is sworn to the seed. Wherefore also, that phrase *Christ died for men*, is by no means to be deflected in its ecclesiastical usage to be synonymous with the notion : Christ died with the intention that His death should not only be available to the elect for their salvation, but also to others for their great advantage ; or with this, Christ died with the intention that He might be a sufficient Saviour to all and every one, provided they believe (as if Christ procured a CONDITIONAL SALVATION, and not an actual salvation, by the gift of faith): or with this, Christ died with the intention that He might be the true object of faith, to be required of all men indiscriminately." The great mistake of the entire theory is that it does not represent the death of Christ as securing its own application, or AS OBTAINING THE FAITH which unites men to Himself.

The Amyraldist type of universal grace was imported into Scotland about the beginning and middle of last century. This tendency was promoted by the posthumous publication, in 1749, of a work on faith, alleged to have been found prepared for the press by the Rev. Mr Fraser of Brea. It found supporters; but the Marrow men, as they were called, were strenuously opposed to the universalist opinions.[1] Along with a firm maintenance of a special atonement, they preached the free invitations of the Gospel to all men indiscriminately. Perhaps the best refutation which is to be found in English of Amyraldism, or of the double satisfaction,—the one effectual and the other ineffectual, is in Rev. Adam Gibb's display of the Secession-testimony (vol. ii. pp. 131-190, and pp. 273-298).

NOTE M, p. 413.—*Historical Sketch of Doctrine of Atonement.*

The primitive doctrine of the atonement, as I have elsewhere proved at large from the testimony of the Fathers,[2] was that the immediate design or end contemplated by the death of Christ was the remission of sins. The connection between these two things, the death of the Lord and forgiveness, was from the first accepted as a causal connection. Nor was this ever formally denied during the fifteen centuries that preceded the rise of Socinianism, if we except the theory of Abelard, whose theology was as faulty as his character. Though the constituent elements of the atonement were not for many ages made matter of dis-

---

[1] Principal Hadow, in his attack on the "Marrow of Modern Divinity," laboured to fasten upon it the charge of universalism, based mainly on the quotation which it gives from Dr. Preston, "Go teach every man without exception here is good news for him, Christ is dead for him" (Mar. p. 120). Riccalton, in his masterly reply, entitled "A Sober Inquiry," meets this as follows (p. 102): "To which one may easily reply by reading out the sentence, *Christ is dead for him,* (but how? was it to purchase salvation for him whether he believes or not? No such thing; but so far as no man shall ever perish for want of a Saviour to die for them). *If he will take Him,* dead as He is, *and accept of His righteousness,* which by His death He has wrought out, *he shall have Him.*"

[2] See Appendix to the *Apostles' Doctrine of the Atonement,* 1870.

cussion, and though the connection between the death of Christ and remission of sins was simply accepted as a fact by all Christians, one thing is certain: the Fathers, with perfect uniformity, considered the death of Christ as a sacrifice for the sins of the world. Christ was regarded as effecting the remission of sins, not by His doctrine alone, nor by His example alone, but by the efficacy of His incarnation and death viewed as a sacrifice. It is true, opinion cannot be said to have been settled or very definite on points which were never subjected to investigation; and this holds true of some parts of their doctrine as to the design and effect of the Lord's death. The Fathers were content to extol the greatness of redemption and its importance, though they did not very minutely canvass the way in which the Saviour effected our redemption. They accepted the statement that He was incarnate, suffered, and died for man's salvation.

I refer to this fact, because an unfair use has been made of it by some modern writers opposed to the vicarious satisfaction, who wish to find the Fathers speaking their views. This holds true of Bähr's treatise (*die Lehre der Kirche vom Tode Jesu in den ersten drei Jahrhunderten*, 1832), in which the writer quotes from most of the Fathers of the first three centuries, as if they held his opinions. Priestley, during last century, attempted in a very unscrupulous and offensive manner to prove that the doctrine of the atonement was one of the corruptions of Christianity. Nothing can be imagined more groundless and unjust. When we examine how Priestley proceeded with the task imposed on himself, we find, that instead of inquiring whether the early Christians believed the doctrine of the atonement or not, whether they asserted the forgiveness of sins for Christ's sake, or for the sake of good works, he merely quotes passages where the Fathers speak of holiness, of virtue, and of good works in a way of commendation. He adduces various passages from the Fathers down to Augustin, and after him, to prove that they regarded the forgiveness of sins as flowing from the free mercy of God. But the question is, did they consider forgiveness as obtained independently of Christ's sufferings and merits. If the Fathers considered the sufferings of Christ merely as an example, and if they regarded repentance and contrition as the sufficient ground of salvation, one would have plainly perceived it in their writings. Many expressions of the Holy Scriptures which refer to the doctrine of the atonement must necessarily have been explained by them in a metaphorical way. Basnage, quoted by Priestley, says that the ancients generally speak sparingly on Christ's atonement, and ascribe much to good works. The explanation has been already mentioned. But I must further add, that Priestley was not the man to enter into this field. He only betrayed his ignorance of the Fathers, which Horsley and others sufficiently exposed. He quoted passages which served his purpose, and was silent on all the testimonies which ran counter to his preconceived opinions. If we consult the writings of the Fathers, it will be found that they regarded Christ as the meritorious cause of salvation, and alluded to His sufferings as expiatory and vicarious. Anselm, from whose work extracts have already been given, is the sort of transition stage between the patristic theology and the later ecclesiastical system.

I. The oldest doctrine accepted in the Church, in a more or less developed form, was, that Christ was the substitute for sinners, who would have been subjected to merited punishment, if a satisfaction had not been offered in their stead. This is undoubtedly the oldest doctrine, and worthy of being called the accepted doctrine of the Church, both in the Greek and Roman section of it. No intelligent and honest investigator can entertain any doubt on this point, though the doctrine came to be more developed in the eleventh century, when men were led to discuss the nature of the connection between the death of Christ and the forgiveness of sins. To give an exact statement of the most widely accepted view of this connection, let it be remarked that they held that men were under obligation to bear the punishment which sin deserved; that Christ took their place to expiate sin; that His death was a satisfaction to divine justice, and the endurance of the punishment of sin in their stead; and that this vicarious suffering on the part of Christ, who united the divine and the human nature in His person, *won forgiveness for the guilty.* The connection, then, is a meritorious and causal connection. This was the most ancient and the received view, sometimes less fully, sometimes more fully, developed.

There were subordinate diversities of view among this class. Some, as Anselm and the Reformation theology, deduced this provision more from an absolute inner necessity. Origen, Athanasius, Augustin, and, latterly, Grotius, and those who followed in his track, deduced it more from God's free will, regarding the satisfaction, not as indispensably necessary but as a free and gracious arrangement, adapted to display the faithfulness, wisdom, and love of God. The one placed it more *in God*, who could not but insist on the satisfaction of His justice; the others placed it more in that which is *without God.* Anselm and the Reformers insisted on the *equivalent;* Grotius and his school allowed an *acceptatio gratuita*, or a *relaxatio* or *dispensatio legis.* They were, however, at one as to the meritorious or causal connection. Some ascribed all the effects produced by the atonement to the *passive obedience* of Christ alone,—such as Piscator, and those who followed him in his conclusions; while the great body of the Lutheran and Reformed Churches, ascribed the validity and efficacy of the atonement to the *active obedience* of Christ, as well as to His sufferings, combining both as equally essential to one joint result. There was also a diversity of opinion as to the persons for whom the atonement was offered; the Reformed Church maintaining that the atonement was for an elect company; the Lutheran Church making the atonement general. But notwithstanding these subordinate points, to which we have adverted in the body of this work, there is a perfect unanimity on the causal connection between the death of Christ and the remission of sins. That is the grand truth which has always been held in all the great sections of the Christian Church, both in the east and west: and to this Protestantism also unequivocally confesses.

II. Another opinion is, that the death of Christ is only the occasion of forgiveness, not its meritorious cause. Under this division may be classified the distinctive peculiarities of the old Socinian doctrine, as well as the various phases of modern speculation,—all uniting in one point, that forgiveness is either given *absolutely*, or on the ground of some *inner amendment* or renovation, but that the death of Christ has no causal connection with it. And in one respect they are all identical: they discover no adequate idea of sin. We may say of them as Anselm said to his pupil: "*non consulerasti quanti ponderis sit peccatum*." They who maintain this second opinion, which cannot be said to express the ECCLESIASTICAL CONSCIOUSNESS of any epoch of Church history, appeal to a number of texts. It will be found, indeed, to the surprise of the investigator in this field, that all the biblical testimonies which are adduced in defence of the first and oldest doctrine on the subject of the atonement, are adduced by the defenders of the second view, with a wholly different explanation. The sayings of Jesus, which we have expounded as proper expressions of the true nature, scope, and effect of His vicarious death, they hold to be merely *figurative* or *metaphorical* representations, the import of which must be translated into strict and honest speech, before their meaning can be ascertained. They make the entire language of our Lord a vast magazine of *metaphors*, which the expositor must distil or filter into proper speech, and exact thought. And when this is done, they maintain that nothing else is taught by all that vast array of testimonies, but simply this, that Jesus died in some indefinite way, which cannot be apprehended or explained, for man's benefit, and to make them partakers of the remission of sins. They explain the death of Christ as a morally operative means of the same nature with His doctrine and example.

I must now advert to the various shades and modifications of this opinion. While they have their diverging peculiarities, they coincide in asserting the absolute forgiveness of sins, and in rejecting the idea of a vicarious satisfaction to the justice and law of God. Here I would willingly make an intermediate classification for those who maintain Trinitarian sentiments; for every one who has learned to weigh opinions, will readily admit that a wide line of demarcation separates the Trinitarian from the Unitarian in everything; that the one is within the pale of biblical Christianity, and that the other has very questionable claims to such a recognition, and that the opinions held by the one differ in their whole character, scope, and tendency from those which are maintained by the other. But I find it impossible to make this intermediate classification, partly because a Trinitarian, such as Mr. Maurice and Mr. Davies, finds a place among the opponents of the vicarious satisfaction, only by extreme inconsistency; partly because the supporters of this second opinion uniformly allow a veil to rest upon their Trinitarianism at this point; and partly because in this matter they socinianize, and cannot be sundered from the sentiments and opinions of the school with which they symbolize.

(I.) The Socinians or Unitarians must first be named in this division, because, in point of fact, they first asserted the opinion that Christ's death had no causal connection with forgiveness. They were the first to oppose the doctrine of vicarious satisfaction; and from them, with various modifications, it passed over to other sections of the Church. There are four points which must be noticed as to their mode of explaining the connection between the death of Christ and forgiveness. (1.) They held that He confirmed, by His death, the doctrine or message which He taught, and particularly the promise of the remission of sins contained in it. They were in the habit of appealing to the words which speak of the blood of the new covenant, but affirmed that the message which that martyr-death confirmed, was the message of absolute forgiveness. (2.) Another reason, according to Socinus and his followers, why remission of sins is commended to us in connection with the death of Jesus, was, that He gave us, in His death, a bright example of spotless virtue, that we might follow His steps; and they appeal to such passages as connect the enforcement of His example with His career of suffering (1 Pet. ii. 21). (3.) A further reason, according to the Socinian school, why remission of sins is put in connection with Christ's sufferings, was, that His death, followed as it was by His resurrection, confirms us in the faith and hope of eternal life. (4.) Another reason is drawn from His resurrection, the frank recognition of which was the only thing that entitled the Socinian or Unitarian body to stand within the pale of Christianity in any sense of the word. They approximate to Christianity in this one respect that they suppose Him to have won power by His death, to be Lord both of the dead and living (Rom. xiv. 9). The Gospel, according to them, is an enforcement of virtue and a proclamation of absolute forgiveness, independently of any atoning sacrifice. In a word, they hold that the death of Christ confirms our confidence in God's grace, and tends, as a moral means, to form men to virtue. In a word, there is little in the whole system beyond naturalism. Thus Priestley limited himself to the point that the death of Jesus confirmed our hope of eternal life, and our faith in the resurrection. The author of *The Apology of Benjamin Ben Mordecai for embracing Christianity*, represents Him as obtaining power to save sinners and bring them to glory, apart from any work of substitution. Wolzogen represented Christ as a sacrifice for sin in the strange sense of showing what a punishment was due to sin; a theory which reduces Christianity to the same rank with the law (Rom. vii. 7). All these writers with one consent repudiate substitution and vicarious punishment.

There is no necessity to dwell at any length on the Socinian positions, as they are the direct antithesis of what we have asserted throughout this volume. The system goes little further than Deism, and in many of its features is allied to the Mahommedan Monotheism. The chief point of attack was the position maintained by the Christian Church from the first, that a satisfaction was made to divine justice, and that this obtained the remission of sins. Socinus says: "having got rid of this justice, had we no other argument, that human fiction of the satisfaction of Jesus Christ must be thoroughly detected and totally vanish."

From this first principle all the other positions followed in due course. Though he allowed the threefold offices of Christ, he neutralized the priestly office in two ways. He asserted that the Lord exercised only the prophetical office in the days of His flesh; that He was not a priest on earth; and that the execution of the office in heaven was coincident with the kingly office, and not different from it (see Socinus, *de offic. Christi;* Racov. Cat. *de munere Christi;* Smalcius, *de div. Christ.*). The adherents of this school call Christ a SAVIOUR only in the sense that He confirmed the truth of the promises; a theory which would preclude Him from being a Saviour to those who lived before His birth, on the ground of performing a work by which others are accepted.

When we more particularly inquire into the Socinian objections, they are the following. They maintain that God has power to forgive sins without exacting any satisfaction; that He is pleased so to act in all cases of pardon; and that Jesus could not have satisfied divine justice for our sins either by His death or by any other means (see Socin. *de Servatore*, part 3). Crellius adduces these arguments, and they are refuted by Essenius and P. De Witte. These assertions are deduced from the great error of the system—that punitive justice is not necessary in the government of the world. But we have proved that the principal scope of Christ's death was the satisfaction of divine justice by a fulfilment of the law, and by enduring the merited penalty. They permit themselves to say the most harrowing things on this point, as if the ecclesiastical doctrine reflected on the divine perfections, and represented the divine Being as a tyrant or a Moloch; whereas we have fully proved that it puts Him in the most amiable light.

But they further argue, What is more unjust than to punish the innocent in stead of the guilty? So far is this from being against the light of nature, that all nations retain something of the idea (see De Moor, 3, 1025). The reason why such a transaction cannot have place in human law is, that no one has power over his own life, and the Judge has no right to take it. The Lord offered Himself willingly (John x. 18); having absolute power as God over His own humanity. And when it is further objected that in this case God satisfied Himself, the answer is at hand. It was in His humanity, properly speaking, that He obeyed the law and bore the penalty, though the Godhead gave infinite value to the satisfaction. The Supreme God in one capacity provided the ransom, and in another accepted it as adequate. And a judge may require compensation, and yet by means of a gift equal to the necessity, provide the satisfaction. (See Hervey's *Dialogues.*)

The method of interpretation by which the Socinian writers attempted to vindicate their positions, was one that can only be called violent. They invented a vast congeries of metaphor, and hid the whole subject in a dark forest. They took such words as RANSOM, PRIEST, SACRIFICE, SIN-BEARING, REMISSION OF SINS BY BLOOD, and the like, in a secondary or figurative sense, putting everything to hazard. The salvation became a metaphorical rather than a real thing. They came to Scripture with preconceived ideas and prepossessions, and made it speak their sentiments. Besides, they appealed to reason as the ultimate court, when the language of revelation was too explicit to be explained away by any ingenuity. Thus Socinus declares in reference to the theme he so much opposed—the Lord's bearing punishment in our stead: " ego quidem, etiamsi non semel sed sæpe id in sacris monumentis scriptum extaret, non tamen ita rem prorsus se habere crederem" (*Lib. de Servatore*, p. 3, 48).

We now enter on a brief review of the more recent modifications of the same opinion,—all which maintain this in common, that Christ's death was not a substitution in the room of the guilty, or a vicarious satisfaction for sin. Though many may go far in the use of biblical phraseology, and even call His death a sacrifice, and compare it with the Old Testament sacrifices, they will not admit a substitution in either case, but view it as either a casualty in a world of sin, or a sensible representation of the evil of sin, or of the love of God.

Among the many opinions, complexionally different, but substantially identical, in as far as they set aside the vicarious work of Christ as the immediate cause of remission, perhaps the theory of Taylor of Norwich, though he had no higher than Arian sentiments, makes the nearest approach to what we have called the general orthodox doctrine. This opinion sets in the foreground, not the value of Christ's sufferings, but His spotless and unexampled obedience to God, which was so much valued and approved, that it was deemed worthy to be rewarded with the salvation of men. The connection between Christ's death and men's salvation, lies, according to Taylor, in this, that His sublime virtue was deemed worthy of a reward, and was rewarded with the forgiveness of sins, just as an earthly monarch will reward the eminent services of an eminent soldier or citizen upon his family. (See Taylor's *Key to the Apostolic Writings*, chap. viii., before his paraphrase and notes to the Epistle to the Romans, 1746, and his essay on *The Scriptural Doctrine of the Atonement*.) His position is, that God had such complacency in the lofty virtue of Jesus, exercised in life and death, that He, on that ground, accepts sinners. This is Taylor's and Purgold's theory ; and it was much followed. But this is not biblical doctrine. We nowhere find our reconciliation ascribed to the sublime virtue of Jesus, but always traced to His blood or vicarious sacrifice ; His sufferings being considered not as a mere proof of His stedfast virtue, but as a vicarious bearing of sin. Blood cannot be made to mean mere virtue, and we cannot lose sight of the allusion to the Old Testament sacrifices, and of the direct connection of His sacrifice with our redemption. If there is nothing more than an example of lofty virtue and of martyr-stedfastness, approved and commended at the divine tribunal, how are we to understand Christ's words, when He speaks of blood shed for the remission of sins (Matt. xxvi. 28) ? There was no reason for maintaining silence on this, when our Lord instituted the memorial of His love, and pointedly referred to His death or blood shed for the remission of sins, if the ground on which God forgives sin is His satisfaction and pleasure in the lofty virtue of Jesus. On the contrary, He makes no allusion to this.

When we abandon our own reasonings, and place before us the whole series of passages used by our Lord, we at once see how meagre and unsatisfactory is the idea here presented to us. Vicariousness in His sufferings and death is everywhere His grand theme (John x. 11), and vicarious suffering is the meritorious cause of remission.

(II.) We have to notice the new phase of the same tendency presented to us in Rationalism which kept the field from about the year 1770 till near the middle of the present century, desolating most of the Protestant churches. It differed little from Socinianism, of which it was but a new edition; it denied the necessity of satisfying divine justice and everything approaching to a transfer of merit. Nay, carrying out its positions to their legitimate consequences, pronounced Rationalists, such as Steinbart, Eberhard, Bahrt, Henke, and Wegscheider, repudiated the notion of positive divine punishment, and also of the remission of sins, considered as a divine act. According to the rationalistic theory, reason was in all matters the court of last appeal; naturalism always finding expression in rationalism. While there was agreement in these principles, there were various phases or currents of thought among its champions.

In common with the Socinians, the great aim of the Rationalists was to attack the ground on which the atonement rests,—to represent divine justice as unworthy of God. They defined justice as divine goodness directed by wisdom, and sought to explode every attempt to compare the divine Being with worldly princes or judges. Not only so: they maintained against the plainest axioms of human experience that inflictions are always beneficent or a wise application of physical evil for the improvement of mankind. Alleging as they did that the supreme Being never presents Himself in any other light than as a loving Father, and that His laws are, properly speaking, but Fatherly counsels, aiming at the benefit of His children, they denied divine punishments in every sense. To remove them would be the removal of benefits. And thus, according to the rationalistic theory, the notion of satisfaction by a surety falls to the ground as destitute of foundation. (See Dippel's expressions.) They attempted in this way to explode the redemption as resting on wrong notions of God and of punishment. But in these speculations, they were at war with the innate convictions and common sentiments of mankind.

The Rationalists have been wont, down to our day, to lay all emphasis on the universal Fatherhood of God, and to repudiate as intolerably severe and terrible every representation of God as a supreme ruler and judge. This one-sided view of theirs has not even its analogy, where they thought to find it, in man made in the image of

God. For among men the paternal relation does not exclude the judicial function, nor the latter the former; and there could be no human society without both. The Rationalists misrepresented God's character by affirming that He was good-natured, rather than good. They spoke of paternal love and tenderness till they annihilated all idea of punitive justice, and described a being indifferent to the moral character of actions. But, said this school, may not God recede from His rights as man ofttimes recedes from his? To this the reply, as it is well expressed by Howe, is, God's rights are inalienable, whereas man's are not. But it does not hold true, even in man, in all cases. The individual may forego his right of self-defence: but can a judge recede from his right to punish? (See Hervey, Van Alphen.) When we are challenged to say to whom God would be unjust in remitting punishment, the answer is obvious. The great God cannot for the physical comfort of mankind act in contravention of the moral perfections of His nature.

But besides this objection, derived from God's relation to man, the rationalistic school, prolific of all manner of cavils and difficulties, adduce others drawn from the dignity and innocence of the Mediator. It would be tedious to enumerate them; and they have been anticipated under different sections of this volume. Do they allege that it was unworthy of a sinless being to be treated as a sinner? I answer: Sin-bearing differs from personal transgression, and was so divine a work, that it could be consummated only by a God-man. Do they demand, How this could be? The answer is: Man was saved by the same constitution and by the same representative system by which he fell. Do they allege that the Lord Jesus was not subjected to proper punishment whether we have respect to the corporeal effects of sin, or to the consciousness of guilt? I answer, He suffered both in Gethsemane and on Golgotha directly from the hand of God (2 Cor. v. 21); and even what came mediately from the hands of men was for sins not His own (Isa. liii. 1-12; 1 Pet. ii. 22; Gal. iii. 13). Do they allege that the Mediator had not the consciousness of guilt? I answer: We distinguish between what was personal and official in the Lord. And He certainly apprehended, more vividly than any ever did, the connection between sin and punishment, between guilt and wrath. Personal disquiet of conscience a sinless being had not, and could not have.

As to a third class of objections propounded by the rationalistic school, based on the condition of those for whom Christ is supposed to have atoned, they are as follows. It is argued that the deliverance from punishment and restoration to divine favour cannot be ascribed to the death of Christ, because He has not taken away the natural punishments either as to body or soul. I answer, though sickness, suffering, and death remain for a time, they cease to be punishments. The moral connection between sin and punishment is broken. (See our remarks on the ransom, Matt. xx. 28.)

Before passing from this rationalistic school, it may be proper to notice a speculation which found much favour both in Germany and Holland. Some maintained that the Lord and His apostles in their teaching, accommodated themselves to the prejudices of the Jews; that the Jews of that age regarded God as a severe and arbitrary monarch, or a terrible avenger who was easily offended, and who could not forgive without the shedding of blood, which served to propitiate Him. They maintained that our Lord and His apostles accommodated themselves to these severe ideas of wrath and punishment, atonement and sacrifice, though the great aim kept before them was to represent God as love. This entire theory was well refuted by Storr, Heringa, and Lotse. It implied a reflection, of the most offensive kind, on the Lord. If the world held false and unworthy conceptions of God, however difficult it might be to recall men from them,—the first task of a divine teacher was to correct what was amiss, and not accommodate His teaching to their perverted views, and this our Lord did at all points. How could it be harmonized with the wisdom and fidelity of the Lord that He appointed two sacraments for His Church, the scope of which was calculated to remind Christians of remission by blood, if these ideas were not comprehended in His teaching?

Other rationalistic champions maintained that Jesus was commissioned to restore the obscured truths of natural religion, and thus became the victim of His own zeal, as He incurred the resentment of an ungodly people. But they would not allow that His death was vicarious or made God more ready to forgive sin; because they argued, forgiveness is an absolute gift irrespective of atonement.

(III.) A third school having much in common with the two former, but making a considerable advance upon it, consists of those who take rank as the advocates of THE SPIRITUAL LIFE, or of A MORAL REDEMPTION, irrespective of the forensic element in theology. It began with Hasenkamp and Menken, and pervades the views of Flatt, Steudel, and Klaiber. But it owes its wide circulation to a far greater name, whose commanding influence, as one of the most bold and original thinkers in the Christian Church, went far to reconstruct the theology of his country. I refer to Schleiermacher, who repudiated all allusion to law or divine wrath, and merged the judicial aspect of theology in the ethical. The watchword of this tendency—wherever it extends —in Germany, Holland, England, and France, is spiritual life, not expiation, the renewal of the nature, not the acceptance of the person; in a word, a mere moral redemption. The thread on which it crystallized itself was the principle of fellowship in the Redeemer's life. But it was accompanied with a marked tendency to deny or ignore many precious doctrines; and it discovered an erratic tendency on the subject of sin, Satan, and the fall of men, on divine justice and the punishment due to us for sin, on a proper substitution and expiation, on imputed righteousness, nay, on imputation in any form, as well as on the incarnation, which was more Sabellian than Trinitarian. The Groningen School in Holland, the theory of Maurice and Robertson of Brighton, and several of Pressensé's positions, are but echoes of this German tendency. We must therefore notice more particularly the theory on the atonement emanating from the modern German believing school, which deviates from the teaching of the symbolic books. It belongs to a much higher type than those already mentioned under this division, both as to the doctrine of CHRIST'S PERSON, and evangelical religion in general. Not a few of them are Trinitarian, though others are no higher than Sabellians or Arians. We may describe their views of the atonement by two marked features,—one of which is more prominent in some writers, and the other more prominent in others. They coincide in OPPOSING THE VICARIOUS SATISFACTION, and in setting aside the forensic side of theology in favour of that which is properly mystical, but lay emphasis on the fellowship of CHRIST'S LIFE, or communion with Christ in His life (*Lebensgemeinschaft mit dem Erlöser*), and on LOVE. (I gave a description of this school, in an article on Neander in the *British and Foreign Evangelical Review* for 1853.)

a. The theory of Schleiermacher was to this effect, that Christ, as the completed creation of human nature, redeems men by receiving them into the fellowship of His life or blessedness. To exhibit Schleiermacher's opinions, the best method will be to translate a few paragraphs of his dogmatic work, entitled *Der Christliche Glaube*, 1842. He says (secs. 101, 102): " As the redeeming work of Christ founds for all believers a common collective activity *corresponding to the being of God in Christ*, so the *atoning element, that is, the blessedness of the indwelling of God in Him*, founds a blessed collective feeling for all believers, and for every one in particular. In this their former personality at the same time expires, so far as it was the isolation of feeling in an unbroken life of sense, subordinating to it every sympathetic feeling for others and for the general body. That which still remains of personal identity is the peculiar mode of conception and feeling which works itself as an individualized intelligence into this new common life; so that as regards this point, too, Christ's agency is person-forming, inasmuch as an old man is put off, and a new man put on." He adds a little below his objection to the view which we have maintained (p. 107): "Those conceptions of the atoning work, which make the impartation of Christ's blessedness independent of the reception into the fellowship of life with Him, appear only as magical; that is, *the forgiveness of sin* is derived from the *punishment* which Christ underwent, and the salvation of men is represented as a reward which God gives to Christ for that penal suffering. Not as if the thought that our salvation is a rewarding of Christ were wholly to be rejected, just as little as all connection between the sufferings of Christ and the forgiveness of sins is to be denied. But both become MAGICAL as soon as they are not effected by the fellowship of life with Christ; for in this fellowship the communication of salvation, as we have already explained the matter, is natural, while, without it, the rewarding of Christ is but a divine arbitrariness. And even this is somewhat magical, when a matter so absolutely internal as salvation is supposed to be produced from· without, without being based internally; for if it is independent of the life of Christ, it can only be in some way infused in each individual, since man has not the source of salvation in himself. *The forgiveness of sins is also magically effected, if the consciousness of guilt is thought to cease because another has borne the punishment.* We can suppose that the expectation of punishment might be thus removed. But this is only the external element (sinnliche) of forgiveness; and there would still remain the properly ethical, *the consciousness of guilt, which would thus be removed and charmed away without any ground.* How far something of this has passed over into the Church doctrine will be discussed below."

"If we compare the connection here assigned with the opposite views just mentioned, they certainly lead us to the remark, that in our view no account whatever is taken of the sufferings of Christ; so that we have not had the opportunity to raise the question, whether or how far they belong to redemption or atonement. But it can only be inferred from this delay, that there was no reason to adduce them as a primary element, either in the one place or in the other; and this is the correct state of the case, because otherwise *no perfect reception into the fellowship of life with Christ*—from which redemption and atonement can be fully understood—*would have been possible anterior to the suffering and death of Christ.* As an element of the second order, however, they belong to both, but immediately to atonement, and indirectly to redemption. The agency of Christ in founding the new collective life could only appear in its perfection—though the belief in this perfection might have existed without this—if it gave way to no opposition, not even to that which could cause the destruction of the person. The perfection, then, does not properly and directly consist in the suffering itself, but only in the resignation to it ; and of this it is a sort of caricature, when any one, isolating this culminating point, and disregarding the founding of the collective life, regards the resignation to suffering for suffering's sake, as the actual sum of Christ's atoning work. But as to the atonement, our representation takes for granted that, in order to effect the reception into the followship of His blessedness, the longing desire of such as were conscious of their misery, must be first directed to Christ by the impression which they received of His blessedness. The fact is, that the belief in this blessedness might have existed without this, but that the blessedness only appeared in its perfection, as it was not overcome by the fulness of suffering."

He adds (p. 110) : " But that the preceding explanation may serve in every respect as a standard for judging of the ecclesiastical formulas, we must apply it to our general formula of the creation of human nature being completed in Christ, in order to convince ourselves that this, too, is carried out in the twofold agency of Christ. For what is thus received into the fellowship of Christ's life, is received into the fellowship of an activity determined by the vigour of the consciousness of God (Gottesbewustseyn), adapted to all occasions, and exhausting their demands ; and also into the fellowship of a complacency resting in this activity, and that can be shaken by no other movements from what quarter soever. That every such reception is nothing else but a continuation of the same creative act, the temporal manifestation of which began with the person of Christ ; that each intensive advancement of this new life is such another continuation in its relation to the diminishing collective life of sin ; and that in this new life the original destiny of man is attained, and that nothing beyond and above this can be conceived or attempted for a nature such as ours,—needs no further proof."

These quotations will show the theory of the atonement held by this remarkable man. He uses language on the sufferings of Christ, as a vicarious sacrifice, which is audacious and repulsive in the last degree. He makes the whole atoning element to consist in the indwelling of God in Him, which Schleiermacher asserted, more in a Sabellian than in a Trinitarian way. But the atoning element could not be effected without the human in Christ, as well as the divine. In reference to this notion, Krabbe, *die Lehre von der Sünde und vom Tode*, 1836 (p. 287), says, happily, " Er auf dem Seyn Gottes in Christo seine ganze erlösende Thätigkeit ruhen lässt, da wir doch namentlich seine

Ueberwindung der Sünde, welche wesentlich zu seiner erlösenden Wirksamkeit gehört, nicht dem Seyn Gottes in ihm beimessen dürfen, sondern dem, was mensch in ihm war." But we must subject this theory to a more particular analysis, chiefly on account of the vast influence exercised by its author over a large class of minds.

A false conception of SIN which with him is something merely negative vitiated the entire theory. According to Schleiermacher sin is a mere defect of the consciousness of God, and the atonement is a mere readjustment of the natural and divine consciousness of man. Wherever sin is considered as a free personal act by which the majesty of the divine law has been violated and the transgressor is handed over to the award of punitive justice, such a theory can find no place. Schleiermacher would not allow that sin involved any thing penal, in consequence of which the sinner not only forfeits fellowship with God, but becomes a captive needing a ransom to deliver him. Nay, the idea of guilt as an objective fact cannot be said to have had any existence for Schleiermacher. Hence no guilt, no sacrifice of expiation. Sin and redemption were with him alike subjective. Not only so : the sufferings of Jesus, divested of every thing vicarious, had no objective significance ; and he goes so far as to say that these sufferings of the Lord are but a SECONDARY matter. How then did he explain what occupies so large a place in the delineations of the prophets, evangelists and apostolic epistles ? He reduced them to the idea of sympathy with human misery. That is much too trivial and evacuating a theory to do justice to the language of Scripture. The SYMPATHY of Christ WITH US is too low and insignificant to explain what Scripture signifies, when it asserts His suffering FOR US and exhibits the various elements of the agony in Gethsemane and Golgotha.

On the contrary, the great doctrine of the atonement takes for granted the dread reality of objective guilt, for which it is the divinely provided remedy. There is not only the consciousness of guilt, but objective guilt, demanding an adequate expiation, if destruction is to be warded off. Considered as a revolt from God and the transgression of this law (1 John iii. 4), sin imposes a demand too stern and inflexible to be discharged at the bar of God, or to be silenced in the human conscience by any theory such as this as to a defective consciousness of God. That will not satisfy the divine Judge nor yet the human conscience : for nothing will satisfy the latter that does not pacify the former. There must be expiation in order to remission and a restoration to fellowship with God.[1]

The only thing to which Schleiermacher attaches any weight is the

[1] See Schleiermacher's *Lehre von der Versöhnung* by Dr. C. G. Seibert, Wiesbaden, 1855.

fellowship of life with Christ, as if this constituted the redemption, and not, as the Bible everywhere puts it, the result, *reward*, and fruit of the ransom offered.   It is nothing but mysticism, where all the great doctrines connected with God as a Lawgiver and Judge are ignored, and where the restoration of life, absolutely considered—nay, such as it was in the person of Christ Himself—is supposed to be repeated in every Christian, without any appreciation of the specially meritorious ground of our acceptance before the Judge of all the earth, or any provision made for the expiation of sin.

b. A second phase of German theology, not excluding the element of spiritual life, but adding something distinctive and peculiar, is the theory that the atonement is only a manifestation of HOLY LOVE.   Most of the modern supporters of the mystic theory of the atonement powerfully dilate on love, and will see love alone in the sufferings of Christ. Klaiber, Hasenkamp and Menken express their view of the atonement in this formula: " dass Gott die Liebe ist, und was nicht Liebe ist, auch nicht in Gott ist." (See Menken's *Schriften*, vi. Band, *über die Eherne Schlange.*)   The same view was strongly urged by R. Stier, in his *Beiträge zu Biblischen Theologie*, Leips. 1828.   He expresses his concurrence with the English mystic, W. Law.   It is well known that Law, while he enforced with great zeal and ardour the spiritual life, held low opinions on the atonement,—views, which can only be called disparaging, inasmuch as they assigned it a very secondary importance.[1]

[1] As Law has been so much lauded by the supporters of the mystic theory of the atonement in Germany, and especially by Stier, the following reference to him, in the life of the admirable Henry Venn, may be appropriately quoted.   " Mr. Law," says the biographer (p. 19), "was, indeed, now his favourite author ; and from attachment to him, he was in great danger of imbibing the tenets of the mystical writers, whose sentiments Mr. Law had adopted in the latter periods of his life.   Many writings of this class discover, indeed, such traces of genuine and deep piety, that it is not at all wonderful that a person of exalted devotional feelings should admire them.   From a too fond attachment, however, to Mr. Law's tenets, he was recalled by the writings of Mr. Law himself.   When Mr. Law's *Spirit of Love*, or *Spirit of Prayer* (I am not sure which), was about to be published, no miser waiting for a rich inheritance devolving on him, was ever more eager than he was to receive a book, from which he expected to derive so much knowledge and improvement.   The bookseller had been importuned to send him the first copy published.   At length the long-desired work was received one evening ; and he set himself to peruse it with avidity.   He read till he came to a passage wherein Mr. Law seemed to represent the blood of Christ as of no more avail, in procuring our salvation, than the excellence of His moral character. 'What ! ' he exclaimed, 'does Mr. Law thus degrade the death of Christ, which the apostles represent as a sacrifice for sin, and to which *they* ascribe the highest efficacy in procuring our salvation ?   Then, farewell, such a guide !   Henceforth I will call no man master.'"

c. Frequent reference has been made by us to V. Hofmann's *Schrift-beweis*—by far the ablest attempt ever made on exegetical grounds, by one reputed an evangelical theologian, to overthrow the vicarious satisfaction. It is proper here to give a connected outline of his views. He thus winds up a discussion occupying a large portion of his first volume (p. 332, first edition) :—" We have come to an end of our examination of all the apostolic sayings in which the fact of the sufferings and death of Jesus is anywhere made use of, and its significance either mediately or immediately mentioned or delineated in any side, and we have found no passage, to the understanding of which anything else was necessary, or from the exposition of which anything else resulted, than what we have gathered from the Gospel history of the sufferings and death of Jesus. We have found that the substance of the apostolic declarations in all the numerous references in which they speak of the death of Christ, whether with or without the use of Old Testament delineations, is always the same as we have expressed in our system, viz., that according to God's purpose the life and work of Jesus issued in an event in which the relation between God and man ceased to be conditioned by sin, because His communion with God stood the test even to the end, even in the uttermost opposition which sin and Satan were able to direct against the work of salvation. Although it does not belong to my task, yet I think I ought not to neglect to show, that the confession of the Church, even when moving in the formulæ of a theory which is not contained in the above, yet does not stand in opposition to what has been advanced, —nay, more, does not contain or purport ought that is wanting in our exposition.

" The idea of the Church, when she speaks of Christ's vicarious obedience, active and passive, by which satisfaction was rendered to the righteousness of God offended by sin, will be recognized in the four following propositions : (1) that the state of alienation between God and mankind has been at once and for ever converted into a communion of peace ; (2) that this change is not in the conduct of man, but in the relation of God to man and man to God ; (3) that this change was produced, not by mankind of themselves, but by God in Christ ; and (4) that God effected this change in such a manner, that He manifested in it actually His will of love, and at the same time His hatred of sin. We need scarcely remind the reader that the first three points are contained in our declaration, and that consequently the fundamental doctrine of our Church concerning justification by faith alone is not endangered. But the fourth point is contained in it, as well as in the traditional mode of representation, only with this difference, *that in the latter the injured holiness of God demands a corresponding satisfaction which had to be offered first, before God could be gracious;* while, according to our view, what was done in Christ combines both elements, the actual manifestation of the love of God to man, and of His hatred of sin, because the creative beginning of a new relation of God to man did not take place without the termination of the previous relation, conditioned by sin. This termination begins, so that the beginner of a new humanity develops His life under the conditions of human nature, which were introduced by sin ; it continued in the righteous One, exercising His life's task in conflict with sin ; and is consummated in His voluntarily enduring whatever the enmity of sin against God determined against Him. The sufferings and death of Jesus form the consummation of this termination ; and their essentially destructive significance is this, that in them only was realized the utmost that the Mediator of salvation could endure and do, that the sin-conditioned relation between God and mankind might issue in an end corresponding to it, and to the divine decree of love, and thus compensating for sin. As, *according to our mode of viewing the subject, it is not the sinner, or the Son of God in his stead, that performs what had been omitted, or suffers what had been deserved,* we are not tempted to present Christ's work as a collective act of the human race, which is not the fact ; and as Christ's work does not appear as a satisfaction for the offence committed against God, which must first be effected, that God might be gracious, the manifestation of God's grace is not merely rendered possible by means of it, but it is itself the realization of the divine will of grace, which it also is. We do not divide human sin into omission and transgression, nor the obedience of Christ into active and passive, in a way which does not correspond to reality, but is merely abstract and notional ; but this one termination of sin, as a whole, is the obedience of Christ in work first, and suffering afterwards. Nor are love and righteousness in God separated in such a manner that the demands of the latter are realized separately from the will of the former ; nor do Father and Son ever stand in such opposition that the Son becomes the object of punitive justice ; but what is done, is the one deed of the love of God to mankind, which is at the same time hatred of sin, and is the united act of Father and Son, for the realization of this will of love, which is a will of hatred to sin. Yet, whether the expression of our system is more appropriate than that of the traditional ecclesiastical, I leave others to judge. I think I have shown that it is more in accordance with Scripture."

This extract will give a just idea of Hofmann's opinions. In his

controversial pamphlets he acknowledges three deviations from the
ecclesiastical doctrine : (1) that He does not speak of Christ's fulfilling the law ; (2) that he does not consider Christ as rendering a vicarious obedience or suffering, but only as verifying His Sonship amid
endurance ; (3) that he apprehends the whole history of Jesus, from
His incarnation to His death, as the carrying out of the plan to which
the three-one God resorted to change or alter the *relation of man* to
Him. He regards the Church doctrine as not having equal claims to
recognition, because it leads to an arithmetical reckoning and counter-
reckoning between the divine claims and Christ's performance. He
thinks, too, that it does not put divine grace in its proper light, to say
that sin must be expiated before God can be gracious.

The whole theory of this able man, who in many points follows
Menken and Schleiermacher, proceeds on the supposition that the
atonement makes no change on God's relation, but simply on man's.
He allows no wrath as a principle of action in God, and acknowledges
only love in God. The whole effect of Christ's death, according to
him, is to initiate a new humanity, or a new starting-point which shall
renovate the nature. Agreeably to this representation, justification is,
with him, not a forensic act, and complete at once: it grows and is
never perfect. All that he says of the mystic union is good. But as
to reconciliation, it is not THROUGH Christ's finished work, but IN Him.
The objective is thus merged in the subjective.

In a word, it makes another Gospel. All that this theory maintains is in the ecclesiastical doctrine of the Protestant Confessions, but
the converse is not true. All that is in them is not reproduced in
Hofmann's theory. He acknowledges Christ's obedience, but it is
neither A FULFILMENT OF THE LAW, nor a work performed in OUR ROOM
and stead. (See his controversial *Abweisung* in reply to Philippi.)
It is a mere self-verification as the Son of God : and the sufferings are
a fortuitous OCCURRENCE, not a vicarious PUNISHMENT or the endurance
of the CURSE in our stead. As compared with the theory of Taylor of
Norwich above mentioned, I may say that, as a theory of the atonement, it has almost everything in common with it.

Since the controversy to which Hofmann's work gave rise, nothing
of much moment has occurred in German theology bearing on the
atonement. On the part of those who will not accept the ecclesiastical
doctrine, the chief peculiarity of their position appears in the attempt
to explain away THE WRATH OF GOD. Many who have advanced a
considerable way, refuse to acknowledge that wrath or PUNITIVE JUSTICE
can be affirmed of God from the impression that this would be incompatible with His Love. This holds true of Ritschl, who makes wrath

only future and contingent on a rejected gospel; a position which neutralizes substitution (see Ritschl's above-named articles in the *Jahrbücher*, and his recent work *Lehre von der Rechtfertigung und Versöhnung*, 1870). What this writer wants is a frank recognition of covenant suretyship, of substitution, of imputation, and of the infliction of the curse on the Redeemer. But having advanced so far from the school of Baur, to which he once belonged, it is to be hoped, he will yet come to occupy the only tenable ground. Without naming those who are anchored on well tried Lutheran ground, such as Kahnis in his Lutheran dogmatics, I may remark that some otherwise sound divines seem disposed to lay all the emphasis on divine love. But though that appeals to the human HEART it does not rectify the evil CONSCIENCE. This is only done by a suffering law-fulfilling substitute (Heb. ix. 14). As to Schenkel of Heidelberg he has so unmistakeably avowed Unitarian sentiments that no theory of the atonement higher than that of Abelard could be expected of him.

When we trace the influence of German thought on other lands we see that the leaven of their sentiments has spread far and wide. In Holland the Groningen school, while still asserting the spiritual life and fellowship with Christ in His life, is most pronounced in its opposition to substitution and imputation. This will be seen from Doedes' sketch of the school, and more fully from their periodical, *Waarheid in Liefde*. When we turn to French Protestantism in France and Switzerland, we find the same leaven at work. Thus Pressensé has committed himself to the theory of moral redemption. Though asserting the spiritual life as warmly as could be wished, he allows himself to speak in the style of the new theology, which allows that Christ is only a Redeemer as He has revealed the divine love, and by that revelation kindled in our hearts the flame of love to God. I may here refer to the work of M. Pozzy, *Histoire du dogme de la Rédemption*, 1868, in which he proves against Pressensé that the fathers, reformers, and the leaders of the French revival, Vinet, Ad. Monod, and others, were all asserters of the propitiatory sacrifice.

When we come to our own country, the most eminent advocates of the same views may be said to be Mr. Maurice and Mr. Robertson of Brighton. The former, in his theological essays and in his *Doctrine of Sacrifice*, the latter in his discourses, which have had a wide circulation, permit themselves to speak in the most offensive way of the satisfaction of divine justice and of Christ's atoning sacrifice in the room of His people; while, at the same time, they proclaim in a style far from either Socinianism or Rationalism the spiritual life or the moral redemption. With all that is said on this latter point the ecclesiastical doctrine is fully compatible, but they subvert the only foundation on which the spiritual life can be bestowed. It is not necessary to quote from these works, as they are so well known. I may only add that the terms in which they extol the incarnation and the person of the only Son, valuable so far as they go, betray a profound insensibility to the infinite evil of sin, the authority of law and the justice of God, and that the views which they advocate only throw men back on a mystic legalism; a piety which makes no account of the acceptance of the person in the righteousness of another, and no provision for securing Christian liberty. A proof of this may be read in Mr. Maurice's *Faith of the Liturgy and the Doctrine of the Thirty-nine Articles*, 1860. (See too Rigg's *Modern Anglican Theology*.)

IV. A fourth theory in the same direction is THE THEORY OF MORAL INFLUENCE, to which most of the American and English divines confess who have deviated from the ecclesiastical doctrine of the vicarious satisfaction. This seems to find favour with the English-speaking errorist, while the previous school finds most acceptance with German minds that have broken with the views of the confessions. Jowett, Bushnell, Young, Davies, Campbell, belong to this tendency fully more than to the former. Thus the death of Christ is only intended to have a subjective effect, and to pacify our fears, by affording a great manifestation of divine love. Reconciliation is something wholly on man's side, not on God's side. It is sometimes said that the Supreme Being needs no reconciliation to Himself. They thus ignore the fact of sin in His universe. They deny that He must deal with it; forgetting that though justice and mercy are not opposed to each other, as equally attributes in the same all-perfect God, yet the terrible evil of sin brings to light a relation of a wholly new kind to the creature. This theory of moral influence has many phases, and to some of the most prominent of these we must now refer.

One phase was to the effect that His death must be considered as an example of God's aversion to sin, and as paving the way for a general proclamation of forgiveness. This theory was advocated by Professor Koopman in the twenty-first volume of the publications of Teyler's Society in Holland. It was argued, that as the ancient sacrifices were meant to imbue the mind with a deep sense of the hatefulness of sin and of its guilt, and to impress the heart of men with reverence, abhorrence of evil, penitence, trust, and an eager pursuit of holiness, so Christ was set forth to be still more fully the means of the same result, and the example of God's displeasure against sin. This theory opposes the vicarious atonement, but insists on an example of the divine displeasure against sin. We may well ask, would it not be an intolerable anomaly in God's moral government, a contradiction to every divine perfection, to be made an example of God's displeasure against sin, and yet have no sin, personal or by imputation? That would be a difficulty indeed, which would defy solution. But if examples of indignation had the effect for which this theory pleads, why could not the blood of bulls and goats take away sin? and amid many examples of the divine displeasure against sin, why do we nowhere read that remission was ascribed to such displays of indignation? But the faith by which we obtain forgiveness extends to the person of Jesus, as the procurer of forgiveness by His death; and we are not only summoned to receive the forgiveness which is preached, but to have faith in His person as crucified. (See *Godgeleerde Bijdragen*, ii. Stuk. 1828.)

Another theory is, that the death of Christ is *a confession of sin*. This is the great burden of Mr. MacLeod Campbell's book on the atonement, who holds that Christ's confession of sin was *a perfect amen in humanity to the judgment of God on the sin of man* (p. 134). He goes on to say, in the following terms, that a true repentance, and a confession of sin, are all that are required to expiate sin: "That due repentance for sin, could such repentance, indeed, be found, would expiate guilt, there is a strong testimony in the human heart, and so the first attempt at peace with God is an attempt at repentance; which attempt, indeed, becomes less and less hopeful, the longer and the more earnestly and perseveringly it is persevered in, but that not because it comes to be felt that a true repentance would be rejected even if attained, but because its attainment is despaired of,—all attempts at it being found, when taken to the divine light, and honestly judged in the sight of God, to be mere selfish attempts at something that promises safety; not evil, indeed, in so far as they are instinctive efforts at self-preservation, but having nothing in them of the nature of true repentance, or a godly sorrow for sin, or pure condemnation of it, because of its own evil; nothing, indeed, that is a judging sin, and confessing it in true sympathy with *the divine judgment upon it*" (p. 143). He then goes on to say that Christ in humanity has repented of and confessed our sin; and this according to Mr. Campbell, is all the expiation for sin rendered or required. To show that this is his precise meaning, let me quote his words: "That we may fully realize what manner of an equivalent to the dishonour done to the law and name of God by sin, an adequate repentance and sorrow for sin must be—and how far more truly than any penal infliction such repentance and confession of sin must satisfy divine justice,—let us suppose that all the sin of humanity was committed by one human spirit, in whom is accumulated the immeasurable amount of guilt, and let us suppose this spirit, loaded with all this guilt, to pass out of sin into holiness." Such change would imply an absolute and perfect repentance, a confession of its sin commensurate with the evil." " We feel that such a repentance as we are supposing, would, in such a case, be the true and proper satisfaction to offended justice, and that there would be more atoning worth in one tear of true and perfect sorrow, which the memory of the past would awaken in this now holy spirit, than in endless ages of penal woe" (p. 144).

What reply is to be made to this extravagant and strangely constituted theory of Christ's confessing sin, and repenting of it? It might be enough to say, without canvassing or discussing it, that it has no warrant or foundation in Scripture, the phraseology and ideas of which alone can direct us in our theological thinking and theological nomenclature. But it is plain that the author cannot intend the words *repentance* and *confession*, which are personal acts, to be understood in their ordinary acceptation. Not only so; anything like vicarious suffering or representative action is wholly opposed to the writer's scheme of thought. The theory explains nothing, and only palters in a double sense. It is only meant to convey to the reader that the action of Christ, though it had no efficacy God-ward, had a something in it calculated to produce a moral influence on men's minds. But the same theory of moral influence comes to light in the writings of others, and with a brief allusion to these I shall conclude this volume.

Thus Professor Jowett expresses himself (*Epistles of Paul*, p. 477): " Not the sacrifice, nor the satisfaction, nor the ransom, but the greatest moral act ever done in the world—the act, too, of one in our likeness —is THE ASSURANCE TO US that God in Christ is reconciled to the world." To the same effect writes Bushnell (*Vicarious Sacrifice*, p. 533): " The facts are impressive; the person is clad in a wonderful dignity and beauty; the agony is eloquent of love, and the cross is a very shocking murder triumphantly met; and if then the question rises, How we are to use such a history so as to be reconciled by it? we hardly know in what way to begin. How shall we come unto God by help of the martyrdom? How shall we turn it, or turn ourselves under it, so as to be justified and set at peace with God. Plainly there is a want here; and this want is met by giving A THOUGHTFORM to the facts which are not in the facts themselves." In a word, the death of Christ has no other effect, according to this theory, except as it is an impressive spectacle to influence men's minds. It effects nothing in reference to God according to Bushnell.

The same thing appears in the sketch of Dr. John Young (*Life and Light of Men*, p. 301): " The sacrifice," says he, " was not offered by men to God, but was made by God for men and for sin, in order that sin might be for ever put down and rooted out of human nature. This stupendous act of divine sacrifice was God's method of conquering the human heart, and of subduing a revolted world, and attaching it to His throne—pure love, self-sacrificing love, crucified dying love." This is the style, and well-nigh the language, in which Stier and Klaiber express themselves on the moral influence of the atonement. It proceeds on the supposition that the reconciliation is only on man's side, and that the death of Christ was meant to calm a groundless fear.

Reconciliation, it is said, is wholly on man's side, and we must entertain comforting views of God. If that mean that God has no hostility to lay aside, and that we have filled our mind with dark suspicious fears of God, it may be accepted on the footing of an accomplished expiation for sin. But if it means that no satisfaction was necessary as the ground on which that message. of reconciliation is made, which is the meaning of those who propound it, nothing can be more at variance with gospel doctrine ; and the section of the Pauline Epistles which most forcibly exhibits reconciliation, puts it wholly on the ground of an atonement (2 Cor. v. 18-21). When it is further objected that the atonement is always represented as the proof or effect or fruit of God's love, but never as its cause, the answer is at hand. The atonement did not, and could not, originate divine love in God, which is an eternal perfection of the divine nature, seeking an adequate object on which to expend its riches ; the atonement emanated from this divine love (see sec. vi.). But if we speak of the actual exercise of grace to sinful men, or of its manifestation to its actual objects, then the doctrine of the gospel is, that grace is capable of being exercised only through the atonement, and that Jesus is the foundation or meritorious cause of its exercise to such objects.

Was the death of Christ merely intended to calm a certain fear, or to satisfy an important moral want in man ? This means, that it was but an assurance of forgiveness, or an imposing manifestation fitted to give peace and confidence. It is said it would be much simpler to set forth the death of Christ as a striking evidence and manifestation of divine love, without maintaining the necessity of any atoning sacrifice.

I might quote all the texts bearing upon the atonement, and ask : Do they, can they, on any principles of interpretation, convey the idea that the atonement is but an open declaration of divine love, and the removal of the slavish fear of divine wrath ? If the death of Christ did nothing but convey an idea of God's love, without effecting anything more, then our Lord stands on the same footing with any of His apostles, who taught that God is love, and died martyr-deaths in confirmation of their testimony. But no teacher, however eager to extol forgiving love, could ever pretend to the titles, *Saviour, Redeemer, Shepherd,* that belong to him. If, according to this theory, the Lord's sufferings were merely intended to remove from us a slavish but groundless fear of punishment, we naturally ask, where is this ever stated in Scripture? On the contrary, our sins are uniformly referred to as the cause of the death of Jesus (Rom. iv. 25 ; Isa. liii.). And when we hear of redemption from iniquity, and from an actual curse, and from the wrath to come, how can that be a mere deliverance from ground-less fear? The Scripture never represents the death of Christ as intended merely to assure us of divine love. And if according to this theory Jesus has freed us from all our groundless fears of divine punishment, and assured us of divine love, how can we explain those terrible threats still connected with impenitence and unbelief (John iii. 18, 36 ; Rom. ii. 4 ; 1 Cor. vi. 9, 10.; Heb. x. 29)?

INDICES.

I. INDEX TO THE TEXTS MORE OR LESS ELUCIDATED.

II. INDEX TO SUBJECTS.

III. INDEX TO AUTHORS MOST FREQUENTLY ADDUCED.

IV. INDEX TO GREEK WORDS ELUCIDATED.